PEARSON CRIMINAL JUSTICE

Criminal Behavior

Custom Edition for Miami Dade College

Pearson Learning Solutions

New York   Boston   San Francisco
London   Toronto   Sydney   Tokyo   Singapore   Madrid
Mexico City   Munich   Paris   Cape Town   Hong Kong   Montreal

Senior Vice President, Editorial and Marketing: Patrick F. Boles
Sponsoring Editor: Debbie Coniglio
Marketing Manager: Kathleen Kourian
Development Editor: Annette Fantasia
Operations Manager: Eric M. Kenney
Production Manager: Jennifer Berry

Cover Art: Police Car: Courtesy of Veer/Alloy Photography. Gavel: Courtesy of iStockphoto/Christine Balderas. Behind the Bars: Courtesy of iStockphoto/Simon Podgorsek.

Printed in the United States of America.
37
Please visit our website at *www.pearsoncustom.com*.

Attention bookstores: For permission to return any unsold stock, contact us at *pe-uscustomreturns@pearson.com*.

Pearson Learning Solutions, 501 Boylston Street, Suite 900, Boston, MA 02116
A Pearson Education Company
www.pearsoned.com

ISBN 10: 0-558-72003-X
ISBN 13: 978-0-558-72003-2

Contents

1

Introduction to Criminal Behavior

CHAPTER OBJECTIVES

- Define criminal behavior and juvenile delinquency.
- Stress that such behavior has multiple causes, manifestations, and developmental pathways.
- Introduce various theories that may help explain crime.
- Identify the different perspectives of human nature that underlie the theoretical development and research of criminal behavior.
- Emphasize that the study of criminal behavior and delinquency, from a psychological perspective, has shifted from a personality focus toward a more cognitive and developmental focus.
- Introduce the reader to the various measurements of criminal and delinquent behavior.

Crime is commonly defined as conduct or failure to act in violation of the law forbidding or commanding it, and for which a range of possible penalties exist upon conviction. Criminal behavior, then, is behavior in violation of the criminal code. To be convicted of crime, a person must have acted intentionally and without justification or excuse. For example, even an intentional killing may be justified under certain circumstances, as in defense of one's life. Although there is a very narrow range of offenses that do not require criminal intent (called strict liability offenses), the vast majority of crime requires it. Obviously, this legal definition encompasses a great variety of acts, ranging from murder to petty offenses.

Crime intrigues people. Sometimes it attracts us, sometimes it repels us, and occasionally, it does both at once. It can amuse, as when we hear about capers and practical jokes that presumably do not harm anyone. It can frighten, if we believe that what happened to one victim might happen to us. Crime can also anger, as when a beloved community member is brutally killed, a child is subjected to heinous abuse, or individuals have been deprived of their life savings by fraudulent schemes.

While interest in crime has always been high, understanding why it occurs and what to do about it has always been a problem. Public officials, politicians, "experts," and many people in the general public continue to offer simple and incomplete solutions for obliterating crime: more police officers on the streets, video cameras and state-of-the-art surveillance equipment, street lights, sturdy locks, self-defense classes, stiff penalties, speedy imprisonment, or capital punishment. Some of these approaches may be effective in the short term, but the overall problem of crime persists. As in most areas of human behavior, there is no shortage of experts and opinions, but there are few all-encompassing and effective solutions.

Our inability to prevent crime is partly because we have trouble understanding criminal behavior and identifying its many causes. Because crime is complex, explanations of crime require complicated, involved answers. Psychological research indicates that most people have limited tolerance for complexity and ambiguity. People apparently want simple, straightforward answers, no matter how complex the issue. Parents become impatient when psychologists answer questions about child rearing by saying, "It depends"—on the situation, on the parents' reactions to it, on any number of possible influences. This preference for simplicity helps to explain the popularity of do-it-yourself, 100-easy-ways-to-a-better-life books. Today, the preference for simplicity is aided by the vast array of information available on the Internet. Search engines provide instant access to a multitude of both reputable and questionable sources. The discerning student is well served by this information explosion; he or she can find up-to-date research on virtually all topics covered in this text, for example. However, many people acquire information—but not necessarily knowledge—by clicking links, entering chat rooms, reading blogs, and following friends who may or may not be providing legitimate data. Thus, the selective and careful use of information technology is a critical skill for all students to acquire.

This text presents criminal behavior as a vastly complex, sometimes difficult-to-understand phenomenon. Readers looking for simple solutions will have to either reorient their thinking, set the text aside, or read it in dismay. There is no all-encompassing psychological explanation for crime, any more than there is a sociological, anthropological, psychiatric, economic, or historic one. In fact, it is unlikely that sociology, psychology, or any other discipline can formulate basic "truths" about crime without help from other disciplines and well-designed research. Criminology needs all the interdisciplinary help it can get to explain and control criminal behavior. An integration of the data, theories, and general viewpoints of each discipline is crucial. To review accurately and adequately the plethora of studies and theories from each relevant discipline is far beyond the scope of this text, however. Our focus is the *psychological perspective*, although other viewpoints are also described.

Our primary goal is to review and integrate recent scholarship and research in the psychology of crime, compare it with traditional approaches, and offer some strategies for the prevention and modification of criminal behavior. We cannot begin to accomplish this task without first calling attention to philosophical questions that underlie any study of human behavior, including criminal behavior.

THEORIES OF CRIME

In everyday conversation, the term *theory* is used loosely. It may refer to personal experiences, observations, traditional beliefs, a set of opinions, or a collection of abstract thoughts. Almost everyone has personal theories about human behavior, and these extend to criminal behavior. To illustrate, some people have a personal theory that the world is a just place, where one gets what one deserves. "Just-worlders" believe that things just do not happen to people without a reason that is closely related to their own actions; for example, individuals who experience financial difficulties probably brought these on themselves. In 2008–2009, when many homeowners in the

United States were facing foreclosure because they could not afford high mortgage payments, a just-worlder would be likely to say this was more their own fault than the fault of bank officers who enticed them into paying high interest rates. Just-worlders also believe good people are ultimately rewarded and bad people are ultimately punished. If you work hard and honestly, good things will happen to you. Laziness and dishonesty, on the other hand, will lead to limited success and potential poverty. In reference to crime, just-worlders may believe that rape victims must have behaved seductively, or that battered spouses must have provoked their beatings, especially if there is no other available reason for explaining such behaviors.

The above beliefs represent individual theories or assumptions about how the world works. However, psychologists have also developed a somewhat more elaborate scientific theory based on just-world ideas and developed a scale to measure one's just-world orientation (Lerner, 1980; Lerner & Miller, 1978). A variety of hypotheses—sometimes discussed under the umbrella term **just-world hypothesis**—have been proposed and tested. For example, just-worlders have been hypothesized and shown to favor capital punishment and to be politically conservative. Interestingly, the most recent research on just-world theory has also identified two tracks: belief in a general just-world—described above—and belief in a personal just-world (Dalbert, 1999; Sutton & Douglas, 2005). Belief in a personal just-world ("I usually get what I deserve") is considered adaptive and helpful in coping with dire circumstances in one's life. For example, Dalbert and Filke (2007) found that prisoners with a high personal just-world orientation evaluated their prison experiences more positively and reported better overall well-being than those without such an orientation.

Scientific theories like the above are based on logic and research, but they vary widely in complexity. A scientific theory is "a set of interrelated constructs (concepts), definitions, and propositions that present a systematic view of phenomena by specifying relations among variables, with the purpose of explaining and predicting the phenomena" (Kerlinger, 1973, p. 9). A scientific theory of crime, therefore, should provide a general explanation that encompasses and *systematically* connects many different social, economic, and psychological variables to criminal behavior, and it should be supported by well-executed research. Moreover, the terms in any scientific theory must be as precise as possible, their meaning and usage clear and unambiguous, so that it can be meaningfully tested by observation and analysis. The process of theory testing is called **theory verification**. If the theory is not verified—indeed, if any of its propositions is not verified—the end result is falsification (Popper, 1968). For example, a theory that includes the proposition that all sex offenders were sexually abused as children would be falsified as soon as one nonabused sex offender was encountered.

The primary purpose of theories of crime is to identify the causes of criminal behavior. Some are broad and encompassing, whereas others are narrow and specific. Basically, theories of criminal behavior are summary statements of a collection of research findings. Perhaps more importantly, theories provide direction for further research. If one component of a theory is falsified or not supported, the theory is not necessarily rejected outright, however. It can be modified and re-tested. In addition, each theory of crime has implications for policy or decisions made by society to prevent crime.

Theories of crime have been around for centuries. During the eighteenth century, the Italian professor Cesare Beccaria (1738–1794) developed a theory that human behavior is fundamentally driven by a choice between the amount of pleasure gained over the amount of pain or punishment experienced. Beccaria argued that in order to reduce or stop criminal offending in any given society, the punishment should be swift, certain, and severe enough to deter people from the criminal (pleasure-seeking) act. If people realized in advance that severe punishment would be forthcoming regardless of their social status or privileges, they would choose not to engage in illegal behavior. This theoretical thinking, which emphasizes free will as the hallmark of human behavior, has become known as **classical theory**. Both criminal and civil law are rooted in the theory that individuals are masters of their fate, the possessors of free will and freedom of choice. As one federal appellate court put it, "our jurisprudence . . . while not oblivious to deterministic components, ultimately rests on a premise of freedom of will" (*U.S. v. Brawner*, 1972, p. 995). It should be noted that many crime prevention approaches are consistent with classical theory. For example, surveillance cameras on the streets and harsh sentences assume that individuals choose to commit crime but may be persuaded not to under the threat of being discovered or being punished with long prison time.

Another thread of theoretical thought is called **positivist theory**, which is closely aligned with the idea of determinism. It is the theory that antecedents—prior experiences or influences—determine present behavior. According to this line of theoretical thinking, human behavior is governed by causal laws, and free will is undermined. In its extreme form, determinism asserts that all behavior is determined by antecedent events and that all human behavior, therefore, is fundamentally lawful. "Lawful" in this context refers to predictability and not the laws established by society. Many contemporary theories of criminology are positivist because they search for causes beyond free will.

In summary, the classical view of crime and delinquency holds that the decision to violate the law is largely a result of free will. The positivist or deterministic perspective argues that most criminal behavior is a result of social, psychological, and even biological influences. This latter perspective is more concerned with identifying causes and predicting and preventing criminal behavior.

Theoretical Perspectives on Human Nature

All psychological theories of crime—and many sociological ones as well—have underlying assumptions about or perspectives on human nature. Three major ones can be identified. The **conformity perspective** views humans as creatures of conformity who want to do the "right" thing. To a large extent, this assumption represents the foundation of the humanistic perspectives in psychology. Human beings are basically "good" people trying to live to their fullest potential.

An excellent example of the conformity perspective in criminology is the **strain theory** of Robert K. Merton (1957). Merton's strain theory argues that humans are fundamentally conforming beings who are strongly influenced by the values and attitudes of the society in which they live. In short, most members of a given society desire what the other members of the society desire. The "right" thing, therefore, is what a society or a group within a society says is the "right" thing. American society, according to strain theorists, advocates that the accumulation of wealth or status is all-important and represents the symbols that all members should strive for. Strain theorists contend that humans, being fundamentally conformists, readily buy into these notions. However, access and the means for reaching these well-advertised goals are not equally available to everyone. Some have the education, the social network, personal contacts, and family influence to attain these goals. The socially and economically disadvantaged, however, do not have the opportunities, the education, or the necessary social network for attaining material wealth and economic or political power. Thus, the strain theory predicts that crime and delinquency occur when there is a perceived discrepancy between the materialistic values and goals cherished and held in high esteem by a society and the availability of the legitimate means for reaching these goals. Under these conditions, a strain between the goals of wealth and power and the means for reaching them develops. Groups and individuals experiencing a high level of this strain are forced to decide whether to violate norms and laws to attain some of this sought-after wealth or power, or give up on the American dream and go through the motions, withdraw, or rebel. In more recent years, strain theorists have emphasized that crimes of the rich and powerful also can be explained by strain theory. Even though these individuals have greater access to the legitimate means of reaching goals, they have a continuing need to accumulate even greater wealth and power and maintain their privileged status in society (Messner & Rosenfeld, 1994).

A second perspective—the **nonconformist perspective**—assumes that human beings are basically undisciplined creatures who, without the constraints of the rules and regulations of a given society, would flout society's conventions and commit crime indiscriminately. This perspective sees humans as fundamentally "unruly" and deviant if allowed to do what they feel like doing. Good illustrations of this perspective are found in biological and neurobiological theories, and in Travis Hirschi's (1969) social control theory. **Social control theory** contends that crime and delinquency occur when an individual's ties to the conventional order or normative standards are weak or largely nonexistent. In other words, the socialization that normally holds one's basic human nature in check is incomplete or faulty. This position perceives human nature as fundamentally "bad" or "antisocial," an innate tendency that must be *controlled* by society.

The third perspective—the **learning perspective**—sees human beings as born neutral (neither inherently conforming nor unruly). This perspective argues that humans learn virtually all their behavior, beliefs, and tendencies from the social environment. The learning perspective is exemplified most comprehensively by **social learning theory**, and Edwin H. Sutherland's (1947) **differential association theory**. Social learning theory emphasizes such concepts as imitation of models and reinforcements one gains from one's behavior. According to differential association theory, criminal behavior is learned, as is all social behavior, through social interactions with other people. It is not the result of emotional disturbance, mental illness, or innate qualities of "goodness" or "badness." Rather, people learn to be criminal as a result of messages they get from others who were also taught to be criminal. Consequently, an excess of "messages" favorable to law violation over unfavorable messages promotes criminal activity. The conventional wisdom that bad company promotes bad behavior, therefore, finds validity in differential association theory. **Table 1** summarizes these three perspectives and provides examples of each.

Another way of looking at human nature is the **difference-in-kind** and the **difference-in-degrees** perspective. The difference-in-degrees perspective holds that human beings may be placed along a continuum consisting of all the animals in the known universe. According to this perspective, humans are intimately tied to their animal ancestry in important and significant ways. For example, this perspective might argue that human aggression and violence is a result of innate, biological needs to obtain sufficient food supplies, territory, status, or mates. In many ways, this approach is similar to the nonconformist point of view. Also, the rapidly developing field of evolutionary psychology generally subscribes to this approach. Evolutionary psychology claims that human cognitive and emotional processes have been selected in our evolutionary environment as devices for solving particular adaptive problems faced by the Pleistocene hunter-gatherers (Bereczkei, 2000; Buss & Shackelford, 1997). Evolutionary psychologists stress that Darwinian theory provides ultimate explanations of many types of antisocial behavior (Quinsey, Skilling, Lalumière, & Craig, 2004).

The difference-in-kind perspective, on the other hand, argues that humans are distinctly different from other animals—spiritually, psychologically, and mentally. Noteworthy neurobiologists

TABLE 1   Perspectives of Human Nature

Perspectives of Behavior	Theory Example	Humans are . . .
Conformity Perspective	Strain Theory (Merton)	Basically good; strongly influenced by the values and attitudes of society
Nonconformist Perspective	Social Control Theory (Hirschi) Biological Theories of Crime	Basically undisciplined; individual's ties to social order are weak; innate tendencies must be controlled by society
Learning Perspective	Differential Association Theory (Sutherland) Social Learning Theory (Rotter, Bandura)	Born neutral; behavior is learned through social interactions with other people

and pioneer brain researchers, such as Sir John Eccles (Eccles & Robinson, 1984), Roger Sperry (1983), and Wilder Penfield (1975), have concluded that humans differ radically in kind from all other animals. According to the difference-in-kind viewpoint, we will understand crime better if we study and build theories based on those human qualities that differ significantly from subhuman features. Consequently, this perspective sees antisocial or criminal behavior as a unique human attribute generated primarily by human cognitive processes.

PERSPECTIVES IN CRIMINOLOGY

Criminology is the multidisciplinary study of crime. Many disciplines are involved in the collection of knowledge about criminal action, including psychology, sociology, psychiatry, anthropology, biology, neurology, political science, and economics. Over the years, the study of crime has been dominated by three disciplines—sociology, psychology, and psychiatry—but other disciplines or subdisciplines, such as economics and the biological sciences are becoming more actively involved.

Although our main concern is with *psychological principles,* concepts, theory, and research relevant to criminal behavior, considerable attention is placed on the research knowledge of the other disciplines, particularly sociology, psychiatry, and biology. Again, criminology needs all the help it can get in its struggle to understand, explain, prevent, and change criminal behavior.

It is not easy to make sharp demarcations between disciplines, because they overlap considerably in focus and practice. For example, what distinguishes a given theory as sociological, psychological, or psychiatric is sometimes simply the stated professional affiliation of its proponent. The reader should also realize that condensing any major discipline into a few pages hardly does it justice. To obtain a more adequate overview, the interested reader should consult texts and articles within those disciplines. **Table 2** summarizes these perspectives.

Sociological Criminology

Sociological criminology has a rich tradition in examining the relationships of demographic and group variables to crime. Variables such as age, race, gender, socioeconomic status, and ethnic-cultural affiliation have been shown to have significant relationships with certain categories and

TABLE 2 Major Perspectives in Criminology

Perspective	Influence	Focus
Sociological Criminology	Sociology	Examines relationships of demographic and group variables to crime; focuses on groups and society as a whole and how they influence criminal activity
Psychological Criminology	Psychology	Focuses on individual criminal behavior; the science of the behavior and mental processes of the criminal
Psychiatric Criminology	Psychiatry	The contemporary perspective examines the interplay between psychobiological determinants of behavior and the social environment; traditional perspective looks for the unconscious and biological determinants of criminal behavior

patterns of crimes. Sociological criminology, for example, has allowed us to conclude that young African American males from disadvantaged backgrounds are disproportionately overrepresented as both perpetrators and victims of homicide. The many reasons for this overrepresentation are reflected in the various perspectives and research findings here. Sociological criminology also probes the situational or environmental factors that are most conducive to criminal action, such as the time, place, kind of weapons used, and the circumstances surrounding the crime.

A major contribution of sociological criminology, however, is the attention it directs to topics that reflect unequal distribution of power in society. This often takes the form of examining how crime is defined and how laws are enforced. It also addresses the underlying social conditions that may encourage criminal behavior, such as inequities in educational and employment opportunities. Conflict theories in sociology are particularly influential in questioning how crime is defined, who is subject to punishment, and in attempting to draw attention to the crimes of the rich and powerful.

Psychological Criminology

Psychology is the science of behavior and mental processes. **Psychological criminology**, then, is the science of the behavior and mental processes of the person who commits crime. While sociological criminology focuses primarily on groups and society as a whole, and how they influence criminal activity, psychological criminology focuses on individual criminal behavior—how it is acquired, evoked, maintained, and modified.

In the psychology of crime, both social and personality influences on criminal behavior are considered, along with the mental processes that mediate that behavior. Personality refers to all the biological influences, psychological traits, and cognitive features of the human being that psychologists have identified as important in the mediation and control of behavior. Recently, psychological criminology has shifted its focus to a more *cognitive, neuropsychological,* and *developmental* approach to the study of criminal behavior, although interest in personality differences among offenders continues. **Cognitions** refer to the attitudes, beliefs, values, and thoughts that a person holds about the social environment, interrelations, human nature, and him- or herself. In serious criminal offenders, these cognitions are often distorted. Beliefs that children must be severely physically disciplined or that victims are not really hurt by burglary are good examples of cognitions that may lead to criminal activity. Prejudice is also a cognition that involves distortions of social reality. They include erroneous generalizations and oversimplification about others. Hate crimes are generally rooted in prejudice and cognitive distortions held by perpetrators. Serial rapists also distort social reality to the point where they may assault only victims who "deserve it." Offender cognitions are important in understanding criminal behavior.

The neuropsychology of criminal behavior is a specialty that combines the scientific study of the nervous system with psychology and crime. This perspective studies to what extent damage, deficits, or abnormality of the brain may be related to antisocial behavior, particularly violent behavior. Compromised neuropsychological functioning may be associated with aggression and violent behavior. For example, a traumatic brain injury (TBI), such as one that might occur in a traffic accident, may produce personality changes, including increased aggressive behavior (Gurley & Marcus, 2008). In addition, we will learn that practices designed to improve neuropsychological functioning and prevent neuropsychological impairment early in life are likely to be major steps in understanding and reducing antisocial behavior.

Another area that is extremely important in understanding criminal behavior is learning how it develops. A **developmental approach** examines the changes and influences across a person's lifetime that may contribute to the formation of antisocial and criminal behavior, sometimes called "risk factors." Examples are poor nutrition, the loss of a parent, or substandard housing or education. However, the developmental approach also searches for "protective factors," or influences that provide individuals with a buffer against the risk factors. A caring adult mentor and good social skills are examples of protective factors. If we are able to identify those changes and influences that occur across the developmental pathways of life that divert a person from becoming caring, sensitive, and prosocial, as well as those that steer a person away from a life of persistent and serious antisocial behavior, we gain invaluable information about how to prevent and change delinquent and criminal behavior. Consequently, psychological criminology develops, examines, and evaluates strategies and interventions that have the potential to prevent or reduce criminal behavior.

In the past, psychologists assumed that they could best understand human behavior by searching for stable, consistent personality **dispositions** or **traits** that exerted widely generalized effects on behavior. A trait or disposition is a relatively stable and enduring tendency to behave in a particular way, and it distinguishes one person from another. For example, one person may be extroverted and have a consistent tendency to socialize and meet others, while another may be shy and introverted and demonstrate a tendency to socialize with only very close friends. Trait theories hold that people show consistent behavior across time and place, and that these behaviors characterize personality. Many psychologists studying crime, therefore, assumed they should search for the personality traits or variables underlying criminal behavior. They paid less attention to the person's environment or situation. Presumably, once personality variables were identified, it would be possible to determine and predict which individual was most likely to engage in criminal behavior.

As you will learn, the search for any *single* personality type of the murderer, rapist, abuser, or burglar has not been fruitful. Contemporary perspectives in the psychology of crime still include personality or behavior traits in their explanations of crime, but they also include cognitions, neuropsychology, and developmental factors in these explanations. Psychologists who provide law enforcement agencies with profiles of the serial rapist or killer still at large, based *solely on personality variables,* are at best engaging in unvalidated clinical judgment and unsubstantiated hunches. However, psychologists can offer *statistical probability* about some *demographic and behavioral patterns* of certain offenders. For example, they might determine, roughly, that a rapist is *probably* young, white, unemployed, from the area, and so forth. They might also offer possible motives for the attack, based on research findings and accompanied by the necessary warnings that this particular offender may not fit those criteria. This "profile" information, however, is based on the knowledge collected from all sectors of criminology, including psychology, sociology, anthropology, psychiatry, political science, history, and economics.

Thus, while trait psychology standing alone has lost favor, some aspects of this approach have survived, primarily in the profiling endeavor. **Criminal profiling** refers to the process of identifying personality traits, behavioral tendencies, geographic location, and demographic variables of an offender based on characteristics of the crime (Bartol & Bartol, 2008). To a very large extent, the profiling process is dictated by a database collected on previous offenders who have committed similar offenses. Basically, profiling is a form of behavioral assessment and prediction. It should be emphasized early in this text that criminal profiling is not restricted to serial murder or serial sexual assaults, but has considerable value when applied successfully to other crimes, including arson, burglary, shoplifting, and robbery.

Psychiatric Criminology

The terms *psychology* and *psychiatry* are often confused by the lay person and even by professionals and scholars in other disciplines. Many psychiatrists, like psychologists, work in a variety of forensic settings, ranging from providing expert testimony in the courtroom, to offering psychiatric services to correctional facilities and law enforcement agencies. Psychiatrists and psychologists who are closely associated with the courts and other legal arenas are often referred to as forensic psychiatrists or forensic psychologists.

Psychiatric concepts and theories are often believed to be accepted tenets in the field of psychology. However, the two professions often see things quite differently and approach explanations of criminal behavior along a different course. Part of this difference is due to the dissimilarity in the educational requirements for the two professions. Unlike psychologists, who have earned a PhD (doctor of philosophy), PsyD (doctorate in psychology), or, in some cases, an EdD (doctorate in education), and who often complete specialized training in research and some area of psychology, psychiatrists first earn a medical degree (MD or a DO [doctor of osteopathy]) and complete a medical internship, as other physicians do. Then, during a two- or three-year residency program in psychiatry, they receive specific training in psychiatry, often focusing on the diagnosis and treatment of individuals in forensic settings, such as court clinics or mental hospitals with special units for mentally disordered individuals accused of crime. Understandably, this medical training encourages a biochemical and neurological approach to explanations of human behavior, and this is often reflected in the psychiatric theories of criminal behavior.

By contrast, many psychologists receive a one-year internship focusing on clinical training, which is often followed by a one- to three-year postdoctoral program focusing on both research and practice. In a majority of cases, the psychologist completes these training steps before practicing professionally. The emphasis of this training is usually far more on the cognitive (thought processes), developmental, and learned behavior of human action and less on the biochemical or neurological influences.

Traditionally, psychologists have not been permitted by law to prescribe medication to patients. However, this distinction between the two professions is beginning to disappear. In 2002, New Mexico became the first state in the United States to allow psychologists to prescribe psychoactive drugs (drugs designed to treat psychological problems). Twelve states have rejected such privileges, however. Several other states currently have pending legislation on prescription privileges for psychologists. This is a controversial issue on which even psychologists themselves disagree, but it is likely that in the years to come, properly trained psychologists will be able to prescribe psychoactive drugs in other states.

Psychoanalytic Tradition

American psychiatric criminology has *traditionally* followed the Freudian, psychoanalytic, or psychodynamic tradition. The father of the psychoanalytical theory of human behavior was the physician-neurologist Sigmund Freud (1856–1939), whose followers are called Freudians. Many contemporary psychoanalysts subscribe to a modified version of the orthodox Freudian position and are therefore called neo-Freudians. Still other psychoanalysts follow the tenets of Alfred Adler and Carl Jung, who broke away from Freud and developed different theories about the human condition. A very influential psychoanalyst in recent times is Erik Erikson, who developed a theory of development that included eight stages. According to Erikson, ego identity is gradually achieved by facing positive goals and negative risks during eight stages across the life span. The degree of achievement in ego identity—or the progress one has made in reaching the various stages—may influence the tendency to commit crime.

Collectively, all psychoanalytic positions form the psychodynamic approach, which explains behavior in terms of motives and drives. This perspective views human nature as innately antisocial, similar to the noncomformist perspective and the difference-in-degree orientation discussed earlier. That is, humans are biologically driven to get what they want when they want it unless they are held in check by internal (conscience) and external (society) forces. Without an organized society with rules and laws, humans (especially men because of their biology) would aggress, plunder, steal, and even kill at will.

The psychoanalytic position assumes that we must delve into the abysses of human personality to find unconscious determinants of human behavior, including criminal behavior. Consider the following comments by two forensic psychiatrists: "The criminal rarely knows completely the reasons for his conduct" (Abrahamsen, 1952, p. 21). "Every criminal is such by reason of unconscious forces within him" (Roche, 1958, p. 25). Psychoanalytic and psychodynamic theories acknowledge that behavior varies across situations. However, they conclude that there are enduring and generalized underlying dynamic or motivational dispositions that account for this diversity. "Surface" behaviors indirectly signal or symbolize dynamic, underlying attributes. Psychological defenses distort and disguise the "true" meaning of external or observed behaviors. The trained clinician, therefore, must interpret the significance of these external behaviors, since the actor is not aware of their purpose.

The Freudian, psychoanalytic, and psychodynamic positions strongly endorse the view that the prime determinant of human behavior lies within the person, and that after the first few years of life, the environment plays a very minor role. Consequently, criminal behavior is believed to spring from within, primarily dictated by the biological urges of the unconscious. The environment, culture, or society cannot be held responsible for crime rates; biopsychological needs and urges within the individual are the culprits.

It would be unfair, however, to simply classify *contemporary* psychiatric criminology or forensic psychiatry as heavily Freudian, psychoanalytical, or psychodynamic in perspective. Contemporary **psychiatric criminology** is far more diverse, increasingly research based, and is considerably less steeped in the traditional belief that criminals are acting out their uncontrolled animalistic, unconscious, or biological urges. Therefore, *traditional* psychiatric criminology is distinguished from *contemporary* psychiatric criminology throughout the text. The traditional psychiatric view represents the biologically unconscious urges that drive humans, whereas the contemporary psychiatric view of crime represents the diverse and rich knowledge gained through research and clinical experience. Whenever possible, we rely on the more contemporary view of psychiatric criminology.

DEFINING AND MEASURING CRIME

As defined at the beginning of the chapter, *criminal behavior is intentional behavior that violates a criminal code, intentional in that it did not occur accidentally or without justification or excuse.* Since crime encompasses so many types of behavior, should we restrict ourselves to a legal definition and study only those individuals who have been convicted of behaviors legally defined as crime? Or should we include individuals who indulge in antisocial behaviors but have not been detected by the criminal justice system? Perhaps our study should include persons predisposed to be criminal, if such persons can be identified. As a review of criminology textbooks and literature attests, there is no universal agreement as to what group or groups should be targeted for study.

If we abide strictly by the legal definition of crime and base research and discussion only on those people who have committed crimes, do we consider only those who have been convicted and incarcerated or serving a sentence in the community, or do we include those who have "probably" broken the criminal law but have not been convicted? Even by conservative estimates, 16 percent to 18 percent of the total U.S. population has arrest records for nontraffic offenses (U.S. Department of Justice, 1988). While some of these individuals are "truly criminal," an undetermined number of others were arrested but were not truly guilty. Furthermore, how can we include individuals who violate the law but escape detection or those who come to the attention of law enforcement officials but are never arrested?

Trying to study criminal behavior on the basis of incidence presents other problems for social scientists. The incidence of crime is usually measured in one of three ways:

1. Official police reports of reported crime and arrests, such as those tabulated and forwarded to the Federal Bureau of Investigation for publication in its annual national statistical report on crime, the **Uniform Crime Reports**
2. Self-report studies, whereby members of a sample population are asked what offenses they have committed and how often
3. National or regional victimization studies, which sample a population of households or businesses asking respondents how often they have been victims of specified crimes

Uniform Crime Reporting System

The Federal Bureau of Investigation's (FBI) **Uniform Crime Reporting (UCR)** Program, compiled since 1930, is the most-cited source of U.S. crime statistics. The UCR Program publishes an annual document containing accounts of crimes known to police and information on arrests received on a voluntary basis from local and state law enforcement agencies throughout the United States. The UCR data are available on the FBI Web site (www.fbi.gov). Interestingly, federal law enforcement agencies do not report through the traditional UCR Program, although a newly revised reporting system has been implemented that requires federal agencies to report. This new system—called the *National Incident-Based Reporting System*—is described shortly.

The first UCR data were published with fewer than a thousand agencies reporting. The 2007 UCR data collection was based on nearly eighteen thousand city, county, and state law enforcement agencies, representing about 95 percent of the U.S. population (Federal Bureau of Investigation, 2008). The UCR Program is the only major data source permitting a comparison of national data broken down by age, sex, race, and offense. A *Supplementary Homicide Report* contains data on victim and offender demographics, the offender-victim relationship, the weapon used, and the circumstances surrounding the homicide. Additionally, the FBI provides special reports on hate crimes, campus crimes, and law enforcement officers killed in the line of duty. A special report was also prepared to cover the events of September 11, 2001.

The UCR provides a variety of information relating to crimes that come to the attention of police, including the age, gender, and race of persons arrested, and the city and region where the crime was committed. Prior to 2004, the UCR labeled serious crimes as **index crimes** or **Part I crimes**, and nonserious crimes as **nonindex crimes** or **Part II crimes**. Index crimes were considered to be "indicators" of the crime problem in the United States. However, this distinction was found to be misleading. For instance, larceny-theft, which includes shoplifting, was categorized as an index crime, whereas fraud and drug offenses were classified as nonindex crimes. Moreover, larceny-theft makes up 60 percent of the total reported crime, and the enormous volume of these offenses overshadows more serious but less frequently committed offenses (Federal Bureau of Investigation, 2008). Consequently, since 2004, the term *index crime* has disappeared, but the Part I and Part II designations have remained (see **Table 3** for definitions of these crimes). Part I crimes are subdivided into violent and property offenses.

Violent crime comprises four offenses: murder and nonnegligent manslaughter, forcible rape, robbery, and aggravated assault. Each of these offenses involves force or the threat of force. Property crime includes burglary, larceny-theft, motor vehicle theft, and arson. The primary objective of the offender in property crime is the taking or destruction of money or property. Arson is included in property crime because it involves the destruction of property, but it may result in the loss of life or serious injury.

For all Part I crimes, the UCR provides information on the crime known to police (reported crime), as well as arrests. Only arrest data are provided for Part II crimes. Thus, in order to appear in the UCR as a Part I crime, a crime must, at a minimum, meet the following requirements:

- Be perceived by the victim or by someone else
- Be defined as a crime by the victim or the observer
- In some way become known to a law enforcement agency as a crime
- Be defined by that law enforcement agency as a crime
- Be accurately recorded by the law enforcement agency
- Be reported to the FBI compilation center

It should be emphasized that the UCR provides crime rate data on the eight Part I crimes listed above. The crime rate is the percentage of crime known to police per 100,000 population. For example, in 2007, the murder rate was 5.6, meaning there were 5.6 murders known to police for every 100,000 population. Part II offenses, for which only arrest data are provided, encompass all crimes, except traffic violations, which are not classified as Part I offenses. If a victim reports a simple assault (a Part II crime), that assault would not be included in the *crime rate*. However, the *arrest* of one or more individuals for that simple assault would appear in the UCR.

TABLE 3   Definitions of Part I and Part II Crimes in Uniform Crime Reports

Part I Crime

Murder and nonnegligent manslaughter	The willful (nonnegligent) killing of one human by another
Forcible rape	The carnal knowledge of a female forcibly and against her will
Robbery	The taking or attempting to take anything of value from the care, custody, or control of a person or persons by force or threat of force or violence and/or by putting the victim in fear
Aggravated assault	An unlawful attack by one person on another for the purpose of inflicting severe or aggravated bodily injury; attempts to inflict injury are also included
Burglary	The unlawful entry of a structure to commit a felony or theft
Larceny-theft	The unlawful taking, carrying, leading, or riding away with of property from the possession or constructive possession of another; includes crimes such as shoplifting, pocket picking, purse snatching, thefts from motor vehicles, and bicycle thefts
Arson	Any willful or malicious burning or attempt to burn, with or without intent to defraud, a dwelling house, public building, motor vehicle or aircraft, or personal property of another

Common Part II Crimes

Simple assaults	Assaults and attempted assaults in which no weapon is used and which do not result in serious or aggravated injury to victim
Forgery and counterfeiting	Making, altering, uttering, or possessing, with intent to defraud, anything false in the semblance of that which is true
Fraud	Fraudulent conversion and obtaining money or property by false pretenses
Embezzlement	Misappropriation or misapplication of money entrusted to one's care, custody, or control
Stolen property	Buying, receiving, and possessing stolen property, including attempts to do so
Offenses against the family and children	Unlawful nonviolent acts by a family member that threaten the physical, mental, or economic well-being or morals of another family member; does not include assault or sex offenses
Sex offenses	Statutory rape, offenses against chastity, common decency, and morals
Drug abuse violations	State and/or local offenses relating to the unlawful possession, sale, use, growing, and manufacture of drugs
Gambling	Promoting, permitting, or engaging in illegal gambling
Vandalism	Willful or malicious destruction, injury, disfigurement, or defacement of any public or private property, real or personal, without the consent of the owner or persons having custody or control

Source: Federal Bureau of Investigation (2008).

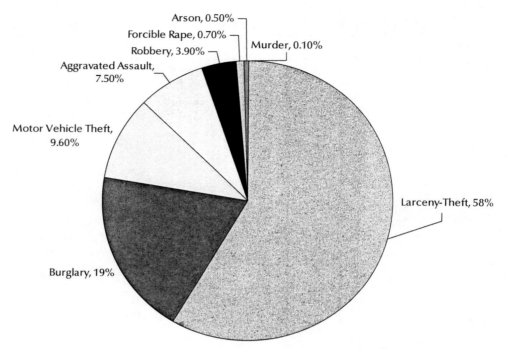

FIGURE 1   Percent Distribution of Part I Crimes, 2007   *Source*: Federal Bureau of Investigation, 2008.

On a regular yearly basis, if we look at crimes known to police, the property crime of larceny-theft, which usually comprises approximately 60 percent of the Part I crimes, is the most frequently occurring of all Part I crimes (see **Figure 1**). The violent crime of murder occurs the least frequently of all Part I crimes, accounting for only 0.1 percent of the total Part I crimes.

The UCR also reports the **clearance rate** of all Part I crimes. An offense is cleared when at least one person is arrested, charged with the commission of the offense, and remanded to the court for prosecution (Federal Bureau of Investigation, 2005b). An offense may also be cleared by exceptional means when something happens to an offender outside the control of the reporting law enforcement agency. For example, if a person about to be arrested for rape commits suicide, the crime will likely be cleared. As another example, when someone under the age of 18 is required to appear in juvenile court or before other juvenile authorities, the incident is considered cleared by arrest, even though a physical arrest may not have occurred. In 2007, 44.5 percent of violent crime in the United States and 16.4 percent of property offenses were cleared by arrest or exceptional means. Usually, murder has the highest clearance rate. In 2007, law enforcement agencies cleared 61.2 percent of murders (see **Table 4** for an illustration of clearance rates).

UCR Problems

UCR data are not without problems. One of the most frequently mentioned shortcomings is the **hierarchy rule**, which stipulates that when a number of offenses have been committed during a series, only the more serious offense is included in the UCR data. For example, if an offender robs

TABLE 4   2007 Clearance Rates for Part I Crimes

Violent Crime	**44.5%**
Murder	61.2%
Rape	40.0%
Robbery	25.9%
Aggravated assault	54.1%
Property Crime	**16.5%**
Burglary	12.4%
Larceny-theft	18.6%
Motor vehicle theft	12.6%
Arson	18.0%

Source: Federal Bureau of Investigation (2008).

a bank, murders the bank security officer, viciously assaults a bystander, and steals a car, only the murder will appear in the UCR.

The compilation center also relies on the accuracy and compliance of local and state agencies to report crime statistics. The data also do not consider early discretionary decision making by law enforcement officers, such as a decision not to "found" a crime when it is reported by a member of the public or a decision not to arrest an individual. In addition, the Part I category emphasizes street crime to the neglect of the equally serious "white-collar" crime, which includes a wide variety of offenses such as corporate, political, and professional crimes.

Official crime statistics, like those of the UCR Program, are generally believed to underestimate most criminal offenses and are routinely criticized for errors and omissions. The overall number of criminal offenses that go undetected or are unknown by law enforcement agencies, known as the **dark figure**, is difficult to estimate, but data from an early victimization survey conducted by the U.S. Census Bureau suggest that out of every 100 offenses committed, 72 are never recorded in the official statistics (Skogan, 1977). However, Skogan also notes that most unreported violations appear to be minor property offenses rather than more serious crimes. As we see shortly, though, more recent victimization studies indicate that many serious crimes are not reported to police.

The National Incident-Based Reporting System

During the late 1970s, the law enforcement community called for the expanded use of the UCR and more detailed information on crime than the statistics offered in the UCR. In response, the UCR reporting system was evaluated under federal contract by ABT Associates of Cambridge, Massachusetts. Recommendations of the research firm are reported in *A Blueprint for the Future of the Uniform Crime Reporting System,* published in 1985. These recommendations formed the basis of the **National Incident-Based Reporting System (NIBRS)** under the Uniform Federal Crime Reporting Act passed by the U.S. Congress in 1988 (Public Law No. 100-690, 102 Stat. 4181). In this act, Congress required all federal law enforcement agencies, including those agencies within the Department of Defense, to collect and report data to the FBI on two categories of offenses: Group A, which includes 46 serious offense categories such as arson, assault, homicide, fraud, embezzlement, larceny-theft, and sex offenses; and Group B, which includes 11 less serious offenses, such as passing bad checks, driving under the influence of alcohol, engaging in disorderly conduct, drunkenness, nonviolent family offenses, and liquor law violations (see **Table 5** for a list of Group A offenses).

In the *Group A Incident Report* information, a crime is viewed along with all its aspects. For example, the report of a crime includes information about the victim, weapon, location of the crime, alcohol/drug influence, type of criminal activity, relationship of victim to alleged offender, residence of victims and arrestees (if someone was arrested), and a description of property and its value. Presumably, this added information is an indispensable tool for law enforcement agencies

---

TABLE 5   National Incident-Based Reporting System (NIBRS) Group A Offenses

Arson	*Homicide offenses*
Assault offenses	Murder/nonnegligent manslaughter
Aggravated assault	Negligent manslaughter
Simple assault	Justifiable homicide
Intimidation	*Kidnapping/abduction*
Bribery	*Larceny-theft offenses*
Burglary/breaking and entering	Pocket picking
Counterfeiting/forgery	Purse snatching
Destruction/damage/vandalism of property	Shoplifting
Drug/narcotic offenses	Theft from building
Drug/narcotic violations	Theft from coin-operated machines
Drug/equipment violations	Theft from motor vehicle
Embezzlement	Theft of motor vehicle parts/accessories
Extortion/blackmail	Motor vehicle theft
Fraud offenses	Pornography/obscene materials
False pretenses/swindle/confidence game	*Prostitution offenses*
Credit card/ATM fraud	Prostitution
Impersonation	Assisting or promoting prostitution
Welfare fraud	*Robbery*
Wire fraud	*Sex offenses, forcible*
Gambling offenses	Forcible rape
Betting/wagering	Forcible sodomy
Operating/promoting/assisting gambling	Sexual assault with an object
Gambling equipment violations	Forcible fondling
Sports tampering	*Sex offenses, nonforcible*
	Stolen property offenses
	Weapon law violations

Source: The National Center for the Analysis of Violent Crime, Annual Report, 1992 (Quantico, VA: FBI Academy, 1992), p. 22.

and researchers because it provides them with detailed data about when and where specific types of crime take place, what forms they take, and the characteristics of their victims and perpetrators. Like the Part II crimes in the UCR, the crimes in Group B include only information about the arrestee and the circumstances of the arrest.

States were also invited to participate in the project. State and federal agencies participating in the NIBRS use automated systems to report information on Group A and Group B offenses to the FBI on a monthly basis. In 2004, 5,271 law enforcement agencies participate in the NIBRS program, representing 20 percent of the U.S. population. Eventually, the NIBRS is expected to replace the FBI's traditional UCR that simply provides summary crime statistics.

The benefits of the NIBRS are primarily through the more precise information it provides to researchers and investigators about when and where crime takes place, its form, and the characteristics of its victims and offenders. Another primary objective of NIBRS is to get a better handle on the nature and extent of crimes involving illicit drugs.

Among the additional crime categories now followed by the FBI but not *traditionally* included in the Uniform Crime Reporting System or the NIBRS reports are hate crimes and terrorism.

Hate Crimes

In recent years, hate crime legislation and policy making has become prominent in many nations. In 1990, the U.S. Congress mandated that the U.S. Attorney General collect data on "hate" or bias crimes. Known as the **Hate Crime Statistics Act**, it requires data collection of violent attacks, intimidation, arson, or property damage that are directed at a person or group of persons because of race, religion, sexual orientation, or ethnicity. As we note below, additional categories have been added since that time. The Attorney General delegated the responsibilities of developing the procedures for implementing, collecting, and managing hate crime data to the Director of the FBI. The FBI defines a hate crime as "a criminal offense committed against a person, property, or society which is motivated, in whole or in part, by the offender's bias against race, religion, disability, sexual orientation, or ethnicity/national origin" (Federal Bureau of Investigation, 2002, p. 59). Note that this law pertains only to the gathering of statistics, not to the penalties prescribed for persons convicted of hate crimes.

In September 1994, the Violent Crime Control and Law Enforcement Act amended the Hate Crime Statistics Act to add disabilities, both physical and mental, to the hate crimes category. The disability bias data collection began in January 1997. Also, in 1994, Congress passed the Hate Crimes Sentencing Enhancement Act, which provides for longer sentences when the offense is determined to be a hate crime. Although the Hate Crimes Statistics Act of 1990 (amended in 1994 and 1996) defines a hate crime against a person or property as motivated by bias against race, religion, ethnicity/national origin, or sexual orientation, the FBI does not have any federal jurisdiction to *investigate* hate crimes motivated by a sexual orientation bias. Also, while the amended law covers disability bias, the FBI's authority to *investigate* these crimes is limited to incidents interfering with the victim's housing rights (Title 42, U.S.C., section 3631).

The Church Arson Prevention Act, signed into law in 1996, amended the Hate Crime Statistics Act by extending the type of data collected. The alarming increase of arson of churches prompted the passage of the Church Arson Prevention Act. Between October 1991 and May 1996, 110 incidents of church arson were reported to federal authorities, with 33 of them occurring during the early part of 1996. Although the burnings included synagogues, mosques, and church congregations, more than half involved African American places of worship located in the southeastern sections of the United States. In an effort to further extend hate crime statutory provisions, Congress passed the Hate Crime Prevention Act of 1999, which allows more authority for the federal government to investigate and prosecute hate crime offenders who committed their crime because of perceived sexual orientation, gender, or disability of the victim. Yet to be passed, though, is the Matthew Shepard Act, which will be discussed below.

In addition to the above federal laws, over 40 states and the District of Columbia have hate or bias crime statutes (Bartol & Bartol, 2004; Wessler & Moss, 2001). Almost all state jurisdictions that have these laws cover bias based on race, religion, ethnicity, and national origin, but significantly fewer states have statutes that cover bias based on gender, disability, or sexual orientation. Nearly all the state and federal statutes provide an enhancement of penalties once a person has been convicted of a bias or hate crime (Bartol & Bartol, 2004).

In accordance with the Hate Crime Statistics Act, hate crime data are collected for 11 traditional offense categories and are divided into two major classifications: crimes against persons and crimes against property. Crimes against persons include murder and nonnegligent manslaughter, forcible rape, aggravated assault, simple assault, and intimidation. Crimes against property include robbery, burglary, larceny-theft, motor vehicle theft, arson, and destruction/damage/vandalism of property. The data are submitted to the UCR by city, county, and state law enforcement agencies.

A victim of a hate crime may be a person, a business, or an institution, but hate crimes against individuals receive the most attention. These crimes often have long-term psychological and social repercussions that are extremely destructive to victims and their families. In 2007, nearly two out of every three hate crimes (57%) were crimes against persons, with intimidation being the most frequently reported (29%) (Federal Bureau of Investigation, 2008). Thirty-seven percent were property crimes motivated by bias against individuals or groups. Recent available data (2007) indicate that a majority of hate crimes are motivated by racial bias (52.5%), followed by ethnic/national origin bias (13.9%), religious bias (16.4%), sexual orientation bias (16.2%), and disability bias (0.9%) (Federal Bureau of Investigation, 2008) (see **Figure 2**). Vandalism was the most frequent hate crime against property, accounting for 60.7 percent of the total hate crime against property.

A vivid example of a hate crime occurred in early June 1998 in Jasper, Texas. James Byrd Jr., a 49-year-old African American, was walking home from a family party when he was offered a ride by three white men, all of them known white supremacists. The men drove Byrd to a remote dirt road where they severely beat him. Then Byrd was chained to their pickup truck by the ankles and dragged along the road, which tore his body to pieces. Police found Byrd's head, neck, right arm, torso, shoes, a wallet, and other personal items scattered along the route. A mile-long blood trail on the road marked the gruesome scene. Another high-profile hate crime was the 1998 murder of Matthew Shepard, a young gay man who was kidnapped, beaten, tied to a fencepost, and left to die. Shepard was found and hospitalized in a comatose state and died shortly thereafter. The two men responsible for his death, Aaron McKinney and Russell Henderson, are serving terms of life imprisonment without parole. In response to Shepard's death, a federal hate crime bill protecting individuals from hate crimes based on sexual orientation wound its way through Congress but was stalled under a threat of veto by then-President George W. Bush. President Barack Obama has indicated that passage of the Matthew Shepard Act will be a priority in his administration. In Spring 2009, during a debate in Congress over versions of the bill, one member of Congress insisted—with Matthew Shepard's mother in the audience—that this was an unfortunate robbery gone wrong, not a hate crime.

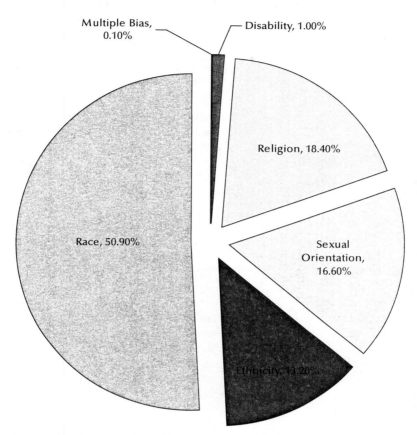

FIGURE 2   Bias-motivated Offenses Percent Distribution, 2007
Source: Federal Bureau of Investigation, 2008.

The Matthew Shepard Act would strengthen existing federal hate crime laws in three ways:

1. Expand the law to authorize the Department of Justice to investigate and prosecute certain bias-motivated crimes based on the victim's actual or perceived sexual orientation, gender, gender identity, or disability.
2. Eliminate the limitation in existing law which restricts the Department of Justice to investigating and prosecuting only bias motivated crimes that occur when the victim was engaged in a specifically federally-protected activity, such as voting, serving on a jury, or attending school.
3. Add the words "gender" and "gender identity" to the Hate Crime Statistics Act. (Recall that the HCSA does not now "count" hate crimes motivated by bias against a victim's gender.)

The Byrd and Shepard cases were publicized nationally and served to focus public attention on the problem of hate crimes against African Americans and gays and lesbians. Other groups and populations also are targeted by hate or bias crimes, however, and some are covered by the legislation under the ethnicity provision. Since the attacks of September 11, 2001, people of Arab or Muslim descent, or anyone with a "Middle Eastern look" (Rabrenovic, 2007), have increasingly been victims (Hendricks, Ortiz, Surgie, & Miller, 2007). Jews, women, veterans, Native Americans, and persons with physical and mental disabilities are examples of other group members victimized by prejudice.

Self-Report Studies

Many researchers believe that self-report (SR) studies provide a more accurate estimate of actual offenses than do UCR statistics, which are based on data provided by law enforcement. In self-report research, people report their own criminal or otherwise antisocial activity to researchers. Although respondents may inflate or deflate reports of their own criminal activity, proponents of this research strategy maintain that self-report offers a better approximation of criminal activity. In a dated but revealing SR survey (Wallerstein & Wyle, 1947), 1,698 persons were asked to indicate on a list of 49 criminal offenses which, if any, they had committed. The list included felonies and misdemeanors but excluded traffic violations. Of the nearly 1,700 respondents, 91 percent admitted they had committed one or more offenses for which they might have received jail or prison sentences. The average number of offenses for each person was 18. None of the sample had served an actual prison sentence. This study suggests that most people have broken the criminal law at some point in their lives.

In another classic study by Short and Nye (1957), three thousand high school students, with a guarantee of anonymity, were administered questionnaires about their unlawful actions. Results confirmed the high incidence of unlawful behavior such as was reported by the Wallerstein and Wyle study. Additionally, the study demonstrated that the unlawful conduct was evenly distributed across all socioeconomic classes. Even if the offenses were not serious ones, if these SR studies are representative, violations of the law are common across all levels of society, at least among young people. The Wallerstein and Wyle study did not address the issue of social class.

Most SR investigations focus on delinquency rather than adult offending. One study that is receiving extensive research attention is the National Longitudinal Study of Adolescent Health, which collected initial data on some 19,000 students in grades 7–12 at 132 schools. The self-reported information related to a variety of health issues, including those associated with criminal activity (e.g., illegal drug possession and use). A subgroup of the original participants, about 15,000, were recontacted as young adults aged 18–26.

When SR studies are done with adults, however, they are primarily adults who are incarcerated, although there are exceptions. In a study of employee theft, for example, researchers found that about one-third of employees who returned surveys admitted to stealing from their employers (Hollinger, 1986). A self-report survey of income tax evasion found 10 percent of the respondents admitting to cheating on their taxes (Tittle, 1980).

Self-report data are gathered either through interviews (personal or telephone) or questionnaires. In most SR measures, subjects are asked to indicate whether they have engaged in any of the listed illegal activities and, if so, how often. Nettler (1984), in a review of the SR research, concluded the following:

- Almost everyone, by his or her own admission, has violated some criminal law.
- The amount of "hidden crime" (the dark figure) is enormous.
- Most of the infractions are minor.

The last point is an important one because it is the basis for much of the criticism directed at SR studies. Most of the offenses included in a majority of SR questionnaires are relatively minor ones—so minor that they are likely to distort one's impressions of criminal offending unless the content of the questions is known. For example, the questionnaire used by Short and Nye was a 23-item delinquency scale that included such questions as whether one has ever defied his or her parents' authority (to their face). Other items included whether one had ever skipped school without a legitimate excuse; taken little things (worth less than $2); bought or drank beer, wine, or liquor; had sexual relations with persons of the opposite sex or the same sex; run away from home; or gone hunting or fishing without a license. Note that some of the above items (e.g., skipping school and running away) relate to offenses that are against the law only for juveniles, called "status offenses." More "serious" violations listed were engaging in fist fights, gang fights, taking a car for a drive without the owner's (including parents') knowledge, use of narcotic drugs, theft (over $50), and vandalism.

Recent SR studies, responding to the criticisms of earlier investigations, have directed their questions at more serious criminal activities. Still, we must be careful about drawing far-reaching conclusions based on the information from SR research unless the nature of the questions is known, as well as who was asked, why, and how. Most importantly, because some people are likely not to be honest in reporting their own antisocial activities, we must be guarded in reviewing the data obtained from SR studies. The best studies recognize this problem themselves and include reliability checks in their methodology—such as by cross-checking the information against other sources. At this point, SR studies do suggest that minor criminal activity is extensive and widespread, at least among youth. Furthermore, SR studies continually show that the number of individuals involved in serious crimes is relatively small, but those few who do engage in serious criminal activity commit many crimes. Moreover, persistent, repetitive offenders do not specialize in any one crime (such as larceny) but show considerable versatility in criminal involvement, committing a wide variety of offenses, violent as well as nonviolent.

Drug Abuse Self-Report Surveys

Several nationwide self-report surveys collect data on drug abuse in the United States. The major surveys are the National Household Survey on Drug Abuse (NHSDA), the Monitoring the Future Study (MFS), and the Arrestees Drug Abuse Monitoring Program (ADAM).

NHSDA is an ongoing survey of the noninstitutionalized population of the United States, 12 years old or older. The survey has been conducted by the federal government since 1971, and is the primary source of statistical information on the use of illegal drugs in the United States. It is designed to estimate the rates of drug use, the number of users, and other aspects related to illicit drugs, alcohol, and tobacco products. The survey collects data by administering questionnaires to a representative sample of the population at their places of residence across all 50 states and the District of Columbia. The sample includes residents of households, noninstitutional group quarters (e.g., shelters, rooming houses, dormitories), and civilians living on military bases. Beginning in 1999, the NHSDA interview has been carried out using a computer-assisted interviewing methodology. Computers are used both for personal interviewing conducted by the interviewer and audio computer-assisted self-interviewing. Nationally, nearly 69,000 persons were interviewed in 2001.

The MFS is a nationwide survey of high schoolers in the United States conducted at the Institute for Social Research at the University of Michigan and sponsored by research grants from the National Institute of Drug Abuse. Each year, since 1991, a total of fifty thousand 8th, 10th, and 12th grade students are surveyed. The MFS also conducts a follow-up survey of each graduating class for a number of years after their initial participation. The mission of the MFS is to predict future trends of drug abuse based on current youth drug use.

The ADAM collected data from adult males and females who were arrested in 33 metropolitan areas (or sites) in the United States. In addition, data are collected from male and female juvenile detainees in nine metropolitan areas. The ADAM utilizes both urinalysis and self-report data to identify the level of recent drug use by the arrestees and juvenile detainees. The urinalysis provides a validity check on the openness of the arrestees in providing information about their drug abuse. The urine tests are provided for 11 drugs and self-report information is collected for 15 drugs. The ADAM project offers invaluable insight into drug use of alleged offenders nationwide.

Victimization Surveys

Additional sources of data on criminal offending are victimization surveys. The main source of victimization data on crime is the **National Crime Victimization Survey (NCVS)**, originally called the National Crime Survey (NCS). Workers for the Bureau of the Census interview—in person or by phone—a large national sample of households (approximately 42,000) representing over 76,000 persons over the age of 12. The same households are interviewed every six months for a period of three years, and during each session, they are asked about crime they had experienced over the past six months. Crimes committed against children below age 12 are not counted for privacy reasons and because the designers of the survey believe that younger respondents, compared with adults, are not as likely to provide accurate information. Additionally, because young children may be victims of crime within their own households, the topic would be too sensitive to broach. The NCVS provides the largest national forum for victims to describe the impact of crime and characteristics of violent offenders.

The original impetus for the NCVS came from the President's Commission on Law Enforcement and the Administration of Justice in 1966. The commission wanted to supplement the UCR because of the widespread dissatisfaction with and distrust of the accuracy of this source. After considerable experimentation and a variety of pilot projects to test methods and their feasibility, the NCVS (then called the NCS) was fully implemented in July 1973. While the survey has generally been regarded as an effective instrument for measuring crime victimization, the National Academy of Sciences concluded that the survey's methodology and scope could be improved. Consequently, the NCVS has undergone several changes and improvements since it was begun in 1973. The most recent significant changes in the NCVS occurred in 1992 when a redesigned interview method was put into place to improve survey methods and collect previously unreported data. This redesign and other ongoing developments of the NCVS have significantly changed the way in which the survey gathers data and information on victimization. The effects of these methodological changes on data are described in a report published by the Bureau of Justice Statistics, titled *Effects of the Redesign on Victimization Estimates* (BJS Technical Report, April 1997 [NCJ-16438]).

The survey is currently designed to measure the extent to which households and individuals are victims of rape and other sexual assault, robbery, aggravated assault, simple assault, household burglary, motor vehicle theft, and theft. It also provides many details about the victims (such as age, race, sex, marital status, education, income, and whether the victim and the offender were related to each other) and about the crimes themselves. Among other things, the NCVS interviewer wants to know the following:

- Exactly what happened
- When and where the offense occurred
- Whether any injury or loss was suffered

- Whether the crime was reported to the police and if not, why
- The victim's perception of the offender's gender, race, and age

According to the NCVS, residents age 12 or older experienced approximately 23 million crimes during 2002 (Rennison & Rand, 2003). Of that total, 17.5 million (76%) were property crimes (burglary, motor vehicle theft, and household theft), and 5.3 million (23%) were violent crimes (rape or sexual assault, robbery, aggravated assault, and simple assault). Approximately 0.18 million (1%) were personal thefts (pocket picking and purse snatching).

If we examine the *rates* (victimizations per 1,000 persons age 12 or older), we find that the NCVS data reveals that victimization in 2002 reached the lowest per capita rates in nearly 30 years (Rennison & Rand, 2003). For example, violent victimization rates fell 54 percent in the past 10 years, from 50 to 23 victimizations per 1,000 persons 12 years old and older. The *number* of violent victimizations fell from 10.5 million in 1993 to 5.3 million in 2002. The property crime victimization rate fell 50 percent, from 319 crimes per 1,000 households to 159 per 1,000. In fact, the rate of every major violent and property crime declined from 1993 through 2002. Specifically, rape/sexual assault declined 56 percent, robbery dropped 63 percent, aggravated assault was down 64 percent, simple assault was down 47 percent, motor vehicle theft dropped 53 percent, household burglary was down 52 percent, and property theft was down 49 percent.

The NCVS data consistently show demographic differences in victimization rates. Males and blacks are victims of violent crime at rates greater than those of whites and persons of other races (Rennison & Rand, 2003). Persons age 12 to 24 sustained violent victimization at rates higher than individuals of all other ages. The 16 to 19 age group is especially vulnerable. Persons age 16 to 19 experienced overall violence, rape/sexual assault, and assault overall at rates higher than rates for persons in other age categories. Persons in households with an annual income under $7,500 were more likely to be victims of overall violence than members of households with higher incomes. And persons who had never married were victims of violent crime at rates higher than those for married, widowed, or divorced/separated persons.

Relationship patterns are important in understanding victimization also, particularly violent victimization. Females were most often victimized by someone they knew, while males were more likely to be victimized by a stranger in 2002 (Rennison & Rand, 2003). More specifically, female victims reported that 40 percent of the offenders were friends or acquaintances, 20 percent were intimates, and 7 percent some other relative. Thirty-one percent of the offenders were strangers. Male victims indicated that 37 percent of the offenders were friends or acquaintances, 3 percent were intimates, and 4 percent were described as some other relative. Strangers committed 56 percent of the violence against males. Robbery was the crime most likely to be committed by a stranger for both male and female victims.

Every year, about 1 million violent crimes are committed against persons by their current or former spouses, boyfriends, or girlfriends (Rennison & Welchans, 2000), a crime designated **intimate partner violence**. Intimate partner violence is committed primarily against women. Women are victims in about 85 percent of reported intimate partner violence; 22 percent of *all* violent crime committed against women is intimate partner violence. Women between the ages of 20 and 24 were most likely to be victimized by an intimate partner (21 per 1,000 women). Black women are subject to intimate partner violence at a rate 35 percent higher than white women and approximately 2.5 times higher than the rate for women of other races. About two-thirds of the victims of intimate partner violence said they were *physically attacked*, and about one-third reported being victims of threats or attempted violence. Approximately one-half of all victims of intimate partner violence (both male and female victims) reported the violence to law enforcement authorities.

The NCVS, similar to all national surveys, has its problems in accurately portraying victimization data. As described earlier in this section, the NCVS samples households and therefore does not usually include the experiences of homeless individuals or those living in institutional settings such as homeless or battered persons' shelters (Rennison & Welchans, 2000). Consequently, the extent of intimate partner violence experienced by the homeless or those persons residing in shelters remains largely unknown. For example, a survey conducted by the U.S. Conference of Mayors indicated that intimate partner violence was the primary cause of homelessness for women (U.S. Conference of Mayors, 1998). Another study suggested that as many as 50 percent of homeless women and children became homeless after fleeing abuse (Zorza, 1991). If these individuals are not represented in the NCVS, the prevalence of intimate partner violence is underestimated.

Despite their shortcomings, victimization surveys are considered a good source of information about crime incidents, independent of data collected by law enforcement agencies throughout the country. Often the offending trends reported through NCVS data procedures differ substantially from those found in police data (Ohlin & Tonry, 1989). Although we have focused on the government-conducted NCVS to illustrate victimization data, be aware that independent researchers also survey victims of crime, often with grants from government agencies or private foundations. One noteworthy example is the National Violence Against Women Survey, conducted by the Center for Policy Research (Tjaden, 1997), which included an examination of the extent and nature of stalking in American society. That survey and others like it will be covered later in the text.

JUVENILE DELINQUENCY

The definitions of crime and the methods of gathering crime data discussed above relate to both adults and juveniles. Juveniles commit a disproportionate amount of crime, but it is not necessarily the most serious offenses. Furthermore, crimes committed by juveniles may be treated very differently from those committed by adults. It is important to mention a few other preliminary distinctions.

First, not all offenses committed by juveniles are technically crimes. Some behaviors—referred to as **status offenses**—are forbidden only to juveniles because of their age. The prime examples are running away from home, curfew violations, underage drinking, skipping school on a regular basis (truancy), and—in some states—"incorrigibility." Many criminologists argue that status offenses should not be criminalized in the same way that true crimes are for various reasons. For example, status offenses label children delinquents for behavior that is not harmful to others, and they are often indicative of problems in the child's environment (e.g., the runaway child may be running away from victimization). Other criminologists argue that it is important to keep track of status offenders in order to provide them with help that they may need; additionally, some, though not all, status offenders commit "real crimes" like burglary and theft. What to do with status offenders is a controversial area.

Another distinction between adult and juvenile criminal behavior is that data gathering on juvenile offending is even more imperfect than data gathering on adult crime. The nature and extent of delinquent behavior—both what is reported and what is unreported to law enforcement agencies—is essentially an unknown area (Krisberg, 1995). Nonetheless, information from a variety of sources, including the UCR, self-report, court records, and data from juvenile corrections provides us some insight into the nature and extent of juvenile offending.

Third, much of the crime (and status offenses) committed by juveniles may be regarded as a "rite of passage" to adulthood. Self-report data indicate that offending among juveniles is more widespread than among adults but—as with adult offending—most people eventually stop. In the case of juveniles, most juveniles stop committing crime once they reach adulthood and have a stake in prosocial behavior. Juveniles may act out in high school or slightly beyond, but then they get full-time jobs, go to college, get married, join the military. From a psychological perspective, however, we need to be particularly concerned with two groups of juveniles: those who continue offending, particularly serious offending, well into their adult years; and those who commit a very serious crime during their juvenile years. Although the latter group receives extensive media attention (e.g., juvenile school shooters or juvenile murderers), this type of one-time offending is rare. Continued serious offending, though, is more problematic. Many theories of crime describe antisocial behavior as having its origins in childhood. Over the past few decades, developmental psychologists in particular have conducted extensive research on children and adolescents who begin offending early and continue into adulthood.

RECAP: DEFINING CRIME AND DELINQUENCY

A major challenge faced by the authors in preparing this text has been striking the balance between antisocial behavior and criminal behavior, or between antisocial individuals and legally defined criminals. Some scholars have argued (e.g., Sellin, 1970; Tappan, 1947)—and the law agrees—that one who engages in undetected criminal activity is not a criminal in the strictest or operational sense, because a criminal is by definition one who has been detected, arrested, and convicted. However, from a psychological point of view, we encounter problems when we limit ourselves to studying persons legally defined as criminals or behavior legally defined as crime. Legal classifications are determined by that which society, at some point in time, considers socially harmful. It may or may not also be considered morally wrong. Therefore, because each society has a different and changing set of values, what may be judged a criminal act in one may not meet the criteria in another, or even in the same society at a later time. Many states in the United States differ significantly in their criminal codes and are continually revising them. Chemical (drug) possession, prostitution, and dissemination of obscene material are examples of activities that generate ever-changing statutes, and if not changing statutes, selective enforcement. In recent years, use of cell phones or text messaging while driving has been banned in some jurisdictions, with criminal penalties sometimes prescribed. Although we do not condone text messaging while driving, we are not interested in focusing on the psychology of the text messager. The more serious crimes, those we are most concerned with in this text, are more likely to be universally recognized as unacceptable. Nevertheless, we also pay attention to offenses that may not be seen as serious or even wrong, but that can have psychological implications. Shoplifting, minor fraud, and prostitution are examples.

Furthermore, members of every society (and consequently every society's legal system) perceive and process violators of the criminal code with some disparity, so that the offender's background, social status, personality, motivation, sex, age, race, and legal counsel, as well as the circumstances surrounding the offense, may all affect the criminal justice process. It is highly likely that individuals who have been arrested, convicted, and punished represent a distinctly different sample from those who participate in illegal activity but avoid detection, conviction, or punishment.

Approximately one-fifth of those arrested go to trial, according to Sarbin (1979), who describes the legal process of becoming a criminal. First, the agents of social control (usually the police) label the individual as a suspect. Next, the agents may decide that the suspect should be arrested. Third, the arrested party may be charged with a crime, at which point he or she becomes a defendant. Fourth, the defendant may plead guilty or be tried and convicted, at which point he or she becomes an offender (a felon or a misdemeanant, depending on the seriousness of the crime). Finally, the offender may be incarcerated in a correctional facility and be labeled a convict, inmate, prisoner, or criminal. Alternately, the offender may be placed on probation, effectively serving a sentence in the community. At each step in the process, there is a funneling effect that shows that fewer and fewer individuals reach each subsequent step in the criminal justice process. This funneling process is prominently displayed in numerous criminal justice texts to illustrate how the system operates.

One reason is the error and subjectivity that cannot realistically be removed from determinations of guilt or innocence. Both judges and juries can be influenced by factors other than the strength of the evidence. For example, it has been demonstrated that the characteristics of the victim may influence how much punishment is assigned to the offender. Landy and Aronson (1969) report evidence that if the victim is a respectable citizen (i.e., successful and altruistic), the offender will receive a stiffer sentence than if the case involves an "unrespectable" victim (i.e., despicable and dishonest). Jones and Aronson (1973) found that defendants who raped a married woman or virgin were more likely to receive longer sentences than defendants who raped a divorced woman. Although these were early experiments in social psychology, later studies also confirmed that subjective factors have considerable influence on judge and jury decision making (Bartol & Bartol, 2004). Such discrepancies in sentencing have led to widespread demands for determinate sentencing, where the punishment is carefully calibrated to the offense and there is less room for discretion on the part of judges or juries. Nevertheless, it is impossible to remove discretion completely from the criminal justice process; restricted in one area, it is almost guaranteed to appear in another.

It is generally acknowledged, therefore, that those individuals sentenced to prison are not representative of the "true" criminal population, because many true criminals go undetected and/or unpunished. Furthermore, as we have long suspected but only recently documented with the increasing availability of DNA evidence, convicted persons are not even necessarily true criminals. Yet, researchers studying the "criminal mind" often use as participants those individuals who have reached the final stage of the legal process—inmates in correctional institutions or convicted offenders serving their sentences in the community. Consequently, if we discuss only legally determined criminals, we will be neglecting a considerable segment of the population that actually breaks the law. To some extent, we have little choice but to do just that. Because this text is based on research, the kinds and amounts of available empirical data dictate to a great extent what will be covered.

Additionally, if we discuss only behavior that is legally defined as crime, we omit a sizable segment of behavior that is clearly relevant to our concerns. For example, a vast body of psychological research deals with topics like aggression and antisocial behavior. Because of their implications for the eventual development of behavior that is legally defined as crime, we will be covering these areas in the text.

The great majority of crime in the United States and other countries is neither serious nor violent. The great majority of offenders are not serious, chronic offenders. Psychological criminology, however, is most concerned about the minority. Therefore, the main focus of the text is the persistent, repetitive *offender*—or the persistent, repetitive antisocial *behavior*—whether detected or undetected by the criminal justice system. In other words, in this text, we concentrate on the individual who has frequently committed serious crimes or antisocial acts over an extended period of time (at least several years). Nevertheless, we also spend time on the one-time serious offender—the mass murderer, for example, or the juvenile offender who commits a heinous crime.

For all of the above reasons, many psychologists and other mental health professionals prefer the term *antisocial behavior* to *crime* or *criminal behavior* to refer to the more serious habitual actions that violate personal rights, laws, and/or widely held social norms. **Antisocial behavior** includes both the legal designation delinquency and criminal behavior, and the actions that violate standards of society but are undetected by law enforcement. Although arrest *may be* a valid indicator of antisocial behavior, it isn't enough. Many antisocial behaviors—probably most—go undetected or escape the attention of law enforcement. Consequently, we use antisocial behavior frequently throughout the text, especially when discussing the development of behavior that has not yet been legally designated delinquent or criminal behavior but is likely to lead to such designation.

Key Concepts

Antisocial behavior
Classical theory
Clearance rate
Cognitions
Conformity perspective
Criminal profiling
Criminology
Dark figure
Developmental approach
Difference-in-degrees
Difference-in-kind
Differential association theory
Dispositions
Hate Crime Statistics Act

Hierarchy rule
Index crimes
Intimate partner violence
Just-world hypothesis
Learning perspective
National Crime Victimization
   Survey (NCVS)
National Incident-Based
   Reporting System (NIBRS)
Nonconformist perspective
Nonindex crimes
Part I crimes
Part II crimes

Positivist theory
Psychiatric criminology
Psychological criminology
Social control theory
Social learning theory
Sociological criminology
Status offenses
Strain theory
Theory verification
Traits
Uniform Crime Reporting
   (UCR)
Uniform Crime Reports

Review Questions

1. Briefly explain the difference between psychological criminology and sociological criminology.
2. What are the three perspectives of human nature? Define each briefly.
3. Identify and provide one example of each of the three predominant methods of measuring crime.
4. How does the NIBRS differ from the UCR?
5. List the strengths and weaknesses of self-report surveys.
6. What are status offenses and how do they differ from other juvenile offenses?
7. Compare and contrast the FBI's Uniform Crime Reports and the National Crime Victimization Survey, focusing on (a) how the data are obtained, and (b) what type of information is available from each.

2

Origins of Criminal Behavior: Developmental Risk Factors

Origins of Criminal Behavior: Developmental Risk Factors

CHAPTER OBJECTIVES

- Identify social, family, and psychological developmental risk factors that lead to delinquency and crime.
- Demonstrate how early preschool experiences can lead to a life of antisocial behavior.
- Emphasize the overriding influence of peer rejection on child and youth behavior.
- Stress the connection between cognitive abilities and delinquency and crime.
- Introduce ADHD and conduct disorders as possible contributors to delinquent behavior.

As a preschooler, Josh was the child most known for shoving other children, stepping on their toes, and refusing to comply with the instructions of his teachers. In grade school, he became the classroom bully; at age eight, he began to steal—from other children, from storekeepers, from teachers, and from his parents. By middle school, he was experimenting with drugs. He was suspended from high school on four separate occasions, all relating to violent behavior. Josh was convicted of robbery at age 19.

Antisocial behavior, including criminal behavior, in adults can often be traced to their childhoods. If we look back at the childhoods of offenders, for example, we typically see signs portending problems in adulthood, although this is not invariably so. Many theories of criminology propose that the roots of serious criminal behavior appear in childhood or early adolescence. This highlights the importance of identifying both factors that put children at risk of becoming antisocial and those that might protect otherwise vulnerable children from this fate.

Each person follows a different **developmental pathway**, the characteristics of which often can be identified at a very early age. The developmental perspective views the life course of all humans as following a pathway (or trajectory) that may be littered with risk factors. Some risk factors can be described as experiences that are common factors in the background of offenders, such as school failure, abuse of alcohol, or childhood victimization. In studies of both adult and juvenile offenders, researchers are beginning to identify a number of different pathways. For example, some children follow a pathway leading to serious delinquency and crime, while others follow a pathway that may lead to minor juvenile offending. For some children, there is no offending at all. Along each developmental path, a child may be exposed to a variety of risk factors, and some children are exposed to many more than others. Some experts believe that the more risks a person is exposed to, the greater the probability that person will participate in antisocial behavior throughout his or her lifetime (Wasserman & Seracini, 2001).

It is important to note that children also may be exposed to protective factors, characteristics, or experiences that can shield them from serious antisocial behavior. Warm and caring parents and a high-quality educational experience are examples. Though we recognize the importance of these factors, the goal in this chapter is to pinpoint the origins and causes of delinquency and criminal behavior; thus, the focus is on factors that place individuals at risk for offending. Nevertheless, when we discuss intervention approaches later in the text, protective factors will be carefully considered.

The risk factors we are most concerned with are individual attributes and developmental social and family experiences that are believed to increase the probability that an individual will engage in persistent criminal behavior. Examples of *social risk factors* are poverty and impoverished resources, antisocial peers, peer rejection, and preschool or school experiences. *Parental and family risk factors* include faulty or inadequate parenting, sibling influences, and child maltreatment or abuse. Examples of *psychological risk factors* are inadequate cognitive and language ability, a troublesome temperament, inadequate self-regulation skills, and poor interpersonal and social skills.

It is important that we learn about these risk factors and how they influence the developmental pathway, especially during the early stages of development. Early identification will help improve the effectiveness of prevention and intervention programs designed to eliminate or, at least, reduce delinquent and criminal behavior. As noted by Terrie Moffitt (2005), we know that certain risk factors are closely linked to delinquency and criminal behavior, but how or why they are linked is largely unknown.

We must be careful not to imply that all criminal behavior has its origins in childhood, however. Pathways researchers emphasize that some individuals begin their criminal offending in adulthood (Farrington, Ttofi, & Cold, 2009) and that this may or may not be precipitated by childhood experiences. For example, some researchers have documented a pathway consisting of adult-onset female offenders whose criminal careers began when they engaged in dysfunctional relationships with male offenders (Salisbury & Van Voorhis, 2009). Nonetheless, risk factors are so often present in the childhoods of both juvenile and adult offenders that we must give them careful attention.

SOCIAL RISK FACTORS

Poverty

Poverty refers to a situation in which the basic resources to maintain an average standard of living within a specific geographic region are lacking. This typically includes the absence of sufficient income to meet basic necessities of life. There is little doubt that poverty has a strong connection to persistent, violent offending, as measured by official, victimization, and self-report data on both adult and juvenile offenders. The connection between poverty and nonviolent offending is not quite as strong, but still existent. Accumulating research evidence indicates that poverty is one of the most robust predictors of adolescent violence for both males and females (Beyers, Bates, Pettit, & Dodge, 2003; Stouthamer-Loeber, Loeber, Wei, Farrington, & Wikström, 2002), and the indigence of defendants processed in criminal courts is well documented. However, we must be extremely careful both in interpreting these data and in making decisions about how to prevent future offending. Furthermore, it should be emphasized that this strong connection holds whether we are referring to victims or offenders. Children and youth living under dire economic conditions are more likely to be victims as well as offenders. Preschool children living in a low-income family characterized by poor housing and unemployment are especially at high risk to become delinquent and/or to become victimized (Dodge, 1993b; Farrington, 1991). Adults living in substandard housing are more likely to be victims of crime than those living in more advantageous conditions.

The exact nature of the relationship between poverty and violence is not well understood. For example, poverty is often accompanied not only by inequities in resources, but also by discrimination, racism, family disruption, unsafe living conditions, joblessness, social isolation, and limited social support systems (Evans, 2004; Hill, Soriano, Chen, & LaFromboise, 1994; Sampson & Lauritsen, 1994). Youth living under poverty conditions are more likely to attend inadequate schools, to drop out of school, to be unemployed, to carry a firearm, to be victimized, and to be a witness to a variety of violent events. Therefore, many factors other than one's economic situation come into play.

Poverty influences the family in many ways, not the least of which is the impact on parents' behavior toward children. For instance, the stress caused by poverty in urban settings is believed to diminish parents' capacity for supportive and consistent parenting (Dodge, Greenberg, Malone, and Conduct Problems Prevention Research Group, 2008; Hammond & Yung, 1994). This situation may lead to coercive and highly aggressive methods of child control. Living in conditions where lack of social support, lack of resources, and lack of opportunity are prevalent make it difficult for some parents to avoid harsh and inconsistent discipline with their young children. Coercive methods of child control are more direct, immediate, and easy to administer. They require less time and energy to administer, compared with parenting that emphasizes sensitivity, interpersonal skills, and patient understanding. It is much "easier" to slap a child than it is to utilize more thoughtful parenting strategies, but the consequences of slapping can be severe. A pattern of slapping or hitting a child to punish or to maintain control promotes a negative self-concept in the child. Furthermore, parenting that utilizes aggressive and violent tactics often provides models and a violent context that can carry the cycle of violence into the next generation. Living in a disadvantaged environment accompanied by physical punishment may also lead to the belief that economic survival and social status depend greatly on being aggressive and violent to others.

Important caveats must be offered in any discussion of serious delinquency and economic status, however. First, the connection between low socioeconomic class and delinquency does not mean that poverty causes or inevitably leads to serious, chronic offending. The great majority of poor children and adults are law-abiding citizens, and children and adults from families of high economic status do engage in serious delinquency and crime. Both self-report and victimization data indicate that sexual assault, serious drug use, theft, and fraud are perpetrated by juveniles and adults across all social classes. Second, in many communities, children from the lower socioeconomic class are targeted by law enforcement practices more than are children of the middle and upper classes. They are more likely to be taken into custody by police, referred to juvenile courts, and adjudicated delinquent. Thus, they appear in the government statistics that serve as the official measures of crime. Additionally, children of the poor are taken into a system that may itself promote delinquent behavior or adult crime, particularly when they are institutionalized with other offenders. Children of the middle and upper classes, by contrast, are more likely to be handled informally, provided with legal assistance, or placed by their parents in private facilities for the treatment of their problem behavior (Chesney-Lind & Shelden, 1998; Schwartz, 1989).

Peer Rejection and Association with Antisocial Peers

Developmental researchers have continually found that children's peer relations make unique and essential contributions to each child's social and emotional development (Bagwell, 2004; Newcomb, Bukowksi, & Pattee, 1993). During adolescence, there is an increase in susceptibility to peer influence and a decline in susceptibility to parental influence (Mounts, 2002). In addition, numerous investigators have found that peer influence is a strong predictor of adolescent substance use and delinquent behavior (Coie & Miller-Johnson, 2001; Mounts, 2002). Not surprisingly, many members of most societies believe that this connection is obvious. The folk wisdom to "avoid bad companions" has long been the traditional admonishment from parents and other concerned adults. The link between childhood peer *rejection* and antisocial behavior and delinquency is not so obvious, however, and requires a closer examination.

One of the strongest predictors of later involvement in antisocial behavior is early rejection by peers (Dodge, 2003; Parker & Asher, 1987). In elementary school, being liked and accepted by the peer group is a crucial developmental task, generally leading to healthy psychological and social development (Rubin, Bukowski, & Parker, 1998). Social rejection by peers in the elementary school grades, on the other hand, presents a very powerful risk factor for delinquency in adolescence and antisocial behavior throughout the life course (Laird, Jordan, Dodge, Pettit, & Bates, 2001). Research has consistently demonstrated that peer rejection by first-grade peers is significantly linked to the development of antisocial behavior by the fourth grade (Cowan & Cowan, 2004; Miller-Johnson *et al.*, 2002). Furthermore, those children who were rejected for at least two or three years by second grade had a 50 percent chance of displaying clinically significant antisocial behavior later in adolescence, in contrast with just a 9 percent chance for those children who managed to avoid early peer rejection (Dodge & Pettit, 2003).

Interestingly, the quality of parent-child and marital relationships seems to play a significant role in whether a child is rejected or not by peers early in his or her life. Research by Cowan and Cowan (2004) demonstrates that "negative qualities in marital- and parent-child relationships in both prekindergarten and kindergarten are risk factors for low social skills, aggressive behavior, and rejection in the early years of elementary school" (p. 173).

Peer-rejected children frequently interact with one another or gravitate to antisocial peers (Laird, Pettit, Dodge, & Bates, 2005). During the adolescent years, involvement with antisocial peers shows a robust and consistent relationship to delinquency, drug use, and a range of other problematic behaviors (Laird *et al.*, 2005). Consequently, we would expect that both peer rejection *and* involvement with antisocial peers would be characteristic of those youngsters exhibiting antisocial or delinquent behavior early in their social development.

WHY ARE SOME CHILDREN REJECTED BY THEIR PEERS?   Children are often rejected by their peers for a variety of reasons, but their own aggressive behavior appears to be a prominent reason. Children tend to reject those peers who frequently use forms of physical and verbal aggression as their preferred way of dealing with others. These findings prompted many social scientists to conclude that aggressive children are more likely than nonaggressive children to be rejected by peers. Ongoing research indicates, however, that the relationship may not be that straightforward. First, peers also may reject peers whom they perceive as shy and socially withdrawn. Second, not all aggressive children are rejected by peers; some are liked, accepted, and sought as friends. In fact, research finds that many popular youngsters are often dominant, arrogant, and physically and relationally aggressive (Cillessen & Mayeux, 2004; Rose, Swenson, & Waller, 2004). Thus, if the children are rejected, it is not *always* because they are aggressive.

On the other hand, aggression *combined with* peer rejection does appear to lead to serious antisocial or delinquent behavior. Children who are *both* physically aggressive and socially rejected by their peers have a high probability of becoming serious delinquents during adolescence and violent offenders during early adulthood. Researchers Coie and Miller-Johnson (2001), for example, conclude from their extensive review of the research literature that "those aggressive children who are rejected by peers are at a significantly greater risk for chronic antisocial behavior than those who are not rejected" (p. 201).

WHICH CHILDREN ARE PRONE TO PEER REJECTION?   An important question still remains: Why are certain aggressive children rejected in the first place? Coie (2004) points out that there are three important differences between peer-rejected boys and nonrejected boys. First, peer-rejected, aggressive boys are more impulsive and have problems sustaining attention and staying on task. Consequently, they are more likely to be disruptive of ongoing activities in the classroom or during group play. Second, peer-rejected, aggressive boys are aroused to anger more readily and probably have more difficulty calming down. This emotional rage is more likely to result in physical and verbal attacks on peers, which in turn encourages peers to avoid them altogether. Third, rejected, aggressive youngsters have fewer social and interpersonal skills for making friends and maintaining positive relationships with peers. In addition, they probably have acquired fewer social and interpersonal skills because they have had limited opportunities to practice these skills on nonrejected peers.

In summary, peer-rejected children often, though not invariably, are aggressive, but they also tend to be more argumentative, inattentive, and disruptive than others, and generally have poorer social skills. These behaviors are characteristic of attention deficient/hyperactivity disorder (ADHD), to be discussed in more detail later in the chapter under psychological risks. The observation that peer-rejected boys demonstrate inattentive, impulsive, disruptive behavior suggests that ADHD may contribute to some of the peer rejection. A study by Erhardt and Hinshaw (1994) underscores this possibility.

The study involved 25 boys with ADHD and 24 other boys who participated in a summer school program, all of whom did not know one another at the beginning of the program. The boys ranged in ages from 6 to 12 years old. As early as the first day of social interactions between the two groups, the ADHD and comparison boys showed clear differences in social behaviors, with the ADHD youngsters displaying socially noxious and noncompliance-disruptive behaviors. More important, within the first day, the ADHD youngsters were overwhelmingly rejected by their peers. Other studies have found similar results, with ADHD symptoms and aggression showing a close link to eventual antisocial behavioral patterns (Coie, 2004; Miller-Johnson *et al.*, 2002). Again, this topic is discussed in more detail later in the chapter.

GENDER DIFFERENCES IN PEER REJECTION   It should be noted that, to date, most of the research and theoretical work examining the effects of peer rejection, aggression, and delinquent behavior has focused on boys. Among girls, little is known about the combined effects of aggression and peer rejection. In one of the few studies focusing on girls, Prinstein and La Greca (2004) found that the development of antisocial and delinquent behavior in girls, as in boys, can be predicted by early involvement in aggressive behavior with peers. There is also some evidence to suggest that relationally aggressive girls are more likely than nonaggressive girls to be peer rejected (Crick, 1995). Relational aggression is the tendency to hurt others and diminish their social status by words, shunning, or other nonphysical methods. Prinstein and La Greca discovered—as did Crick—that peer rejection among girls in elementary school increased aggression but also was associated with increased substance abuse and other delinquent behaviors during adolescence. On the other hand, peer acceptance reduced and even eliminated the risk of aggression and other delinquent behaviors later on. More specifically, the effects of childhood aggression and antisocial behavior were mollified under conditions of high acceptance by peers.

GANG OR DEVIANT GROUP INFLUENCES ON REJECTED YOUTH   There are three major perspectives on the influence of peer groups on antisocial and delinquent behavior. One perspective argues that youngsters become delinquent as a direct result of association with deviant peer groups. According to this view, almost any child is susceptible to the negative influences of participating in a deviant peer group. A second perspective contends that antisocial, peer-rejected youths seek out greater contact with similar peer-rejected and socially unskillful peers. A third perspective is somewhat between these two positions. Peer-rejected, antisocial children are drawn to deviant groups with members similar to themselves, and this encourages and amplifies *already existing* antisocial tendencies. Current research evidence is in favor of the third perspective. It appears that childhood peer rejection encourages children to participate in deviant peer groups that then *amplify* tendencies to become more deviant and antisocial. Put another way, deviant group membership or gangs encourage and increase the already existing antisocial patterns in children and adolescents. As noted by Coie (2004), "The impact of deviant peer group influences on the *crystallization of an antisocial developmental trajectory* [emphasis added] has been solidly documented" (p. 257).

Although the bulk of the evidence supports the third perspective of amplification of already existing deviant tendencies, there is some evidence that deviant group membership appears to encourage some nondelinquent children to participate in *minor* delinquent actions. For example, while following the social development of youngsters, ages 11–17, Elliott and Menard (1996) discovered that nondelinquent youths were more inclined to engage in minor delinquent activity after joining a deviant peer group than before. And Thornberry, Krohn, Lizotte, and Chard-Wierschem (1993) report that nondelinquent youths who joined gangs were more likely to engage in minor delinquent behavior while gang members but decreased or terminated their delinquent behavior when they left the group.

Preschool Experiences

Over the past 30 years, children as a group have been shifted gradually from home to center-based day care or nursery school. The proportion of mothers participating in the workforce has increased substantially in recent years; because mothers have traditionally been the primary caretakers, this is a significant change. The percentage of mothers with children under age six working outside the home increased from 12 percent in 1947, to 31 percent in 1975, to 64 percent in 1997 (Tran & Weinraub, 2006). In 2003, more than half the mothers with infants less than one year old were in the labor force (Tran & Weinraub, 2006). The most recent data indicate that over 60 percent of children under the age of five are in some form of day-care or nonparental care on a regular basis (Morrissey, 2009; U.S. Bureau of the Census, 2002). About 15 percent of young children are in two or more child-care arrangements during a typical week (Morrissey, 2009).

Today, more American children are cared for by paid providers than by relatives (Scarr, 1998). In 1995, there were nearly 21 million children under the age of five who were not yet enrolled in school. Of these, about 40 percent were cared for regularly by parents, 21 percent by other relatives, 45 percent in child-care centers or family day-care centers, and 4 percent by sitters in the child's home. While there are obviously numerous exceptions, out-of-home child care in the United States is, on average, mediocre. The quality of child care provided by day-care centers is highly variable, in large part due to low wages and high staff turnover in many facilities. Nonetheless, licensed day-care centers, which are expected to meet minimal standards for nutrition, programming, and staffing, are often more adequate than individual care providers whom some parents must rely upon. However it occurs, poor-quality child care has been reported to put children's development at risk for poorer language, cognitive development, and lower ratings of social and emotional adjustment (Tran & Weinraub, 2006). Unfortunately, children from families with single employed mothers and low incomes were more likely to be found in lower-quality care (Howes & Olenick, 1986).

The reality of multiple child-care arrangements has only recently come to attention. The nation's economic crisis of 2009 resulted in many parents assuming second jobs—such as low-paying part-time work on weekends—to keep the family financially afloat. This may necessitate "juggling" child care duties among day-care centers, relatives, babysitters, and neighbors. Unfortunately, recent research suggests that these multiple arrangements have negative impacts on children's social adjustment (Morrissey, 2009). Being placed in different homes, day-care centers, classrooms, or peer groups on a weekly basis increases problem behavior and decreases prosocial behavior. This is especially the case for young children with difficult temperaments and young girls.

More encouragingly, there is evidence that improving out-of-home care for children can have long-term beneficial effects. Low-income children who experience high-quality infant and preschool care show better school achievement and socialized behavior in later years than similar children without child-care experience or with experience in lower-quality care. For low-income children, quality child care offers learning opportunities and social and emotional supports that many would not experience at home. Again, this is not to say that low-income parents do not or cannot offer these opportunities to their children; however, the stress associated with maintaining the household under stringent economic conditions may make it difficult to do so.

According to Goldstein Arnold, Rosenberg, Stowe, and Ortiz (2001), day-care teachers worry about aggression in their toddlers more than any other behavioral problem, and they report disruptive behavior as their greatest classroom challenge. These concerns may be important, as aggressive tendencies at three years of age predict aggressive behavior later in life (Goldstein *et al.*, 2001). Accumulating evidence indicates that the amount of exposure that a child has to aggressive peers in day care or preschool is predictive of later child aggressive behavior, perhaps because of modeling effects (Dodge & Pettit, 2003).

After-School Care

The quality of after-school care has been closely associated with the development of antisocial behavior (Flannery, Williams, & Vazsonyi, 1999; Posner & Vandell, 1999; Vandell & Posner, 1999). In the 1990s, the term *latch-key* children was applied to children who returned from school to an empty house and remained on their own until their parents or guardians finished their own work day. Children who spend fairly large amounts of time in unsupervised after-school self-care in the early elementary grades are at elevated risk for behavior problems in early adolescence (Pettit, Laird, Bates, & Dodge, 1997). Moreover, such children are more likely to spend time in unsupervised activity with peers in early adolescence (Colwell, Pettit, Meece, Bates, & Dodge, 2001). Antisocial children seek out niches that involve association with antisocial peers and environments with minimal adult supervision (Snyder, Reid, & Patterson, 2003). Day-care centers that open their doors to children after school hours or community groups that offer after-school programs in troubled neighborhoods can make a positive difference.

School Failure

Early school failure is also linked to antisocial development and delinquency (Dodge & Pettit, 2003). Interestingly, research indicates that retention in kindergarten and in the early school grades has long-term detrimental effects on development, in spite of its immediate academic benefits (Dodge & Pettit, 2003; Holmes, 1989; Sameroff, Peck, & Eccles, 2004). On the other hand, delaying entry into kindergarten does not appear to have the same effects. It is the "staying back" label that prompts retained children to be seen negatively and socially rejected and ridiculed by their peers (Plummer & Graziano, 1987).

In fact, early school failure seems to be more strongly associated with delinquency than low intelligence (Hinshaw, 1992). Some researchers discovered that the odds of severe delinquent behavior in eight-year-old male children who were failing in school were nearly double those of other male children (Loeber, Farrington, Stouthamer-Loeber, & Van Kammen, 1998).

Regardless of race or ethnic background, reading achievement appears to play a prominent role in school failure. In fact, not only is poor reading achievement closely associated with school failure, but it also predicts later arrest and criminal activity in boys (Petras *et al.*, 2004). On the other hand, a high level of reading achievement seems to prevent at-risk youth from engaging in later antisocial behavior. More specifically, a high level of reading achievement brings more acceptance from mainstream peers, greater attachment to school, enhanced job prospects in young adulthood, and better cognitive resources for anticipating the negative consequences of engaging in criminal activity (Petras *et al.*, 2004).

In summary, the most prominent social risk factors that have been identified in the development of criminal behavior include the many disadvantages of living in poverty, peer rejection combined with association with antisocial peers, poor-quality child care during the preschool years, and school failure. The more social risk factors a child experiences during his or her early life, the higher the probability a child will follow a developmental pathway toward delinquent and criminal behavior. Parental and family risk factors may play an even more prominent role in the development of antisocial behavior.

PARENTAL AND FAMILY RISK FACTORS

Single-Parent Households

It is estimated that over 12 million American families with children are maintained by only one parent (U.S. Bureau of the Census, 2001). Early studies based on official data found that delinquents were more likely than nondelinquents to come from homes where parents were divorced or separated (Eaton & Polk, 1961; Glueck & Glueck, 1950; Monahan, 1957; Rodman & Grams, 1967). This led to conclusions that the single-parent home—or the "broken home" as it was called—could be blamed for much delinquency and thus could be considered a risk factor. Beginning in the 1970s, when self-report data indicated that delinquent behavior was widespread, criminologists began to question these conclusions. Today, researchers are more likely to examine accompanying factors such as the quality of the parent–child relationship, the family's economic status, and the degree of emotional support provided to the family by other adults, such as extended family members or community agents.

A wide variety of circumstances can lead to a single-parent home. The home may have started that way, as when an unmarried woman gives birth to or adopts a child. Additionally, two-parent homes may be "broken" by a wide variety of circumstances—death, desertion, divorce, or separation. Such separations do not affect all families the same way. Furthermore, there is evidence that children from single-parent homes that are relatively conflict-free are less likely to be delinquent than children from conflict-ridden "intact" homes (Gove & Crutchfield, 1982). The composition of the home (e.g., grandparents, stepparent, relatives, significant others, or friends) also must be considered. The "nontraditional" family has become a fixture in today's society. Many researchers define family as individuals related by blood or by legal arrangements (i.e., adoptions, legal guardianships, civil unions). Others point out that individuals who live together in long-term committed relationships—either as friends or as sexual partners—and who may be caring for their own or other people's children, are also family.

While the relationship between single-parent homes and delinquency continues to be commonly reported, we are far from explaining it—and it may be pointless to try. If the single-parent home is a risk factor, it is probably influenced by other interacting variables. Rather than concentrating on the *structure* of the family, a focus on the *process* is far more desirable. As Flynn (1983, p. 13) asserts, "One point is indisputably clear in the literature: A stable, secure, and mutually supportive family is exceedingly important in delinquency prevention." However family is defined, it should include at least one competent, caring adult with primary responsibility for the well-being of the child.

Parental Styles and Practices

Parental styles and practices pertain to the ways in which parents or caregivers interact with their children. Some parental (or caregiver) styles and practices appear to be more likely than others to lead to delinquency, and thus can be called risk factors. **Parental practices** are strategies employed by parents to achieve specific academic, social, or athletic goals across different contexts and situations (Hart, Nelson, Robinson, Olsen, & McNeilly-Choque, 1998). That is, when parents use parenting practices, their focus is on affecting some particular aspect of the child (Mounts, 2002). Giving a child a weekly allowance with the hope of teaching her to manage money is an example of a practice. Reading with children, attending their sports events, or serving as room parents in school are other examples. Parenting practices have a direct effect on the development of specific child behaviors (from table manners to academic performance) and characteristics (such as acquisition of particular values or high self-esteem).

While parental practices refer to parental behavioral patterns, **parental styles** refer to parent-child interactions characterized by parental *attitudes* toward the child and the emotional climate of the parent-child relationship (Baumrind, 1991a; Mounts, 2002). Behaviors such as gestures, tone of voice, or the spontaneous expression of emotion are examples of parental style. For example, responsive parent-child interactions are described as warm, playful, accepting, and engaging. Studies reveal that a responsive parenting style often leads to social competence, peer acceptance, and less antisocial behavior (Hart *et al.*, 1998).

FOUR TYPES OF PARENTAL STYLES   Diana Baumrind (1991a) identified four parental styles: (1) authoritarian; (2) permissive; (3) authoritative; and (4) neglecting (see **Table 1**). Those parents who use an **authoritarian style** try to shape, control, and evaluate the behavior of their children in accordance with some preestablished, absolute standard. The authoritarian household has numerous rules and regulations which must be rigidly observed, often without question or explanation. Authoritarian parents discourage any verbal exchanges that imply equality between parent and child; the parent is the authority in all important matters, as well as many unimportant ones. Authoritarian parents expect their children to be obedient and unquestioningly respectful of authority. These parents are often referred to as "running a tight ship."

TABLE 1	**Summary of Baumrind's Parental Styles**
Style	**Intend**
Authoritarian	To shape and control child's life
Permissive	No control and extremely few restrictions
Authoritative	To be rational and apply reasonable restrictions
Neglecting	Detached and unengaged in child's life

Deviations and transgressions are met with punitive, forceful measures, which may or may not include physical punishment.

Years ago, a student who was the youngest in a family of five children, revealed to the class one of the most memorable experiences of his childhood. An older brother—then a high school junior—had arrived home shortly after midnight, heavily under the influence of alcohol. The father of the family woke each of the younger children and had them watch as he placed the oldest son face down across a chair and whipped his backside. He then told the other children, "This is what will happen to you if I ever see you come home like this." Asked about the outcome of this incident, the student said, "We all turned out fine; we knew our father loved us and we still know it now." Obviously, many of us would not agree with this approach, but despite this, the authoritarian parent is not the one most closely associated with criminal behavior in his or her offspring.

Parents who adopt a **permissive style** display tolerant, nonpunitive, accepting attitudes toward their children's behavior, including expressions of aggressive and sexual impulses. Permissive parents generally avoid asserting authority or imposing social controls or restrictions on the child's behavior. In this type of family, parents see themselves as "resource persons" to be consulted if needed. Permissive parents allow children to set their own time schedule for eating, sleeping, watching television, playing video games, leaving the home, and meeting with friends, and they employ little parental monitoring. They are, in essence, ineffectual in their socializing roles. While this may seem a harsh appraisal, and while these parents may suggest that children learn from their own mistakes, research indicates that permissiveness is not the recommended approach (Jackson & Foshee, 1998).

In the **authoritative style**, parents try to direct their children's activities in a rational, issue-oriented manner. There are frequent decision-making exchanges and a general spirit of open communication between parents and children. The hallmark of the family led by authoritative parents is reasoned discussion punctuated with social controls. Authoritative parents expect age-related "mature" behavior from the child, and they apply firm, consistent enforcement of family rules and standards. At the same time, they encourage independence and individuality. In the illustration given above, an authoritative parent might have allowed the high school junior to go to bed—perhaps even tucked him in—but would likely have reasoned with the son the next day and applied some penalty to the unacceptable behavior.

Finally, in the **neglecting style**, parents demonstrate detachment and very little involvement in their children's life or activities. They are neither demanding nor responsive. "They do not structure or monitor, and are not supportive, but may be actively rejecting or else neglect their childrearing responsibilities altogether" (Baumrind, 1991b, p. 62). Basically, the parent or parents respond minimally to either the child's needs or the child's behavior (Brenner & Fox, 1999). They are far more than permissive; they simply have no interest in controlling the child's behavior or monitoring the child's activities. In its extreme form, this style of parenting qualifies as child neglect. It should come as no surprise that Hoeve *et al.* (2007) found neglecting parenting was one of the strongest risk factors identified with delinquency and a life of crime. Baumrind (1991b) found that adolescents from unengaged families were far more likely than their adolescent peers to be antisocial, lacking self-regulation, social responsibility, and cognitive competence.

Baumrind's parenting types are not without their problems. Many parents, for example, vacillate between permissiveness and authoritativeness, and some vary their styles according to the age of the child. Authoritative parents may allow their children to set their own eating and sleeping schedules and choose their modes of dress, but may demand extensive input into decisions related to school, careers, or work. Likewise, some parents may be generally permissive in style, but suddenly erupt into anger and demand that their children abide by a newly announced rule. Despite its shortcomings, "Baumrind's conceptualization of parenting style has produced a remarkably consistent picture of the type of parenting conducive to the successful socialization of children into the dominant culture of the United States" (Darling & Steinberg, 1993, p. 487).

ENMESHED AND LAX PARENTAL STYLES   James Snyder and Gerald Patterson (1987) conclude that two parental styles contribute directly or indirectly to delinquency. They label the two styles "enmeshed" and "lax," and these are very similar to Baumrind's authoritarian and permissive styles. In the **enmeshed style**, parents see an unusually large number of minor behaviors as problematic, and they use ineffective, authoritarian strategies to deal with them. "These parents don't ignore even very trivial excessive behaviors. They issue more and poorer commands, use verbal threats, disapproval, and cajoling more frequently, but fail to consistently and effectively back up these verbal reprimands with nonviolent, nonphysical punishment" (Snyder & Patterson, 1987, p. 221). The ineffective use of coercive punishment sets up a reverberating pattern of family interactions "which elicits, maintains, and exacerbates the aggressive behavior of all family members" (p. 221). When one family member in this coercive interaction acts aversively, other family members react the same way, escalating the exchange. Cathy reacts strongly to her brother's loud music by suddenly screaming to him to turn it off. He screams back at her to "stick it." Cathy bangs violently on his door. He screams louder. The father screams at both, telling them to "shut up" or else. Cathy screams louder and proceeds to kick in her brother's door. She throws a vase at him, just missing. He runs after her, throwing a book. Eventually, the child sometimes "wins" this escalating confrontation when parents "give in" to demands, reinforcing this highly aversive interpersonal strategy. For example, father kicks a chair and "orders" the brother to turn the loud music off. Thus, parents and children "teach" each other that this harsh tactic works in social interactions, a pattern that soon extends to members outside the family.

Enmeshed parents also sometimes dispense authoritarian, harsh punishment, although it is inconsistent and ineffective. However, they probably do not have the energy to apply punishments to each and every behavior they perceive as problematic. Consequently, there are many instances where aversive behavior goes unpunished, such as in the preceding example. This pattern results in an intermittent, inconsistent punishment schedule that, in the long run, does little to discourage antisocial behavior.

The **lax style** employs strategies that are the opposite of the above. According to Snyder and Patterson (1987), lax parents are not sufficiently attuned to what constitutes problematic or antisocial behavior in children. Consequently, they allow much of it to slip by, without disciplinary actions. For a variety of reasons, they fail to recognize or accept the fact that their children are involved in deviant, antisocial, or even violent actions. They simply do not believe it is happening, or they convince themselves that there is very little they can do about it. Lax parents may pretend they are unaware that their son is hosting a drug fest in the back field or fail to see the danger in the weaponry he is collecting.

It appears that overcontrolling parental behaviors—those associated with enmeshed and authoritarian styles—are closely connected to the development of aggression and antisocial behavior in children and adolescents (Blitstein, Murray, Lytle, Birnhaum, & Perry, 2005; Ruchkin, 2002). By contrast, an authoritative style has the opposite effect. Blitstein *et al.* (2005) report evidence that violent behavior and antisocial behavior among girls may be buffered by the presence of a warm, responsive (i.e., authoritative) mother, although the same result was not found for boys. In short, authoritative mothers seem to play a more significant role for the prevention of antisocial behavior in girls than in boys (Hollister-Wagner, Foshee, & Jackson, 2001).

Of all the parenting styles discussed in this section, neglecting style is most closely associated with antisocial behavior and delinquency. Although this is not surprising, having a neglecting parent does not automatically lead to serious antisocial behavior. Alternative adult role models, such as relatives, teachers, coaches, or mentors, may be available. Other parental styles, though, are also tied to delinquency. These include Baumrind's permissive and Snyder and Patterson's lax style. The children brought up with these styles often have very low levels of self-reliance and great difficulty controlling their impulses. Permissive parents have long been faulted both for lack of discipline and lack of supervision. They may treat their children as adults, pushing them into adult behaviors or responsibilities far before they are ready and without needed direction from adult authority figures.

Parental Monitoring

Closely related to parental styles and antisocial behavior is the issue of parental supervision or monitoring. **Parental monitoring** "refers to parents' awareness of their child's peer associates, free-time activities, and physical whereabouts when outside the home" (Snyder & Patterson, 1987, pp. 225–26). The amount and quality of parental monitoring is influenced by a number of things. For example, divorce, serious financial distress, loss of job, parental psychological disorders, substance abuse, or death may significantly affect family dynamics and parental or caregiver monitoring. Monitoring appears to be especially important from about age nine to mid-adolescence, an observation that has received substantial support from several studies (Laird, Pettit, Bates, & Dodge, 2003). Parental anecdotes often support this as well. As one mother expressed, "I couldn't afford to be a stay-at-home Mom throughout my kids' childhoods, so I chose to do it when my oldest got to middle school. That's when they needed me home the most." However, monitoring does not necessarily require the physical presence of the parent. Other adult caretakers or after-school programs also could provide suitable monitoring. The working mother in the above example could still be an effective monitor by being aware of her child's activities and alert to his or her needs.

The bulk of the available research also has concluded that the amount and quality of parental monitoring is a strong predictor of antisocial behavior during later childhood and adolescence (Kilgore, Snyder, & Lentz, 2000). Other studies have found significant evidence that poor parental monitoring and supervision are related to higher levels of violent behavior (Singer *et al.*, 1999) and drug abuse (Webb, Bray, Getz, & Adams, 2002). Some studies have indicated that poor parental monitoring and supervision increase the risk of delinquency two and a half times over those youth who experienced better supervision (Browning & Loeber, 1999).

Interestingly, still more research reports that some children and adolescents are easier to monitor and supervise than others, largely because of their willingness to cooperate in the monitoring process (Kerns, Aspelmeier, Gentzler, & Grabill, 2001). Although this in itself is not surprising, the researchers did document that youths who have a secure and responsive relationship with parents are more willing to be monitored, highlighting once again the importance of a positive parent-child relationship.

Influence of Siblings

Siblings imitate each other, and most often younger children imitate their older siblings rather than the reverse (Garcia, Shaw, Winslow, & Yaggi, 2000). Since siblings generally spend so much time together, it is reasonable to assume that they play a role in shaping the development of aggression and antisocial behavior. This area has not been researched as heavily as other peer influences, but the few studies available indicate that adolescents with high rates of delinquency are also more likely to have siblings with high rates of delinquency (Coie & Miller-Johnson, 2001). Rowe and Gulley (1992) suggest that older siblings who engage in delinquent behavior reinforce antisocial behavior in younger siblings when there is a close and warm relationship between the youths. If the siblings are not close, the opposite effect may occur. That is, the nonaggressive younger sibling may make it a point not to be like his or her older aggressive or antisocial sibling. In addition, the risk of delinquency is higher when the delinquent sibling is closer in age than those siblings spaced further apart (Rowe, Rodgers, & Meseck-Bushey, 1992).

Parental Psychopathology

Children of parents—especially mothers—who are clinically depressed are at increased risk for a range of socioemotional and behavioral problems, including antisocial behavior, emotion dysregulation, and poor cognitive development (Bennett, Bendersky, & Lewis, 2002; Mazulis, Hyde, & Clark, 2004; Nelson, Hammen, Brennan, & Ullman, 2003). As they grow older, children whose mothers were depressed during their infancy continue to display behavioral problems and often engage in various kinds of criminal behavior. Mothers are singled out because they tend to be the dominant caretakers. However, the risk for developing problem behaviors appears to be magnified if both parents are depressed during early childhood.

Parental alcoholism elevates risk for a variety of negative child outcomes, including behavioral difficulties, antisocial behavior, and subsequent alcoholism (Loukas, Zucker, Fitzgerald, & Krull, 2003; Zucker *et al.*, 2000). Interestingly, Loukas and her colleagues (2003) found that the presence of paternal alcoholism in the family may be more important than maternal alcoholism in contributing to a son's antisocial behavior and maladjustment.

The aggressive behavior that is demonstrated in domestic violence is clearly a form of parental psychopathology.

Lack of Attachment

According to John Bowlby (1969), the early relationship between an infant and a caregiver largely determines the quality of social relationships later in life. Bowlby's **attachment theory** has been discussed extensively in the psychological literature and may be extended to the study of criminal behavior. It fits in well with the family and parental issues discussed above.

Some infants, when placed in a strange and unfamiliar environment, show *secure attachment*. They play comfortably in their mother's presence and demonstrate curiosity about their new and challenging environment. When the mother leaves, the child becomes distressed, but when she returns, the child beams with sheer delight. These infants use their mother or caregiver as a secure base from which to explore. Other infants may show an *insecure attachment*, which is often divided into two attachment styles: *anxious/ambivalent* and *avoidant*. The anxious/ambivalent-attached child becomes intensely distressed and anxious by separation, and in new environments, they often cling anxiously to their mother without much exploration (Ainsworth, 1979). When the mother returns after separation, they may become indifferent and even hostile toward the mother. These infants may push the returning mother away, stiffen up, or cry when picked up. The *avoidant attachment* style is characterized by little distress on the part of the infant, whether the mother is present or not. They rarely cry during separation or reunion. Avoidant attachment in infancy and childhood is associated with dismissing attachment in adulthood (Adshead, 2002).

Mary Ainsworth (1979) observed that caregivers who are sensitive, affectionate, and responsive, and who create in their babies a basic trust of the world, typically have securely attached infants. Children with a secure attachment base usually develop into psychologically healthy children. As adults, they form good relationships, empathize with others, and generally show good self-regulation (Ansbro, 2008). "Later on, they emerge as more competent and more sympathetic in interaction with peers" (Ainsworth, 1979, p. 936). Most infants in the United States are regarded as having a secure attachment to their mothers or caregivers (Thompson, 1998). It is also commonly believed that our attachments in infancy play a powerful role in romantic relationships as adults.

According to Ainsworth and her colleagues (1979), infants with avoidant attachment style often have parents who are aloof, distant, and prefer to avoid intimacy with their children. Consequently, these children as adults have difficulty forming intimate relationships. Infants with anxious/ambivalent attachment usually have parents who are overbearing and inconsistent in their affection and intimacy. These infants never know when and how their parents will respond to their needs. As adults, they want to have close relationships but continually worry about their partners and relationships returning the affection. They tend to become obsessive and preoccupied with their relationships, especially spouses and partners.

Ward and his associates (Ward, Hudson, Marshall, & Siegert, 1995) hypothesize that many sex offenders probably had parents who were inconsistently affectionate and poor at identifying their child's needs. In essence, the sex offenders demonstrate the dismissing (avoidant) attachment style in their adult relationships. Gwen Adshead (2002) reports evidence for insecure attachment in her study of violent offenders. She notes that many victims of interpersonal violence are part of the violent offender's attachment network: a child, a parent, a partner, or expartner. Fear of loss or separation can generate strong feelings of anxiety and rage in the offender, often resulting in violent actions. Adshead found that a majority of offenders showed a dismissing attachment style, suggesting a diminished capacity for empathy toward their victims or relationships.

Discussion of the attachment process serves as a good link between the social risk factors reviewed in this section and the psychological factors about to be covered. (For a summary of all of the developmental risk factors, see **Table 2**). While it has a connection with parenting styles, the attachment process also reflects a characteristic of the individual offender. Although attachment may be an important component, it is only one of many and is unlikely to be a major factor. Furthermore, the factors covered below have received more research attention with respect to the development of antisocial behavior.

TABLE 2   Developmental Risk Factors for Delinquency

Social Risk Factors
  Poverty*
  Early peer rejection
  Association with antisocial peers
  Inadequate preschool child care
  Inadequate after-school care
  School failure
Parental and Family Risk Factors
  Single-parent household*
  Permissive or lax parental style
  Minimal parental monitoring
  Parental psychopathology
  Physical and emotional abuse/neglect
  Domestic violence and/or substance abuse
  Antisocial siblings
Psychological Risk Factors
  Cognitive and language deficiencies
  Low IQ scores or psychometric intelligence
  Attention deficit hyperactivity disorder* (ADHD)
  Conduct disorder (CD)

*Must be accompanied by other factors in order to be considered strong risk.

PSYCHOLOGICAL RISK FACTORS

Lack of Empathy

Anyone observing a group of children playing together can notice differences among them if one child gets hurt and begins to cry. Some children will ignore the crying child and continue with their play; others will become solicitous and want to be sure the child is alright. Although this is a simplistic example, we might say that the children in the second group are more empathetic than those in the first.

In practice and research, empathy is perceived as existing along two dimensions: affective and cognitive. Affective empathy is "an emotional response characterized by feelings of concern for another and a desire to alleviate that person's distress" (Young, Fox, & Zahn-Waxler, 1999, p. 1189). Cognitive empathy refers to the ability to understand a person from his or her frame of reference or point of view rather than simply from one's own point of view. Jolliffe and Farrington (2007) note that affective empathy is the ability to *experience* another person's emotions, whereas cognitive empathy is the ability to *understand* another's emotions. These terms are not mutually exclusive, however. In other words, one can possess both affective and cognitive empathy.

Deficiencies in empathy have long been considered characteristic of persistently aggressive and antisocial individuals (Cohen & Strayer, 1996; Hastings, Zahn-Waxler, Usher, Robinson, & Bridges, 2000). For example, low affective empathy is hypothesized to be a central ingredient of psychopathy, which is a combination of psychological and behavioral factors related to an increased tendency to engage in antisocial and violent behavior. Interestingly, psychopaths are believed to be able to understand the emotions of others (cognitive empathy), but show a remarkable inability to experience them.

Girls generally show both dimensions of empathy earlier than boys, beginning in the second year of life and continuing at least through adolescence (Eisenberg & Fabes, 1998; Hastings et al., 2000). The relationship between a lack of empathy and antisocial or excessively aggressive behavior is discernible in children during the early to middle elementary school years (Hastings et al., 2000; Tremblay, Vitaro, Gagnon, Piche, & Royer, 1992), and seems to become stronger with age (Miller & Eisenberg, 1988). Children who demonstrate little empathy in the third grade exhibit even less in the eighth grade.

Researchers who have distinguished between the two dimensions of empathy have generally found that a deficiency in affective (or emotional) empathy appears to be most strongly related to violence and persistent criminal behavior (Jolliffe & Farrington, 2007; de Kemp, Overbeek, de Wied, Engels, & Scholte, 2007; Schaffer, Clark, & Jeglic, in press). "It . . . appears that it is the inability to experience the emotions of others which is related to violence for both males and females rather than the inability to understand other people's emotions" (Jolliffe & Farrington, 2007, p. 281). In addition, "Both high-frequency male and female offenders showed lower affective empathy (but not cognitive empathy) than low-rate offenders" (Jolliffe & Farrington, 2007, p. 281). Essentially, people who engage in violence and/or a large variety of serious offenses appear to have a significant inability to feel the pain of their victims.

Some research has shown an interesting association between lack of empathy and animal cruelty. We recently noticed a bumper sticker on the car ahead of us: "People who abuse animals rarely stop there." Research supports this aphorism with respect to both children and adults. Cruelty to animals, defined as "socially unacceptable behavior that intentionally causes unnecessary pain, suffering, or distress to and/or death of an animal" (Guymer, Mellor, Luk, & Pearse, 2001, p. 1057) is a behavior that demonstrates a lack of empathy; if it occurs in childhood, it can signify serious problem behavior. The swatting of flies or the destruction of insects does not qualify as cruelty (although torture of insects may qualify), but cruelty to dogs, cats, and other household pets is considered significant. Cruelty as defined here does not refer to chasing the family cat and playfully pulling its tail, but swinging the cat by the tail or setting its ears on fire is another matter.

Several studies have found a strong association between animal cruelty and violent behavior toward humans. For example, Stouthamer-Loeber and her associates (2004) followed young males from the ages of 13 to 25 and discovered that cruelty to animals was one of the strongest predictors of serious, violent criminal behavior. Wright and Hensley (2003) found a possible link between childhood cruelty to animals and later serial murders. In fact, the five serial murderers studied by Wright and Hensley, which included the infamous Jeffrey Dahmer, used the same method of torture and killing on their human victims as they had used on their animal victims. Merz-Perez, Heide, and Silverman (2001) reported a similar finding.

Cognitive and Language Deficiencies

Cognitive and language impairments increase the risk of antisocial behavior, at least in boys (Brownlie et al., 2004). For example, a high percentage of children and adolescents diagnosed and treated for antisocial behavior and conduct disorders demonstrate language impairments (Cohen *et al.*, 1998; Giddan, Milling, & Campbell, 1996). **Language impairment** usually refers to problems expressing or understanding language, and some research has even traced these problems as far back as very early childhood. In an important study of Swedish children, Stattin and Klackenberg-Larson (1993) discovered that poor language development during the second year of life was a significant predictor of adult criminal behavior. Brownlie *et al.* (2004) also found that boys diagnosed with a language impairment at age five were far more likely to exhibit delinquent behavior at age 19 than a group of boys without early indications of a language impairment. This relationship held even when controlling for verbal IQ, demographic, and family variables. Brownlie *et al.*, speculated, though, that the association may be largely due to the negative impact that language impairments have on the child's schooling and academic performance in general. In addition, language-impaired children are often rejected by peers and are frequently viewed negatively by their teachers. In essence, language deficiency often makes school a painful and unappealing enterprise, leading to poor or disinterested performance on academic tasks.

Language problems also increase frustration levels in children who have difficulty expressing their points of view, which is so necessary for reasonable resolutions of conflict. This frustration, if not self-regulated, is likely to lead to aggressive and disruptive behavior at home and at school.

Intelligence and Delinquency

For some time, criminologists (and many psychologists) have been eager to label the relationship between intelligence and delinquency and crime as misguided and unsubstantiated. Even to mention the connection may prompt a derisive reaction. As Hirschi and Hindelang (1977, p. 572) wrote some years ago, "Textbooks in crime and delinquency ignore IQ or impatiently explain to the reader that IQ is no longer taken seriously by knowledgeable students simply because no differences worth considering have been revealed by research." Hirschi and Hindelang maintained that these textbooks were misleading, because the delinquency literature consistently reported that delinquents do, as a group, score lower on standard intelligence tests than nondelinquents.

In their 1977 paper, Hirschi and Hindelang hypothesized that an *indirect* causal relationship exists between IQ and delinquency. That is, a low IQ leads to poor performance and negative attitudes toward school, which in turn leads to school failure and ultimately to delinquency. Low IQ does not directly lead to delinquency. A high IQ, on the other hand, leads to good performance and positive attitudes toward school, which in turn leads to the internal acceptance of conventional values and conformity (nondelinquency). The essential point, according to Hirschi and Hindelang, is that the inverse relationship between IQ scores and delinquency continues to be documented by research.

Why does this relationship exist? To address this question, it is necessary to consider the meaning of IQ and to stress that it is not identical to "intelligence." The term *IQ* is an abbreviation of *intelligence quotient,* derived from a numerical score on a so-called *intelligence* test. The term *IQ* originated out of what is now called the **psychometric approach**. The word "psychometric" means "psychological measurement." Traditionally, the psychometric approach has searched for unique differences in persons through the use of psychological tests, including intelligence tests, scholastic aptitude tests (e.g., SAT), school achievement tests, personality inventories, and other specific abilities tests. The various tests are used for many purposes, such as selection, diagnosis, and evaluation. The psychometric approach continues to be widely used by practicing psychologists and mental health professionals. However, the term *psychometric intelligence* (**PI**)—which was preferred by some psychologists (Neisser *et al.*, 1996) in the 1990s—has not caught on. Consequently, the traditional term *IQ* continues to be used with great frequency today.

Satisfactory performance on a vast majority of intelligence tests depends greatly on language acquisition and verbal development. Usually, a person must have considerable experience using and defining words—particularly English words—to do well on most IQ tests. The examinee must be able to make conventional connections and see distinctions between verbal concepts. The examinee must also know the facts that the test designer deems important to know within mainstream culture. At the very least, almost all intelligence tests measure some aspect of academic skills that are taught in school or that predict success in school. A vast majority of psychologists today would agree that IQ scores are strongly influenced by social, educational, and cultural experiences. In short, all intelligence tests are culturally biased.

More importantly, IQ scores and the concept of intelligence should not be confused. The term *IQ* merely refers to a standardized score from a test. *Intelligence, on the other hand, is a broad, all-encompassing ability that defies any straightforward or simple definition.* It means many things to different people. Intelligence includes ability ranging from musical talent to logical mathematical skills. The term may also include wisdom, intuition, judgment, and even humor. While delinquents, as a group, do score lower on intelligence *tests,* this observation should not be construed as documenting that delinquents are less intelligent than nondelinquents. For example, Brazilian street children are masters at doing the math required for survival in their street business even though they have failed mathematics in school (Carraher, Carraher, & Schliemann, 1985; Neisser *et al.*, 1996). Likewise, institutionalized delinquents often display artistic and verbal skills and a sense of humor that are not tapped by traditional IQ scores.

Nevertheless, the relationship between IQ test scores and school performance is strong and consistent. "Wherever it has been studied, children with high scores on tests of intelligence tend to learn more of what is taught in school than their lower-scoring peers" (Neisser *et al.*, 1996, p. 82). Schools help develop certain intellectual skills and attitudes. Quality schools generally have positive effects on IQ. Preschool programs (e.g., Headstart) show significant positive effects on children during their early school years, and recent research shows that these gains do not fade when the program is over, provided there is periodic intervention during the child's middle school years.

IQ AND ETHNICITY   Average IQ scores do vary among racial and ethnic groups. For example, many studies using different tests and samples typically show African Americans scoring significantly lower than whites (Neisser *et al.*, 1996). Studies show, however, that this IQ gap has been consistently decreasing since 1980 (Nisbett, 2005; Vincent, 1991). Asian Americans and whites, on average, score about the same on IQ tests; Native Americans score slightly lower than other groups on verbal skills, but this slight difference may be the result of chronic middle-ear infections common among Native American children (McShane & Plas, 1984a, 1984b). Latinos, who make up the second largest and fastest-growing minority group in the United States, typically score somewhere between African Americans and whites. It is unclear what these reported differences mean, but there is no evidence to support the view that racial or ethnic differences in psychometric intelligence are due to genetics or biological factors. Although genetics may play a role in *individual* differences in psychometric intelligence, there is little evidence for ethnic *group* differences.

Group differences in IQ are most likely due to a combination of factors, dominated by cultural and social influences. According to Boykin (1986, 1994), for instance, the African American culture is not quite in synchronization with the values and expectations of the American school system. To varying degrees, the black culture "includes an emphasis on such aspects of experience as spirituality, harmony, movement, verve, affect, expressive individualism, communalism, orality, and a socially defined time perspective" (Neisser *et al.*, 1996, p. 95).

If schools do not recognize and celebrate these positive aspects, African American children may feel left out of the mainstream. According to Boykin, black children often find their cultural background in conflict with the culture of the school system, and consequently they become alienated from both the process and products of that educational system. Equally problematic, however, is the fact that many black children attend inner-city schools, where the quality of education and services is below par. It is not surprising, then, that performance on standardized tests would reflect this inequity.

In the decade since these studies were published, considerable change has occurred, though the quality of many inner-city schools is still deplorable. Furthermore, the election of an African-American U.S. President and the accompanying conversations on race and ethnicity should have positive effects on the cultural mainstream. That is, children from various racial and ethnic groups should be increasingly less likely to feel alienated from what may have been perceived as the dominant culture.

Other factors—such as poor nutrition, inadequate prenatal care, lack of adequate child-care facilities, and inaccessibility to occupational and training opportunities—also play critical but largely unknown roles on intelligence. IQ scores are crude indices of mainstream language skills that are heavily influenced by experience. In general, rich and varied experiences increase IQ scores, and limited experience decreases them (Garbarino & Asp, 1981; Neisser *et al.*, 1996). School experiences, if positive, may increase language skills; if negative, they may stagnate, or even decrease, language skills. IQ scores are also strongly influenced by the type of test used, its content, the many characteristics of testing situations, and the training and skill of the examiner.

Still, even with these many variations, the inverse relationship between IQ scores and the tendency toward delinquency is consistently reported (e.g., Binder, 1988; Quay, 1987; White, Moffitt, & Silva, 1989). As IQ scores go down, the probability of misconduct increases, and vice versa. Children with low IQ scores are at a higher risk for delinquent behavior, and as Anne Crocker and Sheilagh Hodgins (1997, p. 434) write, "To our knowledge, no study has failed to confirm this relation." The relationship is particularly strong for verbal IQ scores (Culberton, Feral, & Gabby, 1989; Kandel *et al.*, 1988). Furthermore, as noted by Crocker and Hodgins (1997), the relationship between low IQ scores and delinquency appears to be independent of socioeconomic status, race, and detection by the police (Lynam, Moffitt, & Stouthamer-Loeber, 1993; Moffitt, 1990b). Moreover, it should be emphasized that this relationship is not specific to delinquency; the relationship is equally robust for adult offenders. Interestingly, it has been suggested that many adult onset offenders had low intelligence but did not offend as juveniles because they were protected by supportive families or schools. As these cognitively limited individuals reached adulthood, they were unable to transition successfully to adult roles (Thornberry & Krohn, 2005).

IQ AND ADULT OFFENDERS   Very low IQ scores, those that indicate mental disability, are of particular concern. Recent estimates indicate that at least 4 percent of the U.S. prison population qualify as being mentally disabled (Ashford, Sales, & Reid, 2001). **Jails** are believed to hold an even higher percentage. It should be noted that mental disability (also referred to as deficiency or retardation) is distinct from mental disorder or mental illness; mental disability is cognitive impairment, whereas mental disorder or illness is emotional.

Crocker and Hodgins (1997) examined the criminality of mentally deficient (disabled) men and women in a Swedish birth cohort composed of over fifteen thousand subjects. The subjects were followed from birth to age 30. Subjects who were placed in special classes for the mentally retarded (both at the elementary and high school level) were compared with normal subjects. Subjects considered mentally disabled were more likely to have been convicted for criminal offenses, including violent ones, than normal subjects. Crocker and Hodgins also found that, similar to mentally normal subjects, conduct problems in childhood (before age 12) were predictive of adult antisocial behavior in both mentally deficient male and female groups.

SUMMARY   What does the relationship between IQ scores and delinquency and crime mean exactly? It probably means that delinquents *as a group,* particularly serious delinquents, have had limited experiences in mainstream society, ineffective parenting, restricted cognitive and language development, and poor school experiences, but it does not necessarily mean that they are not intelligent. An undetermined proportion of delinquents are cognitively impaired to the extent that they could be called "mentally deficient" or "developmentally challenged," but so many factors are involved in an ultimate IQ score that a simple causal connection between low IQ and delinquency is unwarranted.

Related to the IQ question is the issue of learning disabilities, a term that is also not synonymous with intelligence. Educational psychologists have identified a variety of learning disabilities, including some that may be associated with brain injuries and perceptual difficulties. Many, if not most, children with learning disabilities are not cognitively impaired. However, there is considerable empirical evidence that juvenile delinquents have a far greater incidence of learning disabilities than nondelinquents (Brier, 1989; Lombardo & Lombardo, 1991; Scaret & Wilgosh, 1989). While learning disabilities clearly exist, it is believed that they are overdiagnosed or misdiagnosed in many children who then acquire a label that may follow them through the educational system. Like the IQ question, it is very unclear what the relationship between delinquency and learning disability truly means.

Attention Deficit Hyperactivity Disorder

Children are born with a wide range of genetic influences, neurological predispositions, and different temperaments, although the social and physical environments may alter them. These are all biological factors, and some appear to play a major role in the development of crime and delinquency. Chief among them is attention deficient disorder/hyperactivity disorder, commonly abbreviated ADHD.

The term *hyperactive syndrome* (also called minimal brain dysfunction, hyperkinesis, attention deficit disorder, or currently **Attention Deficit Hyperactivity Disorder [ADHD]**) includes a variety of behaviors. The central three are (1) inattention (does not seem to listen, or is easily distracted); (2) impulsivity (acts before thinking, shifts quickly from one activity to another); and (3) excessive motor activity (cannot sit still, fidgets, runs about, is talkative and noisy).

ADHD is the leading psychological diagnosis for American children (Cowley, 1993; Staller, 2006). Educators note that ADHD children have difficulty staying on task, remaining cognitively organized, sustaining academic achievement in the school setting, and maintaining control over their behavior. Although the common belief is that one eventually outgrows hyperactivity, the evidence is that the key symptomatic features of hyperactivity persist into adulthood (Klinteberg, Magnusson, & Schalling, 1989; Thorley, 1984). It should be emphasized, however, that many children diagnosed with ADHD grow up to lead highly successful lives, and most do not follow a life course of serious delinquency and crime. There is a long list of scientists, entertainers, politicians, artists, musicians, athletes, and other public figures that were once diagnosed with or are now suspected of having had ADHD, including Albert Einstein, Dwight D. Eisenhower, Whoopi

Goldberg, Bill Gates, Bill Cosby, Michael Phelps, Steven Spielberg, Walt Disney, John Lennon, Ann Bancroft, Terry Bradshaw, Richard Byrd, Andrew Carnegie, Robin Williams, Agatha Christie, and Ludwig Beethoven

ADHD affects an estimated 3 percent to 5 percent of school age children (Stern, 2001), and occurs more often in boys than girls, usually in a ratio of 5 to 1. Furthermore, ADHD is diagnosed more frequently in children who have a close biological relative with ADHD than in the general population, suggesting there may be a significant biological component involved. Boys with ADHD are at increased risk for engaging in delinquent and antisocial behavior. "As they grow older, children with untreated ADHD . . . may abuse drugs or alcohol, engage in antisocial behavior, and suffer physical injury at higher rates that the general population" (Stern, 2001, p. 1).

ADHD is a puzzling problem, the cause of which is largely unknown. Some scientists contend that ADHD children are born with a biological predisposition toward hyperactivity; others maintain that some children are exposed to environmental factors that damage the nervous system. Rolf Loeber (1990) demonstrates how exposure to toxic substances during the preschool years often retards children's neurological development or otherwise influences it in a negative way, often resulting in symptoms of ADHD. For example, children exposed to low levels of lead toxicity (e.g., from paint or contaminated soil) are more hyperactive and impulsive, and are easily distracted and frustrated. They also show discernible problems in following simple instructions. The causal factors of ADHD are probably multiple and extremely difficult to identify.

Some researchers observe that ADHD children do not possess effective strategies and cognitive organization with which to deal with the daily demands of school. ADHD children also seem to lack cognitively organized ways for dealing with new knowledge. The core problem appears to center around executive functions, or what can be termed self-regulation skills (Douglas, 2004). **Self-regulation** refers to the ability to control behavior. According to Virginia Douglas (2004), it is not so much "not knowing" as "not doing." Attention, inhibition, and organizing are ways of "doing" or working on cognitive processes. Stimulant drugs, Douglas argues, enable ADHD children to improve on self-regulation processes. These drugs themselves, though, are extremely controversial and are themselves widely believed to be overprescribed.

Although many behaviors have been identified as accompanying ADHD, another overriding theme is that ADHD children are perceived as annoying and aversive to those around them. Although ADHD children are continually seeking and prolonging interpersonal contacts, they eventually manage to irritate and frustrate those people with whom they interact (Henker & Whalen, 1989). They are often rejected by peers, especially if they are perceived as aggressive (Henker & Whalen, 1989). This pattern of peer rejection appears to continue throughout the developmental years (Reid, 1993). As noted earlier in the chapter, peer rejection is a strong predictor of delinquent behavior.

ADHD and Criminal Behavior

Some researchers (e.g., Pfiffner, McBurnett, Rathouz, & Judice, 2005) estimate about one-fourth of all children with ADHD engage in serious antisocial behavior during childhood and adolescence and criminal behavior as adults. Terrie Moffitt (Moffitt, 1993b; Moffitt & Silva, 1988) observes that a very large number of ADHD children self-report delinquent behaviors by early adolescence. She also found that children between the ages of five and seven who demonstrate the characteristics of both ADHD and delinquent behavior not only have special difficulty with social relationships but also have a high probability of consistent serious antisocial behavior into adolescence and beyond (Moffitt, 1990b). Experts generally agree that the most common problem associated with ADHD is delinquency and substance abuse. The data strongly suggest that youth with symptoms of both ADHD and antisocial behavior are at very high risk for developing lengthy and serious criminal careers (Moffitt, 1990b; Satterfield, Swanson, Schell, & Lee, 1994). David Farrington (1991), in his well-cited research, also found that violent offenders often have a history of hyperactivity, impulsivity, and attention-deficit problems.

Conduct Disorder

ADHD frequently co-occurs with a diagnostic category called "conduct disorders" (Offord, Boyle, & Racine, 1991; Reid, 1993), but the two should be considered separate entities. The term *conduct disorder* (CD) represents a cluster of behaviors characterized by persistent misbehavior. Examples of this misbehavior include stealing, fire setting, running away from home, skipping school, destroying property, fighting, frequently telling lies, and cruelty to animals and people. According to the *Diagnostic and Statistical Manual-IV-Revised* (DSM-IV-R), published by the American Psychiatric Association (2000), the central feature of conduct disorder is the *repetitive* and *persistent* pattern of behavior that violates the basic rights of others.

Behavioral indicators of a conduct disorder can be observed in the context of interactions with parents well before school entry (Reid, 1993). For instance, children who are aggressive, difficult to manage, and noncompliant in the home at age three often continue to have similar problems when entering school. Furthermore, these behaviors show remarkable consistency through adolescence and into adulthood. CD children frequently have significant problems with school assignments, a behavioral pattern that often results in their being mislabeled with a "learning disability." It is important to note that genuinely learning-disabled students are not necessarily conduct disordered, however. In other words, the two designations may overlap, but each is also a distinct categorization. Aggressive CDs are at high risk for strong rejection by their peers (Reid, 1993). This rejection generally lasts throughout the school years and is very difficult to change (Reid, 1993). Children who are consistently socially rejected by peers miss critical opportunities to develop normal interpersonal and social skills. Lacking effective interpersonal skills, these youths are forced to get their needs met through more aggressive means, including threats and intimidation.

The *DSM-IV-R* identifies two subtypes of conduct disorders based on the onset of the repetition and persistence of the misbehavior: the *childhood-onset type* and *adolescent-onset type*. According to the *DSM-IV-R*, childhood-onset type occurs when the pattern begins prior to age 10. The adolescent-onset type, on the other hand, is characterized by the absence of any pattern before age 10. The *DSM-IV-R* also notes that if the CD pattern begins before age 10, the prognosis is not good, compared with a more favorable prognosis for a later onset. In fact, Hodgins, Cree, and Mak (2008) found that if a CD pattern is present prior to age 15, it is strongly associated with an increased risk of violent behavior into middle age. This finding holds for both males and females.

There is some recent research suggesting that individual maladjustment and family influences are more highly associated with childhood-onset conduct disorders, whereas ethnic minority status and exposure to deviant peers is more highly associated with adolescent-onset conduct disorders (McCabe, Hough, Wood, & Yeh, 2001). The researchers also found that those children who exhibit childhood-onset conduct disorders are more likely to commit more serious or aggressive offenses than adolescent-onset conduct disorders, although the results were not as strong as the first finding.

Overall, between 2 percent and 6 percent of children and adolescents in the United States show behavioral patterns that may be diagnosed as a conduct disorder (Eddy, 2003). The prevalence in girls ranges from 4 percent to 9.2 percent (Cohen, Cohen, & Brook, 1993; Zoccoulillo, 1993). In addition, CD is the diagnostic label most often placed on youths who appear before the juvenile courts (Lahey *et al.*, 1995). A study by Anna Bardone and her colleagues (Bardone, Moffitt, & Caspi, 1996) found that CD patterns in girls are a strong predictor of a lifetime of problems, including poor interpersonal relations with partners/spouses and peers, criminal activity, early pregnancy without supportive partners, and frequent job loss and firings. Similar to CD boys, CD girls appear destined for a life of interpersonal conflict with the social environment.

Summary and Conclusions

In recent years, developmental psychologists have been extremely active in studying the life course of individuals who participate in persistent juvenile and adult offending. They have examined developmental pathways or trajectories that lead to little or no offending, minor juvenile offending that ends around mid to late adolescence, or serious offending into adulthood, among others. Researchers can now point with confidence to a large list of risk factors associated with juvenile delinquency and criminal behavior. No single variable is particularly at fault. In this chapter, we began to examine some of the social and psychological risk factors associated with crime and delinquency, including peer and family influences, preschool and school influences, cognitive ability, ADHD, and conduct disorders.

Many theories of criminology trace the roots of offending to childhood and early adolescence. An adverse economic environment must be considered within the context of the many influences that impinge on young lives. Features often associated with poverty—discrimination, inadequate schools, unsafe living conditions, joblessness, social isolation, and opportunities to learn law-violating behaviors from peers—all play roles in the formation of crime and delinquency.

One risk factor that appears increasingly in the literature on delinquency is early peer rejection, even during the elementary school years. This can occur regardless of a child's socioeconomic status. Children who are rejected by peers are often aggressive, but aggression alone is not the major explanation. Rather, they also tend to be disruptive, impulsive, and/or have few interpersonal skills. Research has demonstrated consistently that antisocial adolescents, particularly those who displayed highly aggressive behavior, experienced significant peer rejection during their childhoods. In girls, substance abuse and other delinquent behaviors in adolescence has been associated with peer rejection in elementary school.

Preschool experiences are also increasingly being recognized as possible risk factors. Poor-quality child care places children at risk for poorer language and cognitive development, as well as deficiencies in social skills. Unfortunately, inadequate child care is often associated with low socioeconomic class. On the other hand, high-quality day care has been shown to improve the chances that children from economically deprived families will do well both behaviorally and in school settings.

It is important to stress that delinquency is clearly not limited to youths from the lower class. Self-report data suggest that social class differences become smaller when youths are asked to report their own offending. If poverty and the conditions it generates are not an issue for these youth, we must look to other risk factors, such as parenting styles and practices, the influence of antisocial peers, and the more individual factors such as conduct disorders, ADHD, intelligence, and gender.

Among the parental and family risk factors discussed in the chapter are single-parent households, which have too often been blamed for antisocial behavior of children. We stressed process variables rather than structure variables were more likely risk factors. For example, researchers have found associations between certain parental styles and antisocial behavior in children. Styles are typically identified as authoritarian, permissive, authoritative, or neglecting (Baumrind, 1991a) or as enmeshed or lax (Snyder & Patterson, 1987). Although many parents may well vary their styles across situations and as children get older, in general, one style dominates. The permissive and lax styles—characterized by little or no control over the children and extremely few restrictions—are highly correlated with delinquent behavior. In similar fashion, parental monitoring or supervision of the child's activities, particularly from the ages of nine to midadolescence, is crucial to the development of prosocial behavior.

We covered psychological risk factors—those that are unique to the child—as factors on the road to delinquency. Low IQ scores have consistently been associated with delinquency, not necessarily directly but more likely because children with low scores do not do well in school, and school failure is also commonly associated with antisocial behavior. We stressed, though, that a low score on an "intelligence" test does not mean that a child is not intelligent. In addition, we know not only that many delinquents are intelligent despite scoring below normal on IQ tests, but also that other delinquents score high on IQ tests. Therefore, the IQ-delinquency connection must be expressed very cautiously.

Children with ADHD are at some risk of antisocial behavior both as juveniles and adults. This disorder apparently affects 3 percent to 5 percent of school-aged children, though in some communities the percentages are even higher, leading to questions about misdiagnoses. ADHD appears to be a disorder affecting social relationships; the children have difficulty staying on task, they get easily distracted, are impulsive, display excessive motor activity, and are annoying to others. These features often lead to peer rejection. Although ADHD is routinely treated with medication, this in itself is a controversial issue, and critics recommend the use of other approaches, including physical exercise and outdoor activities. Untreated, ADHD children are at risk for delinquency and substance abuse.

Conduct disorder is somewhat of a catch-all category that is characterized by persistent misbehavior, including stealing, running away, fighting, telling lies, and cruelty. Signs of conduct disorder may occur as early as age three; when children reach school age, they are often mislabeled with a "learning disability" or with ADHD, but the three are distinct categories. Not surprisingly, conduct disorder is also associated with peer rejection.

Key Concepts

Attachment theory	Enmeshed style	Parental practices
Attention Deficit Hyperactivity Disorder (ADHD)	Jails	Parental styles
	Language impairment	Permissive style
Authoritarian style	Lax style	Psychometric approach
Authoritative style	Neglecting style	Psychometric intelligence
Conduct disorder	Parental monitoring	Self-regulation
Developmental pathways		

Review Questions

1. What three categories of risk factors are covered in this chapter? Name and explain briefly any two factors falling into each category.
2. Explain the difference between ADHD and conduct disorder.
3. Describe the features of ADHD that create problems for the child who has this disorder.
4. In what ways may preschool experiences influence a life of delinquency and crime?
5. Describe each of Baumrind's four parental styles.
6. What is attachment theory, and how may it relate to juvenile delinquency and adult criminal behavior?

3

Origins of Criminal Behavior: Biological Factors

From Chapter 3 of *Criminal Behavior: A Psychological Approach*, Ninth Edition. Curt R. Bartol and Anne M. Bartol.

Origins of Criminal Behavior: Biological Factors

CHAPTER OBJECTIVES

- Explore the genetic and biological aspects of criminal behavior.
- Provide an overview of twin and adoption studies and their relation to theories of crime.
- Identify environmental risk factors that play a role in the psychobiological aspects of criminal behavior.
- Discuss temperament and its effects on the behavior of children and their caretakers.
- Present Eysenck's theory of crime as an interactionist perspective and to emphasize the role of conditioning in acquiring behavior.

Cross the threshold of any preschool or kindergarten classroom, and you are likely to encounter a flurry of activity—little people scurrying or trying to scurry around the room, or restless and energetic tykes eager to move to a different location or position. You are also likely to observe a fair amount of pushing and shoving, despite a teacher's efforts to keep these behaviors under control.

A common research finding is that many if not most children exhibit high levels of physical aggression in preschool or kindergarten, but in most cases, they typically show significant reductions of these behaviors during the early school years due to the effects of socialization and parenting (Bongers, Koot, van der Ende, & Verhulst, 2003; Séguin, Nagin, Asaad, & Tremblay, 2004). The pushing and shoving observed in kindergarten should dissipate within the next few years. Another common finding, however, is that certain brain and biochemical abnormalities appear to *predispose* some children to exhibit higher levels of aggression than that exhibited by their peers, and if these abnormalities are not neutralized by socialization and competent parenting, many of these children grow up to follow a life path characterized by high levels of aggression and violence. Youngsters who follow an early onset of persistent antisocial behavior often exhibit biological/neurological abnormalities, while late onset offending appears to be more influenced by social factors (Moffitt, Lynam, & Silva, 1994; Rutter, 1997; Rutter, Giller, & Hagell, 1998).

Thus, many—perhaps most—contemporary criminologists would agree with the following statement: "Genetics may play a role in criminality, but it is only an insignificant one. There is little doubt that environment, as well as individual or group values, are important determinants and causes of criminal behavior." Greed, desire for power, the glorification of violence, poverty, high unemployment, poor education, faulty parenting, and group values that deviate from society's norms are often considered the major culprits in producing crime. Heredity-based physiological components have been traditionally scoffed at, and their possible role as causal agents in criminality is often dismissed.

Why so? Perhaps because accepting heredity or biological factors as causal factors in criminal behavior implies that criminal acts are unavoidable, inevitable consequences of the "bad seed," "bad blood," or "mark of Cain." Heredity is destiny. Little can be done to prevent the ill-fated person from becoming a criminal. Most behavioral scientists today—and many social scientists—recognize, however, that behavioral traits result from an *interaction* of hereditary and environmental factors. We no longer ask whether behavior is strictly due to heredity or environment; we agree that both are involved in a complex way. However, researchers usually focus on one or the other for intensive study. In this chapter, we discuss the work of psychologists who study heredity and biopsychology as factors in the genesis of criminal behavior.

Biopsychologists (psychologists who study the biological aspects of behavior) try to determine which genetic and neurophysiological variables play a part in criminal behavior, how important they are, and what can be done to modify them. In recent years, molecular biology has focused on specific genes as foundations for certain patterns of behavior. Further, "a central precept of molecular biology is that all the information needed to construct a mammalian body, whether human or mouse, is contained in the approximately 100,000 genes of mammalian DNA and that a set of master genes activates the DNA necessary to produce the appropriate proteins for development and behavior" (Cacioppo, Berntson, Sheridan, & McClintock, 2000, p. 833).

Biopsychologists do not believe that genetic or neurophysiological components are the sole or even primary causal agents of human behavior. Most would say that understanding the social environment is as important as understanding the biological one. In the words of one group of biopsychologists, "—The social world, as well as the organization and operation of the brain, shapes and modulates genetic and biological processes, and accordingly, knowledge of biological and social domains is necessary to develop comprehensive theories in either domain" (Cacioppo *et al.*, 2000, p. 833). In this chapter, we concentrate on the biological relationships to criminal behavior, while, at the same time, continually appreciating the enormous influence of the social environment on the neurological and biological processes. More than 100 studies have addressed the question of genetic influences on antisocial behavior (Moffitt, 2005). Although we cannot examine these investigations in detail here, we present a summary of their findings.

The chapter first explores the genetic aspects of crime, including findings from twin and adoption studies, and then moves on to discuss physiological and environmental health factors that can affect one's behavior. The chapter ends with one of the major theories and research areas in the psychology of crime—Eysenck's theory of personality. The theory is covered in detail because it offers a compelling view of how personality, biological factors, and the social environment work together in developing criminal behavioral patterns.

GENETICS AND ANTISOCIAL BEHAVIOR

According to Adrian Raine (2002), a prominent biopsychologist, "There is now clear evidence from twin studies, adoption studies, twins reared apart, and molecular genetic studies to support the notion that there are genetic influences on antisocial and aggressive behavior" (p. 312). The more challenging issues, Raine notes, are determining if and how genetic processes interact with environmental factors in predisposing individuals to antisocial and violent behavior. So far, twin studies provide more support for the heritability of antisocial behavior than adoption studies. As we will see, when one identical twin demonstrates antisocial behavior, there is a significant probability that the other twin will demonstrate similar behavior, even when they are reared apart. Nevertheless, both twin and adoption studies have the potential of providing a more convincing case for the relative influence of genetic and environmental factors.

Twin Studies

One way to determine the role of genetics in criminality is to compare the incidence and type of delinquency or criminal convictions among identical (monozygotic) and fraternal (dizygotic) twins. **Dizygotic DZ twins** (also called **fraternal twins**) develop from two different fertilized eggs and are no more genetically alike than nontwin siblings. **Monozygotic (MZ)twins** (or **identical twins**) develop from a single egg; they are always the same sex and share the same genes. Presumably, then, if genes are determinative, identical twins should display highly similar behavior. Because MZ twins share 100 percent of their genes, it can be inferred that a child's genetic risk for antisocial behavior is high if his or her cotwin shows antisocial behavior and low if the MZ cotwin does not.

However, to complicate matters a bit, approximately two-thirds of monozygotic twins are monochorionic (share the same chorion), and one-third of the monozygotic pair is dichorionic (two different chorions) (Rhee & Waldman, 2002). The chorion is the outer membrane enclosing the embryo. Therefore, some identical twins develop in slightly different prenatal environments, which may contribute to some individual differences that may emerge as the twins develop into maturity. In fact, several studies have found that monochorionic, monozygotic twins are more similar in personality and cognitive ability than dichorionic, monozygotic twins (Rhee & Waldman, 2002). Theoretically, however, by comparing fraternal twins and identical twins, researchers should be able to identify the relative contributions of genes compared with environmental factors in the development of personality, cognitive ability, and behavior in general.

SHARED AND NONSHARED ENVIRONMENTS   Two important concepts need to be recognized before a good understanding of twin studies can be achieved: **shared environments** and **nonshared environments**. Shared or common environments include prenatal and life experiences affecting both twins in the same way. For example, twins raised by the same biological parents share a common hereditary and home environment. Shared environments in this sense are apt to promote high trait or behavioral similarity between twin pairs, especially for identical twins. Nonshared environments, on the other hand, include living experiences that are different for each twin, such as being raised in a different home environment, participating in different activities, or even attending different schools. Parents sometimes want to preserve the uniqueness of each twin by encouraging them to join separate groups or pursue separate hobbies. Therefore, in order to determine the relative influence of genes on behavior, compared with the environment, shared and nonshared aspects must be considered.

Twin research indicates that, for a variety of traits, the magnitude of genetic and nonshared environmental influences increases as a person gets older, whereas the magnitude of shared environmental influences decreases (Loehlin, 1992; Plomin, 1986; Rhee & Waldman, 2002). That is, as the child begins to spend more time outside the family circle, especially when he or she becomes a young adult, the influence of the shared environment (family) tends to wane, whereas the influence of genetics and nonshared environments (e.g., peers) becomes more discernible. Rhee and

Waldman (2002) describe a longitudinal study by Matheny (1989) which revealed that the temperaments (e.g., emotional tone, fearfulness, approach or avoidance toward others) became more similar for identical pairs than for fraternal pairs as they grew older. Thus, we might expect that developmental age of the subjects in any twin study may play an important role in determining the influences of genetics compared with the environment. We return to this point shortly.

Some investigators suggest that identical twins are so physically alike that they probably elicit similar social responses from their environment (shared environment), more so than fraternal twins. In this sense, they are more likely to develop similar personalities. There may be merit to this viewpoint, but research does not yet support it. Rather, some research has found that identical twins reared apart are more alike in some personality attributes than are identical twins reared in the same home environment (Canter, 1973; Shields, 1962). When reared together, identical twins or their parents may make a conscious effort to accentuate their individual identities, whereas when reared apart, they may have less need to be different.

A key concept in twin study research, **concordance** is the genetics term for the degree to which related pairs of subjects both show a particular behavior or condition. It is usually expressed in percentages. Assume that we want to determine the concordance of intelligence among 20 pairs of identical twins and 20 pairs of fraternals. If we find that 10 pairs of the identical twins have approximately the same IQ score, but only five pairs of the fraternals obtain the same score, our concordance is 50 percent for identicals and 25 percent for fraternals. The concordance for identicals would be twice that of fraternals, suggesting that hereditary factors play an important role in intelligence. If, however, the two concordances were about the same, we would conclude that genetics is irrelevant, at least as represented in our sample and measured by our methods.

Numerous early twin studies using this concordance method have indicated that heredity may be a powerful determinant of intelligence, schizophrenia, depressions, neurotic disorders, alcoholism, and criminal behavior (Claridge, 1973; Hetherington & Parke, 1975; McClearn & DeFries, 1973; Rosenthal, 1970, 1971). The first such study relative to criminality was reported by the Munich physician Johannes Lange (1929) in his book *Crime as Destiny* (Christiansen, 1977; Rosenthal, 1971). The title reflects Lange's conviction that criminal conduct is a predetermined fate dictated by heredity. He found a criminality concordance of 77 percent for 13 pairs of adult identical twins and only 12 percent for 17 pairs of adult fraternal twins. Auguste Marcel Legras (1932) then found a 100 percent criminal concordance for five pairs of identicals. Note that both of these studies used small samples. Subsequent studies, using more sophisticated designs and methods of twin identification and sampling, continued to find a substantially higher criminal concordance for identical twins when compared with fraternals. The levels were not as high as those reported by either Lange or Legras, however. **Table 1** summarizes relevant investigations of criminal concordance. Although these tabulated investigations differed in method and definitions of criminality, the combined concordance levels demonstrate that, where criminal behavior is concerned, identical twins seem better matched than fraternal twins.

Hans Eysenck reviewed other twin studies, found similar concordances, and concluded, "Thus concordance is found over four times as frequently in identicals as in fraternals, a finding which seems to put beyond any doubt that heredity plays an extremely important part in the genesis of criminal behaviour" (Eysenck, 1973, p. 167). Rosenthal, however, injects a word of caution, stressing the many pitfalls of the concordance twin method and the ramifications of using different legal definitions of criminality. Nevertheless, he allows, "It is clearly not possible to rule out the potential fact that genetic factors may indeed be the primary source of the higher concordance rate in MZ (identical) as compared to DZ (fraternal) twins" (Rosenthal, 1975, p. 10).

TABLE 1   Summary of Twin-Criminality Studies Showing Pairs and Concordance Rates

Researchers	Identical Twins			Fraternal Twins		
	No. of Pairs	Pairs Concordant	Percentage	No. of Pairs	Pairs Concordant	Percentage
Lange (1929)	13	10	77	17	2	12
Legras (1932)	4	4	100	5	0	0
Rosanoff et al.(1934)	37	25	68	60	6	10
Kranz (1936)	31	20	65	43	20	53
Stumpfl (1936)	18	11	61	19	7	37
Borgstrom (1939)	4	3	75	5	2	40
Rosanoff et al. (1941)	45	35	78	27	6	18
Yoshimasu (1961)	28	17	61	18	2	11
Yoshimasu (1965)	28	14	50	26	0	0
Hayashi (1967)	15	11	73	5	3	60
Dalgaard & Kringlen (1976)	31	8	26	54	8	15
Christiansen (1977)						
Males	71	25	35	120	15	13
Females	14	2	21	27	2	8
Total	339	185	55	426	73	17

Eysenck further complicates the issue by suggesting that twin studies may actually have deflated the true concordance rate, since it is likely that identical twins were often confused with fraternal twins, especially in the earlier studies. If the twins are of the same sex, it is difficult to distinguish identicals from fraternals from appearance alone. Today, blood type, fingerprints (which are highly similar but not identical), and various genetically determined serum proteins allow differentiation. Since these methods were not available to earlier investigators, Eysenck contends that mix-ups may have confounded the results. However, the concordance rates may just as easily have been inflated as deflated.

As **Table 1** shows, twin studies have not invariably found high criminal concordance rates in favor of identical twins. One study by Dalgaard and Kringlen (1976) found no significant difference between identicals and fraternals. The Dalgaard-Kringlen sample included all the registered male twins born in Norway between 1921 and 1930. However, 32 percent of the sample was deleted from the analysis for various reasons, which might have affected the results. Also, the label "criminal" was applied to traffic violations, military offenses, and treason during World War II, as well as to all actions against the penal code. This was a broader definition than was used in most twin studies. The late Karl O. Christiansen, who devoted much of his research work to twin studies, could not explain the lack of significant differences reported by Dalgaard and Kringlen. He advocated an additional study to determine whether "some special conditions exist in Norway that would dampen the expression of genetic factors" (Christiansen, 1977, p. 82).

Overall, despite procedural and definitional problems and except for the Dalgaard-Kringlen data, the studies examining concordance rates among twins have consistently indicated higher concordance for identical twins. More recent research, however, indicates that these higher concordance rates may hold only for adult nonviolent offending and not for juvenile offending (Blackburn, 1993). In a careful review of the literature, Adrian Raine (1993, p. 79) concludes, "Summary statistics from 13 twin analyses show that 51.5 percent of MZ twins are concordant for crime compared to 20.6 percent for DZ twins, indicating substantial evidence for genetic influences on crime."

Twin Studies and Criminal Behavior: Recent Research

The twin data clearly suggest that it might be wise to consider heredity a significant component in criminality. However, it should also be emphasized that the research cited above favors the heritability of nonviolent crime, but not violent crime (Dodge & Pettit, 2003; Raine, 1993). Most of early concordance research either did not define criminal behavior clearly, or utilized nonviolent criminal behavior largely to the exclusion of violent criminal behavior. In addition, "Although specific genes . . . may have special relevance for the development of conduct problems, the genetic base for most problem behaviors likely reflects combinations of genes that are expressed in different ways at different points of life" (Dodge & Pettit, 2003, p. 351). Thus, some combination of genes does appear to render certain children at risk for developing delinquent or antisocial behavior, but environmental factors play prominent roles in the formation of that behavior also (Dodge & Pettit, 2003; Rhee & Waldman, 2002). Continuing contemporary research indicates, however, that genetics cannot be overlooked (Beaver, Ratchford, & Ferguson, 2009).

One of the most closely-watched series of twin studies is the longitudinal research now being conducted in the United Kingdom with a large sample of twins born in 1994, 1995, and 1996 in England and Wales. Called the Twins' Early Development Study (TEDS), it explores behavior problems as well as problematic development in language, cognition, and academic abilities from early childhood through adolescence (Oliver & Plomin, 2007; Tourton et al., 2002). Although there has been some attrition since data were first collected, over 13,000 pairs of twins have remained involved in the research.

As we have indicated throughout this chapter, both nature and nurture contribute to human behavior, and—not surprisingly—this is supported in TEDS research studies. However, TEDS research indicates that nature has considerable influence over some behavior problems or disorders (e.g., ADHD; autism spectrum disorder). With respect to antisocial behavior, which is our main concern, heritability plays a very modest role. Nevertheless, at least one personality feature that has been associated with antisocial behavior—the callous-unemotional personality—shows very high heritability and little shared environmental influence (Oliver & Plomin, 2007; Viding, Blair, James, Moffitt, & Plomin, 2005).

In a recent study facilitated by the TEDS data base, Jaffee and her colleagues (2005) used monozygotic (MZ) and dizygotic (DZ) twin pairs to study the interplay between genetic and environmental risks on the development of antisocial behavior in a cohort of 1,116 five-year-old twin pairs and their families. These participants are members of the Environmental Risk (E-Risk) Longitudinal Twin Study. The Jaffee researchers ascertained the children's antisocial behavior through interviews with parents, assessments of the children, and questionnaires administered to teachers. The environmental risk factor in the study was the amount of maltreatment the child reportedly received from parents, because research shows that early maltreatment often leads to antisocial behavior (Lansford *et al.*, 2002). Not surprisingly, Jaffee *et al.* (2005) discovered that the effect of maltreatment on the risk to develop antisocial behavior was strongest among those at higher genetic risk. In other words, those children with a genetic predisposition to become troublesome and antisocial were especially likely to be that way if they were mistreated. These findings and the findings of many other studies support the general consensus that environmental changes turn genetic influences on and off during the developmental years, and that biological factors and environmental influences do interact (Raine, 2002). In fact, there is emerging evidence that suggests the social environment (e.g., parenting) can affect people who are at genetic risk more strongly than previously appreciated (Moffitt, 2005).

These environmental influences seem to wane somewhat as a person moves into adulthood, however. For example, there is emerging evidence that the magnitude of familial or parental influences on aggressive behavior decreases with increasing age, and genetic factors increasingly play a prominent role in the stability of aggression and antisocial behavior across the life span (Rhee & Waldman, 2002; van Beijsterveldt, Bartels, Hudziak, & Boomsma, 2003). This effect seems to be particularly strong in males. Female aggressive behavior, on the other hand, seems to be more strongly affected by the family environment (van Beijsterveldt *et al.*, 2003). In other words, family influences appear to be more powerful in the inhibition of antisocial behavior in girls than in boys, particularly as the girls approach adolescence and early adulthood.

Another longitudinal research project is the Twin Study of Child and Adolescent Development (TCHAD), using data from the Swedish Twin Registry. Tuvblad, Eley, and Lichtenstein (2005), studying 1,226 twin pairs, employed a well-researched behavioral scale to measure parental-reported aggression in children ages 8 and 9. They then asked the same group of children to report their own delinquent behavior eight years later. The researchers used both monozygotic and dizygotic twins in their effort to disentangle genetic factors from environmental factors. They found that genetic factors played an important role in the early onset of aggressive behavior in children, but appeared to play a less important role in the development of delinquent behavior as reported by male adolescents. A similar finding was reported by Taylor, Iacono, and McGue (2000), who found that genetics played a more prominent role in early-onset delinquency (life-course-persistent offenders), whereas the social environment (e.g., delinquent peers) was more influential in late-onset delinquency (adolescent-limited offenders). The subjects in the study were all boys. Surprisingly, genetics appeared to play a much more prominent role in development of *both* aggressive behavior and delinquency in girls in the Tuvblad *et al.* (2005) study. These results appear to be in contrast to the study of Rhee and Waldman (2002), who concluded that the magnitude of genetic and environmental influences on antisocial behavior is equal for both genders. It is clear from these two contrasting studies that further research on the relative influence of genes on gender differences in antisocial behavior is warranted.

Adoption Studies

Another method used to identify crucial variables in the interaction between heredity and environment is the adoption study, which helps identify environments most conducive to criminality. There have been exceedingly few such investigations, however, and those few have been fraught with methodological problems.

One of the first adoption studies was carried out in Denmark by Schulsinger (1972), who explored the incidence of psychopathy in the biological relatives of adopted adults. Schulsinger compared 57 adopted adults whom he diagnosed psychopathic to a control group of 57 nonpsychopathic adopted adults. The two groups were matched for sex, age, social class, and age of transfer to the adopting family. The study's direct implications for criminal behavior are questionable, because Schulsinger defined psychopathy by his own loose criteria. Individuals who were impulse-ridden and who exhibited acting-out behavior qualified. These descriptions do not necessarily connote either psychopathy or criminality. Nevertheless, impulsivity is associated with some forms of criminal behavior, so the study has some relevance.

Schulsinger found that 3.9 percent of the biological relatives of psychopathic adoptees could also be classified as psychopathic, whereas only 1.4 percent of the control group's biological relatives could. The results just failed to reach statistical significance, indicating that we should be very cautious about accepting their implications. It is interesting, though, that psychopathy—even given its loose definition—was about two and a half times greater in the family backgrounds of acting-out adoptees.

Crowe (1974) conducted a better-designed study, a follow-up of 52 persons relinquished for early adoption by female offenders. Ninety percent of the biological mothers were felons at the time of the adoptive placement, the most common offenses being forgery and passing bad checks. Twenty-five of the adoptees were female, and all were white. Another 52 adoptees with no evidence of criminal family background were selected as a control group and matched for sex, race, and age at the time of adoption.

For the follow-up phase of the study, Crowe selected 37 index and 37 control subjects who had by then reached age 18. (Index subjects in research are those subjects who are of major concern.) Seven of the index adoptees had arrest records: As adults, all seven had at least one conviction, four had multiple arrests, two had multiple convictions, and three were felons. Of the 37 matching controls, two had adult arrest records and only one of these had been convicted. Each subject's personality was diagnosed by three clinicians based on test results and data gathered in an interview; no family background was included. The clinicians made their diagnoses independently of one another and without knowing the subject's group. Six of the adoptees born of female offenders were labeled "antisocial personality"; one control group subject was labeled "probable antisocial personality."

Crowe found a positive correlation between the tendency of the index group to be antisocial and two other variables: the child's age at the time of adoptive placement, and the length of time the child had spent in temporary care (orphanages and foster homes) prior to that placement. The older the child of an offender upon adoptive placement and the longer the temporary placement, the more likely the child would grow up antisocial. The control group members were not affected by these conditions. This suggests either that the two adoptee groups responded differently to similar environmental conditions or that the adoption agency placed the offspring of female offenders in less desirable homes—and there was no indication that this selective placement had occurred.

Hutchings and Mednick (1975) also conducted a study examining the effects of genetics and environment. They reasoned that if there is a genetic basis for criminality, then there should be a significant relationship between the criminal tendencies of biological parents and those of their children who were adopted by someone else. In 1971, using Copenhagen adoption files, Hutchings and Mednick identified 1,145 male adoptees, who were by then 30 to 44 years old. They were matched with an equal number of nonadoptee controls on sex, age, occupational status of fathers, and residence. The researchers learned that 185 adoptees (16.2%) had criminal records, compared with 105 nonadoptees (8.9%). A check on the biological fathers of the adoptees revealed that they were nearly three times more likely to be involved in criminal activity than were either the adoptees' adoptive fathers or the fathers of the nonadopted controls. Furthermore, there was a significant relationship between the criminality of the sons and that of the fathers. Where the biological father had a criminal record and the adoptive father had none, a significant number of adoptees still became criminal (22%), but where the biological father had no record and the adoptive father had a criminal record, the number of adoptees who pursued criminal activities was lower (11.5%). If both the biological and adoptive fathers were criminal, the chances were much greater that the adoptee would also be criminal than if only one man was criminal. Hutchings and Mednick concluded that genetic factors continue to exert strong influences in the tendency toward criminality, even though environmental factors also play important roles.

One serious limitation to the Hutchings-Mednick data, as well as to any adoption study, is that agencies often try to match the adopted child with the adoptive family on the basis of the child's biological and sometimes socioeconomic background as well. The Crowe study involving the children of offenders found no evidence of this, but the Danish agency used in the Hutchings-Mednick investigation confirmed that this was done. To their credit, the researchers not only recognized this problem, but also admonished that extrapolations to American society should be made cautiously, since Danish society at the time was more homogeneous in cultural values and race.

The most comprehensive adoption study to date was conducted by Mednick, Gabrielli, and Hutchings (1984, 1987). These researchers compared the court convictions of 14,427 adoptees (adopted between the years 1927 and 1947) in a small European country with conviction records of their biological and adoptive parents. The study showed a significant relationship between the conviction history of the adoptees (for both males and females) and their biological parents. Specifically, if either biological parent had been convicted of a crime, the risk of criminality in the adoptee (the biological child) increased significantly. This relationship was especially strong for male adoptees who were chronic or persistent offenders. As we might expect, chronic offenders accounted for a disproportionate share of the total offending for the entire cohort. Interestingly, there was no evidence that the type of crime committed by the biological parent had any relation to the type of crime committed by the biological child. Both the biological parent and biological child tended to engage in crime but selected different kinds of crime. There was also no indication that the adopted children knew about the criminality of their biological parents. The researchers concluded that some factor transmitted by criminal parents increased the probability that their children would engage in criminal behavior. Elsewhere, Gabrielli and Mednick (1983, p. 63) commented, "It is reasonable . . . to conclude that some people inherit biological characteristics which permit them to be antisocial more readily than others."

In summary, twin and adoption studies suggest that genetic components may contribute moderately to a tendency to become criminal, especially pertaining to nonviolent crime, but they have also found that environment is highly important (Raine, 2002). According to biopsychologists, the available data so far indicate that some people may be born with a biological predisposition to behavior that runs counter to social values and norms, but environmental factors may either inhibit or facilitate it. Genes may not influence criminal behavior directly, but genes may act to influence people's susceptibility or resistance to environmental risk factors.

PSYCHOPHYSIOLOGICAL FACTORS

Psychophysiology is the study of the dynamic interactions between behavior and the autonomic nervous system. The autonomic nervous system is the subdivision of the peripheral nervous system that regulates involuntary functions, such as heartbeat, blood pressure, breathing, and digestion, and is closely connected to the genetic makeup of the individual. Heart rates (cardiovascular activity) and electrical conductance in the skin (electrodermal activity) are the usual measures of psychophysiological investigations examining the relationship between antisocial behavior and autonomic activity. Autonomic arousal theory of crime hypothesizes that persistent, chronic offenders compared with those with no or little offending history, will exhibit low levels of autonomic arousal across a wide variety of situations and conditions. Presumably, low levels of arousal predispose a person to crime because this produces some degree of fearlessness, and also because it encourages antisocial stimulation (excitement) seeking (Raine, 2002). That is, persistent offenders experience little anxiety and fear, and are not troubled about getting caught and punished. Furthermore, they find certain aspects of crime exciting and challenging. On the other hand, high levels of autonomic arousal, in light of the amount of fear and anxiety involved, encourage childhood socialization because of fear of disapproval and punishment.

Some studies reveal that antisocial boys and criminal psychopaths do appear to have lower levels of physiological arousal (as measured by electrodermal and cardiovascular activity) than their non-antisocial counterparts (Raine, 2002; Raine, Venables, & Williams, 1995, 1996).

TEMPERAMENT

A child's **temperament**—defined as a "natural" mood disposition determined largely by genetics and biological influences—may offer important clues about criminal behavior. How we approach and interact with our social environment influences how that environment will interact with us. This is true even of infants and very young children. Parents, teachers, physicians, and caretakers know very well that infants and young children differ in activity, emotionality, and general sensitivity to stimuli. A smiling, relaxed, socially interactive child is apt to initiate and maintain a different social response than a fussy, tense, and withdrawn one. A consistently ill-tempered child—assuming the ill temper cannot be attributed to physical discomfort such as hunger or pain—may become so frustrating to his parents that they feel overwhelmed and helpless in dealing with him. The parents' resulting irritability may feed into the behavior of the child in a reciprocal fashion, producing a serious disruption in the parent–child relationship. Frustration may progress into physical or emotional abuse or neglect by the parent(s). In essence, parents (or caregivers) and the child are active agents, who, by continuous transactions, cocreate their emerging relationship (Kochanska, Friesenborg, Lange, & Martel, 2004). The overwhelming consensus among experts is that parental responsiveness, nurturance, and warmth have emerged as critical core determinants of the early parent–child relationship (Kochanska *et al.*, 2004).

One of the most influential perspectives on temperament was developed by Thomas and Chess (1977). They contend that temperament is an innate readiness to respond to events and objects across a variety of situations. In addition, it is continually evolving and is strongly influenced by family, parental styles, and the social environment in general. Thomas and Chess systematically studied temperament by asking parents to report on nine characteristics of their infants: (1) rhythmicity of biological functions, such as regularity of bowel movements, sleep cycles, and feeding times, (2) activity level, (3) approach toward or withdrawal from new stimuli, (4) adaptability, (5) sensory thresholds, (6) predominant quality of mood, (7) intensity of mood expression, (8) distractibility, and (9) attention span or persistence. Based on these data, the researchers were able to classify child temperament into three styles: (1) the easy child, (2) the difficult child, and (3) the slow-to-warm-up child.

Table 2 summarizes the characteristics of each style. The easy child is characterized by high rhythmicity, positive moods, high approachability, high adaptability, and low intensity of mood expression. The difficult child shows the opposite patterns: irregular biological functioning, initial

TABLE 2   Thomas-Chess Categories of Child Temperaments

Behavioral characteristics	Easy child	Difficult child	Slow-to-warm-up child
Rhythmicity	Regular	Irregular	Regular
Moods	Positive	Negative	Negative
Approach to others	High	Low	Low
Adaptability	Rapid	Slow	Slow
Intensity	Low	High	Low

Source: Thomas & Chess (1977).

aversion, and slow adaptability to environmental changes, high intensity of emotional expression, and generally a negative mood. The slow-to-warm-up child displays high activity, withdrawal from new stimuli and people, low adaptability, negative mood, and low intensity. Difficult children, according to Thomas and Chess, represent a specific cluster of inborn temperamental attributes that make child rearing more challenging for many parents or caregivers.

It is suggested here that temperament increases or decreases the *probability* of antisocial behavior, not that it determines directly whether an individual will or will not engage in antisocial behavior. That is, the concurrence of these temperaments and certain kinds of family environments and parenting style may lead to delinquent or criminal outcomes. Studies have continually discovered significant *links* between children's "difficult" temperament and the occurrence of persistent antisocial behavior (e.g., Bates, Pettit, Dodge, & Ridge, 1998; Rubin, Burgess, Dwyer, & Hastings, 2003; Shaw, Owens, Giovannelli, & Winslow, 2001).

Three Things That Define Temperament

As it is currently used in the research and scholarly literature, "temperament" is assumed to: (1) have a constitutional or biological basis, (2) appear in infancy and continue throughout life, and (3) be influenced by the environment (Bates & McFadyen-Ketchum, 2000). Most developmental experts today believe that temperament has biological underpinnings that are best identified at birth (Bates, Pettit, Dodge, & Ridge, 1998; Dodge & Pettit, 2003; Lahey & Waldman, 2003). Else-Quest, Hyde, Goldsmith, and Van Hulle (2006) write, "Temperament reflects biologically based emotional and behavioral consistencies that appear early in life and predict—often in conjunction with other factors—patterns and outcomes in numerous other domains such as psychopathology and personality" (p. 33). Most of the contemporary research on temperament, therefore, focuses on the infant, because the connection between temperament and behavior seems uncomplicated at this stage and becomes more complex as the child matures and interacts with the psychosocial environment.

Currently, most developmental experts agree that activity and emotionality are two of the behaviors that are strong indicators of temperament. Activity, the most widely studied, refers to gross motor movement across a variety of settings and times, such as the movement of arms and legs, squirming, crawling, or walking. Emotionality refers to such features as irritability, sensitivity, soothability, and general intensity of emotional reactions. Self-regulation (a technical term for controlling impulsivity) is another behavior which is often included in descriptions of temperament. Self-regulation refers to the extent that a child controls his or her own behavior, independent of the control of others and the social environment. Highly impulsive and unmanageable children (poor self-regulators) move into (and often against) their environments at a higher pace and more aggressively than less impulsive children. Recent research (see Olson, Sameroff, Kerr, Lopez, & Wellman,

2005) has shown a strong connection between poor self-regulation and antisocial behavior across different social situations.

Failure to acknowledge these dispositional or temperamental variables may leave researchers and practitioners with an incomplete picture of the development of antisocial behavior, especially in cases of individuals who demonstrate a persistent pattern of violent or serious offending. Else-Quest *et al.* (2006) report that girls temperamentally seem better able than boys to manage and regulate their attention and inhibit their impulses (self-regulation). Henry, Caspi, Moffitt, and Silva (1996) found that children considered temperamentally explosive and lacking in self-control were more likely to become violent adolescents compared with their more temperamentally stable peers. However, although temperament is present at birth, it must be emphasized that its manifestations can be modified by the social environment, especially by parents and significant caregivers. As noted in this section, difficult temperaments can be challenging, but a nurturing and warm parenting style, in which rules are firmly laid out and appropriate self-regulation is encouraged, can prevent, change, or eliminate antisocial behavior in children (Moffitt, 2005; Veenstra, Lindenberg, Oldehinkel, De Winter, & Ormel, 2006). On the other hand, a difficult temperament combined with parental rejection or parental coercion offers a high risk for antisocial behavior (Dekovic, Janssens, & Van As, 2003; Veenstra *et al.*, 2006).

Likewise, the temperament of parents must also be considered as a possible component in the development of the criminal behavior. Moffitt (1993b) suggests that parents and their offspring often resemble each other in temperament and personality. An irritable, temperamental child may have a high probability of being born to highly irritable, temperamental parents. Thus, parents of difficult children often lack the necessary psychological and emotional resources to cope effectively with a difficult child. Cultural differences may also play a role in the interaction between parenting and temperament, but the research on the parent-child-temperament interaction is relatively too recent to make advanced, even tentative, conclusions (Porter *et al.*, 2005; Russell, Hart, Robinson, & Olsen, 2003).

In the next section, we will take a closer look at additional environmental factors that may facilitate or inhibit antisocial tendencies. These factors include prenatal influences, postnatal diseases, and inadequate nutrition and medical care.

ENVIRONMENTAL RISK FACTORS

In addition to genetic factors, in utero experiences may also play a role in the predisposition toward criminal behavior. During pregnancy, the fetus is exposed to various influences that may adversely affect development, leading to potential risks for serious antisocial behaviors later in life. Exposure to a toxic or diseased prenatal environment is one example. "Fetuses exposed to opiates or methadone are at heightened risk for conduct problems 10 to 13 years later, as are fetuses exposed to alcohol, marijuana, and cigarette by-products during pregnancy" (Dodge & Pettit, 2003, p. 351). Also, before and after birth, lead poisoning found in old paint can lead to long-term conduct problems in adolescence and young adulthood (Dodge & Pettit, 2003). Lead has also been found in a variety of other products, including toys, fuel, writing instruments, and products that come into contact with food. During the years 1999–2002, approximately 2 percent of children aged 1–5 had blood lead levels above 10 micrograms per deciliter (Federal Interagency Forum on Child and Family Statistics, 2005). Children aged 1–5 are particularly affected because of frequent hand-to-mouth behavior. Although 10 micrograms per deciliter is considered elevated according to federal safety standards, significant and troubling behavioral and health effects have been shown to occur at lower levels (Federal Interagency Forum on Child and Family Statistics, 2005). Childhood exposure to chips or dust from lead-based paint has been shown to contribute to learning and cognitive development problems (e.g., Braun *et al.*, 2006; Canfield *et al.*, 2003), which increases the risk for antisocial and delinquent behavior. Fortunately, since the 1970s, lead exposure has declined primarily because of the removal of lead from gasoline and the drastic reduction in the use of lead-based paint. Nevertheless, lead can also be present in soil, air, and water (Narag, Pizarro, & Gibbs, 2009). It is estimated that 1.7 million youth in their teenage years have blood lead levels greater than the level of safety established by the Centers for Disease Control (CDC) (Narag *et al.*, 2009).

Many children have blood lead levels at or above 5µg/dl, and these children are predominantly in homes with incomes below poverty level (Dietrich, Ris, Succop, Berger, & Bornschien, 2001; Needleman, McFarland, Ness, Fienberg, & Tobin, 2002). Some racial and ethnic groups may be particularly susceptible (e.g., African American children, 19%; Mexican American children, 7%). Bone lead levels have been shown to be related to antisocial behavior in adolescents (Dietrich *et al.*, 2001; Needleman *et al.*, 2002; Stretesky & Lynch, 2001, 2004). To what extent lead exposure leads *directly* to antisocial behavior is unknown, and the data so far are only suggestive. Still, parents and caregivers are urged to avoid exposing young children to paint chips, dust, and other substances containing lead if at all possible. Airborne lead or lead in water systems or soil is an environmental hazard that needs broader public attention.

Birth Complications

Birth complications are also associated with violent and persistent offending, but usually the relationship is most significant when *combined* with other psychosocial risks. The most common psychosocial risks are maternal separation, maternal rejection, marital discord, parental mental health problems, and paternal absence. For example, Raine, Brennan, and Mednick (1997) followed the criminal offending history of over four thousand Danish babies to age 34. Birth complications, when combined with early maternal rejection, predicted careers of violent crime. Interestingly, the relationship did not hold for *nonviolent* criminal careers, such as burglary, theft, shoplifting, and drug distribution. Another study (Neugebauer, Hoek, & Susser, 1999) found that maternal malnutrition during pregnancy in combination with adverse caregiving conditions may also be closely linked to violent behavior in the offspring.

The relationship between birth or pregnancy complications and a disadvantaged familial environment found in the Denmark study has also been replicated in four other countries (Sweden, Finland, Canada, and the United States) (Raine, 2002). It should be emphasized that birth or pregnancy complications by themselves are not be enough to trigger violent crime and serious antisocial behavior. The relationship seems to require the presence of negative environmental circumstances and heightened psychosocial risks in general. For example, one study (Arseneault, Tremblay, Boulerice, & Saucier, 2002) discovered that obstetrical complications (preeclampsia, chronic fetal hypoxia, placenta problems, umbilical cord prolapse, and induced labor) increased the risk of being violent at both 6 and 17 years of age among boys who grew up in highly adverse familial environments (early maternal rejection or a disadvantaged familial environment).

Birth and pregnancy complications, in combination with a faulty psychosocial environment, are most likely to have a negative impact on children's abilities to learn to self-regulate their behavior. Neurological deficits (such as brain damage) due to birth and pregnancy problems—if not modified and buffered by a stable home environment—are apt to lead to antisocial behaviors characterized by poor impulse or self-control and limited verbal ability because the child lacks the patience to develop socially appropriate verbal skills.

Nicotine, Alcohol, and Drug Exposure

There is substantial literature on the effects of prenatal exposure to drugs on child development. However, the prenatal effects of substance and alcohol abuse on antisocial behavioral development have received relatively little attention. A few studies have examined these effects, however. According to Raine (2002, p. 317), "The effects of fetal exposure to alcohol in increasing risk for conduct disorders is well known, but recently a spate of studies has established beyond reasonable doubt a significant link between smoking during pregnancy and later conduct disorder and violent offending." The evidence for the relationship between maternal smoking during pregnancy and antisocial behavior in her children is quite strong for boys, but weak for girls (Wakschlag & Hans, 2002). One study (Brennan, Grekin, & Mednick, 1999), using a birth cohort of 4,169 males, found a strong connection between adult violent offending and smoking by their mothers during their pregnancy. On average, the mothers smoked 20 cigarettes a day. This relationship was especially strong (increasing by fivefold) when the offspring were exposed to both nicotine and birth complications. In another study that used a large sample from the general population of Finland, Räsänen et al. (1998) found that, compared with the sons of mothers who did not smoke, the sons of mothers who smoked during pregnancy had more than a twofold risk of having committed a violent crime or having repeatedly committed crimes. This finding held even when other biopsychological risk factors were controlled. The available evidence suggests that smoking during pregnancy may contribute to brain deficits that have been frequently found in adult offenders (Raine, 2002).

Maternal substance abuse during pregnancy does show a link to substance abuse by their offspring during adolescence, but it is difficult to determine whether this link is due to a shared genetic predisposition between parent and child, the child modeling the parents' behavior, or the in utero effects of the substances themselves (Allen, Lewinsohn, & Seeley, 1998). Identifying the differential effects of maternal substance abuse of specific drugs is also daunting because the drug-abusing mother rarely uses a drug in isolation. That is, abusers usually use multiple substances. Nonetheless, there is some strong evidence to suggest that prenatal cocaine use by mothers adversely affects emotional and attention regulation in infants and preschool-aged children (Mayes, 1999). This finding is significant because cocaine or crack continued to be used by some pregnant women at least into the 1990s. For example, in some inner-city populations, nearly 50 percent of women giving birth reported or tested positive for cocaine use at the time of delivery (Mayes, 1999).

Brain Development

Neurological and brain dysfunction due to faulty brain development is clearly linked to serious and violent antisocial behavior (Ishikawa & Raine, 2004). It appears this connection is particularly relevant in the case of pathological violence (such as impulsive violence occurring in the context of emotional arousal and provocation) (Siever, 2008). The link is especially strong if the brain dysfunction is located in the frontal lobe, which comprises about one-third of the front part of the human brain. Organized thought, planning, and self-regulation are located in this area.

The importance of the frontal portion of the brain was revealed in the classic case of Phineas Gage. In September 1848, Gage worked as a construction foreman for the Rutland & Burlington Railroad in Vermont. The work crew was blasting rock while clearing the roadbed for a new rail line outside the town of Cavendish. But during the preparation for the next blast, something suddenly went wrong. A premature explosion sent an iron rod, used for tampering the gunpowder into the blasting hole, into Gage's head. The 3-foot iron, which Gage was using, entered the side of his face, shattering the upper jaw, passing through the frontal lobe, out the top of his head, and flew another fifty feet in the air. The frontal lobe area of his brain was badly damaged. Surprisingly,

Gage spoke within a few minutes after the blast, walked with little or no assistance, and sat in a cart that took him to the town doctors. Although Gage lived for another 12 years, the accident dramatically changed his personality. Prior to the accident, Gage was controlled, playful, friendly, and competent. He was a responsible and dependable employee for the railroad. After the accident, he became hostile, ill-tempered, profane, highly unreasonable, and showed poor social judgment. He demonstrated uncontrolled anger, a pattern which led to his inability to hold down a job.

We do not have to go back more than a century to find other examples of individuals with frontal lobe damage and subsequent personality change, however. Traumatic brain injury (TBI) is widely believed to affect one's personality, not infrequently leading to increased aggression (Barash, Tranel, & Anderson, 2000). Researchers studying Vietnam war veterans found that those with head injuries scored higher than those without such injuries on tests of violence (Grafman, *et al.*, 1996). In recent years, it has been clearly established that individuals with frontal lobe damage are far more likely to use physical intimidation and violence in conflict situations (Grafman *et al.*, 1996; Siever, 2008). This is especially the case in impulsive violence, where self-regulation and self-control appear to be lacking.

While brain damage due to accidents and physical trauma can result in a propensity toward impulsive violence, the quality of the prenatal environment is also clearly important in brain development. The brain is highly vulnerable to intrinsic hazards (cell development gone wrong) and to external insults resulting from viral infection, drug or alcohol exposure, malnutrition, or other teratogens. Nutritional adequacy is crucial for both prenatal and postnatal brain development because of the growing brain's reliance on folic acid, iron, vitamins, and other nutrients. Malnutrition is a biological hazard to which the developing infant brain is especially vulnerable. Other hazards include fetal exposure to maternal viruses like HIV and rubella, illicit drugs such as cocaine and heroin, maternal alcohol ingestion, exposure to environmental toxins (e.g., DDI, lead, mercury, and PCB) and other teratogens. The developing brain's vulnerability to many of these hazards continues throughout the early years after birth. As we learned in the beginning of this section, unsafe lead levels found in the paint of older homes or in the environment may be a contributing factor in the development of serious antisocial behavior.

Another area of the brain, the *limbic system*, which consists of a diverse group of loosely connected brain structures and circuitry, has also emerged as an important component associated with impulsive violence. The most important brain structure in the limbic system involved in aggressive behavior is the *amygdala*. The amygdala is a small, almond-shaped group of nerve cells that appears to play a major role in learning, memory, and the experience of emotions. Impulsive aggression and violence appear to be related to activity in the amygdala (DeLisi, Umphress, & Vaughn, 2009; Jones, Laurens, Herva, Barker, & Viding, 2009; Siever, 2008). Developmental influences that adversely affect the amygdala (and the limbic system generally) are very likely to affect various emotional responses, especially anger.

BRAIN PLASTICITY   After birth, early experiences are crucial in shaping the cultivation and pruning of neural synapses that underlie the functional capabilities of the developing brain (Thompson & Nelson, 2001). Recent studies of humans and other species have made it clear that the developing brain is profoundly responsive to experience (Nelson & Bloom, 1997). Both structure and function are affected by experience, a phenomenon known as **plasticity**. In fact, the plasticity and compensational capacities of the developing brain is perhaps the most remarkable discovery found in the developmental sciences to date (Lidzba & Staudt, 2008).

Among the most important of early experiences in the developing infant is nurturant, sensitive care. Although there are few relevant human neuroscience data, parents and caregivers are encouraged to talk and sing to, play with, read to, and sensitively nurture young children because of how these contingent sensory experiences provide stimulation for the brain (Thompson & Nelson, 2001). On the other hand, when caregivers are unable to provide these multisensory stimulations, brain development is likely to be delayed, either temporarily or permanently depending on the timing and quality of the intervention.

The first three to four years of life are significant in the prevention of antisocial behavior and persistent, serious criminal behavior throughout life, but other developmental periods are also important. There is some evidence, for example, that by the fourth year of life, the plasticity of the brain for language development begins to decrease (Chilosi *et al.*, 2008), suggesting that language stimulation of the developing brain is most important during the first four or five years of life. But this does not mean that brain stimulation after age five is not necessary for brain growth and development. Research demonstrates that the brain retains its capacity to grow throughout life (Thompson & Nelson, 2001). Brain development can be facilitated not only during the first four years but also at other developmental stages. This point suggests that early deprivation and harm can be treated and modified during later years, even in adults.

Neuropsychological Factors

Neuropsychological deficits, especially those associated with executive function problems (e.g., problems associated with self-regulation and planning), are reasonably well-established risk factors for antisocial behavior in children, adolescents, and adults (Raine, 2002). Moffitt (1993a) has argued that neuropsychological deficits in combination with certain family risk factors are often found in persistent, serious, violent offenders. Liu, Raine, Venables, and Mednick (2004) report from their investigations that malnutrition at age three predisposes a child to neurocognitive deficits, which in turn predispose a child to persistent antisocial behaviors throughout childhood and adolescence. The authors believe that early malnutrition negatively affects brain growth and development and that the brain impairments may promote antisocial and violent behavior by affecting cognitive executive functions. Morgan and Lilienfeld (2000) concluded after an extensive review of the research literature that there is a robust and statistically significant relationship between antisocial behavior and executive function deficits. However, the relationship between executive function and neuropsychological deficits was far from clear and will require far more research for any firm conclusions to be made on this topic.

Hormones and Neurotransmitters

Neurotransmitters are chemicals, manufactured in the brain, that are intimately involved in biochemical activity and transmission of messages in the nervous system. Research has consistently suggested that the neurotransmitter **serotonin** may play the most significant role in aggression and violence (Coscina, 1997; Lesch & Merschdorf, 2000; Loeber & Stouthamer-Loeber, 1998; Moffitt *et al.*, 1997; Vaughn, DeLisi, Beaver, & Wright, 2009). Serotonin exists in large amounts in the frontal lobe, which we have learned is involved in planning and self-regulation. The evidence to date suggests that deficiencies of serotonin in the frontal regions of the brain result in disinhibition of aggression upon provocation (Siever, 2008). There is also some evidence that levels of serotonin may explain to some extent the general differences in physical aggression between men and women (Verona, Joiner, Johnson, & Bender, 2006).

Some additional preliminary but inconclusive findings suggest that humans who become violent after drinking alcohol (Virrkunen & Linnoila, 1993), and children who torture animals

(Kruesi, 1979; Kruesi *et al.*, 1990), appear to be abnormally low in concentrations of serotonin. Other research suggests that low levels of brain serotonin encourage impulsive forms of aggressive or violent behavior (Kruesi & Jacobsen, 1997).

If certain neurotransmitters are implicated in aggressive behavior, it is not too far-fetched to consider drug regimens for control. Neurotransmitters are strongly affected by drugs. However, since neurotransmitters are the basic chemicals for all behavior, any modification of their levels in the nervous system is likely to affect a large range of behavior and emotions, not only the behavior that researchers are seeking to control. Therefore, although the considerable potential of drugs in controlling and reducing aggression cannot be overlooked, their peripheral effects must be considered.

Some researchers believe that the differential hormonal effects may partly explain why males overwhelmingly display higher levels of aggression and commit more violent crimes than do females. Some studies report that high testosterone levels in males may be associated with violent crimes, such as murder (Dabbs, Carr, Frady, & Riad, 1995; Dabbs, Riad, & Chance, 2001). Despite the progress in the last few years, the link between hormones and violence remains largely speculative and inconclusive (Ramirez, 2003). We underscore, however, that learning and social expectations and cognitions play an extremely powerful role in any statistics that indicate gender or age differences in criminal behavior.

Heredity and the XYY Chromosome

Some early investigators believed that criminal behavior and predispositions to be violent were a result of heredity. The most prominent proponent of this view was Lombroso, who was convinced that a criminal "type" could be identified by specific physical characteristics, such as an unsymmetrical head and jaw, a low forehead, protruding ears, and bushy, connected eyebrows.

Later, mid-twentieth century inquiries on the relationship between genetics and criminality focused on the so-called XYY chromosomal syndrome. The impetus for this research was a study by Jacobs, Brunton, Melville, Brittain, and McClemont (1965), who reported that the presence of an extra Y chromosome in the male is significantly associated with the triad of tall stature, mental retardation, and an unusually high level of aggressive behavior. The Jacobs study was not replicated, but nevertheless after it was released, some investigators hypothesized that the XYY chromosomal anomaly was closely related to violent criminal activity in males.

Chromosomes are chains of genetic material known as DNA that contain hereditary instructions for the growth and production of every living cell in the organism. Within each chromosome there are numerous genes; in fact, each cell contains between 30,000 and 40,000 genes (Andreasen, 2001). Chromosomes and their genes control physical traits such as eye and hair color and height, and they may have substantial influence on many psychological predispositions and temperaments (see, generally, DeLisi, 2009). For example, chromosomes may account for a predisposition to depression. Each cell in the human body normally possesses 46 chromosomes, or 23 pairs. One pair in each cell is responsible for sex determination and sex characteristics. One member of the pair is always an X, but the other member may be either an X or a Y, depending on the sex of the individual. They are named after their appearance under a microscope. Each cell of a normal woman has two X chromosomes, while each cell of a man has an X and a Y. In rare instances, however, a genetic anomaly occurs in males, in that two Y chromosomes pair with a single X—hence the phenomenon XYY. Rather than the usual 46 chromosomes, the individual has 47.

The principal characteristics associated with the presence of an extra Y chromosome include unusual height, episodes of violent aggression, and borderline intelligence—although there are many exceptions. Severe acne or scars from acne are also a characteristic. Obviously, this is not to imply that someone with severe acne or of unusual height possesses the XYY chromosome.

However, a number of infamous murderers apparently had the XYY abnormality. One was Robert Peter Tait, who was convicted of beating to death a 77-year-old woman in Australia (Fox, 1971). The XYY characteristic was discovered after his trial but did not delay his execution. The XYY genotype was first used as a basis for criminal defense in 1968, at the trial of Daniel Hugon in Paris. Hugon was charged with the brutal murder of an elderly prostitute. Although convicted, he received only seven years' imprisonment. It is not certain that the court considered the XYY abnormality a mitigating factor in determining his sentence, however (Fox, 1971). In the United States, criminal defendants have not used the defense successfully. "Big Bad John" (Sean) Farley, a 6-foot, 8-inch, 240-pound individual, who murdered and mutilated a Queens, New York, woman in 1969, was convicted in spite of his plea of insanity due to chromosomal imbalance. Finally, Richard Speck, who murdered eight student nurses, possessed some of the physical features associated with the XYY chromosome. After his conviction, researchers examined his chromosomal structure. Although there was considerable confusion at the time the results were released, it has been concluded that Speck's genetic structure does not include the abnormality.

Although XYY has not been successful as a criminal defense, there is some empirical support for its relationship with crime. So far, however, there is little evidence that violence and XYY go hand in hand. After an extensive review of the world literature, Jarvik, Klodin, and Matsuyama (1973) concluded that the presence of the XYY configuration in the general population averages between 0.11 percent and 0.14 percent; among mental patients it is significantly higher, averaging between 0.13 percent and 0.20 percent. However, in criminal populations, Jarvik found that XYY occurred in 1.9 percent of the cases. Jarvik's research combined information from 26 studies, including 5,066 criminal subjects. The 1.9 percent figure for the presence of the XYY chromosome, however, constitutes a very small percentage of the total prison population and seems to represent very little of the violence in our society. In another study, XYY prisoners were found to have fewer assault incidents than comparable groups of "normal" XY prisoners (Price & Whatmore, 1967). A great majority of the XYY crimes were against property.

Contemporary researchers have not pursued the extra-Y theory, because this particular chromosome does not appear to be a powerful explanatory factor for human violence. However, there is widespread recognition that—as a general principle—the numerous genes contained within a person's chromosomes influence not only one's physical characteristics but perhaps even one's behavior (Comer, 2004). Thus, there may be genetic *susceptibilities* to mood disorders, including severe depression, schizophrenia, and other mental disorders, and these susceptibilities may facilitate aggressive, impulsive, or callous behavior, including crime.

Epilepsy and Violence

During the 1970s, medical researchers implied that there was a relationship between temporal lobe epilepsy and violence (Goldstein, 1974; Pincus, 1980). Before that time, between 1889 and 1970 there were only 15 court cases in the United States in which epilepsy had been used as a defense against charges of murder, homicide, manslaughter, or disorderly conduct (Delgado-Escueta, Mattson, & King, 1981). The new implied relationship resulted in a rash of diminished responsibility or insanity defenses for violent acts beginning in 1977. Presumably, the person plagued with this disorder is prone to uncontrollable periods of violence and destruction. However, available research fails to support any relationship between violence and epilepsy in general or violence and psychomotor epilepsy in particular (Blumer, 1976; Valenstein, 1973).

Although angry, irritable behavior between seizures is commonly reported in individuals with chronic temporal lobe seizures, they rarely inflict physical harm (Blumer, 1976). In rare cases, some violence may occur in the confusional state that takes place immediately after an epileptic seizure, if the individual is provoked. During this brief rage attack, the person appears to lose control and may even destroy some furniture or strike a family member. Rarely is there actual physical injury, and rarely are criminal charges brought. Furthermore, it is not clear whether aggression occurs because of the seizure itself, because of associated brain damage that often accompanies psychomotor seizure activity, or is independent of the seizure itself (Herzberg & Fenwick, 1988). Available evidence (e.g., Wong, Lumsden, Fenton, & Fenwick, 1994) indicates that if violence does occur during the seizure episode, the violent behavior is probably due to a long-standing response pattern of the individual and is not directly related to the seizure itself. Overall, researchers have concluded that *if* there is a relationship between seizures and aggression and violence, it is *extremely* rare (Marsh & Krauss, 2000).

EYSENCK'S THEORY OF PERSONALITY AND CRIME

We will spend some time on the late Hans J. Eysenck's theory of crime in this section not only because it has been one of the most influential psychological perspectives on crime in recent years (Cale, 2006), but also because it exemplifies many of the principles and issues discussed in this chapter, especially how genetic, psychobiological factors play an important role in the understanding of criminal behavior. The reader is encouraged to take Eysenck's measure of personality, the *Eysenck Personality Questionnaire—Revised,* which takes only about 15 minutes to complete, and which is helpful in understanding the theory. The theory itself is summarized in **Table 3**.

Eysenck (1977, 1996; Eysenck & Gudjonsson, 1989) proposed that criminal behavior is the result of an **interaction** between certain environmental conditions and features of the nervous system. Eysenck believed that a comprehensive theory of criminality must allow for an examination of the neurophysiological makeup and the unique socialization history of each individual. Theories that argue that crime is caused by social conditions such as poverty, poor education, or unemployment are as misleading as theories that rely exclusively on hereditary and biological explanations. Crime cannot be understood in terms of heredity alone, but it can also not be understood in terms of environment alone (Eysenck, 1973, p. 171). Eysenck also suggested that different combinations of environmental, neurobiological, and personality factors give rise to different types of crime (Eysenck & Eysenck, 1970). This position implies that different personalities are more susceptible to certain crimes than others, an issue we will return to shortly.

Unlike most contemporary theories of crime, Eysenck's theory places heavy emphasis on genetic predispositions toward antisocial and criminal conduct. Eysenck (1996, p. 146) asserted "genetic causes play an important part in antisocial and criminal behaviour. This simple fact is no

TABLE 3   Summary of Eysenck's Theory

Personality Trait	Neurobiological Influence	High Scores	Low Scores
Extraversion	RAS, CNS	Stimulation seeking	Stimulation avoidance
Neuroticism	Autonomic NS	Nervous, unstable	Stable, calm
Psychoticism	Excessive androgen	Tough minded	Tender minded

longer in doubt." It is important to note at the outset that he was not suggesting that individuals are born criminal, but rather that some people are born with nervous system characteristics that are significantly different from the general population and that affect their ability to conform to social expectancies and rules. "It is not crime itself or criminality that is innate; it is certain peculiarities of the central and autonomic nervous system that react with the environment, with upbringing, and many other environment factors to increase the probability that a given person would act in a certain antisocial manner" (Eysenck & Gudjonsson, 1989, p. 7). Eysenck isolated features of the central and autonomic nervous systems to account for a substantial portion of the differences found in personality in general. The way each individual's nervous system functions may be as unique as his or her personality characteristics. Carrying this one step further, we could posit that some nervous systems are more likely to engage in criminal activity because of their reactivity, sensitivity, and excitability.

Based on a series of empirical studies and statistical analyses, Eysenck argued that there are four higher order factors of personality—one higher order factor for ability called "g" (general intelligence), and three higher order factors for temperament, called **extraversion, neuroticism,** and **psychoticism**. Eysenck believed that the ability factor is an important factor in the cause of criminality, but is less important than the temperament factors. He wrote, "We may conclude that intelligence is a factor in the causation of criminality but that its contribution is probably smaller than one might have thought at first" (Eysenck & Gudjonsson, 1989, p. 50).

Most of the research on crime and personality has focused on extraversion and neuroticism, which are essentially the core concepts of Eysenckian theory. Eysenck did not identify psychoticism until he found a need to account for behaviors not fully explained by extraversion or neuroticism.

Eysenck visualized each of the three temperament or personality factors on a continuum, with the neuroticism and extraversion lines at right angles and intersecting. Psychoticism is on a separate continuum. Most people fall in the intermediate or midpoint area of each, and people are rarely at either extreme (see **Figure 1**). Most people fall within the square. The extraversion dimension runs from the extreme pole extraversion to the extreme pole introversion, with the middle range called **ambiversion**. Thus, depending on where a person falls on this dimension, that person may be an extravert, introvert, or ambivert. The neuroticism continuum runs from the polar ends of neuroticism to stability, with no middle label. Psychoticism runs from tough-mindedness (high psychoticism) to tender-mindedness (low psychoticism), also with no label for the middle majority. The extraversion dimension is believed to reflect basic functions of the central nervous system (CNS), which consists of the brain and spinal cord, while neuroticism represents functions of the peripheral nervous system (nerve pathways outside the central nervous system). As yet, neither Eysenck nor other researchers have postulated a nervous system mechanism for psychoticism.

Measurement of Eysenck's Theory

Eysenck developed several self-report questionnaires to measure these personality variables, the best-known being the British Maudsley Personality Inventory (MPI) and its American editions, the Eysenck Personality Inventory (EPI) and the Eysenck Personality Questionnaire (EPQ). More recently, the Eysenck Personality Questionnaire-Revised (EPQ-R) has been published. The questionnaires have stimulated extensive research to explore both their validity and Eysenck's concept of personality. Overall, worldwide research has supported the general theory, but when it is applied to criminality, the support is a bit more mixed. We will review some of this research later in this chapter, after examining more closely the basic concepts behind each dimension.

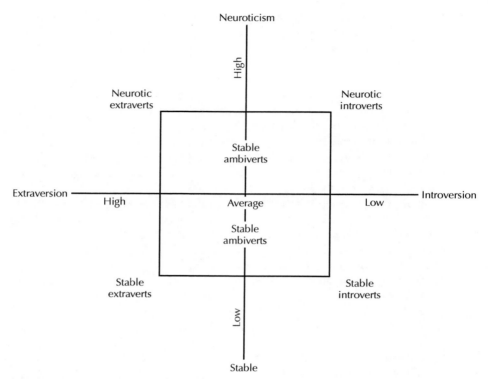

FIGURE 1 Illustration of Eysenck's Personality Dimensions for Neuroticism and Extraversion

Extraversion

BEHAVIORAL CHARACTERISTICS AND INCIDENCE   Usually, two out of every three people will score in the "average" range on the extraversion dimension, thus disqualifying them from studies based on extraversion and introversion. Roughly 16 percent of the population are extraverts, and another 16 percent introverts, and the remainder (68%) are ambiverts.

According to Eysenck, the typical extravert is sociable, impulsive, optimistic, and has high needs for excitement and for a varied, changing environment. Extraverts tend to lose their temper quickly, become aggressive easily, and be unreliable. They like to have people around, enjoy parties, and are usually very talkative. The typical introvert, on the other hand, is reserved, quiet, and cautious. He or she keeps feelings under close control and generally tries to avoid excitement, change, and most social activities. Introverts tend to be reliable and unaggressive and to place great value on ethical standards (Eysenck & Rachman, 1965). Ambiverts exhibit some features of both extraversion and introversion, but not to the same degree or consistency as extraverts and introverts.

Think of the extraversion dimension as a continuum representing a progressive need for stimulation, which can be defined as the impact stimuli have on areas of the brain. The impact is analogous to the taste of food. Some people have a relatively consistent tendency to prefer spicy, hot foods (e.g., Szechuan cuisine) that have more impact on their taste centers, while others more often choose bland foods (e.g., macaroni and cheese) because they do not desire the high taste impact. Some people prefer and actively seek out more stimulation or stimulus impact from other areas of their lives as well—they like rousing music, perpetual bustle, and stimulant drugs. Eysenck maintained that people at the extraversion end of the dimension require high levels of stimulation from their environment because of their biological makeup.

If you conceptualize the dimension this way, you may find that the popular term *extrovert* (note the spelling) takes on added meaning. Extroverts are sociable creatures who like to be around people and to be immersed in activity because of the stimulation this provides them. It is important to note, though, that our everyday usage of the nouns *extrovert* and *introvert* are not identical to Eysenck's polar classifications.

Because extraverts have higher needs for excitement and stimulation to break the daily boredom, they are also most likely to run counter to the law. They tend to be impulsive, fun-loving, thrill-seeking people who are willing to take chances and stick their necks out. They enjoy pranks and practical jokes, and find challenge in opportunities to do the unconventional or even to found that extraverts are more likely to use dramatic, powerful firearms when committing crime, whereas introverts have a strong tendency to use less dramatic weapons, such as knives. Some features of the extraverted nervous system not only encourage stimulation seeking but also inhibit the acquisition and internalization of society's rules, as we will see shortly.

Physiological Bases of Extraversion-Introversion

Eysenck (1967) hypothesized that people differ along the extraversion-introversion axis because of genetic differences in certain mechanisms in their central nervous system, particularly the tiny but complex network of neurons located in the central part of the brain stem called the reticular activating system (RAS) (see **Figure 2**). The RAS

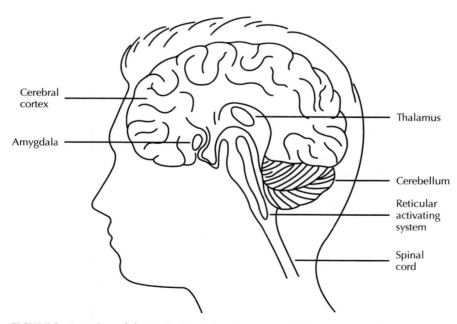

FIGURE 2   Location of the Reticular Activating System (RAS) Relative to Other Brain Structures

is believed to act as a sentinel that awakens and keeps alert the portion of the brain called the cerebral cortex. All higher level functions, like thinking, memory, and decision making, occur in the cerebral cortex (French, 1957). The RAS arouses the cerebral cortex and keeps it alert to incoming stimuli. Nerve pathways communicating information to the cerebral cortex branch off into collateral pathways traveling to the RAS. In effect, these collaterals "tell" the RAS to alert the brain to incoming information.

Eysenck postulated that both extraverts and introverts inherit an RAS that handles cortical arousal in a unique way, differently from the RAS of the general population. The extravert's RAS does not seem to generate cortical excitation or arousal effectively. In fact, it appears to reduce the impact of stimulation and the arousal properties of stimuli before they can reach the cortex. The introvert, on the other hand, apparently has inherited an RAS that amplifies stimulation input, keeping cortical arousal at relatively high levels. So we have the extravert, who is cortically underaroused, seeking additional stimulation to achieve an optimally aroused cortex, and the introvert, who is cortically overaroused, trying to avoid stimulation. The ambivert, who obtains an intermediate level of arousal, is generally content with moderate amounts of stimulation.

There is also the concept of optimal level of stimulation or cortical arousal. One motivation behind human behavior is the desire to achieve a just-right level of stimulation and cortical arousal. Too much stimulation becomes aversive and even painful, while too little results in boredom and eventual sleep. It is assumed that the extravert, because of the dampening effect of the RAS, needs higher levels of stimulation to maintain that just-right or optimal level of cortical arousal. The introvert, because of the amplifying effect of the RAS, desires relatively lower levels of stimulation. This explains the typical extravert's attraction to spicy foods, loud music, and vividly colored objects, and the introvert's preference for bland foods, soft music, and cool or dark-colored objects.

The extravert's stimulation needs are well documented (see Eysenck, 1967, 1981). As mentioned previously, the greater tendency of extraverts to seek sensation is presumably more likely to put them in conflict with the law. Eysenck suggested that most people involved in criminal activity are cortically underaroused and have a strong drive to obtain stimulation or sensation from their environment. They are thus drawn to risk taking, joy riding, and illegal activities that have high stimulation value.

Before leaving the section on extraversion, let's digress for a moment on the effects of alcohol on cortical arousal. Alcohol is a general central nervous system depressant. It lowers cortical arousal to the point that one may pass out or fall asleep. The extravert without alcohol is already "half in the bag," and with alcohol, he or she is even less alert. For introverts, however, alcohol has the effect of lowering a normally high cortical arousal to a point where they become more extraverted, behaviorally and physiologically. Thus, the usually quiet, reserved person may become boisterous or perform a soft shoe routine on the coffee table after a few drinks. The drunk introvert now has an extraverted arousal level and seeks more stimulation.

Eysenck supposed that the active, aroused cortex is a better inhibitor of activity than the poorly aroused one. Therefore, high cortical arousal leads to inhibition, while low cortical arousal allows subcortical regions of the central nervous system to function without restraint. Alcohol lowers the alertness of the cortex, which presumably lessens its censorship over the primitive, subcortical regions of the nervous system. This facilitates inappropriate, antisocial behaviors usually held in check by the cortex. Thus, according to the Eysenckian perspective, under the influence of alcohol, introverts will do things they normally would not do. On the other hand, even relatively small quantities of alcohol influence the extravert, who already functions at a low level of cortical arousal, toward even more uninhibited behavior. The correlation between alcohol and crime is a strong one.

By now you should have a basic understanding of one of Eysenck's personality dimensions. We will now move on to consider the second dimension, which is equally important.

Neuroticism

Like extraversion, neuroticism is a significant variable in the relationship between personality and crime. Sometimes called emotionality, this dimension reflects an innate biological predisposition to react physiologically to stressful events. Basically, neuroticism deals with the intensity of emotional reactions. It is believed to occur in the general population in the same frequencies as extraversion, with 16 percent of the population falling above and below one standard deviation from the mean.

A person high on the neuroticism scale reacts intensely and lastingly to stress. In fact, even under low-stress conditions, the person is likely to be moody, touchy, sensitive to slights, and anxious, and likely to complain of various physical ailments such as headaches, backaches, and digestive problems. He or she tends to overreact to stress and has difficulty returning to a normal, calm state. People high in emotionality also have a strong propensity to develop neurotic features such as phobias and obsessions. Their opposites, persons at the other end of the continuum, display emotionally stable, calm, and even-tempered behavior. They tend to keep their wits about them under stress and intense excitement and to select appropriate reactions to emergencies. Researchers testing Eysenckian theory refer to high emotionality individuals as neurotics and their counter opposites as stables.

Recent research has revealed a similar trait dimension referred to as callous-unemotional (CU) traits (see Frick & White, 2008). However, "unemotional" in this context is not the same as "stable" or low in emotionality. In fact, this dimension is more akin to Eysenck's concept of psychoticism—discussed below—than his concept of neuroticism. CU traits include lack of emotional responsiveness, lack of guilt, absence of empathy, and the callous use of others for one's own purposes. A growing amount of research has discovered that these traits seem to be stable across the life span and are often found in groups of individuals with particularly severe, aggressive, and persistent patterns of antisocial behavior (Frick & White, 2008).

Neurophysiological Bases of Neuroticism-Stability

Whereas the extraversion-introversion dimension is linked to the central nervous system, the neuroticism-stability continuum relates to the autonomic nervous system, which can be divided into the sympathetic and parasympathetic nervous systems (see **Figure 3**). The *sympathetic system* activates the body for emergencies by increasing heart rate, respiration flow, blood flow, pupil dilation, and perspiration. The *parasympathetic system* counterbalances the sympathetic; it brings the body back to its normal arousal state. According to Eysenck, differences in emotionality are due to variances in the sensitivity of these subdivisions, which are both under the control of the so-called visceral brain or limbic system. In addition to a complicated array of neuronal circuitry, the *limbic system* includes the neurological structures known as the hippocampus, amygdala, cingulum, and hypothalamus. The hypothalamus appears to exert the greatest amount of control over the autonomic nervous system and thus represents the central mechanism in emotionality.

Neurotics are believed to have unusually sensitive limbic systems, so they achieve emotionality quickly, and for longer periods of time. Theoretically, it may be that their sympathetic system is activated quickly while their parasympathetic system is slow in counterbalancing this. Stables, low in emotionality, may possess an underactive sympathetic system and an overactive parasympathetic system.

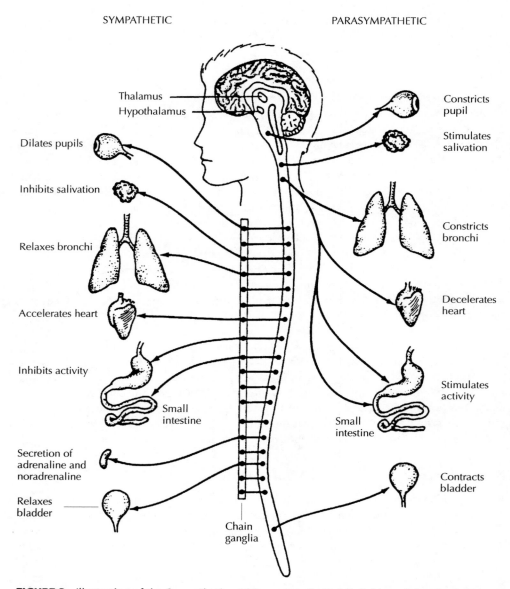

FIGURE 3   Illustration of the Sympathetic and Parasympathetic Subdivision of the Autonomic Nervous System

Although autonomic activation appears to produce a generalized arousal state in everyone, there is good reason to believe that each person reacts to the stress in unique ways. Some of us tense the muscles in our neck, forehead, or back; others breathe more heavily; for others, the heart pumps faster. This tendency for response specificity may account for the various forms of neurotic behaviors displayed by humans reacting to stress. Some complain of headaches, others of digestive problems or backaches. (And again, we are not suggesting that everyone who suffers these ailments is neurotic.)

Eysenck assumed that the person high on emotionality is more likely to engage in criminal activity than the person low on that dimension. He based this assumption on the consistent research finding that emotionality can serve as a drive, pushing an individual to resort to habitual ways of behaving. Under high emotionality (high drive), a person is more vulnerable to his or her habits—good or bad. Thus, if the individual has acquired antisocial habits, he or she will be more driven to commit them under high-drive than low-drive conditions. Neuroticism, therefore, encourages whatever mindless or habitual behaviors the person has acquired. Furthermore, because habits are usually not as well ingrained in the young as they are in the old, we would expect neuroticism to be an important factor with respect to adult criminals, less so with adolescents, and least so with young children (Eysenck, 1983).

The two dimensions we have looked at thus far are usually combined in classifying an individual's personality. That is, based on Eysenck's personality inventories, a person will be a neurotic introvert, a stable extravert, a neurotic ambivert, and so forth. If we accept Eysenck's views up to this point, we should agree that the neurotic extravert is the most likely of the possible personality types to be involved in criminal behavior.

Psychoticism

No neurophysiological mechanism has been established to explain the characteristics of psychoticism, Eysenck's most recently formulated dimension. Eysenck (1996) does suggest, however, high levels of the male hormone testosterone combined with low levels of the enzyme monoamine oxidase and the neurotransmitter serotonin may play a significant role in the formation of psychoticism. A neurotransmitter is a chemical that carries information from one neuron to another across the space between neurons called the synaptic cleft.

Psychoticism seems to be highly similar to primary psychopathy. Behaviorally, psychoticism is characterized by cold cruelty, social insensitivity, unemotionality, disregard for danger, troublesome behavior, dislike of others, and an attraction to the unusual. "Psychotics" are hostile toward others and enjoy duping or ridiculing them. It is important that we distinguish between Eysenck's psychotics and persons who are psychotic in the clinical sense of being out of touch with reality. Although this latter label is losing favor among clinicians, it appears frequently enough in literature to warrant making the distinction.

Eysenck's psychoticism dimension has not received the research attention that extraversion and neuroticism have. However, he hypothesizes that, like extraversion and neuroticism, psychoticism will prove to be a striking characteristic of the criminal population. He suggests that psychoticism will be especially prominent in hard-core, habitual offenders convicted of crimes of violence (Eysenck, 1983). Furthermore, unlike neuroticism, it apparently is important at all stages of development, from childhood through adolescence to adulthood.

Thus far, we have only defined Eysenck's dimensions, and, in the case of neuroticism and extraversion, we have isolated the physiological mechanisms that control them. None of this explains, however, why neurotics, extraverts, and psychotics are more likely to be criminal. The reason has to do with some very basic psychological principles to which we now turn our attention.

Crime and Conditionability

A basic premise of this text is that criminal behavior is learned. Traditionally, psychologists have delineated three major types of learning: **classical** or **Pavlovian conditioning, instrumental**

learning or **operant conditioning**, and **social learning**. It is important now to examine these processes more carefully if we are to approach an understanding of why some people engage in crime or other antisocial behavior.

The reader with a background in introductory psychology will recall Ivan Pavlov's famous experiments with dogs who learned to salivate at the sound of a bell. Pavlov discovered that pairing a neutral stimulus (in this case a bell) with a significant stimulus (e.g., food) would result in the dogs' eventually learning to associate the sound of the bell with that of food. How do we know the dogs learned to make that association? Because they salivated at the mere sound of the bell, a response they usually reserved for food. The process of learning to respond to a formerly neutral stimulus (bell) that has been paired with another stimulus that already elicits a response (salivation) is basically *classical* or *Pavlovian conditioning*. In classical conditioning, animals (or persons) have no control over the situation, even over what happens to themselves. The animal is "forced" to take the consequences. The bell will ring, and food will appear shortly afterward, regardless of what the animal does. In anticipation, and without any effort on its part, the animal salivates. This learning occurs not because of any reward or gain, but merely because of the association between the bell and the food.

In *instrumental learning* (or operant conditioning), the process is quite different. The learner must do something to the environment in order to obtain a reward or, in some cases, to avoid punishment. Instrumental learning is based on learning the consequences of behaving a certain way: If you do something, there is some probability that a certain rewarding event (or at least an avoidance of punishment) will occur. A child may learn, for example, that one parent will give her a piece of candy to quell a temper tantrum; the other parent will not yield. The child will eventually learn to use temper tantrums when Dad's around, but not to use them in front of Mom (or vice versa).

One important aspect of instrumental learning should be stressed: There must be a goal driving the animal or person to operate on the environment. That is, the individual must have a purpose or expectation for his or her behavior, and must expect a reward for the response. A reward or reinforcement is the event that increases the likelihood of a response. Classical conditioning, by contrast, results from an association between stimuli and takes place without reward.

Social learning is more complex than either classical conditioning or instrumental learning, because it involves learning from watching others and organizing social experiences in the brain.

Eysenck (1977) turns the question of criminal behavior around from the usual, "Why do people become criminal?" to "Why don't more people engage in criminal behavior?" To answer this with the adage, "Crime doesn't pay" is nonsense, since there is evidence that for much of the criminal population, crime does pay. After all, one of the chief motivators of behavior may be the desire to gain reward and pleasure (referred to as hedonism). "It would seem . . . that a person may, with a fair degree of safety, indulge in a career of crime without having to fear the consequences very much" (Eysenck, 1964, p. 102). According to Eysenck, those detected, convicted, and incarcerated often represent that portion of the criminal population who are of lower intelligence, poorly taught, unable to afford an influential attorney, or simply unlucky. So, if instrumental learning is a major factor, there should be substantially more crime, because people would be more often than not rewarded for operating criminally on their environment. Moreover, when punishment does occur, it is so long in coming that it cannot reasonably be considered a deterrent. Eysenck suggests, in fact, that delayed and sometimes arbitrary punishment may actually encourage criminal activity. This is reminiscent of the classical school of criminology, which suggested that punishment should occur swiftly and with certainty in order to be effective as a deterrent.

To explain why more people do not become criminal, Eysenck contends that classical conditioning has a stronger effect on most people than instrumental learning. That is, most people behave themselves because they have been classically conditioned during childhood about the rules of society. That guiding light, superego, conscience, or whatever it is that makes us feel uncomfortable before, during, and after a socially and morally disapproved act is, according to Eysenck, a *conditioned reflex*. In the family or educational environment, children may be verbally reprimanded or physically punished for behavior that is against the social mores. Immediately after engaging in a socially or morally frowned-upon act, say, punching a friend, a child finds that punishment quickly follows.

Let's return to Pavlov's dog experiments for a moment, and substitute the food with painful shock. Immediately following the sound of the bell, the dog receives a severe electrical shock (punishment) through the grids in the floor of the cage. After a number of trials (bell followed by shock) the dog, rather than salivating at the bell, begins to shake in fear. The animal has been classically conditioned to fear the sound of the bell, even when shock no longer follows it. The dog now associates shock with the bell rather than food.

Eysenck asserts that basically the same sequence occurs in childhood—inappropriate behavior followed by reprimand. For example, child punches another child, mother reprimands. Following a few repetitions of this sequence, the thought of punching stimulates fear of the consequences. In essence, "by punishing antisocial behavior numerous times, parents, teachers, and others concerned with the upbringing of the child, including his or her peers, perform the role of the Pavlovian experimenter" (Eysenck, 1983, p. 60). The child associates punching with punishment, and this bonding between the behavior and the aversive consequences should deter him or her from performing the act. Moreover, the closer the individual comes to performing the act, the stronger the association (fear) becomes.

Most people, Eysenck believes, do not participate in criminal activity (he prefers the term antisocial behavior) because after a series of trials, they have made strong connections between deviant behavior and aversive consequences. On the other hand, those persons who have not made adequate connections, either because of poor conditionability (e.g., extraverts) or because the opportunity to do so was not presented (socialization), are more likely to display deviant or criminal behavior. According to Eysenck, these people do not anticipate aversive events strongly enough to be deterred, since the association has not been sufficiently developed.

Pavlov observed that dogs differ widely in their conditionability to the sound of a bell and theorized that these differences come from properties of their nervous systems. Eysenck also made this observation, commenting that "German Shepherds are very law abiding: They are easily conditioned and are well known to animal fanciers and shepherds for this property. Basenjis, however, are natural psychopaths, difficult or almost impossible to condition, disobedient and antisocial" (Eysenck, 1983, p. 61). Eysenck advanced the same observation concerning humans: Extraverts condition less readily than introverts due to biological differences in their nervous systems. Introverts condition better and therefore are less likely to engage in behavior contrary to society's laws and mores.

The principles of conditioning have been firmly established in the field of psychology as a valid explanation for many forms of behavior. The conditioning process appears to be a powerful force in the socialization of children, particularly in the suppressing of undesirable behaviors. There is every reason to believe that it may be a critical process in determining who becomes involved in deviant or criminal behavior. However, there is also evidence that conditioning can serve as an instigator of such behavior. The association between pleasurable events and specific behavior is also an extremely powerful motivator of criminal activity.

According to Eysenck, the conditioned conscience has two effects on behavior: it may prevent us from indulging in forbidden activities, or it may make us feel guilty after we commit them. The conditioned conscience inhibits us from engaging in antisocial activities by its association with prior adverse consequences. In addition, once we have committed the act, we tend to feel uncomfortable about our transgressions. Eysenck (1983) supposed the difference rests in the timing of the aversive consequences. Reprimanding a child before or during an act would produce different effects than reprimanding a child after the act. The former situation would result in feelings of discomfort before the act (or while committing it), whereas the latter would produce discomfort (guilt) after the act.

What part does neuroticism or emotionality play? As noted earlier, Eysenck predicted that neuroticism functions as a drive strongly encouraging the performance of behavior previously acquired during childhood. That is, neuroticism amplifies existing habits in a person's repertoire of responses. If a neurotic extravert has not been properly conditioned to avoid stealing and has engaged in frequent, successful stealing in the past, neuroticism will function as a strong force or drive toward the old habit—stealing. In other words, behavior (inappropriate or appropriate) equals prior conditioning or learned habits times (intensified by) emotionality.

According to Eysenck (1983, p. 65), "The general growth in permissiveness in homes, schools, and courts has led to a significant reduction in the number of conditioning contingencies to which children are exposed. It would follow as a direct consequence that they would grow up with a much weaker conscience, and consequently that many more children would be led to engage in criminal and antisocial activities." In essence, Eysenck is asserting that increases in crime may be traced directly to conditions within the home or schools that are not conducive to the development of a conditioned conscience toward avoiding antisocial conduct.

The Evidence for Eysenck's Theory

Now that we have scrutinized Eysenck's theory of criminality, the relevant question becomes, "Can we find research to support it?" Eysenck's theory of criminality predicts that criminals, as a group, will demonstrate lower levels of cortical arousal (high extraversion), higher levels of autonomic (sympathetic) arousal (high neuroticism), and be more tough-minded (high psychoticism). In short, he postulates that criminals will score high on the E-, N-, and P-scales of the Eysenck Personality Questionnaire (EPQ-R), and that these dimensions are more than merely correlated with crime; they are causally related to it. It should also be mentioned that the EPQ-R also contains a Lie (L) scale, which measures trying to look "too good," or as Eysenck called it, "faking good." He also believed that the scale measures a stable personality dimension of a person's response to social expectations. Low L scores indicate that the respondent is indifferent to social expectations and is not well socialized (Carrasco, Barker, Tremblay, & Vitaro, 2006; Kemp & Center, 2003). Consequently, we may hypothesize that those persons prone to be criminal will not only score high on E-, N-, and P-scales, but also will demonstrate a low L-scale score.

Overall, recent research strongly supports Eysenck's position that people likely to commit delinquent and criminal behavior will score high on the P-scale (Cale, 2006; Carrasco et al., 2006; Center, Jackson, & Kemp, 2005; Heaven, Newbury, & Wilson, 2004; Kemp & Center, 2003; Levine & Jackson, 2004; van Dam, Janssens, & De Bruyn, 2005; Walker & Gudjonsson, 2006). This is to be expected since high scorers are generally described as cold, hostile, aggressive, and insensitive to the needs of others, features that lend themselves well to criminal activity. Heaven et al. (2004) report that the P-scale is effective in identifying those adolescents likely to commit delinquent offenses of all kinds, but it appears to be most effective in identifying serious offending and physical aggression in young adults. More specifically, the P-scale predicted those involved in sex crimes and crimes of violence, but it was not highly predictive of nonviolent crimes, such as crimes of theft, vandalism, and other economic or property offenses.

Neuroticism has generally shown a significant relationship with offending, although not as strong as the P-scale (Cale, 2006). The N-scale does well in predicting serious crimes (Kemp & Center, 2003) and is somewhat successful in predicting recidivism (van Dam *et al.*, 2005). We might expect the N-scale to do better at predicting recidivism since Eysenck hypothesized that high N scorers tend to be driven to continue their habitual behaviors and be unusually impulsive.

It should be noted that *low* L scores do show some ability to identify respondents likely to be involved in self-reported delinquency (Center *et al.*, 2005; Gudjonsson, Einarsson, Bragason, & Sigurdsson, 2006; Walker & Gudjonsson, 2006). These results suggest that the L-scale may indeed measure a personality trait, such as conventionality. A high score on the lie scale may reflect those traits that protect some people against offending (Gudjonsson *et al.*, 2006).

The power of the E-scale is more in question, as several studies have found only a weak connection to offending (Cale, 2006; Center, Jackson, & Kemp, 2005; Kemp & Center, 2003). Gudjonsson, Einarsson, Bragason, and Sigurdsson (2006) found a significant relationship between E-scale and criminal offending for both males and females but the nature of the relationship is undoubtedly influenced by the type of crime committed and the person's age. For example, the older a person becomes, the less prominent the need for excitement and stimulation. Consequently, criminal behavior of an exciting nature lessens.

Eysenck (1977) pointed out that incarcerated persons cannot properly answer the social activity questions which are part of the E-scale (see van Dam *et al.*, 2005, p. 16). Eysenck recognized this early in the formulation of his theory, when he commented (1971, p. 289) that "not all crimes are likely to be equally highly correlated with extraversion, and some types of criminals, such as the recidivist 'old lag,' lacking entirely in the social skills needed to make a success of living outside an institution, may in fact show introverted tendencies." Therefore, low E-scales of offenders might be due in part to the effects of incarceration. Furthermore, many murderers and sex offenders do show strong introverted behavior, as we shall see later in the text. Thus, researchers must make distinctions between the various types of offenders and crimes they commit when using the E-scale in their studies. In addition, scores on the E-scale, compared with the P- and N-scales, are more strongly influenced by such factors as age and gender of the respondent; the scale may be measuring more than one dimension of personality, such as sociability, needs for stimulation, and impulsiveness.

To demonstrate the complexity of predicting antisocial behavior on the basis of Eysenckian personality traits, Carrasco *et al.* (2006) emphasized that different *combinations* of Eysenck's personality dimensions show far greater significance to antisocial behavior than any single personality trait by itself. They believe, for example, that psychoticism taps characteristics of empathy and impulsivity, whereas extraversion consists of energy, venturesomeness, and sensation seeking. Correspondingly, they reported in their research that physical aggression is significantly related to impulsiveness and low empathy, and theft and vandalism is related to high venturesomeness. Center and Kemp (2002) also recognize the complexity of the theory; they state that we need to go beyond simply suggesting that antisocial behavior is a direct result of scores on the four personality scales. The scales—which include a version adapted for use with children—are very useful in understanding antisocial behavior, especially for identifying at-risk children during the early school years, but they represent more complexity than originally supposed. We will encounter many other scales formulated by other researchers to identify possible predictors of antisocial tendencies or behaviors.

Although Eysenck's theory continues to be in a state of flux, we have given it a considerable amount of attention here for three reasons. First, the theory is one of the few comprehensive statements about the role of genetics in antisocial behavior, as stated at the beginning of this section. We still have much to learn from this attempt, and perhaps some modifications will strengthen its explanatory potential. Second, Eysenck's theory recognizes the interaction of the environment—specifically via classical conditioning—with characteristics of the nervous system. Of particular importance is the attention Eysenck gives to individual differences in the nervous system as a biological basis for personality in general. Criminology cannot afford to discount the existence of biological factors in antisocial behavior, even if these factors account for the behavior of only a small percentage of the population. At this point, however, it appears that Eysenck's emphasis on classical conditioning as a primary explanation of criminality and his tendency to ignore other forms of learning and mediational (cognitive) processes may be the theory's most damaging weaknesses. In addition, Gordon Trasler (1987) notes that even the concept of conditionability is fraught with difficulties and encourages much debate among contemporary psychologists. There is even considerable debate about what the term means, and the empirical evidence examining the concept remains elusive and conflicting. Finally, Eysenck's theory is unique because it represents one of the few attempts by a psychologist to formulate a general, universal theory of criminal behavior.

Summary and Conclusions

Realizing that crime, like all human behavior, may result from an interaction among heredity, neurophysiology, and the environment, we have in this chapter looked at the research on the genetic and biological makeup of persons who become criminal. The biopsychological approaches of today are far more sophisticated compared with very early efforts to link biology with criminal behavior. These early efforts, which we mentioned only briefly in the chapter, associated criminal activity with (for example) the size of one's skull or one's physique. Contemporary researchers assert that, while some people may be predisposed toward aggressive behavior or behavior that indicates a need for stimulation, socialization or medication can keep inappropriate expressions of those behaviors in check. However, many other criminologists, including some from a psychological orientation, resist any notion of biological or genetic predispositions. Some, while veering away

from predispositions, do agree that factors like toxins, hormones, or brain injuries can influence one's behavior, however.

The genetic factor has been explored in twin and adoption studies. There have been more than 100 of these studies of antisocial behavior (Rhee & Waldman, 2002). Yet, it is difficult to draw firm conclusions concerning the magnitude of genetic and environmental influences on antisocial behavior on the basis of current research. Some empirical studies, however, have found a high concordance rate between identical twins engaged in crime, lending some credence to genetic predisposition. These studies have shown that even when separated at birth, identical twins tend to be similar in their pursuit of criminal careers. However, researchers continually have difficulty separating the social environment (shared or nonshared) from the nature-nurture equation, and it is becoming increasingly clear that the social and biological approaches to understanding human behavior are complementary rather than antagonistic (Cacioppo *et al.*, 2000). There have been relatively few adoption studies conducted, primarily because of the inaccessibility of records. Researchers in this area, who say their research supports the genetic viewpoint, admonish that the social environment can either stimulate or inhibit any inborn tendency toward criminality.

Considerable research has explored temperament, a mood disposition determined largely by genetics and biological influences, and its relationship with antisocial or criminal behavior. Temperament appears in infancy and continues throughout one's life. An irritable baby, according to these researchers, is a challenge to parents or caretakers who may become highly frustrated dealing with him. Likewise, a child who is impulsive is a poor self-regulator who often comes into conflict with the environment. On the other hand, nurturing and warm caretakers can override the effects of such difficult temperaments.

We discussed a number of environmental factors that can significantly affect brain development, which has been linked to serious and violent antisocial behavior. The frontal lobe of the human brain is the location for organized thought, planning, and self-regulation. Such factors as pregnancy and birth complications, exposure to toxic substances (including nicotine, alcohol, and drugs), and malnutrition all can be detrimental to healthy brain development. An environmental hazard of great concern is lead, which can be found in soil, air, or water as well as in some commercial products.

We covered Eysenck's theory, highlighting distinctions between extraverts and introverts in some detail. Eysenck proposed an interaction theory of crime, seeing it as the result of environmental conditions (primarily classical conditioning) working on inherited features of the nervous system. The essence of Eysenckian theory is that individuals with certain types of nervous systems (introverts) condition better, or learn the mores of society much more readily than individuals with other types (extraverts and ambiverts). In other words, introverts link transgressions with

disapproval much sooner than others do. Some people would say introverts have a stronger conscience and experience more fear prior to their transgressions and more guilt after committing them. However, this quick associative or conditioning ability also means that introverts are more likely to acquire sexually deviant behavior.

Eysenck hypothesized that neuroticism or emotionality intensifies existing habits, which in some cases may be antisocial ones. Individuals with high emotionality may be more driven toward antisocial habits than individuals with low emotionality. Psychoticism, a dimension that has received less research attention, appears to correlate with features of the psychopath and frequent offenders. It may also correlate with callous-unemotional (CU) traits, a concept receiving contemporary research attention.

It is obvious that the Eysenckian position needs revision and refinement. As it now stands, the theory has flaws that could be damaging to its construct validity. One glaring weakness is its reliance on classical conditioning to the exclusion of mediational (cognitive) factors and social learning. Despite these problems, Eysenck's work represents a broad, testable theory of criminality that continues to stimulate research. More important for our purposes, the theory integrates nicely the biopsychological perspective with the social environmental perspective in the formation of antisocial behavior. However, as we will see shortly, other contemporary approaches are doing this as well.

We emphasize that most studies in this area focus on violent crime or aggressive antisocial behavior. A considerable body of contemporary research explores the relationship between "violence and the brain." However, assigning a major role in the causation of such behavior to diverse neurological deficits and nervous system functioning is unwarranted. While biopsychology and neurophysiological factors may play some role in the formation of criminal behavior—specifically by affecting brain development—it is far more likely that violent and nonviolent antisocial behavior develops as a result of a series of complicated interactions with significant others in the social environment.

Key Concepts

Ambiversion

Biopsychologists

Concordance

Extraversion

Fraternal twins (dizygotic
  twins)

Identical twins (monozygotic
  twins)

Instrumental learning

Interaction

Neuroticism

Neurotransmitters

Nonshared environments

Operant conditioning
  (instrumental learning)

Pavlovian conditioning (classical
  conditioning)

Plasticity

Psychophysiology

Psychoticism

Serotonin

Shared environments

Social learning

Temperament

Review Questions

1. Briefly describe Eysenck's theory of criminality.
2. What aspects of Eysenck's theory of criminality are supported by research and what aspects are not? In general, how strong is the support?
3. Summarize the findings of adoption studies on the interaction between heredity and environment.
4. Define the following concepts: concordance, RAS, plasticity, ambiversion.
5. What is meant by the term "shared environment" and why is it important in genetic research on crime?
6. Explain how temperament plays a role in the development of antisocial behavior.
7. Provide examples of any three environmental hazards that have been linked with aggressive behavior.

4

Origins of Criminal Behavior: Learning and Situational Factors

CHAPTER OBJECTIVES

- Present learning and cognitive factors as key elements in the development of delinquent and criminal behavior.
- Review the historical background of behaviorism and its contributions to understanding human learning of delinquent and criminal behavior.
- Define and describe operant conditioning and learning.
- Review the fundamental principles of social learning and its contributions to understanding antisocial behavior.
- Introduce frustration-induced crime.
- Describe the power of the social situation, authority, and deindividuation in instigating criminal actions.

When someone has had a brain injury or suffers a seizure or a stroke, it is not unusual for the individual to experience short-term memory loss. The person may, for example, continue to ask the same question repeatedly, both not realizing that he or she just asked it and not knowing the answer. Individuals with dementia, of course, also experience memory loss. As a general principle, though, people do not come into situations empty-headed. They remember what just happened and what has happened in the past. They also have an infinite store of living experiences and an extensive repertoire of strategies for reacting to events. Up to this point, we have not highlighted these strategies, concentrating instead on various individual, family, and social risk factors during the development of criminal behavior.

Genetic and biological factors appear to account in part for individual differences in suscepti- bility to classical conditioning. Since the capacity to be conditioned strongly affects fear of reprisal, it contributes to the inhibition of socially undesirable criminal behavior. However, the classical condi- tioning perspective presumes that the human being is an automaton; that is, humans act in a monot- onous routine manner without active intelligence. Pair a neutral stimulus with a closely following painful event and the alert, intact robot will eventually, and automatically, connect the stimulus with the pain. This sequence is probably a very powerful factor in many behaviors, but certainly not in all or even most. Conditioning is only one of several factors involved in the acquisition (or avoidance) of criminal behavior.

In order to understand criminal behavior in some depth, it is crucial that we regard all individuals—whether or not they violate the rules of society—as *active* problem solvers who perceive, process, interpret, and respond uniquely to their environments. For the moment, consider unlawful behavior as subjectively adaptable rather than deviant. In this sense, unlawful conduct or antisocial behavior is a response pattern that a person has found to be effective, or thinks will be effective, in certain circumstances.

Violent crimes like aggravated assault and homicide are sometimes called "irrational," "uncontrollable," "explosive," or "motiveless," and therefore are believed to resist or defy analysis (e.g., President's Commission on Law Enforcement and Administration of Justice, 1967). By the early twenty-first century, it had become chillingly clear to the public that some violence, specifically that violence associated with terrorism, was carefully controlled and motivated. Later in this text, we will find that different types of violence can be placed into different theoretical frameworks. The decision to act violently may be a quick one, but the violent behavior—including but not limited to terrorist acts—is usually not irrational or uncontrollable. If we consider individual violence, such as a domestic assault, we can say that some people have poor self-regulation skills, but most individuals can be taught to control their behavior, regardless of their excuses. Furthermore, it is almost impossible to determine what is rational or irrational unless we examine the psychological processes of the offender.

Engaging in criminal behavior might be one person's way of adapting or surviving under physically, socially, financially, or psychologically dire conditions. Even behavior that can be attributed to a severe mental disorder may be adaptive, though it may not be legally culpable. Another person might decide that violence is necessary to defend honor, protect self, or reach a personal goal. In either case, the person is choosing what he or she believes is the best alternative for that particular situation (although real choice may be illusory in the case of the person who is severely mentally disordered). It is not, of course, necessarily the alternative that others would choose, nor what society condones. Besides susceptibility to classical conditioning, what accounts for the difference? In a very general sense, learning—both operant (or instrumental) and social learning—is an extremely important component in the equation. In the following pages, we will expand the concept of conditioning to include these two distinct forms of learning, which play a major role in the acquisition and maintenance of criminal behavior. Later, we will introduce situational factors that appear to affect the learning process. Since each of these topics springs from the school of psychological thought called behaviorism, we will begin our discussion there.

BEHAVIORISM

Behaviorism officially began in 1913 with the publication of a landmark paper by John B. Watson (1878–1958), "Psychology as the Behaviorist Views It." The paper, which appeared in the journal *Psychological Review*, is considered the first definitive statement on behaviorism, and Watson is thus acknowledged as the school's founder. However, Watson was by no means the first to discuss the basic elements of behaviorism. Its roots can be traced back at least to Aristotle (Diserens, 1925). Watson's behaviorism represents a recurring phase in the cyclical history of psychology. A psychology of consciousness or mind is followed by a psychology of action and behavior (behaviorism), from which a psychology of mind and consciousness reemerges. Today psychology is immersed once again in a psychology of mind, especially cognitive processes. **Cognitive processes** are those internal mental processes that enable humans to imagine, to gain knowledge, to reason, and to evaluate information. For the moment, let's return to Watsonian behaviorism, which has heavily influenced psychological interpretations of criminal behavior.

Watson frequently declared that psychology was the science of behavior. He believed that psychologists should eliminate the "mind" and all of its related vague concepts from scientific consideration because they could not be observed or measured. He was convinced that the fundamental goal of psychology was to understand, predict, and control human behavior, and that only a rigidly scientific approach could accomplish this.

Watson was greatly influenced by Ivan Pavlov's famous research on **classical conditioning**. Pavlov (1849–1936) was a Russian physiologist interested in studying the digestive system. His subjects were dogs, which he strapped in a harness, placed different types of food in their mouths, and then measured the flow of saliva through a tube he surgically placed in their cheek. During these experiments, he began to notice a curious fact. The dogs began to salivate *before* they received the food. He observed that some began to salivate at the mere sight of the container where their food was kept, and some salivated at the sight of the caretaker who normally fed the dogs. Dog owners will easily recognize this pairing. A dog will become excited and start slobbering as you begin opening a bag of dog chow or shaking a box of dog biscuits. Pavlov quickly recognized the importance of this connection and spent the rest of his life studying it.

Pavlov expanded his laboratory conditions by controlling the dog's associations between events or things and the delivery of food. He began to present a neutral event (an event not previously associated with food) just before food delivery. In his well-known laboratory conditions, he presented a bell just before meat powder. The meat powder was termed the *unconditioned stimulus* because its ability to produce salivation was innate and did not depend on the dog's having to learn the response. Likewise, the salivation was an unconditioned response because it too does not depend on learning. The bell became the *conditioned stimulus*, because the dog quickly learned that the sound of the bell (or even the presence of the bell) preceded the treat. Similarly, salivation to the bell became the *conditioned response* because the association was learned. The importance of classical conditioning will be discussed in more detail as we cover various criminal behaviors here.

Watson thought that psychology should focus exclusively on the interplay between stimulus and response. A **stimulus** is a person, object, or event that elicits behavior. A response is the elicited behavior. Watson was convinced that all behavior—both animal and human—was controlled by the external environment in a way similar to that described by Pavlov in his initial study—stimulus produces response (sometimes called S-R psychology). Therefore, for Watson, classical (or Pavlovian) conditioning was the key to understanding, predicting, and controlling behavior, and its practical applicability was unlimited.

The chief spokesperson for behaviorism for several decades was B. F. Skinner (1904–1990), who was the most influential psychologist in the United States in the twentieth century. The Skinnerian perspective especially dominated the application of behavior modification or behavior therapy in the correctional system and in many institutions for the mentally handicapped or disturbed. Some contemporary theories on criminal behavior (e.g., Akers, 1985) try to integrate Skinnerian behaviorism with sociological perspectives. It is worthwhile, therefore, to spend some time sketching the Skinnerian approach to human behavior in general before assessing its impact on the study of criminal behavior.

Skinner's Theory of Behavior

Like Watson, Skinner believed that the primary goal of psychology is the prediction and control of behavior. And like Watson, he believed that environmental or external stimuli are the primary—if not the sole—determinants of all behavior, both human and animal. The environmental stimuli become **independent variables**, and the behaviors they elicit the **dependent variables**. In the behavioral sciences, a **variable** is any entity (or behavior) that can be measured. A behavior (or response) is called "dependent" because it is under the control of (or dependent on) one or more independent variables. The consistent relationships between independent and dependent variables (stimulus and response) are scientific laws. Thus, according to Skinner, the goal of behavioristic psychology is to uncover these laws, making possible the prediction and control of human behavior, including criminal behavior.

Unlike Watson, Skinner did not deny the existence and sometimes usefulness of private mental events or cognitive processes. He emphasized, however, that these stimuli are not needed by a *science* of behavior, since the products of mental activity can be explained in ways that do not require allusion to unobserved mental states. Specifically, mental activity can be explained by observing what a person does, and it is what a person does that counts. Watson, remember, insisted that consciousness and mind simply do not exist. Thought, to Watson, was little more than tiny movements of the speech apparatus. To Skinner, thought and cognitive processes existed, but studying them is unlikely to lead to the "hard" science of behavior. Consequently, in order to understand and modify criminal behavior, the thoughts, values, decisions, and intentions of a criminal mind are irrelevant. According to Skinner, to understand the development of delinquency and criminal behavior, we must focus on environmental stimuli, observable behavior, and rewards.

BEHAVIORISM AS A METHOD OF SCIENCE   At this point, we must emphasize the need to distinguish between behaviorism as a *perspective on human nature* and a *method of science*. As a method of science, behaviorism posits that knowledge about human behavior can be best advanced if scientists use referents that have a physical basis and can be *publicly observed* by others. Since private events that happen inside our heads cannot be seen by others, they cannot be subjected to the rules of science. According to Skinner, behavioral science data must be comparable to be verified or disconfirmed. Otherwise, psychology would remain a philosophical exercise steeped in armchair speculation and untestable opinions. Self-proclaimed experts could continue to assert that shoplifting is an addiction, just like alcoholism, without being taken to task about the validity of their statements. Only a well-executed, systematic study in which the terms *shoplifting* and *addiction* are clearly spelled out and rigorously tested will advance our knowledge about the accuracy of the shoplifting-addiction connection. Therefore, every psychological experiment, every sentence written into a psychological report, should be anchored to something that we can all observe, or that is testable by another professional. Rather than merely saying that someone is anxious or angry, we must identify the precise behaviors that prompt us to make these interpretations. This offers a basis for others, including the person being observed, to agree or disagree with us.

BEHAVIORISM AS A PERSPECTIVE OF HUMAN NATURE   Concerning behaviorism as a perspective of human nature, Skinner—and a majority of psychologists with a strong behavioristic leaning—embraced the view that humans differ only in degree from their animal ancestry. The behavior of humans follows the same basic natural laws as that of all animals. Like Darwin, Skinner saw no radical differences between humans and animals. Even human language and conceptual thinking are nondistinctive. Verbal behavior "is a very special kind of behavior, but there is nothing by way of processes involved that would distinguish it from nonverbal behavior and hence [verbal behavior] would not distinguish man from the [other] animals" (Skinner, 1964, p. 156). To Skinner, therefore, research on subhumans such as monkeys, rats, and pigeons has great value; if carefully done, it will reveal lawful relationships between all organisms and their environments.

By recognizing how behaviorism views human nature, we are better able to understand the basic framework behaviorism employs in studying and explaining criminal behavior. It also helps us understand the fundamental recommendations advocated by this perspective for reducing or changing criminal behavior, such as might be found in the management policy of certain correctional facilities.

Clearly, Skinner was also a strong situationist. **Situationism** refers to the belief that all behavior is at the mercy of stimuli in the environment, and individuals have virtually no control or self-determination. Independent thinking and free will are myths. Animals, including humans, react, like complicated robots, to their environments. The environmental stimuli and the range of reactions are complex and infinite, but with careful research, this complexity is not unmanageable. Complex human behavior can be broken down into more simple behavior, a procedure sometimes referred to as **reductionism**. In other words, complicated behavior can be best understood by examining the simplest stimulus-response chains of behavior. This point brings us to the issue of operant conditioning.

OPERANT LEARNING   Skinner accepted the basic tenets of classical conditioning, but asserted that we need an additional type of conditioning to account more fully for all forms of behavior. Ivan Pavlov conducted a series of experiments on classical conditioning with hungry dogs during the turn of the twentieth century. The dogs did not operate on their environments to receive rewards; the event (food) occurred regardless of what they did. Skinner called this "responding conditioning" and contrasted it with a situation in which a subject does something that affects the situation. In other words, subjects behave in such a way that reinforcement is forthcoming. To uncover this operant conditioning principle, Skinner established an association between *behavior* and its *consequences*. He trained pigeons (apparently less troublesome and less expensive than dogs) to peck at keys or push levers for food. The pecking or pushing are operations on the environment. **Operant conditioning**, then, is learning to either make or withhold a particular response because of its consequences. Operant conditioning (or operant learning) is a fundamental learning process that is acquired (or eliminated) by the consequences that follow the behavior. For example, a temper tantrum by a toddler at the checkout counter when she wants some candy from the nearby shelves may prompt the parent to give in and provide the child with the candy. Next time, at the same or similar checkout aisle, the temper-tantrum strategy will be tried again since it worked the first time. The child has learned the consequences of timely temper tantrums.

The learning that comes about through operant conditioning was described before Skinner's time, but he is credited with drawing contemporary attention to it. In the early nineteenth century, for example, the philosopher Jeremy Bentham observed that human conduct was controlled by the seeking of pleasure and the avoidance of pain. In essence, this is what is meant by operant learning. It assumes that people do things solely to receive rewards and avoid punishment. The rewards may be physical (e.g., material goods, money), psychological (e.g., feelings of importance or control over one's fate), or social (e.g., improved status, acceptance).

REINFORCEMENT   Skinner called rewards **reinforcement**, defining that term as anything that increases the probability of future responding. Furthermore, reinforcement may be either positive or negative. In **positive reinforcement**, we *gain* something we desire as a consequence of certain behavior. We spend hours practicing a difficult piece on the keyboard or perfecting a ski jump and are rewarded by praise from listeners or a gold medal in the Olympics. In **negative reinforcement**, we *avoid* an unpleasant event or stimulus as a consequence of certain behavior. For example, if as a child you were able to avoid the unpleasantness of certain school days by feigning illness, your malingering was negatively reinforced. Therefore, you were more likely to engage in it again at a future date, under similar circumstances—high school dress-up day, class discussion day in a difficult college course, or the day the district supervisor was scheduled to visit the office. Thus, both positive and negative reinforcement can increase the likelihood of future behavior.

PUNISHMENT AND EXTINCTION   Negative reinforcement is to be distinguished from punishment and extinction. In **punishment**, an organism receives noxious or painful stimuli as consequences of behavior, such as being slapped or hit for "being bad." In **extinction**, a person or animal receives neither reinforcement nor punishment (see **Table 1**). Skinner argued that punishment is a less effective way to eliminate behavior, because it merely suppresses it temporarily. At a later time, under the right conditions, the response is very likely to reoccur. Extinction is far more effective, because once the organism learns that a behavior brings no reinforcement, the behavior will be dropped from the repertoire of possible responses for that set of circumstances.

According to Nietzel (1979), C. R. Jeffrey (1965) was one of the first criminologists to suggest that criminal behavior was learned according to principles of Skinnerian operant conditioning. Shortly afterward, Burgess and Akers (1966) agreed with this, and further hypothesized that criminal behavior was both acquired and maintained through operant conditioning. But, as Nietzel points out, most of the direct evidence for this claim comes from experiments with nonhuman animals. Evidence that the same occurs in humans is scarce and replete with possible alternate interpretations.

Nevertheless, neither Jeffrey nor Burgess and Akers relied exclusively on Skinnerian theory. Rather, they combined sociologist Edwin Sutherland's principles of social learning with operant conditioning, particularly the reinforcement aspect, to suggest explanations for criminal behavior (Williams & McShane, 2004). We will return to Sutherland's theory shortly.

OPERANT LEARNING AND CRIME   The premise that operant conditioning is the basis for the origin of criminal behavior is deceptively simple: Criminal behavior is learned and strengthened because of the reinforcements it brings. According to Skinner, human beings are born neutral—neither good nor bad. Culture, society, and the environment shape behavior. Therefore, behavior will be labeled good, bad, or indifferent, as society chooses. What is judged "good" behavior in one society or culture may be labeled "bad" in another. Members of one group in a society may

TABLE 1   Skinner's Basic Principles of Operant Learning

	Goal	Action
Positive reinforcement	Increases a desired behavior	Introduction of a pleasant stimulus following a desired behavior
Negative reinforcement	Increases a desired behavior	Removal of aversive stimulus following a desired behavior
Punishment	Decreases undesired behavior	Introduction of aversive stimulus following undesired behavior
Extinction	Eliminates undesired behavior	No reinforcement or punishment for undesired behavior

believe that it is "bad" for a child to masturbate or to pretend that a block of wood is a toy truck and "good" to hit the child to stop these behaviors. To others, the behavior of the adults who hit the child is "bad." Depending on the severity of the punishment, it may also be aggravated assault.

Skinner was convinced that searches for individual dispositions or personalities that lead to criminal conduct are fruitless, because people are ultimately determined by the environment in which they live. He does not completely discount the role of genetics in the formation of behavior, but he sees it as a very minor one; the dominant player is operant conditioning. According to Skinner and his followers, if we wish to eliminate crime, we must change society through behavioral engineering based on a *scientific* conception of humans. Having agreed on rules and regulations (having defined what behaviors constitute antisocial or criminal offenses), we must design a society in which members learn very early that positive reinforcement will not occur if they transgress against these rules and regulations, but will occur if they abide by them.

This is a tall order, since the reinforcements for antisocial behavior are already occurring, are not always obvious, and may actually be highly complex. Property crimes such as shoplifting and burglary, or violent crimes such as robbery, appear to be motivated in many cases by a desire for physical rewards. However, they may also be prompted by a desire for social and psychological reinforcements, such as increased status among peers, self-esteem, feelings of competence, or simply for the thrill of it. It is a safe bet that much criminal behavior is undertaken for reinforcement purposes, positive or negative. The problem then becomes, how do we identify those reinforcements and how do we prevent them from happening, or at least minimize their value?

Contemporary psychology still embraces a behavioristic orientation toward the *scientific* study of behavior, but has grown very cool toward the Skinnerian perspective of human nature. All behaviorists are not Skinnerians. Many (if not most) find Skinner's brand of behaviorism too limiting (e.g., Bandura, 1983, 1986). While they agree that a stimulus can elicit a reflexive response (classical conditioning) and that a behavior produces consequences that influence subsequent responding (operant conditioning), they are also convinced that additional factors must be introduced to explain human behavior. **Cognitive learning** is also extremely important, for example. Cognitive learning involves the formation of concepts, schemas, theories, attitudes, beliefs, and other mental or abstract versions of the world. Cognitive psychologists, for example, would argue that mental processes are as crucial—if not more so—in understanding criminal action as behavior itself.

This brings us to the topic of mental states and cognitive processes, which Skinner urged all behavioral scientists to shun. In recent years, many psychologists have been examining the roles played by self-reinforcement, anticipatory reinforcement, vicarious reinforcement, and all the symbolic processes that occur within the human brain. To avoid confusion, we must now begin to distinguish Skinnerian behaviorism from other forms, including social behaviorism (social learning) and differential association-reinforcement.

SOCIAL LEARNING

Early learning theorists worked in the laboratory, using nonhumans as their primary subjects. Pavlov's, Watson's, and Skinner's theories, for example, were based on careful, painstaking observations and experiments with animals. The learning principles gleaned from their work were generalized to a wide variety of human behaviors. In many cases, this was a valid process. Few psychologists would dispute the contention that the concept of reinforcement is one of the most soundly established principles in psychology today.

However, behaviorists also suggested that since all human behavior is learned, it can also be changed, using the same principles by which it was acquired. This generated a plethora of behavior therapies or behavior modification techniques. Use learning principles to establish conditions that change or maintain targeted behaviors and voilà! Therapeutic success! The apparent simplicity of the procedures and methods was especially appealing to many clinicians and other professionals working in the criminal justice system, and behavior modification packages sometimes guaranteed to modify criminal behavior were rushed to correctional institutions, including facilities for juveniles. Prisoners (and juveniles) would be rewarded for good behavior with such incentives as cigarettes, canteen privileges, or an extra shower.

But oversimplification is dangerous when we deal with human complexity. Human beings do respond to reinforcement and punishment, and behavior therapy based on learning principles can change certain elements of behavior. Moreover, humans can be classically conditioned, although there are individual differences in their susceptibility. When we lose sight of the person and overemphasize the environmental or external determinants of behavior, however, we may be overlooking a critical level of explanation. Remember that human beings are, in large part, active problem solvers who perceive, encode, interpret, and make decisions on the basis of what the environment has to offer. Thus, internal factors, as well as external ones, may play significant roles in behavior. This is the essence of **social learning theory**, which suggests that to understand criminal behavior we must examine perceptions, thoughts, expectancies, competencies, and values. Each person has his or her own version of the world and lives by that version.

To explain human behavior, social learning theorists place great emphasis on cognitive processes, which are the internal processes we commonly call thinking and remembering. Classical and operant conditioning ignore what transpires between the time the organism perceives a stimulus and the time it responds or reacts. Skinnerian behaviorists claim, "If we can account for the facts by using observable behavior, why worry about the labyrinths of internal processes?" Social behaviorists, however, counter that this perspective offers an incomplete picture of human behavior.

The term *social learning* reflects the theory's strong assumption that we learn primarily by observing and listening to people around us—the social environment. In fact, social learning theorists believe that the social environment is the most important factor in the *acquisition* of most human behavior. Humans are basically social creatures. These theorists do accept the necessity of reinforcement for the *maintenance* of behavior, however. Criminal behavior, for example, may initially be acquired through association and through observation, but whether or not it is maintained will depend primarily upon reinforcement (operant conditioning). For example, if a boy sees someone he admires (i.e., a role model) successfully pilfering from the local sporting goods store, the boy may try some pilfering of his own. Whether he continues that behavior, however, will depend on the personal reinforcement or value it assumes. If no reinforcement is forthcoming (he fails to pocket a baseball because someone else walked into the store, or he finds that the gym shorts he stole do not fit), then the behavior will probably drop out of his response repertoire (extinction). If the behavior brings aversive results (punishment), this will inhibit or suppress future similar behavior.

Several clusters of psychologists are enrolled in the social learning school of thought. Additionally, the discipline of sociology has its own social learning school. We will focus first on the work of two prominent representatives, psychologists Julian Rotter and Albert Bandura, since they seem to have the most to offer to the study of criminal behavior from the social learning perspective.

Expectancy Theory

Julian Rotter is best known for drawing attention to the importance of expectations (cognitions) about the consequences (outcomes) of behavior, including the reinforcement that will be gained from it. In other words, before doing anything, we ask, "What has happened to me before in this situation, and what will I gain this time?" According to Rotter, whether a specific pattern of behavior occurs will depend on our expectancies and how much we value the outcomes. To predict whether someone will behave a certain way, we must estimate that person's expectancies and the importance he or she places on the rewards gained by the behavior. Often, the person will develop "generalized expectancies" that are stable and consistent across relatively similar situations (Mischel, 1976). **Expectancy theory**, therefore, argues that a person's performance level is based on that person's *expectation* that behaving in a particular way will lead to a given outcome.

The hypothesis that people enter situations with generalized expectancies about the outcomes of their behavior is an important one for students of crime. Applying Rotter's theory to criminal behavior, we would say that when people engage in unlawful conduct, they *expect* to gain something in the form of status, power, security, affection, material goods, or living conditions. The violent person, for example, may elect to behave that way in the belief that something will be gained; the serial murderer might believe that God has sent him on a mission to eliminate all "loose" women, and thus by doing so he pleases God; the woman who poisons an abusive husband looks for an improvement in her life situation. Simply to label a violent person impulsive, crazy, or lacking in ego control fails to include other essential ingredients in the act. Although self-regulation and moral development are involved, people who act unlawfully perceive and interpret the situation and select what they consider to be the most effective behavior under the circumstances. Usually, when people act violently, they do so because that approach has been used successfully in the past (at least they believe it has been successful). Less frequently, they have simply observed someone else gain by employing a violent approach, and they try it for themselves. This brings us to Bandura's imitational model of social learning.

Imitational Aspects of Social Learning

An individual may acquire ways of doing something simply by watching others do it; direct reinforcement is not necessary. Bandura (1973b) introduced this idea, which he called **observational learning** or **modeling**, to the social learning process. Bandura contends that much of our behavior is initially acquired by watching others, who are called models. **Models** are those significant persons in the social environment that provide cues for how to do something. For example, a child may learn how to shoot a gun by imitating television or video characters. He or she then rehearses and fine-tunes this behavioral pattern by practicing with toy guns. The behavior is likely to be maintained if peers also play with guns and reinforce one another for doing so. Even if the children have not pulled the triggers on real guns, they have acquired a close approximation of shooting someone by observing others do it. It is likely that just about every adult and older child in the United States knows how to shoot a gun, even if they have never actually done so: "You aim and pull the trigger." Of course, shooting safely and accurately is much more complicated, but the rudimentary know-how has been acquired through **imitational learning** (also called modeling or observational learning). The behavioral pattern exists in our repertoires, even if we have never received direct reinforcement for acquiring it.

According to Bandura, the more significant and respected the models, the greater their impact on our behavior. Relevant models include parents, teachers, siblings, friends, and peers, as well as symbolic models like literary characters or television, video, or movie personages. Rock stars and athletes are modeled by many young people, which is one reason we are exposed to so many public figures touting everything from cosmetics to a drug-free life to beer. Interestingly, the commercial and public service advertisements often miss the point. In observational learning, it is not so much what the model says as what the model does that is effective. If sports stars actually avoided the use of drugs in their daily lives, their messages to youth might be more effective. Conversely, the messages that young people do get from sports and entertainment figures encourage, rather than discourage, criminal behavior. Media accounts of popular public figures allegedly engaging in domestic violence, rape, child molestation, assault, tax evasion, illegal gambling, drug abuse, and the use of steroids or other muscle enhancing drugs suggest that such behavior is normative.

The observed behavior of the model is also more likely to be imitated if the observer sees the model receive a reward, such as fame plus millions of dollars per year. It is less likely to be imitated if the model is punished. Thus, according to social learning principles, convictions of sports and entertainment figures charged with the crimes mentioned above would suggest that the behaviors will not be imitated. On the other hand, if they serve little or no time and write a widely purchased book about their experiences, an observer might not perceive this as a punishment. Bandura believes—much like Rotter—that once a person decides to use a newly acquired behavior, whether he or she performs or maintains it will depend on the situation and the expectancies for potential gain. This potential gain may come from outside (the praise of others, financial gain) or it may come from within (self-reinforcement for a job the individual perceives as well done).

Much of Bandura's research was directed at the learning of aggressive and violent behavior. A substantial body of experimental findings gives impressive support to his theory. In a classic study, preschool children who watched a film of an adult assaulting an inflated plastic rubber doll were significantly more likely to imitate that behavior than were a comparable group who viewed more passive behavior (Bandura & Huston, 1961; Bandura, Ross, & Ross, 1963). Many studies employing variations of this basic procedure report similar results, strengthening the hypothesis that observing aggression leads to hostility in both children and adults (Walters & Grusec, 1977). In recent years, this research has been extended to viewing media violence and playing violent video games (Dodge & Pettit, 2003). While the research in these areas is not totally conclusive, the growing evidence is that people who observe aggressive acts not only imitate the observed behavior but also become generally more hostile and aggressive themselves (Bryant & Zillman, 2002; Huesmann, Moise-Titus, Podolski, & Eron, 2003).

To some extent, social learning, as it is discussed by Rotter and Bandura, humanizes the Skinnerian viewpoint, since it provides clues about what transpires inside the human brain (or mind). It draws our attention to the cognitive aspects of behavior, while classical and operant conditioning focus exclusively on the environment. Social learning theorists use environment in the social sense, which includes the internal as well as the external environment. Skinnerians prefer to limit relevant stimuli to external surroundings.

Differential Association-Reinforcement Theory

Ronald Akers (1977, 1985; Burgess & Akers, 1966) proposed a social learning theory of deviance that tries to integrate the core ingredients of Skinnerian behaviorism, the social learning theory as outlined by Bandura, and the differential association theory of criminologist Edwin H. Sutherland (1947). Akers called his theory **differential association-reinforcement (DAR)**. Briefly, the theory states that people learn to commit deviant acts through interpersonal interactions with their social environment.

To understand DAR theory, we must grasp Sutherland's differential association theory, which dominated the field of sociological criminology for over four decades. It was first set forth in the third edition (1939) of Sutherland's *Principles of Criminology* and restated in 1947. Although Sutherland died in 1950, the theory was left intact in Donald R. Cressey's subsequent revisions of the original text (Sutherland & Cressey, 1978; Sutherland, Cressey, & Luckenbill, 1992).

Sutherland believed that criminal or deviant behavior is learned the same way that all behavior is learned. The crucial factors are with whom a person associates, for how long, how frequently, how personally meaningful the associations, and how early they occur in the person's development. According to Sutherland, in our intimate personal groups, we all learn definitions, or normative meanings (messages or values), favorable or unfavorable to law violation. A person becomes delinquent or criminal "because of an excess of definitions favorable to violation of law over definitions unfavorable to violation of law. This is the principle of differential association" (Sutherland & Cressey, 1974, pp. 80–81).

Note that criminal behavior does not invariably develop out of association or contacts with "bad companions" or a criminal element. The messages, not the contacts themselves, are crucial. Furthermore, in order for the person to be influenced toward delinquent behavior, the deviant messages or values from the "bad companions" must outweigh conventional ones. Therefore, Sutherland also believed that criminal behavior may develop even if association with criminal groups is minimal. For example, law-abiding groups—such as parents—may communicate subtly or bluntly that it is all right to cheat, or that everyone is basically dishonest. This is an extremely important point that will be reiterated when we discuss moral disengagement later in the chapter. Nevertheless, contemporary reviews of differential association theory emphasize that the associations with deviant peer groups have a major effect on illegal behavior (Williams & McShane, 2004). What is not known is which comes first: the behavior or the associations (Williams & McShane, 2004).

Sutherland's theory is probably popular among social scientists because, as one writer put it, "it attempts a logical, systematic formulation of the chain of interrelations that makes crime reasonable and understandable as normal, learned behavior without having to resort to assumptions of biological or psychological deviance" (Vold, 1958, p. 192). However, the theory is also ambiguous; because of this feature, it did not at first draw much empirical research (see Gibbons, 1977, pp. 221–228). How are a person's contacts to be measured and weighed? Also, as Cressey (Sutherland & Cressey, 1974) admits, the theory does not specify what kinds of learning are important (e.g., operant, classical, modeling). Neither does it adequately consider individual differences in the learning process. Among some sociologists, however, differential association theory remains popular and continues to attract research interest (Williams & McShane, 2004).

Akers (1985) tries to correct some of the problems with differential association theory by reformulating it to dovetail with Skinnerian and social learning principles. He proposes that most deviant behavior is learned according to principles outlined in Skinner's operant conditioning, with classical conditioning playing a secondary role. Furthermore, the strength of deviant behavior is a direct function of the amount, frequency, and probability of reinforcement the individual has experienced by performing that behavior in the past. The reinforcement may be positive or negative in the Skinnerian meanings of the terms.

Crucial to the Akers position is the role played by *social* and *nonsocial reinforcement*, the former being the more important. "Most of the learning relevant to deviant behavior is the result of social interactions or exchanges in which the words, responses, presence, and behavior of other persons make reinforcers available, and provide the setting for reinforcement" (Akers, 1985, p. 45). It is also important to note that most of these social reinforcements are symbolic and verbal rewards for participating or for agreeing with group norms and expectations. For example, doing something in accordance with group or subcultural norms is rewarded with "Way to go," "Great job," "Good going," a pat on the back, or a friendly grin. Nonsocial reinforcement refers primarily to physiological factors or material acquisition that may be relevant for some crimes, such as drug-related offenses or burglary.

Deviant or antisocial behavior, then, is most likely to develop as a result of social reinforcements given by significant others, usually within one's peer group. The group first adopts its own *normative definitions* about what conduct is good or bad, right or wrong, justified or unjustified. These normative definitions become internal, cognitive guides to what is appropriate and will most likely be reinforced by the group. In this sense, normative definitions operate as **discriminative stimuli**—social signals transmitted by subcultural or peer groups to indicate whether certain kinds of behavior will be rewarded or punished within a particular social context.

According to Akers, two classes of discriminative stimuli operate in promoting deviant behavior. First, positive discriminative stimuli are the signals (verbal or nonverbal) that communicate that certain behaviors are encouraged by the subgroup. Not surprisingly, they follow the principle of positive reinforcement: The individual engaging in them gains social rewards from the group. The second type of social cue, *neutralizing* or *justifying discriminative stimuli*, neutralizes the warnings communicated by society at large that certain behaviors are inappropriate or unlawful. According to Akers, they "make the behavior, which others condemn and which the person himself may initially define as bad, seem all right, justified, excusable, necessary, the lesser of two evils, or not 'really' deviant after all" (Akers, 1977, p. 521). Statements like "Everyone has a price," "I can't help myself," "Everyone else does it," or "She deserved it" reflect the influence of neutralizing stimuli.

The more people define their behavior as positive or at least justified, the more likely they are to engage in it. If deviant activity (as defined by society at large) has been reinforced more than conforming behavior (also defined by society), and if it has been justified, it is likely that deviant behavior will be maintained. In essence, our behavior is guided by the norms we have internalized and for which we expect to be continually socially reinforced by significant others.

Akers accepts the validity of Bandura's modeling as a necessary factor in the initial acquisition of deviant behavior. But its continuation will depend greatly on the frequency and personal significance of *social reinforcement*, which comes from association with others.

Akers's social learning theory has received its share of criticism. Some scholars consider it circular and difficult to follow: Behavior occurs because it is reinforced, but it is reinforced because it occurs. Kornhauser (1978) asserted that there was no empirical support for the theory. During the 1980s and 1990s, though, Akers himself—along with research colleagues—published a number of studies supportive of his theory, particularly as it related to drug use (e.g., Akers & Cochran, 1985; Akers & Lee, 1996; Krohn, Akers, Radosevich, & Lanza-Kaduce, 1982). Like Sutherland's differential association theory, Akers's approach retains respectability within sociological criminology.

FRUSTRATION-INDUCED CRIMINALITY

Several learning investigators (e.g., Amsel, 1958; Brown & Farber, 1951) have noted that when organisms—including humans—are prevented from responding in a way that had previously produced rewards, their behavior often becomes more energetic and vigorous. Animals bite, scratch, snarl, and become irritable; humans may snarl and become irritable and rambunctious (and may also bite and scratch). Researchers assume that these aroused responses result from an aversive internal state of arousal that they call **frustration**.

Thus, when behavior directed at a specific goal is blocked, arousal increases, and the individual experiences a drive to reduce it. Behavior is energized, but more significantly the responses that lead to a reduction in the arousal may be strengthened or reinforced. This suggests that people who employ violence to reduce frustration will, under extreme frustration, become more vigorous than usual, possibly even resorting to murder and other violent actions. It also suggests that violent behavior directed at reducing frustration will be reinforced, since it reduces unpleasant arousal by altering the precipitating event or stimuli.

The Socialized and Individual Offender

Leonard Berkowitz (1962) conducted numerous studies relating frustration to criminality. He divided criminal personalities into two main classifications: the **socialized** and the **individual offender**. You have already met socialized offenders. We have discussed them throughout this chapter as products of learning, conditioning, and modeling. They offend because they have learned to, or expect rewards, as a result of their interactions with the social environment. The individual offender, by contrast, is the product of a long, possibly intense series of frustrations resulting from unmet needs. According to Berkowitz, both modeling and frustration are involved in the development of criminal behavior, but one set of life experiences favors a particular criminal style. "Most lawbreakers may have been exposed to some combination of frustrations and aggressively antisocial models, with the thwartings being particularly important in the development of 'individual' offenders and the antisocial models being more influential in the formulation of the 'socialized' criminals" (Berkowitz, 1962, p. 303).

Berkowitz adds an important dimension to frustration, suggesting that it is particularly intense if an individual has high expectancy of reaching a goal (Berkowitz, 1969). People who anticipate reaching a goal, and who feel they have some personal control over their lives, are more likely to react strongly to interference than those who feel hopeless. In the first case, delay or blockage may generate intense anger and even a violent response, if the frustrated individual believes that type of response will eliminate the interference. The power of frustration may well have been what Maslow (1954) was referring to when he stated that crime and delinquency represent a legitimate revolt against exploitation, injustice, and unfairness. The frustration hypothesis also fits neatly into theories offered by radical or conflict criminologists. Individuals who feel suppressed by the power elite and feel they have a right to reap society's benefits may well experience intense frustration at continuing domination. These criminologists would prefer, though, that the focus be on those who hold the power rather than on those who commit crime out of possible frustration.

Frustration-Induced Riots

The frustration-induced theory helps to explain the behavior of looters during unexpected events like floods, fires, urban riots, or electrical blackouts. For example, between April 30 and May 3, 1993, businesses in Los Angeles were burned and looted largely but not only by African Americans who were frustrated by a jury's acquittal of four white LA police officers in the March 1991 beating of African American motorist Rodney G. King. Fifty-eight people were killed in the four days of rioting, and damage was estimated to be at least $1 billion. People of all ages and racial or ethnic backgrounds were stealing everything from food and alcohol to firearms and stereos. The rioting triggered smaller uprisings in several other cities, including San Francisco, Atlanta, Seattle, Las Vegas, and Miami. Authorities concluded that the riots were brought on by frustrations with economic, social, and political inequalities found in many sectors of American society, including the court system. The Los Angeles riot was similar to the August 1965 uprising of the Watts section of LA, when 34 were killed and one thousand were injured. The riot was prompted by deeply felt frustrations with the same perceived inequalities in American society. Since 1980, there have been at least five major city riots in the United States, mostly started in the wake of reports of police violence and perceived inequities.

Following Hurricanes Katrina and Rita in 2005, there were many reports of property crime and some violence. Many commentators noted that this was a reflection of the frustration residents of New Orleans and other communities felt at the failure on the part of federal and state agencies to provide a quick, humane, and efficient response to this natural disaster.

The frustration-induced theory also would suggest that individuals who commit larceny under these situations have materialistic goals (e.g., their fair share of middle-class goods) that they have not yet attained. Society blocked the goals, and the individuals became impatient and frustrated. When the opportunity to loot arises, they are there to take it. Demographic profiles of the 2,706 adults arrested and charged with looting during the New York City blackout of 1977 support this theory. The defendants had stronger community ties and higher incomes than the average defendant in the criminal justice system (*New York Times*, August 14, 1977). Only about 10 percent were on welfare; approximately half were gainfully employed. Sixty-five percent of those arrested were African American and 30 percent were Hispanic. These data indicate that these defendants were, in general, eager to eliminate further delays in meeting their expectancy for a better life.

On the other hand, there have been numerous accounts of peaceful demonstrations and protests after a perceived injustice, even when major disruptions or even riots had been feared.

Frustration and Crime

Berkowitz hypothesizes that the more intense and frequent the thwartings or frustrations in a person's life, the more susceptible and sensitive the person is to subsequent frustration. Thus, the individual who frequently strikes out at society in unlawful or deviant ways may have encountered numerous severe frustrations, especially during early development, but has not given up hope. In support of this argument, Berkowitz cites the research findings on delinquency (e.g., Bandura & Walters, 1959; Glueck & Glueck, 1950; McCord, McCord, & Zola, 1959), revealing that delinquent children, compared with nondelinquents, have been considerably more deprived and frustrated during their lifetime.

Berkowitz also suggests that parental neglect or failure to meet the child's needs for dependency and affection are internal, frustrating circumstances that germinate distrust of all others within the social environment. This generalized distrust is carried into the streets and school, and the youngster may exhibit a "chip on the shoulder." The frustration of not having dependency needs met prevents the child from establishing emotional attachments to other people. The individual may thus become resentful, angry, and hostile toward other people in general. Current psychological approaches to delinquency would not disagree, but would place far less blame on the parent. They are more likely to recognize the restrictions that parents face as a result of social problems like racism and economic inequality. In addition, contemporary psychologists recognize the influences of other social systems in the juvenile's life, including peers and the educational system.

SITUATIONAL INSTIGATORS AND REGULATORS OF CRIMINAL BEHAVIOR

Most contemporary theories and research support the view that human behavior results from a mutual interaction between personality and situational variables. However, several behavioral and social scientists (e.g., Alison, Bennell, Ormerod, & Mokros, 2002; Gibbons, 1977; Mischel, 1976) complain that much crime research and theory neglects situational variables in favor of dispositional factors. They contend that criminality in many cases may simply reflect being in the wrong place at the wrong time with the wrong people. For example, Gibbons comments, "In many cases, criminality may be a response to nothing more temporal than the provocations and attractions bound up in the immediate circumstances out of which deviant acts arise" (Gibbons, 1977, p. 229). Skinner, of course, exemplifies the position that behavior is controlled by environmental contingencies and events.

Haney (1983) discusses **fundamental attribution error**, which refers to a common human tendency to discount the influence of the situation and explain behavior by referring to the personality of the actor instead. Fundamental attribution error is a concept that applies to making attributions about others, not ourselves. For example, when correctional counselors were asked why inmates had committed the crimes that put them in prison, the counselors attributed the causes almost exclusively to dispositional or personality factors (such as laziness, or meanness) rather than to environmental factors (such as upbringing, poverty, or social factors) (Saulnier & Perlman, 1981). The inmates, on the other hand, said that factors they believed landed them in prison were largely external in nature, such as poverty, poor employment opportunities, and physical and sexual abuse. When it comes to ourselves, we engage in **self-serving biases**, in which we tend to attribute good things about ourselves to dispositional factors, and bad things to events and forces outside ourselves. For example, when we do well on an exam, we tend to attribute the cause to our intelligence and study habits. On the other hand, when we do poorly, we tend to attribute the cause to a poorly designed, unfair, or "tricky" exam.

Haney believes that personality or internal states account very little for how we act. He contends that the important determining influence is the situation in which we find ourselves. In essence, Haney is arguing that, given the appropriate circumstances, anyone might engage in culpable criminal behavior—that we all have our price.

Situations are rarely static. Our behavior influences them to some extent, and they in turn influence our behavior. This reciprocal interaction between person and environment is one reason students of crime are beginning to pay more attention to victimology—victims often influence the course of criminal actions, particularly violent ones. **Victimology** is the scientific study of the causes, circumstances, individual characteristics, and social context of becoming a victim of a crime. Although victimologists are very careful not to blame victims for the crimes perpetrated against them, they do note that certain actions can facilitate, precipitate, and sometimes even provoke others to commit crime (Karmen, 2001). At this point we will turn our attention to two situational factors that seem to play a particularly important role in antisocial behavior: obedience to authority, and deindividuation.

Authority as an Instigator of Criminal Behavior

Sometimes, people behave a certain way because someone with power told them they must, even though the actions do not "set right" with their own principles. Kelman and Hamilton (1989) refer to this phenomenon as **crimes of obedience**. "A crime of obedience is an act performed in response to orders from authority that is considered illegal or immoral by the larger community" (Kelman & Hamilton, 1989, p. 46). The classic example of the influence of authority is the military order to kill indiscriminately or to commit some other atrocity, such as Lieutenant William Calley's carrying out the massacre of villagers at My Lai in the Vietnam War. An example of crimes of obedience in a political/bureaucratic context is the Watergate scandal, when, on June 17, 1972, a group of men under the auspices of the Nixon administration burglarized the Democratic National Headquarters in the Watergate apartment complex. The concept also comes to mind as the nation is in the midst of scrutinizing the interrogation tactics and the treatment of detainees in the wake of September 11. Crimes of obedience also appear to be widespread in the corporate world.

In an attempt to delineate some of the variables involved in obedience to authority, Stanley Milgram (1977) designed a series of experiments, using as subjects persons who volunteered (for money) in response to a newspaper ad. The experiments, which eventually received intensive public scrutiny and are now cited in nearly every introductory psychology textbook, studied the amount of electrical shock people were willing to administer to others when ordered to do so by an apparent authority figure.

The subjects were adult males, ages 20–50, who represented a cross section of the socioeconomic classes. They were told that the researchers were studying the effects of punishment on memory. The experiment required a "teacher" and a "victim." Unknown to the volunteers, the victim was part of the experiment, a confederate who had been trained to act in a certain manner as part of the experimental design. In a rigged coin toss, the naive subject (the volunteer) always became the teacher and the confederate the victim. The victim-learner was taken to an adjacent room and strapped into an "electric chair" in the presence of the "naive" teacher.

Next, the teacher was led back to a room where he saw a simulated shock generator—a frightening apparatus with thirty toggle switches presumably capable of delivering thirty levels of electric shock to the learner in the adjacent room. Each level was marked in volts ranging from 15 to 450 and accompanied by a switch. In addition, labels indicated "slight shock," "danger: severe shock," and beyond, to an "XXX" level. Each time the learner gave an incorrect answer to a learning task, the teacher was instructed to administer a stronger level of shock. The victim, who did not of course receive any shock at all, purposefully gave incorrect answers; he had also been trained to scream in agony, plead with the subject to stop, and pound on the wall when the higher levels of shock were administered.

Milgram wanted to discover how far people would go under the orders of an apparent authority figure (the experimenter). He may have found more than he bargained for. Almost two-thirds of the subjects obeyed the experimenter and administered the maximum shock levels. In subsequent experiments, using similar experimental conditions but different subjects (including both males and females), Milgram continued to find similar results. Interestingly, when Milgram originally asked mental health experts to predict the outcome of this experiment, the majority of them thought that only a pathological few would obey the experimenter's commands to incrementally increase the shock to dangerous levels (Tsang, 2002). The experts apparently discounted the enormous pressures that the experiment placed on subjects and committed the fundamental attribution error, assuming that "the obedient person who obeys evil commands is sadistic and ill" (Tsang, 2002, p. 27).

Many of Milgram's subjects, while obeying the experimenter's instructions, demonstrated considerable tension and discomfort. Some stuttered, bit their lips, twisted their hands, laughed nervously, sweated profusely, or dug their fingernails into their flesh, especially after the victim began pounding the wall in protest (Milgram, 1963). After the experiment, some reported that they wanted to stop punishing the victim but continued to do so because the experimenter would not let them stop. Milgram (1977, p. 118) concluded, "The individual, upon entering the laboratory, becomes integrated into a situation that carries its own momentum."

In subsequent studies, Milgram modified the procedure to include women and to determine more precisely what conditions inhibited or promoted this extreme obedience. For example, he varied the psychological and physical distance between the subject and the victim. To increase the psychological distance between the two, Milgram eliminated the cries of the victim that had been programmed into the original experiment. In another experiment, to minimize the physical and psychological distance between them, the subject sat next to the victim.

In general, Milgram found that the subjects obeyed the experimenter less as physical, visual, and auditory contact with the victim increased. However, the nearer the *experimenter* got to the "teacher," the more likely the teacher was to obey. Milgram found no evidence of significant personality or gender differences in the studies as far as shocking behavior was concerned, but he did find that female teachers were more distressed about their task than their male counterparts.

The psychological and physical distance variable suggests some interesting implications. If we were to analogize between Milgram's studies and violent actions, we would expect that the more impersonal the weapon or situation (psychological and physical distance), the greater the likelihood for destruction and serious violence. Certainly, killing someone with a firearm at a distance versus killing someone point-blank are two different tasks. And both methods differ from choking someone to death with one's bare hands. It would appear that the firearm offers a more impersonal and possibly easier way to eliminate someone, and thus is more likely to lead to violent behavior. Admittedly, this suggestion makes some quantum jumps from a psychological experiment in an artificial setting, but it is a point worth considering.

In assessing the profound influence of commands from an authority figure, we should also pay close attention to the reactions of the subjects in Milgram's study. As noted above, individual differences were detected in the way the subjects reacted to the situation, but not in their actual willingness to shock. Although some subjects refused to continue with the experiment when they believed that they were hurting the victim, most (about 65%) administered the full range of shock levels. Most also displayed anxiety and conflict.

Milgram noted a curious dissociation between word and action. Many subjects said they could not go on, but nevertheless they did. Some justified their action by concluding that the experimenter would not permit any harm to come to the victim. "He must know what he is doing." Other subjects expressed different interpretations and expectancies, such as the belief that the scientific knowledge gained in the experiment justified the method. It is interesting to note that people who have not undergone the ordeal are quite convinced that they would be members of the defiant group who refused to deliver the extreme levels of shock. Later studies conducted both in the United States and abroad confirmed Milgram's findings, however (Burger, 2009; Penrod, 1983).

Milgram hypothesized that the subject's obedient behavior could be explained by a shift in the perceived role played by the subject. He referred to this shift in role as an "agentic state," where "a person sees himself as an agent for carrying out another's wishes" (Milgram, 1974, p. 133). In other words, the subject believes he is no longer acting on his own accord but for another authorized agent. Tsang (2002, p. 28) notes that Bandura (1999) also theorizes "that many individuals in an obedient situation have a shift in attention from their responsibility as moral agents to their duty as obedient subordinates." Similar points of view have been expressed by Kelman and Hamilton (1989) and Blumenthal (1999).

Milgram suggested that our culture may not provide adequate models for disobedience to authority. Likewise, Kelman and Hamilton (1989) argued that it was important for schools to provide *all* children with opportunities to develop leadership skills and encourage them to be critical thinkers and to question authority in an effective manner. Milgram admonished (1977, p. 120) that his studies raise the possibility that human nature or, more specifically, the kind of character produced in American democratic society, cannot be counted on to insulate its citizens from brutality and inhumane treatment at the direction of malevolent authority. A substantial proportion of people do what they are told to do, irrespective of the context of the act and without limitations of conscience, so long as they perceive that the command comes from a legitimate authority.

Recently, Jerry Burger (2009) replicated Milgram's study in an effort to discover if people today would still obey commands from authority figures if they were uncomfortable about doing what was asked. He discovered that obedience rates were only slightly lower than those Milgram had found 45 years earlier. In addition, contrary to expectations, participants who witnessed another person refusing to obey the experimenter's instructions obeyed just as often as those who did not witness another person refusing to obey. Moreover, men and women did not differ in their rates of obedience. The findings suggest that the same situational factors appear to be operating today. Burger also found that individuals who were high in empathy expressed a reluctance to continue to obey earlier than those who were low in empathy. However, even though they expressed reluctance, these participants continued to follow procedure nonetheless.

Milgram's original experiment was controversial for a number of reasons, but most particularly for deceiving its participants and not adequately deprogramming them after the experiment had ended. Over the years, some participants have stated that they suffered emotionally as a result of their willingness to harm others, even though they were told the shocking had been a ruse. In his replication, Burger (2009) took a few additional precautions. He excluded people with a history of psychological or emotional problems from the study. He also stopped the experiment at 150 volts for all participants. In addition, participants who had at least three college-level psychology classes were excluded because there was high probability they would know the results of the original experiment.

Milgram's theory—supported by Burger's research—may account to some extent for immoral or despicable acts committed under the influence of authority. At this writing, U.S. president Barack Obama has ordered the closing of the military detention center at Guantanamo Bay in Cuba. We know that a variety of tactics were used to elicit information from detainees at Guantanamo and other locations, and that some of these involved torture, both physical and psychological. We also know that some of the soldiers who were guards have begun to come forward to reveal actions they took under orders from supervisors. We know that some lower-level military persons are serving prison time, but we do not know whether charges will be filed against those higher in the chain of command. The U.S. Attorney General has appointed an independent counsel to investigate possible instances of abuse by CIA personnel during interrogations. Although generalizations from the psychological laboratory to the real-world scenarios of destructive or violent obedience must remain tentative for the time being, the relevance of these studies to actual situations cannot be overlooked.

Milgram appeared convinced that situational factors normally override individual factors, and he would probably find personality or the morality of the individual fundamentally irrelevant in the explanation of the behavior. Other theorists, however, argue that it is precisely personality or moral development that account for resistance to authority. Kelman and Hamilton (1989) suggested that one's behavior in high authority situations most likely is a result of an interaction between one's personality characteristics and the roles played. Philip Zimbardo (1970, 1973; Haney & Zimbardo, 1998), on the other hand, is more closely aligned with Milgram, believing that the situation—including the overwhelming power of roles—is the most likely determinant of the behavior. Zimbardo demonstrated this in the famous Stanford Prison Experiment, and more broadly in his concept of deindividuation, to which we now turn our attention.

Deindividuation

Deindividuation theory is based on the classic crowd theory of Gustave Le Bon. The theory, formulated in Le Bon's book *The Crowd: A Study of the Popular Mind* (1885/1995) was introduced into mainstream social psychology by Festinger, Pepitone, and Newcomb in 1952 (Postmes & Spears, 1998). Deindividuation, according to Festinger, Pepitone, and Newcomb (1952), refers to the observation that in crowds or groups, many people lose their sense of individuality, remove self-imposed controls, and neutralize their internalized moral restraints. Thus, "deindividuation was closely associated with the feeling of not being scrutinized or accountable when submerged in the group" (Postmes & Spears, 1998, p. 240). Philip Zimbardo (1970) extended and further developed deindividuation theory in a number of well-known research projects. For Zimbardo, deindividuation involved feelings of reduced self-observation, and he sought to identify the things that could induce that state (Postmes & Spears, 1998).

Deindividuation, Zimbardo hypothesized, usually follows a complex chain of events. First, the presence of many other persons encourages feelings of anonymity. Then the individual feels he or she loses identity and becomes part of the group. Under these conditions, he or she can no longer be singled out and held responsible for his or her behavior. Apparently, this feeling then generates a "loss of self-awareness, reduced concern over evaluations from others, and a narrowed focus of attention" (Baron & Byrne, 1977, pp. 581–582). When combined, these processes lower restraints against antisocial criminal behavior and appear to be basic ingredients in mass violence. However, they also may be at work in nonviolent offenses, such as looting.

In one early experiment, Zimbardo (1970) purchased two used cars, left one abandoned on a street in Manhattan, New York, and the other on a street in Palo Alto, California (about 55,000 population in the late 1960s). Zimbardo's deindividuation hypothesis predicted that, due to the large population of New York, people would more likely lose their identity and feel less responsible for their actions. Consequently, New Yorkers would be more likely to loot the abandoned vehicle. This is exactly what happened. Within 26 hours, the New York car was stripped of battery, radiator, air cleaner, radio antenna, windshield wipers, side chrome, all four hubcaps, a set of jumper cables, a can of car wax, a gas can, and the only tire worth taking. Interestingly, the looting was not done by delinquents or members of a criminal subculture; all the looters were well-dressed, middle-class whites. On several occasions, the looting was done by entire families: children and parents together in a family enterprise.

On the other hand, the car in Palo Alto was untouched during the seven days it was left abandoned. At one point during a rainstorm, a passerby actually lowered the hood to prevent the motor from getting wet. Why such a dramatic difference?

Zimbardo suggests that the anonymity of the New York residents worked in combination with situational cues, implying that they could get by without repercussions. Zimbardo's hypothesis contends that in high population areas, who cares what you are doing as long as you are not bothering others or damaging a concerned party's property? Passersby in New York even stopped and chatted with the looters. In Palo Alto, people could be more easily identified. Moreover, a person engaging in this kind of behavior would expect to be the target of social disapproval or gossip.

Deindividuation is a commonly used concept to explain various expressions of collective behavior such as violent crowds, mindless hooligans, and the lynch mob, as well as social atrocities such as genocide (Postmes & Spears, 1998). As we saw from the car experiment, deindividuation is not necessarily associated with crowds. Nor is a massive population required. The effect may be achieved by a disguise, a mask, or a uniform also worn by others, or it may be achieved by darkness (Zimbardo, 1970). Research data suggest that people may be more abusive, aggressive, and violent when their identity is hidden. This phenomenon *might* explain why, throughout history, war paints, masks, and costumes have been donned by warriors preparing for battle (Watson, 1973). Even contemporary soldiers, guerrillas, and military advisors are deindividuated by their uniforms. Deindividuation also helps explain the apparent ease with which members of groups such as the Ku Klux Klan regressed from being apparently respectable citizens by day to violent, hooded terrorizers by night. Again, however, it is too simplistic to assume that no dispositional or other factors are at work.

In one widely cited experiment, Zimbardo manipulated two variables: feelings of anonymity and features about the victim. He randomly assigned female college students to deindividuation and "identifiable" groups. Subjects in the deindividuation group wore shapeless white lab coats and hoods over their heads and worked in dimly lit conditions. The experimenters avoided using their names. By contrast, participants in the identifiable groups felt anything but anonymous. They wore large name tags, were greeted by name, worked under fully illuminated conditions, and wore their own clothes with no added lab coats or hoods.

Subjects were told the project was set up to study empathy. The real purpose, of course, was to study the relationship between deindividuation and aggression. Each subject listened to a five-minute recorded interview between her future "victim" and the experimenter. Some victims were portrayed as warm, sincere, honest persons, while others were obnoxious, self-centered, conceited, and critical. After each interview, the subjects were allowed to administer shock to the interviewees they had heard on tape. They were allowed to observe the reactions of their victims by way of a one-way mirror. Aggressive behavior of the subjects was measured by the length of time a painful electrical shock was administered. "Victims"—who actually received no shock—were trained to writhe, twist, and grimace.

Recall now that Zimbardo was manipulating two variables: anonymity (loss of personal identity) and features of the victim (environmental stimuli). Thus, some subjects were hooded, others were well identified. Some victims were pleasant and likable, others were obnoxious. Zimbardo reasoned that members of the deindividuation group would administer shocks of longer duration because of the diffusion of responsibility and loss of personal identity. He also hypothesized that victim features would be irrelevant, because the heightened arousal experienced under deindividuation would interfere with the ability to discriminate between the victims. Put another way, the excitement and resulting arousal engendered by shocking someone without the threat of any repercussions would prevent discernment of the target (the person receiving the shock).

One additional hypothesis was tested. Zimbardo predicted that subjects in the deindividuation group would administer longer shocks as the experiment progressed. He believed the act of administering shock without responsibility would be exciting and reinforcing for its own sake (what he called "affective proprioceptive feedback"). Zimbardo predicted that members of the deindividuation group would increase the duration of shock administered to the victim as the experiment progressed. In brief, the person finds that doing the antisocial behavior feels "so good" each time she does it that the behavior builds on itself in intensity (vigor) and frequency.

Results of the experiment supported all three hypotheses. The deindividuation group shocked victims twice as long as the identifiable group. The deindividuation group also administered the same levels of shock, regardless of the victim's personality features. And, finally, this group shocked for longer periods as the experiment progressed. "Under conditions specified as deindividuating, these sweet, normally mild-mannered college girls shocked another girl almost every time they had an opportunity to do so, sometimes for as long as they were allowed, and it did not matter whether or not that fellow student was a nice girl who didn't deserve to be hurt," Zimbardo concluded (1970, p. 170) Essentially, Zimbardo argued that deindividuated aggression is not controlled by the social environment; it is unresponsive to both the situation and the state or characteristics of the victim.

Zimbardo's research design, like that of Milgram, has been criticized extensively for its questionable use of subject deception and shock (albeit simulated) and its focus on the negative aspects of human behavior. In a sense, these types of experiments constitute a form of psychological entrapment. Would people really act this way if not prompted by an experimenter? In the wake of such experiments, the National Institute of Mental Health, the American Psychological Association, and other organizations have adopted ethical guidelines that are applied to the funding and approval of research. Experiments like Zimbardo's, therefore, are unlikely to be replicated, although we learned above that Milgram's experiment was replicated with modifications that rendered it more ethically acceptable. Moreover, the possible implications of the results of these research studies cannot be ignored.

STANFORD PRISON STUDY

The disguise aspect of deindividuation was vividly illustrated in still another sobering Zimbardo experiment (1973) known as the Stanford Prison Experiment. Zimbardo and his colleagues simulated a prison environment in the basement of the psychology building at Stanford University, with physical and psychological trappings supposedly representative of an actual prison: bars, prison uniforms, identification numbers, uniformed guards, and other features that encouraged identity slippage. (The facility actually represented a jail more than a prison. Furthermore, as critics of the experiment have noted, the simulation lacked authenticity in a number of ways, including the sack-like uniforms and stocking caps worn by the "prisoners" and the mirrored sunglasses worn by "guards" [Johnson, 1996]. Corrections officers in real prisons and jails also undergo training and are not given the unlimited power that Zimbardo placed in the hands of his experimental subjects.)

Student volunteers were screened through clinical interviews and psychological tests to ensure that they were emotionally stable and mature. According to Zimbardo, the subjects finally selected were "normal," intelligent college students from middle-class homes throughout the United States and Canada. They were paid $15 a day for participating.

The experiment required two roles, guard and prisoner, which were assigned by random coin toss. The randomization assured that there were no significant differences between the two groups. The "prisoners" were unexpectedly "arrested" and brought to the simulated prison in a police car. There they were handcuffed, searched, fingerprinted, booked, stripped, "deloused," given a number, and issued a prison uniform. Each prisoner was then placed in a six-by-nine-foot cell with two other inmates.

The guards wore standard uniforms and mirrored sunglasses to encourage deindividuation, but as noted, they were not representative of the attire worn by real correctional officers. In addition, they carried symbols of power: a night stick (which many real officers do not carry), keys to the cells, whistles, and handcuffs. Before the prisoners could do even routine things (e.g., write a letter, smoke a cigarette), they had to obtain permission. Guards drew up their own formal rules for maintaining law and order in the prison (16 rules in all) and were free to improvise new ones.

Within six days, both guards and prisoners had completely absorbed their roles:

Three prisoners had to be released during the first four days because of hysterical crying, confusion in thinking, and severe depression. Many others begged to be paroled, willing to forfeit the money they had earned for participating in the experiment.

About a third of the guards abused their power and were brutal and demeaning. Other subjects did their jobs as tough but fair correctional guards, but none of these supported the prisoners by urging the brutal guards to ease off. The realism of the prison was apparently striking. "The consultant for our prison . . . an ex-convict with sixteen years of imprisonment in California's jails, would get so depressed and furious each time he visited our prison, because of its psychological similarity to his experiences, that he would have to leave" (Zimbardo, 1973, p. 164).

The situation became such that Zimbardo decided to terminate the experiment during the sixth day, instead of proceeding through the planned two weeks.

The experiment prompted him to conclude, "Many people, perhaps the majority, can be made to do almost anything when put into psychologically compelling situations—regardless of their morals, ethics, values, attitudes, beliefs, or personal convictions" (1973, p. 164). Much the same conclusion had been reached by Milgram with respect to the influence of authority figures. Although the Stanford Prison Experiment underscores the crucial importance of situational variables in determining behavior, there were still significant individual differences in the way the subjects responded to the conditions. For example, only one-third of the guards became brutally enthralled with their power. Rather than making far-reaching conclusions on the basis of how a total of twenty-one subjects (both guards and prisoners) responded, it would be much more fruitful to give some attention to individual variables. For example, it would have been helpful to examine the values, expectancies, competencies, and moral development of the participants, in combination with the situational factors. What developmental factors most likely predisposed individuals to act the way they did, and exactly how did they perceive the situation? What did they expect to gain by their behavior?

Moral Disengagement

Bandura (1990, 1991) has proposed a theory of **moral disengagement** to explain why people do immoral or heinous acts against their own moral judgment when ordered to do so by some higher authority or under high social pressure. According to Bandura, individuals, through social learning, internalize moral principles that bring self-worth when they are maintained and self-condemnation when they are violated. Consequently, it is not simply the power of the situation that determines a person's actions. Additionally, people's moral principles and the ease with which they can become detached from them strongly influence the extent to which they will follow immoral or illegal orders. Bandura further supposes that before a person can engage in behaviors that violate their moral principles, he or she has to *disengage* his or her own moral sanctions to avoid self-condemnation. Specifically, "effective moral disengagement . . . frees one from the restraints of self-censure experience as anticipative guilt from detrimental conduct" (Bandura, Caprara, Barbaranelli, Pastorelli, & Regalia, 2001, p. 125). For example, Bandura, Barbaranelli, Caprara, and Pastorelli (1996) found that delinquents used various methods of moral disengagement, relying most heavily on moral justification and dehumanization of victims. The delinquents could justify certain antisocial behavior by relying on habitual and various forms of moral disengagement from the social standards of conduct. Dehumanization refers to the process of maintaining beliefs that strip people of human qualities or invests them with demonic or bestial qualities (Bandura *et al.*, 2001). "The victims are then seen as subhuman, without the same feelings or hopes as the perpetrators, and thus one can rationalize that normal moral principles do not apply" (Tsang, 2002, p. 41).

In a more recent study, Bandura and associates (Bandura *et al.*, 2001) discovered that male adolescents, compared with female adolescents, were "more prone to disengage moral self-sanctions from detrimental conduct, were quicker to rouse themselves to anger through hostile rumination, and were less prosocially oriented" (p. 131). These results, the researchers conclude, lend support to the influence of social learning as a major determinant of the frequently reported gender differences in detrimental or immoral conduct. "Girls are substantially more consoling, sharing, helpful, and affectionately demonstrative" (Bandura *et al.*, 2001, p. 131). Boys, on the other hand, tend to be far less likely to engage peers in discussions of their negative feelings and hostility toward others. Bandura's studies underscore the importance of considering the situation *and* the personal attributes of the person in understanding why people do what they do.

DEINDIVIDUATION AND CROWD VIOLENCE

The powerful effects of crowds on individual behavior has interested social scientists since the early 1900s. Crowd influence is usually studied under the rubric *collective behavior*, which includes riots, gang rapes, panics, lynchings, demonstrations, and revolutions. For our purposes, we are concerned with collective behavior only as it affects the instigation and maintenance of violence.

One of the first theorists of collective behavior was Gustave Le Bon. As noted earlier, his 1896 book *The Crowd* is regarded as the classic study of groups. Because his views were colored by the French Revolution, Le Bon did not take kindly to individual behavior swayed by the crowd. Humans in a crowd are like a herd of animals, he said, easily swayed or frightened. Le Bon believed that those who normally are nonviolent and law abiding are still capable of excessive violence, intolerance, and general cruelty. The person enmeshed in the mob loses sensibility and the ability to reason, and forfeits his or her own mind to the crowd. The collective mind is dangerously brutal and destructive to people and property. According to Le Bon, even educated people become simpleminded and irrational under its influence. Essentially, Le Bon claimed, each person comes under the control of the reflexive "spinal cord" rather than the cerebral cortex.

Most of us have seen dramatizations of a "berserk" mob clamoring for the destruction of some political, social, or physical institution or for swift "justice" for an individual or group. Descriptions of mob actions often liken them to brush fires that grow in intensity and are quickly out of control. However, since true mob actions are naturally occurring and spontaneous events, it is difficult to place them under the scrutiny of scientific, systematic investigation. The processes involved in mob action are still not well understood. Some social psychologists (e.g., Diener, 1980; Zimbardo, 1970) have attempted laboratory studies of mob or group violence, generally by approximating conditions that might bring out aggression and positing that, if allowed to continue, the aggression would likely result in violence. Obviously, they must stop far short of actual violence, so whether it would have occurred remains speculative. The procedure of trying to mimic an event under laboratory conditions is called a **simulation**.

Zimbardo (1970) believed that deindividuation accounts for much of the tendency of otherwise "tame" individuals to engage in antisocial, violent behavior. Recall that deindividuation includes a reduction in feelings of personal distinctiveness, identifiability, and personal responsibility. Furthermore, in a crowd, the threshold of normally restrained behavior is lowered. In other words, people feel anonymous, less responsible for their behavior, and less inhibited. According to Zimbardo, these conditions encourage the antisocial behavior associated with selfishness, greed, hostility, lust, cruelty, and destruction.

Diener's (1980) perspective is a bit different. According to Diener, because deindividuated individuals do not pay attention to their internal processes, including their self-regulatory capabilities, they depend more on environmental cues for behavioral direction. Thus, when aggressive and violent cues are present, they are far more likely than usual to engage in violence. It is Diener's contention that if the victim of a mob action could, in some way, be "humanized," the crowd might stop its brutality. In other words, the perpetrators' attention should be directed toward the suffering or fear expressed by the victim rather than the violence being displayed by other actors. Diener also believes that participants in a mob action can be made to pay closer attention to their own internal regulation norms. His hypothesis deserves to be tested by further research. Of course, whether the cries and pleas of the victim during an attack actually could alter the crowd behavior is a question unlikely to be answered by laboratory research. Furthermore, because the theories of Zimbardo and Diener are based on laboratory studies, we cannot conclude that they generalize to actual situations. They do, however, suggest possible explanations for violent mob behavior.

Summary and Conclusions

This chapter has led us away from biologically oriented approaches to the perspective that all behavior, including antisocial behavior, is learned as a result of interactions with the environment—after, not before birth. According to the theories discussed in this chapter, people are not born with a predisposition to violence or deficient conditionability; rather they become that way as a result of social experiences. Furthermore, criminal behavior, again like all behavior, is an individual's way of adapting to his or her environment.

We have reviewed Skinnerian behaviorism, a theory based on the psychology of J. B. Watson and Ivan Pavlov. Together, Skinnerian, Watsonian, and Pavlovian psychology provided the field with some of its most fundamental concepts, such as classical conditioning, operant conditioning, reinforcement, punishment, and extinction. Today, most behaviorists may applaud the basic premise that stimuli elicit responses (classical conditioning), and behavior produces consequences that influence subsequent responses (operant conditioning). However, they also believe other factors must be introduced to explain human behavior. Thus, social learning theorists have focused on cognitions, attitudes, beliefs, and other mental processes that must be taken into consideration.

We covered the expectancy theory of Rotter, the observational learning theory of Bandura, and the social learning theories of Sutherland and Akers to illustrate these mental processes. Sutherland, a sociologist with antipathy toward psychology, probably would not want to be included in this group, but his is still a learning theory. Berkowitz's frustration theory, and

Zimbardo's concept of deindividuation and accompanying research were also discussed. Each of these emphasizes to varying degrees the importance of learning in the development *and maintenance* of criminal behavior. Most of them also outline the external reinforcements involved in this maintenance, or alternately, its cessation. People who engage in persistent antisocial behavior get tangible rewards, as well as social and psychological ones. Collectively, external reinforcements that bring us material, social, or psychological gain are called positive reinforcements. Behaviors that enable us to avoid unpleasant circumstances are negatively reinforced.

Also included in the regulation of behavior is vicarious reinforcement, which consists of both observed reward and observed punishment. When we observe others (models) receiving rewards or punishments for certain behavior, we tend to alter our behavior correspondingly. Models are extremely important in the acquisition and regulation of criminal behavior. They are reference points for what we should and can do in a particular set of circumstances. Therefore, models may act as inhibitors or facilitators of behavior. People internalize the actions and philosophies of significant models, thereby making them part of their own behavioral repertoire and cognitive structure. Research in recent years has focused extensively on the models available in the media, violent video games, and Internet sites. There is growing evidence that some individuals who observe aggressive acts to a great degree themselves become more violent and aggressive.

In addition to models, situational factors can be important contributors to criminal behavior. To some theorists, frustration plays a significant role in violent criminality. When children are frustrated at not having their needs met by parents or caretakers, for example, this promotes distrust of other adults and prevents the forming of emotional attachments. Individuals who strike out at society have encountered severe frustration, according to this approach.

We also discussed the influence of authority figures and the environmental factors involved in the process of deindividuation. People sometimes engage in illegal or violent conduct because they are told or ordered to do so, as Milgram's classic shocking experiment demonstrated. It is interesting that Burger (2009) found results very similar to Milgram's. There are many anecdotal illustrations as well in the military, in law enforcement, and in places of business. Some psychologists have searched for individual differences that might predict the extent to which a person will or will not obey an order perceived to be immoral or illegal, such as differences in personality or moral development. On the other hand, others point to the powerful influence of roles, illustrated by Zimbardo's Stanford experiment. In still other instances, one's personal sense of identity appears to be lost in the excitement of the crowd. Under these deindividualized conditions, people—again, not all—may do things they normally would not do.

Key Concepts

Behaviorism
Classical conditioning
Cognitive learning
Cognitive processes
Crimes of obedience
Deindividuation
Dependent variable
Differential association-reinforcement (DAR)
Discriminative stimuli
Expectancy theory
Extinction

Frustration
Fundamental attribution error
Imitational learning
Independent variable
Individual offender
Models
Moral disengagement
Negative reinforcement
Observational learning (modeling)
Operant conditioning
Positive reinforcement

Punishment
Reductionism
Reinforcement
Self-serving biases
Situationism
Social learning theory
Socialized offender
Stimulus
Variable
Victimology

Review Questions

1. Describe the process of operant conditioning and give an example of how criminal behavior is acquired.
2. Explain the difference between differential association theory and differential association-reinforcement theory.
3. Explain the concept of deindividuation and illustrate by describing any one experiment in social psychology.
4. What is "frustration-induced criminality"? Provide an illustration.
5. Briefly explain Bandura's theory of moral disengagement.
6. Compare and contrast the behaviorism promoted by B. F. Skinner with the modern behaviorism promoted by Bandura.
7. Describe and discuss the situational factors that can influence criminal behavior. In addition to those mentioned in this chapter, what others might be identified?
8. What is meant by crimes of obedience? Give examples.
9. Give three illustrations of fundamental attribution error.

5

Human Aggression and Violence

From Chapter 5 of *Criminal Behavior: A Psychological Approach*, Ninth Edition. Curt R. Bartol and Anne M. Bartol.

Human Aggression and Violence

CHAPTER OBJECTIVES

- Explore the vast array of problems in defining and identifying aggressive behavior.
- Review the major theories on the development of aggression and violence.
- Emphasize the importance of cognitive processes in aggressive behavior.
- Explore the interactions of biology and cognitive processes in aggressive behavior and violence.
- Outline the important key concepts in understanding aggression and violence, such as hostile attribution bias, weapons effect, contagion effect.
- Illustrate common occurrence of aggression with a discussion of road rage and aggressive driving.
- Review the effects of electronic and other media on aggression and violence.

There is ample evidence of the long history of human involvement in aggression and violence. The 5,600 years of recorded human history, for example, include 14,600 wars, a rate of more than 2.6 per year (Baron, 1983; Montagu, 1976). Today, many people fear a terrorist attack such as occurred in 2001 or on public transportation systems in Spain and England in 2005 and India in 2006. In reality, violence is more likely to occur in people's homes or in high-crime areas on the streets. Some writers argue that aggression has been instrumental in helping people survive. Through centuries of experience, humans learned that aggressive behavior enabled them to obtain material goods, land, and treasures; to protect property and family; and to gain prestige, status, and power. Although some might wonder whether the human species could have survived had it not used aggression, others are quick to point out that both historically and in the present, aggressive behavior is at the root of numerous social and individual problems.

Aggression—a psychological concept that we will define shortly—warrants an entire chapter because it is the basic ingredient in violent crime. By studying aggression, psychologists have made substantial contributions to society's efforts to understand both violent and nonviolent crime, as well as violent behavior that may not necessarily be defined as crime (e.g., legitimate uses of force). Is human aggression instinctive, biological, learned, or some combination of these characteristics? If it results from an innate, biological mechanism, the methods designed to control, reduce, or eliminate aggressive behavior will differ significantly from methods used if aggression is learned.

Perspectives of human nature emerge very clearly from the scholarly and research literature on aggression. Some writers and researchers believe that aggressive behavior is basically biological and genetic in origin, a strong residue of our evolutionary past. This physiological, genetic contention is accompanied by compelling evidence that explanations of human aggressive behavior may be found in the animal kingdom from which it originated. On the other hand, researchers who subscribe to the learning viewpoint believe that, while some species of animals may be genetically programmed to behave aggressively, human beings learn to be aggressive from the social environment. The learning position also offers cogent evidence to support its theory. Other researchers remain on a theoretical fence, accepting and rejecting some aspects of each argument. Research does indicate, however, that the level of aggressive behavior demonstrated by an eight-year-old appears to remain largely unchanged well into adulthood for many children, regardless of gender (Kokko & Pulkkinen, 2005).

If aggression and violence represent a built-in, genetically programmed aspect of human nature, we may be forced, as Baron (1983) suggests, toward a pessimistic conclusion. At best, we can only hope to hold our natural, aggressive urges and drives temporarily in check. Furthermore, we should design the environment and society in such a way as to discourage violence, including administering immediate and aversive consequences (punishment) when it is displayed. Even better—and setting aside ethical or legal considerations for the moment—we might consider psychosurgery, electrode implants, and drug control—all effective methods for the reduction, if not the elimination, of violence.

If, on the other hand, we believe that aggression is learned and is influenced by a wide range of situational, social, and environmental variables, we can be more optimistic. Aggression is not an inevitable aspect of human life. Once we understand what factors play major roles in its acquisition and maintenance, we will be able to change human behavior by manipulating these factors. There are, of course, both positive and negative aspects of human aggression. Many individuals who play in competitive sports, hunt for sport, serve in the military, and work for law enforcement engage in socially permissible forms of aggression that may be necessary or that enhance their quality of life as well as that of others. The focus in this chapter is on the negative aspects, or the forms of aggression that are not socially permissible.

By most accounts, animal aggression reflects the biological programming carried in the genes to ensure the survival of the species. Humans, with their enormously complex and sophisticated brain (cerebral cortex), rely heavily on thought, associations, beliefs, and learning; these become primary determinants of behavior. Theorists differ over the degree to which genetic programming contributes to human behavior. Thus, are people aggressive and violent because their animal instincts continue to promote this particular behavior? And, if the evolutionary aggressive drives still reside within the subcortical structures of the brain (below the cortex in the "old" brain), as some writers tell us they do, are they modifiable? If not, how can we best prevent people from attacking and killing one another? On the other hand, a difference-in-kind perspective suggests that genetic predispositions, or biological precursors of aggression, have a minimal influence on human behavior, if they have any influence at all. After defining aggression, we will return to these different points of view.

DEFINING AGGRESSION

The task of defining human aggression is surprisingly difficult, as many social psychologists have discovered. Forcibly jabbing someone in the midsection is certainly defining it by example—or is it? Now what about jabbing someone more softly, in jest? Would everyone consider football and boxing aggressive behaviors? If someone pointedly ignores a question, is that an example of aggression? What if someone spreads malicious gossip? If a burglar breaks into your home and you reach for your trusty but rusty rifle, aim it at the intruder, and pull the trigger, is yours an act of aggression? Is it any less so if the rifle does not fire? If someone sits passively on a doorstep and blocks your entry, is this aggression?

Some social psychologists define aggression as the intent and attempt to harm another individual, physically or socially, or, in some cases, to destroy an object. This definition seems adequate for many situations, but it has several limitations. Refusing to speak does not fit well, since it is not an active attempt to harm someone, nor is blocking someone's entry. Most psychologists place these two behaviors in a special category of aggressive responses and call them **passive-aggressive behaviors**, since they are generally interpreted as aggressive in intent, although the behavior is passive and indirect.

As fascinating as passive-aggressive behavior may be, it is generally irrelevant when we discuss crime, since the aggression we are concerned about is the type that manifests itself directly in violent or antisocial behavior. We might stretch the point by suggesting that the doorstep sitter is trespassing, in which case he or she might be charged with a criminal offense. Likewise, there are other situations in which passive-aggressive behavior could lead to various types of crime. Refusing to file income tax because one is intensely dissatisfied with the policies of the current administration is one example. In general, however, the aggressive behavior we wish to focus on in this chapter is not of the passive-aggressive kind.

In an effort to conceptualize the many varieties of human aggression, Buss (1971) tried to classify them based on the apparent motivation of the aggressor (see **Table 1**). You may easily find exceptions and overlapping categories in the Buss scheme, but that emphasizes how difficult it is to compartmentalize human aggressive behavior. It also epitomizes the many definitional dilemmas that hamper social psychologists studying aggression.

Hostile and Instrumental Aggression

Before finally settling on a satisfactory definition of aggression (and we will get there), it may be useful to recognize two types of aggression, **hostile** and **instrumental**, a distinction first made by

TABLE 1   Varieties of Human Aggression

	Active		Passive	
	Direct	**Indirect**	**Direct**	**Indirect**
Physical	Punching Hitting	Practical joke Booby trap	Obstructing passage	Refusing to perform a necessary task
Verbal	Insulting the victim	Malicious gossip	Refusing to speak	Refusing consent

Source: Buss (1971).

Feshbach (1964). They are distinguished by their goals, or the rewards they offer the perpetrator. Hostile (or expressive) aggression, which we are most concerned with in this chapter, occurs in response to anger-inducing conditions, such as real or perceived insults, physical attacks, or one's own failures. The aggressor's goal is to make a victim suffer. Most criminal homicides, rapes, and other violent crimes directed at harming the victim are precipitated by hostile aggression. The behavior is characterized by the intense and disorganizing emotion of anger, with anger defined as an arousal state elicited by certain stimuli, particularly those evoking attack or frustration. Angry at the economic system that deprived him of a job, a sniper may open fire on passing motorists and feel satisfaction at having lashed out "successfully" at society.

Instrumental aggression begins with competition or the desire for some object or status possessed by another person—jewelry, money, territory. The perpetrator tries to obtain the desired object regardless of the cost. Instrumental aggression is usually a factor in robbery, burglary, larceny, and various white-collar crimes. The perpetrator's obvious goal in a robbery is to obtain items of value. Usually, there is no intent to harm anyone. However, if someone or something interferes with the perpetrator's objective, he or she may feel forced to harm the victim or risk losing the desired goal. In that sense, a robbery may lead to murder, but the aggression represented is still instrumental. Instrumental aggression is also usually a feature of calculated murder committed by a hired, impersonal killer. Although psychologists make the distinction between hostile and instrumental aggression, the law does not, insofar as responsibility for the crime is concerned. However, certain factors associated with hostile aggression (e.g., if the crime is committed in a particularly heinous fashion) can affect the criminal sentence. On the other hand, a contract killer's instrumental aggression may also bring a longer sentence if information about prior offenses comes to light at sentencing.

It should be mentioned, however, that some scholars (e.g., Bushman & Anderson, 2001) find fault with a strict hostile-instrumental dichotomy. Bushman and Anderson point out that this two-category division fails to take into account that many aggressive acts have multiple motives. Furthermore, they say, aggressive acts can be better understood if they are placed somewhere along a continuum that runs from controlled aggression at one pole to automatic (impulsive or thoughtless) aggression at the other pole. Bushman and Anderson believe that, although the dichotomy was useful during the early stages of theory development, it is time to move to a more cognitive approach to understanding the various types of aggressive behavior. This is discussed more fully in the section on the cognitive models of aggression later in the chapter.

Interpretation by Victim

As Bandura (1973a) noted, most definitions of aggression imply that aggression revolves around the behaviors and intentions residing within the perpetrator (or performer). Going a step further, he suggests that an adequate definition of aggression must consider both the "injurious behavior" of the perpetrator and the "social judgment" of the victim. Thus, a soft poke in the belly may qualify as aggression if it is both done derisively and the recipient interprets it that way. A textbook on criminal behavior, however, must focus on aggression as manifested in conduct, not as it is perceived by a victim; it is the actions of the perpetrator that are critical. For our purposes, therefore, we define aggression as *behavior perpetrated or attempted with the intention of harming another individual physically or psychologically (as opposed to socially) or to destroy an object.* The psychological harm would cover aggressive actions that do not involve physical force but are still criminally accountable, such as intimidation, threats, or stalking. This definition encompasses all the behaviors described in Buss's typology. Note, however, that aggressive behavior will not *always* qualify as criminal. A law enforcement officer using *reasonable* force against a criminal suspect is displaying aggressive behavior, but it is not criminal. A hunter shooting a deer (in season) falls into the same category.

Furthermore, we define violence as *destructive physical aggression intentionally directed at harming other persons or things.* Violence may be methodical or random, sustained or fleeting, intensive or uncontrolled. It always harms or destroys the recipient or is intended to do so (Daniels & Gilula, 1970). Therefore, all violent behavior is aggressive behavior, but not all aggressive behavior is violent. Spreading malicious, false information about someone or stalking are cases in point. Both are aggressive, one is also criminal in most jurisdictions, but neither is violent.

THEORETICAL PERSPECTIVES ON AGGRESSION

Behavioral and social scientists have debated for over a half century whether humans are born aggressive and naturally violent, or born relatively free of aggressive tendencies. Several theories have been developed that try to provide some answers to the debate. A **theory** is an integrated set of principles that describes, predicts, and explains some phenomena. It also guides research. The aggression debate, part of a wider controversy about the respective merits of nature and nurture, touches every school of thought in human behavior. According to the first perspective, humans are programmed aggressive to defend themselves, family, and territory from intruders. According to the second, humans become violent by acquiring aggressive models and actions from society. In this section, the topics will move from the instinctive and biological perspectives to the more learning-based perspectives.

Psychoanalytical/Psychodynamic Viewpoint

Psychodynamic theorists assume that humans, by their very nature, will always be prone to aggressive impulses and hence are likely to commit violent acts if these impulses are not appropriately managed or held in check. Sigmund Freud, the father of psychoanalysis and a physician by training, was convinced that human beings are susceptible from birth to a buildup of aggressive energy, which must be dissipated or drained off before it reaches dangerous levels. This is known as the **psychodynamic or hydraulic model** since it bears a close resemblance to pressure build-up in a container. If excessive pressure accumulates in the container—the human psyche—an explosion is likely to occur, as demonstrated by tirades that may involve violence. According to the traditional Freudian perspective, people who have tirades are blowing off the excess steam of aggressive energy.

Freud suggested that violence in all of its forms is a manifestation of this aggressive energy discharge. Internal energy accumulates to dangerous levels when people have not discharged it appropriately through a process called catharsis, one of the most important concepts in psychoanalytic psychotherapy. Catharsis may be accomplished by actual behavior (e.g., playing football) or may occur vicariously (watching football). The Freudian-psychodynamic position predicts that children who participate in or avidly watch school sports will ultimately be less aggressive than children who do not. Freudian psychodynamic followers also maintain that people who engage in violent crime (particularly hostile aggression) have not had sufficient opportunity to "blow off steam" and keep their aggressive energies at manageable levels.

According to the psychoanalytical viewpoint, if violent crime is to be controlled, the human animal must be provided with multiple but appropriate channels for catharsis (e.g., adequate recreational facilities). In this way, children and adults presumably learn to dissipate aggression in socially approved, appropriate ways. Psychotherapy is one such channel, encouraging catharsis under the guidance of a therapist.

Ethological Viewpoints

Ethology is the study of animal behavior in relation to the animal's natural habitat, and it compares that behavior to human behavior. In the mid-1960s, a number of ethologists published books and articles about aggression that interested and appealed to the general public. Three especially popular books were Konrad Lorenz's *On Aggression* (1966), Robert Ardrey's *The Territorial Imperative* (1966), and Desmond Morris's *The Naked Ape* (1967). Before his death, Lorenz was the chief spokesperson for a theoretical formulation of ethology as it relates to aggression.

A Nobel laureate in biology, Lorenz believed that aggression is an inherited instinct of both humans and animals. One of its main purposes is to enable the animal—and the human being—to defend "staked out" territory, a territory that ensures sufficient food, water, and space to roam and reproduce. If this space is violated, Lorenz argued, the instinctive or genetically programmed response is to attack, or at least to increase aggressive behavior toward the intruder, thus preventing further territory violation. The tendency to attack space violators is referred to as **territoriality**. Lorenz believed it is an innate propensity developed through the lengthy, complex process of evolution. This innate aggressive behavior among members of the same animal species (intraspecific aggression) prevents overcrowding and ensures the best and most powerful mates for the young.

The more deadly the animals' evolutionarily developed weaponry (e.g., fangs, claws, size, and strength), the more intense the innate inhibitions against engaging in physical combat with members of its own species. This innately programmed inhibition is a form of insurance for species survival, Lorenz believed, since constant intraspecific physical combat would eventually extinguish the species. Intraspecies aggression is accomplished, therefore, not by actual combat but by complicated displays of force and superiority, such as a show of teeth, size, or color array. These displays are referred to as **ritualized aggression**. Through an intricate communication system not yet understood by scientists, the animals transmit signals, after which the more powerful, dominant animal generally wins out. The losing animal demonstrates defeat by various appeasement behaviors, such as rolling over on its back (characteristic of puppies), lowering its tail or head, and emitting cries of defeat. The weaker animal then leaves the territory of the dominant one.

What does all of this have to do with human aggression? Lorenz and other ethologists believe that it is important to understand animal aggression before we try to understand human aggression, since humans are part of the animal world and probably follow many of its basic principles. In other words, ethologists subscribe to the **difference-in-degree** Darwinian perspective. Efran and Cheyne (1974), for example, observed after studying invasion of personal space among humans that "human society may operate through mechanisms which are less uniquely human than is currently fashionable to suggest" (p. 225).

Lorenz raises another issue that, if valid, is more significant to criminal behavior, however. He maintained that human beings have outdistanced the evolutionary process of inhibiting aggression. Instead of developing natural weapons and the species-preserving function of ritualized aggression, humans have developed technological weaponry. Thus, he and many other ethologists believe they can provide at least a partial answer to why human beings wantonly maim and kill members of their own species: They have not developed the ability to engage in the species-preserving behavior of ritualized aggression. Instead, through superior learning ability, they have developed the capacity to annihilate.

The ethological position is intriguing, but it has not been supported by human aggression research (Bandura, 1983; Montagu, 1973; Zillmann, 1983). Zoologists, biologists, and psychologists have tried with little success to apply the Lorenzian tenets to humans. One problem is that the ethological position relies on a strong analogy between animals and humans. Lorenz argued, for example, that the Greylag goose is remarkably similar to the human species (Berkowitz, 1973). However, the human brain makes us remarkably unlike the Greylag goose and considerably less likely to rely on instinct for determining behavior. Research has yet to delineate any instinctive or invariant genetically programmed behavior determinant in humans. Furthermore, "the capacity to exercise control over one's own thought processes, motivation, and action is a distinctively human characteristic" (Bandura, 1989, p. 1175).

Ethologists also fail to acknowledge and interpret the vast body of existing scientific research that has tested their position and found it wanting. This curious response—or nonresponse—undermines the validity of their whole presentation. Some critics have referred to ethological theorizing as "scientific-sounding misinformation" (Leach, 1973). To date, therefore, there is little evidence to justify portraying humans as *innately* dangerous and brutal or as controlled by instinct. Some contemporary theories do adopt a biological perspective on violence, however, as we discuss later in the chapter.

The ethological perspective has evolved into what is referred to today as **evolutionary psychology**. Evolutionary psychology is the study of the evolution of behavior using the principles of natural selection. It argues that human evolutionary history provides the fundamental framework for understanding human cognition and behavior. An important point to remember here is that evolutionary psychology does not see aggression as pathology, but something that is normal, especially for men (Spallone, 1998).

Frustration-Aggression Hypothesis

Around the time of Freud's death in 1939, a group of psychologists at Yale University proposed that aggression is a direct result of frustration (Dollard, Doob, Miller, Mowrer, & Sears, 1939). According to John Dollard and his colleagues, people who are frustrated, thwarted, annoyed, or threatened will behave aggressively, since aggression is a natural, almost automatic response to frustrating circumstances. Moreover, people who exhibit aggressive behavior are frustrated, thwarted, annoyed, or threatened. "Aggression is always a consequence of frustration" (Dollard *et al.*, 1939, p. 1).

Because of its simplicity and important implications, the **frustration-aggression hypothesis** drew much research, along with much criticism. Psychologists found it difficult not only to decide what frustration was, but also to determine how it could be measured accurately. Researchers also learned that aggression was a much more complex phenomenon than Dollard and his associates had postulated. Frustration does not always lead to aggression, and aggressive behavior does not always signify "frustration." Experiments indicated that people respond to frustration and anger differently. Some do indeed respond with aggression, but others display a wide variety of responses.

Led by Leonard Berkowitz (1962, 1969, 1973), whose general views on some of the causes of criminality, researchers began to propose a revised, contemporary version of the frustration-aggression hypothesis. According to Berkowitz, frustration increases the probability that an individual will become angry and soon act aggressively. In short, frustration facilitates the performance of aggressive behavior. The behavior may be overt (physical or verbal) or implicit (wishing someone dead). Anger, however, is not the only emotion that potentially leads to aggression. Aversive conditions, such as pain, or pleasant states, such as sexual arousal, may also lead to aggressive behavior (Berkowitz, 1973). We will return to this subject shortly.

An important component of the revised frustration-aggression hypothesis is the concept of anticipated goals or expectations. When a behavior directed at a specific goal is thwarted, frustration is likely to result. Thus, the person must have been expecting or anticipating the attainment of a goal or achievement. Mere deprivation of goods will not necessarily lead to frustration. People who are living under deprived conditions may not be frustrated unless they actually expect something better. "Poverty-stricken groups who have never dreamed of having automobiles, washing machines, or new homes are not frustrated because they have been deprived of these things; they are frustrated only after they have begun to hope" (Berkowitz, 1969, p. 15).

Aggression, Berkowitz says, is only one possible response to frustration. The individual may learn others, like withdrawal, doing nothing, or trying to alter the situation by getting out of the situation completely or by compromising. With this approach, Berkowitz not only emphasizes the importance of learning but also stresses the role of individual differences in response to frustrating circumstances.

The revised frustration-aggression hypothesis, therefore, suggests the following steps: (1) the person is blocked from obtaining an expected goal, (2) frustration results, generating anger, and (3) anger *predisposes* or readies the person to behave aggressively. Whether the person actually engages in aggressive actions will depend in part on his or her learning history, interpretation of the event, and individual way of responding to frustration. It will also depend, however, on the presence of aggression-eliciting stimuli in the environment.

WEAPONS EFFECT   Berkowitz notes that the presence of aggressive stimuli in the external environment (or internal environment represented by thoughts) increases the probability of aggressive responses. A weapon is a good example of such a stimulus. Most people in our society associate firearms with aggression. Consider the public outrage that erupted in the summer of 2009 when a man carried a handgun to a speech by President Obama. Berkowitz (1983) likens the firearm to a conditioned stimulus in that the weapon conjures aggressive associations, facilitating overt aggression. A gun, even when not used, is more likely to generate aggressive action than is a neutral object. "The mere sight of the weapon might elicit ideas, images, and expressive reactions that had been linked with aggression in the past" (Berkowitz, 1983, p. 124).

In one experiment designed to test this hypothesis (Berkowitz & LePage, 1967), angry male subjects were more likely to engage in aggressive action in the presence of a gun than a comparable group of angry subjects in the presence of a badminton racket. This suggests that a visible weapon (such as a law enforcement officer might carry) may actually facilitate, rather than inhibit, a violent response in some people.

The Berkowitz-LePage finding generated much controversy as to whether weapons actually do provoke aggressive behavior. A number of studies tried to replicate the finding, but failed to find evidence of a **weapons effect** (Penrod, 1983). Some researchers believed that many of the subjects used in some of the studies "saw through" the purpose of the study, a research flaw called demand characteristics. However, a comprehensive review of the research literature found strong evidence that the weapons effect does—in fact—exist (Carlson, Marcus-Newhall, & Miller, 1990). Carlson *et al.*, concluded, "Aggression-related cues present in experimental settings act to increase aggressive responding. This cue effect occurs more strongly when subjects have been negatively aroused before their exposure to aggression-facilitating cues" (p. 632). The weapons effect has also been found in other countries, including Belgium, Croatia, Italy, and Sweden (Berkowitz, 1994).

Berkowitz (1989) emphasized two important components to the frustration-aggression equation. Aggressive behavior will be generated (1) to the extent that a person perceives the mistreatment as intentional and (2) to the degree that the frustration experienced is aversive. According to Berkowitz, people " . . . are much more likely to become openly aggressive at someone's blocking their goal attainment if they believe their frustrater had deliberately and unjustifiably attempted to keep them from reaching their goal than if they think the thwarting had not been intentional or had not been directed at them personally" (Berkowitz, 1989, p. 68). Thus, self-restraint comes into play when people think they have not been deliberately mistreated or that the blocking of the goal was legitimate. On the other hand, people become angry and aggressive when they perceive that they have been treated unfairly or were personally attacked.

Berkowitz also postulates that thwartings or frustrations generate a negative affect, which refers to an emotional state people typically seek to lessen or eliminate. Furthermore, an unexpected interference is more apt to provoke an aggressive reaction than is an anticipated barrier to goal attainment, because the former is usually much more unpleasant. That is, an unexpected interference has a more negative effect.

Cognitive-Neoassociation Model

In his reformulation of the frustration-aggression hypothesis, Berkowitz has emphasized the importance of cognitive factors. Currently, it is called the **cognitive-neoassociation model**. It operates in the following manner: During the earlier stages, an aversive event produces a negative affect (discomfort). This negative affect may be due to physical pain or psychological discomfort. Physical pain as an aversive circumstance is clear, but psychological discomfort needs further elaboration. Being verbally insulted is a good example. While there is no physical pain, personal insults or demeaning comments engender anger, depression, or sadness—all negative affects—in just about everyone. Unpleasant feelings or negative affects presumably then give rise, almost automatically, to a variety of feelings, thoughts, and memories that are associated with flight (fear) and fight (anger) tendencies. During this early stage, mediating cognitive processes have little influence beyond the immediate appraisal that the situation is aversive. Some people may act quickly on the basis of these initial emotions without further deliberation or forethought, sometimes engaging in violence. Berkowitz emphasizes that any unpleasant feeling or arousal can evoke aggressive, even violent responses. A depressed person can murder his or her family, or a thwarted teenager may violently lash out at authority.

Most of us get past the initial stages, however. During the later stages, cognitive appraisal may go into operation and substantially influence the subsequent emotional reactions and experiences after the initial, automatic responses. These cognitions mediate and evaluate a proper course of action. During the later stages, roused people make causal attributions about the unpleasant experience, think about the nature of their feelings, and perhaps try to control their feelings and actions. Thus, what began as an angry reaction to someone's critical comments develops into a careful consideration of their merits or a conclusion that they are not worth being concerned about.

Excitation Transfer Theory

Zillmann (1988) has proposed a theory to explain how physiological arousal can generalize from one situation to another. Called **excitation transfer theory**, it is based on the assumption that physiological arousal, however produced, dissipates slowly over time. For example, a person who receives some anger-producing criticism at work is likely to have some residual arousal from that criticism when he or she arrives home later that evening. Encountering some annoying event at home, the person is apt to "fly off the handle" and overreact to the minor home incident. "You're taking it out on me," or "You're taking it out on the kids" are familiar statements in some homes.

Consequently, the combination of preexisting arousal, plus anger generated by the irritation at home, may increase the likelihood of aggression. The transfer of arousal from one situation to another is most likely to occur if the person is unaware that he or she is still carrying some arousal from a previous situation to a new, unrelated one.

Displaced Aggression Theory

Closely related to the excitation transfer theory is **displaced aggression theory**, especially the recent model proposed by Bushman, Anderson, Miller, and their colleagues (Anderson & Bushman, 2002; Bushman, Bonacci, Pederson, Vasquez, & Miller, 2005; Miller, Pedersen, Earleywine, & Pollack, 2003). According to Bushman *et al.* (2005), "Aggression is *displaced* when the target is innocent of any wrongdoing but is simply in the wrong place at the wrong time" (p. 969). Displaced aggression can occur when an individual cannot aggress against a source of provocation, such as a boss at work, but feels less constrained about being aggressive toward an innocent, nonprovoking, or mildly provoking individual (or pet). The displaced aggression is probably more likely to be directed at a person (or pet) who emits a mildly annoying act—the cat that tips over the water dish, for example. Bushman *et al,*. refer to this phenomenon as *triggered displaced aggression*. "Following an initial provocation, the target commits a minor provocation, the triggering event, which in turn prompts an aggressive response" (p. 970). The "displaced" aggressive response is usually far in excess of what might be expected to be directed at the minor provocation but probably is in proportion to the perceived severity of the initial provocation. One may believe the boss deserves a good kick for not appreciating one's hard work on a project; since one can't kick the boss, the cat bears the brunt of the anger.

Bushman *et al.* (2005) take the model one step further by working into the equation the concept of rumination. **Rumination** refers to self-focused attention toward one's thoughts and feelings. In other words, the person keeps thinking about the incident long after it is over. More importantly, ruminative thought can harbor and maintain angry feelings over a period of time, far removed from the initial provocation. It is, according to Bushman *et al.*, the ruminative thoughts that can promote subsequent aggression against someone who is mildly annoying but not highly deserving of an aggressive attack.

Aggressive Driving and Road Rage

Aggressive driving and road rage illustrate the previous displaced aggression-arousal theory very well. Before we proceed, however, it is important to note that although aggressive driving and road rage are sometimes used interchangeably, many experts consider them distinct phenomena (Asbridge, Smart, & Mann, 2006). **Road rage**, a term coined by the media in the late 1980s (Roberts & Indermaur, 2005), is defined as an incident in which an angry, impatient, or aroused motorist *intentionally* injures or kills, or tries to injure or kill, another motorist, passenger, or pedestrian, in response to a traffic dispute, altercation, or grievance (Joint, 1995; Mizell, 1995). The provocation may be real or imagined. It is also considered road rage when an aroused, upset motorist drives his or her vehicle into a building or other structure or property (Mizell, 1995). Additional examples include chasing another vehicle, driving straight at another vehicle when angered, extreme tailgating, and trying to edge another car off the road (Galovksi & Blanchard, 2004).

Aggressive driving, on the other hand, is usually considered less serious. Generally, aggressive driving is the result of a motorist becoming impatient or frustrated, and it is often not the direct result of the behavior of another motorist. In other words, aggressive driving is often the result of the triggered displaced aggression discussed in the previous section. The aggressive driver was already angry at someone or something and "takes out" this anger on the road.

Common examples of aggressive driving include tailgating, cutting in and out of lanes, excessive speed, illegal passing, horn blowing, flashing headlights, refusing to yield right of way, slow driving with intent of blocking other vehicles, and running red lights. In contrast, road rage is most often the result of interpreting the actions of other motorists as personal affronts which require retaliating to vindicate one's self-esteem (Neighbors, Vietor, & Knee, 2002). Aggressive driving, on the other hand, is most often caused by traffic congestion, travel impedance, and time urgency (Neighbors *et al.*, 2002). Both aggressive driving and road rage are particularly problematic in the United States, but they appear to be growing worldwide problems (Asbridge *et al.*, 2006; Junger, West, & Timman, 2001; Krahé, 2005). It is estimated that an average of over 1,500 men, women, and children are injured or killed each year in the United States as a direct result of aggressive driving or road rage, and this is increasing at a rate of about 7 percent per year (Yu, Evans, & Perfetti, 2004).

An interesting survey of drivers in 20 major U.S. cities was conducted by Prince Market Research for Auto Vantage, an automobile membership club offering travel services (Associated Press, 2006). Two thousand adult drivers who regularly commuted within each city were asked to rate the amount of road rage and "rude" driving in their metropolitan area. The survey found that Miami drivers reported the most incidents of road rage and rude driving during 2006. Phoenix was second in the road rage and rude driving, followed by New York City, Los Angeles, and Boston. Nashville and Minneapolis reported the fewest incidents. The drivers were also asked what driving behavior most incites road rage in themselves. Thirty-nine percent said being "cut off," 30 percent said tailgating, and 23 percent reported slow driving. There were no significant gender differences in the survey.

WHO ARE THE ROAD RAGERS?   A growing number of studies reveal that the majority of road ragers are young males (ages 18–35) who have criminal and violent histories, psychiatric problems, and drug or alcohol problems (Asbridge *et al.*, 2006; Mizell, 1995; Smart, Asbridge, Mann, & Adlaf, 2003). For example, Galovski and Blanchard (2002) report that nearly half of the motorists referred by a traffic court to a program specifically designed for highly aggressive drivers (mostly road ragers) had one of more convictions for driving under the influence of alcohol. In reference to the relationship between criminal history and aggressive driving, Junger *et al.* (2001) examined the criminal histories of a random sample of 1,531 persons involved in traffic accidents in the Netherlands. The researchers discovered that those motorists involved in traffic accidents due to risky or highly aggressive driving (according to the police) were far more likely to have a police record for violent crime, vandalism, property crime, and similar traffic accidents in the past. However, aggressive drivers and road ragers come from all walks of life, across a variety of socioeconomic levels and occupations. Celebrities are not immune. "In California, Oscar winner Jack Nicholson believed that a driver of a Mercedes-Benz cut him off in traffic. The [then] 57-year-old actor grabbed a golf club, stepped out of his car at a red light, and repeatedly struck the windshield and roof of the Mercedes" (Mizell, 1995, p. 5).

WEAPONS USED   The weapons most commonly used by road ragers are firearms (37%) and the vehicle itself (35%). In fact, some research suggests that having a gun in the car is linked to high levels of aggressive behavior behind the wheel (Miller, Hennenway, & Solop, 2002). Other weapons used are tire irons, jack handles, baseball bats, hurled projectiles, defensive sprays, fists, and feet. Mizell (1995, p. 8) writes, "While the event that sparks the incident may be trivial, in every case there exists some reservoir of anger, hostility, or frustration that is released by the triggering incident." In one case, a man was attacked by fellow motorists because he could not turn off the antitheft alarm on his rented jeep. Surprisingly, it is not unusual for angry drivers to use their motor vehicles to attack law enforcement personnel and vehicles.

PRECIPITATING FACTORS IN ROAD RAGE   Domestic violence or domestic disputes are very common factors in both aggressive driving and road rage, when upset spouses and intimate partners vent their anger on the highway. Under these conditions, the gender differences in aggressive driving are not as great as might be expected. In one survey, 54 percent of the women admitted to aggressive driving behavior compared with 64 percent of men (Joint, 1995). In that survey, respondents reported that aggressive tailgating (62%) was the most common form of aggressive driving, followed by headlight flashing (59%), obscene gestures (48%), deliberately obstructing other vehicles (21%), and verbal abuse (16%).

However, the immediate, precipitating causes of road rage are largely minor misunderstandings that are perceived and interpreted by the other drivers as aggressive, aversive, or directed personally at them. It also appears that a major factor in the road rage reaction is frustration, followed by emotional arousal that detaches the angry driver from his or her usual cognitive control of appropriate behavior. In many instances, the road rager is already primed for aggressive or violent action due to an incident that happened before reaching the highway (Connell, 1996). A quarrel with a loved one, some difficulty on the job, problems making financial ends meet, or any number of previous events can contribute to the arousal factor. The stimulus that sets off the aggression, as Berkowitz might argue in his cognitive-neoassociation model, is the annoying behavior of another driver. The available weapon is the motor vehicle. Thus, the necessary components of a negative affect and the appropriate stimuli are in place for aggression to occur. Obviously, not all drivers in these circumstances react with rage. In the following section, we focus more on the factors that might distinguish one person's reactions from another's.

SOCIAL LEARNING FACTORS IN AGGRESSION AND VIOLENCE

Why do some people behave aggressively when intensely frustrated, while others change their tactics, withdraw, or seem not to be affected? One major factor may be past learning experiences. The human being is very adept at learning and maintaining behavior patterns that have worked in the past, even if they only worked occasionally. This learning process begins in early childhood. Children develop many behaviors merely by watching their parents and significant others in their environment, a process we have called modeling or observational learning. A child's behavior pattern, therefore, is often acquired through the modeling or imitation of other people, real and imagined, in the child's environment (Bandura, 1973a). In fact, available research reveals that the conditions most conducive to the learning of aggression are those in which the child (1) has many opportunities to observe aggression, (2) is reinforced for his or her own aggression, or (3) is often the object of aggression (Huesmann, 1988).

Suppose Harris's father returns home feeling harried after a hot and humid day during which he accomplished nothing (frustration). He finds an official-looking letter from the IRS in the mailbox. He opens it, perhaps muttering mild obscenities under his breath, and finds that the IRS apparently suspects he has shortchanged the U.S. government by several hundred dollars, although he knows he has not (more frustration). He is invited for an audit (even more frustration). In response, he slams his fist on the table, exclaims "Damn it!" or some colorful variation, and kicks the nearest chair (just enough not to damage his toe, since he has learned the painful consequences from past similar episodes). Unknown to father, Harris has observed this whole scenario. Several hours later, when his block tower crumbles, little Harris pounds his fist, kicks the living room chair, and curses, "Damn it!"

Modeling

Many years ago, Albert Bandura (1965) conducted what is now considered a classic study in psychology. Sixty-six nursery school children (33 girls and 33 boys) were divided into three groups and shown one of three five-minute films. All three films depicted an adult verbally and physically assault a Bobo doll, a large plastic, inflatable clown with a sand base which bounces back after being pushed down. (A common household toy in the 1950s and 1960s, the Bobo doll has now morphed into inflatable Superman or Spiderman characters that are available on the toy market of today.) In the film, the adult punched, kicked, and hit the clown with a mallet. One group saw the adult model being rewarded with candy and a soft drink after displaying aggressive behavior. A second group observed the model being spanked (with a rolled-up magazine) and reprimanded verbally. A third group witnessed a situation in which the model received neither punishment nor reward.

After the children saw the film, they were permitted to free play for 10 minutes in a playroom of toys, including a Bobo doll. The group that had witnessed the adult model being rewarded for aggressive behavior exhibited more aggression than the other two groups. In addition, boys were more aggressive than girls. The group that saw the adult model being punished exhibited the lowest amount of aggression in the playroom.

Bandura's subsequent research, which included variations on this basic study design, consistently demonstrated this modeling effect. Furthermore, numerous follow-up studies not only replicated his findings but also suggested that media violence (TV, movies, video games) may have a strong influence on real life in many situations (Baron, 1977).

When a child's imitative behavior is reinforced or rewarded by praise and encouragement from significant models, the probability that the behavior will occur in the future is increased. There is evidence that American parents (consciously or inadvertently) encourage or reinforce aggressive behavior in their children, particularly in their sons. For example, the behavior of Harris described above might have been reinforced if Dad or Mom drew attention to it—"Isn't that cute?"—or if they laughed. In a future episode, the kicking behavior might be directed at the family cat. Furthermore, while kicking chairs and towers (or even the family cat, in the minds of some readers) may seem relatively mild, the same behavior becomes very sobering if the parent's anger is taken out on a family member, as too many Harrises in our society have observed. Other children are "merely" expected or encouraged to be hard-hitting linebackers and to hold their own against neighborhood bullies, providing they are approximately the same size. They learn that the child who aggresses successfully against others is often rewarded by status, prestige, and the most attractive toys or material goods.

Types of Models

Bandura (1983) identifies three major types of models: family members, members of one's subculture, and symbolic models provided by the mass media. Family members, particularly parents, can be very powerful models up until early adolescence. Beginning in early adolescence, peer models are likely to dominate. Not surprisingly, the highest incidence of aggression is found in communities and groups in which aggressive models abound and fighting prowess is regarded as a valued attribute (Bandura, 1983; Lacourse, Nagin, Tremblay, Vitaro, & Claes, 2003; Thornberry & Burch, 1997).

The mass media, including television, movies, magazines, newspapers, and books, provide abundant symbolic models. Video games and the Internet have vastly expanded this collection. Television pervades the life of the growing child, even the very young one, and offers hundreds of potentially powerful aggressive and violent models in a variety of formats, ranging from Saturday morning cartoon film festivals to triple-X-rated cable movies. The effects these models have on children are a highly debated issue, and one we cover later in this chapter.

Since parents are powerful models, we would expect aggressive or antisocial parents to have aggressive or antisocial children. In an old but classic study, Sears, Maccoby, and Levin (1957) interviewed four hundred mothers of kindergarten children about their disciplinary techniques, their attitudes about children's aggressiveness, and the children's expressions of aggression toward peers, siblings, and parents. One of the major findings was that physical punishment by parents was related to aggressiveness in the children. This was especially true when physical discipline was supplemented by high permissiveness toward aggression. In support of this finding, some researchers found that preschoolers played more aggressively when they were watched by a permissive adult than when no adult was visible (Siegel & Kohn, 1959).

Bandura (1973a) argues persuasively that aggressive behavior can be most productively understood and modified if we give attention to the learning principles like those alluded to earlier. As psychologists learn more about human behavior, many are beginning to agree with him.

Social learning theory hypothesizes that the rudiments of aggressive behavior are initially acquired through observing aggressive models or on the basis of direct experience; aggression is then gradually refined and maintained by reinforcement. Therefore, people may have an aggressive behavioral pattern, but may rarely express it if it has no functional value or is not condoned by significant others in their social environment. The social learning system acknowledges that biological structures can set limits on the types of aggressive responses that can be learned, and that genetic endowment influences the rate at which learning progresses (Bandura, 1973a). Biology does not program the individual to specific aggressive behavior, however. These behaviors are learned by observation, either deliberately or inadvertently; they become refined through reinforced practice.

Observation Modeling

In addition, mere exposure to aggressive models does not guarantee that the observer will try to engage in similar aggressive action at a later date. First, a variety of conditions may prevent observational learning from even taking place. Individuals differ widely in their ability to learn from observation. Some people may fail to notice the essential features of the model's behavior or may have a poor symbolic or visual memory. Alternately, they may not wish to imitate the model. Bandura suggests also that one important component of observational learning may be the motivation to rehearse what has been observed. He notes that a mass murderer, for example, may get an idea from descriptive accounts of another mass killing. The incident remains prominent in his mind long after it has been forgotten by others. He continues to think about the crime and to rehearse the brutal scenario mentally until, under appropriate conditions, it serves as a script for his own murderous actions.

Another restriction on observational learning is what happens to the observed model. If the model is reprimanded or punished either during or immediately after an aggressive episode, this will probably inhibit the observer's behavior. The "bad guy" should not get away with violence, if we are to discourage antisocial behavior via the entertainment media.

If aggressive behavior is to be maintained, it needs periodic reinforcement. According to social learning theory, aggression is maintained by instrumental learning. In the initial stage of learning, observation is important, but in the later stages, reinforcement is essential. The reinforcement may be positive, as when the individual gains material or social rewards, or it may be negative, if it allows the individual to alter or avoid aversive conditions. If aggressive behavior brings rewards in either of these ways, the person is likely to continue it. Research has consistently discovered that aggressive children anticipate more positive outcomes and fewer negative outcomes following their aggressive acts (Hubbard, Dodge, Cillessen, Coie, & Schwartz, 2001). "When compared with average peers, aggressive children are more likely to believe that aggression will produce tangible rewards, reduce aversive treatment by others, make themselves and peers feel good, increase self-esteem, and help to avoid a negative image" (Hubbard *et al.*, 2001, p. 268).

A youngster subjected to unmerciful harassment or bullying because of his unusual name or where he lives may be able to stop the teasing with his fists. The reinforcement he gets from his newly found aggressive behavior is negative, but it is still rewarding. Aggression can also allow the individual to feel in control of a situation if things have not been going his or her way. A more extreme example is when a student who is constantly bullied by peers decides to put a stop to the aversive circumstances by using a firearm on all those who are perceived as participants. The psychological reinforcement offered by feeling in control is an extremely powerful component in any human behavior, especially aggressive or violent behavior.

COGNITIVE MODELS OF AGGRESSION

Recent cognitive models for learning aggression have hypothesized that, while observational learning is important in the process, the individual's cognitive capacities and information processing strategies are equally important. Two major cognitive models have emerged in recent years. One that has been proposed by Rowell Huesmann (1997) is a hypothesis called the **cognitive scripts model**. The other model has been developed by Kenneth Dodge and his colleagues (Dodge, 1986; Dodge & Coie, 1987), and is called the **hostile attribution model**.

Cognitive Scripts Model

According to Rowell Huesmann (1988), social behavior in general, and aggressive behavior in particular, is controlled largely by cognitive scripts learned and memorized through daily experiences. "A script suggests what events are to happen in the environment, how the person should behave in response to these events, and what the likely outcome of those behaviors would be" (Huesmann, 1988, p. 15). Scripts may be learned by direct experience or by observing significant others (Bushman & Anderson, 2001). Once learned, the script is usually followed. Each script is different and unique to each person, but once established it becomes resistant to change and may persist into adulthood. For a script to become established, it must be rehearsed from time to time. With practice the script will not only become encoded and maintained in memory, but also it will be more easily retrieved and utilized when the individual faces a problem. Furthermore, the individual's "evaluation of the 'appropriateness' of a script plays an important role in determining which scripts are stored in memory, in determining which scripts are retrieved and utilized, and which scripts continue to be utilized" (Huesmann, 1988, p. 19). The evaluation process includes the confidence that one has in predicting outcomes of the script, the extent to which an individual judges himself or herself capable of executing the script, and the extent to which the script is seen as congruent with the person's self-regulating internal standards. Scripts that are inconsistent or violate one's internalized standards are unlikely to be stored or utilized. An individual with poorly integrated internal standards against aggression, or who is convinced that aggressive behavior is a way of life, is more likely to incorporate aggressive scripts for behavior. Importantly, the aggressive child is apt to instigate aggressive reactions from others, confirming his or her beliefs about the aggressiveness of human nature in a circular, perpetuating fashion.

Hostile Attribution Bias

Kenneth Dodge and his colleagues discovered that highly aggressive youth often have a **hostile attribution bias**. That is, youth (and adults) prone toward violence are more likely to interpret ambiguous actions as hostile and threatening than are their less aggressive counterparts (Dodge, 1993b). For example, a foot casually and innocently positioned near a school desk may be interpreted as a deliberate attempt to trip. As Dill, Anderson, Anderson, and Deuser (1997, p. 275) put it, people described as having hostile attribution bias "tend to view the world through blood-red tinted glasses." Children with a hostile attribution bias are twice as likely as average children to see aggressive actions from others where there is none (Hubbard *et al.*, 2001). In addition, the bias is present in both boys and girls (Vitale, Newman, Serin, & Bolt, 2005).

Research consistently indicates that violent youth "typically define social problems in hostile ways, adopt hostile goals, and seek few additional facts, generate few alternative solutions, anticipate few consequences for aggression, and give higher priority to their aggressive solutions" (Eron & Slaby, 1994, p. 10). Similarly, Serin and Preston (2001, p. 259) conclude, "Aggressive juvenile offenders have been found to be deficient in social problem-solving skills and to espouse many beliefs supporting aggression. Specifically, they tend to define problems in hostile ways, adopt hostile goals, seek less confirmatory information, generate fewer alternative solutions, anticipate fewer consequences for aggressive solutions, and choose less effective solutions."

Research indicates that this hostile attribution bias begins to develop during the preschool years and seems to be a stable attribute that is still present into adulthood (Dodge *et al.*, 2002; Nigg & Huang-Pollock, 2003). Dodge (1993b) reports that when children were followed from elementary school to middle school, a child's tendency to attribute hostile intentions to others showed a significant relationship between peer rejection during elementary school and increased aggression during middle school. Coie (2004) asserts, "The fact that rejected, aggressive males show persistently higher tendencies toward hostile attribution biases, as well as other social cognitive deficits related to aggression, fits with their pattern of higher involvement in violent delinquent acts in adolescence and their tendency to persist in violent behavior into the early adult years" (p. 255).

There is further research to suggest that some children are especially primed to develop hostile expectations of peers because of earlier exposure to family abuse and maltreatment (DeWall, Twenge, Gitter, & Baumeister, 2009; Dodge, Bates, & Pettit, 1990; Hubbard *et al.*, 2001). Studies have revealed that children exposed to maltreatment early in their lives become "hypervigilant toward hostile social cues, perceptually ready to perceive hostility in others' intentions, and quick to generate aggressive retaliatory responses to even mild provocations" (Dodge, 2001, p. 65). In addition, peer-rejected children with hostile attribution bias are frequently targets of physical assault by others, prompting them to be more suspicious of the motives of others (Coie & Miller-Johnson, 2001). These children appear to be especially quick at developing hostile attribution biases against a wide range of peers, including new acquaintances. "These children come to have a generalized set of social cognitions that dispose them to draw hostile inferences from the behavior of new peer acquaintances more quickly than their peers do" (Hubbard *et al.*, 2001, p. 277). Some other children, although prone to hostile attribution bias, tend to be specific in who they identify as hostile, probably due to certain behavioral patterns or interests they find threatening.

Ronald Blackburn (1998) also reports research evidence that suggests that persistent law-breaking by adults represents attempts to master a social environment perceived as hostile and threatening. Blackburn hypothesizes that highly criminal offenders approach the world with a well-developed hostile-dominance interpersonal style. That is, rather than be simply a reflection of deficits in conscience or self-control, frequent criminal behavior may represent an ongoing attempt to control and dominate others in the social environment. According to Blackman, chronic criminality can be understood as "an attempt to maintain status or mastery of a social environment from which they feel alienated" (1998, p. 174). The well-rehearsed cognitive script of persistent, lifelong offenders, therefore, is to dominate—often in a hostile manner—social environments they perceive as hostile.

Blackburn's observations have been recently supported by research by Vitale *et al.* (2005) who investigated the amount of hostile attribution in 150 incarcerated males. The researchers discovered that psychopaths were significantly more likely to exhibit hostile attribute bias than nonpsychopaths in a variety of situations. The study also supported the hypothesis that there may be different antisocial pathways associated with hostile attributions. That is, hostile attribution bias was also prevalent in those prisoners who held negative thoughts about themselves, other people, and the world in general.

In summary, hostile attribution bias involves the tendency to view the behavior of others as provocative, harmful, hostile, or wrongful. Some individuals demonstrate this tendency more strongly than others. Consequently, attribution bias or style should be viewed as existing along a continuum. At its extreme level, the bias represents a cognitive deficit in processing that distorts social information so dramatically that the individual is literally unable to process that information accurately (Fontaine, 2008). In some cases, some people may engage in extreme violence toward others they interpret as trying to do them harm. In the chapters on criminal homicide, we will return to this topic as it applies to murder, including serial and mass murder.

Aggressive Behavior: Simple and Easy to Use

Aggression is a simple, direct way of solving immediate conflicts. If something is not going your way, approaching the social environment in a threatening, hostile manner is the most direct way (not necessarily the most effective in the long run) of confronting your tormentors. On the other hand, prosocial solutions and alternative nonaggressive scripts are less direct and more complex than aggressive solutions. In essence, they are more difficult to apply. Theoretically, the more cognitively "simple" individual would be more inclined to pursue simplistic and direct solutions to problems. In addition, because prosocial solutions are more complicated and more difficult to apply, they also require effective social skills. However, the development of effective social skills takes time, and those skills will have a spotty reinforcement history until perfected. Aggressive behavior, on the other hand, often receives immediate reinforcement for the aggressor, and therefore is more likely to be retained in one's arsenal of strategies for immediate solutions of conflictful situations.

After a 22-year longitudinal study, Eron and Huesmann (1984) concluded that diminished intellectual competence and poor social skills have an early effect in increasing the likelihood that a child will adopt characteristically more aggressive styles of behavior to conflict resolution. For example, research has repeatedly documented the fact that juveniles who are serious sexual offenders have significant deficits in social competence, such as inadequate social skills, poor peer relationships, and social isolation from peers (Righthand & Welch, 2001). Further, the evidence indicates that this aggressive style will persist across situations and time and become a preferred style throughout adulthood. But the relationship is not simply one-way, with limited intellectual competence and inadequate skills promoting aggressive behavior. Rather it appears to be interactive. Aggressive behavior may interfere with positive social interactions with teachers and peers for intellectual and social advancement, perpetuating a chain of mutually influencing events: aggressive behavior influencing the social environment, and the social environment, in turn, influencing aggressive behavior.

Dolf Zillmann (1988) proposes a similar idea to the cognitive script theory, but, like Berkowitz, emphasizes the importance of physiological arousal and its interaction with cognitions. Zillmann agrees with Hebb (1955, p. 249) that arousal "is an energizer, but not a guide, an engine but not a steering gear." Cognition provides the steering and direction to the energizing effects of anger, fear, or frustration. A long-standing observation in the study of animal and human aggression is that when the organism recognizes or perceives a threat to its welfare and well-being, it can either fight or flee. Following this "recognition of endangerment," physiological arousal quickly sets in, preparing the organism for fight or flight. The "recognition of endangerment," Zillmann reminds us, can be immediate, and the response can be reflex-like. What happens then is also highly dependent on cognition, especially in humans. Very likely, this is when cognitive scripts come in.

If the arousal is moderate, the individual with skills and well-integrated standards of prosocial values will probably pursue nonaggressive scripts, even though the person may have been angry or threatened at first. However, very *high* levels of arousal interfere with the complex cognitive processes that mediate our consideration of our internal codes of conduct, as well as our ability to assess the intentions of others and the mitigating circumstances around the incident (Zillmann, 1988). Think of a very stressful or frightening situation that has happened to you, and how difficult it was to think clearly. Or think of a time when you became extremely angry and said or did things you wish you hadn't. At high levels of arousal, our cognitions seem to become narrower and more restricted, almost incapacitated at times. Generally, under these high states of arousal, we resort to strongly established habits to guide and dominate our behavior. In essence, we become "impulsive" and largely unthinking, and cognitions that mediate the diminution of hostile or even violent actions are substantially reduced. However, if we have practiced or rehearsed nonviolent or nonaggressive behaviors as solutions, these cognitive scripts are likely to be the habits we resort to under high stress, fear, and high arousal.

OVERT AND COVERT ACTS OF AGGRESSION

Rolf Loeber and Magda Stouthamer-Loeber (1998) recommend that researchers on aggression and violence be mindful of two types of aggressive actions: overt and covert. According to Loeber and Stouthamer-Loeber, the two forms of aggression are different in (1) behavior patterns, (2) emotions, (3) cognitions, and (4) development. Behaviorally, overt aggression usually involves direct confrontation with victims and the administration of physical harm or threats of physical harm. Covert aggression, on the other hand, does not involve direct confrontation but relies on concealment, dishonesty, or sneaky behavior. It is similar to the passive-aggressive behavior discussed earlier in the chapter. In many instances, overt aggression decreases with age, while covert aggression increases with age (Loeber, Lahey, & Thomas, 1991; Stanger, Achenbach, & Verhulst, 1997). However, children who exhibit serious forms of overt aggression (violence) tend to increase their violence as they get older, and often commit both violent and property crimes as adults (Loeber & Stouthamer-Loeber, 1998).

Emotionally, anger is usually an important ingredient in most overt acts of aggression, while more neutral emotions are characteristic of covert actions. Violent actions are usually accompanied by high levels of arousal brought on by anger. Covert actions, on the other hand, tend to be less emotional in nature, such as fraud, theft, embezzlement, burglary, and other white-collar or property offenses (see **Table 2**).

Covert and overt aggression can also be distinguished on the basis of the cognitions that accompany them. As we explained in this chapter, violent persons (overt aggression) tend to have cognitive deficiencies that make it difficult for them to come up with nonaggressive solutions to

TABLE 2   Overt and Covert Aggressive Actions

Aggression	Behavior Patterns	Emotions	Cognitions	Development
Overt	Direct confrontation with victims; generally decreases with age	Anger, high level of arousal and violence	Lacks social cognitions for coming up with nonaggressive solutions	Aggression begins early, especially in boys
Covert	Concealment, dishonesty, sneaky behavior, increases with age	Less emotion; crimes such as fraud, larceny, and theft	Relies on cognitive capabilities, such as planfulness, deceitfulness	Can evolve as well-learned strategy to escape punishment

interpersonal conflicts and disputes. Overt aggressors also have hostile attributional biases that contribute to violence-prone cognitive processing. On the other hand, people who use covert aggression as a preferred strategy do not demonstrate the degree of cognitive deficiencies in solving their interpersonal problems, nor do they manifest a hostile attributional bias. "Instead, it is postulated that most covert acts are facilitated by specific cognitive capabilities, such as planfulness (i.e., casing situations prior to theft), preoccupations with consumables and property, and lying to escape detection" (Loeber & Stouthamer-Loeber, 1998, p. 250). Occupationally-related crimes, for instance, such as theft of company property, the misuse of information, or software piracy, are often committed with planning and forethought. Some crime committed through the use of computers, called **cybercrime**, is also a good example of covert actions of aggression. Examples are cyberstalking and cyberbullying.

Developmentally, overt aggression generally begins early, especially in boys, as seen, for example, in the case of life-course-persistent offenders. However, Loeber and Stouthamer-Loeber suggest that development of overt aggressive behavior does not necessarily parallel the development of covert actions. Instead, "some children have never been socialized by their parents to be honest and to respect the property of others. This is common among neglectful parents or parents who hold an indistinct or a weak moral stance in these respects" (1998, p. 251). Honesty and respect for the property of others are instilled by parents' teaching and the prosocial models they offer their children. Some covert actions, especially lying, can also evolve as a well-learned strategy that serves to minimize the chances of detection and punishment by adults.

It should be emphasized that not all overt aggressors who engage in violence start early. As Loeber and Stouthamer-Loeber note, "It is necessary to account for the emergence of violence in individuals during adulthood who do not have a history of aggression earlier in their lives" (1998, p. 246). These *late-onset types* represent a minority of adult violent offenders, but the hypothesis does suggest that not all highly aggressive and violent individuals manifested aggression in childhood.

Reactive and Proactive Forms of Aggression

Kenneth Dodge and his colleagues (Dodge, Lochman, Harnish, Bates, & Pettit, 1997) have suggested that another way of classifying aggression in children (and adults) is to make a distinction between reactive aggression and proactive aggression. **Reactive aggression** includes anger expressions, temper tantrums, and vengeful hostility, and more generally "hot-blooded" aggressive acts. **Proactive aggression**, on the other hand, includes bullying, domination, teasing, name-calling, and coercive acts—in other words, more "cold-blooded" aggressive actions. Reactive aggression appears to be a reaction to frustration and is associated with a lack of control due to high states of arousal. In general, reactive aggression is a hostile act displayed in response to a perceived threat or provocation. Proactive aggression, by contrast, is less emotional, and more driven by expectations of rewards. "Proactive aggression is unprovoked, deliberate, goal-directed behavior used to influence or coerce a peer" (Hubbard *et al.*, 2001, p. 269). Reactive aggression has its theoretical roots in the frustration-aggression model proposed by Berkowitz (1989) discussed earlier. The theoretical roots of proactive aggression are found in social learning theory which, as we learned previously, states that aggression is acquired behavior that is controlled and maintained by reinforcement. It is highly similar to the concept of instrumental aggression. Reliable observations of these two forms of aggression have been found in children (as young as 3 to 6 years of age) through teacher ratings, peer ratings, clinical psychiatric records, and direct observations of peer interactions by researchers (Dodge & Coie, 1987; Dodge *et al.*, 1997; Poulin & Boivin, 2000).

Reactively aggressive children, compared with proactively aggressive children, display greater problems in social and psychological adjustment (Dodge *et al.*, 1997). Psychological adjustment problems include a lack of emotional control when angry, accompanied by sleep disorders, depressive symptoms, and personality disorders. On average, these problems emerged around age 4–5. In addition, reactive aggression is related to the tendency to over-attribute hostile intent to peers in ambiguous provocation situations (hostile attribution bias) (Hubbard *et al.*, 2001). That is, when a reactive aggressive child interprets a peer's behavior as intentionally harmful or aggressive, he is far more likely to respond with angry retaliation or even violence.

Dodge (1991) proposed that reactive and proactive aggression originate from different social experiences and develop independently. According to Dodge, reactive aggression develops in reaction to a harsh, threatening, and unpredictable environment or abusive or cold parenting (Vitaro, Brendgen, & Barker, 2006). Proactive aggression, on the other hand, develops as a result of exposure to aggressive role models who value the use of aggression to resolve conflict or advance personal interests (Vitaro *et al.*, 2006). However, Vitaro *et al.* are quick to point out that proactive and reactive aggression may not only be fostered by different social environments but may also be influenced by differences in temperamental and genetic factors. That is, reactive aggression appears to be associated with a temperamental disposition toward anxiety, angry reactivity, emotional impulsiveness, and inattention. Proactive aggression appears to be less affected by temperament and is more based on beliefs that aggressive behavior will bring rewards and positive outcomes. Furthermore, preliminary research results suggest that reactive aggression develops earlier in the life span than proactive aggression, and the two types of aggression seem to follow different developmental trajectories (Vitaro & Brendgen, 2005).

Gender Differences in Aggression

While boys engage in more overt aggression and direct confrontation as they grow up, it is not clear if boys are generally more aggressive than girls. It is clear that *physical* aggression is more prevalent among males than females and that this consistent finding holds across hundreds of studies and across nations (Archer, 2004; Campbell, 2006), but what about other forms of aggression?

The current work of cognitive psychologists suggests that there may be socialized differences in the way girls and boys construct their worlds. Social learning theorists have long held that girls are "socialized" differently than boys, or taught not to be overtly aggressive. Anne Campbell (1993, p. 19) argues that "boys are not simply more aggressive than girls; they are aggressive in a different way." Other researchers concur with this observation (Hawkins, Pepler, & Craig, 2001;

Lumley, McNeil, Herschell, & Bahl, 2002; Wood, Cowan, & Baker, 2002). According to Campbell, boys and girls are born with the potential to be equally aggressive, but girls are socialized not to be overtly aggressive, whereas boys are encouraged to be overtly aggressive "to defend" themselves.

Interestingly, research supports the observation that boys and girls are equally physically aggressive toward their peers when they are toddlers, but that this pattern soon changes as they get older and enter their elementary school years (Xie, Farmer, & Cairns, 2003). Loeber and Stouthamer-Loeber (1998, p. 253) conclude from their review of the research that "in general, gender differences in aggression, as expressed by frustration and rage, are not documented in infancy." They note that only in the preschool period (3–5 years of age) do observable gender differences begin to emerge, with boys displaying more overt aggression than girls. Overt aggression becomes especially prominent in boys from elementary school age onward. Boys are taught to be tough, not to cry, to take on the bullies and physically defend themselves. However, many researchers report that girls are more likely to engage in relationship or interpersonal forms of aggression rather than the physical forms of pushing and hitting (Casey-Cannon, Hayward, & Gowen, 2001; Crick & Zahn-Waxler, 2003; Prinstein, Boergers, & Vernberg, 2001). For example, researchers (Björkqvist, Lagerspetz, & Kaukianinen, 1992; Cairns, Cairns, Neckerman, Ferguson, & Gariépy, 1989) find that girls and women tend to use more covert, indirect, and verbal forms of aggression, such as character defamation and ostracism. Other researchers report that girls are far more likely to employ *relational aggression*, such as abandoning one friend in favor of another, spreading malicious gossip, or ridiculing another's physical traits (e.g., their facial features, weight, or general demeanor) (Crick, 1995; Crick & Grotpeter, 1995; Crick & Zahn-Waxler, 2003; Garside & Klimes-Dougan, 2002; Loeber & Stouthamer-Loeber, 1998).

In conclusion, there is growing recognition that gender differences in aggression are not simply due to biology, but are primarily due to cultural and socialization processes that promote different kinds of aggression. Environmental cues are also important in cognitive scripts and in the aggressive strategies individuals employ for various situations. Which script or strategy an individual employs is dependent on which environmental cues are present.

EFFECTS OF MEDIA VIOLENCE

American youth are growing up in a media-saturated environment (Gentile & Walsh, 2002), and much of this environment has a violence theme. Surveys estimate that the average American youth between the ages 2 and 18 spends nearly 6 hours per day with electronic media (e.g., television, music, computers, movies, and video games) and 44 minutes per day with print media (Gentile & Walsh, 2002). Although television still dominates the electronic media (averaging around 25 hours per week), video games are becoming increasingly popular. With the variety of portable, wireless devices available today, youth and adults have access to games at all times, unless they are in a location where use is restricted.

Violence is a common theme in the movie, TV, and video game media. Some surveys estimate that the average American child sees more than 100,000 violent episodes and some 20,000 murders on television before reaching adolescence (Myers, 1996). Other studies estimate there are four scenes of violence portrayed on network television to every one scene expressing affection. Note that this does not include the huge range of "non-network" programming that offers an increasing number of options for viewers. A three-year study (1994–1997) by four universities on violence on American television revealed that 90 percent of movies shown on television include violence (National Cable Television Association, 1998). Violence was found most frequently on subscription television (85% on premium cable and 59% on basic cable), while the lowest incidence of violence

(18%) was found on Public Broadcasting Service (PBS) stations. Across three years of the study, nearly 40 percent of the violent incidents on television were initiated by "good" characters, who are likely perceived as attractive role models. In 67 percent of the programs, violence was portrayed within a humorous context. In general, the study found that most media violence is glamorized and that the long-term negative consequences of violent behavior are rarely depicted. Nearly three-quarters of violent scenes contain no remorse, criticism, punishment, or emotional reactions from the perpetrators. Overall, the survey found that the percentage of programs on television that contain some violence remained unchanged over the three-year period of study.

It is clear that video games have become one of the favorite activities of youth in America. Today, approximately 90 percent of American children between the ages of 8 and 16 play video games at home (Anderson *et al.*, 2008). In addition, there are age and gender differences in video playing time. Adolescent girls play video games for an average of 5 hours per week, whereas boys average 13 hours a week (Gentile, Lynch, Linder, & Walsh, 2004). The most popular game category is fantasy violence and other human violence games (Anderson & Dill, 2000; Funk & Buchman, 1996). Dietz (1998) examined 33 popular Sega and Nintendo games and discovered that nearly 80 percent of the games were violent in nature. Dietz also found that 21 percent of the violent games depicted violence toward women.

The research community is sharply divided on the long-term effects of violent media on aggressive behavior. To date, the overwhelming bulk of the research suggests that portrayals of violence on television and movies may have a significant effect on the frequency and type of aggressive and violent behavior expressed by America's youth. Over the past 45 years, research has periodically demonstrated that media violence viewing is a contributing factor on the development of aggression and violence in children, adolescents, and young adults (Huesmann, Moise-Titus, Podolski, & Eron, 2003). Moreover, media violence appears to influence children more strongly than adults, as they seem to be more susceptible to its long-term effects. Interestingly, the Huesmann *et al.* (2003) study discovered that violent films and TV programs that have the most deleterious effects on children are not always the ones that adults perceive as the most violent. Research suggests that violent scenes in which children can identify with the perpetrator of the violence, and those in which the perpetrator gets rewarded for the violence, have the greatest negative impact on children. It is not necessarily the level of violence per se.

Although the largest body of research on media violence has concentrated on televised violence, the research community in recent years has shifted its attention to violent video games (Murray, 2008). Similar to studies on violent film and TV programs, recent research consistently suggests that heavy exposure to violent video games may be significantly linked to increases in aggressive behavior, aggressive thoughts, aggressive feelings, and decreases in helping behavior (Anderson 2004; Anderson & Bushman, 2001; Anderson *et al.*, 2008; Dill & Dill, 1998). As we see shortly, not all researchers agree with these conclusions.

Before proceeding with this discussion, it is important to distinguish between short-term and long-term effects of violent media on aggressive behavior. Research indicates that different cognitive processes are involved (Huesmann, 2007). Although there is compelling evidence that exposure to violent electronic media has both short-term and long-term effects, we are particularly concerned here about long-term effects. They occur as a result of observational learning, desensitization, and storing violent and aggressive material into the thought process. Young children are especially open to new learning, and these early experiences often have a greater impact during the early development years than learning events that occur during adulthood. Thus, if young children learn that violence or aggressive behavior is acceptable, this information is likely to follow them to and through adulthood. To this effect, Huesmann *et al.* (2003) write, "In recent theorizing, long-term relations have been ascribed mainly to acquisition through observation learning of three social-cognitive structures: schemas about a hostile world, scripts for social problem solving that focus on aggression, and normative beliefs that aggression is acceptable" (p. 201). Over time, and with frequent exposure to aggressive behavior, children develop beliefs (schemas) that the world is basically a hostile place, that aggression is an acceptable social behavior, and that the best way to solve conflicts and to get things is to be aggressive. These aspects may actually become part of the personality over the long run.

Research by Krahé and Möller (2004) supports these hypotheses. They found that adolescents were more likely to condone aggression and to display hostile attribution bias toward ambiguous cues if they were frequently exposed to violent electronic games. Another study (i.e., Funk, Baldacci, Pasold, & Baumgardner, 2004) demonstrated that high exposure to violent electronic games is associated with lower levels of empathy and more positive attitudes toward violent behavior in general. This study also indicated that violent video games may have greater impact than other forms of violent entertainment media, such as films or television programs. This is likely due to the interactive component of video games, whereby the individual is a virtual participant rather than a passive observer of the violence.

Huesmann and his colleagues (2003) report strong long-term effects of media violence observed in early childhood appears to carry over into adulthood. They conclude:

> Overall, these results suggest that both males and females from all social strata and all levels of initial aggressiveness are placed at increased risk for the development of adult aggressive and violent behavior when they view a high and steady diet of violent TV shows in early childhood. (p. 128)

The effects of violent video or electronic games on the development of aggressive behavior received considerable scrutiny after a series of school shootings by avid players of such games occurred during the late 1990s and early 2000. In April 1999, public concern was especially strong after 13 persons were murdered and 23 were wounded during a shooting spree by two students at Columbine High School in Colorado. The two assailants were considered social outcasts and seemed preoccupied with the violence presented in the media, music, and video games. Reports indicated that the two were especially fascinated by the bloody video game *Doom*, one of the earliest and most successful of all electronic games. It is interesting to note that the Marine Corps in 1998 adapted *Doom II* to train soldiers for combat, and called it *Marine Doom*. The video game, consisting of a team leader, two riflemen, and a machine gunner, was designed to teach teamwork, coordination, and effective decision making. Although the game is no longer used by the military, it has been released for public use.

Lt. Col. (Ret.) David Grossman, a former Airborne Ranger, West Point psychology professor, and a leading expert on the psychology of killing, has written several books that pertain to the subject of violence in the media. The school shootings prompted the books *On Killing* and *Stop Teaching Our Kids to Kill*. In the latter, Grossman and DeGaetano (1999) point out that the training methods used by the military, which includes brutalization, classical conditioning, operant conditioning, and role modeling, can be found in many of the violent video games found on the market today. They argue that video game publishers unethically train children in the use of weapons and, more importantly, harden them emotionally to the act of murder by simulating the killing of hundreds or thousands of opponents.

The impact of violent electronic games is not restricted to the United States. It occurs in other countries also, such as Japan (Anderson, 2004; Anderson *et al.*, 2008). In another example,

Krahé and Möller (2004) describe an incident that occurred in Germany in April 2002, in which 17 people were killed in a shooting spree by an expelled student who had spent much of his time playing violent electronic games.

However, similar to the effects of TV and movies, the research community is divided about the long-term effects of violent video games, and the empirical evidence has been challenged at many levels. Some scholars argue that many of the studies on video games are inconclusive and can be criticized on methodological grounds (Ferguson *et al.*, 2008; Grimes & Bergen, 2008; Gunter, 2008; Savage, 2008; Savage & Yancey, 2008). Certainly, the overwhelming majority of individuals who play violent video games do not commit violent acts. Therefore, the oversimplified position that violent video media or games cause or even promote violence must be tempered. It may well be that exposure to media violence does increase violence and aggressive behavior for individuals who are already aggressive and prone toward violence. Media violence may not do the same for those individuals less prone toward physical aggression and violence.

In October 2002, ten people in Washington, D.C., were killed at random over a 23-day period. One of the shooters was 17-year-old Lee Malvo. Malvo's defense team argued that the youth had been brainwashed and trained to kill while playing violent video games depicting sniper attacks, such as *Halo*, *Tom Clancy's Ghost Recon*, and *Tom Clancy's Rainbow Six: Covert Ops* (Olson, 2004). While this may appear to be anecdotal evidence that extensive exposure to violent video games is harmful, it should also be noted that Malvo had been exposed to a wide variety of risk factors throughout his early life, including apparent rejection by his biological father and instability in his home life. He had also demonstrated a variety of antisocial actions, such as cruelty to animals, including apparently killing at least 20 cats (Olson, 2004).

Thus if there is a research consensus emerging, it is that violent video games may be one risk factor, and when coupled with other risk factors, it may contribute to antisocial or even violent behavior. It is unlikely that video games contribute directly to make a child grow up to be a killer or even become excessively aggressive. "A review of both aggregate studies and experimental evidence does not provide support for the supposition that exposure to media violence causes criminally violent behavior" (Savage & Yancey, 2008, p. 786).

Contagion Effect

To this point we have focused upon the effects of violence in the entertainment media. However, even news reports of violence may be problematic. Like entertainment media, the news media may provide aggressive models or may produce a **contagion effect or copycat effect**. This is a tendency in some people to model or copy an activity portrayed in the entertainment or news media. Contagion effect is said to occur when action depicted in the media is assessed by certain individuals as a good idea and then mimicked. An ingenious bank robbery, dramatized on television, might be imitated. The contagion effect is not simply restricted to media portrayals of violence, however. For example, a study by Joiner (1994) illustrates how depression in a college classmate may be contagious. A classmate who is depressed can lower the mood of friends, family, and others who associate with the depressed person and try to help. The contagion effect also has been cited in reports of teen suicide, as in a recent case in which four girls from one high school committed suicide over the course of an academic year.

Another tragic illustration of the copycat effect can be found in a series of school shootings, discussed briefly above, that began in 1997. In October of that year, a 16-year-old, having just stabbed his mother to death, arrived at the high school in Pearl, Mississippi, and began randomly shooting his classmates, killing two and wounding seven. Less than two months later, a 14-year-old boy opened fire on a group of fellow high school students participating in a prayer circle in West Paducah,

Kentucky. He killed two schoolmates and wounded five others. The West Paducah incident received worldwide media coverage for several weeks, accompanied by extensive stories about the shooter. A few months later, on March 24, 1998, two boys, ages 13 and 11, armed with seven handguns and three rifles, opened fire on their classmates as they gathered on the school playground in Jonesboro, Arkansas, killing four very young girls and their teacher and wounding 10 others. Of the 15 killed or wounded, only one was male, suggesting that the young shooters were aiming specifically at girls.

After Jonesboro and exactly one month later, a 14-year-old male student in Edinboro, Pennsylvania, began shooting during a school dance, killing a teacher. This incident was followed by another shooting less than a month later in Fayetteville, Tennessee, resulting in the death of a student. A week later, a 15-year-old male in Springfield, Oregon, walked into the high school cafeteria and began randomly shooting at fellow students, firing 50 rounds from a .22-caliber semiautomatic rifle in less than a minute. As he stopped to reload, the young shooter was tackled and disarmed by a varsity wrestler. During that one minute, however, he managed to kill two classmates and wounded 22 others. He had also shot both his parents prior to leaving for school. Less than two weeks later, on June 15, 1998, a 14-year-old student, armed with a .32-caliber semi-automatic handgun, opened fire in the hallway of a high school as students took final exams, wounding a basketball coach and a volunteer aide. All of these young shooters had an inordinate interest in guns, had troubled backgrounds, knew the details of the previous school shootings, and had a strong fascination with violence presented through the media. Thus, both media violence and the contagion effect seem to be implicated. And as mentioned earlier, on April 20, 1999, two teenagers, Eric Harris and Dylan Klebold, in Littleton, Colorado, entered Columbine High School and killed 13 people and injured dozens of others before taking their own lives.

In summary, exposure to media-portrayed violence does not automatically promote aggression. Some individuals are affected more than others. Children from low-income families are apparently more influenced by media violence than middle-class children (Eisenhower, 1969); it is not clear whether this reflects exposure to the violence itself or other factors as well. It is clear that no one causal factor alone accounts for more than a small proportion of variance of individual differences in aggressive behavior (Bartholow, Sestir, & Davis, 2005; Huesmann, 1998). Researchers have found evidence that positive parental models are likely to override violent models on television (Goldstein, 1975; Huesmann *et al.*, 2003). Moreover, television violence seems to have substantially less effect on families in which the parents do not rely on aggressive behavior for solving problems (Wright *et al.*, 2001).

Nevertheless, hundreds of research articles conclude that *heavy* exposure to violent media is one of the most significant causes of violence in American society (American Psychological Association, 2003a). The evidence is especially strong on the effects of violent electronic games, where the participant learns aggressive schema and practices new aggression-related cognitive scripts that become more and more accessible for use when real-life conflict situations arise (Anderson & Dill, 2000).

Summary and Conclusions

In this chapter, we reviewed the major psychological perspectives on aggression and violence. Answers to what can be done about aggression and violent crime rest ultimately on one's perspective of human nature. If one believes that aggression is innate and part of our evolutionary heritage, a position held by mainstream psychoanalytic and ethological thought, then the conclusion must be that aggression is part of life, and that little can be done to alter this basic ingredient of human nature. Clues for reducing aggression are found in the behavior demonstrated throughout the animal kingdom. If, on the other hand, one believes that human aggression is acquired, then the key becomes principles of human learning and thought, and hope that one can change this acquired behavior for the betterment of humankind. The distinction between the innate and learning viewpoints has been somewhat oversimplified, but most contemporary theories on aggression fall within one or the other camp. At this point, the learning perspective has garnered considerably more empirical support than the innate perspective. Cognitive factors are especially important in explanations of human aggression.

Complicating the above, though, is the increasing amount of research being done in the biological sciences, most particularly relating to the brain and to human genetics. Ninety-five percent of everything we know about the human brain has been learned within the last 15 years. Researchers are acquiring extensive information about the contribution of genes to physical characteristics and susceptibility to medical problems. Many believe that they will eventually link genes to a variety of behavioral problems and mental disorders as well. It is crucial to keep in mind, though, that although some genes may *predispose* individuals to certain disorders that may lead to violence or other antisocial behavior, genes do not *determine* behavior.

Furthermore, as more research data are published, even the *learning* perspective becomes increasingly complex, and additional factors must be considered. For one thing, physiological arousal certainly plays a major role in aggressive and violent behavior, as suggested by Berkowitz (1989). High levels of arousal seem to *facilitate* (again, not cause) aggressive behavior in certain situations. Extremely high arousal seems to interfere with our sense of self-awareness and internal control, rendering us more susceptible to environmental cues and to mindless or habitual behaviors. In this sense, under very high arousal, we may not stop to consider the consequences of our violent behavior. The discussion of road rage and aggressive driving in the chapter illustrates this very well.

The different classifications of aggressive behavior were also emphasized in this chapter.

Overt and covert forms of aggression must be considered in any discussion of crime. Overt aggressors are more likely to be involved in violent crimes, whereas covert aggressors are more prone to be involved in property offenses. And although the conventional wisdom has been that boys are more likely to commit highly aggressive crimes, the evidence suggests that girls may be equally involved in aggressive behavior of a different kind. Gender differences in aggressive behavior are believed to be mainly due to socialization factors.

Situational and neurophysiological factors also contribute significantly to aggressive behavior. Aggressive stimuli, including weapons, crowds, pollution, temperature, smells, and central nervous system pathology all must be entertained as possible contributors. Social learning theorists also note that the media and the models they provide substantially affect our attitudes, values, and overall impressions about violence as well as our behavior. Attitudes, beliefs, and thoughts refer to the cognitive processes that are beginning to emerge as contenders for a leading role in the psychological explanation of criminal behavior. Operant and classical conditioning remain important, but they do not adequately address the many intricacies of criminal behavior.

The controversial topic of violence in the entertainment and news media was addressed. In light of rapid developments in technology, it is impossible to shelter children and adolescents from violent images in a realistic manner, though it is possible to place limits on that exposure. Media violence, though, is only one of many risk factors in the development of violent behavior. Nevertheless, for some children, excessive exposure to such images can have significant negative effects on their development.

We end the chapter with a concise summary statement by Rowell Huesmann who, after reviewing the research literature, concludes, "No one causal factor by itself explains more than a small portion of individual differences in aggressiveness" (1997, p. 70). He hastens to add, however, that "early learning and socialization play a key role in the development of habitual aggression" (1997, p. 70).

Key Concepts

Aggressive driving
Cognitive-neoassociation
    model
Cognitive scripts model
Contagion effect (copycat effect)
Cybercrime
Difference-in-degree
Displaced aggression theory
Evolutionary psychology
Excitation transfer theory

Frustration-aggression
    hypothesis
Hostile aggression
Hostile attribution bias
Hostile attribution model
Instrumental aggression
Passive-aggressive behaviors
Proactive aggression
Psychodynamic model
    (hydraulic model)

Reactive aggression
Ritualized aggression
Road rage
Rumination
Territoriality
Theory
Weapons effect

Review Questions

1. What physiological factors have been associated with aggression?
2. What accounts for gender differences in aggression? Cite relevant research findings.
3. Define cognitive scripts and how they may be applied in situations where spontaneous violence could occur.
4. Define weapons effect and discuss how it may account for some of the violence in today's society.
5. Define hostile attribution bias and discuss how it might explain chronic aggression in young children.
6. Explain the difference between each of the following: overt and covert acts of aggression, cognitive scripts model and hostile attribution model, and reactive and proactive aggression.
7. Review the research presented in this chapter on the effects of the mass media on violence.

6

Criminal Psychopathy

CHAPTER OBJECTIVES

- Present a special type of offender (the criminal psychopath) who is different emotionally, cognitively, and behaviorally from other offenders.
- Review the various measures of psychopathy.
- Examine the neurobiological aspects of psychopathy.
- Review the evidence for juvenile psychopathy.
- Identify the ethical dilemmas that juvenile psychopathy presents.

> Given its relation to crime and violence, psychopathy is arguably one of the most important psychological constructs in the criminal justice system. (Porter *et al.,* 2000, p. 227)

It is no surprise, then, that psychopathy has become a central focus of research in psychology, particularly as it relates to criminal behavior. Most recently, *juvenile* psychopathy has become the subject of considerable interest and debate. Some researchers question its validity and implications, while others believe it is crucial that we identify psychopathic characteristics in juveniles in order to intervene at an early age. As we will see in the chapter, the psychopath is not identical to the person with an antisocial personality disorder, but some researchers and clinicians continue to confuse the two terms (Gacono, Nieberding, Owen, Rubel, & Bodholdt, 2001). Because psychopathy is such an important topic in criminal psychology, we devote an entire chapter to describing the research and clinical characteristics of this interesting behavior.

WHAT IS A PSYCHOPATH?

The term "psychopath" is currently used to describe a person who demonstrates a discernible cluster of psychological, interpersonal, and neurophysiological features that distinguish him or her from the general population. Psychologist Robert Hare (1993), one of the world's leading experts on psychopathy, describes psychopaths as "social predators who charm, manipulate, and ruthlessly plow their way through life, leaving a broad trail of broken hearts, shattered expectations, and empty wallets. Completely lacking in conscience and empathy, they selfishly take what they want and do as they please, violating social norms and expectations without the slightest sense of guilt or regret" (p. xi).

Hare (1970) proposed a useful scheme to outline three categories of psychopaths: the primary, the secondary or neurotic, and the dyssocial. Only the **primary psychopath** is a "true" psychopath. The primary or "true" psychopath has certain identifiable psychological, emotional, cognitive, and biological differences that distinguish him or her from the general or criminal population. We discuss these differences in some detail throughout the chapter. The other two categories meld a heterogeneous group of antisocial individuals who comprise a large segment of the criminal population. **Secondary psychopaths** commit antisocial or violent acts because of severe emotional problems or inner conflicts. They are sometimes called acting-out neurotics, neurotic delinquents, symptomatic psychopaths, or simply emotionally disturbed offenders. The popular entertainment media often refer to these persons as "psychopathic killers," or utilize some other attention-getting terminology designed to conjure a bloodthirsty disturbed person indiscriminately killing all those whom he meets. The third group, **dyssocial psychopaths,** display aggressive, antisocial behavior they have *learned* from their subculture, like their gangs or families. In both cases, the label "psychopath" is misleading, because the behaviors and backgrounds have little if any similarity to those of primary psychopaths. Yet, both secondary and dyssocial psychopaths are often incorrectly called psychopaths because of their high recidivism rates.

Another term that should be distinguished from primary psychopathy is **antisocial personality disorder (APD).** This term is used by psychiatrists and many clinical psychologists to describe "a pervasive pattern of disregard for, and violation of, the rights of others that begins in childhood or early adolescence and continues into adulthood" (American Psychiatric Association, 1994, p. 645). Antisocial personalities (ASPs) are further described as those persons who "fail to conform to social norms with respect to lawful behaviors. They may repeatedly perform acts that are grounds for arrest, such as destroying property, harassing others, stealing or pursuing illegal occupations" (American Psychiatric Association, 1994, p. 646). As we noted, the descriptions of the psychiatric term *antisocial personality disorder* follow very closely the descriptions of the psychological term *psychopathy*. However, the definition of APD is more narrow than primary psychopathy because it restricts its definition to behavioral indicators. Hare's definition of primary psychopathy also includes emotional, neurological, and cognitive aspects. Nevertheless, with each new publication of the American Psychiatric Association's *Diagnostic and Statistical Manual of Mental Disorders*, the characteristics used to describe the antisocial personality (ASP) are increasingly similar to Hare's primary psychopathy in behavioral terms. It is easy to understand why clinicians often confuse the terms.

This text adopts Hare's scheme, considering "primary psychopath" an empirically and clinically useful designation. It is distinguished from secondary or neurotic psychopaths in its behavioral, cognitive, and neurophysiological features. From this point on, when we refer to the psychopath, we mean the primary psychopath. He or she is unique: not neurotic, psychotic, or emotionally disturbed, as commonly believed and portrayed by the entertainment media. Primary psychopaths are usually not volcanically explosive, violent, or extremely destructive. They are more apt to be outgoing, charming, and verbally proficient. They may be criminals—in fact, in general, they run in perpetual opposition to the law—but many are not. The term **criminal psychopath** will be used to identify those primary psychopaths who do engage in repetitive antisocial or criminal behavior.

An Example of a Psychopath

The late Ferdinand Waldo Demara Jr., the "Great Impostor," who forged documents and tried dozens of occupations without stopping to obtain a high school education, is a good example of a primary psychopath. A brief description of some of his exploits may help put the psychopath in perspective (see Critchton, 1959, for a more complete version).

Demara frequently came into contact with the law, primarily because he persisted in adopting fake identities. He once obtained the credentials of a Dr. French, who held a Harvard PhD in psychology. Demara was in the U.S. Navy at the time, awaiting a commission on the basis of other forged documents, but when he realized he was in danger of exposure via a routine security check, he decided he would prefer the Dr. French identity. He dramatized a successful suicide by leaving his clothing on the end of a pier with a note stating that "this is the only way out." Navy officials accepted his "death," and Demara became Dr. French. With his impressive credentials in hand, he obtained a dean of philosophy position in a Canadian college, successfully taught a variety of psychology courses, and assumed administrative responsibilities.

He developed a friendship with a physician, Joseph Cyr, and learned the basics of medicine from their long conversations. He eventually borrowed and duplicated Cyr's vital documents—birth, baptism, and confirmation certificates, school records, medical license—and obtained a commission in the Royal Canadian Navy as Dr. Cyr. He read extensively to nurture his growing knowledge of medicine.

During the Korean War, Demara/Cyr was assigned to a destroyer headed for the combat zone. The ship met a small Korean junk carrying many seriously wounded men, who were brought on board for emergency medical care. Three men were in such critical condition that only emergency surgery could save their lives. Although Demara had never seen an operation performed, he hurriedly reviewed his textbooks. With unskilled hands, he operated through the night. By dawn, he had not only saved the lives of the three men, but had also successfully treated 16 others.

Demara/Cyr's deeds were broadcast over the ship's radio and disseminated, along with his photo, by the press. The real Dr. Cyr, shocked to see Demara's visage over his own respected name, immediately exposed him. Demara was discharged from the Canadian Navy which, to save itself from additional embarrassment, allowed him to leave without prosecution. Demara's biography represents an example of a psychopath who did not engage in serious or lifelong violent crime.

Many psychopaths do commit violent crimes, though, some of them heinous and brutal. Neville Heath—charming, handsome, and intelligent—brutally and sadistically murdered two young English women (Critchley, 1951; Hill, 1960). Like Demara, Heath had an extraordinary career, much of it in the armed forces. Unlike Demara, his brushes with the law were serious and occasionally ended in imprisonment. He was commissioned and dishonorably discharged on three separate occasions, once each in the British Royal Air Force, the Royal Armed Service Corps, and the South African Air Force. He flew in a fighter squadron in the RAF until he was court-martialed for car theft at age 19. He then committed a series of thefts and burglaries and was sentenced to Borstal Prison. Pardoned in 1939, he joined the Royal Armed Service Corps but was dismissed for forgery. On his way home to England, he jumped ship and eventually managed to obtain a commission in the South African Air Force until his past caught up with him. When not in trouble, Heath was regarded as a daring, confident, and highly charming officer—and a rake. After the third court-martial, he developed a taste for sadistic murder.

You may be able to identify other examples of psychopaths at their worst. The notorious Charles Manson, who in the 1960s exhibited an uncanny ability to attract a devout cluster of unresisting followers, is one probable example. The fictional Hannibal Lechter, whose sadistic offenses and deadly charm have captivated readers and screen audiences, is another. It is not advisable, though, to see psychopaths around every corner, despite the frequent usage of this designation in popular media. As we note below, it is more likely that psychopathy exists on a continuum and that "full blown psychopaths" are rare. Throughout the remainder of this chapter, we examine in more detail their behavioral patterns, cognitive processes, interpersonal features, neuropsychological characteristics, and general backgrounds.

BEHAVIORAL DESCRIPTIONS

One pioneering authority on the behavioral characteristics of the psychopath was Hervey Cleckley, a well-known psychiatrist from Augusta, Georgia, who died in 1984 at the age of 79. A large part of Cleckley's professional recognition came as a result of the nonfiction book, *The Three Faces of Eve*, which he coauthored with Corbett Thigpen. The book, which is about the phenomenon of "multiple personality," was made into a very popular 1957 movie with the same title. However, his major professional contribution to the field of psychiatry can be found in his often-quoted text, *The Mask of Sanity* (first published in 1941). The book describes in clear and empirically useful terms the major behaviors demonstrated by the full-fledged or primary psychopath, as distinct from the other psychopathic types referred to previously. Cleckley was able to identify 16 characteristics he felt described the typical psychopath (see **Table 1**). We discuss some of these psychological characteristics identified by both Cleckley and Hare in more detail below.

Charming and Verbally Fluent

Superficial charm and average to above-average intelligence are two of the psychopath's main features, according to Cleckley, and they are both especially apparent during initial contacts. It

TABLE 1   Psychopathic Behaviors Identified by Hare and Cleckley

Hare PCL Checklist	Cleckley's Primary Psychopath Description
Glibness/superficial charm	Superficial charm and good intelligence
Grandiose sense of self-worth	Pathological egocentricity
Pathological lying	Untruthfulness and insincerity
Cunning/manipulative	Manipulative
Lack of remorse or guilt	Lack of remorse or guilt
Shallow affect	General poverty of affective reactions
Callous, lack of empathy	Unresponsiveness in interpersonal relationships
Failure to accept responsibility for actions	Unreliability
Promiscuous sexual behavior	Impersonal sex life
Lack of realistic, long-term goals	Failure to follow any life plan
Poor behavioral controls	Impulsive
High need for stimulation/prone to boredom	Inadequately motivated antisocial behavior
Irresponsibility	Poor judgment
	Absence of delusions
	Absence of anxiety
	Bizarre behavior after drinking alcohol

should be emphasized, however, that a large portion of the psychopaths Cleckley worked with were well educated and from middle- or upper-class backgrounds (Hare & Neumann, 2008). Many psychopaths usually impress others as friendly, outgoing, likable, and alert. They often appear well educated and knowledgeable, and they display many interests. They are verbally skillful and can talk themselves out of trouble. In fact, their vocabulary is often so extensive that they can talk at length about anything (Hare, 1991). However, systematic study of their conversation reveals that they often jump "from one topic to another and that much of their speech is empty of real substance, tending to be filled with stock phrases, repetitions of the same ideas, word approximations, abstract terms and jargon used in a superficial or inappropriate fashion, logically inconsistent statements and phrases, and half-formed sentences" (Hare, 1991, p. 57). As Hare (1996, p. 46) notes, "In some respects, it is as if psychopaths lack a central organizer to plan and keep track of what they think and say." However, since psychopaths are so charming and manipulative, these language shortcomings are not readily apparent.

Readers should not conclude that psychopaths as a group are usually verbally and socially skillful at *successfully* manipulating others and the system. In a revealing study that followed a large number of psychopaths from age 8 to 48 (Ullrich, Farrington, & Coid, 2008), it was found that psychopathic traits did not lead to status or wealth, or successful intimate relationships. Apparently, the charm, deception, and impression management used by psychopaths does not lead to success in life.

Psychological Testing Differences

Psychometric studies (studies that use standard psychological tests as measures) indicate that psychopaths usually score higher on intelligence tests than the general population (Hare, 1970, 1996), particularly on individually administered tests. In fact, Hare wryly comments, the psychopaths who were the sample for his studies were probably the least intelligent of their ilk, since they were not quite bright enough to avoid being convicted for their offenses. (Hare has conducted much of his research on imprisoned psychopaths.) Recent research (e.g., Ishikawa, Raine, Lencz, Bihrle, & Lacasse, 2001) has found that a useful dichotomy of psychopathy may be to divide psychopaths into "successful" psychopaths (those who have committed crimes but avoided arrest and conviction for offenses) and "unsuccessful" psychopaths (those who have been convicted and imprisoned). Overall, available research indicates that many psychopaths are bright, but some are not (Hare & Neumann, 2008).

Psychopaths and Mental Disorders

Psychopaths usually do *not* exhibit mental disorders, either mild or severe. Most lack any symptoms of excessive worry and anxiety, psychotic thinking, delusions, severe depressions, or hallucinations. Even under high pressure conditions, they remain cool and calm, as did Ian Fleming's fictitious James Bond, probably a prime example. Feasibly, the doomed psychopath might enjoy a steak dinner (*au poivre*) with gusto just before being executed. The infamous multiple murderer Herman W. Mudget, alias H. H. Holmes, retired at his normal hour the evening before his execution, fell asleep easily, slept soundly, and woke up completely refreshed. "I never slept better in my life," he told his cell guard. He ordered and ate a substantial breakfast an hour before he was scheduled to be hanged. Until the moment of death, he remained remarkably calm and amiable, displaying no signs of depression or fear (Franke, 1975).

Not everyone agrees with the view that psychopaths do not suffer from some mental disorder. Some clinicians argue that psychopathy and schizophrenia are part of the same spectrum of disorders (Hare, 1996), and Cleckley briefly considered psychopathy as a form of masked psychosis. Some forensic clinicians maintain that they occasionally see a mentally disordered offender who qualifies as both a psychopath and a schizophrenic (Hare, 1996). There is some evidence to suggest that it is not uncommon to find psychopaths who seem mentally disordered in maximum security psychiatric units for highly violent or dangerous patients. Other researchers have reported similar findings (Quinsey, Harris, Rice, & Cormier, 2006; Tengström, Hodgins, Grann, Längström, & Kullgren, 2004; Vitacco, Neumann, & Jackson, 2005). Tengström *et al.* found that individuals diagnosed with schizophrenia and who demonstrated many of the features of psychopathy had more severe histories of offending and violence than those persons diagnosed with schizophrenia alone.

Do Psychopaths Ever Commit Suicide?

Cleckley was under the impression that psychopaths rarely—if ever—committed suicide. Recent research and clinical experiences, however, have put Cleckley's observation in doubt. Hare, for instance, knows of several psychopaths who took their own lives when it became clear to them there was no other way out of what they perceived as an intolerable situation (Hare & Neumann, 2008). Intolerable situations include a very long prison term, incurable illness, or being surrounded by the police. "We suspect that at least some cases of 'suicide by cop' involved psychopaths who were trapped and wished to go out in a 'blaze of glory' " (Hare & Neumann, 2008, p. 228).

Verona, Patrick, and Joiner (2001) found that, among male inmates, psychopaths who were especially aggressive and impulsive did show some indicators of suicidality. *Suicidality* is a term used by clinicians to indicate there is a risk of suicide, usually inferred from suicidal thoughts or intent. In another study that examined psychopathy and suicidality in psychiatric patients, youthful offenders, jail detainees, and prison inmates, the researchers also found a significant relationship between psychopathy and suicidality (Douglas, Herbozo, Poythress, Belgrage, & Edens, 2006). However, the researchers also warned that the suicide–psychopathy relationship was highly complex and multifaceted, and required much more research to confidently establish it. In sum, research and clinical experience are beginning to find that some psychopaths who find themselves in desperate situations do commit suicide, especially if they are highly impulsive and violent.

Other Principal Traits

Other principal traits of the psychopath are selfishness and an inability to love or give affection to others. According to Cleckley, egocentricity is *always* present in the psychopath and is essentially unmodifiable. The psychopath is unable to feel genuine, meaningful affection for others. Psychopaths may be likable, but they are seldom able to keep close friends, and they have great difficulty understanding love in others. They may be highly skillful at pretending deep affection, and they may effectively mimic appropriate emotions, but true loyalty, warmth, and compassion are foreign to them. Psychopaths are distinguished by flat emotional reaction and affect. And since psychopaths have so little need to receive or give love, psychopaths, as a group, have relatively little contact with their families, and many change their residences frequently (Hare, 1991). In addition they do not usually respond to acts of kindness. They show capacity only for superficial appreciation. Paradoxically, they may do small favors and appear considerate. One prototype mowed the lawn for his elderly neighbor and brought her schnapps when she was ill—the next morning he stole her car.

Psychopaths have a remarkable disregard for truth and are often called "pathological liars." They seem to have no internalized moral or ethical sense and cannot understand the purpose of being honest, especially if dishonesty will bring some personal gain. They have a cunning ability to appear straightforward, honest, and sincere, but their claims to sincerity are without substance.

Psychopaths are unreliable, irresponsible, and unpredictable, regardless of the importance of the occasion or the consequences of their impulsive actions. Impulsivity appears to be a central or cardinal feature of psychopathy (Hart & Dempster, 1997). This pattern of impulsive actions is cyclical, however. Psychopaths may, for months on end, be responsible citizens, faithful spouses, and reliable employees. They may experience great successes, be promoted, and gain honors, as did Demara and Heath. Skillfully as they have attained these socially desirable goals, they have an uncanny knack of suddenly unraveling their lives. They become irresponsible, and may pass bad checks, sabotage the company computers, or go on a drunken spree. They also tend to have a "bad temper" that flares quickly into an argument and attack. Psychopaths may later say they are sorry and plead for another chance—and most will probably get it. Invariably, if the psychopath is a young adult, the irresponsible behavior will return.

Even small amounts of alcohol prompt most psychopaths to become vulgar, domineering, loud, and boisterous and to engage in practical jokes and pranks. Cleckley noted that they choose pranks that have no appeal for most individuals, and that seem bizarre, inappropriate, and cruel. They lack genuine humor and, not surprisingly, the ability to laugh at themselves.

Although often above average in intelligence, psychopaths appear incapable of learning to avoid failure and situations that are potentially damaging to themselves. Some theorists suggest that the self-destructive, self-defeating deeds and attitudes reflect a need to be punished to mitigate the guilt they subconsciously experience, or more simply, that they are driven by a masochistic purpose. Evidence refuting these explanations is offered later in this chapter.

When a psychopath drifts into criminal activity, impulsivity will usually prevent him or her from performing like a professional criminal. Psychopaths are more likely to participate in capers and hastily planned frolics, or in spontaneous, serious crimes for immediate satisfaction. The professional criminal has purpose and a plan of action; the psychopath is impulsive and lacks long-range goals.

A cardinal fault of psychopaths is their absolute lack of remorse or guilt for anything they do, regardless of the severity or immorality of their actions and irrespective of their traumatic effects on others. Since they do not anticipate personal consequences, psychopaths may engage in destructive or antisocial behavior—such as forgery, theft, rape, brawls, and fraud—by taking absurd risks and for insignificant personal gain. When caught, they express no genuine remorse. They may readily admit culpability and take considerable pleasure in the shock these admissions produce in others. Whether they have bashed in someone's head, ruined a car, or tortured a child, psychopaths may well remark they did it "for the hell of it."

Psychopaths have little capacity to see themselves as others perceive them. Instead of accepting the facts that would normally lead to insight, they project and externalize blame onto the community and family for their misfortunes. Interestingly, educated psychopaths have been known to speak fluently about the psychopathic personality, quoting the literature extensively and discussing research findings, but they cannot look into their own troublesome antics or mount a reasonable attack on their actions. They articulate their regrets for having done something, but the words are devoid of emotional meaning, a characteristic Cleckley calls **semantic aphasia.** Johns and Quay (1962) remarked that psychopaths "know the words but not the music." Similarly, Grant (1977) notes that the psychopath knows only the book meaning of words, not the living meaning. Hare (1996, p. 45) concludes, "In short, psychopaths appear to be semantically and affectively shallow individuals."

Another important behavioral characteristic of psychopaths noted by Blair, Peschardt, Budhani, Mitchell, and Pine (2006) is their *excessive* use of instrumental aggression. Instrumental aggression is purposeful and goal-directed aggression used to achieve a specific goal, such as the possessions of another person. It is distinguished from reactive aggression, which is considered spontaneous, unplanned, and done in response to an event or an action by another individual.

Finally, an important behavioral distinction underlying much of Cleckley's description is what Quay (1965) refers to as the psychopath's profound and pathological stimulation seeking. According to Quay, the actions of the psychopath are motivated by an excessive *neuropsychological* need for thrills and excitement. It is not unusual to see psychopaths drawn to such interests as race car driving, skydiving, and motorcycle stunts. We will examine this alleged need for stimulation in the pages to follow.

In recent years, it has become useful for research purposes to focus on psychopaths who repeatedly commit crimes, collectively called criminal psychopaths. Concentrating on psychopaths who are violent or chronic offenders provides invaluable information about their backgrounds, learning history, and behavioral patterns. Such research also might offer key strategies for how to deal and potentially treat this challenging group of individuals.

THE CRIMINAL PSYCHOPATH

As stated repeatedly above, many psychopaths have no history of serious antisocial behavior, and persistent, serious offenders are not necessarily psychopaths. For our purposes here, the term *criminal psychopath* will be reserved for those psychopaths who demonstrate a wide range of *persistent* and *serious* antisocial behavior. As a group, they tend to be "dominant, manipulative individuals characterized by an impulsive, risk-taking and antisocial lifestyle, which obtain their greatest thrill from diverse sexual gratification and target diverse victims over time" (Porter *et al.*, 2000, p. 220). As noted at the beginning of this chapter, Porter and his colleagues consider psychopathy "one of the most important psychological constructs in the criminal justice system" (p. 227).

Contemporary theory and research consider psychopathic traits and predispositions as existing on a continuum. The entertainment media often portray the psychopath as an inhuman, vile, despicable person who enjoys violence (Consider, for example, the eerie protagonist in the film *No Country for Old Men*). One is left with the impression that an individual is either a psychopath or a nonpsychopath. However, psychopathic traits and characteristics in adults and adolescents are best viewed today as occurring along a dimension, with some people demonstrating more psychopathic tendencies than others. As we will see shortly, someone is labeled as a psychopath after attaining a given cutoff score on tests to measure the construct. The accumulation of psychopathic characteristics is what determines the final diagnosis, and not everyone agrees on the required cutoff point. Therefore, the best perspective to take when studying the following material is that psychopathy exists on different levels rather than viewing people as either psychopaths or nonpsychopaths. Nevertheless, when we refer to percentages of psychopaths in a population, we are referring to the percentages that have met the cutoff criteria as defined by a particular research study.

Prevalence of Criminal Psychopathy

Overall, Robert Hare (1998) estimates that the prevalence of psychopaths in the general population is about 1 percent, whereas in the adult prison population, estimates range from 15 percent to 25 percent. Some researchers (e.g., Simourd & Hoge, 2000) wonder, however, whether these estimates are not somewhat inflated. Simourd and Hoge report only 11 percent of their inmate population could be identified as criminal psychopaths. The inmates used in the Simourd–Hoge study were not simply inmates in a medium security correctional facility. All 321 were serving a current sentence for violent offending, more than half of them had been convicted of a previous violent offense, and almost all of them had extensive criminal careers. Even so, few qualified as criminal psychopaths. Therefore, percentage estimates of criminal psychopathy within any given prison population should be tempered by the type of facility, as well as the cultural, ethnic, gender, and age mix of the targeted population. Interestingly, the American Psychiatric Association (1994) estimates that the overall prevalence of *antisocial personality disorder* (APD) in the community at large is about 3 percent in males and about 1 percent in females. In clinical samples (those receiving therapy for various disorders), the prevalence estimates vary between 3 percent and 30 percent, depending on the characteristics of the sample surveyed. Keep in mind, though, that APD is *not* identical to psychopathy.

Offending Patterns of Criminal Psychopaths

Criminal psychopaths are believed responsible for a disproportionate amount of crime in society, and they are considered to be the most violent and persistent offenders (Forth & Burke, 1998; Hart & Hare, 1997; Newman, Schmitt, & Voss, 1997; Saltaris, 2002). Gretton, McBride, Hare, O'Shaughnessy, and Kumka (2001, p. 428) point out that criminal psychopaths generally "lack a normal sense of ethics and morality, live by their own rules, are prone to use cold-blooded, instrumental intimidation and violence to satisfy their wants and needs, and generally are contemptuous of social norms and the rights of others." Hare (1996, p. 38) posits, "The ease with which psychopaths engage in . . . dispassionate violence has very real significance for society in general and for law enforcement personnel in particular." Hare refers to a report by the Federal Bureau of Investigation (1992) that found that nearly half of the law enforcement officers who died in the line of duty were killed by individuals who closely matched the personality profile of the psychopath. Moreover, the unlawful acts of psychopathic sex offenders are likely to be more violent, brutal, unconventional, and sadistic than those of other sex offenders (Hare, Clark, Grann, & Thornton, 2000; Porter, Birt, & Boer, 2001; Woodworth & Porter, 2002). Psychopathic sex offenders appear to be more motivated by thrill seeking and excitement rather than simply sexual arousal (Porter, Woodworth, Earle, Drugge, & Boer, 2003). Psychopaths as a group also appear to be significantly more sadistic than violent nonpsychopaths (Holt, Meloy, & Stack, 1999), and commit more diverse and severe forms of sexual homicides (Firestone, Bradford, Greenberg, & Larose, 1998; Porter *et al.*, 2003). Porter and his colleagues (2003) found that in a sample of the male offenders incarcerated in two Canadian federal prisons for homicide, nearly half could be classified as sexual homicide offenders. (In order to be classified as a sexual homicide, there had to be physical evidence of sexual activity with the victim before, during, or after the homicide.)

Murderers described as excessively sadistic and brutal tend to have many psychopathic features (Hare *et al.*, 2000; Stone, 1998). Serial murderers who exhibit psychopathic features are especially sadistic and brutal in their murders. Collectively, the research suggests that psychopaths may be more likely than other offenders to derive pleasure from both the nonsexual and sexual suffering of others (Porter *et al.*, 2003).

Many of the murders and serious assaults committed by nonpsychopaths occurred during domestic disputes or extreme emotional arousal, thereby qualifying as reactive aggression. This pattern of violence is rarely observed for criminal psychopaths (Hare, Hart, & Harpur, 1991; Williamson, Hare, & Wong, 1987). Criminal psychopaths frequently engage in violence as a form of revenge or retribution, or during a bout of drinking. Many of the attacks of nonpsychopaths are toward women they know well, whereas many of the attacks of criminal psychopaths are directed toward men who are strangers. Hare *et al.* (1991, p. 395) observe that the violence committed by criminal psychopaths was callous and cold-blooded, "without the affective coloring that accompanied the violence of nonpsychopaths." Research also indicates that rapists who have psychopathic characteristics are more likely to have "nonsexual" motivations for their crimes, such as anger, vindictiveness, sadism, and opportunism (Hart & Dempster, 1997).

PSYCHOLOGICAL MEASURES OF PSYCHOPATHY

Currently, the most popular instrument for measuring criminal psychopathy is the 22-item **Psychopathy Checklist (PCL)** (Hare, 1980) and its 20-item revision (**PCL-R**) (Hare, 1991). The PCL-R has been published in a second edition, which includes new information on its applicability in forensic and research settings. The second edition also has been expanded for use with offenders in other countries, and includes updated normative and validation data on male and female offenders. A 12-item short-form version has also been developed, called the **Psychopathy Checklist: Screening Version (PCL:SV)** (Hart, Cox, & Hare, 1995; Hart, Hare, & Forth, 1993). Other additions are the **Psychopathy Checklist: Youth Version (PCL:YV)** and the **P-Scan: Research Version.** The PCL:YV is beginning to be researched more extensively and is covered in more detail in the section on juvenile psychopathy. The P-Scan is a screening instrument that serves as *rough* screen for psychopathic features and as a source of working hypotheses to deal with managing suspects, offenders, or clients. It is designed for use in law enforcement, probation, corrections, civil and forensic facilities, and other areas in which it would be useful to have some information about the possible presence of psychopathic features in a particular person. Of course, the P-Scan needs much more research before its results can be considered definitive. All five checklists are conceptually and—with the exception of the P-Scan—psychometrically similar.

The PCL scales are largely based on Cleckley's (1976) conception of psychopathy, but are specifically designed to identify psychopaths in male prison, forensic, or psychiatric populations. Cleckley's work was based primarily on psychiatric patients. Although several other personality scales for measuring psychopathy have been developed in recent years, the PCL-R is currently the most frequently used instrument for both research and clinical application; it will be the center of attention for the remainder of this section.

The PCL-R assesses the affective (emotional), interpersonal, behavioral, and social deviance facets of criminal psychopathy from various sources, including self-reports, behavioral observations, and collateral sources, such as parents, family members, friends, and arrest and court records which can help to establish the credibility of self-reports (Hare, 1996; Hare, Hart, & Harpur, 1991). In addition, item ratings from the PCL-R, for instance, require some integration of information across multiple domains, including behavior at work or school; behavior toward family, friends, and sexual partners; and criminal behavior (Kosson, Suchy, Mayer, & Libby, 2002). Typically, highly trained examiners use all this information to score each item on a 0–2 scale, depending on the extent to which an individual has the disposition described by each item on the checklist (0 = consistently absent; 1 = inconsistent; 2 = consistently present). Scoring is, however, quite complex and requires substantial time, extensive training, and access to a considerable amount of background information on the individual. In recent years, some researchers have been obtaining PCL-R scores from detailed records, without the interview component. Although there is some support for conducting such reviews (Gretton *et al.*, 2001), it appears that lower scores may result from using this approach (Hare, 2003).

A score of 30 or above usually qualifies a person as a primary psychopath (Hare, 1996). In some research and clinical settings, cutoff scores ranging from 25 to 33 are often used (Simourd & Hoge, 2000). Hare (1991) recommends that persons with scores between 21 and 29 be classified as "middle" subjects who show many of the features of psychopathy but do not fit all the criteria. As mentioned above, psychopathy is best conceptualized as occurring on a continuum; scores below 21 are considered "nonpsychopaths."

So far, the research has strongly supported the reliability and validity of the PCL-R for distinguishing criminal psychopaths from criminal nonpsychopaths, and for helping correctional and forensic psychologists involved in risk assessments of offenders (Hare, 1996; Hare & Neumann, 2008; Hare, Forth, & Stachan, 1992). In addition, the instrument provides researchers and mental health professionals with a universal measurement for the assessment of psychopathy that facilitates international and cross-cultural communication concerning theory, research, and eventual clinical practice (Hare *et al.*, 2000). Currently, the PCL-R is increasingly being used as a clinical instrument for the diagnosis of psychopathy across the globe, although it appears to be most powerful in identifying psychopathy among North American white males (Hare *et al.*, 2000).

Interestingly, Scott Lilienfeld and his colleagues (Lilienfeld, Gershon, Duke, Marion, & de Waal, 1999) have developed a psychopathy scale for chimpanzees, called the Chimpanzee Psychopathy Measure (CPM). Preliminary data indicate that the scale appears to be a reliable measure of psychopathic-like behavior in chimpanzees. According to the researchers, the psychopathic behavior of chimps include excessive displays of sexual activity, daring behaviors, teasing, silent bluff displays, and temper tantrums. While we do not suggest that chimp research is akin to research with humans, these data underscore the potential neuropsychological basis for psychopathy in humans.

Core Factors of Psychopathy

From the research on the PCL-R, it has become clear that psychopathy is multidimensional in nature. One statistical procedure designed to find different dimensions or factors in test data is **factor analysis.** When expert ratings of psychopathy on the PCL-R were submitted to a factor analysis, at least two behavioral dimensions or factors emerged (Hare, 1991; Harpur, Hakstian, & Hare, 1988; Hart, Hare, & Forth, 1993). Many researchers note that more have been identified, and the two-factor position is becoming less accepted as a complete portrayal of psychopathy.

THE TWO-FACTOR POSITION   In the two factor scheme, **Factor 1** reflects the interpersonal and emotional components of the disorder and consists of items measuring remorselessness, callousness, and selfish use and manipulation of others. The typical psychopath feels no compunctions about using others strictly to meet his or her own needs. **Factor 2** is most closely associated with a socially deviant or antisocial lifestyle, as characterized by poor planning, impulsiveness, an excessive need for stimulation, proneness to boredom, and a lack of realistic goals. Some researchers have found that Factor 1 appears to be associated with planned predatory violence, while Factor 2 appears to be related to spontaneous and impulsive violence (Hart & Dempster, 1997). Factor 1 is also linked to resistance and inability to profit from psychotherapy and treatment programs (Seto & Barbaree, 1999). Factor 2 appears related to socioeconomic status, educational attainment, and cultural/ethnic background, whereas Factor 1 may be more connected to biopsychological influences (Cooke & Michie, 1997). Research also suggests that Factor 1 *may* be a more powerful indicator of psychopathy than Factor 2 (Cooke, Michie, Hart, & Hare, 1999). In addition, while it is quite clear that Factor 1 does a better job of identifying psychopathy in general, there is some evidence that Factor 2 does a better job of predicting general recidivism and violent recidivism (Walters, 2003).

THE THREE-FACTOR POSITION   Psychopathic behavior may be too diverse to be captured in only two dimensions. With increasing sophistication of statistical methods (e.g., confirmatory factor analysis and model-based cluster analysis), contemporary research indicates that there may be at least three core behavioral or personality dimensions that best describe psychopathy (Cooke & Michie, 2001; Cooke, Michie, Hart, & Clark, 2004; Vitacco *et al.*, 2005). In an influential paper, Cooke and Michie (2001) challenged the traditional two-factor explanation of psychopathy, and recommended that psychopathy be divided into the following core dimensions:

1. An arrogant and deceptive interpersonal style, which includes a grandiose sense of self-worth, glibness, superficial charm, lying, conning, manipulation, and deceitfulness. (This dimension is also referred to as impression management.)
2. Deficient affective or emotional experience characterized by low remorse, low guilt, a weak conscience, the absence of anxiety, fearlessness, callousness, little empathy, and a failure to accept responsibility for one's actions.
3. An impulsive and irresponsible behavioral style, including failure to think before acting, a lack of long-term goals, stimulation seeking, unsatisfactory work habits, and a parasitic lifestyle (living off others, including spouses, intimate partners, friends, and parents).

THE FOUR DIMENSIONS POSITION Some researchers (e.g., Hare, 2003; Hare & Neumann, 2008; Salekin, Brannen, Zalot, Leistico, & Neumann, 2006; Vitacco, *et al.*, 2005) have asserted that, in addition to disturbances in interpersonal, affective, and behavioral functioning, the definition of psychopathy should also include a fourth factor or dimension: antisocial behavior. Hare and Neumann (2008) write, "A number of recent studies . . . provide considerable support for a four-factor model of psychopathy across diverse and primarily very large samples of male and female offenders" (p. 232). The four-factor model has also been supported across various cultures, ethnic groups, young and adult offenders, and forensic patients (Jackson, Neumann, & Vitacco, 2007; Jones, Cauffman, Miller, & Mulvey, 2006; Neumann, Hare, & Newman, 2007; Neumann, Kosson, Forth, & Hare, 2006).

The argument for a four-factor model is based on the finding that individuals manifesting psychopathic traits often exhibit violence and a large collection of other antisocial behavioral patterns that are more than the poor planning and impulsivity associated with Factor 2. Consequently, the argument contends that researchers and clinicians are missing a critical ingredient in the understanding and definition of the psychopath if measures of antisocial behavior are left out of the equation. It is also argued that much of the predictive power of psychopathy is enhanced if we take into consideration past criminal behavior (Salekin *et al.*, 2006). According to the four-factor perspective, the factors are: (1) interpersonal, such as pathological lying and conning, (2) impulsive lifestyle, such as irresponsible behavior, sensation seeking, and impulsiveness, (3) affective (shallow affect or emotional reactions, lack of remorsefulness for their actions), and (4) antisocial tendencies, such as poor self-regulation and a wide array of antisocial behavior. Table 2 summarizes these four factors.

TABLE 2 Summary of the Four Hypothesized Core Factors of Psychopathy

Factor	Core Features
Interpersonal (F1)	Lying, conning, manipulating others; superficial charm; promiscuous sexual behavior
Impulsive lifestyle (F2)	Irresponsibility; sensation seeking; lack of realistic goals, poor planning
Affective (F3)	Shallow emotions, callousness, little empathy; grandiose self-worth
Antisocial tendencies (F4)	Poor self-regulation; persistent criminal activity; antisocial behavior

Recidivism

Research studies report that the recidivism rate of psychopaths is very high. **Recidivism** refers to the tendency to return to criminal offending, although studies differ in how it is measured (e.g., arrests, convictions, self-reported crime). In other words, psychopaths commit crimes again and again, regardless of the methods used to stop or rehabilitate them. According to Porter *et al.* (2000), research suggests psychopaths reoffend faster, violate parole sooner, and perhaps commit more institutional violence than nonpsychopaths. In one study (Serin, Peters, & Barbaree, 1990), the number of failures of male offenders released on unescorted temporary absence programs (furloughs) was examined. The failure rate for psychopaths was 37.5 percent, while none of the nonpsychopaths failed. The failure rate during parole was also examined. While 7 percent of nonpsychopaths violated parole conditions, 33 percent of the psychopaths violated their conditions. In another study (Serin & Amos, 1995), 299 male offenders were followed for up to eight years after their release from a federal prison. Sixty-five percent of the psychopaths were convicted of another crime within three years, compared with a reconviction rate of 25 percent for nonpsychopaths. Quinsey, Rice, and Harris (1995) found that within six years of release from prison, more than 80 percent of the psychopaths convicted as sex offenders had violently recidivated, compared with a 20 percent recidivism rate for nonpsychopathic sex offenders. Recidivism was measured by either arrests or convictions for a violent offense. Richards, Casey, and Lucente (2003) found the PCL-R and the PCL:SV measures of persistent offending history, in conjunction with high scores on the PCL-R, are probably two of the most powerful predictors of violent recidivism available anywhere. In fact, the PCL-R is a strong predictor of recidivism even when the offender's criminal history is not known to the examiner (Hemphill & Hare, 2004; Hemphill, Hare, & Wong, 1998).

High recidivism rates are also characteristic of psychopathic adolescent male offenders. Shortly, though, we will discuss the controversy over whether juvenile psychopathy even exists. According to Gretton *et al.* (2001), these offenders are more likely than other adolescent offenders to escape from custody, violate the conditions of probation, and commit nonviolent and violent offenses over a five-year follow-up period. The high recidivism rates among adult and juvenile offenders have prompted some researchers to conclude that there is "nothing the behavioral sciences can offer for treating those with psychopathy" (Gacono *et al.*, 1997, p. 119). This is partly because psychopaths tend to "be unmotivated to alter their problematic behavior and often lack insight into the nature and extent of their psychopathology" (Skeem, Edens, & Colwell, 2003, p. 26). As we note below, other researchers are more optimistic.

THE FEMALE PSYCHOPATH

Overall, research suggests that there are significantly fewer female than male psychopaths, both in the general population and among persons convicted of crime (Bolt, Hare, Vitale, & Newman, 2004; Rogstad & Rogers, 2008). In the general population, the estimated prevalence of psychopathy among males is 1 percent (Hare, 2003), but the prevalence is significantly less among females (Nicholls, Ogloff, Brink, & Spidel, 2005). Salekin, Rogers, and Sewell (1997) reported that the prevalence rate of psychopathy for female offenders in a jail setting was 15.5 percent, compared with the 25 percent to 30 percent prevalence rate estimated for male offenders. In another study, Salekin, Rogers, Ustad, and Sewell (1998) found, using a PCL-R cutoff score of 29, that 12.9 percent of their sample of 78 female inmates qualified as psychopaths. In a more recent investigation involving 528 adult women incarcerated in the state of Wisconsin, Vitale, Smith, Brinkley, and

Newman (2002) report that only 9 percent of their participants could be classified as psychopaths, using the recommended cutoff score of 30 on the PCL-R. Finally, Hare (2003) found that about 7.5 percent of female offenders and 15 percent of male offenders meet the recommended cutoff score of 30 on the PCL-R. All these studies consistently indicate that females generally score lower on the PCL-R than males.

Hare's PCL and PCL-R have been developed almost exclusively on male criminal psychopaths. Some studies using the PCL-R suggest that female criminal psychopaths may demonstrate different behavioral patterns than male criminal psychopaths (Nicholls & Petrila, 2005; Vitale, Smith, Brinkley, & Newman, 2002). Although the data are far from conclusive, female psychopaths, compared with male psychopaths, appear to demonstrate a lack of realistic long-term goals, have numerous marital relationships, engage in a wide range of crime, and show a greater tendency to be sexually promiscuous (Grann, 2000; Salekin et al., 1997; Warren et al., 2003). We urge caution in interpreting this last characteristic, because men and women are often judged differently on this criterion. Female psychopaths also may not express the same emotional processing abnormalities as male psychopaths (Sutton, Vitale, & Newman, 2002). It appears that the affective features of psychopathy are especially important in identifying female psychopaths, with high levels of callousness and low levels of empathy clearly distinguishing them from nonpsychopathic women (Jackson, Rogers, Neumann, & Lambert, 2002; Rogstad & Rogers, 2008).

There is also some evidence that female psychopaths are less aggressive and violent than male psychopaths (Mulder, Wells, Joyce, & Bushnell, 1994) and may begin their offending careers later than male psychopaths (Hart & Hare, 1997). Female psychopaths may also recidivate less often than male psychopaths (Salekin et al., 1998). In fact, the evidence suggests that psychopathic female inmates may have recidivism rates that are no different than the recidivism rates reported for nonpsychopathic female inmates (Salekin et al., 1998).

Similar to gender differences in criminality on the whole, the reported gender distinctions in psychopathy are probably due to a number of social influences and neuropsychological differences that occur across the developmental trajectory of males and females. Women and men arrive at crime via different pathways, and we must often look for different explanations for their crimes (Salisbury & Van Voorhis, 2009). As a result of these differences, females with psychopathic characteristics might rely on different tactics than males to reach the same goals (Nicholls & Petrila, 2005).

The more recent research utilizing the PCL-R shows considerable promise in identifying gender differences in psychopathy, but many researchers and experts urge caution before the instrument is adopted for clinical or diagnostic use with women (Nicholls et al., 2005). Rogers (2000) admonishes that "psychologists are on safest ground if they limit their risk predictions on the PCL-R to White males with criminal histories" (p. 600). For the most part, however, there is emerging evidence that psychopathy as measured by the PCL-R has a significant relationship with antisocial behavior in adult females. To date, though, the research on female juvenile psychopaths is less convincing, as we will see shortly.

RACIAL/ETHNIC DIFFERENCES

Kosson, Smith, and Newman (1990) noticed that most measures of psychopathy have been developed using white inmates as subjects. In their research, they found that psychopathy, as measured by Hare's PCL, does exist in African American male inmates in a pattern that resembles white male inmates. However, Kosson et al. found one important difference. The African American criminal psychopaths tended to be less impulsive than white criminal psychopaths. This finding raises some questions as to whether the PCL is entirely appropriate to use with African American inmates. On the other hand, Jennifer Vitale *et al.* (2002) found no significant racial differences in the scores and distributions of female psychopaths. More specifically, Vitale *et al.* report that 10 percent of the 248 incarcerated Caucasian women who participated in their study reached the cutoff scores of 30 or higher on the PCL-R compared with 9 percent of the 280 incarcerated African American women who had similar scores.

A meta-analysis by Jennifer Skeem, John Edens, Jacqueline Camp, and Lori Colwell (2004) supports the conclusion that the differences between blacks and whites are minimal. They concluded that "Our finding that Blacks and Whites do not meaningfully differ in their levels of core psychopathic traits is consistent with community-based findings for self-report measures of psychopathy and clinical diagnoses of antisocial personality disorder" (p. 505). Questions remain, however, as to the potential differences among other minority or disadvantaged groups.

Some researchers have raised the intriguing and serious issue of whether the stigmatizing diagnosis of psychopathy is likely to be used in a biased manner among minority or disadvantaged groups (Edens, Petrila, & Buffington-Vollum, 2001; Skeem, Edens, & Colwell, 2003; Skeem, Edens, Sanford, & Colwell,2003). In essence, the consequence of being diagnosed with psychopathy is becoming more serious (Skeem, Edens, *et al.*, 2003). As pointed out by Skeem, Edens, and Colwell (2003), Canada and the United Kingdom use the diagnosis of psychopathy to support indeterminate detention for certain classes of offenders. Furthermore, "there is evidence that psychopathy increasingly is being used as an aggravating factor in the sentencing phase of U.S. death penalty cases, where it has been argued that the presence of these personality traits renders a defendant a 'continuing threat to society' " (Skeem *et al.*, 2003, p. 17). Edens, Petrila, and Buffinton-Vollum (2001) suggest that perhaps the PCL-R should be excluded from capital sentencing until more solid research on its ability to predict future dangerousness in minority and disadvantaged individuals is established.

JUVENILE PSYCHOPATHY

As we have seen, one of the serious shortcomings of the extensive research conducted on psychopathy is that it has focused almost exclusively on white, adult males (Frick, Bodin, & Barry, 2000). Consequently, research on juvenile (adolescent and child) psychopathy is limited, but it is rapidly growing. There is substantial evidence that male criminal psychopaths begin their offending patterns at a very early age (Rutter, 2005). However, attempts to apply the label "psychopathy" to juvenile populations "raise several conceptual, methodological, and practical concerns related to clinical/forensic practice and juvenile/criminal justice policy" (Edens, Skeem, Cruise, & Cauffman, 2001, p. 54). Some debate has focused on whether psychopathy can or should be applied to juveniles at all. Can features of adult psychopathy be found in children and adolescents in the first place? Others are concerned that—even if psychopathy can be identified in adolescents—the label may have too many negative connotations. More specifically, the label implies that the prognosis for treatment is poor, a high rate of offending and recidivism can be expected, and the intrinsic and biological basis of the disorder means little can be done outside of biological interventions. This may lead those working in the juvenile justice system to give up on the juveniles so labeled. A third debate contends that psychopathy assessments of youths must achieve a high level of confidence before they can be employed in the criminal justice system (Seagrave & Grisso, 2002). We will discuss these assessments shortly.

Can Juvenile Psychopathy be Identified?

Another major problem of identifying juvenile psychopaths is that psychopathy—if it exists in this age group—may be very difficult to measure reliably because of the transient and constantly changing developmental patterns across the life span. Many clinicians and researchers have resisted any trend to search for psychopathy in juveniles, noting that features of the adult psychopath simply represent normal adolescent development. In other words, adolescents often appear callous and narcissistic, sometimes to hide their own fear and anxiety. They are often impulsive and engage in sensation-seeking behaviors, and many are not particularly good at long-range planning. In reality, these and other psychopathic-like characteristics represent either a passing phase in the difficult transition to adulthood and/or the adolescent's "cover" to make himself or herself appear noncaring. For other children, psychopathic-like characteristics might be indicative of physical or sexual abuse. Children in abusive homes often demonstrate an abnormally restricted range of emotions that are similar to the emotional characteristics of psychopathy. Actually, these symptoms are the child's way of coping with a very stressful home environment (Seagrave & Grisso, 2002). Furthermore, "Some adolescent behavior may . . . appear psychopathic by way of poor anger control, lack of goals, and poor judgment, but is actually influenced by parallel developmental tasks encountered by most adolescents" (Seagrave & Grisso, 2002, p. 229). Going against the rules is part of many adolescents' attempts to gain autonomy from adult dominance, such as found in adolescent-limited offending.

Nevertheless, certain problem characteristics in children and adolescents—for example, conduct problems, hyperactivity, impulsivity, and attention difficulties—resemble features of the adult psychopath and suggest that the term *juvenile psychopath* may have some validity. On the other hand, these characteristics may simply represent disorders such as conduct disorder (CD) or oppositional defiant disorder (ODD) that are distinct from psychopathy. As Cruise, Colwell, Lyons, and Baker (2003) have emphasized, to be useful, the construct of juvenile psychopathy must be distinguished from other diagnoses. It appears, though, that current research is rapidly approaching a distinct construct. For example, a multidimensional model that identifies callous and unemotional traits (C/U), narcissism, and impulsivity has been proposed and tested as indicative of childhood psychopathy (Barry, Barry, Deming, & Lochman, 2008; Fite, Stoppelbein, & Greening, 2009; Pardini & Loeber, 2008).

Ethical Considerations

On the whole, though, there is considerable concern about misuse of labels suggesting psychopathy by juvenile justice professionals, including judges, youth detention workers, and treatment providers. Because of the widespread assertion that psychopaths are highly resistant to treatment, an adolescent "psychopath" accused of a crime—or even a youth demonstrating psychopathic characteristics—is more likely to be transferred to the adult court system rather than kept in the juvenile system. In the latter, treatment is more likely to be available once the youth has been adjudicated delinquent. Until very recently, a 16- or 17-year-old juvenile labeled a psychopath also was more likely to be sentenced to death in some states (Edens, Guy, & Fernandez, 2003). However, in 2005, the U.S. Supreme Court ruled that juveniles who committed their crimes at these ages could not be sentenced to death (*Roper v. Simmons*). The court had previously set 16 as the minimum age at which juveniles were eligible for the death penalty (*Thompson v. Oklahoma,* 1989). Nevertheless, juveniles who are tried in criminal courts continue to be subjected to punitive criminal sanctions, including life sentences.

Even when juveniles are kept in the juvenile system and placed in treatment centers, though, the label "psychopath" can become a self-fulfilling prophecy with treatment providers who may be unlikely to expend considerable effort on a seemingly hopeless case. However, supporters of the construct of juvenile psychopathy argue that treatment providers should have that information at their disposal, both to make management decisions regarding custody and programming and to fashion the type of treatment that could be effective. Researchers are beginning to identify such treatment (e.g., Spain, Douglas, Poythress, & Epstein, 2004), as we discuss later in the chapter. In essence, if there is a distinct difference between psychopathic youth and nonpsychopathic youth, supporters claim it is critical that knowledge of this difference be communicated to those who work most closely with them. Additionally, it is helpful to identify and promote "protective factors" in a child's developmental sequence that might help insulate him or her from psychopathy (Salekin & Lochman, 2008). Supporters also believe there is wisdom in targeting for early intervention in a subgroup of adolescents who otherwise might become career criminals (Skeem & Cauffman, 2003). This presumes, of course, that youth are correctly identified, which leads to the issue of reliability and validity.

Psychopathic assessments of youths must achieve a high level of confidence before they can be used in the criminal justice system, where individuals face dire consequences (Seagrave & Grisso, 2002). For example, if an assessment instrument is designed to measure juvenile psychopathy, then there must be considerable research to demonstrate that it, in fact, does measure what it says it measures. Many experts maintain that, with reference to "juvenile psychopathy," we are not near that point yet.

Even so, over the past 15 years, knowledge regarding the theoretical and empirical applicability of juvenile "psychopathy" has expanded at a fast pace (Salekin, Leistico, Trobst, Schrum, & Lochman, 2005). The research has demonstrated that the diagnostic label is linked to conduct disorder (Forth & Burke, 1998; Frick, 1998; Lynam, 1998) and higher levels of delinquency and police contacts (Corrado, Vincent, Hart, & Cohen, 2004; Falkenbach, Poythress, & Heide, 2003; Murrie, Cornell, Kaplan, McConville, & Levy-Elkon, 2004; Salekin, Ziegler, Larrea, Anthony, & Bennett, 2003). Only about 25 percent of juveniles with conduct disorders show psychopathic tendencies (Blair *et al.*, 2006). Forth and Burke (1998) report that children and adolescents with psychopathic traits differ from other antisocial youngsters in terms of the age of onset of their behavior problems, the number of violent acts committed, the seriousness of their offenses, and their recidivism rates. Consequently, it appears that those youth who demonstrate psychopathic characteristics also seem to be heavily involved in antisocial behavior, at least hinting that the psychopathic label may have some validity.

Psychopathic Traits in Juvenile Delinquents

A number of researchers have reported finding the traits associated with psychopathy in children and adolescents, particularly juvenile delinquents. In a study examining the prevalence rate of psychopathic tendencies in children, Skilling, Quinsey, and Craig (2001) found that 4.3 percent of a sample of over 1,000 boys in grades 4–8 could be classified as psychopathic on every measure employed in the study. Dåderman and Kristiansson (2003) found that 59 percent of their sample of violent juvenile offenders qualified as psychopaths. Similarly, Brandt, Kennedy, Patrick, and Curtain (1997), using a sample of incarcerated adolescents with persistent violent offending histories, reported that they could identify 37 percent of the sample as psychopathic. By contrast, Campbell, Porter, and Santor (2004) discovered that only 9 percent of their sample of incarcerated adolescent offenders could be classified as psychopaths. These authors note, though, that the juveniles they studied were primarily nonviolent in nature, with only 15 percent having a history of violent offending. It is clear, therefore, that the sample used in a study, as well as the measuring instrument itself, will strongly influence the number of identifiable psychopathic traits within a given group of adolescents.

Measures of Juvenile Psychopathy

It is not surprising that the avid interest in psychopathy, including juvenile psychopathy, would lead to the development of a variety of instruments designed to measure it, or at least psychopathic characteristics. Several instruments for measuring juvenile psychopathy have been developed in recent years, including the *Psychopathy Screening Device* or the PSD (Frick & Hare, 2001; Frick, O'Brien, Wootton, & McBurnett, 1994), the *Childhood Psychopathy Scale* or the CPS (Lynam, 1997), the *Youth Psychopathic Traits Inventory* or YPI (Andershed, Kerr, Stattin, & Levander, 2002), and the *Psychopathy Checklist: Youth Version* or the PCL:YV (Forth, Kosson, & Hare, 2003). Although originally developed as research instruments rather than for diagnosis purposes in clinics or for the courts, they are rapidly becoming available to forensic clinical examiners for use in their private practice and their consulting work with the courts and the juvenile justice system.

All the measures have some difficulty because juvenile psychopaths—if they exist—are unlikely to give accurate or honest self-reports about their emotions, thoughts, or behavior. The PCL:YV relies on an interview that has some specific questions to ask, plus collateral and other written data. Because of the interview and collateral data requirement, the PCL:YV requires extensive training to administer and is time consuming. In addition, the PCL:YV is more research based and measures four dimensions of psychopathy. In contrast, the PCS and the YPI rely heavily on self-reports, while the APSD and CPS are designed to obtain information from teachers, parents, and the child or adolescent himself or herself.

The PCL:YV (youth version) is a 20-item rating scale adapted from the adult PCL-R (Hare, 1991, 2003) for use with juveniles. It adopts the four-factor model approach, scoring individuals on interpersonal, affective, behavioral, and antisocial factors. The PCL-YV has been subjected to extensive research, which suggests that it has adequate reliability and validity (for a review, see Vincent, 2006). However, caution is urged in its use. In particular, it appears to have limited ability to identify a meaningful relationship to psychopathy and antisocial behavior in adolescent girls (Odgers, Reppucci, & Moretti, 2005; Sevecke, Pukrop, Kosson, & Krischer, 2009; Vincent, Odgers, McCormick, & Corrado, 2008). It appears, therefore, that further investigations into the capacity of the PCL:YV to distinguish psychopathy in girls is critical before it can become a useful forensic tool.

There have been several attempts to compare various measures of juvenile psychopathy in terms of their validity and reliability (Farrington, 2005a). Preliminary research so far indicates that the measures do not have much in common, but more research needs to be done before conclusions can be drawn. One recent study shows considerable promise. Lynam and his colleagues (2007) were interested in discovering whether psychopathy scores on the CPS at age 13 predicted psychopathy scores on PCL:SV (short or screening version) at age 24. Surprisingly, the researchers determined that the CPS did a decent job of predicting PCL:SV scores. These results suggest that psychopathy not only appears stable across stages of development but also implies that juvenile psychopathy appears similar to adult psychopathy in many ways.

BIOLOGICAL FACTORS AND PSYCHOPATHY

There is belief among the general public that psychopathic tendencies are caused exclusively by social factors, such as abuse and poor upbringing. However, researchers have implicated a variety of biological factors as well. Contemporary research favors the view that psychopathic behavior results from a complex interaction between neuropsychological and learning or socialization factors.

Genetic Factors

There is emerging evidence that genetics may play a role in the development of psychopathy (Blonigen, Carlson, Krueger, & Patrick, 2003; Blonigen et al., 2005; Viding, Blair, Moffitt, & Plomin, 2005). For example, some evidence suggests that temperament linked to low arousal and fear responses is associated with psychopathy (Frick & Morris, 2004). A temperament of this nature may disrupt the formation of guilt, conscience, or concern about punishment.

The overall influence of genetics on psychopathy is not large, but it seems large enough to draw the increasing attention of developmental and genetic researchers, especially those investigators interested in twin studies. Blair et al. (2006) believe that genetic contributions may play a significant role in the emotional dysfunction frequently found in psychopaths. That is, heredity may contribute significantly to the underarousal and low emotional responsiveness of psychopaths. However, at this point in our knowledge, we appear to be a long way off from a genetic account of psychopathy.

Neurophysiology and Psychopathy

Although the research on psychopaths in recent years has focused on the psychometric characteristics of psychopaths, the current trend in psychopathy research is the investigation of neuropsychological factors involved in determining their behavior (Vien & Beech, 2006). Neuropsychological indicators (called **markers**) have been repeatedly found in psychopaths, as reflected in electrodermal (skin conductance) measures and cardiovascular and other nervous system indices (Fishbein, 2001; Morgan & Lilienfeld, 2000). It is important, therefore, to become familiar with additional neuropsychological vocabulary and basic structures of the nervous system.

BASIC NEUROPHYSIOLOGICAL CONCEPTS AND TERMINOLOGY   The human nervous system can be divided into two major parts, either on the basis of structure or function. The structural division—the way it is arranged physically—is perhaps the clearest distinction. The central nervous system (CNS) and the peripheral nervous system (PNS) are the two principal parts. The CNS comprises the brain and spinal cord, and the PNS comprises all nerve cells (called neurons) and nerve pathways located outside the CNS (see **Table 3**). In other words, those nerves that leave the spinal cord and brain stem and travel to specific sites in the body belong to the peripheral (outside) nervous system. This includes all the nerves connecting the muscles, skin, heart, glands, and senses to the CNS.

The basic function of the PNS is to bring all the outside information to the CNS, where it is processed. Once the CNS has processed information, it relays the interpretation back to the PNS if action is necessary. When you place your finger on a hot object, the PNS relays this raw data (it is not yet pain) to the CNS, which interprets the datum as the sensation of pain, and in return, relays a command to the PNS to withdraw the finger. The PNS cannot interpret; it only transmits information to the CNS and carries communications back. In the following pages, we will consider the significance of each of these systems to the diagnosis of psychopathy.

TABLE 3   Divisions of the Human Nervous System

I. Central nervous system (CNS)
  A. Brain
  B. Spinal cord
II. Peripheral nervous system (PNS)
  A. Skeletal nervous system (communicates with voluntary muscles)
  B. Autonomic nervous system
    1. Parasympathetic nervous system (relaxes and deactivates after emergencies)
    2. Sympathetic nervous system (activates for emergencies)

Central Nervous System Differences

Structurally, the CNS consists of the brain and spinal cord. Interpretation, thoughts, memories, and images all occur in the cerebral cortex (the highest center of the brain). It is the processing center for stimulation and sensations received from the outside world and the body via the PNS. The cerebral cortex, which is the outer surface of the human brain, contains more than 100 billion nerve cells (called neurons) (Hockenbury & Hockenbury, 2004; *Scientific American,* 1999). Each neuron has a complicated communication link to numerous other neurons, creating an extremely complex and poorly understood communications network. Although the physical structure of the brain does not directly concern us, the electrical circuitry and arousal properties of the cortex are relevant in understanding the neuropsychological characteristics of the psychopath.

Hemisphere Asymmetry and Deficiency

The human brain can be divided anatomically into two cerebral hemispheres—a right and a left. These two cerebral hemispheres seem to coexist in some sort of reciprocally balancing relationship in cortical functioning and information processing. For most individuals, the right hemisphere specializes in nonverbal functions, whereas the left specializes in verbal or language functions. Furthermore, the left-hemisphere processes information in an analytical, sequential fashion. Language, for example, requires sequential cognition, and the left seems to be the best equipped for this operation. The right hemisphere, on the other hand, seems to process information holistically and more globally. For example, the right is involved in the recognition of faces, a complicated process requiring the processing of information all at once or simultaneously. Thus, the right and left hemispheres are two functionally differentiated information processing systems.

In addition to information processing, research is now finding that these two cerebral hemispheres also make different contributions to human emotions (Jacobs & Snyder, 1996; Tomarken, Davidson, Wheeler, & Doss, 1992). The right hemisphere appears to be particularly important in the understanding and communication of emotion (Kosson, *et al.,* 2002; Wheeler, Davidson, & Tomarken, 1993). The left seems to be closely tied to self-inhibiting processes, in contrast with the right which appears to be more spontaneous and impulsive (Tucker, 1981). Furthermore, the two hemispheres must have a balance of contribution from each for normal judgment and appropriate self-control (Tucker, 1981), and self-regulation of emotion (Tomarken *et al.,* 1992). These control and judgment processes are especially prevalent in the frontal lobes (front sections of the brain).

Hare (Hare, 1998; Hare & Connolly, 1987; Hare & McPherson, 1984) hypothesizes that criminal psychopaths manifest an abnormal or unusual balance between the two hemispheres, both in language processing and in emotional or arousal states, which he calls **hemisphere asymmetry.** Hare notes that criminal psychopaths are often strikingly inconsistent with their verbalized thoughts, feelings, and intentions. Criminal psychopaths seem to be highly peculiar in the organization of certain perceptual and cognitive processes. Their left hemisphere seems, in some ways, deficient in linguistic processing because they do not rely on the verbal sequential operations to the extent that a majority of individuals do. Hare (1998) also hypothesizes that as the language task increased in complexity, nonpsychopathic persons rely more and more on the left hemisphere to process the information, while psychopaths rely more on the right hemisphere. Recent research supports this hypothesis (Lorenz & Newman, 2002).

There is also some research indicating that psychopaths are less accurate than nonpsychopaths at reading emotional expressions portrayed by faces. More specifically, psychopaths appear to be less accurate than nonpsychopaths in facial emotional recognition under conditions designed to promote reliance on left-hemisphere processing (Kosson et al., 2002). These data are in support of the *left-hemisphere activation hypothesis* (Kosson, 1998), which states that psychopaths exhibit deficits on a variety of tasks that require activation of the left hemisphere.

Since language plays a very important role in the self-regulation of behavior, one of the contributing factors in the extremely impulsive, episodic behavior of psychopaths may reside in some deficiency in their use of internal language. This characteristic was pointed out some time ago by Flor-Henry (Flor-Henry, 1973; Flor-Henry & Yeudall, 1973), who was convinced that psychopathy is closely linked to left-hemispheric language dysfunction. There has been some research to suggest that the right hemisphere of psychopaths may be deficient as well (Herpertz & Sass, 2000). Research by Day and Wong (1996) and Silberman and Weingartner (1996), for example, suggests that many psychopaths have impairments in the right hemisphere that prevents them from experiencing emotions as strongly as the nonpsychopath population. Other researchers have found evidence that psychopaths exhibit an **emotional paradox.** "That is, psychopaths demonstrate normal appraisal of emotional cues and situations in the abstract (i.e., verbal discussion), but they are deficient in using emotional cues to guide their judgments and behavior in the process of living" (Lorenz & Newman, 2002, p. 91). In other words, psychopaths seem to be able to talk about emotional cues but lack the ability to use them effectively in the real world. This deficiency seems to be due to processing problems located in the left hemisphere (Bernstein, Newman, Wallace, & Luh, 2000; Lorenz & Newman, 2002). Nachshon (Nachshon, 1983; Nachshon & Denno, 1987) points out that many studies have found that a disproportionate percentage of violent, repetitive offenders have left-hemispheric dysfunction. Researchers in Germany had found similar results (Pillmann et al., 1999).

Frontal Neuropsychological Studies

Some studies suggest that psychopaths may also suffer from frontal lobe problems or dysfunctions (Kiehl, 2006; Morgan & Lilienfeld, 2000; Sellbom & Verona, 2007). The frontal lobe refers to that section of the cerebral cortex we commonly call the forehead. The frontal lobes (there are two) are believed to be responsible for the "higher level" cognitive functions of abstraction, decision making, cognitive flexibility, foresight, the regulation of impulses, and the control of appropriate behavior (Ishikawa et al., 2001). In other words, the frontal lobes perform the "executive functions" of the human brain. **Executive functions** refer to higher-order mental abilities involved in goal-directed behavior. Executive functions include organizing behavior, memory, inhibition processes, and planning strategies. Research has been consistent in demonstrating that prefrontal damage results in poor decision making, reduced autonomic functioning, and a psychopathic-like personality (Yang *et al.*, 2005).

Gorenstein (1982) and Newman, Patterson, and Kosson (1987) report findings that indicate psychopaths may have defects in frontal lobe processing. On the other hand, research by Hare (1984), Hoffman, Hall, and Bartsch (1987), and Sutker and Allain (1983) failed to support the frontal lobe hypothesis. These equivocal results prompted Ishikawa *et al.* (2001, p. 423) to assert, "Clearly, research on the frontal dysfunction hypothesis in psychopaths is far from conclusive." However, a recent meta-analysis of the extant research on the topic by Morgan and Lilienfeld (2000) *suggests* that psychopaths, as a group, do show executive function deficits, which may result in faulty impulse control, judgment, and planning under certain conditions.

Cathy Widom (Widom, 1978; Widom & Newman, 1985) points out that the mixed research results may stem from differences in the population of psychopaths being tested. Specifically, Widom (1978) found that psychopaths recruited from newspaper advertisements did not demonstrate the same level of frontal lobe deficits as incarcerated psychopaths. Widom speculated that "successful psychopaths" (community-based psychopaths who escaped conviction of their offenses and who answered the ad) probably had better functioning frontal lobes for controlling their behavior than the "unsuccessful" institutionalized psychopaths. Consistent with Widom's results, Ishikawa *et al.* (2001) discovered that successful psychopaths do not show the same psychophysiological or neuropsychological deficits as unsuccessful psychopaths. Overall, the researchers found that successful psychopaths exhibited stronger and better-organized executive functions than either the unsuccessful psychopaths or the controls used in the study. Interestingly, the *unsuccessful* psychopaths did show most of the neuropsychological characteristics reported in the previous studies conducted over the past 30 years.

At this point, the evidence suggests that the frontal lobes may play an important role in explaining some of the observed behavioral differences between psychopaths and nonpsychopaths. Furthermore, frontal lobe dysfunction may not be simply limited to psychopaths but may be a feature that is characteristic of many other types of offenders (Raine, 1993).

Amygdala Dysfunction

Psychopaths clearly demonstrate some problems in emotional processing. The frontal lobe is most often associated with this observation, as we have seen. Some researchers are beginning to believe that another neurological structure responsible for this dysfunction may be the amygdala (Crowe & Blair, 2008; Kiehl, 2006). The amygdala is an almond-shaped cluster of neurons in the brain responsible for emotions such as fear, anger, and disgust. The amygdala is also involved in learning and short-term memory, especially in those learning situations involving high emotions.

Kiehl *et al.* (2001) found that psychopaths exhibited lower amygdala activity during an emotional processing task when compared with criminal nonpsychopaths and noncriminal controls. Similar findings were reported by Müller *et al.* (2003). With further research, the relationship between amygdala and learning might emerge as a highly significant factor in understanding the emotional behavior of the psychopath.

Stimulation Seeking

Herbert Quay (1965) suggested that much of the psychopath's behavior represents an extreme form of stimulation seeking. He hypothesized that psychopaths do not receive the full impact of sensations from the environment and thus are always craving more. Therefore, in order to get the optimal amount of stimulation necessary to keep the underaroused cerebral cortex satisfied, they must engage more frequently in various forms of excitement than the normal person.

Several early studies have supported Quay's hypothesis. For example, Wiesen (1965) found that psychopaths worked harder for visual (colored lights) and auditory (music on a radio) stimulation than did a group of nonpsychopaths. In a second experiment that provided continued bombardment of lights and music, Wiesen also demonstrated that nonpsychopaths worked harder than psychopaths to obtain three seconds of silence and relative darkness.

Skrzpek (1969) delineated psychopaths and "neurotic delinquents" on the basis of a behavior rating list for psychopathy and neuroticism developed by Quay (1964). He found that conditions that increased "cortical arousal" (e.g., where the subject was required to make difficult auditory discriminations) decreased preference for visual complexity in both the psychopathic and neurotic groups, but was most pronounced in the latter. On the other hand, a brief period of stimulus deprivation (presumably low cortical arousal) increased preference for complexity in both groups, but a significantly greater increase was shown by the psychopaths.

In an attempt to test Quay's hypothesis that deficient responsivity of the nervous system might account for pathological stimulation seeking, Whitehill, DeMyer-Gapin, and Scott (1976) conducted an experiment using 103 boring slides of "concrete facades of a modern college campus building." As subjects, the researchers used 55 institutionalized "disturbed" preadolescent boys. The professional staff at the institution rated eight boys psychopathic (antisocial) and eight neurotic. A group of seven "normal" noninstitutionalized adolescent boys, matched with the index subjects for age, were used as controls. The average age was 11.5 years. Results showed that the psychopathic and normal boys looked at the slides significantly less than the neurotic group. More important, the psychopathic preadolescents showed a significant decrease in viewing time earlier than the other groups, suggesting that they became bored more quickly than the other groups. Whitehall concluded that the data support the pathological stimulation-seeking hypothesis and favored a physiological ingredient in the formulation of psychopathy. In another project, Orris (1969) found that, compared with nonpsychopaths, psychopathic boys performed more poorly on a boring task requiring continuous attention and that they engaged more in boredom-relieving activities like singing or talking to themselves.

Optimal Arousal of the Cerebral Cortex

A number of theorists have postulated (e.g., Berlyne, 1960; Hebb, 1955; Fiske & Maddi, 1961) that organisms seek to maintain preferred or optimal levels of stimulation, with stimulation referring to the amount of sensation and/or information processed by the cortex. In effect, their theories argue for an inverted U-shaped function, with intermediate levels of stimulation most preferred and the extremes least preferred (see **Figure 1**). Insufficient amounts of stimulation lead to boredom, which can be reduced by an increase in stimulation-seeking behavior. On the other hand, exceptionally high levels of stimulation are also aversive and may promote behavior designed to avoid stimulation in an effort to bring the stimulus input to a more pleasurable level.

Cortical arousal appears to have a direct relationship with the amount of stimulation received by the cortex. Low stimulation produces a relatively low level of cortical arousal, whereas high levels of stimulation initiate high cortical arousal. To fall asleep, we must lower the cortex's

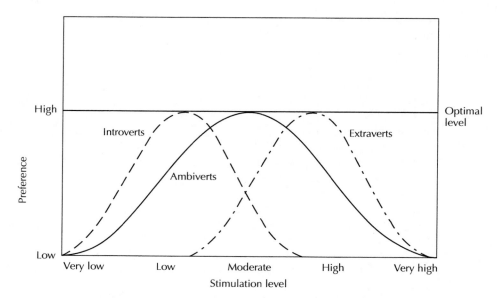

FIGURE 1 Optimal Levels of Stimulation for Ambiverts, Introverts, and Extraverts

arousal level by minimizing external and internal stimulation (noises, lights, thoughts). If we do not wish to fall asleep, but our cortical arousal is low (e.g., during a boring lecture), we seek excitement to increase the arousal level. On the other hand, if stimulation becomes excessive, such as via a blaring radio or the pandemonium of rush-hour traffic, we are distressed if unable to control the stimulus input. Some psychologists argue that much behavior can be explained as an attempt by the person to maintain optimal or just-right levels of stimulation—levels that are the most comfortable and pleasurable to the individual.

It is generally agreed that there are individual differences in the quality and quantity of stimulation necessary for each person to reach the optimum level of stimulation. Some of this individual difference may be attributed to certain physiological structures, particularly those found in the brain stem. Eysenck (1967), you will recall, hypothesized that personality differences are largely due to differential needs for stimulation, which are dictated by functional properties of the reticular formation.

The reticular formation can be conveniently divided into several anatomical areas. Chief among these is the reticular activating system (RAS), a tiny but complex nerve network located in the central portion of the brain stem. The RAS underlies our attentiveness to the world and acts as a sentinel that activates the cortex and keeps it alert. Sensory signals or inputs from all parts of the body must travel through the brain stem on their way to the processing center, the cortex. Inside the brain stem, they branch into two major pathways. One major pathway goes through a relay station known as the thalamus; the other travels through the RAS, which, in turn, alerts the cortex to incoming information being routed through the thalamic pathway. The RAS-generated arousal is nonspecific, in that it energizes the entire cortex and not any specific area. Therefore, any particular stimulation or sensation, from the outside world or from inside the body, has both a coded message (which travels through the thalamus) and a nonspecific arousing effect (which travels through the RAS).

The RAS can also decrease cortical arousal. If certain incoming stimuli are no longer significant or relevant, the cortex "tells" the RAS to filter out that particular group of stimuli. That process is called adaptation or **habituation.** Therefore, repetitive and insignificant stimuli are prevented by the RAS from unnecessarily bombarding the cortex with meaningless detail.

Contemporary research and theory suggest that the psychopath has a pathological need for excitement and thrills because of some deficiency in or excessive habituation property of the RAS. We emphasize the word *suggest* because, while the research seems consistent in demonstrating that psychopaths appear to have a strong need for stimulation, research has not clearly identified what neurophysiological mechanisms are involved. However, mainstream theory concerning the neurophysiological processes is as follows: The RAS either does not activate the cortex sufficiently to receive the full impact of the incoming information, or else it adapts too quickly, thereby shutting down the cortex's activation before it receives complete information. Either way, the psychopath is unable to reach optimal arousal levels with the same amount of stimulation that nonpsychopaths find adequately arousing. So, the psychopath engages in behaviors that society refers to as thrill-seeking, chancy, antisocial, or inappropriate, in order to reach satisfying optimal cortical arousal.

The general concept of arousal has been used interchangeably with cortical arousal throughout this chapter. In discussing psychopathy, many investigators refer to other forms of arousal, like autonomic (anxiety) or behavior arousal. Basically, these terms mean the same thing. Many states of activation or arousal involve overlapping systems (Korman, 1974). Thus, although there may be slightly different processes and mechanisms involved in different states of arousal, all must involve the heightened arousal levels of the cortex.

In an interesting experiment, Chesno and Kilmann (1975) tested the arousal hypothesis of psychopathy by manipulating stimulation variables (aversive white noise and shock) and personality variables (psychopaths, neurotics, and normals). Ninety male offenders incarcerated in a maximum security penitentiary were selected for the experiment by various criteria. Psychopaths were classified according to Cleckley's criteria. The procedure involved an avoidance learning task, with electric shock being administered for certain incorrect choices by the subject. During the avoidance learning task, each subject received 35, 65, or 95 decibels of white noise through earphones. (White noise is an auditory stimulus that sounds like a hissing radiator.)

If the arousal hypothesis is correct, the underaroused psychopath under low levels of stimulation should require some form of increased stimulation. Since errors in avoidance learning led to electric shock, psychopaths would be most likely to commit errors and benefit by the stimulation provided by the electric shock. Accordingly, as external stimulation increases (higher levels of white noise), the psychopath should have a decreased need for stimulation and, therefore, should learn to avoid the shock more effectively. The results of the study supported the hypothesis. Psychopaths made significantly more avoidance errors than the other groups as the stimulation decreased, which suggests that they prefer punishment to boredom. The finding may explain the well-known inability of psychopaths to benefit from punishment in situations low in stimulation, like prisons or even classrooms. It might even be that imprisoned psychopaths would "learn better" if the conditions under which they were incarcerated were more stimulating.

Therefore, psychopaths apparently do not learn to avoid aversive circumstances because of underarousal. However, if their arousal is increased, their avoidance learning should correspondingly increase. Furthermore, there is evidence that if incentives (e.g., money or other rewards) are used, avoidance learning in psychopaths also increases. In summarizing the research on this topic, Newman and his colleagues (Newman, 1987; Newman & Kosson, 1986; Newman, Patterson, Howland, & Nichols, 1990) have studied how rewards or incentives change the avoidance learning patterns of psychopaths. Their research suggests that, with adequate incentives, psychopaths become highly motivated to learn certain tasks and requirements. In fact, psychopaths under incentive conditions may learn better than nonpsychopaths. Raine (1993, p. 228) writes, "Psychopaths do indeed learn poorly when the reinforcer is physical or social punishment, but they do appear to learn well when (1) their arousal is increased, or (2) they are sufficiently motivated by financial incentives."

Peripheral Nervous System (PNS) Research

The PNS is subdivided into a *skeletal division,* comprising the motor nerves that innervate the skeletal muscles involved in body movement, and an autonomic division, which controls heart rate, gland secretion, and smooth muscle activity. Smooth muscles are those muscles found in the blood vessels and gastrointestinal system; they look smooth under a microscope in comparison with the skeletal muscles, which look striped or textured.

The autonomic segment of the PNS is extremely relevant to our discussion of the psychopath, because here, too, research has consistently uncovered a significant difference between the psychopath's and the general population's reactivity or responsiveness to stimuli. The autonomic division is especially important, because it activates emotional behavior and responsivity to stress and tension. It can be subdivided into the *sympathetic* and *parasympathetic systems.*

The sympathetic system is responsible for activating or arousing the individual for fight or flight before (or during) fearful or emergency situations. As you will recall, the psychopath displays a James Bond–like coolness, even in stressful situations. We might explain this in one of two ways. Either the sympathetic nervous system does not react sufficiently to stressful stimuli, or the parasympathetic system springs into action in the psychopath more rapidly than in nonpsychopaths. There is research support for both of these positions.

Before discussing in more detail the psychopath's autonomic nervous system, we should note the principles and techniques of measuring autonomic activity. Emotional arousal, which is largely under the control of the autonomic nervous system, can be measured by monitoring the system's activity, such as heart rate, blood pressure or volume, and respiration rate. The most commonly used physiological indicator of emotional arousal, however, is *skin conductance response* (SCR), also known as the *galvanic skin response* (GSR). Since SCR is the label most advocated by contemporary researchers (Lykken & Venables, 1971), it will be used throughout this chapter.

SCR is simply a measure of the resistance of the skin to conducting electrical current. Although a number of factors in the skin influence its resistance, perspiration seems to play a major role. Perspiration corresponds very closely to changes in emotional states and has, therefore, been found to be a highly sensitive indicator of even slight changes in the autonomic nervous system. Other things being equal, as emotional arousal increases, perspiration rate increases proportionately. Small changes in perspiration can be picked up and amplified by recording devices, known as polygraphs or physiographs. An increase in perspiration lowers skin resistance to electrical conductance. In other words, skin conductance (SC) increases as emotional arousal (anxiety, fear, and so on) increases.

We noted earlier that psychopaths lack the capacity to respond emotionally to stressful or fearful situations. Essentially, they give the impression of being anxiety-free, carefree, and cool, and they display a devil-may-care attitude. We would expect, therefore, that compared with the normal population, the psychopath has a comparatively underactive, underaroused autonomic nervous system. What has the research literature revealed? Consistently, investigators have reported low SC arousal in psychopaths (Fishbein, 2001). "Deficits in measures of SC arousal are believed to be associated with low autonomic arousal levels which are, in turn, related to low emotionality, poor conditionability, lack of empathy and remorse, and ability to lie easily" (Fishbein, 2001, p. 51). There is also some evidence that juvenile psychopaths show low SC arousal levels (Fung *et al.*, 2005). We now turn our attention to the division of the nervous system most responsible for SC arousal.

Autonomic Nervous System Research

In a pioneering study, Lykken (1957) hypothesized that since anxiety reduction is an essential ingredient in learning to avoid painful or stressful situations, and since the psychopath is presumed to be anxiety free, then the psychopath should have special difficulty learning to avoid unpleasant things. Recall that two characteristic features of psychopaths are their inability to learn from unpleasant experiences and their very high recidivism. Lykken carefully delineated his research groups according to Cleckley's criteria. His psychopaths (both males and females) were drawn from several penal institutions in Minnesota and were classified as either primary or neurotic psychopaths. College students comprised a third group of normals.

Lykken designed an electronic maze that subjects were expected to learn as well as possible in twenty trials. There were 20 choice points in the maze, each with four alternatives, with only one being the correct choice. Although three alternatives were incorrect, only one of these would give the subject a rather painful electric shock. Lykken was primarily interested in discovering how quickly subjects learned to avoid the shock, a process called **avoidance learning.** He reasoned that avoidance learning would be rewarded by the reduction of anxiety on encountering the correct choice point, but since psychopaths are presumably deficient in anxiety, their performance should be significantly worse than that of normals. The hypothesis was supported.

Prior to the maze portion of the experiment, Lykken measured the skin conductance changes of each subject while he or she tried to sit quietly for 30 to 40 minutes. During this time, the subjects would periodically hear a buzzer and occasionally receive a slight, brief electric shock several seconds after the buzzer. Eventually, the buzzer became associated with the shock. In normal individuals, the sound of the buzzer itself produced an anxiety response in anticipation of the electric shock (classical conditioning) and was reflected by a substantial increase in SCR. Psychopaths, however, were considerably less responsive to this stress. Furthermore, psychopaths were incapable of learning to avoid the painful electric shocks, while the normals learned significantly better.

Lykken's data indicate that psychopaths do in fact have an underresponsive autonomic nervous system and, as a result, do not learn to avoid aversive situations as well as most other people. More recent research continues to support these findings (Gottman, 2001; Ogloff & Wong, 1990). Does this provide at least a partial explanation for why psychopaths continue to get into trouble with the law, despite the threat of imprisonment?

Schachter and Latané (1964) followed up on Lykken's work by using similar apparatus and basic procedures, with the exception of one major revision. Each subject was run through the maze twice, once with an injection of a harmless saline solution, once with an injection of adrenaline, a hormone that stimulates physiological arousal. Subjects were prisoners selected on the basis of two criteria: how closely they approximated Cleckley's primary psychopath and how incorrigible they were, as measured by the number of offenses and time in prison. Prisoners high on both criteria were psychopaths; prisoners relatively low were nonpsychopaths.

Injections of adrenaline dramatically improved the performance of the psychopath in the avoidance learning task. In fact, with adrenaline injections, the psychopaths learned to avoid shocks more quickly than did normal prisoners with similar injections. On the other hand, when psychopaths had saline injections, they were as deficient in avoidance learning as Lykken's psychopaths.

Since anxiety is presumed to be a major deterrent to antisocial impulses, the manipulation of arousal or anxiety states by drugs may suggest policy implications for the effective treatment of convicted psychopaths. Specific drugs apparently have the potential to increase the emotional level of psychopaths to a point equivalent to the level of the general population.

Subsequent research by Hare (1965a, 1965b) found that primary psychopaths have significantly lower skin conductance while resting than do nonpsychopaths. Other researchers have reported similar results (Herpertz & Sass, 2000; Lorber, 2004). In a major study, Hare (1968) divided 51 inmates at the British Columbia Penitentiary into three groups—primary psychopaths, secondary psychopaths, and nonpsychopaths—and studied them under various conditions, while constantly monitoring their autonomic functioning. The experimental conditions also permitted the observation of a complex physiological response known as the *orienting response* (OR).

The OR is a nonspecific, highly complicated cortical and sensory response to strange, unexpected changes in the environment. The response may take the form of a turning of the head, a dilation of the eye, or a decrease in heart rate. It is made in an effort to determine what the change is. Pavlov referred to the OR as the "what-is-it" reflex. It is an automatic, reflexive accompaniment to any perceptible change, and it can be measured by various physiological indices. The OR produces, among other things, an increase in the analytical powers of the senses and the cortex.

Hare found that not only did psychopaths exhibit very little autonomic activity (skin conductance and heart rate), but also that they gave smaller ORs than did nonpsychopaths. His data suggest that psychopaths are less sensitive and alert to their environment, particularly to new and unusual events.

Hare later reported intriguing data relating to the heart or cardiac activity of the psychopath. The aforementioned conclusions were based on skin conductance data. When cardiovascular variables are considered, however, some apparent anomalies appear. While skin conductance is consistently low, cardiac activity (heart rate) in the psychopath is often as high as that found in the nonpsychopathic population (Hare & Quinn, 1971). Hare comments, "The psychopaths appeared to be poor electrodermal [skin conductance] conditioners but good cardiovascular ones" (Hare, 1976, p. 135). That is, although psychopaths do not learn to react to stimuli as measured by skin variables, it appears that they learn to react autonomically as well as nonpsychopaths when the heart rate is measured. Hare suggests that the psychopath might be more adaptive to stress when "psychophysiological defense mechanisms" are brought into play, thereby reducing the impact of stressful stimuli.

Hare and his colleagues designed experiments in which the heart rate could be monitored throughout the experimental session. In one experiment, a tone preceded an electric shock by about 10 seconds (Hare & Craigen, 1974). In anticipation of the shock, psychopaths exhibited a rapid acceleration of heartbeat, followed by a rapid deceleration of heart rate immediately before the onset of the noxious stimulus (a "normal" reaction is a gradual but steady increase in heart rate until the shock). However, their skin conductance remained significantly lower than that of nonpsychopaths. Therefore, psychopaths appear to be superior conditioners when cardiac activity is measured, indicating that they do indeed either learn or inherit autonomic adaptability to noxious stimuli. Hare suggests that this accelerative heart response is adaptive and helps the psychopath tune out or modulate the emotional impact of noxious stimuli. This, he speculates, may be the reason that skin conductance responses are relatively low in the psychopath.

Lykken (1955) also conducted experiments testing the performance of psychopaths on polygraph equipment. If psychopaths are generally underaroused, we would expect that lie detectors would be unable to differentiate their deceptive from their truthful responses, since polygraphs rely on physiological reactivity to questions. Also, psychopaths should have no trouble being deceptive, since they are typically adept at manipulating and deceiving others. Lykken's research confirmed these expectancies. Psychopaths emitted similar skin conductance responses, regardless of whether they were lying or telling the truth. Nonpsychopaths displayed significant differences in reactivity; their lie ratios, reflected by skin conductance, were larger than those of psychopaths. Because of the artificial atmosphere of the laboratory compared with real-life situations, particularly stressful ones, Lykken admonished against uncritical acceptance of his findings until further testing.

Few studies have since directly examined the relationship between psychopathy and lie detection. However, Raskin and Hare (1978) did reexamine the Lykken study, using more sophisticated equipment and better standardization for lie detection. Using 24 psychopathic prisoners and 24 nonpsychopathic prisoners, they found that both groups were equally easily detected at lying about a situation involving a $20 mock theft. This contradictory finding underscores the fact that fine-tuning is still needed if we are to understand the neurophysiological characteristics of the psychopath.

There is evidence, for example, that sufficiently aroused or motivated psychopaths will give physiological responses to interesting events that equal the responses of nonpsychopaths (Hare, 1968). On the other hand, when it comes to highly stressful, serious occasions, psychopaths appear to have incomparable skill at attenuating guilt or aversive reactions (Lykken, 1978). The simulated crime scene in the Raskin–Hare experiment was not only relatively unstressful; it may also have been regarded by the psychopath as an interesting "game." The acid test for the lie detection hypothesis will rest with carefully designed experiments under real-life, highly stressful situations. The present data do not justify firm conclusions. Christopher Patrick and his colleagues (Patrick, Bradley, & Lang, 1993) conducted a study designed to test in what ways the startle reflex action in psychopaths differs from that of the normal population. An example of a startle response is the eye-blink reflex in response to a puff of air. These researchers note that psychophysiological research on the psychopath has relied almost exclusively on skin conductance and cardiovascular measures. The researchers found that criminal psychopaths (measured by Hare's PCL-R) exhibited much lower startle responses under aversive conditions than nonpsychopaths. Their findings confirm previous research showing that criminal psychopaths give smaller autonomic responses under aversive conditions than do other nonpsychopathic offenders. Hare (1993, 1996) postulates that psychopaths suffer from a general "hypoemotionality." That is, it appears that psychopaths fail to experience the full impact of any kind of emotion—positive or negative. Psychopaths may be born with this hypoemotionality and that may account for their lack of remorse throughout their lifetimes.

In summary, the research reviewed thus far allows us to make four tentative conclusions about the autonomic functioning of the psychopath. First, psychopaths appear to be both autonomically and cortically underaroused, both under rest conditions and under some specific stress conditions. They are much more physiologically "drowsy" than nonpsychopaths. Second, because they lack the necessary emotional equipment, psychopaths appear to be deficient in avoidance learning, which might account partially for their very high recidivism rates. Third, some data suggest that if emotional arousal can be induced, such as by adrenaline, psychopaths can learn from past experiences and avoid normally painful or aversive situations, such as prison, embarrassment, or social censure. And fourth, with adequate incentives, such as monetary rewards, psychopaths can learn from past experiences and avoid aversive consequences as well as anyone.

Adrian Raine, in his excellent review of the relevant research, finds that many of these psychophysiological indicators discussed for psychopaths may be characteristic of repetitive, violent offenders in general. In fact, in reference to resting heart rate levels in *noninstitutionalized offenders,* he concludes, "This is probably the best replicated and most robust biological finding on antisocial behavior reported to date" (1993, p. 190).

We noted earlier that psychopaths are often profoundly affected by alcohol, even in small amounts. Alcohol is a general CNS depressant, decreasing arousal levels in the nervous system. Research indicates that underaroused psychopaths are already half asleep and "half in the bag"; alcohol has the general effect of "bagging" them completely. Therefore, we would expect not only that the psychopath would get intoxicated more rapidly than the nonpsychopath of comparable weight, but also would probably pass out sooner. We would also expect the psychopath to have few sleep difficulties. Steven Smith and Joseph Newman (1990) found that a higher percentage of criminal psychopaths have been polydrug users when compared with criminal nonpsychopaths. In addition, criminal psychopaths were particularly heavy alcohol abusers, and alcohol may have played a very significant role in prompting their extensive antisocial behavior.

Recent research has shown that adult psychopaths usually exhibit significant antisocial behavior in their childhoods (Seagrave & Grisso, 2002). It is reasonable, therefore, to expect researchers to begin searching the developmental trajectory of psychopathy in order to identify tomorrow's psychopaths. The next section examines what we currently know about the childhood of the psychopath. In light of our earlier discussion of juvenile psychopathy, though, we must be careful not to assume that adult psychopaths were necessarily psychopathic as juveniles.

CHILDHOOD OF THE PSYCHOPATH

We have discussed the behavioral descriptions and biopsychological components of psychopaths. Now, how did they get that way? Criminal behavior and other behavior problems are often assumed to be rooted in the home, usually in homes with conflict, inadequate discipline, or poor models. From our discussion of the biopsychological components of psychopaths, however, it is obvious that the answer is not that simple. Psychopathy seems to be a result of a highly complex interaction of biopsychological, social, and learning factors.

Cleckley (1976) was not convinced that any common precursors exist in the family backgrounds of psychopaths, even though relatively homogeneous classifications of psychopathy do exist. However, even if we accept that neurophysiological factors may be causal factors in the development of psychopathy, this does not mean they are hereditary. In fact, there is little evidence to support a *strong* genetic influence on psychopathy so far. It is possible, though, that psychopaths are born with a biological predisposition to develop the disorder and that this predisposition requires certain psychosocial factors before emerging, such as neglectful or abusive parenting. In line with the Eysenckian view, it could be that psychopaths have a nervous system that interferes with rapid conditioning and association between transgression and punishment. Because of this defect, the psychopath fails to anticipate punishment and, hence, feels no guilt (no conscience). As an alternative to the defect argument, it is possible that certain aspects of the psychopath's nervous system simply have not matured. Another possibility is that genetics, toxicity (e.g., lead paint or other sources of lead or other toxic substances) in utero or early childhood, birth difficulties, temperament, and other early developmental factors may affect certain processes in the nervous system, rendering some children vulnerable to develop conduct problems and psychopathic characteristics. These early contexts are especially prevalent for disadvantaged children. In addition, it should be emphasized that social factors play a major role in affecting these predispositions. "For example, a problematic temperamental predisposition at 6 months of age *and* low socioeconomic status at birth *and* early life experiences of physical abuse *and* peer rejection in early elementary school combine to predict clinically significant conduct-problem outcomes . . . in adolescence" (Dodge & Pettit, 2003, p. 354). Basically, persistent and serious offending that emerges early in life is driven partially by heritable influences that are strengthened or weakened during childhood and adolescence by parenting and other environmental factors (Tengström *et al.*, 2004).

Many researchers believe that psychopathy begins in childhood and continues throughout adulthood (Farrington, 2005b; Forth & Burke, 1998; Lynam, 1998), which has led to the intense interest in juvenile psychopathy (see Salekin & Lochman, 2008). According to the research, the childhood of the psychopath is littered with signals that something is amiss. Marshall and Cooke (1999) found that, compared with nonpsychopaths, psychopaths were more likely to have experienced family difficulties such as parental neglect, abuse, or even antipathy and indifference. They were also more likely to have experienced negative school experiences. Poor parental monitoring and discipline have also been identified in the backgrounds of psychopaths (Tolan, Gorman-Smith, & Henry, 2003). Lynam (1998) reports that children with symptoms of hyperactivity, impulsivity, and attention problems *and* conduct problems closely resemble psychopathic adults. We hasten to add, however, that while it may appear that all psychopaths have experienced all or some of these problems as children, this is not to say that children with similar problems are necessarily fledgling psychopaths.

"Few researchers have tried to investigate early childhood risk factors that might predict, influence, or cause psychopathy" (Farrington, 2005a, p. 493). And very few researchers have conducted prospective longitudinal investigations of those risk factors (Farrington, 2005a). Some retrospective studies (Koivisto & Haapasalo, 1996; Patrick, Zempolich, & Levenston, 1997) and some longitudinal studies (Lang, af Klinteberg, & Alm, 2002; Weiler & Widom, 1996) have found that PCL-R scores appear to be related to early childhood abuse. In one prospective longitudinal study of 400 London boys, ages 8–10 years, it was found that physical neglect, poor parental supervision, a disrupted family, large family size, a convicted parent, a depressed mother, and poverty predicted psychopathy scores at age 48 (Farrington, 2005b).

A fruitful avenue for exploring the childhood of the psychopath would be close examination of the life-course-persistent (LCP) offender described by developmental theorists. Developmental theory postulates that LCP offenders manifest antisocial behaviors across all kinds of conditions and situations in their childhoods. Neurologically, LCPs demonstrate a variety of minor neuropsychological disorders, such as difficult temperaments as infants, attention-deficit disorders or hyperactivity as children, and learning problems as adolescents. Socially, LCPs are rejected by peers during their preteen years and are annoying to adults. Emotionally, these children display virtually no empathy or concern for others, show very little bonding to family, and often are sadistic and manipulative. They are highly impulsive and lack insight. A careful reading of LCPs' developmental histories often shows a striking resemblance to the symptomology of criminal psychopaths. It should be emphasized, however, that only a modest number of LCPs probably qualify as full-blown psychopaths.

TREATMENT OF PSYCHOPATHS

The treatment and rehabilitation of criminal psychopaths has been shrouded with pessimism and discouragement. Hare (1996, p. 41) asserts, "There is no known treatment for psychopathy." A long line of research documents that *adult* psychopaths are not responsive to treatment, whether in prisons, in psychiatric treatment centers, or in the community (e.g., Hare *et al.*, 2000). Some commentary has indicated that psychotherapy or intervention with psychopaths is basically a waste of time. Gacono *et al.* (2001) concluded from their review that "simply stated, at this time there is no empirical evidence to suggest that psychopathy is treatable" (p. 111). O'Neill, Lidz, and Heilbrun (2003) remarked that "to date, there is no treatment for psychopathy that has been established as effective" (p. 300). In fact, some forms of treatment (e.g., milieu therapy) have been linked to higher rates of violent recidivism in psychopaths (Rice, Harris, & Cormier, 1992). Several studies indicate that psychopaths are either completely nonresponsive to treatment or play the treatment game well, pretending to cooperate but in actuality "conning" the treatment provider (Hare, 1996; Rice *et al.*, 1992; Porter *et al.*, 2000). Farrington (2005a) states that "it seems to be generally believed that psychopaths are difficult to treat because (a) they are an extreme, qualitatively distinct category; (b) psychopathy is extremely persistent throughout life; (c) psychopathy has biological causes which cannot be changed by psychosocial interventions; and (d) the lying, conning, and manipulativeness of psychopaths make them treatment resistant" (pp. 494–95).

Indeed, based on the research examining the effectiveness of various treatment programs, there does not appear to be any effective treatment program for adult psychopaths in the criminal justice system today. Hare (1996, p. 41) admonishes, though, "This does not necessarily mean that the egocentric and callous attitudes and behaviors of psychopaths are immutable, only that there are no methodologically sound treatments or 'resocialization' programs that have been shown to work with psychopaths." Other researchers take a decidedly different perspective and believe that untreatability statements concerning the psychopath are unwarranted (Salekin, 2002; Skeem, Monahan, & Mulvey, 2002; Skeem, Poythress, Edens, Lilienfeld, & Cale, 2003; Wong, 2000). There is some evidence that psychopaths who receive larger "doses" of treatment are less likely to demonstrate subsequent violent behavior than those who receive less treatment (Skeem, Poythress *et al.*, 2003). It should be mentioned that a vast majority of the research has focused on recidivism rates of male psychopathic offenders, and very little is known about the recidivism rates of female psychopathic offenders.

It is usually difficult to evaluate properly the effectiveness of programs designed to treat psychopaths because of their ability to manipulate the system. For example, many psychopaths volunteer for various prison treatment programs, show "remarkable improvement," and present themselves as model prisoners. They are skillful at convincing therapists, counselors, and parole boards that they have changed for the better. Upon release, however, there is a high probability that they will reoffend. In fact, there is some evidence to suggest that psychopaths who participate in therapy are more likely to engage in violent crime following the treatment than those psychopaths who did not receive treatment. Rice *et al.* (1992) investigated the effectiveness of an intensive therapeutic community program offered in a maximum security facility. The study was retrospective in that the researchers examined records and files 10 years after the program was completed. The results showed that psychopaths who participated in the therapeutic community exhibited higher rates of violent recidivism than did the psychopaths who did not. The results were the reverse for nonpsychopaths. Nonpsychopaths who received treatment were less likely to reoffend than nonpsychopaths who did not receive treatment.

Some critics of this study have remarked that the therapeutic community referred to was highly atypical of treatment programs in correctional facilities and has limited generalizability. Furthermore, the researchers themselves cautioned that the psychopaths used in the study were an especially serious group of offenders. Eighty-five percent had a history of violent crimes. Whether less serious psychopathic offenders will show similar results is unknown. The researchers conclude, "The combined results suggest that a therapeutic community is not the treatment of choice for psychopaths, particularly those with extensive criminal histories" (Rice *et al.*, 1992, p. 408). Hare (1996) suggests that group therapy and insight-oriented treatment programs—both of which were features of the program reviewed above—may help the psychopath develop better ways of manipulating and deceiving others.

Treatment of Children and Adolescents with Psychopathic Features

As we noted in the previous section, the treatment and rehabilitation of adult criminal psychopaths has been cloaked with pessimism and discouragement. While there are exceptions, very few treatment approaches have been successful. Unfortunately, little is known about the effectiveness of prevention and treatment methods for child and adolescent psychopathy (Farrington, 2005a, p. 494) or, as many researchers and clinicians prefer to say, children and adolescents with psychopathic tendencies or characteristics. Recall from our discussion of juvenile psychopathy that this is an extremely controversial area, with many preferring not to place such a negative label on juveniles.

Logically, it makes sense to hypothesize that children and adolescents with psychopathic features would respond more positively than psychopathic adults to prevention and treatment strategies because of their malleability. Consequently, researchers have begun to evaluate the effectiveness of (a) treatment programs designed specifically for juveniles with psychopathic characteristics, and (b) programs for youthful offenders that include those with psychopathic characteristics.

Studies have underscored the observations that children and adolescents with psychopathic features show distinct sets of emotional and cognitive deficits that lead to their violent and antisocial behavior. According to Salekin and Frick (2005), knowledge about these areas may be important for designing more individualized interventions for youths with psychopathic traits. For example, laboratory studies have revealed that children with conduct problems and high levels of callous-unemotional (CU) traits exhibit tendencies to respond better to reward-driven interventions and respond poorly to punishment-driven or fear-induced forms of intervention (Hawes & Dadds, 2005). These findings imply that children displaying high-reward drive and low fearful inhibitions should, compared with conduct-problem children *without* CU traits, respond well to parents who use reward-based strategies for changing behavior (e.g., praise, rewards, reinforcement tokens), but remain insensitive to other parental disciplinary practices (e.g., time-outs, forms of verbal or behavioral punishments, such as scolding or confiscating a favorite game). "The assessment of CU traits in addition to other established risk factors," Hawes and Dadds (2005) conclude, "may allow such children to be targeted with more individualized intervention" (p. 740).

Juveniles with psychopathic characteristics did not fare well in an outpatient *substance abuse* treatment program, however (O'Neill *et al.*, 2003). In this study, youths with higher scores on the PCL:YV were more likely to be rearrested and demonstrated higher attrition from the program, lower quality of participation, and more frequent use of alcohol and drugs while in the treatment program. The treatment program was based on a cognitive-behavioral model, whereby the adolescents would set goals and learn coping skills. They had daily group therapy sessions and twice-weekly one-hour sessions of individual therapy. While youths who scored low on the PCL:YV did benefit from the program, those with high scores did not. The reasons for the failure in this program are unknown.

On a more promising note, Salekin, Rogers, and Machin (2001) in their survey of over five hundred child clinical psychologists discovered that many of these clinicians reported that they were moderately to significantly successful in treating children and adolescents with psychopathic features. The treatment duration for these psychopathic youth averaged about 12 months. "After nearly 1 year of treatment these youths reportedly made marked improvement on such criteria as violence and recidivism" (Salekin *et al.*, 2001, p. 192). The clinicians estimated that approximately 42 percent of the boys and 45 percent of the girls made moderate-to-marked improvement in reducing their psychopathic symptomatology overall. "These findings are important," Salekin *et al.* conclude, "and indicate that psychopathy, at least in youth, may be less recalcitrant to treatment than previously thought" (p. 192).

Salekin (2002) also published a comprehensive review of 42 studies specifically directed at treating psychopathy. Despite some methodological shortcomings with many of the studies (e.g., small sample size, diverse definitions of psychopathy), cognitive-behavioral, psychodynamic, and eclectic interventions were shown to be effective. The most notable benefits included a reduction in psychopathic characteristics, such as a decrease in lying, an increase in remorse or empathy, and improved relations with others. Salekin specifically noted that one intensive action-oriented program was highly successful (88%) with youngsters showing psychopathic tendencies. Ingram, Gerard, Quay, and Levison (1970) devised a program specifically designed to address psychopathic behaviors in youth. The program was based on the sensation-seeking model that kept the 20 young participants interested in treatment throughout the sessions. The program was able to decrease institutional aggressive behavior and improved overall adjustment in the community. Those psychotherapies that proved most effective tended to be more intensive and often combined with other programs, such as group psychotherapy, pharmacotherapy, or the involvement of family members. "These results indicate, at least preliminarily," Salekin writes, "that for complex problems such as psychopathy, more elaborate and intensive intervention programs involving individual psychotherapy, treatment of family members, and input from groups (other patients/inmates) are beneficial and may enhance their overall effectiveness" (p. 105). The key for success with psychopaths may be the scope, type, intensity, and duration of the treatment, as well as the training of the staff applying the intervention. Salekin points out that those intervention programs that were less successful were characterized by little input by trained mental health professionals and extremely little one-to-one patient–psychologist contact. He further stated that early intervention is particularly important in working with children exhibiting psychopathic traits. Salekin concludes that the therapeutic pessimism that surrounds the treatment of psychopathy and undermines motivation to search for effective modes of intervention for the disorder is unwarranted.

Summary and Conclusions

The primary psychopath should be distinguished from people who may be classified as psychotic, neurotic, or emotionally disturbed. The primary psychopath should also be distinguished from the sociopath, who is similar in many ways. However, the term *sociopath* usually refers to a person who *habitually* violates the law and who does not seem to learn from past experience. Another common term—"antisocial personality disorder" (APD)—also is distinct from "psychopathy," even though

these two terms are often confused by clinicians and researchers. This is understandable, because the diagnostic category "antisocial personality disorder", as defined in the latest editions of the DSM, has many parallels to Robert Hare's concept of criminal psychopathy.

The psychopath as discussed here may or may not run afoul of the law. In addition, psychopaths demonstrate a variety of behavioral and neurophysiological characteristics that differentiate them from other groups of individuals. In this text, we are of course most interested in the psychopath who does run afoul of the law, particularly by way of persistent and/or violent offending. Hare has proposed the term *criminal psychopath* to describe this individual. In this sense, the criminal psychopath, the sociopath, and the person with antisocial personality disorder are very similar in their offending patterns.

Psychopaths most often function in society as charming, daring, witty, intelligent individuals, high on charisma but low on emotional reaction and affect. They appear to lack moral standards or the ability to manifest genuine sensitivity toward others. If criminals, they become the despair of law enforcement officials because their crimes appear to be without discernible or rational motives. Even worse, they show no remorse or ability to be rehabilitated.

We reviewed much of the neurophysiological research suggesting that the psychopath is different from the rest of the population on a number of physiological measures. The psychopath seems to be underaroused, both autonomically and cortically, a finding that may account for his or her difficulty in learning the rules of society. However, there is some evidence to suggest that with adequate incentives, psychopaths may learn societal expectations very well. It is clear that the psychopath would be a stable extravert with high psychoticism. The psychopath, like the extravert, apparently is not aroused enough to profit as easily from the classical conditioning that perhaps sets most of us on the straight and narrow path in childhood. If, in addition to this physiological lack, the psychopath's family situation leaves him or her without appropriate models, then he or she is doubly cursed.

Many psychopaths also apparently have abnormal brain-wave patterns, mostly of a slow-wave childlike variety, which suggests that their nervous system is immature, at least until middle age. There are indications of more than the usual amounts of positive spikes, which are brain-wave bursts that correlate with aggressive episodes and impulsivity. Research has failed to discover, however, whether these abnormalities engender

psychopathic behavior or vice versa. There is also little evidence to support a strong hereditary influence, although we should not overlook the possibility that psychopaths may be born with a biological predisposition to the disorder.

Studies on the childhood of psychopaths strongly suggest that they may have been ADHD as children, causing chaos for parents and teachers. It would be a folly to maintain, though, that the ADHD child of today is the psychopath of tomorrow. Perhaps because they are physiologically underaroused, psychopaths do not respond as well to admonishments, threats, or actual punishment as do their nonpsychopathic peers. They do not learn society's expectations and the rules of right and wrong, possibly because anxiety-inducing disciplinary procedures are not that anxiety-producing for them. In many respects, the criminal psychopath follows a developmental path highly similar to the life-course-persistent offender described by developmental theory.

There are still numerous gaps in our knowledge of the psychopath, one being in the area of gender differences. Research on female psychopaths is scant. Some research suggests that behavioral characteristics for females are generally similar to those of male psychopaths, with slightly more emphasis among females on sexual acting-out behavior. This probably reflects a cultural bias, however, since women have been traditionally chastised more than men for behavior deemed inappropriate according to sexual mores. However, research on female criminal psychopaths using Hare's PCL-R implies that their behavioral patterns may be somewhat different than those of male criminal psychopaths.

A highly controversial area relating to psychopathy is the measurement and existence of juvenile psychopathy. Some researchers are very actively involved in developing scales to assess this construct and in comparing features of juvenile and adult psychopaths. Other researchers prefer to focus on psychopathic "characteristics" in juveniles that may or may not mean they are themselves psychopathic. Many juveniles, for example, are impulsive, seek stimulation, and appear to be noncaring; these features are often part of the normal turmoil of adolescent development. While it is worthwhile to study these characteristics, we must not rush to judgment and assume they are indicative of psychopathy. Others are even more cautious, suggesting that the concept itself simply is not valid when applied to juveniles. However, representatives of each of the above groups have expressed concern that juvenile psychopathy will be misdiagnosed, condemning juveniles to a label that is frequently associated with defeat: Psychopaths do not feel remorse, therefore cannot be helped.

Contemporary research on psychopathy is robust and shows few signs of abating. By now, it is quite clear that Hare's primary psychopath—as measured by the PCL—has many unique features and that it may involve more than the two factors originally identified. The four-factor model is rapidly gaining adherents. At the least, we can say that psychopathy includes distinctive cognitive and emotional styles and physiological indicators. Many psychopaths also had childhoods marked by parental deficiency and conduct problems. These features combine to render the psychopath highly resistant to treatment. This is particularly frustrating to clinicians working with criminal psychopaths, many of whom know how to play the clinical games that will make it appear that they have changed their behavior.

Key Concepts

Antisocial personality disorder (APD)
Avoidance learning
Criminal psychopath
Dyssocial psychopath
Emotional paradox
Executive functions
Factor analysis

Factor 1
Factor 2
Habituation
Hemisphere asymmetry
Markers
Primary psychopath
Psychopathy Checklist (PCL and PCL-R)

Psychopathy Checklist: Screening Version (PCL:SV)
Psychopathy Checklist: Youth Version (PCL-YV)
P-Scan: Research Version
Recidivism
Secondary psychopath
Semantic aphasia

Review Questions

1. Briefly describe the core behavioral characteristics of the criminal psychopath.
2. What differences have been found between male and female psychopaths?
3. Name and describe briefly any five instruments used to measure psychopathy.
4. Define each of the following as proposed by Hare: primary psychopath, secondary psychopath, dyssocial psychopath, and criminal psychopath.
5. What has been learned about (a) recidivism, and (b) treatment of the criminal psychopath?
6. Identify some of the ethical problems created as a result of labeling a child a "psychopath."
7. Describe the three- and four-factor models of psychopathy.
8. How is the psychopath different from the nonpsychopath on psychophysiology? Thoroughly discuss all relevant features.

7

Crime and Mental Disorders

CHAPTER OBJECTIVES

- Define mental disorders.
- Provide an overview of the DSM-IV and the diagnoses that are most relevant to criminal behavior.
- Define and review issues relating to competency to stand trial.
- Review the insanity defense rules and standards.
- Discuss special defenses sometimes raised to absolve defendants of criminal responsibility.
- Discuss the prevalence of mental illness in incarcerated populations.
- Define risk assessment and identify various tests used for this purpose.

On June 20, 2001, a 31-year-old woman in Texas, Andrea Yates, called 911 seeking help. When the police arrived, she confessed that she had drowned her five children, ages 6 months to 7 years, in a bathtub because she had been a bad mother who hopelessly damaged them. Due to the sensational nature of the crime, the case received extensive nationwide publicity. Yates had a history of mental disorder; she had attempted suicide twice and had been hospitalized at least four times, apparently for depression.

At her trial, Yates raised the insanity defense, citing in particular a severe case of postpartum psychosis. Her lawyers said she believed she was possessed by Satan and that her children would suffer in hell because she represented evil. To save them from that fate, she thought it was critical that they die now so that they could go to heaven; she herself would be executed for their deaths, as Satan demanded.

Under Texas law, for the defense to succeed with an insanity defense, it had to be established that Yates could not distinguish right from wrong at the time of the crime, a common requirement for establishing insanity across the country. However, other aspects of the Texas law are among the most restrictive in the nation, and establishing insanity was going to be an uphill battle (Roche, 2006). Experts testified that she was mentally disordered but whether she knew what she was doing at the time of crime was a question left for the jury to answer. Apparently, the jury believed she did; on March 12, 2002, Yates was found guilty of murder for drowning three of her children. The charges did not include the deaths of two of her sons.

The Yates story does not stop there. Her conviction was overturned, primarily because of flawed testimony by a forensic psychiatrist, Park Dietz, who had testified during the trial that Yates may have been influenced by an episode of the television program *Law and Order,* in which a woman suffering from postpartum depression drowned her children in a bathtub and was found **not guilty by reason of insanity (NGRI)**. During their appeal, Yates' lawyers documented that such an episode was never aired, thus doing irreparable damage to the psychiatric testimony. In a later trial, Andrea Yates was found NGRI and is now receiving treatment in a hospital setting.

The Yates case created a national debate over the legal standards for mental disorders. In this, we discuss many of the points and issues brought up by the Yates case, including the various standards for the insanity defense.

Despite the tragedy of the Yates case, brutal, violent, and apparently senseless crimes are not usually committed by people who are mentally ill or "sick." It is a common perception that someone who walks into a business establishment and randomly shoots its customers and employees must be mentally ill. Likewise, someone who sexually assaults, tortures, and kills a 4-year-old child has to be sick. How else could these people do this? An alternate explanation focuses on the subhuman perspective: If not sick, they are less than human. Closely related is the view that these individuals are basically evil. Although these latter approaches are gaining ground, perhaps reflecting public impatience with perceived insanity loopholes in the law, there is still wide public subscription to a presumption of mental illness, particularly in the case of outrageous, inexplicable crimes. And, as we will see in this chapter, mental disorder *is* an issue in some of these crimes—as it was in the Yates case.

The media have been instrumental in developing the connection between mental disorder and crime, particularly serious violent crime. Along with greed and revenge, mental illness is a basic motivation for criminality in the vast majority of crimes on television and other entertainment media (Surette, 1999). John Monahan (1992) cites an early survey (Gerbner, Gross, Morgan, & Signorielli, 1981) showing that on prime-time American television, 73 percent of all individuals characterized as mentally disordered also displayed some violent behavior. In a later analysis (Shain & Phillips, 1991), 86 percent of all print stories dealing with former mental patients focused on the violence of the patients, especially if the topics dealt with serial or mass murder.

The tendency to make the connection between crime and mental disorder is not new, nor is it limited to the media. Throughout the history of civilization, there has been a strong tendency to forge this link (Monahan, 1981). Most societies and their legal systems have been confused about and often frightened by mental disorder. In fact, the first mental hospital in the American colonies was established after Benjamin Franklin argued forcefully that the mentally ill were prone to violence and should be confined, involuntarily if need be, to protect society (Monahan & Geis, 1976).

Those who subscribe to the view that the mentally disordered are a threat assume that these individuals do not play by the rules of society, are unpredictable, and cannot control their own actions. Since they are apt to do anything at any given time, these "crazy people" are potentially dangerous. It should be emphasized, however, that the perception that mental disorder inevitably or even frequently leads to violence is not universal. Surveys suggest that only about one-quarter of the U.S. adult population strongly subscribe to such a view (Monahan, 1992). This more realistic appraisal is at least partly due to the efforts of advocates for the mentally ill, who have waged and supported public information campaigns aimed at disseminating truth and alleviating fear. However, while most people may not believe the mentally ill as a group are dangerous, many do believe that senseless or incomprehensible violent acts are the work of someone who must be "crazy" or "sick." Thus, to some members of the public, mentally ill people are dangerous; to others, people who commit bizarre crimes are mentally ill. Still others would subscribe to both views. For the present, we will set aside the issue of who is and is not dangerous but will revisit it later in the chapter.

DEFINING MENTAL ILLNESS

Mental illness is a disorder (some say a disease) of the mind that is judged by experts to interfere substantially with a person's ability to cope with life on a daily basis. It presumably deprives the person of freedom of choice, but it is important to note that there are degrees to this deprivation. In other words, even a seriously disordered individual has some decision-making ability. Mental illness is manifested in behavior that deviates notably from normal conduct. However, the word *illness* encourages us to look for etiology, symptoms, and cures, and to rely heavily on the medical profession both to diagnose and to treat. It also encourages us to excuse the behavior of persons plagued with the "sickness." The term **mental disorder,** however, need not imply that a person is sick, to be pitied, or even necessarily less responsible for his or her actions. Therefore, although *mental illness* is still used in the psychological, psychiatric, and legal literature, as well as in both civil and criminal law, we prefer the less restrictive *mental disorder.* This is not to say that medication is not needed, however; it may be.

Another term that must be distinguished is **mental retardation,** professionally known as **developmental disability.** This is a cognitive deficiency—measured by "IQ tests"—that cannot be cured. However, many mentally retarded individuals can be provided training and support services to lead productive and independent lives. Even so, they are sometimes charged with primarily minor offenses that result in arrests, being detained in jail, and serving time. Dual diagnoses of mental retardation and substance abuse have been observed in a significant number of these individuals (Day & Berney, 2001). Misperceptions about the mentally retarded are perhaps not as strong as misperceptions about the mentally disordered, but they represent a population whose needs may go unrecognized by the criminal justice system. Thus, while the chapter focuses primarily on issues related to the mentally disordered, we will also give attention to unique problems faced by the developmentally disabled.

Mental disorders are manifested in a variety of behaviors, ranging in severity from dangerous, harmful acts to conduct that is essentially innocuous. Morse (1978) preferred the term *crazy behavior,* which he characterized as behavior that is obviously strange and unusual *and cannot be logically explained.* The person who walks onto the hotel elevator at the lobby level and faces the rear, staring blankly at the elevator's rear wall, while others are facing the front, is exhibiting strange behavior. However, if the elevator subsequently opens at the "back" door, there is a logical explanation: the person is a hotel guest or employee who is familiar with the elevator's setup. In the absence of such an explanation, the behavior becomes disconcerting to the other passengers and, if only mildly, "crazy." In this instance, some clinicians—again in the absence of a logical explanation—might see the behavior as symptomatic of an anxiety disorder or a dissociative disorder, depending on other aspects of the individual's behavior. However, the behavior, as described above, is not dangerous. On the other hand, a person who walks into a hotel lobby in a highly agitated state, brandishing a knife, and stating that hotel employees were all trained by Satan and must die for their sins is exhibiting both "crazy" and dangerous behavior. There is obviously a crucial distinction between the above scenarios.

The DSM-IV

The concept of mental disorder, therefore, connotes a very wide range of bizarre, dramatic, harmful, or mildly unusual behaviors whose classifications are published in the **Diagnostic and Statistical Manual of Mental Disorders (DSM).** Compiled by committees appointed by the American Psychiatric Association, the DSM—now in its fourth edition (DSM-IV)—is the guidebook for clinicians seeking to define and diagnose specific mental disorders. It is used by virtually every mental health professional in the United States to guide diagnosis and to justify third-party reimbursement for treatment. A slightly revised version of the DSM-IV called the DSM-IV-TR (TR stands for "text revision") was published in 2000 and is the most recent edition available. A fifth edition of the DSM (DSM-V) is currently being prepared and is expected to be released in May 2012.

The current version lists approximately 400 mental disorders (Comer, 2004). Interestingly, approximately half of the people in the United States will qualify for a DSM diagnosis at some point in their lifetimes (Comer, 2004). Diagnoses based on the DSM also are provided to courts in a wide range of forensic settings, including evaluations of competence to stand trial, mental state at the time of an offense, sentencing, and assessments of harm suffered by both victims of crime and plaintiffs in civil suits.

The DSM is reviewed and revised periodically to conform to the contemporary, mainstream thinking of psychiatrists and other mental health professionals. A frequently cited illustration is the removal of homosexuality as a disease, a change made in 1973 after protests by gay activist groups and many psychologists. Another is the recognition of post-traumatic stress disorder (PTSD). Today, some proponents are urging that sexual addiction be added. The long-awaited DSM-V is expected to be more based on scientific advancements as well as clinical expertise. According to a recent edition (DSM-IV 1994, p. xxi), a mental disorder

> is conceptualized as a clinically significant behavioral or psychological syndrome or pattern that occurs in an individual and that is associated with present distress (e.g., a painful symptom) or disability (i.e., impairment in one or more important areas of functioning) or with a significantly increased risk of suffering death, pain, disability, or an important loss of freedom. In addition, this syndrome or pattern must not be merely an expectable and culturally sanctioned response to a particular event, for example, the death of a loved one. Whatever its original cause, it must currently be considered a manifestation of a behavioral, psychological, or biological dysfunction in the individual.

As noted by Wakefield (1992), there are two basic principles that guide the DSM-IV definition for mental disorder. *First,* the mental condition must have negative consequences for the person. That is, the person must be experiencing some pain, distress, discomfort, or disability. The *second* principle rests on the assumption that a mental disorder is a dysfunction of some internal process within the person—that is, for some reason, something is wrong. This principle differentiates the disorder from the normal or expected internal processes that result from a trauma or tragedy of daily living, such as the loss of a loved one.

We now turn to the specific disorders identified in the DSM that are most likely to be associated with criminal conduct. It must be stressed, however, that (1) persons with these disorders are not "crime prone," and (2) even if an individual is diagnosed with these disorders, he or she still can be held responsible for criminal conduct.

For the present, the four categories of mental disorders most relevant are (1) schizophrenic disorders, (2) paranoid disorders, (3) mood disorders (serious depression), and (4) the personality disorder called "antisocial personality disorder." Note that the first two fall into what was previously called the "psychotic" category. The third was considered in that psychotic category only if serious enough, such as bipolar depression. The fourth is a separate category under the general label "personality disorders." These four categories of disorders are relevant because they are most likely to be associated with violent, serious criminal, or antisocial behavior and are most often cited to support an insanity defense to criminal charges. We review each of these disorders and then assess their relevance to criminal behavior. However, toward the end of the chapter, we discuss less common disorders that, when cited in courts, attract considerable media attention.

Schizophrenic Disorders

Schizophrenia is the mental disorder that people most often associate with "crazy behavior," since it frequently manifests itself in highly bizarre actions. It is a mental disorder that continues to be extremely complex and poorly understood (Andreasen & Carpenter, 1993; Sitnikova, Goff, & Kuperberg, 2009). The disorder generally begins early in life, often leads to social and economic impairment, and leaves traces on its victims for the rest of their lives (Andreasen & Carpenter, 1993). Behavioral manifestations of schizophrenia are varied, but there are some common characteristics.

Severe breakdowns in thought patterns, emotions, and perceptions are common. Spells of extreme social withdrawal from others are also typical. The thoughts and cognitive functioning of the person with schizophrenia become disorganized and fail to correspond to reality, and his or her speech will reflect this. The most common example is a loosening of associations, in which ideas shift between totally unrelated and only obliquely related subjects. Thought becomes fragmented and bizarre, and **delusions**—false beliefs about the world—are common. An example of a delusion is *believing* some alien from another universe is listening in on your cell phone conversations or sending you text messages and ultimately plotting against you.

The person with schizophrenia is typically inappropriate in emotion or affect (e.g., indiscriminate giggling or crying), or reflects emotional flatness, where very little—if any—emotional reaction is exhibited. The voice is monotonous, the face immobile and expressionless. The major disturbances in perception are various forms of **hallucinations,** which involve sensing or perceiving things or events that others do not sense or perceive. The most common hallucinations are auditory, with the individual hearing voices or sounds that no one else in the vicinity hears.

The proportion of violent crimes committed by people with schizophrenia is small; however, when they do commit violent crimes, the level of violence may be higher than that of the "typical" violent offender, particularly with respect to homicide or aggravated assault. One individual, for example, repeatedly bashed a stranger sitting in a public park on the head. In a study of 125 homicide offenders diagnosed with schizophrenia (Laajasalo & Häkkänen, 2006), one-third were considered excessively violent. Excessive violence was most common among offenders with hallucination and delusions, rather than one or the other. Delusions, particularly persecutory ones, are particularly common in those schizophrenics who commit violent offenses. Other researchers (Marleau, Millaud, & Auclair, 2003; Taylor *et al.*, 1998) also have found that hallucinations alone (without deslusions) are rare at the time of crime among homicide offenders. Interestingly, though, the strongest predictors of excessive violence in Laajasalo & Häkkänen's study were the offender's own history of violence and the presence of a cooffender at the scene.

The DSM-IV outlines five characteristic symptoms of schizophrenia, at least two of which must be manifested before a diagnosis can be entertained: (1) delusions, (2) hallucinations, (3) disorganized speech, (4) grossly disorganized behavior, and (5) inappropriate affect. Furthermore, the social interactions, self-care, and/or occupational life of the individual must show signs of being markedly below the level achieved prior to the onset. In addition, there must be continuous signs of the disturbance for at least six months.

The DSM-IV also recognizes five subtypes of schizophrenia: (1) disorganized, (2) catatonic, (3) paranoid, (4) undifferentiated, and (5) residual. Following is a brief summary of the essential features of each subtype:

1. *Disorganized type:* These individuals show inappropriate affect (flat, incongruous, or silly emotional responses) and marked incoherence and disorganization in thought patterns. Associated features include grimaces, strange mannerisms, complaints of nonexistent physical ailments, extreme social withdrawal, and other oddities of behavior.

2. *Catatonic type:* This type shows severe disturbances in muscular and voluntary movement. Extended periods of mutism are common. Parrotlike and senseless repetition of a word or phrase just spoken by another person is also common. Prominent grimacing is another frequent characteristic. The catatonic may assume a bizarre posture for long periods of time (usually several hours) and then fly into an overactive, agitated state of screaming and throwing things.

3. *Paranoid type:* These individuals are characterized by delusions and hallucinations (usually auditory hallucinations). A person with paranoid schizophrenia may be convinced that the world is inhabited by extraterrestrials who are plotting to take over the world. Another may hear voices commanding him to rid the world of red-haired individuals. Of all the schizophrenic types, the paranoid is the most frequently represented in criminal behavior.

4. *Undifferentiated type:* This type shows psychotic symptoms that cannot be classified into any of the foregoing categories. People with this type display active psychotic features, such as hallucinations, delusions, incoherent speech, or confused and disorganized behavior, but do not meet the specifications of the other types.

5. *Residual type:* These individuals have had at least one episode of schizophrenia, and there is evidence that some of the symptoms are continuing. For example, the person may still display blunted emotions or illogical thinking, but no other symptoms.

The DSM-IV identifies a sixth category, *schizophreniform disorder,* a behavioral pattern that shows at least two indicators of delusions, hallucinations, disorganized speech, grossly disorganized behavior, and emotional inappropriateness. It is a temporary disorder and underscores the difficulty in classifying schizophrenic disorders in general. In order to qualify for schizophreniform disorder, the symptoms must persist for at least one month but less than six months. If the symptoms continue more than six months, the clinician is encouraged to classify the disorder into one of the five longer-lasting types.

Delusional Disorders

The **delusional disorders** (also called **paranoid disorders**) are characterized by the presence of one or more *nonbizarre* delusions that persist for at least one month. The judgment of whether the delusion's systems are bizarre or nonbizarre is especially important in deciding between a delusional disorder and schizophrenia. In delusional disorder, the delusions are reasonably believable and not completely far-fetched. An example of a nonbizarre delusion is the belief that a neighbor is spying and attempting to poison one's dog, when there is no evidence to that effect. Even so, neighbors sometimes spy and sometimes do try to poison dogs. A bizarre delusion—more characteristic of schizophrenia—is the belief that the neighbor has disguised herself as a mosquito and is hovering outside one's window.

Delusional disorders often accompany other disorders like schizophrenia, organic mental disorder, paranoid personality disorder, and depressions. However, the essential feature of all delusional disorders is the delusional system, which most often includes persecutory beliefs about being spied on, cheated, conspired against, followed, drugged, maliciously maligned, harassed, or obstructed. Generally, anger, resentment, and sometimes violence accompany these false persecutory beliefs. Suspiciousness, either generalized or directed at one or more persons, is also common. The DSM-IV recognizes seven different types of delusional disorders, but the persecutory type is the one most closely associated with criminal conduct, especially violent criminal conduct. Thus, the individual who believes he is being followed by someone intending to do him harm may try to kill or otherwise harm his "persecutor."

Depressive Disorders

The disorders described in this section have a variety of names and diagnostic labels, such as affective disorders, mood disorders, and bipolar depressive disorders. The most common label is **major depressive disorder.** The symptoms include an *extremely* depressed state that lasts for at least two weeks and is accompanied by a generalized slowing down of mental and physical activity, gloom, despair, feelings of worthlessness, and perhaps frequent thoughts of suicide. Everyone has up and down periods, but these mood changes are extreme and the depression is deep and usually long-lasting. Persons with major depression describe themselves as down, discouraged, and hopeless. A less common form of depression is bipolar depression in which there are both periods of depression and periods of excessive euphoria called *mania*.

The role of depression in the development of criminal behavior is just beginning to be explored. Preliminary data indicate that depression may be strongly associated with delinquency, especially in teenage girls (Kovacs, 1996; Obeidallah & Earls, 1999; Teplin, 2000). Depression seems to render teenagers—both boys and girls—indifferent to their own personal safety and the consequences of their actions. They just don't care what happens to them, which may increase the likelihood of gravitating toward delinquency. When depressed, people lose interest in life and the activities going on around them, isolating them further from social life and school or work.

Depression also very likely plays a significant role in mass murders, school shootings, workplace violence, and "suicide-by-cop" incidents in which a person sets up a situation wherein police are essentially forced to shoot.

Antisocial Personality Disorder

The DSM-III and the DSM-III-R criteria for the **antisocial personality disorder** (APD) have been among the most frequently criticized because of their vagueness and lack of empirical anchoring (Widiger *et al.*, 1991). The DSM-IV and DSM-IV-TR, however, have tried to address these problems by incorporating into the criteria more empirically based attributes. Many of the new criteria closely follow the Robert Hare definition of the criminal psychopath.

The essential feature of a person with an APD is a history of continuous behavior in which the rights of others are violated. The individual must be at least 18 years of age and must have a history of some symptoms of conduct disorder before age 15. Recall that a diagnosis of **conduct disorder** is reserved for children and adolescents. Before a person can be diagnosed with APD, a pervasive pattern of disregard for and the violation of the rights of others must be indicated by at least three of the following behavioral patterns:

1. Failure to conform to social norms or the criminal law, as reflected by frequent performance of acts that are grounds for arrests
2. Irritability and unusual aggressiveness, as indicated by repeated physical fights or assaults
3. Consistent irresponsibility, as reflected in a poor work history or failure to honor financial obligations
4. Impulsivity or a failure to plan ahead (characteristic at all ages)
5. Deceitfulness, as reflected in frequent lying, use of aliases, or conning others for personal profit or pleasure
6. Reckless disregard for the safety of others or self
7. Lack of remorse or guilt for wrongdoings, as indicated by indifference to or rationalization of having hurt, mistreated, or stolen from another

Additional symptoms, as outlined in the DSM-IV, include stealing, fighting, truancy, and resisting authority—typical childhood symptoms. Antisocial personalities lack empathy and tend to be callous, cynical, and contemptuous of the feelings, rights, and sufferings of others. Furthermore, they frequently exhibit precocious and aggressive sexual behavior, excessive drinking, and the use of illicit drugs. There is a markedly impaired capacity to maintain lasting, close, warm, and responsible relationships with family, friends, or sexual partners.

On average, ASPs fail to become independent, self-supporting adults. They spend most of their lives in institutions (usually correctional facilities) or remain highly dependent on their families. Other accompanying features include restlessness, an inability to tolerate boredom, and a belief that the world is hostile. ASPs often complain of tension and depression, but they do not usually meet the criteria for a diagnosis of depression. They are often impulsive and unable to plan ahead, and show deficits in executive functioning.

Antisocial personality disorder occurs more frequently in males than in females. It is estimated that about 3 percent of the American male population and about 1 percent of the American female population fall into this category (DSM-IV). Furthermore, the disorder is more common in lower-socioeconomic populations, partly because it is connected with impaired earning capacity and partly because of the greater likelihood of being raised in an economically disadvantaged, dysfunctional household with limited adequate role models and resources. Lastly, the DSM-IV concludes that the disorder runs in families, possibly due to a genetic link that predisposes the child to antisocial behavioral patterns. Other perspectives would emphasize that family members share the disorder—not because of a genetic link—but because they also share the economic and social background that facilitates it.

Research dating from the 1970s has indicated that ASP is a common diagnosis of criminal defendants and offenders. In an early study, Henn and his colleagues conducted an extensive series of investigations on all defendants referred by a St. Louis, Missouri, court for psychiatric assessment over a 10-year period (Henn, Herjanic, & Vanderpearl, 1976a). Focusing on a sample of 1,195 defendants accused of a variety of crimes and referred for psychiatric assessment, Henn and colleagues learned that the most frequent diagnosis was personality disorder, accounting for nearly 40 percent of all the diagnoses. Two-thirds of those classified as personality disorders were specifically designated antisocial personality. The second most frequent diagnosis was schizophrenia (which also included those labeled probable schizophrenia), comprising 17 percent of the total. The other diagnostic labels were evenly distributed and of low frequency.

Henn *et al.* also found frequent references to alcoholism, primarily as a secondary diagnosis, in the diagnostic reports. Alcoholism cut across all diagnostic categories, with the notable exception of schizophrenia, where only a few cases were reported. The combination of alcoholism and drug addiction as a secondary diagnosis was common in persons labeled antisocial personality. These findings support those reported by Guze (1976), who found the diagnosis of alcoholism prevalent among offenders with a diagnosis of antisocial personality disorders.

The pervasiveness of this diagnosis continues today. APD is very frequently offered as a diagnosis in criminal courts and in corrections, sometimes serving as a catch-all category. Researchers have noted that when courts press for a diagnosis, many clinicians will oblige by concluding that an individual qualifies for APD (Melton *et al.*, 1997). In correctional facilities, rates of inmates considered APD range from 30 percent to 50 percent, and it is not unusual to find the diagnosis in over 50 percent of the correctional population (Gacono *et al.*, 2001). APD is such a common diagnosis applied to persons both accused of and convicted of criminal offenses that some jurisdictions specifically exclude it from the list of mental disorders that can support an insanity defense.

The validity of the antisocial personality disorder as a meaningful concept has been debated. Blackburn (1988) contends that there is no single type of abnormal personality that is prone to chronic rule violation. Furthermore, he believes the diagnostic label "antisocial personality disorder" remains a mythical entity that fails to be meaningful for theory development, research, clinical communication, or prediction. Such a concept is little more than a moral judgment masquerading as a clinical diagnosis. Given the lack of demonstrable scientific evidence of clinical utility of the concept, it should be discarded (Blackburn, 1988, p. 511). Others have observed that there remains widespread confusion about the distinction between APD and psychopathy, with many clinicians viewing them as synonymous (Gacono *et al.*, 2001). As we noted earlier, the DSM-IV now describes APD in such a way that it is virtually indistinguishable from Hare's concept of psychopathy.

COMPETENCY AND CRIMINAL RESPONSIBILITY

The above psychiatric diagnoses are often those that come into play when decisions must be made as to whether defendants who are mentally disordered are competent to stand trial or, if competent, are culpable enough to be held responsible for the crimes that occurred. In this section, we review these two very important legal constructs.

Incompetency to Stand Trial

Some persons charged with a crime are considered so intellectually and/or psychologically impaired that—were they to be tried—they would be present in body but not in mind. The U.S. Supreme Court has determined that the trial of such an individual violates the Constitution. Specifically, defendants are competent to stand trial if they have "sufficient present ability to consult with their lawyer with a reasonable degree of rational understanding . . . and a rational as well as factual understanding of the proceedings" (*Dusky v. United States*, 1960, p. 402). To protect the rights of the individual and to preserve the dignity of the court process, the law states that a person who is incompetent must not be tried.

The competency issue does not relate only to the actual trial, however. In fact, some scholars now prefer to use the term **adjudicative competence** rather than competence to stand trial (e.g., Bonnie & Grisso, 2000; Mumley, Tillbrook, & Grisso, 2003; Viljoen & Wingrove, 2007). The former term relates to the ability to participate in a wide variety of court proceedings and court-related activities, including plea bargaining, preliminary hearings, and other pretrial hearings related to one's case. It also encompasses two distinct concepts: (1) the competence to proceed (which implies understanding the purpose of the proceedings and being able to help one's attorney), and (2) decisional competence (which implies the ability to comprehend the significance of various decisions to be made) (Mumley *et al.*, 2003). If a criminal defendant is found incompetent to stand trial, the court has essentially determined that he or she cannot understand the process that is occurring or effectively participate in it. Interestingly, the issue of competence also extends to whether a mentally disordered defendant who is competent to stand trial is also competent to represent himself. In a 2008 case (*Indiana v. Edwards*), the U.S. Supreme Court ruled that a unitary standard for deciding these two issues was inappropriate. Although many questions were left unanswered in that case, for our purposes, it must be emphasized that just because defendants are competent to stand trial, this does not mean that they are competent to serve as their own attorney.

The competency issue can be raised at any time during the actual proceedings. For example, a defendant may be competent up to and into the beginning phases of his trial; during a long and protracted trial, he may become incompetent. A defendant also may be competent before and during trial, but may be ruled incompetent at the time of sentencing.

Evaluations for **competency to stand trial** represent the most common referral for criminally related forensic assessments (Cruise & Rogers, 1998). Most typically, defendants referred for competency evaluation have a history of psychiatric care or institutionalization or exhibited signs of mental disorder at arrest or while detained in jail. Data indicate that approximately 25,000 criminal defendants nationwide, or about one in 15, are evaluated each year by state and federal courts for their competency to stand trial (Cruise & Rogers, 1998; Nicholson & Kugler, 1991). About four out of every five of these evaluated defendants are found competent (Grisso, 1986; Nicholson & Kugler, 1991; Roesch, Zapf, Golding, & Skeem, 1999).

Interestingly, mental health clinicians have been criticized extensively in the literature for the poor quality of their assessments, even sometimes confusing competence with criminal responsibility (Skeem & Golding, 1998). In recent years, the quality of the assessments has improved, though examiners are still faulted for not making sufficient use of the competence assessment tools developed by researchers or providing adequate explanations to judges in their reports (Nicholson & Norwood, 2000). In a recent study of 60 clinicians who had conducted a total of 7,000 evaluations, researchers found that individual clinicians varied widely in the rates at which they recommended that defendants be found incompetent (Murrie, Boccaccini, Zapf, Warren, & Henderson, 2008), leading to questions about how these evaluations are conducted and which factors are persuasive to the examining clinician. Most recently, an area receiving considerable research attention is the topic of juvenile competency (e.g., Viljoen & Grisso, 2007; Viljoen & Wingrove, 2007).

It is important to emphasize the distinction between **incompetence to stand trial** (IST) and insanity, the legal concept to be discussed below. Although they may be related, the two concepts are distinct and should be assessed separately—although this is not always done. Criminal responsibility, which is at the core of the insanity defense, and competency to stand trial refer to a defendant's mental state/capacity at *two different points in time*. If a defendant pleads not guilty by reason of insanity, the law asks, "What was the defendant's state of mind at the time the offense was committed?" In competency considerations, the question becomes, "What is the defendant's state of mind at the present time, or at the time of the pretrial proceedings or trial?" An individual who was seriously mentally disordered at the time of an offense and whose criminal responsibility is questionable may have enough mental stability by the time of the trial to be competent to stand trial. On the other hand, a person may be of sound mind during the unlawful act, but may later become disordered or disoriented and be determined incompetent to stand trial.

If found incompetent to stand trial—a decision that must be made by the presiding judge—the defendant is typically sent to a mental institution or, less frequently, to an outpatient therapeutic program, until rendered competent. For those defendants who are restored to competency, some research suggests that the average time needed for restoration is about three months (Hoge *et al.*, 1996). In a survey of mental health program directors across the United States, Miller (2003) found that outpatient treatment to restore competency was rare. Outpatient *evaluations* of competency were on the increase, however.

Until the 1970s, the typical procedure for evaluating competency required that defendants be confined within a maximum security institution for a lengthy psychiatric-psychological evaluation (usually 60–90 days). Following evaluation, the defendant was granted a hearing on the matter of competency. If the court found the defendant unable to understand the charges or the judicial proceedings, or to help counsel in his or her defense, then the defendant would automatically be committed to a secure hospital for an indefinite period of time—until competent. Theoretically, this indefinite time period could extend—and sometimes did—into a lifetime of involuntary commitment.

In 1972, in *Jackson v. Indiana*, the Supreme Court declared that such an indefinite confinement violated the Constitution. While the court allowed the confinement, it specified that if no progress was made toward competence, the individual must be released or must be recommitted under civil, not criminal statutes. Today, individuals found IST with little likelihood of being restored to competency often have their cases dismissed. However, in many jurisdictions, the prosecutor still retains the option of reinstituting charges if the person regains competency at some later time.

In recent years, ISTs have asserted additional constitutional rights in connection with their status, including the right to the "least restrictive or drastic alternative," specifically the right to be treated in a community setting rather than in an institution. As noted earlier, though, recent research suggests that community treatment is not the typical approach (Miller, 2003). In addition, because treatment is often offered in the form of psychoactive drugs, some defendants ruled IST have argued that they should not be forced to take these drugs. Psychoactive drugs are "those drugs that exert their primary effect on the brain, thus altering mood or behavior, or that are used in the treatment of mental disorders" (Julien, 1992, p. xii). Although these drugs have been improved considerably over the past few decades, many have side effects—including in some cases debilitating side effects—and are resisted by many patients.

In a recent Supreme Court ruling on this matter (*Sell v. United States*, 2003), the court ruled that, in a case that did not involve violence, courts must be wary of ordering such medication against a defendant's will. Sell, a former dentist charged with insurance fraud, had been found incompetent and was hospitalized for treatment. He had a history of mental disorder and had prior hospitalizations, during which he had received psychoactive drugs. Psychiatrists again prescribed psychoactive drugs in an effort to render him competent to stand trial, but Sell refused to take them. Both a trial judge and a federal court of appeals ruled against him, but the U.S. Supreme Court did not agree. The court noted that the trial court had not adequately weighed the advantages and disadvantages of the drugs, and it sent the case back to the court to do just that. However, for serious, violent crimes, where the government has a strong interest in bringing a defendant to trial, the court has been less sympathetic to the defendant, refusing to hear an appeal of an order for involuntary medication (*United States v. Weston*, cert. denied). Russell Eugene Weston, Jr. is the individual charged with the lethal shooting of two Capitol police officers in 1998 and the nonlethal shooting of two other individuals. In light of the nature of the crimes, Weston's long history of serious mental illness (he was a diagnosed paranoid schizophrenic with previous hospitalizations), and the government's strong interest in bringing him to trial, courts ruled in favor of the involuntary medication, saying he could be forced to take the medication. It should be noted, though, that the lower court in Weston's case had given careful consideration to the advantages and disadvantages of ordering the medication. Interestingly, over ten years after the incident, Weston apparently remains in a federal psychiatric facility and has yet to be tried.

Research on persons found IST indicates that they are highly similar in background characteristics. Most have limited social and occupational skills and a history of prior criminal charges and psychiatric hospitalizations (Williams & Miller, 1981). Compared with the general population, ISTs are disproportionately unmarried, African American, and poorly educated (less than ninth grade education) (Steadman, 1979). More recent research has continued to support these earlier findings (Nicholson & Kugler, 1991; Roesch et al., 1999). However, these differences do not hold when we compare persons referred for evaluations and ultimately found competent with those referred and ultimately found incompetent. Competent and incompetent defendants do not differ significantly on demographic variables such as race, gender, or marital status (Nicholson & Kugler 1991; Riley, 1998; Rosenfeld & Ritchie, 1998). They do differ, not surprisingly, on clinical variables. Thus, persons found incompetent are more likely to be diagnosed with a psychotic disorder or organic mental disorder (Warren, Rosenfeld, Fitch, & Hawk, 1997) or schizophrenia and affective disorders (Hoge, et al., 1997).

The offense charged seems to play some part in the ultimate competency decision, but the research in this area is quite mixed. A meta-analysis by Nicholson and Kugler (1991) indicated that individuals adjudicated IST are much more likely than other criminal defendants to be charged with violent offenses. However, Warren et al. (1997) found that public order offenses were more likely to yield a finding of incompetence than were serious charges like homicide or sex offenses. Rosenfeld and Ritchie (1998) found that misdemeanor defendants were more likely to be found incompetent than felony defendants. Mumley et al. (2003) surmise that these differences may be due to the clinical diagnosis; in other words, persons with more severe diagnoses may be charged with the less serious offenses. IST defendants are often diagnosed psychotic or with other serious mental disorders. Nicholson and Kugler (1991, p. 364) conclude, "Defendants who manifested disorientation and impaired memory, poor judgment, thought and communication disturbances, hallucinations, delusions, and bizarre, unmanageable behavior were considered unfit to proceed to trial more often than defendants who did not exhibit such symptoms."

In recent years, far more attention has been given to the issue of mentally retarded individuals and adjudicative competence. As Mumley et al. (2003, p. 343) noted, "Unlike psychotic defendants, persons with mental retardation often do not show obvious signs of poor understanding or reasoning, so that attorneys may be less capable of identifying those who are in need of AC (adjudicative competence) evaluation." Consequently, we have little information on the extent to which mentally retarded defendants are referred for competency evaluation, and virtually no information on the proportion of IST defendants who are mentally retarded. However, researchers are developing instruments and guidelines for the assessment of competence in mentally retarded individuals (e.g., Coles, Freitas, & Tweed, 1996; Smith & Hudson, 1995).

Criminal Responsibility

Given the widespread publicity associated with the insanity defense, most people are probably far more aware of defendants found **not guilty by reason of insanity (NGRI)** than those found incompetent to stand trial. Insanity is a legal term, not a psychiatric or psychological one; for our purposes, it should be used only in the context of a criminal offense. Insanity refers to a person's *state of mind at the time an offense was committed.* When an individual is found not guilty by reason of insanity, a judge or jury have determined that he or she was so mentally disordered at the time of the crime that the person should not be held responsible. The law assumes that mental disorder *can* rob an individual of free will or the ability to make appropriate choices. Note that insanity should not be *equated* with mental disorder, even serious mental disorder. That is, a mentally disordered person can still be found responsible for committing a criminal offense. Likewise, an individual who is mentally retarded can still be held criminally responsible.

Insanity defenses, especially if they are successful, receive extensive media coverage and commentary. When John Hinckley, charged with an attempt on the life of President Reagan, was found NGRI by a federal jury, there was widespread public indignation accompanied by numerous demands for repeal of the insanity defense in both federal and state laws. Since the Hinckley acquittal by reason of insanity in June 1982, at least 34 states have made some kind of alteration to their insanity statutes (Steadman *et al.*, 1993). Moreover, in response to the public outcry against the Hinckley acquittal, the U.S. Congress passed the *Insanity Defense Act of 1984,* which is discussed below. Virtually, all these legal changes made it more difficult for defendants who wished to plead not guilty by reason of insanity. Incidentally, to this day, Hinckley remains hospitalized, although he has been allowed to leave the facility for incrementally longer periods.

It is important to note that the number of insanity defenses raised in the United States is believed very small compared with the total number of criminal cases. Furthermore, despite the outcry after the Hinckley verdict, insanity defenses are rarely successful. We often hear that someone is planning to use the insanity defense but this does not necessarily come to pass. Former astronaut Lisa Nowak, charged in 2007 with the attempted kidnapping of another astronaut, initially announced she would raise the insanity defense, but changed to a standard plea of not guilty. Nowak's behavior was bizarre, and allegedly included driving 900 miles over a short period of time after packing a black wig, latex gloves, pepper spray, a hammer drill, and a folding knife among several other items.

Unfortunately, there are no *systematic, nationwide* data on how often the insanity defense is actually used (McGinley & Paswark, 1989). County, state, and federal levels of government rarely share information about these issues (Steadman *et al.*, 1993). Steadman and his colleagues write, "County level information on insanity pleas, for example, is rarely, if ever, aggregated to the state level, meaning almost nothing is known about the earliest stages of the insanity defense process" (1993, p. 3). However, there are some very good estimates based on studies conducted by independent and governmental researchers. These researchers estimate that insanity defenses are used in only 1 percent of all U.S. felony criminal cases (Callahan, Steadman, McGreevy, & Robbins, 1991; Golding, Skeem, Roesch, & Zapf, 1999).

HOW SUCCESSFUL IS THE INSANITY DEFENSE?   Data on acquittals suggest that the defense is typically not successful. In an eight-state study of 9,000 defendants who pleaded not guilty by reason of insanity, Callahan *et al.* (1991) found a 22–25 percent success rate. Other studies have reported wide statewide differences, with a high of 44 percent in Colorado and a low of 2 percent in Wyoming (McGinley & Paswark, 1989). Cirincione and Jacobs (1999) found a mean of only 33.4 insanity acquittals per year across 35 states over the period 1974–1995. More important, acquittals seem to be closely tied to the diagnosis placed on the defendant and, to some extent, on the crime charged (Cochrane, Grisso, & Frederick, 2001; Warren *et al.*, 1997). Cochrane *et al.* found that federal defendants with diagnoses of psychotic disorders, affective disorders, and mental retardation had higher rates of acquittal than those diagnosed with other disorders. Personality disorders were negatively correlated with a finding of insanity. More recently, researchers have found that jurors are favorably disposed toward defendants who provide neurological evidence, particularly evidence of traumatic brain injury (Gurley & Marcus, 2008). Such injury to the brain may be accompanied by increases in aggression, personality changes, and impaired ability to control one's emotions, among other consequences (Gurley & Marcus, 2008).

By contrast, some elements work against a defendant pleading not guilty by reason of insanity. For example, recall that many states specifically exclude antisocial personality disorder as a mental disorder to support an insanity defense. This is often the diagnosis placed on individuals who are believed to be psychopaths. Warren *et al.* (1997) found that defendants charged with violent crimes against others had the highest acquittal rates, while sex offenders significantly are more likely to be *convicted*. Nevertheless, the research literature strongly indicates that the clinical diagnosis, more than the offense, seems to be the critical factor. This also may explain the low acquittal of sex offenders, because these offenders are often not considered by clinicians to be mentally disordered.

In the United States, acquittals are far more difficult to obtain from juries (jury trials) than from judges (bench trials), a pattern that underscores the pervasive negative attitude the American public has toward the insanity defense. For example, in their eight-state study, Callahan *et al.* (1991) found that only 7 percent of the acquittals were handed down by juries. In another study, Boehnert (1989) found that 96 percent of defendants found not guilty by reason of insanity had gone before a judge. Thus, it seems wise for defendants who plan to use the insanity defense to have a bench trial (where the judge decides) rather than a jury trial. On the other hand, research suggests that, if jurors are informed of the consequences of an NGRI verdict—specifically that the defendant will likely be hospitalized for treatment—they may be more likely to acquit the defendant (Wheatman & Shaffer, 2001).

Callahan *et al.* (1991) found that successful NGRI defendants, compared with unsuccessful defendants, tended to be older, female, better educated, and single. They also had a history of prior hospitalization and were considered extremely disturbed. Furthermore, 15 percent of the acquitted defendants had not themselves raised the insanity defense, indicating that they were so disordered that an insanity verdict was essentially imposed on them. The tragic case of Andrea Yates, the Texas woman who drowned her children in a bathtub in 2001, is inconsistent with several of the above criteria, however. Yates had some college education and a history of serious mental disorder, including postpartum psychosis and hospitalization. Despite evidence of disorder—which even the prosecutor acknowledged—Yates was convicted and sent to prison, although as noted in the beginning of the chapter, her conviction was overturned and she was eventually found not guilty by reason of insanity.

WHEN IS THE INSANITY DEFENSE MOST OFTEN USED?   Defense attorneys generally do not recommend that their clients plead not guilty by reason of insanity unless they are charged with a serious offense and the evidence against them is overwhelming. Nevertheless, it is a mistake to think that defendants charged with misdemeanor offenses do not raise this defense; it is sometimes used to obtain treatment for mentally disordered individuals who might not otherwise be eligible for institutionalization. However, when the possible penalty is capital punishment or life imprisonment without parole, an insanity defense becomes more palatable to the defense. In many jurisdictions, however, insanity acquittees are immediately confined to a mental institution, where they are kept for as long as needed to produce substantial improvement in their condition and assure that they are not a danger to themselves or others. In fact, until recently, research indicated that persons found NGRI on average spent at least as much time in mental institutions or treatment facilities as they would have spent in prison if convicted (Golding *et al.*, 1999). More and more, though, persons found NGRI are being institutionalized for shorter periods of time and then released, typically on a conditional basis, into the community where they can receive specialized treatment services (Vitacco *et al.*, 2008). This also allows mental health authorities to monitor their progress and assure that they are taking the medication that presumably keeps them stabilized and their mental disorder in remission. Vitacco *et al.* (2008) found considerable success offering quality services to insanity acquittees in the community. Quality services often included alcohol and drug abuse treatment as well as close monitoring of both mental health symptoms and compliance with medication orders. In other words, someone should assure that the acquittees are "taking their meds" if these have been prescribed. Vitacco *et al.* found that most individuals who were returned to the institution were more likely to be sent back for rules violations than for criminal charges.

Community treatment orders are partially in response to a 1992 U.S. Supreme Court decision, *Foucha v. Louisiana*, which placed some limits on the hospital confinement of persons found not guilty by reason of insanity. In the *Foucha* case, the Court ruled that insanity acquittees may not be held in psychiatric facilities once they are no longer mentally disordered, even if it could be argued that they are dangerous. Foucha had been hospitalized for four years. While a committee of mental health practitioners found his mental illness to be in remission, they could not certify that he was no longer dangerous. Nevertheless, a divided Supreme Court (5–4) ruled that, if no longer mentally ill, he should be discharged. Critics of the *Foucha* decision maintain that the Court did not sufficiently recognize the recurring quality of serious mental disorders. They note that, while mental disorders may go into remission, persons suffering from them are not necessarily cured (Golding *et al.*, 1999). On the other hand, it is difficult to justify holding an individual who is not disordered on the premise that at some point in the future, his or her disorder is likely to reappear.

Thus far, we have discussed the consequences of a finding of not guilty by reason of insanity. In the following section, we cover a variety of standards that courts use to decide whether a person was insane.

INSANITY STANDARDS

The insanity defense has been recognized in English courts for over 700 years (Simon, 1983). Since the American legal system is derived from British law, American courts have generally recognized it as well. Standards or tests to determine insanity vary widely among the states, but they usually center around one of three broad models: the M'Naghten Rule, the Brawner Rule, or the Durham Rule. Moreover, all the insanity standards are fundamentally based on two criteria: **irrationality** and **compulsion** (Morse, 1986). If it can be established that a person was not in control of his or her mental processes (was thinking irrationally) and/or was not in control of his or her behavior (was driven by compulsion) at the time of the offense, then there are grounds for absolving that person of some or all responsibility for the offense. Jurisdictions, however, differ in the extent they accept both these criteria. That is, some jurisdictions accept both criteria, while others will accept only the irrationality component.

The M'Naghten Rule

The **M'Naghten Rule** has been around in some form since at least the nineteenth century. The current rule was formulated in 1843, after Daniel M'Naghten, a Scottish woodcutter, was acquitted of killing a man he believed to be the prime minister. M'Naghten thought he was being persecuted by the Tories and their leader, Prime Minister Sir Robert Peel. He fired a shot into a carriage transporting Peel's secretary, Edward Drumond, thinking Peel himself was in the carriage. There was no question that M'Naghten had committed the act, but the court believed he was so mentally deranged that it would be inhumane to convict him. Applying a "wild beast" test in use at the time, the court concluded it was clear he was not in control of his faculties. He was committed to the Broadmoor Mental Institution, where he remained until his death 22 years later. It was widely believed that M'Naghten "knew" his actions were wrong and that he should have been convicted. Therefore, the law was changed to prevent a similar "miscarriage of justice" in the future. Thus, the rule that bears M'Naghten's name is not the rule under which he was tried.

In 1851, the M'Naghten Rule was adopted in the federal and most state courts in the United States. It is deceptively simple, and therein lies its popularity. It states that a person is not responsible for a criminal act if, "at the time of committing the act, the party accused was labouring under such a defect of reason, from disease of the mind, as not to know the nature and quality of the act he was doing; or if he did know it . . . he did not know he was doing what was wrong" (*M'Naghten,* 1843, p. 718). Essentially, the rule states that if a person, because of some mental disease, did not know right from wrong at the time of an unlawful act, or did not know that what he or she was doing was wrong, that person cannot be held responsible for his or her actions.

Thus, the M'Naghten Rule, sometimes referred to as the **right and wrong test,** emphasizes the *cognitive elements* of (1) being aware and knowing what one was doing at the time of the illegal act, or (2) knowing or realizing right from wrong in the moral sense. The rule recognizes no degree of incapacity. You are either responsible for the action or you are not. There are no in-betweens.

Some states supplement M'Naghten with an irresistible impulse test, which has similarities to the "wild beast" test applied in the original M'Naghten case. The irresistible impulse test recognizes or assumes that people may realize the wrongfulness of their conduct, be aware of what is right or wrong in a particular set of circumstances, but still be powerless to do right in the face of overwhelming pressures from uncontrollable impulses. In other words, there are conditions under which people presumably cannot help themselves. The M'Naghten Rule alone would not cover those circumstances, since it requires that the person did not know right from wrong.

The Brawner Rule and the American Law Institute Rule

The **Brawner Rule,** which is largely based on an insanity rule suggested by the Model Penal Code (MPC), is another rule for determining insanity. The MPC was proposed in 1962 by a group of legal scholars associated with the American Law Institute (ALI). The Code was drafted to serve as a model for legislatures seeking to modernize and rationalize their criminal statutes. According to the Brawner Rule, "A person is not responsible for criminal conduct if at the time of such conduct as a result of mental disease or *defect* [italics added], he lacks substantial capacity either to appreciate the criminality [wrongfulness] of his conduct or to conform his conduct to the requirements of the law" (*United States v. Brawner,* 1972, p. 973). It must be demonstrated that the disease or mental defect *substantially* and directly (1) influenced the defendant's mental or emotional processes, or (2) impaired his or her ability to control behavior. The Brawner Rule, unlike M'Naghten, recognizes *partial* responsibility for criminal conduct, as well as the possibility of an irresistible impulse beyond one's control. It also excludes from the definition of mental disease or defect any repeated criminal or otherwise antisocial conduct, an exclusion we referred to earlier in the chapter. This provision (called the **caveat paragraph**) was intended to disallow the insanity defense for criminal psychopaths who persistently violate social mores and the law. Thus, psychopaths and persons with APDs cannot claim that their abnormal condition is a mental disorder, disease, or defect, even if they have been diagnosed with APD.

The Durham Rule: The Product Test

The **Durham Rule** was created in 1954 in *Durham v. United States* by the same court that later rejected it in favor of the Brawner Rule. Monte Durham, a 26-year-old resident of the District of Columbia, had a long history of mental disorder and petty theft. His crime of the moment was burglary, but he was acquitted because his unlawful act was considered to be "the product of a mental disease or mental defect" (*Durham v. United States*, 1954, p. 874). While the M'Naghten Rule focuses on knowing right from wrong (the mental element in a crime), Durham assumes that one cannot be held responsible if an unlawful action is the product of mental disease or defect.

There is nothing in the Durham Rule that relates directly to the person's mental judgment. If the person has a disease or defect, lack of culpability is easily assumed. The rule was later clarified in *Carter v. United States* (1957), which held that mental illness must not merely have entered into the production of the act, it must have played a necessary role.

Many states were attracted to the apparent simplicity of the Durham Rule, since it seemed more straightforward and comprehensible to juries. However, it soon became apparent that definitions of "mental illness" are vague and subjective, a situation that fostered the widespread discretionary power of psychiatry and considerable misuse of mental health experts during trial. Moreover, virtually any defendant could be excused once mental disease or defect had been established, and the Durham Rule quickly lost its popularity.

Until the 1980s, most jurisdictions adopted one of the above rules, with varying degrees of satisfaction. However, the well-publicized Hinckley acquittal sparked a public outcry for the elimination of the insanity defense and prompted legislative bodies and many professional organizations to reexamine it. The American Bar Association and the American Psychiatric Association, for example, proposed new, more restrictive standards (Steadman *et al.*, 1993). Nearly 100 different reforms in 34 jurisdictions occurred soon after Hinckley's acquittal, the most active insanity reform period in American history. In most instances, these reforms reflected a return to the M'Naghten Rule in a modified, more restrictive form (Steadman *et al.*, 1993). A small minority of states have abolished the insanity defense altogether. Other changes include (1) placing on defendants the burden of proving they were insane (where in the past prosecutors had been required to prove they were not insane), (2) restricting the role of clinical testimony, and (3) requiring persons found NGRI to prove they were no longer mentally ill before being released from a mental institution. Many of these changes were modeled after the federal law discussed below. It should be noted, though, that the U.S. Supreme Court has given wide latitude to the states in defining insanity and crafting their laws relating to it (*Clark v. Arizona*, 2006; DeMatteo, 2007).

The Insanity Defense Reform Act

Amid public clamors to abolish the insanity defense completely after the Hinckley acquittal, Congress passed the **Insanity Defense Reform Act of 1984,** which kept the defense in the federal law but modified it in important ways. Rita Simon and David Aaronson (1988, p. 47) assert, "The Hinckley verdict was unquestionably the decisive influence on congressional modifications to the insanity defense." Essentially, Congress made it more difficult for persons using the insanity defense in federal courts to be acquitted. The Insanity Reform Act changed the Brawner/ALI Rule—the rule that has been most consistently adhered to in all federal circuits (except the Fifth Circuit) since its adoption during the early 1970s—to one patterned more along the lines of the M'Naghten Rule. Specifically, a defendant cannot be held responsible if "at the time of the commission of the acts constituting the offense, the defendant, as a result of a severe mental disease or defect, was unable to appreciate the nature and quality or the wrongfulness of his acts. Mental disease or defect does not otherwise constitute a defense" (18 U.S.C., sec 20[a] [1984]).

In addition, the new federal standard changed the Brawner/ALI Rule in three principal ways (Simon & Aaronson, 1988). First, the act abolished the irresistible impulse test (commonly called the **volitional prong**) of the Brawner/ALI Rule. The inability to control one's actions because of mental defect was no longer acceptable as an excusing condition. Second, the act modified the "cognitive" requirement by replacing the phrase "lacks substantial capacity . . . to appreciate" with "unable to appreciate." The intention was to tighten the requirement to a total lack of ability to appreciate that what they did was wrong (Simon & Aaronson, 1988). Third, under the new law, the mental disease or defect must be severe, to emphasize that certain behavioral disorders (especially personality disorders) do not qualify as a defense. It should be noted that the federal law also bars mental health clinicians from expressing an opinion as to whether the defendant was insane. Clinicians may testify, report on the findings of their evaluations, and provide a diagnosis, but they may not express an ultimate opinion. This is to emphasize that insanity is a legal determination that must be made by the court. **Table 1** summarizes common standards for determining criminal responsibility in mentally disordered defendants.

TABLE 1   Standards for Criminal Responsibility

Standard	Year First Used	Description
M'Naghten Rule	1843	It must be clearly proved that at the time of committing the act, the party accused was laboring under such a defect of reason, from disease of the mind, as not to know the nature and quality of the act he was doing, or if he did know it, that he did not know he was doing what was wrong.
Durham Rule	1954	An accused is not criminally responsible if the unlawful act was the product of mental disease or mental defect.
Brawner/ALI Rule	1972	A person is not responsible for criminal conduct if at the time of such conduct as a result of mental disease or defect he lacks substantial capacity to either appreciate the criminality [wrongfulness] of his conduct or to conform his conduct to the requirements of the law.
Insanity Defense Reform Act	1984	A person charged with a criminal offense should be found not guilty by reason of insanity if it is shown that, as a result of mental disease or mental retardation, he was unable to appreciate the wrongfulness of his conduct at the time of his offense.
Guilty but mentally ill	1975	This holds the defendant blameworthy for the offense, but recognizes the presence of a mental disorder.

Guilty but Mentally Ill

Also in response to disenchantment with the insanity defense, some states have introduced a new verdict alternative, **Guilty but Mentally Ill (GBMI).** Michigan was the first to adopt this alternative in 1975, and by 1992, 11 other states had followed Michigan's lead. The GBMI option is intended as an alternative to, not a substitute for, the NGRI verdict. States differ in the standards and procedures associated with the GBMI verdict, and some use slightly different terminology, such as guilty except insane. In all, though, the major intention of the option is to reduce the number of insanity acquittals, hold the defendant blameworthy, but still recognize the presence of a mental disorder. Thus, GBMI allows the court to render a "middle-ground" verdict in the case of allegedly mentally disordered defendants. The verdict allows juries, for example, to reconcile their belief that a defendant who commits a crime should be held responsible with the belief that he or she also needs help.

Research on the GBMI laws indicates that the intended purposes may not have been accomplished. In Michigan, for example, insanity acquittals have remained stable while guilty verdicts have generally declined (Smith & Hall, 1982). The same findings have been reported in other states that have adopted the GBMI option (McGinley & Paswark, 1989). Furthermore, defendants found GBMI have received longer sentences and had longer confinements than "sane" defendants found guilty of similar charges (Callahan, McGreevy, Cirincione, & Steadman, 1992; Steadman *et al.*, 1993). In addition, research indicates that those individuals found GBMI are no more likely to receive psychotherapy or rehabilitative services than other mentally disordered defendants in the prison system (Morse, 1985; Slobogin, 1985). Thus, the promise of treatment that is implicit in the statutes remains unfulfilled. However, depending upon the wording of the statute, it may be read as creating a *right* to treatment for those defendants found GBMI (Cohen, 2008), although this is not the common approach. Interestingly, there is also evidence that defendants charged with a serious violent crime often elect the GBMI alternative as part of the plea-bargaining process. Defense attorneys may be more willing to accept this option than go to trial and risk their client's life (Steadman *et al.*, 1993). Considering the research strongly suggesting that GBMI statutes do not accomplish what was intended, virtually all of the scholarly writing on this issue has questioned the wisdom and efficacy of these laws (Cohen, 2008).

UNIQUE DEFENSES

Earlier in the chapter, we discussed some of the psychiatric diagnoses that are most likely to accompany a decision that a defendant is incompetent to stand trial or used to bolster an insanity defense. In this section, we discuss additional disorders or diagnoses that are less common but still cited by defense lawyers, either to absolve defendants completely or to support a claim of diminished capacity or responsibility.

Posttraumatic Stress Disorder

According to the DSM-IV, **posttraumatic stress disorder (PTSD)** is "the development of characteristic symptoms following exposure to extreme traumatic stress or involving direct personal experience of an event that involves actual or threatened death or serious injury, or other threat to one's physical integrity; or witnessing an event that involves death, injury, or threat to the physical integrity of another person; or learning about unexpected or violent death, serious harm, or threat of death or injury experienced by a family member or other close associate" (p. 424). The precipitating event would be substantially distressing to almost anyone, and it is "usually experienced with intense fear, terror, and helplessness" (p. 424).

PTSD was formally recognized as a distinct disorder in the 1980 edition of the DSM-III following efforts by veterans' groups to have mental health professionals recognize a "post-Vietnam syndrome" that led to a variety of disabling symptoms (Appelbaum *et al.* 1993). Since being formally recognized, PTSD has been broadly applied to war veterans, survivors of the Holocaust, survivors of major disasters—such as the events of September 11, 2001—and victims and survivors of rape, child abuse, spousal abuse, and sexual harassment. PTSD falls under the broader category of "dissociative disorders" in the DSM-IV-R. Dissociative disorders are marked by major changes in memory not due to physical causes (Comer, 2004). Other examples of these disorders are certain forms of amnesia, fugues, and dissociative identity disorder.

Surveys estimate that between 1 percent and 2 percent of all Americans suffer from PTSD (Sutker, Uddo-Crane, & Allain, 1991). One study estimated that PTSD affected 31 percent of all male and 27 percent of all female Vietnam veterans (Kulka *et al.*, 1991). Veterans of combat in Afghanistan, Iraq, and the Persian Gulf have also been affected. Victims of human rights abuses around the globe are also susceptible to the symptoms associated with PTSD.

The symptoms of PTSD include "flashbacks," recurrent dreams or nightmares, or painful, intrusive memories of the traumatic event. A diminished responsiveness, a don't-care attitude, or psychological "numbing" to the external world are common, particularly during the weeks following the event. On the other hand, some research indicates that the symptoms of PTSD may not emerge until considerable time has elapsed, six months to a year or more. In fact, the DSM-IV-TR distinguishes among acute (symptoms last less than three months), chronic (symptoms last longer than three months), and delayed onset PTSD (when at least six months have passed since the traumatic event). Feelings of alienation or detachment from the social environment are also characteristic, a pattern that leads to difficulty in developing close, meaningful relationships with others. Other symptoms include sleep problems, being easily startled, considerable difficulty concentrating or remembering, and extreme avoidance of anything that reminds them of the event. Even anniversaries of the trauma are often enough to precipitate symptoms. Individuals with a diagnosis of PTSD tend to be moody, depressed, and difficult to be around or work with. They often move from job to job, relationship to relationship.

PTSD has been used to support a defense of NGRI, in both violent and nonviolent cases (Monahan & Walker, 1990, 1994). For example, PTSD has been used as an excusing condition for drug trafficking (e.g., *United States v. Krutschewski,* 1981). Evidence to date, however, shows that—while courts are willing to admit evidence of PTSD—using it to support an insanity defense is no more successful than using other mental disorders (Appelbaum *et al.*, 1993). Moreover, PTSD defendants, as a rule, do not follow the stereotypic images portrayed by the media as "tortured but essentially upstanding veterans, who at some point, become overwhelmed by their symptoms, 'snap,' and commit a violent crime" (Appelbaum *et al.*, 1993, p. 233). Specifically, the research evidence reveals that defendants who use PTSD to support an insanity defense have been in as much trouble and involvement with the criminal justice system as other defendants who use the insanity defense (Appelbaum *et al.*, 1993).

When the PTSD defense has been successful, it usually results in a finding of *diminished responsibility,* rather than the complete absolution of responsibility (NGRI) for the defendant. PTSD has also been cited in plea bargaining and in presentence reports (Monahan & Walker, 1990). That is, prosecutors may be more willing to accept a guilty plea to a reduced charge, and judges more willing to impose a lighter sentence, if evidence of PTSD exists. Appelbaum and colleagues (1993) also found that, in cases involving veterans, PTSD was frequently used as evidence for diminished responsibility in assigning cases to pretrial diversion, in plea bargaining, and in sentencing.

The primary legal argument used by the defense is that the defendant was in a PTSD dissociated state when he committed the act. A **dissociated state** refers to symptoms in which the individual feels detached from themselves and their surroundings and basically loses some contact with reality. While in that state, a person typically does not remember what he or she has experienced or even his or her own identity. In *State v. Felde* (1982), the defendant—a Vietnam veteran who shot a police officer—"claimed that he was in a dissociative state and that he believed that he had been captured by the North Vietnamese at the time he shot the officer" (McCord, 1987, p. 65). In *Miller v. State* (1983), the defendant, charged with a prison escape, argued that he thought he was still in Vietnam and his only intention was to get back to the United States.

PTSD has been used to excuse or mitigate criminal responsibility in cases involving battered women who maintain that they have **battered woman syndrome,** sometimes considered a variant of PTSD (Appelbaum *et al.,* 1993). This is a controversial area for at least two major reasons. First, there is not universal agreement in the psychological literature that there exists a battered woman syndrome. Second, advocates for battered women resist the implication that they have a mental disorder or that they are "insane." When PTSD is used, a battered woman may claim that the abuse was so extensive and brutal that, in a dissociative state brought about by the disorder, she killed the abuser. In this case, she is more likely to claim "temporary insanity" than "insanity," in the hope that acquittal will not be followed by commitment to a mental institution. However, PTSD in a battered woman also may be used to support a claim of self-defense rather than insanity, though courts have not been sympathetic to this approach (Slobogin, 1999). When used in this way, the defendant focuses on other symptoms of PTSD—for example, heightened fear, anxiety, depression—rather than on the dissociative state. In a different context, evidence that an alleged rape victim shows the symptoms of PTSD has been accepted in some courts as proof that the victim has indeed been raped (Appelbaum *et al.,* 1993). Likewise, PTSD has been used in civil suits involving emotional or physical personal injury, such as sexual harassment suits or civil suits against former abusers.

While courts are increasingly accepting PTSD evidence, some legal scholars and researchers remain skeptical. They believe that objective assessment of PTSD lacks solid validity, and the diagnosis depends almost exclusively on self-report. Consequently, critics argue that there is considerable opportunity for malingering or faking the disorder, especially if the individual rehearses and practices the symptoms. Appelbaum *et al.* (1993, p. 230) conclude that the problem of PTSD in the courts as an excusing condition is "particularly acute with something as new, as 'unverifiable,' as potentially useful, and as politically charged as PTSD." Skepticism of PTSD as an excusing condition for crime does not mean that it is not recognized as a major problem in adjustment, though. Moreover, clinicians who encounter these individuals recognize the debilitating effects of traumatic situations on those who have suffered them.

Pathological Gamblers' Syndrome

The syndrome of **compulsive gambling** began with psychoanalytic case studies during the early part of the twentieth century (Cunnien, 1985). Compulsive gamblers, the early case studies concluded, are neurotics with an insatiable, unconscious desire to lose what was gained (Cunnien, 1985). The DSM-IV describes pathological gambling as the inability to resist impulses to gamble, despite the dire consequences to family, interpersonal relationships, and daily living. "The essential feature of Pathological Gambling is persistent and recurrent maladaptive gambling behavior that disrupts personal, family, or vocational pursuits" (DSM-IV, p. 615). It is a progressive and eventually overwhelming urge to engage in gambling behavior. The disorder may afflict as many as 1–3 percent of the adult population, and is more common among males than females (DSM-IV-TR). In a survey of 1,200 residents of Ontario, Insight Canada Research (1998) found that about 8 percent of Ontarians could be classified as "problem gamblers," while 0.9 percent are probable pathological gamblers. Pathological gambling usually begins during adolescence in males, and later in life in females (DSM-IV-TR). Pathological gamblers are often overconfident, very energetic, and easily bored, but sometimes exhibit stress, anxiety, and depression during their losing streaks.

The distinguishing characteristic of pathological gambling from "normal" or social gambling is its "addictive" nature. Addicted gamblers are believed to be unable to walk away from a gamble and are tense and restless if gambling is denied them.

Pathological gambling became fully recognized in the DSM-III in 1980 as a serious mental disorder, and since that time, the disorder has been used by defendants as an excuse for a variety of illegal activities. The crimes with which defendants have been charged are not gambling offenses, but rather crimes committed for monetary gain. The defendants contended that money was necessary in order to support their pathological gambling habit (McCord, 1987). For example, in *United States v. Gillis* (1985), the defendant, who was charged with interstate transportation of stolen vehicles and forged securities, argued that he engaged in these illegal activities to support his gambling habit. The following are additional examples where similar defenses were used: *United States v. Davis* (1984), in which the defendant was charged with forging and converting government checks payable to deceased relatives; *United States v. Gould* (1984), in which the defendant was charged with bank robbery; and *United States v. Lewellyn* (1985), in which the defendant was charged with embezzlement, making a false statement, and mail fraud.

In general, defendants using this defense have been unsuccessful, because they have been unable to demonstrate a connection between "the syndrome and the inability of the defendant to resist the impulse to commit crimes in order to support the gambling urge" (McCord, 1987, p. 67). However, it should be noted that the pathological gambling defense has been occasionally successful, as seen in *State v. Lafferty* (1984) in a case involving embezzlement, and in *State v. Campanaro* (1980) in a case involving forgery.

Cunnien (1985, p. 89) writes, "There are . . . no available data to suggest whether pathological gambling and attendant criminal behavior are uncontrollable or merely uncontrolled." He further concludes, "It remains unproven that impulses to gamble are uncontrollable" (p. 98).

Dissociative Identity Disorder

The essential feature of **dissociative identity disorder (DID)** (formerly called **multiple personality disorder (MPD)**) is "the existence within the person of two or more distinct personalities or personality states that recurrently take control of behavior" (DSM-IV, p. 484). Furthermore, "each personality state may be experienced as if it has a distinct personal history, self-image, and identity, including a separate name" (DSM-IV, p. 484). Periodically, at least two personalities take full control of the individual's behavior. The change or transition from one personality to another is often very sudden (seconds to minutes), and is generally triggered by stress or some relevant environmental stimuli. Often, hypnosis can also bring about this shift into another personality.

According to the DSM-IV, each of the personalities may be aware of some or all the other personalities in varying degrees. There may be as many as a hundred different identities. The disorder occurs about three to nine times more frequently in females than in males. Persons who experience DID are highly suggestible and impressionable, and can be readily hypnotized either by themselves or others. Reported cases of what was then called MPD have historically been extremely rare. However, between 1980 and 1989, the number of cases diagnosed in the United States rose dramatically, from

200 to 6,000 (Slovenko, 1989). Part of this increase is due to the American Psychiatric Association officially recognizing the disorder in the DSM-III.

There is a good deal of controversy surrounding the existence and prevalence of DID, which seemed to have gained more status among clinicians in the 1990s, while researchers were far more skeptical. The concept of individuals having "multiple personalities" or "alter egos" that control their lives is fascinating to many but remains scientifically questionable. While this phenomenon may exist in a very minute segment of the mentally disordered population, it is also highly susceptible to being overdiagnosed.

On occasion, MPD has been used successfully as an excusing condition for criminal responsibility. In *State v. Rodrigues* (1984), a defendant accused of three counts of sodomy and one count of rape of young girls was acquitted on the basis of MPD. In *State v. Milligan* (1978), Billy Milligan claimed he had 24 separate personalities and was found NGRI in criminal charges of raping three women. In general, however, MPD has not been a successful defense (Slovenko, 1989). One of the more well-known cases in which the MPD defense was tried involved serial killer Kenneth Bianchi, known as the Hillside Strangler. The Hillside Strangler was given wide publicity because of the brutality and sadistic quality of his murders. The victims were young, attractive women who were raped and strangled, and whose nude bodies were conspicuously displayed on the hillsides in the Los Angeles area. The Hillside Strangler was responsible for at least a dozen murders during a one-year period (1977–1978).

Much of the following material was acquired from an article written by Martin T. Orne, David F. Dinges, and Emily Carota Orne (1984), and the interested reader is encouraged to study that paper. Throughout his adult life, Bianchi's most consistent career aspiration was to become a police officer, and he even attended a junior college program in police science. Although he repeatedly applied for positions at various police departments, he was not successful at landing a job. However, he did obtain employment as a security guard.

Overall, Bianchi was unable to sustain a successful career pattern, holding at least 12 different jobs during the nine-year period following high school. His background was a series of lies, scams, and illegal activities, ranging from the use of stolen credit cards to the pimping of juvenile prostitutes. During his last year in Los Angeles, Bianchi masqueraded as a psychologist, complete with an office and answering service. He obtained false diplomas and credentials by placing a classified ad in the *Los Angeles Times*, offering a position to a recently graduated psychologist. He requested that the applicants send not only résumés, but also their official university transcripts. From the hundreds of applications he received, he obtained enough information to forge a transcript and diploma with his name on them.

At age 19, Bianchi married a high school girlfriend, but the marriage lasted less than eight months. At age 26, he began to live with a woman in a common-law relationship; she bore him a son. After the birth of his son, his common-law wife moved to Bellingham, Washington, where Bianchi joined her three months later. In Bellingham, he obtained a job as a supervisor for a private security agency. Bianchi, however, was arrested on January 11, 1979, for the murders of two women in Washington—murders that followed a pattern similar to the Hillside Strangler in California.

Despite considerable evidence against him, Bianchi insisted that he was innocent. Eventually, he maintained under hypnosis that his alter personality "Steve" had done the killings. Since Steve did the killings, Ken Bianchi argued he should not be held responsible and pleaded NGRI under the State of Washington's M'Naghten Rule. The court appointed a team of experts to determine if Bianchi really was suffering MPD. The court (*State v. Bianchi,* 1979) posited that if the experts could agree, the insanity defense might prevail. The team of experts, however, after careful examination of his past and present behavior, found no basis for Bianchi's claim of MPD. Although Bianchi knew the "textbook version" of MPD (probably knowledge gained during the time he impersonated a psychologist), he was less than convincing on the more subtle aspects of the disorder recognized by the experts. The team concluded that Bianchi was a psychopath. Bianchi then quickly changed his plea to guilty in order to avoid the death penalty.

There is considerable debate among practitioners and scholars as to whether the syndrome MPD/DID actually exists, and it is sometimes referred to as the "UFO of psychiatry" (Ondrovik & Hamilton, 1991). In some instances, it may be **iatrogenic**—that is, unintentionally caused by clinicians or practitioners themselves. This means that practitioners who firmly believe in and are perceptually sensitive to DID look for and interpret a variety of behaviors as symptoms of the disorder. Some clinicians maintain that the symptoms of DID are very subtle and that the average length of time it takes for the disorder to be diagnosed is seven years (Gelinas, 1993). In effect, the practitioner may develop the syndrome in the patient, and the patient, in turn, learns to believe that he or she is afflicted with it. It has also been argued that implicit and explicit suggestions during hypnosis can shape segments of self into the appearance of MPD (Orne *et al.*, 1984). Regardless of whether the syndrome is iatrogenic or whether it is possible for several personalities to "possess" a physical body, an important point must be made. The syndrome is *often subjectively real* to the patient, and the person who allegedly experiences it often plays each of the roles well and convincingly. Martin Orne and his colleagues (Orne *et al.*, 1984, p. 120) observe, "So striking are the behavioral differences between personalities that the assertion is often made that one would need to have the dramatic skills of Sarah Bernhardt or Sir Laurence Olivier, along with a detailed knowledge of psychiatry, to effectively simulate such radically different persons."

Everyone to some degree hosts a number of subpersonalities (Slovenko, 1989). One aspect of our subpersonalities is our moods: one day we may be cool and withdrawn, and the next day, warm and sociable. The situation also makes a big difference. For example, each person is different when at home with parents than when spending time with friends. At home, parents might treat you like the immature 16-year-old they remember, and you find yourself assuming that role quickly and easily. The old conflicts and squabbles with your parents return, just as they did years ago. It is possible that these changes in moods, together with the fact that some clinics "look hard" for MPD/DID and some patients are happy to oblige, all contribute to the increased prevalence of this disorder.

In summary, the validity of DID as a viable entity is very much open to debate by both the mental health and legal professions. Supporters of the concept maintain that diagnostic procedures among clinicians are more accurate today than in the past, and clinicians have at their disposal specific diagnostic tests to detect the disorder (Comer, 2004). At present, though, there is very little solid evidence that the syndrome, as a bona fide mental disorder in which one personality completely controls the other(s), actually exists, except possibly in very rare situations. Nevertheless, it is not unusual to be in a roomful of clinicians who seem firmly convinced that DID is a significant problem encountered in their practices and one that mental health practitioners still fail to diagnose. According to this perspective, treatment is a highly complex and multistage process. It involves allowing the alter egos to emerge and enabling the client to confront them. Eventually, the "alters" are left behind, a process that can be very frightening to the client. As one therapist commented, after a long period of treatment, the client had successfully confronted her problems and was ready to move on to a normal life. However, she was concerned about how she would handle financial matters, because "Ruth"—one of her alters—was the one who had always balanced the checkbook.

Amnesia

Amnesia refers to complete or partial memory loss of an event, series of events, or some segment of life's experiences, either due to physical trauma, neurophysiological disturbance, or psychological factors. According to the DSM-IV, "Individuals with an amnestic disorder are impaired in their ability to learn new information or are unable to recall previously-learned information or past events" (p. 156). Amnesia is not simply forgetting a name, a date, or an incident, but is reserved for severely impaired ability to remember past material (retrograde amnesia) or to acquire and retain new material (anterograde amnesia).

Some researchers have identified a classification of amnesia called **limited amnesia,** which is "a pathological inability to remember a specific episode, or small number of episodes, from the recent past" (Schacter, 1986b, p. 48). Limited amnesia may be caused by emotional shock, alcohol or drug intoxication, or a blow to the head. Therefore, limited amnesia is not ongoing, nor does it involve extensive memory loss. Rather, the loss is temporary and restricted to a specific event or incident.

In general, the courts have not been receptive to amnesia as a valid condition in either the insanity defense, or as a condition that promotes incompetence to stand trial (Rubinsky & Brandt, 1986). The exception is in cases of brain injury, when a connection can be established between the injury and the memory loss. Paull (1993) notes that there have been cases in at least 20 states and five federal circuit courts where the court has held that amnesia per se does not render a defendant incompetent. One reason for this judicial "hard line" approach to amnesia is the suspicion that the defendant may be faking the memory loss. It is easy for people to simply say they cannot remember committing the crime, and it is difficult for psychologists to determine whether a person can or cannot remember. In recent years, though, psychologists have been able to fine-tune a number of instruments designed to measure malingering—or faking—of various symptoms, including symptoms of amnesia (Rogers, 1997). Additionally, some psychologists believe that amnesia can be evaluated with recognition tests that are tailored to the information that the client claims not to know (Frederick, 2000).

Amnesia associated with alcoholic intoxication presents a favorite excuse for reprehensible behavior, and is the most commonly invoked excusing condition in criminal cases. "When I drink I go blank about some things" is the usual line. It is intriguing to note that 30–65 percent of persons convicted of criminal homicide claim they cannot remember the crime, usually because of alcoholic intoxication at the time of the offense (Schacter 1986b). A similar pattern exists for other violent crimes (e.g., rape) as well.

However, the courts have not been very sympathetic to defendants who rely on excuses based on alcohol or other drug intoxication. This is because the courts hold the person blameworthy since he or she should have known, at the outset, the risks involved in drinking alcohol or taking drugs. Thus, attempts to use amnesia in this way have met with strong judicial resistance. For example, one court held that "insanity is the incapacity to discriminate between right and wrong while amnesia is simply the inability to remember" (Rubinsky & Brandt, 1986, p. 30). Therefore, amnesia per se fails to qualify as a mental disorder that robs a person of the ability to distinguish between right and wrong.

MENTAL DISORDER AND VIOLENCE

While the mental disorders described in this chapter may be associated with a variety of criminal offenses, it is the crimes of violence that are most disturbing. The depressed individual may embezzle funds in an effort to obtain a way out of his dire economic situation. The individual with a delusional disorder may break into a building to seek shelter from those who persecute him. The person with an antisocial personality disorder may perpetrate a series of economic scams on unsuspecting victims. Publicity is most likely to accompany criminal behavior when it is violent, however, and the public is most fearful of these offenses, despite the fact that we are far more likely to be victims of economic crimes than violent crimes. And as we learned above, the mere presence of a mental illness does not guarantee that a defendant will be found incompetent to stand trial or absolved of criminal responsibility. In some jurisdictions, this is even more true when defendants are accused of violent crimes than when they are accused of property offenses.

As a group, individuals who are mentally ill are no more likely to commit crimes than those who are not. Nevertheless, they do appear with some regularity in arrest records, in jails, in prisons, and on probation and parole caseloads. As a matter of fact, the prevalence of mental disorders is more than three times higher in the criminal justice population than in the general population (Skeem, Emke-Francis, & Louden, 2006). Part of this is due to a decrease in the availability of inpatient care for mental health problems.

Long-term inpatient care or hospitalization of the mentally disordered has largely disappeared, particularly in public institutions. While these institutions still exist, they are generally intended for short-term crisis care and treat patients with drugs rather than psychotherapy. They typically do not hold most patients for more than three to six months, although there are exceptions. (One is the sexually violent predator. Persons found not guilty by reason of insanity (John Hinckley, Andrea Yates) or incompetent to stand trial (Russell Weston)—if their crimes or alleged crimes were particularly serious—are other examples.) Although the mentally disordered may be discharged from these institutions with orders to continue taking medication, they are often not well supervised. Consequently, the mentally disordered have become a more visible presence within the community. When problems arise, it is often the responsibility of law enforcement officials to handle the situation.

Research on the Violence of the Mentally Disordered

Early research literature consistently supported the position that mentally disordered individuals—even the severely mentally disordered—are no more likely to commit serious crimes against others than the general population (Brodsky, 1973, 1977; Henn, Herjanic, & Vanderpearl, 1976a; Monahan, 1981; Rabkin, 1979). However, more recent research (Brennan, Mednick, & Hodgins, 2000; Klassen & O'Connor, 1988, 1990; Monahan, 1992) finds that this cannot be said of a certain subset of the mentally disordered population. Specifically, male mentally disordered patients, *who have a history of at least one violent incident,* have a high probability of being violent within a year after release from the hospital. In fact, evidence is beginning to accumulate that individuals with schizophrenia are at increased risk of violent offending and even at higher risk to commit murder (Naudts & Hodgins, 2005). In addition, when offenders with schizophrenia do commit murder, they most often kill relatives, and many are exhibiting hallucinations and delusions at the time of the offense (Häkkänen & Laajasalo, 2006). As we noted earlier, however, delusions that are of a persecutory nature are particularly problematic.

We cannot emphasize enough that a majority of people with mental disorders do *not* commit serious or violent offenses. For example, only 11.3 percent of the men and 2.3 percent of the women who developed schizophrenia committed violent offenses (Tengström, Hodgins, Grann, Långström, & Kullgren, 2004). In addition, those individuals with schizophrenia who commit violent crime constitute a very heterogeneous group. "Some display a history of antisocial behavior from a very early age; others begin engaging in antisocial behavior around the time of schizophrenia onsets; others commit only 1 violent attack in their lives, while others behave aggressively only when acutely psychotic" (Naudts & Hodgins, 2005, p. 1).

Recent research also finds that offenders with schizophrenia who have high scores on the Psychopathy Checklist-Revised (PCL-R) are usually convicted for more violent offenses than those with low scores on the PCL-R (Tengström *et al.*, 2004). The results suggest that PCL-R scores offer the strongest predictor of violent and chronic offending histories. Tengström *et al.* (2004) write, "These results indicated that among offenders with schizophrenia, as among non-mentally ill offenders, high PCL-R ratings are associated with more severe histories of offending and violence" (p. 385).

The Tengström *et al.* (2004) study underscores the fact that males who develop schizophrenia *and* exhibit antisocial behavior at an *early* age often demonstrate persistent and versatile patterns of criminal offending. Essentially, early-onset offenders with schizophrenia show a pattern very similar to life-course-persistent offenders (LCP).

In addition, there is further evidence that men who have both schizophrenia and a substance abuse problem are at an increased risk of violent offending. For instance, Räsänen *et al.* (1998) report evidence that male schizophrenics with alcohol abuse problems are 25 times more likely to commit violent crimes than males with no mental disorders and no alcohol problems. Follow-up studies of patients with schizophrenia and substance abuse problems have frequently found them to be at risk of committing violent offenses (Appelbaum, Robbins, & Monahan, 2000; Tengström *et al.*, 2004).

John Monahan (1992) stresses two things about the research showing a connection between mental disorders and violence. First, the relationship refers only to people *currently* experiencing a *serious* mental disorder. People who have experienced a serious mental disorder in the past and are not showing symptoms currently are unlikely to engage in violent behavior. Second, it is still a fact that a great majority (over 90%) of the currently mentally disordered are not violent. Media portrayals of common psychotic killers driven berserk by bloodthirsty delusions are sensational, frightening, and perhaps entertaining, but in reality the phenomenon is rare. Finally, it must be emphasized not only that the mental disorder–violence link relates to the seriously mentally disordered (e.g., schizophrenics), but also that the relationship is also stronger for individuals who have a history of violent behavior. Recall that Laajasalo and Häkkänen (2006) found that the strongest predictors of excessive violence among their sample of schizophrenics convicted of homicide were a past history of violent behavior and the presence of a cooffender.

Furthermore, it is possible, as some clinicians believe, that the more bizarre violent offenses are committed by the mentally disordered, particularly those categorized as schizophrenic or paranoid. Moreover, the more extreme violence of schizophrenics is typically directed toward family members or acquaintances, and bizarre self-mutilation is more likely than mutilatory murders (Blackburn, 1993). However, Ronald Blackburn (1993, p. 274) admonishes, "Although there appears to be an increased risk in schizophrenia, particularly in paranoid schizophrenia, it must be reiterated that only a small minority of patients in this category are violent, and that the disorder itself is rarely sufficient to account for violent acts in instances where they occur."

Individuals experiencing affective (mood) psychoses are less likely to be violent. When affective psychoses are associated with violence, they are usually manifested in women within the context of extended suicide, in which the offender kills herself as well as others in the environment, including her immediate family (Blackburn, 1993). Mass murders in public settings are often committed by men who feel hopeless and also have the signs of affective psychoses. In most cases, mass murderers plan to die or commit suicide at the site of their crime.

The MacArthur Research Network

Some of the best-known research on the potential violence of the mentally disordered has been conducted by the MacArthur Research Network (Monahan *et al.*, 2001; Steadman *et al.*, 1998). Researchers followed over 1,000 patients discharged from civil psychiatric hospitals in an effort to determine the extent to which they demonstrated aggressive behavior over a one-year period. The patients also had been measured on a wide range of "risk factors"—134 in all—while they were hospitalized. These included such factors as violent fantasies, history of abuse as a child, frequency of parents fighting with each other, and number of negative and positive persons in the social network, to name but a few. The data allowed the MacArthur researchers to develop a risk-assessment instrument, The Multiple Iterative Classification Tree (ICT), which they believe can help clinicians identify low, average, and high-risk individuals. It is worth noting that about half of the discharged patients in this study were in the low-risk group, while the remaining patients were about evenly divided between average and high-risk groups. However, no single risk factor was a significant predictor of violence. As Monahan *et al.* (2001, p. 142) stated, "The propensity for violence is the result of the accumulation of risk factors, no one of which is either necessary or sufficient for a person to behave aggressively toward others."

In sum, then, the research on the mentally disordered and violence allows us to conclude the following:

- Past mental disorder alone, even serious mental disorder, is not necessarily a good predictor of violence.
- The mental disorder most closely associated with violent and serious offenses is schizophrenia.
- Persons with schizophrenia who commit violent crimes consist of a very heterogeneous group.
- Males who have developed schizophrenia and who score high on the PCL-R have an increased risk of being violent.
- Males who develop schizophrenia *and* exhibit antisocial behavior at an *early* age often demonstrate persistent and versatile patterns of criminal offending.
- Violence is associated with *current* serious mental disorder, particularly when a history of violent behavior is also present.
- While researchers have developed some instruments to assess the likelihood that a person will engage in violence, no one factor serves as strong predictor; violent behavior seems to be a result of an accumulation of risk factors, unique to each individual.

Police and the Mentally Disordered

During the last quarter of the twentieth century, researchers focused a good deal of attention on interactions between law enforcement officials and the mentally disordered. An early literature review of the criminal behavior of discharged mental patients is instructive (Rabkin, 1979). Rabkin found that a significant number of studies documented a higher arrest rate for discharged mental patients than for the general population, especially for assaultive behavior. Rabkin suggested two explanations for the disproportionate arrest rates. First, a small subset of patients who had criminal records prior to hospital admission continued their antisocial ways soon after discharge from the mental institution. These habitual offenders significantly inflated the arrest rates for all mental patients. In fact, those discharged patients *without* prior criminal records were substantially below the arrest rates for the general population. Second, most criminal offenses after discharge were committed by individuals who had been diagnosed with alcoholism, substance addiction, or APD, all of which appear consistently in the research. Alcoholism and substance addiction are in the fringe areas of traditional diagnoses because they do not represent what are considered serious or typical mental disorders. With respect to APD, it was often used when clinicians could find no other way to label a person acting antisocially. When these three categories were omitted, Rabkin found that the arrest rates among the discharged patients, *without a criminal history,* were comparable with those reported in the general population. "When patients with arrest histories, primary diagnoses of substance abuse, and personality disorders are considered separately, the remainder of the patient group appears to be considerably less dangerous than are those members of the general public who are not mentally ill" (Rabkin, 1979, p. 26).

Research has also documented that police may be more apt to arrest the mentally disordered (Teplin, 1984). Trained graduate students in psychology observed 1,382 police–citizen encounters (involving 2,555 citizens) and evaluated the mental status of the citizens according to specific criteria (a symptom checklist that listed the major characteristics of severe mental disorders). The police determined that 506 citizens qualified as suspects, and they arrested 148. The graduate students classified 30 of the 506 suspects and 14 of the 148 suspects arrested as exhibiting definite symptoms of mental disorders. Therefore, the police arrested 20 percent more individuals with symptoms than without symptoms. Considering that many disordered individuals tend to have annoying symptoms, such as verbal abuse, belligerence, and disrespect, the slightly higher probability of arrest is hardly surprising. To some extent, police also may have taken some of these individuals into custody in order to provide them with shelter. However, police officers failed to recognize the behavior as representing a mental disorder in a large number of cases, believing the individuals were simply being disrespectful and asking for trouble.

In the 20-plus years since Teplin's now-classic study, significant changes have occurred nationwide relative to law enforcement's handling of mentally disordered individuals. First, police academies are more likely to offer some training in both recognizing and dealing with mental disorders (Fields, 2006). In some communities, police have taken the initiative to appoint specially trained liaison officers to work with the disordered (Smith, 2002). Second, communities across the nation are establishing specialized courts—mental health courts—that provide diversionary options to jailing and prosecuting the mentally disordered—and the mentally retarded—who are charged with nonviolent offenses, or even minor violent crimes, such as simple assault. Rather than being held in jail, they are offered shelter and treatment or training services. Mental health courts are of recent origin and need continuing evaluation before we can conclude that they are effective. However, they offer a promising alternative to the short-term cycles of arrest, jail, court, release, and rearrest that characterize the lives of some mentally disordered individuals.

MENTALLY DISORDERED INMATES

Mental disorders in those incarcerated in prison and jail are sometimes cited as evidence of a link between crime and abnormal behavior. Both the prevalence and the nature of disorder among these populations are difficult to determine, however, because statistics and descriptions vary widely. Furthermore, some data are based on the inmates' own self-report, while other data are based on clinical findings.

The most recent statistics indicate that more than half of all prison and jail inmates have a mental health problem (James & Glaze, 2006). This does not mean that they are seriously mentally disordered—rather, it suggests that they might benefit from mental health treatment. Female inmates have higher rates of mental health problems than male inmates. The most common problem reported is major depression, followed by psychotic disorders (see **Table 2**).

TABLE 2 Inmates Identified as Mentally Disordered, by Gender, Race/Hispanic Origin, and Age

Offender Characteristics	Percent Identified as Mentally Disordered		
	State Inmates	Federal inmates	Jail Inmates
All inmates	56.2	44.8	64.2
Gender			
Male	55.0	43.60	62.8
Female	73.1	61.2	75.4
Race/Hispanic Origin			
White	62.2	49.6	71.2
Black	54.7	45.9	63.4
Hispanic	46.3	36.8	50.7
Other	61.9	50.3	69.5

Source: James & Glaze (2006).

Other researchers have reported that 10–15 percent of persons in jails and federal and state prisons have *severe* mental disorders (Lamb, Weinberger, & Gross, 2004). It is difficult to determine to what extent these data include APDs; it is estimated that 40–80 percent of inmates carry that diagnosis (Steffan & Morgan, 2005). Nevertheless, both researchers and mental health professionals working with jail and prison inmates report significant increases in *serious* mental health problems (Ashford, Sales, & Reid, 2001).

Some research reveals that the rates of serious mental disorders among prison inmates vary widely, ranging from 5 percent to 16 percent psychotic (Teplin, 1990). Among a sample of adult male jail detainees in Cook County (Chicago), Teplin (1990) found 9.5 percent had experienced a severe mental disorder (schizophrenia, mania, or major depression) at some point in their life, compared with 4.4 percent of males in the U.S. general population. Robins and Regier (1991) found that 6.7 percent of prisoners had suffered from schizophrenia at some point in their lives, compared with 1.4 percent of the U.S. population. In the New York correctional system, it was estimated that about 8 percent of the inmates had "severe" mental disorders and another 16 percent had "significant" mental disorders (Steadman, Fabisiak, Dvoskin, & Holobean, 1987). However, it is unclear whether the mental disorders were present prior to incarceration, or developed as a result of being incarcerated. In addition, it is often not clear from the research what percent of the disordered have been diagnosed with APD, the catch-all category we discussed earlier.

In the 1970s and 1980s, it was not unusual for mentally disordered individuals— particularly those serving time in prison rather than jails—to be transferred to secure units of civil mental hospitals. As the number of disordered inmates increased, prison systems across the United States began to open treatment facilities within the prison system. Depending on the jurisdiction, then, a seriously mentally disordered inmate might be treated in a separate mental health wing of the prison, transferred to a prison facility specifically designated for the mentally disordered, or transferred to a civil mental institution. It is also possible that the offender might not receive any treatment, because the extent of his disorder is not recognized or, more soberingly, not acknowledged.

Young offenders—including juveniles—may be more likely than adults to be diagnosed with mental disorder. Linda Teplin (2000) found that two-thirds of juveniles in a sample of more than 1,800 youths held in Chicago's Cook County Juvenile Temporary Detention Center tested positive for at least one drug, and two-thirds were diagnosed with at least one mental disorder. A considerable portion of the mental disorders in these juveniles consisted of major depressions, especially among female juveniles. The Teplin study, known as the Northwestern Juvenile Project, strongly suggests that many mentally disordered juveniles are also abusing drugs and alcohol quite extensively at the time of their arrest.

It is obvious that jail and prison conditions, as well as conditions in juvenile facilities, can have deleterious effects on mental states. Therefore, an individual may become mentally disordered after being institutionalized, which may be reflected in these statistics. However, considerable evidence indicates that many inmates or prisoners were showing signs of mental disorders prior to incarceration (Bureau of Justice Assistance, 2000).

Diagnoses of Mentally Disordered Inmates

It remains difficult to determine, however, the precise clinical diagnoses associated with these mental disorders. Many could have been diagnosed with antisocial personality disorder. Second, some data were collected by asking the inmates themselves about their mental conditions (see **Table 2**). Third, the reliability of psychiatric diagnoses, even in the general population, is often in doubt. Finally, we do not know whether the mental disorders reported are the result of being in prison or jail, or whether the individual entered the system with the existing disorder. Regardless, however, if the disorder exists, it is a problem.

The subgroup of individuals who are transferred to civil mental institutions may be declining with the availability of secure treatment facilities within the prison setting. Because states differ greatly in the treatment and transfer options they provide for mentally disordered prisoners, it is difficult to distinguish a general pattern in either the disorders or the circumstances surrounding the transfers. However, in 1980, the U.S. Supreme Court ruled that the transfer of an inmate to a mental health hospital requires, at a minimum, an administrative hearing to determine whether such transfer is appropriate (*Vitek v. Jones*, 1980). An inmate is entitled to challenge that transfer, and to have legal assistance for that purpose. The Supreme Court recognized the special nature of confinement in a mental health facility and the stigma that often accompanies a commitment (Churgin, 1983). Furthermore, transfer to a mental institution not only entails forced treatment of almost any variety, but also may substantially reduce chances for parole, since parole boards may be reluctant to release into the community a prisoner who was recently in a mental hospital setting. Nevertheless, researchers have observed that transfers to civil mental institutions—or to prison mental hospitals—are not often challenged, despite the due process protections afforded to these inmates by the *Vitek* case (Cohen, 1998). Cohen adds that inmates are less likely to resist a transfer than to face delays in getting timely admission to a hospital setting when it is needed.

In summary, it is very clear that prisons and jails today are facing increasing numbers of mentally disordered inmates whose problems will likely escalate if not sufficiently treated. This may be especially problematic in very high security, supermax facilities where inmates are kept in solitary confinement, sometimes for many years (see, generally, Toch, 2008). Even in the general population of prisons and jails, however, the prevalence of individuals in need of mental health services is sobering.

DANGEROUSNESS AND THE ASSESSMENT OF RISK

Up to this point in the chapter, we have covered a range of situations involving mentally disordered individuals, criminal courts, police, and prisons and jails. In many—but not all—of those situations, the courts and other agents of the criminal justice system were concerned about whether the disordered individual was also a danger to society.

The concept of **dangerousness** pervades much of the criminal law and appears in civil law as well. Defining dangerous behavior is a challenge faced by legislatures, courts, and clinicians. All states and all courts recognize that behavior that is likely to result in *physical harm* is dangerous. They begin to differ when behaviors that lead to property damage or psychological injury are involved. One example of psychological injury is the effect on victims of stalking, who may be continually shadowed, photographed, contacted by phone or e-mail, and otherwise harassed. Some courts have ruled that this type of behavior can cause irreparable emotional damage. They conclude that a threat of "psychological trauma is . . . as much a menace to the health or safety of others as is possible physical injury" (Developments in the Law, 1974, p. 1237). This form of psychological damage has prompted many state legislatures to pass "stalking laws" that state that persons who continually follow and otherwise harass other individuals are dangerous and can be charged with a criminal offense.

It is fair to say, though, that dangerousness is used primarily in conjunction with violent behavior. Defendants charged with violent crimes are sometimes denied bail because they are judged dangerous, violent offenders are sentenced to long prison terms to prevent them from committing more crime, and some are sentenced to death because it is feared they will commit more violence. Decisions on whether to parole prisoners convicted of violent crimes are largely based on whether they are dangerous.

Risk Assessment

Implicit in the above decisions is the belief that it is possible to predict an individual's violent behavior. Although some clinicians believe they can do so with a high degree of confidence, most are far more modest about this ability. Since the 1990s, the research and professional literature have increasingly preferred the term *risk assessment* rather than prediction of dangerousness. **Risk assessment** suggests that clinicians and researchers are more proficient at *assessing the probability* that a given individual—or group of individuals—will engage in harmful behavior than they are at outrightly predicting that someone will be violent. We will return to this change in terminology shortly.

Controversy over the ability to predict, particularly predict violence, has been longstanding. Not surprisingly, it has often been fueled by highly publicized incidents. The April 2008 shootings at Virginia Tech were perpetrated by Seung-Hui Cho, who had a history of psychiatric treatment and periodic episodes of violence. A year later, 12 people were killed by Jiverly Voong, who entered an immigration center in Binghamton, New York, dedicated to helping immigrants adjust to life in the United States. Individuals who knew him said they were "not surprised," because he was isolated, had continuously voiced his disenchantment with his station in life, and complained that people ridiculed his lack of facility with the English language. Nevertheless, the above could characterize numerous individuals who do not go out and kill others.

We do not know whether either Cho or Voong had actually made threats against others. One who apparently did was Charles Whitman, a University of Texas student majoring in architectural engineering, who murdered his wife and his mother in 1966. Shortly thereafter, he carried his personal arsenal in a footlocker to the observation deck of the 307-foot-tall University Tower, where he loaded a number of high-powered, scope-equipped rifles and began randomly shooting at people near the observation deck and on the ground far below. Whitman managed to shoot 44 victims, killing 14, before a police officer and a citizen climbed to the tower and ended the tragedy by shooting Whitman himself.

An investigation revealed that the 25-year-old Whitman had consulted a psychiatrist five months before the incident, and, during a two-hour interview, had described "overwhelming violent impulses" and great fear of his inability to control them. He had also revealed a compelling need to "go up on the tower with a deer rifle and start shooting people." Whitman did not return for further consultation after the initial two-hour session. Nevertheless, when the news of his contact with a psychiatrist was disseminated, there was public outcry and many questions about why he was not treated, confined, or referred to the proper authorities. Similar questions were raised when the public learned that James Huberty, who killed 22 fast-food restaurant patrons in the summer of 1984, had also had contact with a mental health clinic. In Huberty's case, social workers had apparently tried without success to return his telephone calls.

The Tarasoff Case

In another highly publicized case, an outpatient at a University of California, Berkeley, clinic revealed to his psychiatrist his fantasies about harming, or perhaps even killing, a woman whom he had met at a dance. The psychologist, who learned from one of his patient's friends that he planned to purchase a gun, became increasingly concerned. When the patient discontinued therapy, clinic officials wrote to the police requesting their help in getting the individual committed to a mental institution. Police investigated the case, interviewed the patient, warned him to stay away from the woman, but did not pursue the commitment, apparently because California's new civil commitment law was difficult to interpret. Two months later, Prosenjit Poddar—the patient—killed Tatiana Tarasoff by stabbing her, though he was carrying his newly purchased gun. He was charged with first-degree murder. Tarasoff's family sued the university clinic, claiming the psychologist had been negligent in not warning the young woman or the family of the danger.

The *Tarasoff* case, undoubtedly familiar to all clinicians, addressed very directly the question of what duty therapists owe to third parties in warning them of possible harmful behavior from their clients. The California Supreme Court first ruled that when a therapist determines that a patient is a serious danger to another person, the therapist has a **duty to warn** that individual (*Tarasoff v. Regents*, 1974). Two years later (*Tarasoff v. Regents*, 1976), the Court redefined the role as a **duty to protect.** That is, the therapist need not directly warn the individual, but he or she should take some steps to protect the individual from harm. Following the California court's decisions, courts in many other states issued similar decisions, but others rejected the doctrine. In the 1980s, the doctrine was widely applied, but in the 1990s, the doctrine was rejected altogether or severely limited in many states (Felthous, 2001). Whether or not there exists a statutory duty to warn/protect, many practitioners have interpreted the "spirit" of *Tarasoff* as a standard of practice, believing that the clinician has a professional obligation to take some steps to protect an identifiable potential victim (e.g., Litwack & Shlesinger, 1999).

Courts that have adopted duty to warn/protect rules apparently believe that mental health professionals can predict with considerable accuracy who is or will be dangerous and who will not. The law has been relying on predictions of dangerousness for a long time, dating at least as far back as the sixteenth century (Morris & Miller, 1985). Yet, researchers and clinicians have long struggled both to define dangerousness and to predict its occurrence. After the *Tarasoff* case, dangerousness generated more controversy than even the insanity defense (Simon & Cockerham, 1977).

When courts consider this question, they often turn to the psychiatric and psychological professions. However, as noted, many in these professions have resisted the notion that dangerousness could be predicted. Instead, they maintain that, at best, they can offer probabilities based on known factors relating to the individual, often based on data obtained from large groups. (Recall our earlier discussion of the MacArthur Risk Assessment Study with civilly committed psychiatric patients.) Thus, increasingly, the psychological literature has avoided the term prediction of dangerousness and has replaced it with risk assessment. Regardless of the terminology, it is clear that some attempt at assessing/predicting the likelihood that an individual will commit violence is warranted.

There is little doubt that a person who has been violent in the past and indicates by word or deed that he or she plans to do serious harm to others is dangerous. Someone who has committed a series of murders, mutilations, or rapes, and who attests to planning to do more of the same, is certainly—by anyone's definition—a dangerous individual. If a person has no history of violence and threatens harm, however, the situation becomes more problematic. Likewise, if a person has been violent in the distant past but has shown no recent signs of violent behavior, the situation is again problematic. In these contexts, clinicians have difficulty reaching a consensus on who is dangerous and who is not. This is why current thinking favors surveying a list of "risk factors" in an attempt to determine the likelihood that aggressive behavior will occur. Risk assessment is perhaps the most complicated and controversial issue in the entire field of forensic psychology (Borum, 1996). Many researchers and scholars (e.g., Steadman *et al.*, 1993) consider it one of the most important issues in both criminal and civil matters worldwide. A variety of instruments are available for clinicians engaging in the risk-assessment enterprise. As we will see, some of these instruments are chiefly actuarial in nature and may even be filled out just from case files, without an interview, although this is not generally recommended. Other instruments focus more on the interview process, but suggest questions to help the clinician to exercise structured clinical judgment.

Until very recently, the psychological research literature consistently concluded that clinicians are unable to specify the type or severity of harm an individual may cause, or to predict with great accuracy the probability of harm even occurring. That early literature can best be summarized in the words of Alan Stone (1975, p. 33), who wrote,

> It can be stated flatly on the basis of my own review of the published material on the prediction of dangerous acts that neither objective actuarial tables nor psychiatric intuition, diagnosis, and psychological testing can claim predictive success when dealing with the traditional population of mental hospitals. The predictive success appropriate to a legal decision can be described in three levels of increasing certainty: Preponderance of the evidence, 51% successful; clear and convincing proof, 75% successful; beyond a reasonable doubt, at least 90% successful.

The early research on prediction also demonstrated that clinicians had a strong tendency to overpredict dangerousness, a pattern that held for criminal offenders as well as mentally disordered patients (Monahan, 1981, 1984). At a minimum, the most sophisticated predictive methods yield 60–70 percent false positives (people who were predicted to be dangerous but did not engage in harmful behavior) (Kozol, Boucher, & Garofalo, 1972; Rubin, 1972; Wenk, Robison, & Smith, 1972). In a ten-year follow-up investigation of 592 convicted male offenders, mostly sex offenders (Kozol, Boucher, & Garofalo, 1972), two of every three persons predicted dangerous were false positives, even after extensive background data and results of independent clinical exams by psychiatrists had been made available to those doing the predicting. Moreover, because of some flaws in the design of the study, the odds for accurate prediction were very much in the researchers' favor (Dix, 1980; Monahan, 1976; Steadman, 1976).

In the 1970s, classic studies that followed individuals after their release from mental institutions also documented the limitations of prediction. Steadman (1976) followed patients who were released from New York hospitals after a landmark U.S. Supreme Court case, *Baxstrom v. Herold* (1966). These "Baxstrom patients" had first been convicted of crimes and had then been transferred to civil mental institutions without hearings shortly before their prison sentences expired. On average, they had spent eight years in confinement beyond their prison sentence. The Baxstrom patients were predominantly nonwhite, lower socioeconomic class, middle-aged males. Although a vast majority had arrest records and many had previous convictions, only 58 percent had been convicted of violent crimes (Steadman, 1976). On the average, the patients had been institutionalized continuously for 14 years. In its *Baxstrom* decision, the Supreme Court noted that—like other individuals committed to civil mental institutions—the prisoners had a right to a hearing to determine whether they were mentally disordered and dangerous. As a result, many were released, often against the advice of clinicians who predicted that they were dangerous.

The Baxstrom patients were considered some of New York's most dangerous mental patients, but follow-up reports found that predicted dangerousness had been grossly overstated (false positives) (Monahan, 1976). Steadman and Cocozza (1974) followed up 85 Baxstrom patients and discovered that 20 percent were rearrested, but only 7 percent were convicted, usually for minor violations such as vagrancy and public intoxication. An examination of both in-hospital and community behaviors revealed that only 20 percent of the "extremely dangerous" patients were assaultive toward others during the four-year follow-up period (Steadman, 1976). A prominent variable predicting whether Baxstrom patients demonstrated assaultive behavior was age: the younger the patient, the more likely he or she was to engage in assaultive behavior. Even using the Legal Dangerousness Scale (Cocozza & Steadman, 1976), a measure of four criminal background characteristics, there were two false positives for every three patients predicted to be violent, again underscoring the inaccuracy of clinical prediction.

In a similar research project, Thornberry and Jacoby (1979) followed up a group of mentally disordered offenders in Pennsylvania who were transferred from criminal to civil mental hospitals in that state. During a four-year follow-up, about 24 percent were arrested, and only one-quarter of these arrests were for violent offenses.

The ratio of false to true positives deserves some attention. **False positive** is a descriptor we use for persons who are labeled dangerous (positive), but who do not engage in harmful behavior during a specific period of time after release from custody (false). **True positives** are persons predicted to be dangerous (positive) who do engage in subsequent harmful behavior (true). (See **Table 3**.) For example, assume a team of mental health professionals concludes that ten persons are dangerous. If, during a two-year period following release, six do engage in harmful behavior, we have a 60 percent rate of true positives and a 40 percent rate of false positives. On the other hand, the team may predict that 10 people will not engage in violent behavior (negatives). If some of them do, they are called **false negatives.** **True negatives** are those who are predicted not to engage

TABLE 3 Four Possible Outcomes of Prediction

	Criterion Behavior	
Prediction	**Did**	**Did not**
Will	True positive	False positive
Will not	False negative	True negative

in harmful behavior within a certain period of time and who do not. Thus, if the team predicts that 7 out of 10 people will not engage in harmful behavior, and 5 of the 10 do not, the team was wrong in two cases. We therefore have a ratio of 20 percent false negatives to 50 percent true negatives.

In many ways, it is clearly advantageous for mental health professionals to predict more positives than negatives, especially if there is some question about whether a person is dangerous. The *Tarasoff* decision also encourages this trend. Clinicians who fail to warn and protect the community by not detecting persons who eventually commit violent or harmful acts will likely pay a higher social and professional price than clinicians who overpredict dangerousness.

Predictors of Dangerous Behavior

It must be stressed that—although we discuss risk assessment in the chapter on crime and mental disorder—risk assessment is not limited to the mentally disordered. And it must be stressed, again, that the mentally disordered, as a group, are not dangerous. Overall, the best predictor of future behavior is *past behavior,* but even past behavior will not necessarily be repeated. The best predictor of criminal behavior is a history of criminal behavior, and past violence will suggest a probability of future violence. A history of criminal behavior is the best predictor of criminal recidivism regardless of whether the offender is mentally disordered or normal (Bonta, Law, & Hanson, 1998). But again, people change. Furthermore, the more frequently the behavior has occurred in a variety of situations, the more accurate will be the predictions. Someone who frequently manifests violence across many different situations will be far easier to predict than a person who is only occasionally violent in some situations.

Since the 1990s, researchers have made considerable strides in the ability to identify more factors that are associated with violence. In addition to criminal history, recent research strongly indicates that other predictors of criminal recidivism (not limited to violence) include some combination of age, juvenile delinquency, and substance abuse (Andrews & Bonta, 1994; Bonta *et al.*, 1998; Gendreau, Little, & Goggin, 1996). However, researchers have also warned that risk factors are unique for each individual, and that no one factor will necessarily predict violence or serious antisocial behavior in any one individual. We now turn to the types of clinical measures that have been offered to help clinicians assess the likelihood that a person will engage in harmful behavior toward others.

Current Risk Assessment Measures

Many of the *risk assessment instruments* have been developed by Canadian psychologists. These instruments generally require a clinician or assessor to evaluate an individual based on information obtained in interviews or from case files about background and behavioral patterns. The first of these instruments was the Dangerous Behavior Rating Scheme (DBRS) developed by Christopher Webster and Robert Menzies (1993). The scale underwent considerable research development but became a disappointment when it failed to predict dangerousness and violence to a satisfactory level. A second, more promising attempt is the Violence Risk Assessment Guide (VRAG) developed by Grant Harris, Marnie Rice, and colleagues (Webster *et al.*, 1994). The VRAG is based on data from 618 men with prior histories of significant violence who were initially confined at the Oak Ridge Division of the Penetanguishene Mental Health Center in Ontario, Canada. Oak Ridge is a maximum security facility providing assessment and treatment for persons referred from the courts, correctional services, and other provincial psychiatric hospitals (Webster *et al.*, 1994). Twelve variables believed to predict future violence make up the VRAG. The variables include separation of parents by age 16 or younger, schizophrenia, elementary school maladjustment, alcohol abuse history, and symptoms of psychopathy. The 618 violent men in the project were followed for 10 years. Overall, 31 percent of the subjects committed another violent offense, usually within seven years after release (Rice, 1997). The best predictor of violent recidivism was the score of the psychopathy scale (i.e., PCL-R). "It alone predicted better than any combination of other criminal history variables" (Rice, 1997, p. 415). On the other hand, the presence of a mental disorder did not predict violence. Based on preliminary research, Rice concludes, "Our work and that of others on the prediction of violence has shown that long-term criminal violence can be predicted with a considerable degree of accuracy among men who have already been apprehended for a violent criminal offense" (p. 418).

Another instrument for evaluating risk is the Historical/Clinical/Risk Management (HCR-20) scale developed by Christopher Webster and his colleagues (Webster, Douglas, Eaves, & Hart, 1997). The HCR is popular with many clinicians because it is not a purely actuarial instrument; it suggests areas for the clinician to pursue, thus allowing the clinician to use his or her best clinical judgment. The HCR bases its predictive power on three major areas: past or historical factors, clinical or current factors, and risk management factors. It contains 10 historical items, 5 clinical items, and 5 risk management items, for a total of 20 items. The historical items include "previous violence," which, as we have learned, is one of the strongest predictors of future violence. Another historical or "H" item is "young age at first violent incident" (Webster *et al.*, 1997, p. 267). In other words, the younger the person at the time of the first violent incident, the greater the likelihood that a violent pattern will persist into the future. "Early maladjustment" at home, at school, or in the community is another predictive H item. Other H items in the HCR-20 are relationship instability, employment problems, substance use problems, and major mental illness (particularly psychotic or mood disorders). Clinical or "C" items include lack of insight, negative attitudes (antisocial, hostile, angry), and "active symptoms of major mental illness" (Webster *et al.*, 1997, p. 263). Active symptoms of serious mental illness that include delusional systems characterized by sadistic fantasies and homicidal and suicidal ideation are especially related to violence prediction. Risk management or "R" variables are related to the future circumstances of the individual being evaluated—that is, whether the person is likely to have adequate housing, meals, daily activities, and finances. Research suggests that individuals without these basics are at higher risk of violence than those who have these needs managed and taken care of. Examples of R items are lack of personal support, noncompliance with remediation attempts, feasibility of future plans, and stress. The researchers of the HCR-20 find that the historical (H) items are the strongest for predicting future violent behavior (Webster *et al.*, 1997), and C items are second strongest (Borum, 1996).

Two instruments receiving considerable research attention are the LSI-R (Andrews & Bonta, 1994), a 54-item instrument that appraises an individual's risk and criminogenic needs, and the Static-99 (Hanson & Thornton, 2000), which is specifically designed to predict recidivism in sex offenders.

It should be emphasized that risk-assessment instruments, such as those already described, are not invariably supported in the clinical literature. Many mental health practitioners are suspicious of such measures, particularly those that are actuarial or that were developed on specific populations, such as incarcerated violent offenders or persons held in civil mental hospitals. Some scholars also have noted that risk-assessment instruments were developed almost exclusively on male populations, and that different or supplemental measures may be required for female populations (Holtfreter & Cupp, 2007; Manchak, Skeem, Douglas, & Siranosian, 2009). Other scholars have noted that risk-assessment instruments may ignore factors that are specific to the case at hand (Heilbrun, Marczyk, & Dematteo, 2002), or that clinicians often adjust the scores to incorporate their own clinical impressions (Doren, 2002). Heilbrun *et al.* acknowledge the value of risk-assessment instruments, but they also urge clinicians not to undermine the role of clinical judgment. In essence, one should supplement the other, because neither approach, standing alone, is likely to produce consistent, valid results.

Summary and Conclusions

In this chapter, we focused on the relationship between mentally disordered individuals and crime. In order to understand this relationship, we must go beyond labels, which do not explain why someone behaves in a certain way.

Mental illness (or mental disorder) is a disorder or disease of the mind that interferes substantially with a person's ability to cope with life on a daily basis. Although it deprives someone of freedom of choice, this deprivation is rarely total. As noted in the chapter, even severely disordered individuals can have some decision-making ability. Mental illness should be distinguished from retardation or developmental disability. The former can be treated, cured, or held in remission; the latter cannot, although developmentally disabled individuals can be taught to perform many tasks and supported in their desires to be self-sufficient.

We reviewed diagnostic categories that are most often associated with criminal behavior. For example, persons accused of crime may introduce these diagnoses to support an insanity defense. The main categories discussed were schizophrenic disorders, with particular emphasis on the paranoid type that is most frequently represented in criminal behavior; delusional disorders, with emphasis on the persecutory type; depressive disorders, which may play a major role in delinquency, mass murders, and workplace violence, among others; postpartum depression, with emphasis on the very rare postpartum psychosis that can result in serious crime; and antisocial personality disorder, which most courts today do not accept in support of an insanity defense. The juvenile equivalent of APD is conduct disorder, and it is a very frequent diagnosis of adolescents held in detention and treatment facilities.

The chapter also reviewed the legal constructs of competency and insanity. Criminal defendants are found incompetent if they are so disordered that they cannot understand the proceedings or help their attorneys in their own defense. Adjudicative competence is relevant to a wide range of proceedings, including a variety of pretrial hearings and the trial itself as well as the sentencing stage. Basically, the law says that an incompetent defendant is not present; therefore, before proceeding with prosecution, he or she must be rendered competent. As we noted, the common approach with incompetent defendants is to hospitalize them for treatment until they attain competency; alternately, the case against them is dismissed. A major issue today relating to incompetent defendants is the extent to which they can be medicated against their will. Courts have generally ruled that, when the government has a strong interest in bringing the defendant to trial—such as in a very serious crime—medication will be allowed.

Although it is the competency issue that affects the greatest number of defendants, it is the insanity issue that most intrigues the public. The truly insane individual is not responsible for his or her crime. Successful insanity defenses are very rare, but even when they occur, they are no bargain. Persons found not guilty by reason of insanity are typically institutionalized, very often for longer periods of time than they would have served in prison. We reviewed the various standards for establishing insanity, including the M'Naghten (right/wrong) Rule, the ALI/Brawner Rule, and the Durham Rule (product test). Since the 1980s, largely as a result of the acquittal of John Hinckley, many states and the federal government have passed more restrictive insanity statutes, making it even more difficult for defendants to be absolved of criminal responsibility. Some states also have adopted a "guilty but mentally ill" verdict form, which allows a judge or jury to find a defendant guilty, but also acknowledges that he or she needs treatment. Research indicates, though, that the treatment implied is rarely provided in correctional facilities.

We also discussed "special defenses" that are sometimes raised in criminal cases, either to absolve a defendant completely or to support a defense of diminished capacity: PTSD, pathological gamblers' syndrome, dissociative identity disorder (DID; formerly called multiple personality disorder), and amnesia.

Individuals with mental disorders as a group are no more likely than the general population to commit crimes, including violent crimes. If we include the category antisocial personality disorder, the likelihood of committing crime increases somewhat. In addition, recent research documents that the subgroup of *currently* mentally disordered male patients, particularly with schizophrenic diagnoses, and who have a *history of violence,* do demonstrate far more violence than nondisordered members in the general population. According to Monahan (1996), this relationship is especially significant if a current mental disorder is accompanied by three symptoms: (1) feeling that others wish to do one harm, (2) feeling that one's mind is dominated by forces beyond one's control, and (3) feeling that others' thoughts are being put into one's head.

The visibility of the mentally disordered, as well as publicity given to the occasional sensational case in which a severely disordered individual kills a stranger, has led to questions about dangerousness and our ability to predict it. When the criminal justice system deals with a defendant charged with a violent crime or an offender convicted of one, whether or not the individual is disordered, the system wants to know if he or she is dangerous. For many years, mental health practitioners tried to answer this question with very little success. Traditionally, clinicians overestimated the potential violence of this population, engendering debate about the proper criteria for assessing dangerousness. How many persons were forcefully confined, on the basis of dangerousness, without justification?

Recently, this enterprise has shifted to "risk assessment." Rather than trying to predict whether someone is dangerous and will commit a violent act, the clinician is now more likely to identify risk factors that may make it *more likely* that he or she will do so. In other words, the prediction of dangerousness has been transformed to an *assessment of the probability* that violence or other serious offending will occur in the future. Various risk-assessment instruments have been developed and tested for this purpose, but some scholars question their applicability to particular groups of individuals, such as women. Among the risk-assessment instruments are the HCL-20, the Iterative Classification Tree, the VRAG, the LSI-R, and the Static-99. These and other instruments will be discussed again later in the book. Again, although we have discussed this topic in the chapter on the mentally disordered, readers should be aware that risk assessments are conducted on many nondisordered offenders. Overall, the best single predictor available is past behavior. Those who were violent in the past, compared with those without such a history, are more likely to offend in the future. Nevertheless, people change, mature, grow tired, and/or learn from past experiences. It is important to emphasize that no one factor—even past violence—is a foolproof predictor of future violence.

Key Concepts

Adjudicative competence	Battered woman syndrome	Compulsion
Amnesia	Brawner Rule	Compulsive
Antisocial personality	Caveat paragraph	gambling
disorder (APD)	Competency to stand trial	Conduct disorder

Delusional disorders or paranoid disorders
Delusions
Diagnostic and Statistical Manual of Mental Disorders (DSM)
Dissociative identity disorder (DID)
Dissociated state disorder
Durham Rule
Duty to protect
Duty to warn
False negatives
False positives

Guilty but mentally ill (GBMI)
Hallucinations
Iatrogenic
Incompetent to stand trial (IST)
Insanity Defense Reform Act of 1984
Irrationality
Limited amnesia
Major depressive disorder
Mental illness or mental disorder

Mental retardation or developmental disability
M'Naghten Rule
Multiple personality disorder (MPD)
Not guilty by reason of insanity (NGRI)
Posttraumatic stress disorder (PTSD)
Right and wrong test
Schizophrenia
True negatives
True positives
Volitional prong

Review Questions

1. What is meant by a "duty to warn" and a "duty to protect"? And to whom does it pertain?
2. What are the conditions under which mentally disordered people may become violent or seriously criminal?
3. Briefly describe four legal standards for insanity and their requirements.
4. Identify and include symptoms of the four diagnostic categories most relevant to criminal behavior.
5. What are guilty but mentally ill statutes? Why do many legal scholars oppose them?
6. Give an example of iatrogenic effects in counseling or psychotherapy.
7. Describe fully and evaluate any three of the unique defenses discussed in the chapter.
8. Thoroughly explain the difference between incompetence to stand trial (or adjudicative incompetence) and insanity. Include in your answer what researchers have learned about the individuals who receive those legal designations.

8

Homicide, Assault, and Family Violence

CHAPTER OBJECTIVES

- Define criminal homicide, negligent manslaughter, and aggravated assault.
- Review the demographics of homicide victims and offenders.
- Emphasize that criminal homicide is rare compared with other violent offenses.
- Review what we know about juvenile murderers and their victims.
- Present the research on family violence, its dynamics, and its causes.

If the news and entertainment media are reasonably decent barometers of human interest, homicidal violence must be one of the Western civilization's most fascinating subjects and, along with sex, the most marketable. Usually, the more bizarre, senseless, or heinous the murder, the more extensive press coverage it receives, followed shortly thereafter by books, television specials, and movies. Unusual mass murders, serial murders, and so-called motiveless killings are especially popular. On a national level, criminal homicide consistently accounts for only about 1 percent or 2 percent of all violent crimes reported in the FBI's Uniform Crime Reports (UCR).

A total of 14,831 such homicides were reported in 2007 (Federal Bureau of Investigation, 2008). In the same year, an estimated 1.37 million violent offenses were reported to law enforcement agencies. If we consider its percentage distribution among all violent crimes, murder represents only 1.2 percent of the total (see **Figure 1**). Furthermore, a vast majority of these criminal homicides offer very little mystery or intrigue. In many cases, they involve angry friends, spouses, or acquaintances killing friends, spouses, or acquaintances. During 2007, for example, the relationship between the victims and the perpetrators was known in 54 percent of all of the homicides. Within those known relationships, 22 percent of the victims were related to their killer, and 54 percent were acquainted with them. This does not make them less serious. It is simply a reminder that homicidal attacks of strangers are not common.

The disproportionate amount of attention paid to criminal homicides may be explained in a variety of ways. Obviously, this is a highly serious crime, with death being the ultimate victimization. However, another reason for the attention may be related to our fascination with the mysterious and

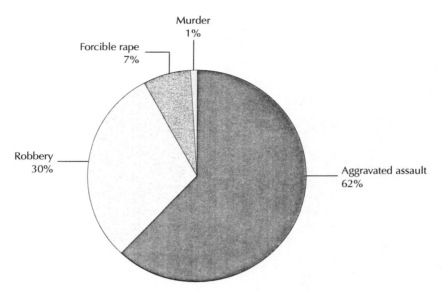

FIGURE 1   Violent Crime Distribution in the United States, 2007
Source: Federal Bureau of Investigation, 2008

the macabre. We crave science fiction, tales of terror, even haunted houses. Perhaps we need a certain amount of excitement and arousal to prevent our lives from becoming too mundane and boring. Psychologists have long known that novelty produces arousal and excitement and breaks monotony (Berlyne, 1960). This human need for stimulation and excitement—which is greater in some people (extraverts) than others (introverts)—may partly explain the appeal of roller coasters, skydiving, race car driving, bungee jumping, and gambling. Extraverts also may enjoy films featuring vampires, werewolves, and heavy violence—or these vicarious pleasures might be enjoyed by ambiverts or introverts not wishing to seek out this type of excitement directly. In any case, tales of murder, fictional or not, add zest to life. For the family that has been touched by murder, however, this vicarious response on the part of others must be difficult to understand and to accept.

The marketability of murder might also be explained by curiosity or exploratory behavior, which is very closely related to excitement and arousal. One purpose of curiosity is to allow organisms to adjust to their environments (Butler, 1954). An individual or an organism explores a new situation to satisfy this curiosity—which is theorized to be a physiological drive state—and in the process of discovering information, adapts to the new situation. Curiosity about murder might help us prepare for the possibility that a similar event might happen to us. Reading about bizarre, seemingly irrational homicides might help us to identify danger signals. Information about the incident gives clues about who murders, who gets murdered, and under what circumstances. To some extent, we can take preventive measures, even though there is no guarantee that such measures will keep us safe. Furthermore, families and close friends of murder victims would say that nothing can prepare someone for the devastation that is experienced when a loved one is murdered.

The above reactions to depictions of violence—experienced vicariously—may be regarded as adaptive or functional. Extensive exposure to violence also has a dysfunctional side, however. Specifically, it may immunize us from the horror of violence. Many social commentators have advanced cogent arguments that Western civilization has become conditioned or jaded to cruelty and inhumane behavior and that people are desensitized to human suffering. In addition, the constant attention that the news media and politicians give to violence also makes it seem more widespread and frequent than it really is. This phenomenon is called the **availability heuristic** by social psychologists. Heuristics refer to cognitive shortcuts that people use to make quick inferences about their world. When the news media continually show graphic and frightening accounts of violence, people are likely to incorporate these vivid details into cognitive shorthand and have them readily available for future reference. When they think of violence at a later time, they remember the most frequently seen and horrific accounts, increasing their fear of violent crime and exaggerating its incidence in their minds.

To speculate about why we are attracted to accounts of murder and violence, or to wonder about the effects of repeated exposure, may not seem to address the main focus of this chapter, which is the violent offender. Speculation becomes relevant, however, when we shift the focus to the individual who is part of a society that seems to have an inordinate need to seek out stimulation or to know details of crimes. When that individual is insensitive to suffering and begins to create his or her own excitement by torturing and murdering, we have a social problem. Psychology, as we will see in this chapter, can offer some suggestions for understanding and solving this problem.

After defining our terms, we examine situational and dispositional factors that occur consistently in homicide and aggravated assault, beginning with statistical data on their incidence and prevalence and their demographic correlates. Thus far in the text, theoretical issues and potential causes of crime have been introduced with minimum application to specific offenses. Beginning here and throughout the remainder of the text, we interweave the research and concepts previously outlined with specific categories of criminal behavior. Thus in this chapter, we focus on family violence.

DEFINITIONS

Criminologists generally study aggravated assault and homicide together, primarily because they view many aggravated assaults as failed homicide attempts (Doerner, 1988; Doerner & Speir, 1986). Dunn (1976) challenges this practice. He notes that the aggravated assault rate is at least 20 times that of homicide. "Given this disparity in rates, it is difficult to imagine that even one-quarter of all aggravated assaults were attempted homicides or would have been homicides except for the intervention of medical care" (Dunn, 1976, p. 10). Therefore, it may be unwarranted to consider aggravated assault as being in the same league as homicide; the two may differ in important variables, including the motives of the perpetrator. A purist, therefore, would try to maintain an aggravated assault–homicide distinction. And, of course, the distinctions are maintained in crime statistics, as well as in criminal law.

For our purposes, it is neither realistic nor desirable to maintain a definitive assault–homicide distinction. Not realistic, since much of the relevant research on offender *characteristics* collapses the categories into one, under the rationale that people who kill usually (but not invariably) have a history of assaultive behavior. It is not desirable, since, from a psychological point of view, the two types of behavior are comparable. Often, the type of weapon used determines the final outcome. The high-powered bullet, as an obvious example, is in most cases far more lethal than the knife. A stabbing or even a beating may represent behavior similar to that displayed in homicide with a small firearm. In law, the distinctions between murder and aggravated assault are crucial; in psychology, they are less so. The individual is displaying highly aggressive behavior in either situation. For this chapter, combining the discussion of homicide and aggravated assault as one form of violent behavior makes sense, although the statistics section will separate them briefly. We discuss other forms of violent behavior, including rape, armed robbery, and arson.

Criminal Homicide

Criminal homicide is causing the death of another person without legal justification or excuse. Legally, it is usually divided into two categories: **murder** and **nonnegligent manslaughter.** The term *murder* is reserved for the "unlawful killing of one human being by another with malice aforethought, either expressed or implied" (Black, 1990, p. 1019). "Malice aforethought" refers to premeditation, or the mental state of a person who thinks ahead, plans, and voluntarily causes the death of another, without legal excuse or justification. However, "premeditation" can occur in a very short period of time (even a minute); it does not require weeks of planning.

Homicide laws in most states have additional gradations or degrees. Even the way in which first-degree and second-degree murder are distinguished varies enormously among the states. In most jurisdictions, murder is divided into two degrees, a statutory provision that allows courts to impose a more severe penalty for some murders than others. The degree system was once a useful and meaningful method of distinguishing between murder that was punishable by death and that which was not (Gardner, 1985). In more recent times, the distinctions between the degrees have been more blurred. Broadly, state statutes generally posit that murder of the first degree is a homicide that was committed with particularly vicious, willful, deliberate, and premeditated intent. Murder of the second degree is characterized by the intentional and unlawful killing of another but without the type of malice and premeditation required for first-degree murder. Examples of second-degree murder include "crimes of passion," such as an enraged father who strangles the drunken driver who just killed his son. Although there was no premeditation, the angry father still wanted to kill him. States that do not distinguish between degrees of murder would call this an example of nonnegligent manslaughter.

The Uniform Crime Reports include both murder and nonnegligent manslaughter under the rubric criminal homicide for reporting purposes. Deaths of others that occur as a result of negligence (negligent manslaughter) are not included. The essential difference between murder and nonnegligent manslaughter is that malice aforethought must be present for murder, whereas it must be absent for nonnegligent manslaughter.

Negligent manslaughter is killing another as a result of recklessness or culpable negligence. Although there is no intent to kill, the law says you should have known that your actions could result in the death of another person. For example, a man who recklessly waves a gun around in jest, and the gun discharges and kills someone, is still responsible for that person's death. A driver who turns to look at her passenger, crosses the center lane, and hits an oncoming car, killing its occupant, displayed negligent (not reckless) behavior, but would still be responsible for the death. What the above two individuals have in common is that they did not intend to kill anyone. Both situations would illustrate negligent manslaughter, as opposed to the nonnegligent manslaughter covered along with murder in the UCR statistics. Nonnegligent manslaughter refers to an action that is more than negligent or reckless, but less than premeditated. It typically occurs in a highly aroused emotional state.

The person charged with murder (first or second degree) or with nonnegligent manslaughter intended that his victim die. In the case of nonnegligent manslaughter, the original intent may not have been to kill the victim. However, the person became so agitated and emotionally upset in a particular situation that he or she lost partial control of his or her self-regulatory system. A man who chokes a woman to death during rough sex would be an example. In some states, nonnegligent manslaughter would be similar to second-degree murder.

The broad parameters of homicide law in the United States are highly similar to the laws of homicide found in other countries and cultures (Morawetz, 2002). This similarity is largely because maintaining some semblance of social order in any given society depends greatly on controlling reckless and widespread homicide. As pointed out by Morawetz (2002), "Homicide law . . . responds to a universal need to identify, deter, and punish intentional and reckless killings, a need that crosses borders. We all fear annihilation" (p. 400).

In line with UCR classifications, we combine both murder and nonnegligent manslaughter under the general term *homicide* in this chapter. We are not concerned with suicides, accidental deaths, negligent manslaughter, or justifiable homicide (e.g., the justifiable killing of a person by a law enforcement officer in the line of duty). In other words, from a psychological point of view, these are not illustrative of the aggressive behavior we are concerned about in a book about criminal behavior. It should be emphasized, however, that the definitions of criminal homicide used in this chapter, and by governmental agencies and researchers in general, do not encompass the many legal definitions found in various jurisdictions.

Aggravated Assault

Assault is the intentional inflicting of bodily injury on another person, or the attempt to inflict such injury. In past years, assault and battery were considered discrete crimes. In many cases, state laws treated the threat of physical injury as an assault, and the completed act of physical contact or unlawful touching as battery. Although many states have gotten away from distinguishing the two, all jurisdictions continue to recognize some form of assault and battery, such as mayhem, malicious wounding, or felonious assault (Bacigal, 2002). An assault or attack becomes **aggravated assault** when the intention is to inflict serious bodily injury. Aggravated assault is often accompanied by the use of a deadly or dangerous weapon, such as a gun, knife, ax, or other sharp or blunt instrument. Simple assault is the unlawful, intentional inflicting of less than serious bodily injury without a deadly or dangerous weapon, or the attempt to inflict such bodily injury, again without a deadly or dangerous weapon. However, even one's fists can become a deadly weapon; thus, if a victim is seriously assaulted in a fistfight, the perpetrator will likely be charged with aggravated assault.

Aggravated assault will be covered in the domestic violence section of the chapter. The beginning sections of this chapter will focus on homicide, particularly homicide dealing with a single offender killing one person. We begin with briefly covering the demographics of homicide offenders and then proceed to the psychological characteristics of people who kill. The demographic characteristics most commonly studied in homicide research are race or ethnic origin, gender, social class, and the victim–offender relationship.

DEMOGRAPHIC FACTORS OF HOMICIDE

Researchers have found that a variety of demographic factors are strongly associated, or correlated, with criminal homicide. These factors may be characteristics of the offenders or the victims. We must emphasize, though, that the factors reported in the literature often refer to *arrests* for murder or nonnegligent manslaughter. Although the minimum standard for an arrest is probable cause that the individual committed a crime or is about to commit a crime, arrests do not necessarily result in conviction, or a finding of guilt. This is an important caveat whenever we consider the official police data which are cited in numerous research studies. As we discuss the demographics of homicide, readers should keep in mind the distinctions between arrests, convictions, and victimizations.

Race/Ethnic Origin

One of the most consistent findings reported in the criminology literature is that African Americans in the United States are involved in criminal homicide—both as offenders and victims—at a rate that significantly exceeds their numbers in the general population. Although African Americans make up about 13 percent of the U.S. population, they accounted for approximately 53 percent of all arrests for homicide in 2007 (Federal Bureau of Investigation, 2008).

The disproportionate representation of African Americans in the arrest and conviction data for homicide probably reflect social inequities, such as lack of employment or educational opportunities, racial oppression in its many forms, discriminatory treatment at the hands of the criminal justice system, and law enforcement practices in inner-city areas where many African Americans reside. There is no evidence to suggest that a racial biological or neuropsychological predisposition plays a role in the consistently reported differences in violence rates over the years.

Although much more research needs to be done on the relationship between racial/ethnic minorities and crime, using rigid categories such as black, Latino/Hispanic, Asian, Native Americans, and white represents an oversimplification of the multiethnic and multicultural mixtures across the nation. Cultures and subcultures are highly complex and multidimensional, and meaningful research on the ethnic/minority differences in violence requires a knowledgeable awareness of and sensitivity to this complexity.

Gender Differences

The relationship between homicide and gender is also robust. UCR data consistently reveal that the annual arrest rates for murder run about 90 percent male, 10 percent female (Federal Bureau of Investigation, 2008). Males are victims 78 percent of the time, and females are victims 22 percent of the time.

Age

With monotonous regularity, national statistics from all sources continue to underscore the fact that about half of all those arrested for violent crime are between the ages of 20 and 29. In 2007, individuals under age 25 made up 47 percent of all violent crime arrestees and comprised 50 percent of all those arrested for murder or nonnegligent manslaughter, and 22 percent were under the age of 18 (Federal Bureau of Investigation, 2008). The young are also the victims.

Socioeconomic Class

Research has consistently shown that children born into an adverse neighborhood and disadvantaged family context are at high risk for violence, either as offenders or victims. Poverty places children at risk for violence because of lack of resources, social support, and opportunity. Some researchers have observed that conditions of poverty make it difficult for parents or caregivers to avoid harsh and inconsistent discipline for their young children (Dodge, Greenberg, *et al.*, 2008). Nonetheless, as a general principle, it is important to remember that warm, supportive parenting exists across all social classes.

Circumstances

The 2007 data, based on known circumstances, indicate that 44 percent of the murders resulted from arguments (including family violence), and 23 percent were committed in the process of committing felonies such as forcible rape, robbery, burglary, arson, or drug trafficking (Federal Bureau of Investigation, 2008). Thirty-three percent involved other types of circumstances—some also involving felonies—such as brawls, sniper attacks, or juvenile and gang killers (see **Table 1**).

TABLE 1   Murder Circumstances by Victim's Gender, 2007

Circumstances	Total Murder Victims	Male	Female	Unknown
Total	**14,831**	**11,618**	**3,177**	**36**
Felony type total	2,184	1,824	358	2
Rape	31	1	30	0
Robbery	924	811	113	0
Burglary	86	63	23	0
Larceny-theft	11	10	1	0
Motor vehicle theft	20	11	9	0
Arson	58	33	25	0
Prostitution	11	3	8	0
Other sex offenses	9	5	4	0
Narcotic drug laws	563	544	38	1
Gambling	4	4	0	0
Other—not specified	447	339	107	1
Suspected felony-type	67	43	24	0
Other than felony-type total	7,105	5,243	1,857	5
Romantic triangle	105	77	28	0
Child killed by babysitter	34	21	13	0
Brawl due to influence of alcohol	117	100	17	0
Brawl due to influence of narcotics	61	45	16	0
Argument over money or property	192	158	34	0
Other arguments	3,645	2,661	981	2
Gangland killings	77	65	12	0
Juvenile gang killings	676	634	42	0
Institutional killings	11	10	1	0
Sniper attack	1	1	0	0
Other—not specified	2,186	1,471	713	2
Unknown	5,475	4,508	938	29

Source: Federal Bureau of Investigation (2008).

WEAPONS USED IN VIOLENCE

Nationwide data indicate that firearms are used in approximately 70 percent of all homicides, while knives or cutting instruments were used in less than 12 percent of the homicides (Federal Bureau of Investigation, 2008; Zawitz & Strom, 2000). Approximately 80 percent of firearm homicides are committed with handguns, 6 percent with shotguns, 5 percent with rifles, and 7 percent with unspecified firearms.

Juvenile Weapon Possession

According to the 2007 UCR data, 29 percent of the total arrests for carrying or possessing a firearm were juveniles, and 11 percent of the total arrestees were under age 15. Males, compared with females, were four times more likely to report carrying a weapon. The weapons most often carried were knives or razors (55%), followed by clubs (24%), and firearms (21%). In a national survey of more than 16,000 students in grades 9–12, 18 percent said they had carried a weapon outside the home in the previous 30-day period (Lizotte & Sheppard, 2001). The percentages were higher (22%) for youths living in inner-city high schools. A more recent survey (PRIDE, 2003) reported that approximately 2 percent of middle-school youths (grades 6–8) carried a gun to school on a regular basis during 2002–2003. Available data (e.g., Decker, Pennel, & Caldwell, 1997) suggest that more than two-thirds of juveniles who carry weapons say they do so primarily for self-protection.

Gun ownership by gang members appears to be a standard feature of many youth gangs (Lizotte & Sheppard, 2001). Gun ownership by juveniles is also related to a wide range of antisocial behaviors, including gun-related crimes, gang membership, and drug selling (Lizotte & Sheppard, 2001). For example, the amount of serious violent crimes these juveniles committed during periods of carrying a gun was more than five times the amount they committed while not carrying a gun.

The Violent Crime Control and Law Enforcement Act of 1974 made it a federal offense for any person to sell or transfer a handgun to a person under age 18; it is also a crime for a juvenile to possess ammunition of a handgun. Yet, there are multiple ways for juveniles to obtain firearms, and they report being able to do so with ease. For example, gangs often have a "community gun" well hidden on the street but easily accessible to gang members if needed. Some juveniles (about 28%) ask others, such as older siblings or friends, to buy guns for them (Braga & Kennedy, 2001). About 11 percent of juveniles buy them from a gun shop or pawnshop. Theft is also an important source of firearms for juveniles. It is estimated that about 500,000 guns are stolen each year, mostly from residences (Braga & Kennedy, 2001). It is further estimated that about 70 percent of the firearms used by offenders are obtained through theft (Wright & Rossi, 1994). As pointed out by Braga and Kennedy (2001), juveniles obtain guns through corrupt licensed dealers, unregulated dealers, gun shows, organized gun rings and fences, and criminal firearms trafficking.

Weapons and Violence

About every 14 minutes, someone in America dies from a gunshot wound. About half of those deaths are suicides, about 44 percent are homicides, and 4 percent are unintentional shootings (*Washington Post,* October 12, 1993; Zawitz & Strom, 2000). Moreover, considerable research, including a study in the *New England Journal of Medicine* (*Washington Post,* October 12, 1993), contradicts the common view that having a gun protects people from violence. The study reported that households with guns are three times more likely to experience the death of a household member than gunless households. Research such as the above suggests that, while guns do not *cause* violent crime, accessibility of guns facilitates it. Hepburn and Hemenway (2004) found that where there are higher levels of gun ownership, homicides are substantially higher. Of course, where homicides are higher, families may be more likely to own guns for protection, but the evidence stills strongly points toward the availability of firearms as the major reason for the higher homicide rates.

Consider the **weapons effect,** where the mere sight of an aggressive stimulus can influence behavior. Because weapons are associated with violence, the visible presence of a handgun, a club, or a knife automatically brings violence-related thoughts (cognitions) to mind. The classic study of Berkowitz and LePage (1967) was among the first experiments to provide evidence of a strong link between aggressive thoughts engendered by the presence of a weapon and subsequent aggressive behavior. Hepburn and Hemenway's discovery that a high number of available weapons within a neighborhood promote more aggression in a vicious circle of violence may be partially due to the widespread presence of aggressive stimuli.

Sniper Attacks

On November 25, 2003, Gail Knisley, while heading to a doctor's appointment, was killed on Ohio Interstate 270 by a sniper. Throughout the year, at least 13 other reports documented shots fired at vehicles along the same highway which surrounds Cleveland. One shot broke a window at an elementary school. The reports began in May. The shots had been fired at different times of the day, piercing cars, trucks, vans, and horse trailers, shattering windows and flattening tires (McCarthy, 2003). Investigators believed that all 14 incidents were related, or caused by the same person or persons. In March 2004, Charles McCoy, Jr., was arrested and charged with 12 shootings, although he was suspected of 12 others. McCoy, who had been diagnosed with paranoid schizophrenia in 1996, stood trial in 2005. The first trial resulted in a hung jury, apparently due to his severe mental illness. Rather than face another trial and a possible death sentence, McCoy pled guilty. He was sentenced to 27 years in prison in August 2005.

Perhaps the most frightening sniper attacks in modern times took place over a 23-day period in October 2002. Ten persons, chosen at random, were killed by sniper fire, the first six killed within the first 27 hours of the incident. The attacks took place in and around the Washington, D.C., area. The two alleged and since convicted snipers, 42-year-old Army veteran John Allen Muhammad and his teenage sidekick, 17-year-old Lee Boyd Malvo, were arrested on October 24, 2002, while sitting in their 1990 Chevrolet Caprice. The beat-up Caprice had been modified to enable the snipers to crawl into the vehicle's trunk from the backseat and shoot a high-powered rifle (a Bushmaster XM-15, a semiautomatic version of the M-16) through a hole sawed just above the license plate. In total, the two men were accused of shooting 19 people, killing 13, and wounding 6, in Alabama, Georgia, Louisiana, Maryland, Virginia, and Washington, D.C., in an attempt to extort $10 million from the government.

Muhammad was convicted of two counts of capital murder on November 17, 2003, after a Virginia jury deliberated for six and one-half hours. A week later, a seven-woman, five-man panel sentenced him to death. He was the first person ever charged and sentenced under Virginia's new post–September 11, 2001, terrorism law. The law outlaws attempts to intimidate the civilian population at large, or to influence the conduct or activities of the government through intimidation. On September 16, 2009, a Virginia judge set a November 10 execution date for Muhammad.

Muhammad was an ex-U.S. soldier who served in the Gulf War and who was an award-winning expert marksman. He was trained as a mechanic, truck driver, and metal worker. He is the father of four children, had been married at least twice, and was involved in bitter custody battles for his children. At least on one occasion, he was accused of abducting the children. Malvo and his mother left Jamaica when he was about 14 years old and moved to the island of Antigua, and then to Fort Myers, Florida. Muhammad and Malvo were very close, with Muhammad referring to the teenager as his son. Malvo, tried separately, advanced an insanity defense, arguing that he was brainwashed by Muhammad and was thus not responsible for the crimes. He was also convicted in December 2003, but a jury recommended that he be sentenced to life imprisonment without parole rather than given a death sentence. Malvo has since testified when Muhammad was prosecuted for additional sniper killings.

The Washington sniper attacks apparently prompted the FBI to study other sniper incidents between 1982 and 2001 (Federal Bureau of Investigation, 2003). Much of the material in the remainder of this section pertains to that study. During this 20-year interval, there were an estimated 327 incidents of sniper attacks in which a total of 379 victims were killed. Although the numbers seem large, research demonstrates that sniper attacks are unique circumstances that occur infrequently. More specifically, of the total 364,648 homicides that occurred during the 20-year period, only 0.1 percent was caused by sniper fire.

Nearly 80 percent of the victims of sniper attacks were males. Although the victims included all age ranges, 14 percent were under the age of 18. In about nine out of the 10 cases, the victim and the sniper were either strangers and/or the relationship was unknown. A breakdown of the data by race indicated that 52.5 percent of the victims were white, 44.1 percent were black, and the remaining 3.4 percent were other races. A handgun was the weapon of choice in two-thirds (63.6%) of the incidents; a rifle or shotgun was used in the remainder. Nearly half of the sniper attacks took place in the Western regions of the country.

In a vast majority of cases (96.9%), the sniper was male, usually between the ages of 18 and 24. Female offenders cut across all age groups with no particular age group emerging as the most prevalent. The youngest female sniper identified was 13, and the oldest fell into the 30- to 34-year-old age group. The youngest male sniper identified was in the 10- to 12-year-old age group. In 54.5 percent of known cases, the offender was white, and 43.7 percent of the time the offender was black. The remainder of the offenders were either American Indian/Alaskan Natives or Asian/Pacific Islanders. Other than demographic data, the psychological characteristics of criminal snipers are largely unknown, other than the characteristics they share with other perpetrators of homicide. It is interesting to note, though, that some psychological characteristics of *military* snipers have been identified (Scholtz, Girard, & Vanderpool, 2008).

PSYCHOLOGICAL ASPECTS OF HOMICIDE

The psychology of murder is a very complex subject. There is no universal set of homicide offenders who present developmental risk factors or personality characteristics which predict they are particularly prone to commit murder. Homicide is multidetermined and is associated with many risk factors. Risk factors include selling drugs, peer delinquency, early indications of conduct disorder, living in poverty, and growing up in violent families and neighborhoods. To a large extent, homicide is also situation specific. That is, it depends on a number of things, including the availability of a weapon, the amount of alcohol consumption, the nature of the provocation, the circumstances, the motivation, and the emotional and mental state of the offender at the time.

Because of the complexity and diversity of homicide offending, a typology of the various types of homicide will aid greatly in presentation of the psychological aspects of homicide. In contemporary psychology, the term *typology* refers to a particular system for classifying personality, motivations, or other behavioral patterns. Usually, the typology is used to organize a wide assortment of behaviors into a more manageable set of brief descriptions. A typology is not perfect and does not always reflect reality, but it does help in understanding an enormously complex phenomenon such as homicide. It should be mentioned that we will also utilize various typologies to explain other crimes throughout the remainder of the text.

The FBI *Crime Classification Manual* (Douglas, Burgess, Burgess, & Ressler, 1992, 2006) is the most widely known and used typology system. The manual describes four major categories of homicide based on the underlying motives of the offender. The manual also lists several subcategories of homicide motives under each category. The manual is the result of a ten-year study conducted by the Federal Bureau of Investigation's National Center for the Analysis of Crime. The four major homicide categories are: (1) criminal enterprise murder, (2) personal cause murder, (3) sexual homicide, and (4) group cause homicide. *Criminal enterprise* murder refers to killings done for material gain, such as money, goods, territory, or favors. The category includes eight subcategories, such as contract killing, gang-motivated murder, kidnap murder, product tampering, insurance-motivated murder, and felony murder. Felony murder refers to a homicide committed during the commission of another serious crime, such as a robbery, burglary, or kidnapping. *Personal cause murder*, usually committed under emotional upheaval, conflict, or passion, is a homicide precipitated by a general altercation or argument. Personal cause homicide subsumes 11 subcategories, including domestic violence, argument murder, revenge killing, and hostage murder. *Sexual homicide* category is defined as a murder that has a sexual component in the situation or dynamic that leads to the murder. This category includes four subtypes: organized crime scene murder, disorganized crime scene murder, mixed crime scene murder, and sadistic murder. In most instances, serial killers represent this category. *Group cause homicide* is committed by two or more individuals who share common ideologies or belief systems. This category includes three subtypes: cult murder, extremists (political, religious, or socioeconomic murder), and group excitement. Terrorist activity most often represents this classification.

Although the *FBI Crime Classification Manual* presents an interesting breakdown of homicide categories and subcategories, it is too overwhelming and complicated to use as a framework for presenting homicide in this chapter. However, we will present many of the unusual types of homicide listed in the manual, particularly homicide involving multiple victims. Although there have been a number of other homicide typologies developed, most have focused on the more sensational, "high class" of murderers known as serial or mass killers. Very few typologies or classification systems have been developed on the "underclass" of homicide offenders—the more mundane, single homicide offender, which is the focus of this chapter. One meaningful exception has been the four distinct categories generated by Roberts, Zgoba, and Shahidullah (2007), who analyzed the patterns and motivations of 336 homicide offenders known to the New Jersey Department of Corrections. The four classifications are as follows:

1. Offenders who committed a homicide that was precipitated by a general altercation or argument, such as an argument over money or property, or verbal disputes that escalate into fight. Escalation of aggression refers to progressive increases of hostile or destructive behavior, often to the point of violence. It often stems from the need to reciprocate after being provoked by aggressive behavior from another person. Roberts *et al.* (2007) discovered that the altercation or argument was often over an exceedingly small amount of money (such as $4) or insignificant value of property (such as a bike). This category represented the largest group, accounting for 45 percent of the total homicide offenders. It is likely that this is the largest group that would be found in other jurisdictions as well.
2. Offenders who committed a homicide during the commission of a felony. In this situation, homicides are committed as a means to commit other crimes, such as robbery, burglary,

grand theft, or kidnapping. Roberts *et al.* (2007) noted that a majority of these offenders had records of past criminal histories.

3. Offenders who committed a domestic violence-related homicide. The perpetrators in these instances were current or ex-spouses, cohabiting intimate partners, or girlfriends or boyfriends. The researchers found that these homicides were precipitated by "the complexities and fragilities in relations involving sex, love, and emotion" (Roberts *et al.*, 2007, p. 499). This group represented the second-largest group, accounting for 25 percent of the homicide offenders.

4. Offenders who were charged with a degree of homicide after an accident, usually involving automobiles. In most cases, the fatality was a result of driving under the influence of alcohol or drugs.

We begin with the first two classifications: (1) offenders who committed a homicide precipitated by a general altercation or argument, and (2) offenders who committed a homicide during the commission of a felony. The third classification, offenders who committed a domestic violence-related homicide, will be covered later in the chapter under family violence. The fourth category, offenders who were charged with a degree of homicide after an accident, will not be considered in this chapter. They are distinct from the other groups in that they did not intend to perpetrate harm against their ultimate victims.

General Altercation Homicide

General altercation homicide is a result of hostile aggression. Hostile aggression is a form of reactive aggression, and it occurs in response to anger-inducing conditions, such as real or perceived insults, threats, physical attacks, or one's own failures. The ultimate goal is to make a victim or victims suffer. This **reactive violence,** as it is sometimes called, " . . . is hot blooded, emotionally charged, and enacted quickly for the purpose of harming a perceived provocateur or defending oneself" (Fontaine, 2008, p. 243). It usually involves little instrumental motivation (Fontaine & Dodge, 2006) and consequently is distinct from instrumental aggression or violence. Reactive violence is essentially identical to the Roberts *et al.* first category which delineates the offender who impulsively and fatally retaliates to a perceived egregious provocation or threat.

Many general altercation offenders probably possess a strong hostile attribution bias which promotes violence whenever they perceive provocations and threats, no matter how benign or minor. Fontaine (2008) describes these individuals as possessing dysfunctional thinking processes in the interpretation of ambiguous social stimuli. They seem to have a "hair trigger" toward others where the slightest and most benign provocation sets them off. Common descriptions of this behavior include impulsiveness and out-of-control behavior. A not atypical illustration is the patron who kills someone during a bar fight.

Impulsivity is a key concept in understanding violence. In most cases, impulsive violence is a result of faulty or inadequate self-regulation (also known as self-control) compounded by a hostile attribution bias and a simplistic belief of how to deal with perceived hostility or threats. Self-regulation is defined as the capacity to control and alter one's behavior and emotions. Note that the definition includes *both* behavioral and emotional control. One of the most important protective factors against developing violent behavior is success in developing self-regulation of emotions, impulses, and behavioral reactions at an early age (Alvord & Grados, 2005).

Fontaine and Dodge (2006) point out that attachment theory is based on the observation that early life events have enduring and considerable influence on beliefs and biases, even more so than do later events. In fact, early events shape the manner in which later events are cognitively represented. It is highly likely that many general altercation offenders demonstrated inadequate self-regulation skills early in their developmental years (Krueger, Caspi, Moffitt, White, & Stouthamer-Loeber, 1996). Clear signs of self-regulation and self-control begin to emerge during the second year of life, as does the concern for others. During the third year, children are expected to become reasonably compliant with parental requests and to internalize the family standards and values for behavior. Girls, on average, tend to show earlier self-regulated compliance during childhood than boys (Feldman & Klein, 2003). Fortunately, most people are able to restrain their aggressive impulses so as to stop violence or severe aggressive behavior. However, alcohol has the property of impairing self-regulation and self-control, even in persons who have a reasonably developed self-regulatory system. Consequently, considerable violence is especially prevalent among those persons who are intoxicated (with alcohol or other substances) and have marginally developed self-regulation skills.

Another key concept in explaining reactive violence is emotional arousal. Cognitive or thinking processes are greatly impaired at extreme levels of emotional arousal (Zillman, 1979, 1983). Under high excitement, such as anger, behavior normally controlled by reasonable thought becomes controlled by biases and habitual responses. If the individual has the well-learned habit of exploding, lashing out, or otherwise acting in a violent manner, he is especially likely to do this under highly emotional circumstances. High arousal inhibits cognitive processing to the point where one may not think before acting. Therefore, at very high levels of emotional upset, violence is apt to become impulsive, a term *Zillman* associated with habit strength. The violent behaviors have been so well learned that they appear quickly and without thought on the part of the individual. They seem to be "mindless" actions.

Felony Commission Homicides

Felony commission killings are motivated by instrumental aggression. Instrumental aggression is aggression for the sake of obtaining some object, rewards, or status possessed by another person—jewelry, money, territory, or influence. It is compared with reactive aggression, which occurs in response to provocation or perceived provocation. When it comes to severe or violent aggression, we will call the term in this section **proactive violence**. Proactive violence is characterized by cold-blooded, nonemotional, and premeditated aggression for the purpose of personal gain, such as a robbery or bullying. This description falls within the category of some offenders who kill during the commission of a felony. However, the term fits only those who anticipated and were accepting of the death of a victim. It does not fit the individual who holds up a liquor store with no intention of killing, but the robbery goes horribly wrong and the robber kills in a state of panic. In that case, the violence is better classified as reactive.

Proactive violence (also called instrumental violence) is typified by insensitive, calculated acts of severe violence enacted in the course of a crime, such as robbery, burglary, and drug acquisition. This form of violence is less emotional compared with reactive violence and more likely driven by the expectation of reward (Dodge, Lochman, Harnish, Bates, & Pettit, 1997). Similar to reactive aggressive patterns, proactive forms of violence appear to start early. Dodge *et al.* (1997) discovered in their research that children who frequently demonstrated reactive aggression seemed not only to have self-regulation problems, but did not expect positive consequences for their behavior. Their reward was in hurting the victim. Proactively aggressive children, on the other hand, anticipated more positive consequences for aggressive actions based on previous social learning. The researchers concluded that " . . . the proactively violent group might be displaying its violence because of an acquired belief that such violence will lead to positive social consequences for them" (Dodge *et al.*, 1997, p. 49). These findings suggest that reactive violence is thoughtless and emotionally driven, whereas proactive violence is self-regulated and stems from a rewarding learning history. The self-regulation process requires the development and refinement of cognitions and concepts which stem from social learning at an early stage of development, but these children also learn that strongly aggressive actions and bullying lead to the acquisition of goods and status from others.

In conclusion, it should be emphasized that the division separating general altercation homicide offenders from felony commission homicide offenders is used here primarily to present some types of homicide into a manageable set of explanations. There is certainly overlap between the two classifications, as some felony commission offenders during a mugging or armed robbery, for example, quickly lose self-control if the victims do not cooperate fully. In addition, we all tend to lose self-regulatory function under certain conditions when we become angry. High levels of emotional arousal take our attention away from our usual internal mechanisms of control. When we become extremely angry, for instance, we often say and do things we later regret. We feel upset, remorseful, and guilty, and we wish we could take back our words or actions. If we had carefully considered and evaluated the consequences of our behavior, we would probably have acted differently. But under the heat of emotion, our self-regulatory system, with all its standards, morality, and values, was held in abeyance. As we get older, however, we generally learn from experience to pay closer attention to our internal control mechanisms, and we engage in fewer impulsive outbursts. This "mellowing" feature may partly account for the lower rates of impulsive violence as age increases.

We should also mention that the Roberts *et al.* classification scheme does not entirely account for those offenders who have mental or behavioral disorders, such as severe depression and psychosis. In Western countries, it is estimated that 10 percent to 15 percent of those persons convicted of homicide have some form of psychotic disorders (Hodgins, 2001; Nordström, Dahlgren, & Kullgren, 2006). It is highly likely, therefore, that a significant proportion of the 336 homicide offenders in the Roberts study had one or more psychological disorders. After all, hostile attribution biases are not far from well-developed delusional thinking, and poor self-control or impulse-control deficits are not far from an assortment of disorders characterized by emotional and mental dysfunction.

JUVENILE MURDER

In January 2001, two male juveniles—Robert Tulloch and Jimmy Parker—arrived at the home of Dartmouth College professors Half Zantop and Susame Zantop under the guise of conducting an environmental survey. Half Zantop invited them in, led them to his study, and proceeded to answer some of their questions, even offering them help in wording them. At some point, the "survey" stopped and the professor was stabbed repeatedly. When his wife came running to his aid, she too was stabbed to death. With the rural New Hampshire community in shock, police began to search for a random killer or possibly even a disgruntled student. Clues at the scene eventually led them to suspect the two juveniles, and a warrant was issued for their arrest. They were located in Michigan after police were notified by a truck driver who had offered them a ride.

The Dartmouth murders—as they have come to be known—were atypical with respect to juvenile murders, most of which are believed to be the result of drive-by shootings or gang-related turf wars. Other juvenile murders are accompanied by severe family dysfunction, such as physical or sexual abuse. In this case, the two boys came from respected families in the community, were involved in school activities and well liked by peers, and were not economically disadvantaged. The murders were planned—although it is not clear that the Zantops were the targets. Neither did robbery appear to be a motive; the boys left the house without taking cash, jewelry, or valuable objects (Powers, 2002). The boys apparently wanted to see if they could successfully carry out a murder; one writer commented that they were going through the "apocalypse of adolescence" (Powers, 2002).

The above incident does not correspond well with what is known about juvenile murder, however. For example, studies (Cornell, 1989; Myers, Scott, Burgess, & Burgess, 1995; Shumaker & Prinz, 2000) reveal that a majority of homicide acts by juveniles took place either during general altercation episodes (64%) or the commission of a felony (36%). These categories, of course, are basically the same as the first two categories outlined by Roberts and his associates.

The 2007 UCR data reveal that only 6 percent of offenders arrested for murder were juveniles; 87 percent were adults, and the ages of 7 percent were unknown (Federal Bureau of Investigation, 2008). A breakdown of the overall data by gender showed that 90.1 percent of the offenders were male and 9.9 percent were female. Two percent of all murders were allegedly perpetrated by juveniles under age 15. Girls accounted for about one in five of the alleged assailants. From 1985 through 2000, the juvenile courts handled 1,700 juvenile murders, but the number of cases has steadily decreased since 1996 (Puzzanchera, Stahl, Finnegan, Tierney, & Snyder, 2004; Sickmund, 2009). To some extent, this reflects nationwide trends to transfer juveniles charged with serious crimes to criminal courts rather than process them in the juvenile system. Tulloch and Parker both pled guilty in adult criminal court, and both are serving lengthy sentences.

Nonetheless, regardless of the courts in which they are processed, the number of juveniles age 15 or younger who murder is relatively small (Snyder, 2001). Between 1980 and 1997, about 2 percent (or 600 cases) of murders involved *child* delinquents (ages 7–12), and the annual rate of these homicides is relatively stable, averaging about 30 homicides per year (Loeber, Farrington, & Petechuk, 2003). Nearly all of the homicides committed by children (94%) involved a single victim, mostly male (70%). More than half (58%) of the murder victims of child delinquents were juveniles under age 18 and more than a third (38%) of the victims were under age 13 (Snyder, 2001). Rarely was the victim a parent. The killing of a parent by a juvenile is often precipitated by child maltreatment, especially psychological abuse and neglect (Heide, 1993). More than half (54%) of the victims of child delinquents were killed with firearms. Gun play is often a contributing factor when children kill other children (Goetting, 1993).

Demographics and Psychological Characteristics of Juvenile Murderers

To obtain more detailed information both about the crimes and about the backgrounds of the offenders, some researchers have conducted studies with small samples of juvenile offenders. In general, these offenders have committed the "typical" homicides, not those of the apparent callousness exhibited in the Dartmouth case. For example, Myers and Scott (1998) examined 18 male juvenile murderers between the ages of 14 and 17 who met the criteria for conduct disorder at the time of their crimes. Their homicides were committed either in relation to criminal activities (72%) or during interpersonal conflict (28%). Half of the victims were strangers, whereas the other half were acquaintances (39%) or family members (11%). The results revealed that 16 of the 18 (89%) juvenile murderers had histories of one or more psychotic episodes (especially paranoid ideation), and other forms of mental disorders. These results were remarkably similar to the prevalence rate in earlier studies examining the psychological characteristics of juvenile murderers (e.g., Lewis *et al.*, 1985, 1988).

Research has also revealed that juvenile murderers—and those juveniles who commit violent crimes in general—tend to have a history of severe educational difficulties compared with nonviolent juveniles (Heckel & Shumaker, 2001). Children who begin school with deficits in social and cognitive skills are at high risk to engage in antisocial and violent behavior (Dodge *et al.*, 2008). Myers,

Scott, Burgess, and Burgess (1995) report that within their sample of 25 juvenile murderers, 76 percent demonstrated a learning disability and 86 percent had failed at least one grade. Verbal abilities evaluated by intelligence tests have also been found to be associated with antisocial behavior (Moffitt & Caspi, 2001). Significant language handicaps appear to be the most prominent learning problems among juvenile murderers (Heckel & Shumaker, 2001; Myers & Mutch, 1992). Again, none of the above was noteworthy in the backgrounds of Tulloch and Parker.

Another prominent factor in the backgrounds of juvenile homicide offenders is lack of parental monitoring. Parental monitoring refers to such things as knowing the child's whereabouts, being involved in the child's school activities and homework, and supervising time allocations for outside activities. Knowing the whereabouts and setting time limits for activities outside the home are especially important during the preteen and teenage years. Roe-Sepowitz (2007) reports that limited parental involvement and lack of supervision were present in many of the adolescent female murderers she followed. Hill, Castellino, et al. (2004) report that lack of parental involvement in school during the middle school years also appears to be critical. In Tulloch and Parker's case, however, lack of parental involvement would be a difficult argument to make. They seemed to be no less supervised than other adolescents inching their way to independence, and the parents were apparently interested in and caring about their activities.

Other studies have reported that juvenile homicide offenders often have high rates of family abuse (Darby, Allan, Kashani, Hartke, & Reid, 1998; Lansford, Deater-Deckard, Dodge, Bates, & Pettit, 2004), substance use and alcohol abuse (DiCataldo & Everett, 2008; Roe-Sepowitz, 2007), and prior delinquency (Loeber et al., 2005; Roe-Sepowitz, 2007) and peer delinquency (Loeber et al., 2005). Many juvenile murderers also appear to have a variety of neurological abnormalities (Heckel & Shumaker, 2001), similar to what has been reported in the medical histories of life course persistent offenders. Myers and his colleagues (e.g., Myers, 1994; Myers & Mutch, 1992; Myers, Scott, Burgess, & Burgess, 1995) have continually noted the high incidence of conduct disorders in his samples of juvenile murderers, ranging from 84 percent to 88 percent. ADHD has also been identified with juvenile murderers with some regularity (Heckel & Shumaker, 2001).

In summary, although researchers have made headway in identifying factors that might explain murder committed by juveniles, some cases defy neat explanations. The complexity of crime is illustrated in the bizarre case introduced at the beginning of this section. Nothing seems to fit, with the possible exception of "juvenile psychopathy."

The Dynamic Cascade Model

The list of risk factors influencing antisocial behavior, as we have discovered throughout the text, is extensive and even overwhelming. Loeber and his colleagues suggest that the probability of individuals committing homicide is enhanced by their exposure to an *accumulation* of different risk factors during early development (Loeber et al., 2005). They contend that violence-producing processes do not suddenly emerge; they accumulate over many years. The implications of the Loeber et al. position are that the higher the number of risk factors a child experiences, the greater the tendency to engage in violent acts during the life course.

Kenneth Dodge and his colleagues (2008) have advanced a theory that goes beyond the risks accumulation perspective, and helps us explain, organize, and understand how youth and adults get to the point of committing a homicide. It is called the **dynamic cascade model.** The model provides a coherent developmental story of how violent behavior grows across childhood and adolescence in a dynamic cascade. The model hypothesizes that each risk-factor group operates on antisocial and violent outcomes by directly influencing the next factor group in a developmental sequence.

Dynamic cascade in this context refers to a succession of developmental skills or deficits, each of which enhances, affects, or determines the next skill or deficit along a life-course trajectory. The term *snowballing* effect could also be used to describing the cascading effect.

To illustrate, the model starts with children who are born into an adverse neighborhood or disadvantaged family context, where parents may feel they need to resort to harsh or inconsistent discipline in a desperate attempt to control their young children. Although a more comprehensive model would also include prenatal experience and temperament, Dodge and his colleagues stated that their research began when the children were age five; they did not examine their lives retrospectively before that time. Harsh and inconsistent parental disciplinary strategies for controlling their children have a high risk of preventing the child from acquiring social and cognitive skills that are necessary for school social and academic success. "These skill deficits include vocabulary deficits, poor social problem solving, hostile attributional biases, and emotion recognition deficits" (Dodge *et al.*, 2008, p. 1921). Lacking the necessary social and academic skills to achieve during the early school years, the child begins to show conduct problems soon after entry into school, signaling the early start of the life-course-persistent offender. Next in the cascade is school social and academic failure as a result of disinterest in school and conduct disorder. Peer rejection sets in during this time. As the youth approaches early adolescence, parental monitoring of his or her activities and whereabouts is virtually nonexistent, accelerating academic failure and poor relationships with nondelinquent peers. Consequently, deviant peer associates become important and highly influential, and this often leads to persistent antisocial and violent behavior. The Dodge *et al.* research team was also able to determine that girls follow largely similar developmental pathways toward violence as boys. The researchers recognized that males are more likely than females to become seriously violent due to biological and socialization differences. However, they found little evidence to support the view that females, as a group, take a different developmental path to violence from males. In other words, they did not find a gender-specific developmental pathway.

After describing the dynamic cascade model, Dodge and his associates conclude with this crucial statement:

> An important implication of the current findings is that it is premature to conclude that an early-starting antisocial 5-year-old is unequivocally destined for a life-persistent path toward violent outcomes. Although the risk is substantial, it is by no means certain. The findings reported here indicate that trajectories can be deflected at each subsequent era in development, through interactions with peers, school, and parents along the way. (Dodge *et al.*, 2008, p. 1922)

This emphasizes that there are many preventive and therapeutic ways to steer a child away from a developmental trajectory of violence and serious delinquency and crime. Thus, psychological treatment of juveniles who kill may be more realistic than treatment of adults who commit these crimes. The dynamic cascade model provides specific targets for prevention at specific periods in development. In addition, because new risks arise with each developmental period, prevention and intervention cannot be deemed completed until the child passes through adolescence.

Treatment of Juveniles Who Kill

Juvenile homicide is a complex if rare phenomenon, and it often defies categorization. Contrast, for example, school shooting cases, the Dartmouth murders, the case of a boy who kills his abusive father, the 13-year-old girl who kills her newborn infant, the gang member in a drive-by shooting, and the

14-year-old who smothers his younger cousin to death in the process of trying to rape her. Some juveniles who kill are mentally disordered or developmentally disabled, and some may have psychopathic traits, but clearly not all do. Very little research is available by which to document the percentages, however. Most of the treatment information of juvenile murderers is from clinical case reports of a few cases referred for treatment (Heide, 2003). Juveniles who commit homicide—if not transferred to criminal courts—generally are placed in a juvenile facility where they do not always receive treatment tailored to the needs of the offender. In addition, the likelihood of juvenile murderers receiving intensive psychological treatment and intervention deceases as they enter adolescence (Heide, 2003; Myers, 1992). Older adolescent murderers are often placed in adult prisons. Mental health care in juvenile facilities is typically minimal because of financial constraints and limited awareness of the psychological needs of this population (Heide, 2003). Psychiatric hospitalization, although commonly used for young children who kill, is rarely done for adolescent murders (Heide, 2003). There are, of course, exceptions.

Overall, young killers appear to make a satisfactory adjustment in a correctional facility and in the community after release from custody (Heide, 2003). This is especially true for those youths who have killed family members as an isolated act of violence (Hillbrand, Alexandre, Young, & Spitz, 1999). On the other hand, hard-core, persistent, violent delinquents who killed in the course of committing other crimes do not make a good adjustment and often continue offending on release. The evidence for successful treatment of those juveniles who committed homicide during an altercation is mixed.

FAMILY VIOLENCE

Family violence (also called domestic violence, intimate partner violence, or spouse abuse) refers to any assault, intimidation, battery, sexual assault, sexual battery, or any criminal offense resulting in personal injury or death of one family or household member by another who is or was residing in the same single-dwelling unit (Wallace & Seymour, 2001). The term *battering* is often used in a slightly more specific fashion to describe *physical violence* in intimate relationships, either during a dating relationship, marriage or partnership, or separation and divorce. In recent years, the term *intimate partner violence* (IPV) is preferred, and this phenomenon will be discussed again later in the chapter. Family violence, which may or may not include IPV, "is an ongoing, debilitating experience of physical, psychological, and/or sexual abuse in the home, associated with increased isolation from the outside world and limited personal freedom and accessibility to resources" (Wallace & Seymour, 2001, p. 4). At the heart of family violence is usually the perpetrator's misuse of power, control, and authority (American Psychological Association, 2003).

The passage of the Violence against Women Act of 1994 (Public Law 103-322, Title IV) represented a substantial change in the nation's efforts to identify, control, and prevent crimes of domestic violence. "The Act explicitly recognizes that domestic violence is a serious crime that harms not only its immediate victims, but also their families, children, and the larger community" (Campbell, 1996, p. 2). The *Violence against Women Act of 2000* (often referred to as VAWA-2) expanded research and services to victims nationwide and focused on the role of courts in combating violence against women through training, education, and technical assistance for judges and other court personnel (Roberts, 2002).

Prevalence

About one of every five murders and nonnegligent manslaughters in the United States—in which the victim–offender relationship is known—involves a family member killing another family member, with a majority (about 50%) involving spouse killing spouse (Durose *et al.*, 2005; Federal Bureau of Investigation, 2005b). Similar statistics have also been reported in Canada (Silverman & Mukhergee, 1987). Homicide within the family accounts for 45 percent of all murders in England and Wales (d'Orban & O'Connor, 1989; Home Office, 1986). A neglected area of research in family violence is homicide followed by suicide, in which a family member kills other family members and then kills him- or herself. One reason for the neglect is that homicide-suicides are relatively rare, accounting for less than 2 percent of all homicides. Yet they are so sobering that they are almost invariably covered by national media. Research has consistently shown, however, that a high proportion of homicide-suicides (usually well over 50%) involve spouses, especially ex-spouses.

Ethnic/Minority Differences

Research on the incidence of family violence among various races and ethnic/minority groups has been largely neglected. Although indications are that family violence is substantially underre-ported at all levels of society, this is especially true for families outside the majority culture (American Psychological Association, 2003). Based on what is known, however, violence within the African American family is similar to that within white families, except that it occurs at higher rates. "As is the case for all types of homicide, African Americans are victimized by lethal violence at the hands of family members at rates that are many times higher than those for other racial groups in the United States" (Mercy & Salzman, 1989). Exceedingly few studies document the prevalence of domestic violence against Latinas (Santiago, 2002), Asian women (Lee, Jackson, Pattison, & Ward, 2002), or other ethnic minorities in general (Roberts, 2002). Very few existing studies on the prevalence of domestic or family violence make reference to race or ethnicity.

Victims

In 1995, approximately 19 percent of all arrests made for aggravated assaults and 68 percent for simple assault involved family members (U.S. Department of Justice, 2000b). Children under 12 comprised 5 percent of victims of family aggravated assault and 4 percent of the victims of family simple assault. Infants (under one year old) are the most vulnerable victims of family violence. **Figure 2** shows the nature of offenses that occurred against infants during the years 2001 to 2003. Most often, the offense committed against infant victims is simple assault, and the second most common is aggravated assault (Federal Bureau of Investigation, 2005). **Figure 3** shows the age of victims who were also present at the time of infant victimizations. Although infants make up the majority of victims, sometimes additional victims of other ages are present at the infant's victimization, demonstrating the multiple aspects of family violence. Infants are rarely the solitary victim in family violence.

Self-report victimization studies also suggest that at least 20 percent of simple or aggravated assaults involve family members (U.S. Department of Justice, 1989). Although these official statistics are woefully incomplete, they still underscore the considerable magnitude of family violence.

Some variant of family violence has probably existed for as long as individuals grouped together as families, both nuclear and extended. However, with the notable exception of intrafa-milial homicide, domestic or family violence has not traditionally been regarded as serious crime or worthy of criminal prosecution in this country. State governments and the courts have long claimed that family relationships require or deserve special immunity, including the views that parents have a right to discipline children physically, that a husband possesses the right to have sexual access to his wife, or that nagging women or disobedient children often provoke and deserve the beatings they receive (Pleck, 1989). This view has been energetically challenged in

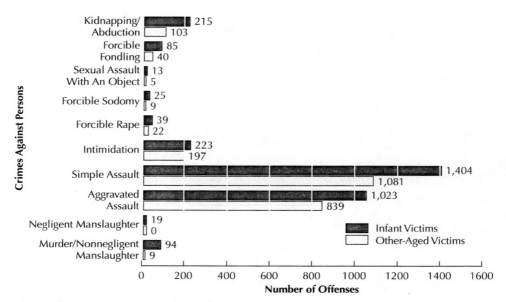

FIGURE 2   Offenses Related to Infant Victims

Source: Federal Bureau of Investigation, 2005, p. 359.

recent years by various interest groups attempting not only to acquaint the public with the problem but also to activate lawmakers and the criminal justice system toward more stringent legal and social sanctions.

Brief History of the Modern Era of Family Violence

The modern era of family violence interest and research began in 1962 when a Denver pediatrician (C. Henry Kempe) and four of his medical colleagues published a paper in the *Journal of the American Medical Association* titled "The Battered Child Syndrome" (Kempe, Silverman, Steele,

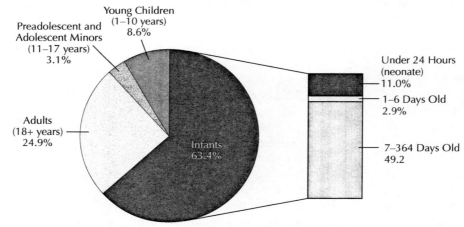

FIGURE 3   Age of Victims Present at Infant Victimization

Source: Federal Bureau of Investigation, 2005, p. 360.

Droegemueller, & Silver, 1962). The paper documented evidence of repeated multiple bone fractures of children suspected of being abused, and the article gradually became instrumental in the "rediscovery" of serious child abuse. The article was certainly not the sole precipitating factor in prompting the reexamination of child abuse. During the 1960s, a very large and influential child welfare movement, bent on drawing public and professional attention to the plight of abused and neglected children, was also taking hold.

In the early 1970s, the women's movement was highly influential in the rediscovery of wife beating, and shortly thereafter drew attention to marital rape. What began as a women's rights issue soon picked up support as a law-and-order issue (Pleck, 1989). The women's movement spawned legislation to increase or establish penalties for wife beating, to strengthen civil remedies, and to make it easier for women victims to file criminal charges against their assailants (Pleck, 1989). During the 1980s, several other types of family violence, from sibling violence to filial abuse of the elderly, have been acknowledged and empirically investigated. Thus, the generic term *family violence* includes spouse or partner abuse, child abuse, sibling violence, abuse of the elderly, and child-to-parent violence. And, as noted above, many researchers now prefer the term intimate partner violence to distinguish the violence that occurs when partners may or may not be "family." Currently, child abuse research is the most advanced, sophisticated, and extensive in the field of family violence (Finkelhor & Lewis, 1988). The problem of child abuse has also been the most widely publicized. Nationwide polls in 1976 revealed that only 10 percent of the general population considered child abuse a serious problem. In 1983, however, over 90 percent of the population considered it a serious problem (Wolfe, 1985).

However, despite the current interest and public concern about family violence and its many variants, we still know very little about it. Systematic study of family violence is new and often poorly designed. Even definitions, terms, and concepts in the field are excessively broad, ambiguous, and applied inconsistently, jeopardizing the comparability, generalizability, and reliability of the research findings (Weis, 1989). For example, it is unclear what behaviors should be included under the rubric family violence. Should verbal threats, shouting, slapping, aggressive gestures, intimidation, or spanking be included as examples of violence? Or only the more serious, physical forms of violence such as punching, stabbing, striking, shooting, and burning? Surveys conducted during the 1960s and 1970s indicated that between 84 percent and 97 percent of all parents used physical punishment at some time to discipline their children (Gelles, 1982). Surely we cannot conclude that 90 percent of the American parents were abusive during that era. Rather, this high incidence of corporal punishment was due to the widespread and firmly held tradition that a spanking now and then did the child some good. Although that tradition is currently shifting toward less or no corporal punishment, there still remains considerable controversy as to whether parental spankings and slaps constitute abuse.

It is also unclear how the term *violence* differs from abuse, maltreatment, neglect, and emotional and social deprivation. As noted by Gelles (1982), the battered child syndrome quickly gave way to the terms *child abuse, child neglect*, and *child maltreatment*. Child abuse, once restricted by Kempe and his associates to physical violence, has become increasingly broad, encompassing an extensive range of behaviors and misbehaviors by parents and caretakers. Furthermore, it also remains unclear what relatives or intimates should be included in family violence. Should lovers, intimate friends, common-law spouses, distant relatives, ex-spouses, or separated spouses also be included? Therefore, a troubling aspect of family violence research is that terms are defined differently and often unclearly, and an assortment of family members are included in the sample, making reliable comparisons between studies difficult and valid conclusions nearly impossible to come by. In addition, each study collects data from a variety of sources and often uses substantially different procedures and methodology to tabulate and analyze the data.

For our purposes, research on family violence will be divided into four major questions: (1) how much family violence is there? (2) What are the common characteristics (or correlates) of the offenders and victims? (3) Is family violence fundamentally different from other kinds of violence (such as street violence)? (4) What are the causes of family violence? We will explore the research in these four areas, keeping in mind the critical problems in definition, sampling, and methodology just described.

Incidence, Prevalence, and Demographics of Child Abuse and Neglect

In the United States, about 1 in 7 children (138 per 1,000) are maltreated at some time during their childhood (Finkelhor, Ormrod, Turner, & Hamky, 2005). Maltreatment refers to all forms of abuse and/or neglect, and can be divided into five types: physical abuse, sexual abuse, emotional abuse, neglect, and family abduction (see **Table 2**). Finkelhor and his associates, in a national survey of over 2,000 children, discovered that emotional abuse (name calling or denigration by an adult) was the most frequent of the five types. Boys and girls experienced similar rates for maltreatment with the exception of sexual abuse. Girls are four times more likely to be sexually abused.

The prevalence of this victimization is approximately 12 per 1,000 children, a rate that has been relatively consistent over the past decade. The data also indicate that child protective services received approximately 2,672,000 reports of *possible* maltreatment in 2001 (U.S. Department of Health and Human Services, 2003). According to the U.S. Department of Health and Human Services (2003), approximately two-thirds (63%) of all victims were neglected, and about one out of five children (19%) experienced physical abuse. Approximately 10 percent were sexually abused, and another 8 percent were emotionally abused. There is a high probability that emotional abuse is substantially underreported. Over one-quarter of the victims were victims of more than one type of maltreatment. Definitions for each of these terms are found in **Table 2**.

TABLE 2   Definitions of Child Abuse and Neglect

Type of Abuse	Definition
Physical abuse	Occurs when a parent willfully injures, causes injury, or allows a child to be injured, tortured, or maimed out of cruelty or excessive punishment
Emotional abuse	Chronic pattern of behavior in which the child is belittled, denied love to promote specific behavior, or subjected to extreme and inappropriate punishment
Emotional neglect	Failure to provide a child with appropriate support, attention, and affection.
Sexual abuse	Exploitation of a child or adolescent for another person's sexual and control gratification
Child neglect	Chronic failure of a parent or caretaker to provide a child with basic needs such as food, clothing, shelter, medical care, educational opportunity, protection, and supervision.
Missing and exploited	Kidnapping a child from a custodial parent, child abduction by strangers, or child sexual exploitation for child pornography, child prostitution.

Source: Adapted from Whitcomb (2001).

The highest victimization rates were for the 0–3 age group, and rates declined as age increased. Child abuse/neglect perpetrators, defined as persons who have maltreated a child while in a caretaking relationship to the child, were mostly female (three-fifths). More than four-fifths (87.1%) of the victims were maltreated by one or both parents. The most common pattern of maltreatment was a child neglected by a female parent with no other perpetrators identified (44.7%). In cases involving sexual abuse, more than half (55.5%) of the victims were abused by known male adults.

Boys and girls are about equally neglected, physically, or emotionally abused, but, as mentioned earlier, girls are four times more likely to be sexually abused. In 2001, an estimated 1,300 children died of abuse and neglect, a rate of approximately 1.81 deaths per 100,000 children in the general population (U.S. Department of Health and Human Services, 2003). This child fatality figure due to maltreatment is very probably an underestimation, however. The figure is probably closer to 2,000 or more. Determining the actual number of children who die each year from maltreatment is exceedingly difficult. Child fatalities due to maltreatment are probably underreported because *some* deaths labeled as accidents, or sudden infant death syndrome (SIDS), might be attributed to child maltreatment if more comprehensive investigations were conducted.

Interestingly, research has found that pet abuse and child abuse commonly occur together in dysfunctional families (Arkow, 1998). Adults who are cruel and inhumane to children (and their spouses) are often cruel and inhumane to the family pet(s) as well. Abusers often threaten to harm or actually kill a pet to frighten a child into secrecy or to punish the child or to keep the spouse from reporting the abuse to authorities. In one study, more than half of the women at a shelter reported that their pets had been harmed or killed by their partner, and they delayed coming to the shelter for fear of harm to their pets (Ascione, 1997).

Missing, Abducted, Runaway, and Thrownaway Children

Each year, thousands of children run away, are abducted, or are thrown away. A thrownaway youth refers to one whom a parent or caretaker "throws" out of the home. Numerous children—some say a majority—who run away do so to escape neglect or abuse from their current home or living arrangement. Most of the nationwide data on these children are reported in the NISMART Bulletins. NISMART is an acronym for the National Incidence Studies of Missing, Abducted, Runaway, and Thownaway Children, a large nationwide survey of households, juvenile residential facilities, and law enforcement agencies conducted by the Office of Juvenile Justice and Delinquency Prevention. NISMART consists of several studies designed to estimate the size and nature of the missing children problem in the United States. The more recent study, the NISMART-2, covers 1997–1999. Much of the information in this section comes from that report (U.S. Department of Justice, 2002a).

In 1999, an estimated 1,682,900 youth had a runaway or thrownaway episode (U.S. Department of Justice, 2002a). In most instances (71%), the runaway/thrownaway youth could have been endangered during the episode by virtue of such "street" factors as substance dependency, use of hard drugs, sexual or physical abuse, and their presence in places where criminal activity is prevalent.

Child abduction is another form of child abuse. In many instances, child abduction by a noncustodial parent from the custodial parent takes place. However, an undetermined number of child abductions are done by a parent who wants to protect the child or children from abuse by the other parent. Even a custodial parent may, in these circumstances, "abduct" the child, if the two parents share joint custody. An estimated 203,900 children were victims of family abduction in 1999, and nearly half were younger than six years of age (U.S. Department of Justice, 2002a).

Abduction of children by nonfamily members is less frequent. In this type of abduction, a nonfamily perpetrator takes a child by use of physical force or threat of bodily harm or detains the child for a substantial period of time (at least one hour) in an isolated place without lawful authority or parental permission. Nonfamily abductions are not typically the "stereotypical" stranger abductions highlighted in the media, however. They also may occur when a child younger than 15 is taken or detained or voluntarily accompanies a nonfamily person who conceals the child's whereabouts, demands a ransom, or expresses the intention to keep the child permanently. This last would include situations where a 20-year-old persuades his 14-year-old girlfriend to leave the state, or where a family acquaintance takes a child to protect the child from abuse. In 1999, approximately 58,200 children were abducted by nonfamily perpetrators, but this covered a very wide range of circumstances.

Stranger abductions—every parent's nightmare—are relatively rare, although any number is too great. In 1999, there were 115 of these stereotypical kidnappings, perpetrated by a stranger or slight acquaintance, and involving a child who was transported 50 or more miles, detained overnight, held for ransom or with intent to keep the child permanently (U.S. Department of Justice, 2002a). Abduction by a stranger is uncommon, but when it occurs, the child's chance for survival is significantly lowered (Whitcomb, 2001). Sexual motivations appear to be a major factor. Nearly half of all child victims of these stereotypical kidnappings were sexually assaulted by the perpetrator, and about one-third required medical attention for injuries (U.S. Department of Justice, 2002a). Over two-thirds of the victims of stereotypical kidnapping were female. In 40 percent of the stereotypical abductions, the child was killed, and in another 4 percent, the child was not recovered (U.S. Department of Justice, 2002a). In the summer of 2009 the nation was riveted to news that an 11-year-old girl abducted 17 years before was alive and living with her alleged abductor and his wife in a bizarre living arrangement that included a sheltered back yard structure. Now 28, the victim had apparently given birth to children fathered by this individual. In another high-profile similar case in the early 2000s, a teen-age boy was found and returned to his family after having lived under an assumed name with his abductor for a number of years. Such returns are rare, however, and they cannot be called happy endings in light of the trauma that has been experienced by the victims.

One out of five nonfamily abductions (21%) and almost half the victims of stereotypical kidnappings (48%) were abducted by multiple perpetrators (U.S. Department of Justice, 2002b). About half of the offenders of nonfamily abductions and one-third of the abductors in stereotypical kidnappings are in their twenties. Most of the abductions took place in the streets, parks, wooded areas, and other public areas, but rarely from the home, backyard, or school environments. Most children were taken into vehicles (45%) or to the offender's home (28%). Ransom is rarely demanded by the perpetrator(s) (less than 5% of all nonfamily or stereotypical abductions).

Munchausen Syndrome by Proxy

An unusual but serious type of child abuse is called **Munchausen syndrome by proxy (MSBP)**. This is a form of child abuse in which the parent (usually the mother), or parents, *consistently* and *chronically* bring a child in for medical attention with symptoms falsified or directly induced by the parent or parents (Murray, 1997). Munchausen syndrome by itself is the chronic and relentless pursuit of medical treatment for combinations of symptoms that are either falsely reported or that are the results of consciously self-inflicted injury. In its proxy form, MSBP, another person, usually a child, is the victim. MSBP cases are found in homes of all socioeconomic levels (Pearl, 1995), and the victims are most often children between infancy and eight years of age (Jones *et al.*, 1986). Both male and female children may be victims. In most cases (about 98% of the time), the mothers are the offending parent, while the father is often unaware of what is happening. There does not seem to be a gender preference for the victim, as both male and female children are represented in equal numbers.

Very often, the offending mother is very knowledgeable about medical issues, has a fascination with medical details, has her own medical history of fabricated illnesses, and may be a health professional herself. In addition, the mother will be unusually attentive to the child and will be reluctant to leave the child's side during medical examination or treatment. Another important symptom of MSBP is the child's series of reoccurring medical conditions that either do not respond to treatment or follow an unusual course that is persistent, puzzling, and unexplained. Another MSBP symptom is a series of physical or laboratory findings that are highly unusual, discrepant with medical history, or physically or clinically impossible. In extreme cases, the parent may initiate starvation in the child, nearly suffocate the child, inflict vaginal/rectal injuries in order to produce bleeding, add fat to stool collection to produce a lab abnormality, put her blood into child's urine sample before lab testing, or even inject contaminated material intravenously into the child's bloodstream (Murray, 1997; Pearl, 1995). The extreme forms of abuse certainly can lead to serious injury or even death. Unfortunately, the prevalence or incidence of MSBP is unknown at this time, probably partly due to the difficulty of identifying actual illnesses as opposed to the fabricated ones.

In some instances, the family pet may be the victim of MSBP, with the pet owner consistently taking the pet to the veterinarian for a variety of vague or fake symptoms. The pet owner often is trying to get sympathy and attention through the pet's misfortune.

Shaken Baby Syndrome

Another form of child abuse is **shaken baby syndrome (SBS),** in which a parent or caretaker, usually in anger, shakes a baby so hard that serious head injury results. Although there are no accurate statistics regarding the frequency of this form of abuse, there is consensus that head trauma is the leading killer of abused children (over 50%) and that shaking is involved in many of these cases (Duhaime, Christian, Rorke, & Zimmerman, 1998; Showers, 1999; Smithey, 1998). Ellis and Lord (2001) estimate that 10 percent to 12 percent of all deaths due to abuse and neglect are attributable to SBS (see also National Information Support and Referral Service, 1998). In addition, available research suggests that 70 percent to 80 percent of the perpetrators of SBS are male, and most of the time they are the parent of the child (Child Abuse Prevention Center, 1998; Ellis & Lord, 2001). Both male and female babies appear to be equally victimized. And, of course, not all baby victims of SBS die, but many suffer significant brain damage, resulting in conditions such as cerebral palsy, blindness, deafness, seizures, learning disabilities, and coma.

Available research indicates that childhood abuse and neglect in general increase the odds of future delinquency and adult criminality by 40 percent. More specifically, being abused or neglected as a child increases the likelihood of arrest as a juvenile by over 50 percent, as an adult by 38 percent, and for a violent crime by 38 percent (Widom, 1992). More recent research by Widom (2000) confirms these data further. She states (2000, p. 5), "The odds of arrest for a juvenile offense were 1.9 times higher among abused and neglected individuals than among controls; for crime committed as adult, the odds were 1.6 times higher." In addition, psychological and emotional problems were prevalent among the abused and neglected sample. Specifically, the abused and neglected individuals were significantly more likely than the controls (a comparison group who had not experienced abuse or neglect) to have attempted suicide and to have met the criteria for antisocial personality disorder.

INFANTICIDE

In this section, the focus is on that form of child homicide that occurs when a person intentionally kills a child or infant, and *intends that the death occur.* That is, the homicide is not accidental or the incidental result of abuse or neglect. Although the term **infanticide** literally means the killing of an *infant,* it has become synonymous with the killing of a child by a parent. Some forms of infanticide can be traced back to ancient societies, including ancient Greece, Rome, China, India, and Europe. "In some instances, it took place as part of socially sanctioned religious sacrifice, was meant to dispose of physically defective infants, was a way to dispose of female infants when males were preferred, or was a form of population control (Smithey, 2002, p. 888).

An estimated 1,200–1,500 children are intentionally killed each year by a parent or other person, representing about 12 percent to 15 percent of the total homicides in the United States (Emery & Laumann-Billings 1998) (see **Figures 2** and **3**). There were 69 children under the age of 18 murdered in Canada, comprising 12 percent of the total homicides in that country in 2001 (Au Coin, 2003b). In the United States and Canada, about two-thirds of murdered children are killed by family members, mostly parents. Child homicide is not randomly distributed, but occurs with greater frequency across the globe in areas characterized by poverty, limited opportunity, and urbanization. A majority of child homicides across the globe are the result of parents killing their own child. Interestingly, the United States ranks fifth in homicides of infants under one year of age (with a rate of 5.4 per 100,000 live births) among 18 developed countries (Smithey, 2002).

Infants aged 12 months or younger have the highest homicide victimization rate of any single group in Australia, England and Wales, Canada, and the United States (Brookman & Nolan 2006). In England and Wales, for instance, children younger than one year old are at least twice as likely to be a victim of homicide as any other age group (Brookman & Nolan, 2006). They are, in most cases, killed by a biological parent.

In Canada, between 1974 and 2001, children under age six were more likely to have been killed as a result of strangulation or a beating than by other methods (Au Coin, 2003b). In England and Wales, two-thirds of the infants are killed as a result of suffocation or nonspecific methods such as shaking (shaken baby syndrome) and physical abuse (Brookman & Nolan, 2006). Older Canadian children, on the other hand, were more likely to be killed by a firearm, with 32 percent of victims age 6–8 years and over 50 percent of victims 15–17 years of age dying of gunshot wounds (Au Coin, 2003b).

Several decades ago, Resnick (1970) recommended that the killing of one's children be divided into two separate categories, **neonaticide,** which refers to the killing of the newborn within the first 24 hours after birth, and **filicide,** which refers to the killing of a child older than 24 hours. Resnick's research indicated that neonaticide was more likely to represent an attempt to dispose of a problem, while filicide was more likely a reflection of parental depression or feelings of being overwhelmed. This distinction has now largely disappeared from the literature, but social concerns about neonaticide continue. An increasing number of jurisdictions, for example, now have laws that bar the prosecution of parents who leave newborns or infants in "safe harbors" such as hospitals, churches, or synagogues. The assumption is that if the parents have no such safe harbor, they might not sufficiently care for the infants or, worse, take the drastic step of ending their lives.

Neonaticide

The extent of neonaticide is difficult to determine because many go undetected and there is no national data depository for these cases (Beyer, Mack, & Shelton, 2008). The same situation holds for filicide (Koenen & Thompson, 2008). It is roughly estimated that approximately 150–300 incidents of neonaticide occur each year in the United States (Meyer & Oberman, 2001). A similar estimate has been advanced by researchers on filicide (Koenen & Thompson, 2008). In their investigation of existing neonaticide data at the FBI National Center for the Analysis of Violent Crime, Beyer and her colleagues (2008) discovered that many of the 40 women in their study gave birth unassisted to infants of normal birth weight. The women then killed the neonate, disposed of the body, cleaned up the crime scene, and remained undetected. "Many of the offenders are then able to engage in routine activities, immediately following the birth of the child, including attending classes, shopping, eating out, dancing, or returning to work" (Beyer *et al.*, 2008, p. 531).

Beyer *et al.* found very little evidence that the women who engaged in neonaticide had serious mental or psychological disorders, a finding consistent with previous studies (Dobson & Sales, 2000; Spinelli, 2001). However, several women did show some bizarre behaviors following the neonaticide, such as placing the infant's body in containers, driving around with the infant's body in the trunk of their car, or breastfeeding the dead infant. Similarly, Spinelli (2001) identified bizarre incidents following the neonaticide, such as returning to bed with the infant's corpse or keeping it under their clothes. In one case, "The putrefied corpse of one infant was found 2 weeks after delivery in a file cabinet in the office the subject shared with others" (Spinelli, 2001, p. 812). Such extreme measures likely were indicative of some mental disorder or postpartum psychosis precipitated by hormonal changes associated with the pregnancy and birth.

Beyer *et al.* report that virtually none of the women in the study had a criminal history, nor were arrested for crime against a child prior to the homicide. It is also interesting to note that several of the offenders had living biological children (ranging in number from one to four additional children) at the time of the homicide. Killing the newborn appears to reflect a desire to rid oneself of a problem. Most of the women who commit neonaticide are described as being sexually submissive, immature, childlike, and passive (Koenen & Thompson, 2008). However, there is so little research specifically on this topic that firm conclusions are unwarranted.

Filicide

Although severe mental disorders and suicide are rare in neonaticide, this is not the case in filicide. Some researchers contend that a majority of the women who commit filicide are demonstrating symptoms of affective disorders, a psychotic disorder, or a combination of the two (Lewis & Bunce, 2003). Traditionally, women who kill their children have been viewed by the legal system and the mental health profession as suffering from severe emotional problems, rendering them either insane (the legal system) or psychotic (the mental health profession). Men who kill their children are more likely to be viewed as evil and cruel (Wilczynski, 1997).

Resnick (1969, 1970) concluded that two-thirds of the mothers who committed filicide were psychotic, compared with only 17 percent of the women in the neonaticide group. As noted, Resnick found that a vast majority of the filicide group suffered from serious depression, while very few women in the neonaticide group exhibited this feature. Furthermore, suicide attempts accompany one-third of the filicides, but rarely accompany neonaticide.

More recent research sheds additional light on maternal murder of their young. In a cross-national comparison of British and Canadian filicidal women by McKee and Shea (1998), the data suggested that women who were charged with murdering their children usually suffered from a diagnosable mental disorder and were contending with many stressful events in their lives at the time of the murder. In another study, results showed that women suffering from a diagnosed mental disorder were more likely to use a weapon to murder their children than filicidal women not suffering from an apparent mental disorder (Lewis, Baranoski, Buchanan, & Benedek, 1998). The Lewis *et al.* study found that guns were used 13 percent of the time and knives 12 percent of the time.

Some studies have indicated that the prevalence of major depression among women who commit filicide is as high as 82 percent (Haapasalo & Petaja, 1999). Most often, the clinical diagnosis is "postpartum depression," a depressive episode thought to be brought on by childbirth. However, it is important to realize that three categories of mental or emotional reactions may be apparent after childbirth: (1) postpartum blues, (2) postpartum depression, and (3) postpartum psychosis (Dobson & Sales, 2000). The most frequent is *postpartum blues*, characterized by crying, irritability, anxiety, confusion, and rapid mood changes. It is estimated that anywhere from 50 percent to 80 percent of women exhibit some minor features of postpartum blues about one to five days after delivery (Durand & Barlow, 2000). The symptoms may last for a few hours to a few days and are clearly associated with childbirth and the hormonal changes that accompany pregnancy and delivery. The connection between postpartum blues and neonaticide or filicide has not been supported by the research literature (Dobson & Sales, 2000).

The second category, *postpartum depression*, occurs during the weeks or months after childbirth. The symptoms include depression, loss of appetite, sleep disturbances, fatigue, suicidal thoughts, apathy about the newborn, and a general loss of interest in daily living. However, in contrast to postpartum blues, postpartum depression does not appear totally related to childbirth. Rather, it is more a clinical form of depression that is present before childbirth and probably is more a recurring depressive disorder that has existed before the delivery; however, it is accelerated by late pregnancy, birth, and the subsequent physical exhaustion and overwhelming responsibility of caring for an infant. This form of mood disorder is usually not linked to filicide.

The third category, *postpartum psychosis*, is a severe mental disorder that is rare, occurring in one out of every 1,000 women following delivery. Usually, the psychotic features are strikingly similar to symptoms of serious bipolar depression and appear directly associated with childbirth. Sometimes, this mental disorder is severe enough to lead to the mother's attempted suicide, together with an attempt to kill the infant (Kendall & Hammen, 1995). Dobson and Sales (2000) report that research indicates that many women (estimates range from 20%–40%) who commit filicide are suffering from postpartum psychosis. In one noteworthy incident that occurred in the 1980s, the new mother had closed the window shades of her home for several weeks after her baby's birth, sitting in darkened rooms, and resisting entreaties of her husband and other family members to get psychological help. On the day of the killing, she shot her infant to death in his crib. The prosecutor dismissed the case, supposedly because he could not find one clinician who would say she was *not* suffering from a severe form of postpartum psychosis.

Overall, though, few filicides are committed by mothers suffering from depression or psychosis, or some other serious mental disorder. Filicides can result from acts of omission, such as neglecting to supervise or monitor the child in a hazardous environment or dangerous situation, or acts of commission, such as shaking an infant or delivering a swift blow to silence persistent crying. The father of the infant or another male figure may also be the responsible party, but research on filicides tends to focus on the mother. In many cases, it is difficult to determine whether the child's death is due to an accident, carelessness, or an intentional act to murder.

Coramae Richey Mann (1993) investigated the patterns and characteristics of maternal filicide in six major U.S. cities (Chicago, Houston, Atlanta, Los Angeles, New York, and Baltimore) between 1979 and 1983. Although the data set for the study consisted of 296 cleared (or solved) homicide cases in which the offender was female, Mann restricted her research sample to 25 maternal filicides of preschool children (ages birth to five years). Because of the small sample size, any far-reaching conclusions must be drawn very cautiously.

Mann found that 40 percent of the women who killed their preschool children had arrest records. One offender had 15 misdemeanor arrests, while another had six felony arrests. Twenty-five percent had arrest records for violent crime. Moreover, 12 of the 25 filicide offenders had recorded child abuse histories where court or social service intervention had taken place. Most of the victims were killed in the bathroom (30%), or the bedroom (26%), usually on Sunday morning. Manual methods were used in 80 percent of the cases—hands or feet (52%), suffocation or strangulation (16%), or drowning (12%). The killing of older children (ages 4 or 5) tended to be more brutal.

While a majority of the offenders in the Mann study were initially charged with murder, only 19 percent were convicted of that charge. Forty percent of the women who killed their preschool children were sent to prison, most often on a conviction of manslaughter, and another 36 percent received a probation sentence. The remaining six cases were either not processed, dismissed, or received special treatment from the court, and their dispositions were sealed. A determination of a mental disorder of the offenders was apparently rare.

Dobson and Sales (2000) conclude, "There is certainly little evidence that women who kill their infant within the first 24 hours of birth are seriously mentally ill, and furthermore, many women who kill their infant after the first 24 hours do not exhibit symptomatology that meets the requirements for diminished capacity or insanity" (p. 1109). However, they also concluded that the potential role of psychosis in *some* women should not be underestimated in filicide. In some instances of filicide, such as observed by Resnick, some mothers are psychotic or otherwise seriously mentally disordered.

PARTNER AND OTHER FAMILY ABUSE

Intimate Partner Abuse: Prevalence, Incidence, and Nature

The National Family Violence Survey of 1995–1996 estimated that the prevalence of women battering in the United States ranged from 6 to 8.7 million annually (Roberts, 2002). It is further estimated that one in three murders every year are intimate partner homicides (Roberts, 2002). According to estimates from the National Crime Victimization Survey (NCVS), there were 691,710 nonfatal violent victimizations committed by current or former spouses, boyfriends, or girlfriends of the victims during 2001 (Rennison, 2003). Eighty-five percent of victimizations by intimate partners were against women. Overall, **intimate partner violence** (IPV) comprised 20 percent of violent crime against women in 2001. In 2002, 32.1 percent of female murder victims were slain by their husbands, ex-husbands, or boyfriends, compared with 2.7 percent of the male murder victims who were killed by their wives, ex-wives, or girlfriends (Federal Bureau of Investigation, 2003).

BATTERED WOMAN SYNDROME   The term **battered woman syndrome** was minted and developed by Lenore Walker (1979), a psychologist who specializes in domestic abuse. Walker has identified a cluster of behavioral and emotional features that, she believes, are often shared by women who have been physically and psychologically abused over a period of time by the dominant male figure in their lives. Feelings of low self-esteem, depression, and helplessness are among the important components that frequently accompany the syndrome.

Research on domestic violence finds that a great majority of battered women either remain in lifelong abusive relationships, leave the relationship, or are killed by their abusers. Very rarely do battering relationships get better. A small minority of abused women kill their abusers. Although evidence for the battered woman syndrome is being admitted into the trials of women who do kill their abusers (Schuller & Vidmar, 1992), it is rarely successful in bringing about an acquittal (Browne, 1987; Ewing, 1990).

Currently, there is considerable debate concerning the reliability, validity, and usefulness of the diagnosis "battered woman syndrome" (Bartol & Bartol, 2004b). One of the major problems with the concept is the tendency for mental health and law professionals to regard it as a *single* entity representing some kind of mental or behavioral disorder displayed by all women who experience a severe abusive relationship. In addition, some theorists prefer to view the psychological effects of battering as a form of posttraumatic stress disorder (PTSD), rather than as a separate syndrome.

However, battered women demonstrate a wide range of behavioral patterns that often reflect survival skills and adaptation to serious, life-threatening situations rather than a psychological disorder. Many women simply do not exhibit discernible clusters of psychological maladjustment, depression, and helplessness as portrayed by the battered women syndrome or by PTSD, even though they may have experienced high degrees of coercion, domination, and abuse during a lengthy relationship (Stark, 2002). Some victims, regardless of the abuse, may not demonstrate any signs of a syndrome or mental health problems at all.

Same-Sex Domestic Violence

In recent years, the nature and extent of same-sex partnerships has received increased attention. With the increasing likelihood that more and more states will recognize the right of gays to marry, these partnerships will come under the same research microscope as heterosexual marriages, including scrutinizing their divorce rates, styles of parenting, and any presence of violence in their relationships. Some researchers (Potoczniak, Mourot, Crosbie-Burnett, & Potoczniak, 2003) already have discovered some strong similarities in the research literature comparing the violence cycles and stages of abuse between same-sex domestic violence (SSDV) and opposite-sex domestic violence (OSDV). For example, similar to OSDV perpetrators, SSDV perpetrators are extremely controlling, threatened by outside influences, are highly selfish, and blame their partners for the abuse. In addition, the SSDV victims show many of the same behavioral and thought characteristics of OSDV victims.

Turrell (2000) examined SSDV among lesbians, gay women, and gay men. In the survey, female participants were able to choose between the designations lesbian and gay women. Turrell found a physical abuse prevalence rate of 44 percent for gay men, 58 percent for gay women, and 55 percent for lesbians in a past or present relationship. With increased attention relating to issues involving civil unions and same-sex marriages across the nation in recent years, it is obvious that a better understanding and skillful research attention to SSDV are important, especially pertaining to providing adequate domestic violence and psychological services to the victims and training criminal justice personnel to handle the incidents in a competent fashion.

Psychological and Demographic Characteristics of Abusers

As the section on battered woman syndrome indicates, most of the research on psychological characteristics in domestic violence has focused on the characteristics of the person being abused, particularly the woman in heterosexual relationships. It has been a traditional belief in some quarters that these battered women allow themselves to be battered (Frieze & Browne, 1989). Others have argued that victims of spouse abuse are masochistic, consciously and unconsciously precipitating the violence to which they are subjected (Megargee, 1982). Still others have depicted battered wives as lacking self-esteem, being highly passive and dependent on their husbands, and willing to place greater value on maintaining the marriage above their safety (Megargee, 1982).

Some researchers, though, have preferred to focus on the characteristics of the abusers. Abusive husbands, for example, have been depicted as extremely possessive and unreasonably jealous men who treat their wives like property coveted by other men. This depiction led to other assumptions about the inadequacy, incompetence, and low self-esteem of these abusive husbands who saw threats to their masculinity everywhere. Christine Rasche (1993) examined 155 "mate" homicides in Florida that occurred between 1980 and 1986. She was able to identify several motives for these intimate homicides, with possessiveness the most prominent. The list of motives and related percentages was as follows:

- Possessiveness (48.9%)
- Self-defense (15.5%)
- Abuse by victim (2.6%)
- Feelings arising out of arguments (20.7%)
- Other motives (9.7%)
- Unknown (7.7%)

Alcohol abuse is also often seen as part of the clinical picture. Similarly, men who abuse their children were seen as incompetent, immature individuals, overwhelmed and frustrated by the responsibilities of parenting. The violence of both the abusive husband and the abusive father was seen as irrational and expressive, precipitated by frustration and extreme anger. Some professionals have suggested that street violence is generally rational and instrumental, whereas family violence is predominately irrational and expressive (see Hotaling & Straus, 1989; Megargee, 1982).

The empirical evidence for these depictions is meager, equivocal, and confusing and no more persuasive than the depictions of battered women as passive and lacking in self-confidence. Some studies find some support for these correlates; others provide no support. Despite several attempts at psychological typologies for wife and child abusers (Megargee, 1982), there does not seem to be any evidence for typical psychological profiles for either the abusers or the abused. However, recent research results look promising for a typology that might help in the prevention, intervention, and treatment of abusers. In an extensive review of the research literature, Holtzworth-Munroe and Stuart (1994) identified three primary types of male spouse batterers: Type 1 batterers who abuse family members only. Type 2 batterers who abuse family members because of emotional problems, and Type 3 batterers who are generally violent toward both family members and persons outside the family. Type 1 abusers are the most common, tend to be less aggressive than the other two, and also tend to be more remorseful for their actions. They are generally inadequate, passive men who are dependent on others. Type 2 batterers tend to be depressed, inadequate individuals who are emotionally volatile and who display indicators of personality disorders and psychopathology. Type 3 batterers are individuals who are antisocial, criminally prone, and violent across situations. They are more likely to abuse alcohol and are generally more belligerent toward almost everyone. They are also most likely to be involved in serious violence toward a spouse.

The search for demographic variables has been equally mixed and inconclusive (Hotaling & Straus, 1989; Weis, 1989). Wife and child abuse appears to cut across socioeconomic, religious, and ethnic lines. Even current research on gender does not reveal clear trends for women or men as assaulters of spouse, child, or parent.

The abuse of alcohol and drugs seems to play a role as an exacerbator, *but not as a cause,* of the family violence. Abusive men with severe alcohol or drug problems are apt to abuse their partners both when drunk and when sober. However, abusive husbands who drink heavily are violent more frequently, and inflict more serious injuries on their partners than do abusive men who do not have a history of alcohol or drug problems (Frieze & Browne, 1989). A similar pattern also holds for men who abuse their children. Many use alcohol as an excusing agent that allows them to escape some culpability for their antisocial or violent actions, as well as to avoid the full impact of legal sanctions. Babcock, Waltz, Jacobson, and Gottman (1993), in some very promising research, examined the interactions of marital power, interpersonal strategies, and communication skills as predictors of marital violence. They reasoned that husbands who are unable to affect their intentions through negotiation or general communication skills are more likely to resort to physical aggression—pushing, slapping, and beating—to achieve their intentions. This is especially the case if the wives are more verbally competent, more educated, or have better jobs than their husbands. For example, previous research suggests that women with jobs that are higher in status than their husband's jobs experience more life-threatening violence than wives who were occupationally similar to their husbands (Hornung, McCullough, & Sugimoto, 1981). Frustrated with some combination of power discrepancy between him and his wife, the husband's only effective expressive retort may be physical aggression. Moreover, husbands who battered their wives were more likely to be in relationships where their demands were met with their wives' withdrawal (e.g., defensiveness, passive inaction, "stonewalling," or the "silent treatment"). The researchers interpreted the withdrawal pattern as one of power (the individual has resources the other partner wants), whereas the demanding role represented a weak position (the individual wants something the other partner has). This research emphasizes the importance of studying the reciprocal interaction of a relationship if we are to understand family violence more fully.

Elderly Abuse: Prevalence, Incidence, and Nature

It is estimated that approximately 2.5 million older Americans are victims of abuse each year (National Center on Elder Abuse, 1999). Elder abuse is characterized by the infliction of physical, emotional, or psychological harm on the older adult, usually defined as age 65 or older (Marshall, Benton, & Brazier, 2000). "The general concept involved in the numerous definitions of 'elder abuse' is that the victim is injured, neglected, or exploited because of vulnerabilities associated with age, such as impaired physical or mental capacities" (Klaus, 2000, p. 13).

Neglect in this instance is "the refusal or failure to fulfill any part of a person's obligation or duties to an elder" (Seymour, 2001, p. 4). More specific elder abuse definitions include "the refusal or failure to provide an elderly person with such life necessities as food, water, clothing, shelter, personal hygiene, medicine, comfort, personal safety, and other essentials included in the responsibility or agreement with an elder" (Seymour, 2001, p. 4). Abandonment may also be included in the definition of neglect, and is characterized by such things as the desertion of an elder at a hospital, a nursing facility, or other similar institution, or desertion of an elder at a public location (see **Table 3**).

TABLE 3   Estimated Incidence of Specific Types of Elder Abuse, 1996

Type of Abuse	Estimated Percentage
Neglect	58.50
Physical abuse	15.70
Financial exploitation	12.30
Emotional abuse	7.30
Sexual abuse	0.04
Other types	5.10
Unknown	0.06

Source: National Center on Elder Abuse (1999).

The elderly appear to be maltreated in much the same way that children are maltreated—with one notable exception: financial exploitation (Pagelow, 1989). The likeliest candidates for elder abuse appear to be white women between the ages of 75 and 85, middle to lower class, Protestant, and suffering from some form of physical or mental impairment (Pagelow, 1989). Only 5 percent of the elderly are placed in institutions or rest homes, although 85 percent of them have at least one chronic illness (Hudson, 1986). Most elderly are living at home or in the homes of relatives. Abusive caretakers tend to lack resources, feel trapped, and may be abusing drugs or alcohol.

Spouses constitute the second-largest abuser category. Male caretakers are more likely to abuse the elderly physically, while female caretakers are prone to abuse them psychologically or neglect them. However, both men and women are equally likely to exploit them financially. The most common abuse is a combination of psychological abuse and neglect (Pagelow, 1989). About 20 percent of elder abuse cases are physical, and 45 percent involve neglect (Marshall, Benton, & Brazier, 2000).

Although there are similarities between the various types of family abuse, elder mistreatment is a more complex phenomenon that encompasses both aspects of interpersonal violence and the aging process (Wolf, 1992). That is, elder abuse and neglect are often a result of long-standing troubled family dynamics and interpersonal processes that have been highly charged when the dependency relationship is altered, either because of illness or financial needs.

Estimates of the proportion of elderly persons (persons 65 or older) who are abused range from 4 percent to 10 percent, but it is difficult to make confident estimates because of a lack of reliable statistics (Klaus, 2000; Pagelow, 1989; Pillemer & Suitor, 1988). The first-ever National Elder Abuse Incidence Study, conducted by the National Center on Elder Abuse (1999), estimated that during 1996, at least one-half million older persons in domestic settings were abused and/or neglected, or experienced self-neglect, and that for every reported incidence of elder abuse, neglect, or self-neglect, approximately five go unreported (Seymour, 2001). The same report found that female elders are abused at a higher rate than males, even after accounting for their larger numbers in the aging population. And two-thirds of the perpetrators of elder abuse are adult children or spouses. While there is no one single causal factor to fully explain why family members abuse their seniors, some explanations have focused on caregiver stress and dependency issues (either the caregiver's or the senior's) (Au Coin, 2003a).

Pillemer and Finkelhor (1988) focused on the Boston metropolitan area and found that 3 percent of the elderly suffered from one of three kinds of abuse: physical abuse, chronic verbal abuse, or neglect. Based on their findings, the researchers extrapolated that about one million elderly persons are similarly abused throughout the United States. A Canadian survey (Podnieks, Pillemer, & Nicolson, 1990) reported that about 4 percent of the elderly population living in private homes in Canada was subjected to abuse and neglect.

The violent crime committed against persons age 65 or older is most likely to be simple assault (Klaus, 2000). Nevertheless, there is ample evidence that they are also victims of more serious violent crimes. Recent statistics from two countries are illustrative. In Canada, 6 percent of the total homicide victims were older Canadians (65 or older), with a family member being responsible for over half of the cases (Au Coin, 2003a). The same statistic (6.4%) was reported in the United States for older Americans (Federal Bureau of Investigation, 2003). The term **eldercide** is usually reserved for the murder of a person age 65 or older. In Canada, when the incident involved a family member, a majority of older women were killed by a spouse or ex-spouse (53%), whereas older men were most often killed by an adult son (43%) (Au Coin, 2003a). The data are similar for American senior citizens (Klaus, 2000). In Canada, the most common cause of death for older victims of family-related homicides was beating (29%) and shooting (28%), followed by stabbing (23%) (Au Coin, 2003a). Although a similar family breakdown is not currently available in the U.S. data, the most common causes of death for all older victims were firearms (45%), followed by stabbing (20%), blunt objects (14%), and beatings with fists or feet (13%) (Federal Bureau of Investigation, 2003).

Sibling-to-Sibling Violence

Violence between siblings is believed to be the most common form of violence within families, but surprisingly little is known about it (Gelles, 1997; Wallace, 1996). The violence and abuse a child or adolescent receives from a sibling is often overlooked and trivialized (Simonelli, Mullis, & Rohde, 2005). Sibling conflicts are generally seen as a normal part of growing up (Underwood & Patch, 1999). Mothers and fathers display a great tendency to deny the seriousness of the aggressive outburst of siblings or their children—including violence toward themselves—in order to perpetuate a "myth of family harmony" (Harbin & Madden, 1979). Yet in many cases, sibling conflict and violence involves punching, choking, beating up, threatening to use a weapon, and actually using a weapon. In addition, sibling violence appears to be linked to violence in dating relationships, family violence in adulthood, and nonfamily adult violence in general (Hoffman, Kiecolt, & Edwards, 2005). More severe forms of child-to-family violence involve murder, and have specific terms, such as **siblicide** (sibling killing sibling), **patricide** (killing one's father), **matricide** (killing one's mother), **sororicide** (killing one's sister), **fratricide** (killing one's brother), and **parricide** (killing one or more of one's parents).

Nearly 30 years ago, Steinmetz (1981) reported that two-thirds of the adolescent siblings in the family sample she studied—a sample characterized by family violence—used physical violence to resolve conflict. These findings have been recently supported by Hoffman *et al.* (2005) who found 70 percent of the adolescents in their sample (students) had committed at least one violent act against their closest-age sibling during their senior year of high school. Families having only sons consistently experience more sibling violence than do families with only daughters (Hoffman *et al.*, 2005). Hoffman *et al.* (2005) found that males perpetrated more violent acts against their brothers than against sisters or sisters against their siblings. In 2002, 72 percent of murders by siblings involved a brother killing a brother, and 14 percent involved a brother killing a sister (Durose *et al.*, 2005). An additional 14 percent of siblicides involved a sister killing a brother or sister. Among the 671 intrafamilial murders reported in 2002, 18 percent (or 119 murders) involved a sibling victim (Durose *et al.*, 2005).

Victims of the more extreme forms of sibling violence tend to be younger siblings. For example, Fehrenbach, Smith, Monastersky, and Deisher (1986) reported that over 40 percent of victims of adolescent sexual assault were younger siblings. Available data also suggest that 85 percent of siblicide offenders and 73 percent of siblicide victims are male (Dawson & Langan, 1994). Approximately one out of every 100 homicides in the United States is a siblicide (Federal Bureau of Investigation, 2005; Underwood & Patch, 1999). In their analysis, Underwood and Patch (1999) reported that the most common circumstance of sibling homicide was some type of argument between the perpetrator and the victim. Interestingly, the same study uncovered very few incidents involving Asian Americans or Pacific Islanders in their data set. African Americans, on the other hand, were overrepresented in the data. In addition, firearms predominated as the weapon of choice in siblicides.

Child-to-Parent Violence

Child-to-parent violence and abuse has also become an important topic. In one early study (Gelles, 1982), approximately four adolescents (ages 15–17) in 100 were reported to kick, bite, punch, hit with an object, beat up, threaten, or use a gun or knife against a parent. Almost one-third of restraining orders issued in Massachusetts were requested by parents against their adolescent children (Pagani *et al.*, 2004). In a study using a nationally representative sample of American children, Ullman and Straus (2003) concluded that 10% of the adolescents (ages 10–17) participated in child-to-parent violence during the previous 12 months. Sixty percent of these youths had witnessed violence between their parents. In one longitudinal study involving 2,524 Canadian adolescents, Pagani *et al.* (2003) affirmed that 13 percent of the teenagers engaged in physical aggression toward their mothers, ranging from pushing and shoving, punching or kicking, throwing objects, to using a weapon.

In 2004, 3 percent of murder victims were killed by their children (Federal Bureau of Investigation, 2005) (see **Figure 4**). The killing of parents, termed **parricide,** is most often committed by sons by a ratio of about 3 to 1 over daughters (Federal Bureau of Investigation, 2005; Lubenow, 1983; Pagelow, 1989). Mothers are killed (**matricide**) far more often than fathers (**patricide**) by both adolescents and adult sons and daughters. Female parricide is exceptionally rare in all countries of the world (d'Orban & O'Connor, 1989). When daughters kill a parent or parents, they often secure the help of a male friend or sibling. In Britain, boys most often kill a parent (or parents) with explosive violence in response to prolonged provocation and parental brutality and abuse (d'Orban & O'Connor, 1989). Heide (1993) identifies three types of youth parricide: (1) the severely abused child, (2) the severely mentally ill child, and (3) the dangerously antisocial child.

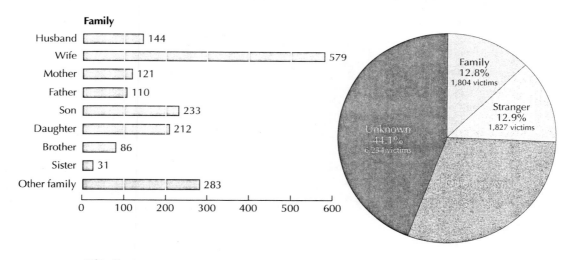

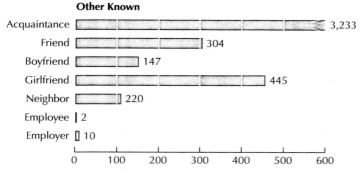

FIGURE 4 Murder by Relationship

Source: U.S. Department of Justice—Federal Bureau of Investigation, 2008.

The complex dynamics of families in which parricides occur often include multiassaultive family patterns, easy access to firearms, alcohol and drug abuse, and the youthful offender's strong feelings of helplessness in coping with the stresses at home. Sometimes the adolescent murderer, as well as other family members, feels a sense of relief that the parent(s) is (are) dead.

Although males predominate in the more extreme forms of juvenile violence toward parents, the gender differences disappear at more moderate levels of violence (Pagani *et al.*, 2004). In addition, the risk of violence toward parents gradually increases during adolescence, peaking at age 15 and diminishing thereafter (Pagani *et al.*, 2004). This pattern corresponds to the peak age of adolescent violence toward nonrelated individuals noted by Loeber and Stouthamer-Loeber (1998). Most violent incidents between child and parents are associated with conflicts about home responsibilities, money, and privilege (Pagani *et al.*, 2004). Children and adolescents who displayed early and chronic forms of aggression and antisocial behavior are most likely to be aggressive toward parents (Pagani *et al.*, 2004). "As adolescents, those described as chronically aggressive by their (annually) different primary school teachers were (9 and 4) times at greater risk of engaging in verbal and physical aggression (respectively) toward their mothers in comparison to their persistently nonaggressive peers" (Pagani *et al.*, 2004, p. 534). In fact, violent predispositions during childhood, measured by teachers, are among the best predictors of later violence toward mothers. "Indeed," Pagani *et al.* (2004) concluded in their study, "teacher-rated disruptiveness during early childhood predicted the risk of engaging in physical aggression toward mothers during adolescence" (p. 220).

Multiassaultive Families

Some families, referred to as **multiassaultive families,** are characterized by continual cycles of intrafamilial physical aggression and violence. Siblings hit each other, spouses hit each other, parents hit the children, and the older children hit the parents. According to the available data, at least 7 percent of all intact families may be considered multiassaultive (Hotaling & Straus, 1989).

Research supports the notion that assault is a generalized pattern in interpersonal relations that crosses settings and is used across targets beyond the immediate family (Hotaling & Straus, 1989). Men in families in which children and wives are assaulted are five times more likely to have also assaulted a nonfamily person than are men in nonassaultive families. A similar pattern holds for women from multiassaultive families, although the relationship is not as strong. Sibling violence is particularly high in families in which child assault and spouse assault are present, with boys displaying significantly more assaultive behavior (Hotaling & Straus, 1989). Moreover, children from multiassaultive families have an inordinately high rate of assault against nonfamily members (Hotaling & Straus, 1989). These children are also more likely to be involved in property crime, to have adjustment difficulties in school, and to be involved with police (Hotaling & Straus, 1989). It should be carefully noted that it is extremely difficult to tell what is causing what in this complicated web of interrelated variables. Nevertheless, it is quite clear that multiassaultive family members are violent and antisocial across a variety of settings, toward both family members and society in general, and may demonstrate this behavioral pattern throughout most of their lifetimes.

The Cycle of Violence

For some time, the scholarly and popular literature has concluded that both abusive parents and abusive spouses have themselves been the victims of family violence during their childhoods (Megargee, 1982). Some research suggests that highly violent offenders may have been subjected to more severe and frequent physical and psychological abuse and punitive parenting during their childhoods than other offenders (Hämäläinen & Haapasalo, 1996). Individuals grow up to be abusive because they were abused themselves, a belief referred to as the **cycle-of-violence** hypothesis.

According to social learning theory, those who receive harsh discipline learn that physical violence can be used to change the behaviors of others (Schwartz, Hage, Bush, & Burns, 2006). **Coercion theory** proposed by Patterson (1982) also posits that coercive and punitive tactics in parenting increase the likelihood of later aggressive behavior and potential domestic violence. Theories that view domestic violence as a tactic for gaining power and control in relationships are highly consistent with coercion theory. As noted by Schwartz *et al.* (2006), "Men involved in intimate violence have been found to have demand and/or withdraw patterns of communication with their partners and perceive themselves as lacking power in their relationships" (p. 212). Consequently, abusing spouses and other family members is one way, in the abuser's eyes, of gaining and maintaining control over those in their immediate social environment. There is also accumulating evidence that males who experience parental neglect during their childhoods are more likely to engage in dating violence, a behavior that is a precursor to spousal abuse (Chapple, 2003; Simons, Lin, & Gordon, 1998).

Nevertheless, violence does not necessarily beget violence. The cycle of violence and the presumed overall consequences of abuse and neglect do not take into account the resilience of human beings, which rules out any simple cause-and-effect relationship between maltreatment and future violent behavior (Garbarino, 1989). In many cases, rather than finding that abusive parenting is the logical consequence of being victimized as children, the opposite sequence is likely to take place. Realizing and sensitive to the enormous psychological and social costs of family violence, many victims of child abuse may be even less likely than their nonabused peers to commit aggressive acts as adults within their families. Garbarino (1989, p. 222), for example, writes, "Many victims of child abuse, probably most, survive it and avoid repeating the pattern in their own child rearing." Nevertheless, the effects of family violence in general on children are devastating, as we see in the following section.

The Effects of Family Violence on Children

Domestic violence is recognized as a serious problem in our society today, but how such violence affects the children who are exposed to it did not appear in the research literature until the 1980s. Children who are exposed to violence between adults in their homes have often been referred to as the "silent," "forgotten," and "unintended" victims of domestic violence. These children were initially referred to as simply "witnesses" or "observers," but recent research literature has discovered that some are not only directly involved victims themselves but also suffer some troubling consequences.

Children experience domestic violence through a bewildering array of events. Most often, children see or hear the violence, and they are often directly targeted, sometimes fatally. In a recent incident, a 13-year-old boy was the only survivor in a family mass shooting during which the father shot his mother and two younger siblings before turning the gun on himself. The father had shot at the 13-year-old, but missed. According to news reports, the boy ran around the garage with his hands lifted in the air in a surrender gesture before fleeing to the home of a neighbor. Other children experience family violence by trying to intervene or calling 911 (Edleson, 1999). Additional examples include the assaulter taking the child hostage to force the mother's return, using a child as a physical weapon against the victim, forcing the child to watch the violence, forcing the child to participate in the abuse, and using the child as a spy or questioning the child about the mother's activities (Ganley & Schechter, 1996). Any of these experiences can leave lasting imprints on a child or adolescent.

Experiencing the aftermath of the violence may be equally traumatic for children (Edleson, 1999). Examples include the child seeing the mother with physical injuries and possibly in need of medical help, observing maternal emotions (such as anxiety, depression, stress), and having the family move to a shelter for battered women to escape further abuse. If the family has pets, leaving the pet behind can be intensely traumatizing for the child—and often the pet is abused as well. The aftermath of violence can also include a father alternating between physical violence and loving care, as well as police intervention that could result in the removal of the father from the home. In some instances, removal of the children from the home by child welfare agencies is also a terrifying possibility.

The number of children exposed to domestic violence in the United States each year is largely unknown. Straus (1991, p. 98) estimates that "at least a third of Americans have witnessed violence between their parents, and most have endured repeated instances." This estimation is based on Straus and Gelles's (1990) national survey that discovered that the 30 percent of parents who admitted domestic violence existed in their home also reported that their children had witnessed at least one violent incident during the length of the marriage.

Research has also found that 13 percent to 27 percent of adults recall witnessing physical violence during their childhood years between their parents (Forrstrom-Cohen & Rosenbaum, 1985). Police arrest data from five U.S. cities revealed that children were directly involved in adult domestic violence incidents about 27 percent of the time (Fantuzzo, Boruch, Abdullahi, Atkins, & Marcus, 1997). Fantuzzo *et al.* also found that younger children were disproportionately represented in households where domestic violence occurred. Another study (Silvern *et al.*, 1995) found that exposure to domestic violence may be even higher in some populations. Silvern and colleagues found that 118 (41.1%) of the 287 college women and 85 (32.2%) of the 263 college men surveyed had witnessed abuse by one parent against the other.

Explanations about how domestic violence affects a child must include an assortment of already existing risk factors. The child's age, the nature and severity of the violence, socioeconomic status, and parental substance abuse all must be entered into the equation.

The child's behavioral and emotional functioning is the area that has received the most attention from researchers. Overall, these studies report the consistent finding that children exposed to domestic violence exhibit many behavioral and emotional problems when compared with other children. For instance, studies using the Child Behavior Checklist (Achenbach & Edelbrock, 1983) and similar measures have found that children who are exposed to domestic violence display more aggressive and antisocial behaviors as well as fearful and inhibited behaviors (Fantuzzo *et al.*, 1991; Hughes, 1988; Hughes, Parkinson, & Vargo, 1989), and show lower social competence and interpersonal skills than other children (Adamson & Thompson, 1998; Fantuzzo *et al.*, 1991; Hughes, 1988). More aggressive and antisocial behaviors are often referred to as "externalized" behaviors, while fearful and inhibited behaviors are referred to as "internalized" behaviors (Carlson, 1991; Edleson, 1999; Stagg, Wills, & Howell, 1989).

Domestic violence has also been shown to have dramatic negative effects on children's emotional health and overall adjustment. Both boys and girls in families with spousal violence demonstrate far more depression and aggression (McClosky, Figueredo, & Koss, 1995; Wolfe, Jaffe, Wilson, & Zak, 1985), and lower self-esteem (Hughes & Barad, 1983) compared with other children. In addition, children who are exposed to violence between parents are more likely to show anxiety, depression, trauma symptoms, and temperamental problems (Hughes, 1988; Maker, Kemmelmeier, & Peterson, 1998).

Another consequence of experiencing violence within the home is the overall effects it has on the child's immediate and long-term cognitive functioning and attitudes about how to deal with violence and conflict resolution in their own lives. Many researchers conclude that children's exposure to adult domestic violence may generate attitudes justifying their own use of violence to solve problems and deal with frustrations. For example, Spaccarelli, Coatsworth, and Bowden's (1995) study found support for such an association by showing that, among a sample of 213 adolescent boys incarcerated for violent crimes, those boys who had experienced family violence were more likely to subscribe to the viewpoint that "acting aggressively enhances one's reputation or self-image" (p. 173). And Carlson (1991) reports that in a sample of 101 adolescents, boys who witnessed domestic violence were significantly more likely to approve of violence than were girls who had witnessed domestic violence.

In conclusion, the empirical evidence reveals that children's exposure to domestic violence is a serious and widespread problem. Such violence affects children indirectly through its effect on the parenting relationship, as well as directly affecting children's behavioral, emotional, cognitive, psychological, and social adjustment.

THE NATURE AND THEORY OF FAMILY VIOLENCE

Once violence has occurred in a relationship, it tends to be repeated (Frieze & Browne, 1989). Over time, violence, if not adequately sanctioned, may also become more severe and more frequent. Furthermore, being violently victimized by an intimate over an extended period of time may result in emotional reactions and psychological scars decidedly different from those incurred by victims of violent crime by strangers.

As noted earlier, some clinicians and writers have suggested that family violence is fundamentally different from general (or street) violence and thus should be examined separately (Megargee, 1982). We are often reminded of this when a battered woman displays continuing attachment to her abuser. Most recently, for example, a woman who was shot in the face by her husband and subsequently received a widely-publicized face transplant said in an interview, "I still love him." Physical violence against children and spouses are considered by some to be "special" cases of violence that require family-based theories to explain them. Wife abusers are psychologically distressed, and their violence is irrational. As also mentioned earlier, child abusers are depicted as incompetent and immature, unable to cope with the responsibilities of parenting and holding unrealistic expectations of children. Similarly, child abusers are extremely emotional and irrational in their assaults. Street offenders, on the other hand, presumably use violence in a deliberate, rational way to gain things, such as material goods, status, or other social reinforcements. General violent offenders utilize violence for a purpose, whereas family violent offenders are lashing out in anger and without discernible purpose. And would a woman shot in the face by a stranger become attracted to him?

Interestingly, empirical evidence for differences between criminal violence in the streets and family violence is weak and equivocal, with most of the studies being unsystematic or seriously flawed methodologically (Hotaling & Straus, 1989). That is to say, the evidence we have so far strongly suggests that the etiology or cause of violent behavior may be very similar, whether it is used against a family member or a nonfamily member. Violent people tend to be violent generally, both within and outside the family context, although they do not necessarily display that violence in all settings. However, there are usually indicators of a more passive aggression, such as not cooperating with others in the work setting. As a general principle, the factors that contribute to violent behavior are more individual than they are situational.

The development of theory requires well-designed and executed research. Without theoretical testing through sound research, speculations and free-floating explanations abound with no empirical anchoring. This describes what is happening in the field of family violence. Gelles and Straus

(1979), for example, were able to identify 15 different theories attempting to explain family violence. Weis (1989, p. 123) observes that "the field is, with few exceptions, characterized by descriptive work, with little hypothesis testing, causal modeling, or attempts to construct and test integrated theories of the different types of family violence."

The systematic study of family violence, however, is a relatively new undertaking. Thus, it suffers from a constellation of uncoordinated research and a matrix of poorly integrated theory, as all new sciences do. Furthermore, the family is a difficult social situation to study. It is a complex social system consisting of many roles, and it is a private social group in which interactions and behaviors are invisible to outsiders. Social interactions are more intense, emotional, and consequential than other interactions (Weis, 1989). In addition, family influences do not flow in one direction; they are apt to be multidirectional, a process called reciprocal influence (Bartol & Bartol, 1998). For example, while the parents affect the development of the child, the child also affects the development and psychological growth of the parents, including their marital relationship, relationships with friends, and even the level of job satisfaction. Reciprocal influence implies that the social environment influences the individual, and the individual, in turn, has an impact on the social environment. Therefore, if family violence is to be treated separately from other violence, theories that are sensitive to the reciprocal interactionism of family dynamics are the best candidates to advance our knowledge.

Cessation of Family Violence

Although theories of family violence are underdeveloped, the effectiveness of various procedures or strategies to reduce family violence can still be tested. Unfortunately, there have been very few systematic evaluations of the effectiveness of particular strategies in combating family violence (Elliott, 1989).

One of the more influential investigations examining the effectiveness of police responses to spouse abuse was the Minnesota Domestic Violence Experiment (Sherman & Berk, 1984). The police officers participating in this project handled marital conflict one of three ways: arrest, separating the parties, or advising (or mediating) the parties. Follow-up of the effectiveness of these approaches over a six-month period indicated that arrest of the suspected abuser was the most effective police response for reducing misdemeanor family assaults. However, the study had serious design problems that undermine both its external validity and internal validity. Subsequent research in other cities failed to replicate the results of the study (Buzawa & Buzawa, 1996). Moreover, there is some evidence that the impact of an arrest wears off over a relatively short period of time (8–12 months), and the assaults return to their original level (Elliott, 1989).

The effectiveness of the legal sanctions of prosecution, conviction, and sentencing in deterring subsequent family violence is also questionable. There are also many unanswered questions about the effectiveness of community services and care for family violence victims (Saunders & Azar, 1989). Skeptics often note, for example, that women who are battered frequently return to the home situation after spending some time in a shelter for victims of domestic violence. Shelter supporters say they are used to this, and that some women return repeatedly. Some women, however, and sometimes the ones who have returned again and again, eventually learn to leave. Therefore, despite the pessimism sometimes associated with this troubling social problem, approaches that combine (1) arrest, (2) supportive services for the victims, and (3) monitoring if the abuser remains in the community offer some hope for decreasing the violence.

Much of the contemporary work and commentary has been directed at reducing wife abuse or male abuse of female intimate partners. Fagan (1989) hypothesizes that a large segment of the rewards and support men receive for abusing women derives from a long-standing cultural stereotype that men must be dominant and show women who is boss. One very "masculine" way of achieving and maintaining this expected dominance is through physical aggression and, if necessary, some violence. Some of the reinforcement comes from the satisfaction of maintaining this physical dominance and the positive social status that accompanies domination over women, particularly wives, advocated by one's peer group and subculture. Accordingly, men subscribing to this subculture socialize together, drink together, and participate in male-oriented recreation activities, generally excluding their wives from these activities. This male subculture provides a social milieu that supports and encourages traditional male dominance in male–female relationships, even if it requires violence now and then. Frequent contacts with this exclusive male subculture by the husband, combined with increasing social isolation of the wife, are particularly associated with the more severe forms of wife abuse (Bowker, 1983; Fagan, 1989). Presumably, the more deeply immersed into this subculture a man is, the more likely he is to batter his wife.

To what extent some women also support this male-dominating tradition is largely unknown, but knowledge about the degree to which women explicitly or implicitly favor this belief system may be extremely important in a deeper understanding of the dynamics of the relationship. This is not to imply that a subculture that supports male domination in a marriage necessarily advocates violence in carrying out this dominance, but research does suggest that many wife batterers manage to isolate their families socially while receiving considerable encouragement and support for physical aggression from their social network of friends.

An effective way of breaking the wife- or female partner–abuse cycle, therefore, is to change the abuser's attitudinal system and social network of friends who support or at least condone physical male domination of family relationships. Obviously, this strategy will not be easy to apply in many abusive behavioral patterns. Abusers have had a lifelong learning experience in developing belief systems, and probably have had considerable reinforcement history for their aggressive actions toward women from their subculture. "Leaving the subculture is not unlike leaving the world of the addict or the alcoholic" (Fagan, 1989, p. 408).

Initiating motivation to change a behavioral pattern of abuse often requires establishing a series of situations where the psychological costs for the abuse outweigh its psychological benefits. Legal sanctions may be one way, but many batterers realize that these sanctions are normally weak and without teeth. However, serious attempts by the criminal justice system to put some bite into these legal sanctions (such as arrests, criminal charges, and conviction) may begin to prove effective over the long haul, provided that they are accompanied by community support systems for the woman. It is important to note that it is unlikely that any one arrest or single event will promote a wish to change. It is more likely that a series of aversive and costly events, such as strong legal sanctions, combined with social sanctions from the community (public disclosure, visits by social agencies) and emotional sanctions from the victim (reporting the abuse to authorities, leaving the home, separating, threatening divorce) will wear the abuser down to a point at which he makes a decision to change his behavioral patterns.

However, the more severe and protracted the violence is, the more difficult it may be to stop, despite formal external interventions—legal or otherwise (Fagan, 1989). Legal and social sanctions for spouse abuse may work for less chronic and severe situations. However, legal sanctions, regardless of the nature and strength of the sanction, may not only be ineffective for the more serious cases, but could possibly lead to escalation in violence. Therefore, social, legal, and emotional sanctions may be more effective with individuals who do not have an extensive history of repetitive and serious violence. One of the most sobering research findings in recent years has been the discovery that a woman's life is in the greatest danger from an abusive partner within the first six months of leaving that partner.

Summary and Conclusions

In this chapter, we began to narrow our focus to consider specific offenses. Chapters were broader, in that they dealt with general theoretical orientations to crime. Here, we reviewed the major sociological data on violence and summarized empirical and clinical research on family violence.

Sociological and official data indicate that homicides are rare compared with the total incidence of violent crime. In the United States, violent crime is often committed by young males living in environments that implicitly or explicitly advocate violence for the resolution of conflict. Guns (especially handguns) are commonly used in the crime. Certain minority groups are overrepresented in violent crime statistics, but there are a number of explanations for this that have nothing to do with racial or ethnically based individual factors. Statistics indicate also that, when the relationship of victim and offender is known, the homicide victim and the offender are usually family members, friends, or acquaintances. The relationship is known in between half to two-thirds of the offenses. While assaults are far more common than homicide, the same sociological features appear, particularly for aggravated assault.

Considering the rapidly expanding research on the topic, family violence undoubtedly deserves a chapter of its own. Family violence is a broad subject that encompasses child abuse, spouse or partner abuse, elder abuse, sibling abuse, and child-to-parent abuse. Some researchers also include intimate partner abuse that occurs when the victim and perpetrator occupy separate households. Abuse comes in many forms, including physical, psychological, or sexual abuse. Family violence is found across ethnic, racial, and socioeconomic classes. Women are disproportionately subject to spousal

violence and the dire economic situations that may lead to both victimization and victimizing. Children are particularly vulnerable targets for family violence and maltreatment, enduring physical maltreatment, sexual exploitation, medical and emotional neglect, and psychological trauma—all of which are usually lifelong in their consequences. In this chapter, we focused not only on "typical" forms of child abuse, but also on statistics and research relating to shaken baby syndrome, Munchausen syndrome by proxy, and infanticide. For the child who survives abuse, the psychological consequences can nevertheless be devastating. Though he or she does not necessarily become an abuser, perpetuating the cycle of abuse, emotional scars relating to one's self-concept and the ability to trust others are often very deep and long-lasting.

In addition to the obvious physical injuries and deaths that result, family violence is often cited in research and clinical studies as contributing to other individual, family, and societal problems. Most of all, family violence and maltreatment highlight the importance of considering a victimological approach for the complete understanding of violent crime, and underscore the fact that the family is far from being a safe haven for many. Factors such as family instability and violence have been consistently found to be prevalent among juveniles who engage in sexually abusive and violent behavior (Righthand & Welch, 2001). Many studies conclude that abused children have trouble recognizing appropriate emotions in others, have less empathy for others, and have difficulty taking another person's perspective (Knight & Prentky, 1993). It is very likely that many of the LCP offenders discussed elsewhere in the text spring from families characterized by abuse, violence, and neglect.

Key Concepts

Assault	Battered woman syndrome	Cycle-of-violence hypothesis
Aggravated assault	Coercion theory	Dynamic cascade model
Availability heuristic	Criminal homicide	Eldercide

Filicide
Fratricide
Infanticide
Intimate partner
    violence
Matricide
Multiassaultive family

Munchausen syndrome
    by proxy (MBP)
Murder
Negligent manslaughter
Neonaticide
Parricide
Patricide

Proactive violence
Reactive violence
Shaken baby syndrome
Siblicide
Sororicide
Weapons effect

Review Questions

1. What is the availability heuristic? How might it account for our perception of violence?
2. What are the psychological effects of (a) child abuse and (b) other domestic violence on children?
3. Define "battered woman syndrome" and briefly state the controversy associated with it.
4. Define each of the following: neonaticide, parricide, infanticide, filicide, eldercide, homicide.
5. Define "weapons effect" and how it might contribute to violence in our society.

6. What is the cycle-of-violence hypothesis?
7. Explain how juvenile homicide is different from adult homicide.
8. Compare and contrast shaken baby syndrome and Munchausen syndrome by proxy as specific forms of child abuse.
9. Discuss eldercide as a form of family violence, including its prevalence, perpetrators, and etiology.

TABLE 1   Profile Characteristics of Organized and Disorganized Murderers as Classified by the FBI

Organized	Disorganized
Average to above-average intelligence	Below average intelligence
Socially competent	Socially inadequate
Skilled work preferred	Unskilled work
High birth order status	Low birth order status
Father's work stable	Father's work unstable
Sexually competent	Sexually incompetent
Inconsistent childhood discipline	Harsh discipline as a child
Controlled mood during crime	Anxious mood during crime
Use of alcohol with crime	Minimal use of alcohol
Precipitating situational stress	Minimal situational stress
Living with partner	Living alone
Mobility (car in good condition)	Lives/works near crime scene
Follows crime in news media	Minimal interest in news media
May change job or leave town	Significant behavior change

Source: Federal Bureau of Investigation (1985), p. 19.

TABLE 2   Crime Scene Differences Between Organized and Disorganized Murderers as Classified by the FBI

Organized	Disorganized
Planned offense	Spontaneous offense
Victim a targeted stranger	Victim/location known
Personalizes victim	Depersonalizes victim
Controlled conversation	Minimal conversation
Crime scene reflects control	Crime scene random and sloppy
Demands submissive victim	Sudden violence to victim
Restraints used	Minimal use of restraints
Aggressive acts prior to death	Sexual acts after death
Body hidden	Body left in view
Weapon/evidence absent	Weapon/evidence often present
Transports victim or body	Body left at death scene

Source: Federal Bureau of Investigation, 1985, p. 19.

Although the organized–disorganized classification system seems intuitively logical, it appears to have very limited usefulness as an investigative tool (Canter, Alison, Alison, & Wentink, 2004; Kocsis, Cooksey, & Irwin, 2002). In fact, Snook, Cullen, Bennell, Taylor, and Gendreau (2008) report that, at this point, there is no convincing evidence to support the dichotomy. It may be more realistic to assume that crime scenes fall along a continuum, with the organized description at one pole and the disorganized description at the other pole (Bartol & Bartol, 2004), but with few crimes being at either pole.

PROFILING

The term *profiling* is used to describe the gathering of various kinds of information about a person or persons. For clarity of presentation, we divide the term into five somewhat overlapping categories: (1) psychological profiling, (2) criminal profiling, (3) geographical profiling, (4) equivocal death analysis, and (5) racial or ethnic profiling. For our purposes, **psychological profiling** will be reserved for the psychological description of a person or persons *in general,* criminal or noncriminal. It was first used by the Office of Strategic Services (OSS) during World War II, primarily to profile enemy leaders and their proclivities (Ault & Reese, 1980). It included their preferred strategies and ways of thinking. After the war, profiling was largely shelved until the FBI started using it again during the early 1970s. Essentially, psychological profiling has its basic scientific roots in psychological testing or psychometrics.

It is important to note, therefore, that psychological profiling is not necessarily designed to describe criminal tendencies, but refers to a broad behavioral realm of tendencies, foibles, faults, likes and dislikes, interests, strengths, and so on. Football coaches, business leaders, political leaders, attorneys, and other professionals often prefer to have some idea or psychological sketch about the psychological characteristics of their opponents or adversaries or about individuals they plan to hire. Consequently, we will not discuss the general category of psychological profiling to any great extent in this text but will focus on those methods that are directly related to crime.

Criminal profiling is the process of identifying personality traits, behavioral patterns, geographic habits, and demographic features of an offender based on characteristics of the crime. It can be considered a skill or an activity that is a part of the investigative psychology described earlier. Therefore, while investigative psychology is the broad application of psychological research and principles to solving crimes, profiling is the narrower activity that focuses on the traits, features, and habits of the offender. Some researchers (e.g., Knight, Warren, Reboussin, & Soley, 1998) have introduced the term *crime scene analysis*, or the more technical term *criminal investigative analysis*, to describe the practice of developing offender descriptions based on the analysis of the crime scene. However, we prefer to use the more straightforward label "criminal profiling."

Geographical profiling is a method of identifying the area of probable residence or the probable area of the next crime of an unknown offender based on the location of and the spatial relationships among various crime sites (Guerette, 2002). Geographical profiling, therefore, can help in any criminal investigation of an unknown offender by locating the approximate area in which he or she lives, or by narrowing the surveillance and stakeouts to places where the next crime by the offender is most likely to occur. This type of profiling basically tries to identify the geographical territory the offender knows well, feels most comfortable in, and prefers to find or take victims in (Rossmo, 1997). Although a *criminal* profile hypothesizes about the demographic, motivational, and psychological features of the crime and offender, a geographic profile focuses on the location of the crime and how it relates to the residence and/or base of operations of the offender. Geographical profiling is useful not only in the search for serial violent offenders but also in the search for property offenders, such as serial burglars.

Equivocal death analysis, also called **reconstructive psychological evaluation,** is the reconstruction of the emotional life, behavioral patterns, and cognitive features of a deceased person. In this sense, it is a postmortem psychological analysis and therefore is frequently referred to simply as a **psychological autopsy** (Brent, 1989; Ebert, 1987; Selkin, 1987). Most often, equivocal death analysis or the psychological autopsy is done to determine whether the death was a suicide, and if it was a suicide, the reasons why the person did it. The psychological autopsy differs from criminal profiling in two important ways: (1) The profile is constructed on a dead person, and (2) the identity of the person is already known.

Racial (or ethnic) profiling is defined as "police-initiated action that relies on the race, ethnicity, or national origin rather than the behavior of an individual or information that leads the police to a particular individual who has been identified as being, or having been, engaged in criminal activity" (Ramirez, McDevitt, & Farrell, 2000, p. 3).

Because the last four forms of profiling are relevant to criminal behavior issues, we will now cover each in some detail in the remainder of this section.

Criminal Profiling

The practice of profiling is utilized by police agencies across the world (Snook *et al.*, 2008). Many police investigators and detectives indicate they find it useful in their investigations of certain crime. In one survey reported by Snook *et al.* (2008), 8 out of 10 police officers in the United Kingdom found criminal profiling helpful in their investigations and said they would seek profiling help again. In an exploratory Internet survey of forensic psychologists and psychiatrists, Torres, Boccaccini, and Miller (2006) found that 40 percent of these professionals thought that criminal profiling was scientifically reliable and valid. As we will see shortly, however, these perceptions are not supported by the research.

Descriptions or profiles of the general characteristics of a person on the basis of a limited amount of information were used long before the OSS or the FBI employed such methods (Canter & Alison, 2000). In fact, the history of profiling can be traced back to Jack the Ripper, the serial killer who brutally murdered five prostitutes in separate incidents in London's East End in 1888. Although the case was never solved, the chief forensic pathologist, Dr. George Baxter Phillips, attempted to help police investigators by inferring personality characteristics based on the nature of the wounds inflicted on the victims (Turvey, 2002). That is, he noticed that the wounds were inflicted with considerable skill and knowledge, suggesting that the killer had a sophisticated knowledge of human anatomy. "In particular, he was referring to the postmortem removal of some of Annie Chapman's organs, and what he felt was the cleanliness and preciseness of the incisions involved" (Turvey, 2002, p. 10). Interestingly, the fictional detective Sherlock Holmes, first created by Sir Arthur Conan Doyle in 1887, consistently employed a form of criminal profiling in his intriguing search for the offender. Since then, virtually every detective or mystery novel has the main characters engaging in some variant of criminal profiling.

The FBI began using criminal profiling when it was introduced by special agent Howard Tegen in 1970 (Turvey, 2002). He taught the first criminal profiling course at the FBI National Academy, called Applied Criminology, and later constructed his first actual profile as an FBI agent in Amarillo, Texas (Turvey, 2002). In 1972, the new FBI Academy was opened and Special Agent Jack Kirsch developed the FBI's Behavioral Science Unit. The Unit was a major contributor to criminal profiling during the 1970s and 1980s. Currently, the Unit operates under the direction of the National Center for the Analysis of Violent Crime (NCAVC) at the FBI Academy in Quantico, Virginia.

Criminal profiling is usually done in three stages. Police officers and detectives collect crime scene data, such as forensic photographs, autopsy results, and all relevant physical evidence relating to the present crime as well as past similar crimes. This information is then turned over to a profiler who analyzes the data and makes an "educated hypothesis" about important characteristics of the offender. The profiler report, including predictions, is then communicated to the police investigating the case.

Criminal profiling "is best viewed as a strategy enabling law enforcement to narrow the field of options and generate educated guesses about the perpetrator" (Douglas *et al.*, 1992, p. 21). Other researchers write that a criminal profile "focuses attention on individuals with personality traits that parallel traits of others who have committed similar offenses" (Pinizzotto & Finkel, 1990, p. 215). In short, criminal profiling is an attempt to identify demographic variables, geographical location, and behavioral patterns of an offender based on characteristics of previous offenders who have committed similar offenses.

Pinizzotto and Finkel (1990) have observed that criminal profiling requires a complex number of tasks that involve a "multilevel series of attributions, correlations, and predictions" (p. 230). However, much profiling is guesswork based on hunches and anecdotal information accumulated through years of experience, and it is full of error and misinterpretation. Currently, profiling is probably at least 80 percent an art and speculation and only 20 percent science, probably in its most sophisticated form. Professional profilers continually provide predictions of some demographic variables (e.g., white male, age 25–35), but rarely do they provide accurate information on psychological variables of the offender. Furthermore, very rarely does profiling provide the specific identity of the offender, nor is it intended to. Criminal profiling basically tries to narrow the field of investigation to a manageable number of potential suspects (Douglas *et al.*, 1986). Broadly, criminal profiling suggests the kind of person who might have committed the crime under investigation, but it is highly unlikely to pinpoint an individual's exact identity. In fact, responsible individuals who are supportive of profiling are careful not to exaggerate its usefulness.

A profile report normally includes the gender, age, marital status, education level, and some broad identification of the occupation of the offender. There is also some prediction or estimation as to whether the offender will strike again, whether he or she likely has a police record, and what types of victims are at risk. In some instances, the profiler will try to identify possible motivational factors for the crime as well as the offender's personality traits.

Experienced profilers assert that profiling of *serial* offenders is most successful when the offender demonstrates some form of psychopathology at the crime scene, such as sadistic torture, evisceration, postmortem slashings and cuttings, and other mutilations (Pinizzotto, 1984). The reasoning behind this conclusion is that such individuals are likely mentally disordered, and mentally disordered individuals show consistency in behavior from situation to situation. Whether mentally disordered persons truly are more consistent in their behavioral patterns than those who are not mentally disordered remains an open question, however. It is likely that some are, and some are not.

Profiling appears to be particularly useful in serial sexual offenses, such as serial rape and serial sexual homicides (Pinizzotto & Finkel, 1990). This is because we have a more extensive research base on sexual offending than we do on homicide. Furthermore, profiling is largely ineffective at this time in the identification of offenders involved in fraud, burglary, robbery, political crimes, theft, and drug-induced crime because of the limited research base, although significant gains in some of these areas have been made in recent years.

Computer-based models of offender profiles developed from extensive statistical data collected on similar offenses hold considerable promise. To date, however, there is very little research on the criminals who specifically set out from their residence to look for victims, searching through the areas in their awareness space that they believe contain suitable targets" (p. 167). The hunters are geographically stable in that their crimes usually occur near the offender's residence or neighborhood. Poachers are more transient, traveling some distance from their neighborhood in their search for suitable victims. The troller, on the other hand, does not specifically search for victims but depends on random encounters during the course of other activities. The trapper creates situations (traps) to entice victims to come to him.

Although geographical profiling was originally designed to help investigations of murder, rape, and arson, it is now being used for serial bombings, bank robbery, and child abductions (Guerette, 2002). Geographical profiling still has a way to go before it establishes its predictive validity across a variety of serial offenses. Much of the available research has been conducted by Rossmo himself, although this is changing (e.g., Bennell & Jones, 2005). To his credit, however, Rossmo warns that the method is essentially an investigative tool that does not necessarily solve crimes, but should help in identifying appropriate areas for surveillance, patrol saturation, stakeouts, and monitoring.

The Psychological Autopsy

The psychological autopsy was first used to help medical officials determine the cause of deaths that were classified as ambiguous, uncertain, or equivocal (Shneidman, 1994). Today, the psychological autopsy is also done to determine what may have been in the mind of the deceased person leading up to and at the time of death—particularly if the death appears to be a suicide (La Fon, 2002). In other words, the individual conducting the autopsy tries to "reconstruct" what was in the mind of the decedent.

La Fon (2002) notes that there are two basic types of psychological autopsies used in modern practice: (1) suicide psychological autopsy (SPA), and (2) equivocal death psychological autopsy (EDPA). The objective of the SPA is to identify and understand the psychosocial factors that contributed to the suicide. The purpose of the EPDA, on the other hand, is to determine the *reasons* (i.e., suicide or otherwise) for the death. In most cases, the EPDA is done for insurance claim purposes. Although some insurance policies compensate beneficiaries if death is determined to be the result of a suicide, many policies do not. In that case, it is important for life insurance companies to have a ruling on the *manner* of death before payment claims are honored.

The reliability and validity of the psychological autopsy, however, has yet to be demonstrated and remains open to debate (Poythress, Otto, Darkes, & Starr, 1993). Poythress *et al.* write, "Persons who conduct reconstructive psychological evaluations should not assert categorical conclusions about the precise mental state or actions suspected of the actor at the time of his or her demise. The conclusions and inferences drawn in psychological reconstructions are, at best, informed speculations or theoretical formulations and should be labeled as such" (1993, p. 12). Selkin (1994) further notes that clear, definitive procedures for carrying out the psychological autopsy have yet to be developed and that investigators still have a long way to go before standardized methods for conducting the psychological autopsy are established.

Racial Profiling

It may seem odd to see racial profiling discussed in this section. Its practice is not condoned—in fact, it is an illegal practice, though difficult to prove that it occurred. We are certainly not interested in researching the effectiveness of an illegal practice. However, racial profiling is a practice that accounts in part for the fact that racial and ethnic minorities are disproportionately represented in arrest statistics. Furthermore, racial profiling illustrates the dangers and inaccuracies of the profiling enterprise that could affect anyone in the population.

As noted earlier, racial profiling is defined as "police-initiated action that relies on the race, ethnicity, or national origin rather than the behavior of an individual or information that leads the police to a particular individual who has been identified as being, or having been, engaged in criminal activity" (Ramirez *et al.*, 2000, p. 3). Such profiling is not new, but it was not until the 1990s that it began to be seen as a nationwide problem. Apparent incidents of racial profiling were experienced so commonly by people of color that they began to label the phenomenon "driving while black" or "driving while brown" (commonly abbreviated DWB), as a play on the legally accepted term DWI (driving while intoxicated or impaired). A Gallup Poll released in 1999 revealed that 72 percent of black men between the ages of 18 and 34 who had been stopped by police believed that police stopped them because of their race. Research supports this belief, as we will see below. By contrast, only 6 percent of white men believed their race played a role in being pulled over by the police. More specifically, members of communities of color say they are being stopped for minor traffic violations, such as underinflated tires, failure to signal properly before switching lanes, vehicle equipment failure, or speeding less than 10 miles above the speed limit. Another common complaint is that police often stop people of color traveling through predominately white neighborhoods because the officers believe that people of color do not belong in the area and consequently suspect them of engaging in criminal activity.

A large segment of racial profiling is based on beliefs by law enforcement that minorities tend to be involved in drug trafficking or carrying contraband, such as illegal weapons. This is a good illustration of the confirmation bias discussed above. Seeking evidence in support of that belief (albeit unconsciously), the officer stops an individual; if the individual is indeed carrying drugs, the belief is confirmed. If the individual is not, the officer continues to seek evidence in support of the belief—by stopping more representatives of minority groups. Meanwhile, any research evidence that minority groups are just as law abiding as others is ignored.

Interestingly, we have evidence both that racial profiling occurs and that the assumptions on which it is based are unjustified. One of the first cases involving the empirical evidence of racial profiling in a court hearing was *Wilkins v. Maryland State Police* (cited in Harris, 1999). *Wilkins* was a class-action lawsuit against the Maryland State Police (MSP) on behalf of Robert L. Wilkins, an African American attorney who was stopped, detained, and searched by the MSP for no apparent reason (Harris, 1999). With the assistance of Dr. John Lambert, a psychology professor at Temple University, the American Civil Liberties Union (ACLU) conducted a survey on traffic violations on Maryland highway I-95. The survey revealed that 74.7 percent of the 5,354 speeders stopped by the MSP were white and 17.5 percent were African American. However, "between January 1995 and September 1996, the Maryland State Police reported searching 823 motorists on I-95, north of Baltimore. Of these, 600, or 72.9 percent were black. Six hundred and sixty-one, or 80.3 percent, were black, Hispanic, or other racial minorities. Only 19.7 percent of those searched in this corridor were white" (Harris, 1999, p. 23). Based on his analysis of these data, Lambert concluded the following:

> The evidence examined in this study reveals dramatic and highly statistically significant disparities between the percentage of black Interstate 95 motorists legitimately subject to stop by Maryland State Police and the percentage of black motorists detained and searched by MSP troopers on this roadway. While no one can know the motivations of each individual trooper in conducting a traffic stop, the statistics presented herein,

representing a broad and detailed sample of highly appropriate data, show without question a racially discriminatory impact on blacks and other minority motorists from state police behavior along I-95.

(Harris, 1999, p. 24)

Closely related to racial profiling is the drug courier profile, developed by law enforcement during the "war on drugs" in the 1970s and 1980s. In 1985, when the war on drugs was intensifying, the Florida Department of Highway Safety and Motor Vehicles issued guidelines for law enforcement on how to identify drug couriers. The guidelines encouraged officers to be suspicious of rental cars, drivers who are scrupulously obeying traffic laws, drivers wearing lots of gold, drivers whose status does not "fit" the vehicle, and drivers who represent *ethnic groups associated with the drug trade.* The unsubstantiated conclusion of various agencies at that time was that African Americans and Latinos were the principal participants in the exploding drug trade business. In 1986, a racially biased drug courier profile was introduced by the Drug Enforcement Administration (DEA) to various law enforcement agencies across the nation. The profile was used extensively in their training methods for officers in "Operation Pipeline" (Harris, 1999). In 1999, a preliminary survey by the San Diego Police Department found that Latino and African American drivers were far more likely to be stopped and searched than other drivers (Dvorak, 2000). Several studies in New Jersey and New York report similar results (Ramirez *et al.*, 2000). In the 1990s, lawsuits alleging racial profiling by law enforcement agencies were brought on behalf of minority motorists in Pennsylvania, Florida, Illinois, and Maryland. In 1996, a New Jersey Superior Court judge threw out 19 drug possession cases, concluding that state troopers patrolling the New Jersey Turnpike had improperly singled out and stopped black motorists. Over a dozen states have passed laws against racial profiling, many of them requiring antibias training and the gathering of statistics on every driver who is stopped (Lewin, 2001), and many other states considered similar laws (Dvorak, 2000). The catastrophic events of September 11, 2001, have led to new forms of racial profiling, as well as ethnic and religious profiling.

International data indicate that racial profiling is not restricted to the United States. A 1998 study by the British Government's Home Office investigated the racial and ethnic demographics of the stop-and-search patterns of police agencies in England and Wales. The study found that blacks were 7.5 times more likely to be stopped and searched, and four times more likely to be arrested than whites (Ramirez *et al.*, 2000). According to 1999 census data, Britain is 93 percent white and 7 percent ethnic minority.

In conclusion, empirical research, anecdotal evidence, and survey data confirm the existence of racial and ethnic profiling as a social problem. It occurs despite the fact that there is no evidence to support a valid profile based strictly on race or ethnicity. Even if there were—and again, there is not—a profile model that revolves around these factors as critical components violates or infringes on civil rights. It is worth repeating that what is psychologically interesting here are the biases and motives of those who engage in the practice, but this is rarely subjected to empirical scrutiny.

MULTIPLE MURDERERS

One of the most frightening and perhaps incomprehensible types of homicide is the random killing of groups of people, either in one episode or individually over a period of time. Although multiple murders are still rare occurrences, when they do happen, they cannot escape attention, and they remain etched in the public consciousness. The slaughter of 21 patrons at a McDonald's restaurant in San Ysidro, California, in July 1984, by James Oliver Huberty is a case in point. Another is the mass murder of 22 patrons at Luby's Cafeteria in Killeen, Texas, on October 16,

1991. Many people still recall the planned, separate murders of 33 young men and boys whose bodies were found in the cellar of the suburban Chicago home of John Wayne Gacy during the late 1970s. Between 1978 and 1991, Jeffrey Dahmer lured at least 17 boys and young men into his apartment in Milwaukee, where he drugged, killed, and dismembered them. The public was shocked to learn the details of how Dahmer ate the victims' flesh and had sex with the corpses. Other notorious multiple murderers include David Berkowitz, known as the infamous Son of Sam; Kenneth Bianci, the Hillside Strangler; Albert DeSalvo, the Boston Strangler; Gary Ridgeway, the Green River Killer; Donald Harvey, the nursing-care killer; Dennis Rader, the BTK killer, and Theodore Bundy.

England was the setting for the notorious Jack the Ripper and, more recently, Peter Sutcliffe, the Yorkshire Ripper who killed 13 women in the red-light districts of Northern England. Dennis Nilsen became England's first serial killer to prey on homosexuals, committing at least 15 known murders (Jenkins, 1988). In 2009, a 19-year-old entered the grounds of a school and killed 16 people, including 13 teachers, in the suburbs of Stuttgart, Germany. In the same week, in the United States, a 28-year-old allegedly killed ten people, including his mother, relatives, and neighbors before killing himself. Two weeks later, a gunman opened fire in a North Carolina nursing home, killing eight and wounding several others. And in Binghamton, New York, a heavily-armed man who had recently lost his job, had relationship difficulties, and claimed to be ridiculed because of his difficulty with the English language, entered a building that served as a community service center for immigrants. He killed 14 people before killing himself. Other individuals barricaded themselves in the basement for several hours before police were able to enter and secure the building and assure that the shooter was no longer at large. These are but illustrations of tragic incidences that occurred over a short period of time; in the United States alone, six mass murders took 47 lives in just four weeks' time. However, as can be seen from the above examples, some of which will be discussed in more detail below, not all multiple murders can be categorized in the same way.

Definitions

Serial murder is usually reserved for incidents in which an individual (or individuals) kills a number of individuals (usually a minimum of three) over time. The time interval—sometimes referred to as the cooling-off period—may be days or weeks, but more likely months or years. The cooling-off period is the main difference between serial murders and other multiple murders (Douglas *et al.*, 1986). The murders are premeditated and planned, and the offender usually selects specific victims. **Spree murder** normally refers to the killing of three or more individuals without any cooling-off period, usually at two or more locations. A bank robber who kills some individuals within the bank, flees with hostages, and kills a number of people while in flight during a statewide chase would be an example of a spree murderer. However, some experts are not convinced that spree murder represents a meaningful separate category of multiple murder (Federal Bureau of Investigation, 2005a). This is understandable; some murders that would be characterized as spree share characteristics of serial murders; others seem to be more like multiple murders, without the single location. **Mass murder** involves killing three or more persons at a single location with no cooling-off period between murders. There are various kinds of mass murder, including those sponsored by some governmental authority, such as genocide designed to exterminate large groups of people, often on the basis of religion or ethnicity. Another type is mass murder by terrorists, such as occurred in New York City on September 11, 2001, when nearly 3,000 persons were killed. Mass murder committed by terrorists will be discussed in more detail. In this section, we focus on mass murder by individuals.

Investigators have traditionally identified two types of mass murder by individuals: classic and family (Douglas *et al.*, 1986). An example of a **classic mass murder** is when an individual barricades himself or herself inside a public building, such as a fast-food restaurant, randomly killing the patrons and any other individual he or she has contact with. The 1984 shootings of patrons at the San Ysidro's McDonald's restaurant in San Diego and 1991 shootings at Luby's cafeteria in Killeen, Texas, mentioned earlier, are examples. Another example is Sylvia Seegrist (nicknamed "Ms. Rambo" because of her military-style clothing), who began shooting people at a Pennsylvania mall in October 1985, killing three and wounding seven (Douglas *et al.*, 1986). The 2007 Virginia Tech murders in Blacksburg, Virginia, the 2008 Northern Illinois University killings in Dekalb, and the 2009 killings in Binghamton, New York, are recent examples of classic mass murder. In these instances, the shooters entered buildings or classrooms claiming most victims at random before killing themselves. To return to the point made above about classification difficulty, however, the Virginia Tech killings could also be classified as spree murders, because they were spread throughout the day, with no "cooling off" period and did not occur in one location. A **family mass murder** is when at least three family members are killed (usually by another family member). Very often, the perpetrator kills himself or herself, an incident that is classified as a mass murder/suicide.

SERIAL MURDERERS

The U.S. Department of Justice estimated that there were about 35–40 serial murderers active at any given point in the United States during the 1970s and 1980s (Jenkins, 1988). Hickey (2006) makes similar estimates on the more recent number of active and unapprehended serial killers. Realistically, though, there are no accurate data on the prevalence and number of serial murderers active at any one time in the United States or internationally (Brantley & Kosky, 2005).

It is equally difficult to estimate the annual number of serial murder victims. Many serial offenders are adept at hiding their victims. Gary Ridgway, the Green River Killer, confessed to killing 48 women, and he skillfully hid their bodies. The long-haul truck driver Keith Hunter Jesperson, known as the Happy Face Killer because of the smile face he drew on his many letters to the media, claimed to have killed 160 persons in multiple states. He took great pride in the fact that he had been killing for over a year before any of the bodies were discovered (Quinet, 2007). In one case of a serial murder described by Wolf and Lavezzi (2007), the offender hid the bodies of eight women in the house inhabited by his parents and sister. Some of the bodies were found in the crawl space of the basement, and others were found comingled in the attic.

Many serial killers select victims that apparently are not missed or, if missed, they are given up as runaways or adults who have left on their own volition. An examination of the victim selection of known serial murderers will reveal that killers prefer the group of people offering easy access, transience, and a tendency to disappear without seeming to cause much alarm or concern. Victims are often prostitutes, especially streetwalkers, street runaways, young male drifters, and itinerant farm workers. Young women in or near a university or college campus or the elderly and solitary poor appear to be the groups next preferred. The strongest determining factor in victim selection for both groups—the factor that victims seem to have in common—is their vulnerability or easy availability. Serial murderers rarely break in and kill middle-class strangers in their homes, for example, despite media portrayals. It should be pointed out, however, that although serial killers begin their murderous careers by selecting highly vulnerable victims, they may, as their killings continue, gain substantially more confidence in their ability to abduct more "challenging" victims. Fortunately, very few serial killers become this successful before they are arrested.

Although serial killers are similar in some background characteristics to the single-victim killers discussed, there are notable differences in the victims they choose and their method of committing the crimes. For example, the victims of single-victim murderers are most often family, friends, and acquaintances. Serial murderers most often kill strangers with no apparent consensual relationship between the offender and the victim. The lack of a relationship in serial murders makes identifying suspects especially difficult.

The preferred method of killing also is often different for the two groups. Serial offenders tend to prefer more hands on killing through strangulation or beating with hands or feet, while single-victim offenders prefer guns (Kraemer, Lord, & Heilbrun, 2004). As we learned, single offenders kill most often out of anger and lack of control stemming from interpersonal conflict and provocation. Some, of course, kill in accordance with a carefully thought-out plan, but this is believed to be the exceptional case. Serial homicides, on the other hand, are often deliberate, premeditated, sexually predatory in nature, and are not usually precipitated by interpersonal disagreements or provocation. Serial homicide offenders also exhibit more planning by moving the victim or body from one location to another, by using restraints, and by disposing of the body in a remote location (Kraemer *et al.*, 2004). Single-victim offenders tend to be much less skillful in disposing of the body.

Psychological Motives and Causes

A frequent question asked is, What causes a person to become a serial murderer? Serial murderers like all human beings are products of their genetic makeup, their upbringing, their social environment, and ultimately the developmental path that circumstances lead them to take. There is no single identifiable causal factor in the development of a serial killer. As we have discussed throughout the text, criminal behavior develops from a complicated mixture of various factors and influences. The same factors and influences that lead to violence very likely play a significant role in serial homicide, although others are certainly added. For example, the motives of many serial killers appear to be based on some combination of psychological rewards, such as control, domination, media attention, and personal or sexual excitement rather than identifiable material gain. Their actions are predictably planned, organized, and purposeful, and they seem to take delight in playing games with the law enforcement community and the public at large.

Many serial homicide offenders are especially drawn to committing murders that attract media interest, send spine-chilling fear into the community, and are incomprehensible to the public. Keith Hunter Jesperson apparently became so irritated that his killings were not highly publicized that he began writing letters to the media in 1994, signing his letters with a smiling happy face, and thus earning the nickname the Happy Face Killer. Dennis Rader, who could be classified as both a serial and mass murderer, also sent letters to police and newspapers. In his communications, he suggested a number of names for himself; one that eventually stuck was BTK, an acronym for "bind, torture and kill."

The evidence does not support any notion that serial killers kill on the basis of some compulsion or irresistible urge. Rather, the murder appears to be more a result of opportunity and the random availability of a suitable victim. It is a mistake, therefore, to assume that serial murderers are seriously mentally disordered or emotionally disturbed according to traditional clinical or psychiatric standards. Some are, but most are not.

Nor should it be assumed that serial killers are social misfits who have trouble fitting into the local community. The BTK killer, Dennis Rader, killed ten victims in and around Wichita, Kansas. He was married for 33 years, had two children, and was a Boy Scout leader. He was a long-time and dedicated church member who had held elected office in his church council. He was employed as a local government official (compliance officer) and served on several community boards. The Green River Killer, Gary Ridgway, who confessed to killing 48 women over a sixteen-year period in the Seattle Washington area, read the Bible at work and tried to save others by talking about religion with coworkers. At one time, he went door to door for a Pentecostal church trying to save souls. He liked to hunt, fish, work around the yard, and take trips with his wife in their RV. He had been married three times, had a son, and was married at the time of his arrest. He worked as a truck painter for a company for thirty-two years. Robert Lee Yates, Jr., who murdered 13 women, worked as a corrections officer in the state Penitentiary in Walla Walla, Washington, and was a well-decorated helicopter pilot during his 19 years of military service.

Although the cognitive processing and values of serial murderers may be considered extremely aberrant when it comes to sensitivity and concern for their victims, a vast majority of serial killers fail to qualify as seriously mentally disordered in the traditional diagnostic categories of mental disorders. As a group—and there are always exceptions—they would not be diagnosed paranoid schizophrenic, delusional, or psychotic, for example. However, some would likely qualify as having "antisocial personality disorder," a category that is virtually indistinguishable from psychopathy. Serial killers have developed versions of the world that facilitate repetitive murder, often in a brutal, demeaning, and cold-blooded manner, but they are not necessarily seriously mentally disordered in the clinical use of this term. This is a difficult concept to comprehend, because most of us are probably attuned to believe that anyone who kills in this manner "must be crazy."

Research on Backgrounds

The backgrounds of serial killers is varied and underscores the importance of the many risk factors discussed earlier in the text. Similar to violent offenders in general, serial killers have frequently experienced considerable abuses and deprivations within their families growing up (Delisi & Scherer, 2006). McKenzie (1995) discovered in her examination of 20 serial killers that 80 percent were reared in homes characterized by family violence and severe abuse, and parental alcoholism; 93 percent had been exposed to inconsistent and chaotic parenting. For example, Henry Lee Lucas, who claimed to be responsible for an unlikely 600 murders, was severely abused as a child. He was regularly beaten by his mother who at one point struck him so hard with a piece of wood that he was in a coma for three days. He eventually killed her. Coral Eugene Watts, who is suspected of killing 100 women, was continually abused and berated by his stepfather, and was persistently bullied and socially rejected in school.

In his study of serial killers in England, Jenkins (1988) found that—unlike the typical violent individual who demonstrates a propensity for violence at an early age—serial murderers generally begin their careers of repetitive homicide at a relatively late age. He concluded that most started their careers between the ages of 24 and 40. Interestingly, the median age of arrested serial murderers in Jenkins's sample was 36. Arrests typically occurred about four years after they began killing. The serial murderers did have extensive police records, though, but the records reflected a series of petty theft, embezzlement, and forgery, rather than a history of violence (Jenkins, 1988). Surprisingly, they did not have extensive juvenile records. Jenkins concluded that the English cases did not provide any early indicators or predictors of eventual murderous behavior. When British serial murderers committed their first murder, about half were married, had a seemingly stable family life, and had usually lived in the same house for many years. A majority had stable jobs, and, disconcertingly, a good number had been former police officers or security guards.

Female Serial Killers

Although relatively rare, there have been at least three dozen female serial murderers in U.S. history. Hickey (1991) identified 34 documented female serial murderers, with 82 percent of them acting after 1900. Moreover, there are some discernible differences between female and male serial murderers. For example, only about one-third of the female offenders killed strangers, in contrast to males who almost exclusively killed strangers (Holmes, Hickey, & Holmes, 1991). Most victims of female serial killers are husbands, former husbands, or suitors. For example, Belle Gunness murdered an estimated 14–49 husbands or suitors in La Porte, Indiana (Holmes *et al.*, 1991). Nannie Doss killed a combination of 11 husbands and family members in Tulsa, Oklahoma.

Perhaps the most notorious female serial killer in our time was Aileen Wuornos, who killed seven men in Florida in 1989 and 1990, when she was in her thirties. Wuornos had a pathetic, devastating childhood and adolescence, littered with the risk factors were discussed here. She was pregnant at 13 and became a prostitute at 15. She had a lengthy criminal record, mostly for nonviolent offenses, but she was also frequently victimized. She was generally well known to the criminal justice system even before her first murder. Wuornos is unusual as female serial killers go, because her victims were strangers or brief acquaintances rather than husbands or persons of whom she was in charge. She argued that the men she killed had raped her or attempted to rape her, or that her crimes were in self-defense. Psychiatrists diagnosed her with borderline personality disorder, but it was almost universally believed that she would be convicted, and she was. Wuornos was executed by lethal injection in October 2002. She was the subject of several documentaries and the movie *Monster*, in which—despite the film's title—she was portrayed somewhat sympathetically by Charlize Theron.

Traditionally, female serial killers murder primarily for material or monetary gain, such as insurance benefits, will allocations, trusts, and estates. Furthermore, the method of killing is through poisons (usually cyanide) or overdoses of pills. Approximately half of the female serial killers had a male accomplice. Some women murdered because of involvements in cults or with a male serial murderer. For example, Charlene Gallego, the common-law wife of serial killer Gerald Gallego helped him select, abduct, and murder at least 10 individuals (Holmes et al., 1991).

Over the past two decades, several female health care workers who have killed patients have been identified, although males—including a physician—have also been identified. Some research suggests that as many as 17 percent of female serial killers are nurses (Stark, Paterson, Henderson, Kidd, & Godwin, 1997). A female health worker may have been responsible for the deaths of 28 patients at two hospitals in The Hague, Netherlands. Her victims were either children or elderly patients, and her method of killing involved injections of various substances. She was arrested in December 2001 and was later convicted of four counts of first-degree murder and three counts of attempted murder.

The motivations of health care workers' serial killings are variable: recognition, attention, revenge, power, and control (Brantley & Kosky, 2005). Some of these health care workers admitted that the killings relieved tension, stress, and frustration (Linedecker & Burt, 1990). Some also maintained that they killed to put the patients out of their misery and that these were essentially mercy killings.

The Victimological Perspective in Understanding Serial Killers

Jenkins (1993) contends that the current popular image of the serial murderer—a white male who kills for sexual motives—may be an inaccurate one. He argues that lack of a **victimological perspective** encourages confusion and distorted information. He suggests that our current knowledge about serial murderers is strongly influenced by two factors: availability of the victims and the attitudes of law enforcement agencies toward those victims. Rather than strictly focusing on individual and personality attributes of the offender, he believes we should also examine the *social opportunity* to kill. In other words, what we know about serial murder may be strongly influenced by the nature and type of the potential victims.

To illustrate, Jenkins (1993) provides the case of Calvin Jackson, who was arrested in 1974 for murder committed in a New York apartment building. Actually, Jackson was a serial murderer, but none of his victims led the police to suspect a serial killer. Jackson's killings took place in a single-occupancy hotel where the guests were poor, socially isolated, largely forgotten, and mostly elderly. Time after time, the police were called to the hotel to deal with cases of death or injury due to alcohol, drugs, or old age. When foul play was suspected, the police never considered it the work of a serial murderer, because the victims did not fit the stereotypic profile. Since there was no evidence of grotesque sexual abuse of the victim (the victim stereotype), there was little reason for the police to entertain the possibility of a serial murderer. Other serial murderers may set up situations where murders resemble drug-related homicides. Therefore, our current knowledge of serial murderers may be restricted to a certain category of offender.

Jenkins (1993) further suggests that dramatic increases in serial murder are directly related to dramatic increases in potential victims, such as severe downturns in the economy or deinstitutionalization of mental patients that result in putting more vulnerable people on the streets.

Geographical Location of Serial Killing

Interestingly, 31 of 52 known cases of serial murders in the United States from 1971 to approximately 20 years later occurred in the western states, especially California (Jenkins, 1993). Over the last 15 years, despite the attention given to this type of crime in the entertainment media, few additional cases have been documented. The reason for this geographical distribution remains largely a mystery, although the answer probably lies in some combination of lifestyles, economic conditions, and the availability of potential victims.

Most serial killers have specific preferences for the location of their killings. They frequently commit their killings within comfort zones that are often defined by an anchor point, such as their residence, employment, or the residence of a relative. Very few serial murderers travel interstate to kill (Federal Bureau of Investigation, 2005a). Those that do travel interstate for their murders are often truck drivers, those in military service, transients, or itinerant individuals who move from place to place. Hickey (1997) estimates that 14 percent of serial killers use their homes or workplaces as the preferred location, whereas another 52 percent commit their murders in the same general location or region, such as the same neighborhood or city. This tendency suggests that geographical profiling may be an invaluable aid in the identification of serial killers.

Perhaps an effective method for reducing serial murder is to identify and protect specific high-risk groups and regions and to take whatever social measures are needed to reduce their vulnerability. Focusing on the offender through criminal profiling and other investigative measures is usually of limited usefulness because most serial killers are apprehended by a mixture of fortuitous events and carelessness by the offender. In the meantime, community leaders and authorities should concentrate on reducing the availability of potential victims.

Ethnic and Racial Characteristics

The widespread belief that only whites are serial killers and blacks and other minorities never commit this type of crime is basically a myth (Walsh, 2005). Walsh found that approximately 21.8 percent of the serial killers in the United States have been black, and was able to document 90 black serial killers during the post–World War II era. Research on Latino and other minority serial killers is virtually nonexistent.

The number of victims black killers admitted killing does not differ significantly from white serial killers either. Jake Bird, for instance, was verified to have killed 44 victims, just 4 victims short of the white killer Gary Ridgeway's (the Green River Killer) record-setting 48. And some are equally chilling. Walsh (2005) describes the methods of black serial killer Maury Travis when he writes, "Travis had a secret torture chamber in his basement, where police found bondage equipment, videotapes of his rape and torture sessions, and clippings relating to police investigations of his murder victims (mostly prostitutes and crack addicts). Travis hanged himself in jail after confessing to 17 murders" (p. 274).

We may have assumed that serial killings are perpetrated almost exclusively by whites because of how serial murder is identified and investigated. For example, law enforcement agencies may be less prone to investigate African American victims as casualties of serial murderers if they are found in a rundown apartment complex located in a poverty-stricken, crime-infested neighborhood. Under these circumstances, law enforcement officials are more likely to conclude that the victim is simply another fatality in the long stream of never-ending violence found in parts of inner cities. This point was made by Jenkins (1993) in the previous section.

Also, as Walsh (2005) has observed, the media tend to cover the sensational serial killings by whites but fail to cover in any detail those offenses committed by blacks and other minorities. "The extensive media coverage of Bundy, Gacy, and Berkowitz cases have made these killers almost household names, but African Americans such as Watts, Johnson, Francois, and Wallace are practically unknown, despite having operated within the same general time framework (1980s and 1990s)" (Walsh, 2005, p. 274). Similar disparity in media coverage of other crimes has occurred. In many communities, it is not unusual to see extensive coverage of the disappearance or murder of a white child and very little attention given to a similar tragedy involving a black victim. Because violent crime, on the whole, is interracial rather than intraracial (Federal Bureau of Investigation, 2005a), it follows that lack of attention might favor the nonwhite perpetrators of these offenses.

Juvenile Serial Murderers

Serial murder by children and adolescents is an exceedingly rare event, and scientific information is extremely sparse. Myers (2004) could only identify six serial cases involving juveniles over the past 150 years, after an exhaustive search of periodicals, newspapers, books, legal references, and Internet sources on crime. According to Myers (2004), serial murders by juveniles are a complex phenomenon, with psychological, family, social, cultural, and biological factors playing a role. Myers believes that many of the same motives manifested by adult serial killers hold for child and adolescent serial killers. Since serial murder by juveniles is such a rare event—in contrast to mass murder—we will concentrate on adult serial murderers for the remainder of this section.

Typologies of Serial Murderers

Efforts to classify any offenders into categories, or typologies, must be made with caution because many individuals do not fit neatly into these divisions. In addition, typologies based on behavior are problematic because behavior is not always consistent from situation to situation. Nevertheless, typologies can be useful in organizing an array of behavioral patterns that would otherwise be confusing—but they need to be subjected to empirical verification.

Holmes and DeBurger (1988) make a gallant attempt to classify serial murderers into a typology based on motive and have accumulated some research evidence in support. They identify four major types: (1) visionary, (2) mission oriented, (3) hedonistic, and (4) power/control oriented. The *visionary type* is driven by voices or visions that demand that a particular group of people be destroyed, such as prostitutes, homosexuals, or derelicts. The visionary killer often operates on the basis of a "directive from God." In many instances, this type qualifies as psychotic or crazy, which is atypical because serial killers—as we learned—are not usually mentally disordered. He (or she) is probably the most difficult to understand for investigators and the public alike. The crime scene is usually chaotic and has an abundance of physical evidence, often including fingerprints and the murder weapon (Holmes & Holmes, 1998).

The *mission-oriented type* determines that there is a particular group of people who are undesirable and who must be destroyed or eliminated. The undesirables may be prostitutes, gays or lesbians, "street people," or members of a particular religious, racial, or minority group. This killer demonstrates no discernible mental disorder. He or she sees no visions, hears no voices, and functions on a day-to-day basis without exhibiting notable psychologically aberrant behavior.

The *hedonistic type* strives for pleasure and thrill seeking, and feels that people are objects to use for one's own enjoyment. Reportedly, the hedonistic killer gains considerable pleasure from the murder event itself. According to Holmes and Holmes (1998), hedonistic killers may be divided into three subtypes based on the primary motive for the murder: lust, thrill, or comfort. The lust killer's primary motive is sexual gratification. The thrill killer is primarily motivated to induce pain or a terrified reaction from the victim. The pain and terror created, in combination with the process of murder itself, are highly stimulating and exciting for the killer. The primary motive for the comfort killer is to acquire activities (business or financial interests) or objects (money or assets) that provide a comfortable and luxurious lifestyle.

The *power/control type* strives to get satisfaction by having complete life-or-death control over the victim. Sexual components may or may not be present, but the primary motive is the extreme power and control over the helpless victim. These killers also tend to seek specific victims who appear especially vulnerable and easy to victimize, such as children.

Despite the extensive media coverage and several books on the subject in recent years, there have been very few well-designed, empirically-based studies on serial murderers during the past 10–15 years done from a psychological perspective. Those that are available have been based on very small samples (e.g., McKenzie, 1995). Much of the available information has been gathered through anecdotes or investigative articles written by journalists. While informative and interesting, they fail to provide a systematic and functionally useful data base for predicting and identifying these offenders.

MASS MURDERERS

Surprisingly, little research has been directed at mass murderers, especially in comparison with the attention directed at serial murderers. Perhaps this is because mass murder, while frightening, is not as intriguing or mysterious as serial murder. Furthermore, mass murder happens quickly and unpredictably without warning—then the killing is usually over. It is often clear who the offender is, and his or her life is usually ended on the spot, either when they kill themselves or when they are shot by the police. If they surrender, they are almost invariably convicted. Serial murders, on the other hand, occur over a period of weeks, months, or years, and the identity of the offender is unknown.

In this section, we will focus on mass murder by the individual. As we referred to earlier in the chapter, there are two types of mass murder by the individual: classic mass murder and family mass murder. This section will concentrate on the classic type.

Classic Mass Murder

Mass murderers tend to be frustrated, angry people who feel helpless about their lives. They are usually between the ages of 35–45, and they are convinced there is little chance that things will get better for them. Their personal lives have been a failure by their standards, and they have often suffered some tragic or serious loss, such as a loss of meaningful employment. George Hennard, for example, the 35-year-old who drove his Ford Ranger pickup into the plate glass window of Luby's Cafeteria in Killeen, Texas, and proceeded to shoot to death 22 patrons, had lost his cherished job as a merchant marine.

In addition, mass murders are usually carefully planned, sometimes over very long periods of time. For example, on November 2, 1991, Gang Lu, a former graduate student at the University of Iowa, sought six specific professors he felt kept him from getting a $1,000 award for his doctoral dissertation. He managed to kill five of the six within 10 minutes before taking his own life. Lu had written five separate letters to people detailing his plans prior to the murder. Likewise, Hennard had apparently planned his onslaught for many months, even studying video documentaries of previous mass murders.

Moreover, the targets selected by mass murderers are either symbolic of their discontent (such as their workplace) or are likely to contain individuals they hate or blame for their misfortunes. George Hennard, for example, had a lifelong hatred of women, and he knew that Luby's Cafeteria during lunch would be filled with them. Hennard moved from victim to victim, frequently selecting women, and methodically shot each victim in the head at close range as he shouted "bitch." Fourteen of the 22 deaths that day were women. Marc Lepine walked calmly through the University of Montreal engineering school (Ecole Polytechnique) with a semiautomatic rifle in search of women to kill. In one classroom he shouted, "I want to kill women!" and as he proceeded to shoot them, he shouted, "You're all a bunch of feminists!" He killed 14 women that day and wounded 13 more people (four of them men) before he took his own life. In his pocket was a three-page suicide note in which he complained that feminists had always ruined his life. James Oliver Huberty, the McDonald's killer, selected a fast-food restaurant in a Hispanic community (San Ysidro) because he apparently disliked Hispanics and children.

Mass murderers often take a very active interest in guns, especially semiautomatics that maximize the number of deaths in a short period of time. In large measure, the availability of high-powered semiautomatic or automatic weaponry accounts for the increasingly large death toll in recent mass murders. Moreover, mass murderers usually plan to die at the scene, either by committing suicide or by being shot down by law enforcement.

Also, mass murderers are often socially isolated and withdrawn people who are without a strong social network of friends or supports. Their isolation is probably due to some combination of an active dislike of people and their inadequate interpersonal and social skills. The mass murder is their chance to get even, to dominate others, to take control, to call the shots, and to gain recognition. The 41-year-old individual who killed at the immigration center in New York had a history of interpersonal and work problems. He was apparently bitter and angry, and had stated that the United States was a terrible place. An immigrant himself, he had obtained his citizenship and had lived in the United States for most of his adult life; however, he had considerable trouble learning English and maintained that people ridiculed his speech. Many who knew him said they were not surprised at his actions.

A Mass Murder Typology

James Alan Fox and Jack Levin (2003) have proposed a five-category typology based on the motivations for mass killings. The five categories are revenge, power, loyalty, profit, and terror.

According to Fox and Levin, many—if not most—mass killings are motivated by *revenge*, either against specific individuals or specific groups. Usually, the killer seeks to get even with a group of people he dislikes. Fox and Levin bring up the concept of "murder by proxy" in which victims are chosen because they are associated, by the killer, with a primary target against whom revenge is sought. For example, 25-year-old Marc Lépine's long-term hatred against feminists ignited his murderous rampage at the Université de Montréal. Although some of his victims may have not considered themselves feminists, he considered all women, by proxy, feminists.

Another recent example of the revenge mass killer occurred on March 10, 2009, when Michael McLendon, age 28, went on a rampage in southern Alabama. The gunman, who killed 11 people including himself, had a list of people he had worked with who had allegedly done him wrong. He began the day of the shooting by burning down his mother's house (her body and four dead dogs were later found inside), and shot most of his victims at a sausage plant where he had stopped working just days before the rampage.

The second type identified by Fox and Levin (2003) is the killer who seeks *power* and domination over his victims. They enjoy and crave the fear in others they engender and the immense control they have over their victims. Usually, the need for revenge and power go together. The power killer is seeking both revenge and control over his tormentors. Fox and Levin observe that the thirst for power and control inspire this type of mass murderer to dress in military fatigues and combat gear, and carry assault weapons packed with considerable firepower. Some investigators refer to them as pseudocommando killers. Another example of this type of mass killer is James Huberty, who could also fit into the revenge category because of his dislike of Hispanics and children.

On July 18, 1984, Huberty, a 41 year-old unemployed security guard, put on his camouflage pants, told his wife that "Society has had its chance. I'm going hunting, hunting for humans." Armed with a 9-mm Uzi semiautomatic, a Winchester pump-action 12-gauge shotgun, 9-mm Browning HP, and hundreds of rounds of ammunition, he set out to wage his "war."

The third type is inspired to kill by a warped sense of love and *loyalty*, usually based on a desire to save their loved ones from misery and hardship. Many family massacres stem from this motivation. "Typically, a husband/father is despondent over the fate of the family unit, and takes not only his own life, but also those of his children and sometimes his wife, in order to protect them from pain and suffering in their lives" (Fox & Levin, 2003, pp. 59–60).

The fourth motivation for mass murder is *profit*. The intention in this murder is to eliminate victims and witnesses to a crime, such as a robbery. Drug wars between organized crime groups is also sometimes involved. This type of mass murder also send the message to other potential witnesses that the same thing could happen to you if you try to testify to authorities.

The fifth and final motivation for mass murder is *terror*. In this situation, the perpetrator wants to send a message through a horrific murder. One of the more infamous examples of this type is represented by Charles Manson, who led a quasi-commune located in southern California in the 1960s. Manson, who likely would qualify as a charismatic psychopath, desired to send a message of terror to communities in southern California. He was a devout listener to Beatles music, and was especially influenced by the song "Helter Skelter," a composition found on the Beatles' *White Album*, which he interpreted as prophesying an apocalyptic war between blacks and whites. Manson apparently wanted to start a race war by having his followers commit horrific mass murders of wealthy whites and have them blamed on angry blacks. Manson had the grandiose delusion of world domination (Deal & Hickey, 2003). He believed that once Helter Skelter started, blacks would eventually kill all whites except for himself and his family because they would hide in the desert (Deal & Hickey, 2003). On August 9, 2009, Manson told four of his followers that it was time for Helter Skelter. He instructed them to commit brutal mass murder and to "leave a sign and do something witchy" to ignite fear and terror within the white community. The site they selected was the home of well-known actress Sharon Tate and film director Roman Polanski, located in a prominent Los Angeles neighborhood. The group brutally murdered five people at the house that night, including Tate, who was eight and one-half months pregnant. Polanski was out of the country at the time. After the killing, they wrote the message "pig" on the front door of the house in the blood of one of the victims.

The next night, six Manson followers set out—again per Manson's instructions—to murder Leno LaBianca, a wealthy supermarket executive, and his wife Rosemary, a successful dress shop co-owner. After Leno was killed, one of the followers carved "war" on the man's abdomen. The group also left frightening messages in three different places in the house, "death to the pigs," "rise," and "Healter (sic) Skelter," all in the victims' blood. Manson was eventually arrested, convicted of accessory to murder, and sentenced to death. However, his sentence was commuted to life in prison in 1976 after the Supreme Court of California temporarily eliminated that state's death penalty. One of Manson's followers, Tex Watson, allegedly found God in prison. Another member, Lynette "Squeaky" Fromme, was paroled and later reimprisoned after threatening the life of President Ronald Reagan. In 2009 she was again released from prison. Still another follower, Susan Atkins, died of cancer in prison in Fall 2009. Other members of the Manson family have been paroled or remain incarcerated.

The Manson slayings demonstrate the power that a charismatic figure—and in this case probably a psychopath—can have over vulnerable individuals. Manson himself was not directly involved in the killings; his followers did precisely what he wanted them to do, providing unquestioned obedience to his commands.

The remainder of the chapter addresses some specific offenses that have been, or possess the strong possibility of becoming mass murder. Product tampering, school violence, and workplace violence do not necessarily result in death, of course, but when they do, the deaths may be multiple. These crimes have drawn extensive media coverage, and some research interest, in recent years.

PRODUCT TAMPERING

Product tampering is the sabotaging of a commercial product, usually for commercial gain. It becomes **product-tampering homicide** when the sabotaging is so serious that it results in the death of one or more individuals. Because the product is typically used by many persons before the tampering is discovered, this crime has the potential of resulting in multiple such deaths. Between 1982 and 1986, there were 12 confirmed deaths directly due to product tampering (Lance, 1988). Thus, this form of homicide is very rare. The offender usually expects financial gain either through litigation on behalf of the victim (wrongful death), through extortion, or through business operations (Douglas, Burgess, Burgess, & Ressler, 1992). The business operation strategy refers to attempts to damage a competing business by tampering with its products. In addition to financial gain, other motives for product tampering include revenge by a disgruntled employee or former employee, attention getting, diversion from a single murder, or malicious mischief (Deal, 2003).

The method most commonly employed in product-tampering homicide is to place cyanide within the product, either before (if the offense involves extortion or business operations) or after purchase (in cases claiming wrongful death). Cyanide is often the poison of choice because of its potency (an ounce can kill 250 people) and its availability (Douglas *et al.*, 1992). Product-tampering incidents have also included liquid mercury, weed killer, syringes, pesticides, glass, fecal matter, hydrochloric acid, razor blades, staples, and straight pins (Deal, 2003). In June 2004, parents in Irvine, California, found threatening notes in Gerber baby food (Ailworth, 2003).

Fortunately, although there are numerous threats to tamper, very few are actually carried out. Nearly two-thirds of the threats are directed at retail stores, and the products threatened are usually well-known national brands (Lance, 1988). News of product tampering sometimes prompts a contagion effect (also known as copycat effect), in which many people either copy or falsely report the offense. For example, when a baby food company was accused by an individual of having glass in its baby food, more than 600 complaints of glass particles were immediately received across the country. A vast majority of the complaints were false claims by consumers seeking monetary reward by claiming that glass in the products had caused them some injury. One individual was arrested for deliberately feeding shards of glass to his developmentally disabled son in an attempt to obtain money from the baby food company. Another example of contagion effect involved Pepsi-Cola. On June 10, 1993, a report came in that a syringe was found in a can of Diet Pepsi. During the next week, over 50 more reports came in from 23 states alleging syringes or needles had been found in cans of Pepsi. The reports could be devastating for the company as Pepsi was selling about 30 million cans of soft drinks per day (Janofsky, 2003). Fortunately, it was discovered to be a hoax. Not one of the reports was found to be authentic.

SCHOOL VIOLENCE

In the later 1990s a rash of school shootings made headlines. The most infamous case was the mass murder of 12 students and one teacher at Columbine High School in Littleton, Colorado, in April 1999. The two teenage boys who did the shootings committed suicide during the incident. Twenty more students were injured. Although there had been a number of school shootings prior to Columbine (there were at least 10 school shootings between 1996 and 1999), the Columbine shooting prompted a great deal of alarm and concern nationwide. In addition, the media and some experts were quick to make gross generalizations about the school violence problem.

However, even prior to these violent incidents, anecdotal and media accounts of children being victimized at school by other children prompted researchers to study the issue to document the magnitude of the problem. Violence in schools is more than school shootings. Violence in schools includes aggravated and simple assaults, sexual assaults, and robbery. As long ago as 1974, the U.S. Congress funded a three-year study to evaluate the nature and extent of crime, violence, and disruption in the nation's schools. The National Institute of Education (NIE), which conducted the study, released its findings in 1977, and Safe School Study (National Center for Education Statistics, 2005) still remains the most comprehensive study available.

The report indicated the following:

- Between 1995 and 2001, the percentage of students who reported being victims of crime at school decreased from 10 percent to 6 percent.
- Victims of theft decreased from 7 percent to 4 percent.
- Victims of violence decreased from 3 percent to 2 percent.

The report also indicates that there was no detectable increase or decease over time in:

- The percentage of students threatened or injured with a weapon.
- The percentage of teachers physically threatened or injured with a weapon.
- Marijuana use, alcohol use, and drug distribution at school.

In the 2002–2003 school year, an estimated 54.2 million students in prekindergarten through grade 12 were enrolled in about 125,000 U.S. elementary or secondary schools (National Center for Education Statistics, 2005). In 2003, violent crimes occurred at a rate of 6 per 1,000 in that student population. Students were more likely to be victims of serious violence or homicide away from school, occurring at a rate of 12 crimes per 1,000 students away from school. For example, in each school year from 1992 to 2002, youths aged 5–19 were over 70 times more likely to be murdered away from school than at school. Still, national statistics indicate that about one out of 10 students in secondary schools fear that they will be attacked or harmed while at school (Verlinden, Hersen, & Thomas, 2000).

School Shootings

Although school shootings are understandably frightening and are of deep concern, statistically they are rare. Between 1992 and 2002, the number of homicides of school-aged youth at school declined from 33 to 14. In addition, violent crime rates in the nation's public and private schools in 2003 remained unchanged and continued at about half those recorded in 1992 (Bureau of Justice Statistics, 2005).

O'Toole (2000, p. 4) lists the usual wrong or unverified impressions of school shooters often promoted by the news media. Among these myths are the following:

- School violence is an epidemic.
- All school shooters are alike.
- The school shooter is always a loner.
- School shootings are exclusively motivated by revenge.
- Easy access to weapons is the most significant factor.
- Unusual or aberrant behaviors, interests, or hobbies are hallmarks of the student destined to become violent.

Investigations of school shooters have consistently found that the two characteristics that emerge are peer rejection and social rejection. The Columbine High School shooter, Dylan Klebold, wrote in his diary how lonely he was without friends and was especially tortured by his failures with girls (Meadows, 2006). The other shooter, Eric Harris, wrote in his diary how everyone continually made fun of him. A vast majority of shooters have poor social and coping skills and felt picked on or persecuted (Verlindene *et al.*, 2000). They expressed anger about being teased or ridiculed and vowed revenge against particular individuals or groups. Moreover, as a group, "they lacked social support and prosocial relationships that might have served as protective factors" (Verlinden *et al.*, 2000, p. 44). Cruelty to animals was prominent in the backgrounds of at least half of the shooters (Verlinden *et al.*, 2000). Their backgrounds also revealed a keen interest in guns and other weaponry, and they often had easy access to firearms (see **Table 3**). Most of these assailants expected to be killed or planned suicide during or immediately after the attacks. All the attacks seemed to be carefully planned and thought out beforehand.

In virtually all school shootings, investigators discovered that the violent intentions of the assailants were repeatedly made clear to others, particularly peers, often including the time and place. It is estimated that at least 50 percent of school shooters let their intentions known to others, a phenomenon that become known by investigators as *leakage*. Documents show that the Columbine school shooters repeatedly dropped hints at school about their murderous intentions (Meadows, 2006). However, peers rarely reported these threats to the authorities. The reasons for this lack of reporting behavior are not well understood, but fear seems to play a major role. A survey by the Safe School Coalition of Washington State (1999) (cited in Verlinden *et al.*, 2000) revealed that fear of not being believed, fear of retribution, or fear for what might happen to the youth threatening the school violence were the most frequently reported concerns of peers. Verlinden *et al.* (2000) concluded that the risk for school violence is high when there are multiple warning signs and risk factors. "The more signs there are and the greater the opportunity, motivation, and access to weapons, the greater the possibility that the child may commit a violent act" (Verlinden *et al.*, 2000, p. 47).

TABLE 3   School Homicides, 1994–1999

Type of weapon	Number	Percent
Total	172	100
Firearm	119	69
Handgun	89	52
Rifle	18	11
Unknown	12	7
Sharp object	31	18
Beating	12	7
Strangulation	5	3
Other	5	3

Source: Perkins (2003), p. 11.

So far, we have talked about school-aged shooters killing classmates and teachers. Adults unaffiliated with the school are also involved in school shootings. In recent years, adult males have barged into school buildings, killing students. Perhaps one of the more horrific occurred in West Nickel, Pennsylvania, where, on October 2, 2006, 32-year-old Charles Carl Roberts carried three guns into Nickel Mines School, an Amish one-room schoolhouse. The gunman took hostages, all girls, and sent the boys and adults outside. He barricaded the doors and then opened fire on a dozen girls, killing five and seriously wounding five before committing suicide. His motivation was unclear, but he indicated that his actions were not directly related to school or the Amish community, but was driven by events in his childhood. More likely, "he may have viewed himself as powerless or his own life circumstances as hopeless and acted out in a school environment that was simple, peaceful—and completely at his mercy" (Gerler, 2007, p. 2).

A week earlier, 53-year-old Duane Roger Morrison, armed with an assault rifle and carrying a backpack full of explosives, walked into Platte Canyon High School located in Bailey, Colorado. He took six female students hostage and sexually assaulted five of them. He then released four of them. When a SWAT team broke into the classroom, Morrison shot and killed 16-year-old Emily Keyes before turning the gun on himself. The other female hostages managed to escape. The motive of this adult attacker remains unclear.

Psychological Characteristics of School Shooters

Leary, Kowalski, Smith, and Phillips (2003) examined the psychological characteristics of juvenile offenders involved in 15 school shootings between 1995 and 2001. They discovered that social rejection was involved in most cases of school shootings. Most of the rejected shooters experienced an ongoing pattern of teasing, bullying, or ostracism, and a few were subjected to a recent romantic rejection. In many cases, the victims of the violence were those who rejected or humiliated the shooter. But social rejection alone did not seem to be enough to ignite killing classmates. In addition to the social rejection, perpetrators showed at least one of the following three risk factors: psychological problems, an interest in guns or explosives, or a morbid fascination with death. The psychological problems centered around low impulse control, lack of empathy for other people, serious depression, aggressiveness, and antisocial behavior. Many of the shooters had been in trouble for aggressive behavior toward peers, and some had abused animals. Depression appears to be especially important in identifying potential school shooters. In one comprehensive study, three-fourths of school shooters had expressed thoughts of suicide or attempts at suicide before the attack (Vossekuil, Fein, Reddy, Borum, & Modzeleski, 2002).

Fascination with firearms, bombs, and explosives is also a common theme. They seem to be comfortable with instruments of destruction. Wike and Fraser (2009) note that police in Plymouth Meeting outside of Philadelphia arrested a 14-year-old school dropout who, with his parents' assistance, had collected swords, guns, grenades, bomb-instructional manuals, black powder used in bomb making, and videos of the Columbine massacre. According to police—who acted on a tip from students—this alienated student had plans to attack his former school.

The third observation is that shooters tend to be highly fascinated with death and dark lifestyles and themes. They are not as horrified by sadistic and brutal carnage as most of their peers. Jeffrey Wiese, a 16-year-old at Red Lake High School in Minnesota, killed his grandfather and his grandfather's girlfriend, and then drove to the high school and fatally shot a security guard, a teacher, and five students. He wounded six others before shooting himself. Weise, who had been hospitalized for suicidal behavior, left many dark themes on web sites, dressed in black, and wrote stories about school shootings and zombies (Weisbrot, 2008). However, these dark themes may be more characteristic of depression, thoughts of suicide, and anger at society than a central lifestyle. Eric Harris and Dylan Klebold, the Columbine High School shooters, are often referred to as devout believers of the macabre, but the evidence does not hold up that this was clearly the case. Rather, it appears that they were both angry young men. In a vast majority of school shootings, the perpetrator apparently had very little attachment or bonding to their schools, teachers, or peers (Wike & Fraser, 2009). School attachment and bonding appear to be crucial in any strategy designed to reduce school violence. Some investigators have found that school attachment plays an important role in producing high levels of academic achievement and in reducing substance use, violence, and high risk sexual behavior (Catalano, Haggerty, Oesterle, Fleming, & Hawkins, 2004; Wike & Fraser, 2009).

In a national study of school violence, Gottfredson, Gottfredson, Payne, and Gottfredson (2005) report that schools in which students find the rules fair and in which discipline is managed consistently experience less violence and disorder. This is regardless of the type of school and community. They also found that schools characterized by high teacher morale, focus, strong leadership, and high teacher involvement are protected from school crime and violence. Their conclusions: The school climate makes a significant difference in reducing the overall crime, disorder, and violence that occur within the school building.

One key conclusion made by Leary et al. (2003) is, "The typical shooter is a male student who has been ostracized by the majority group at his school for some time, and has been chronically taunted, teased, harassed, and often publicly humiliated." Being the victim of vicious and public bullying by peers consistently emerges in the school experiences of shooters. We now turn our attention to the topic of bullying.

School Bullying

School bullying came under intense public and media scrutiny after the shootings at Columbine High School in 1999 and Santana High School in Santee, California, in early 2001 (Ericson, 2001). Considerable research-based literature on the topic has emerged over the past decade, much of it prompted by conclusion that school shooters were often socially rejected and bullied, and eventually took their revenge through violent actions on their schools and peers. Seung-Hui Cho, the shooter who killed 31 students and professors at Virginia Tech in 2007, was said to have been bullied in high school and ridiculed about his accent to the point that he resisted speaking to others.

Bullying is commonly defined as a form of peer aggression in which one or more individuals repeatedly physically, verbally, and/or psychologically harass a weaker victim (Olweus, 1997; Vijoen, O'Neill, & Sidhu, 2005). Examples of physical bullying include hitting, spitting, kicking, punching, pushing, and taking or destroying personal items. Verbal bullying includes name calling, taunting, malicious teasing, and verbal threats. Psychological bullying includes spreading rumors and engaging in social exclusion, extortion, or intimidation.

Bullying is a common and significant problem for a large number of children throughout the world. Over half of school children have reported being victimized and over half have taken part in bullying (Jolliffe & Farrington, 2006). It commonly occurs on playgrounds, on school buses, in school hallways, neighborhoods, and homes. The victims and the bullies themselves are highly disliked and socially rejected by peers (Eslea *et al.*, 2003; Veenstra, Lindenberg, Oldehinkel, De Winter, Verhulst, & Ormel, 2005). While the playground or school bus or school halls is where bullying traditionally has occurred, technology has expanded the problem to the borderless cyberworld (Diamanduros, Downs, & Jenkins, 2008). Cyperbullying is fast emerging as having the same devastating psychological effects on its victims as persistent traditional bullying. It is especially troubling for its intended victim because the perpetrator is often unknown.

It is clear from research that bullying has negative effects on both the victim and the bully. Victims of persistent bullying are more likely to perform significantly more self-destructive actions and are more likely to bring weapons to school to protect themselves (Henry & Sanders, 2007). A deeply troubled youth, however, after many years of being victimized by bullying, may decide he has no alternative but suicide, or worse, a massive school shooting accompanied by suicide (Burgess, Garbarino, & Carlson, 2006). At least two-thirds of school shooters were teased, taunted, or bullied by peers (Vossekuil *et al.*, 2002).

In ending this section, it should be emphasized that chronic bullies themselves and those that have been both bullied and became bullies often demonstrate little empathy for others (Jolliffe & Farrington, 2006), cruelty to animals (Henry & Sanders, 2007), and many engage in a life of antisocial and violent behavior long after they leave school (Henry & Sanders, 2007).

WORKPLACE VIOLENCE

Defining Workplace Violence

Many terms and behaviors have been subsumed under the rubric of workplace violence. In the public mind, workplace violence usually means a worker killing his or her coworkers or supervisors. Commentators, researchers, and experts, on the other hand, have used workplace violence to refer to a wide range of aggressive actions, such as gossip, assaults, sexual assaults, robberies, and murders. For our purpose, it is worthwhile to distinguish between workplace aggression and workplace violence. **Workplace aggression** is "a general term encompassing all forms of behavior by which individuals attempt to harm others at work or their organizations" (Neuman & Baron, 1998, p. 393). Workplace aggression may range from subtle and hidden actions to active confrontations or direct destruction of property (Hepworth & Towler, 2004). **Workplace violence,** on the other hand, refers to incidents in which the offender intends to cause *serious* physical or bodily harm to an individual or individuals within an organization or to the organization itself.

Data collected by the Bureau of Labor Statistics (2004) indicate that an average of 900 people are murdered at work each year, making it the third leading cause of occupational

TABLE 4   Average Annual Workplace Homicide by Victim-Offender Association, 1993–1999

Association of Offender to Victim	Number	Average Annual Number	Percent of total
Worker association	6,316	899	100%
Stranger	5,274	753	84
Work associate	721	103	11
Coworker, former coworker	469	67	7
Customer, client	252	36	4
Intimate	194	28	3
Husband	122	17	2
Wife	3	—	—
Boyfriend	72	10	1
Other relative	38	5	1
Other acquaintance	65	9	1

Source: Critical Incident Response Group, 2001, p. 42.

death in the United States (see **Table 4**). In 2003, 14 percent of workplace fatalities were due to assaults and violent acts. Although the impression derived from media reports over the past two decades is that workplace violence is expanding, it must be emphasized that a large majority of workplace homicides do *not* involve murder between coworkers or supervisors *within* an organization but occur in robberies and related crimes by people *outside* the organization (Neuman & Baron, 1998). That is, young convenience store clerks or fast-food restaurant workers are often the victims of robbery and other forms of violence while working.

The following statistics, compiled in an overview by Gregorie (2000), show how dangerous the workplace can be:

- Each year, about 2 million Americans are victimized while working.
- Approximately 900 workplace homicides occur annually.
- Guns are the primary weapon used in 82 percent of workplace homicides, followed by knives and physical force.
- About one of every six violent crimes experienced by U.S. residents occurs in the workplace.
- Boyfriends and husbands, both current and former, commit more than 13,000 acts of violence against women in the workplace every year.
- The National Institute for Occupational Safety and Health reports that murder is the leading cause of death for women at work.

Examples of Workplace Violence

Gregorie (2000, pp. 2–3) further outlines four types of offenders who commit violence at the workplace, in an effort that is very useful for understanding this phenomenon. The classification system or typology was first identified by the California Division of Occupational Safety and Health in *Guidelines for Workplace Security* (1995). The four types of offenders are as follows:

- *Type I.* This offender has no legitimate relationship to the workplace or the victim and usually enters the workplace to commit a criminal action such as a robbery or theft. Common victims of Type I offenders are small, late-night retail establishments, including convenience stores and restaurants, and taxi drivers. This type of workplace violence also includes terrorist and hate crimes such as the World Trade Center and Alfred P. Murrah Federal Building bombings, as well as abortion clinic attacks.
- *Type II.* This offender is the recipient of some service provided by the victim or workplace and may be either a current or former client, patient, or customer.
- *Type III.* This offender has an employment-related involvement with the workplace. The act of violence is usually committed by a current or former employee, supervisor, or manager who has a dispute with another employee of the workplace. This type of workplace violence offender is usually referred to as the "disgruntled employee" and is often someone who has been fired, demoted, or lost benefits. When death results from the violence, if the victim or victims were of higher authority than the perpetrator, the crime may be called **authority homicide.**
- *Type IV.* This offender has an indirect involvement with the workplace because of a relationship with an employee. The offender may be a current or former spouse or partner, someone who was in a dating relationship with the employee, or a relative or friend. This type of violence follows the employee into the workplace from the outside.

The first of these categories, depicting violence by someone not connected to workplace, accounts for the vast majority of violence and homicides, perhaps as high as 80 percent of the total (Critical Incident Response Group, 2001). The motive is usually robbery, and in many cases, the offender or offenders are carrying a gun or other weapon, greatly increasing the likelihood that the victim (most often, the victims) will be killed or seriously wounded. For example, in May 2000, two men entered a Wendy's in Flushing, New York, with the intent to rob the fast-food restaurant. They left with $2,400 in cash after shooting seven employees. Five of the employees died, and two others were seriously wounded. Convenience store clerks, taxi drivers, security guards, and proprietors of "mom-and-pop" stores are also vulnerable to this type of workplace violence.

Workers who exchange cash with customers as part of the job, work late-night hours, and work alone are at greatest risk for Type I workplace violence. In California, for example, the majority (60%) of workplace homicides involved a person entering a small, night-retail establishment, such as a liquor store, gas station, or convenience food store, to commit a robbery (Southerland, Collins, & Scarborough, 1997).

Type II workplace violence usually involves health care workers, police officers, counselors, schoolteachers, college professors, social workers, and mental health workers. An example of Type II workplace violence is provided by the University of Iowa Injury Prevention Research Center (2001, p. 7):

Rhonda Bedow, a nurse who works in a state-operated psychiatric facility in Buffalo, NY, was attacked by an angry patient who had a history of threatening behavior, particularly against female staff. He slammed Bedow's head down onto a counter after learning that he had missed the chance to go outside with a group of other patients. Bedow suffered a concussion, a bilaterally dislocated jaw, an eye injury, and permanent scarring on her face from the assault.

In the 1970s and 1980s, a number of social workers were assaulted—and sometimes killed—by individuals who were furious because their children were removed from the family home or because they lost custody based on social worker recommendations. These tragedies prompted many state agencies to erect barricades between clients and the workers and, in many cases, to hire private security officers to screen those entering the offices. Likewise, after similar incidences in which family court judges and lawyers were threatened, shot at, or stabbed, family court proceedings—which had traditionally been held rather informally—were formalized and the courtrooms themselves subjected to heightened security.

The Type III workplace violence offender probably is regarded by the media as the most sensational and receives a bulk of its coverage. As noted by the Critical Incident Response Group (2001, p. 11), "mass murders in the workplace by unstable employees have become media-intensive events." An example of Type III violence occurred on August 20, 1986, when a part-time letter carrier, facing possible dismissal after a troubled work history, walked into the Edmond, Oklahoma, post office where he worked and shot 14 people to death before killing himself. In the previous three years, four postal employees were slain by present or former coworkers in separate shootings in South Carolina, Alabama, and Georgia (Critical Incident Response Group, 2001). Similar mass murders in the workplace by emotionally disturbed employees have drawn considerable media scrutiny and—because they initially came to attention with the post office crimes—the term *going postal* was introduced into the American lexicon. The Critical Incident Response Group (2001) has identified a number of additional examples, including four state lottery executives killed in Connecticut by a lottery accountant (1998), seven coworkers killed by a Xerox technician in Honolulu (1999), seven murdered by a software engineer at the Edgewater Technology Company in Massachusetts (2000), four killed by a 66-year-old former forklift driver in Chicago (2001), three killed by an insurance executive at Empire Blue Cross and Blue Shield in New York City (2002), three murdered by a plant worker at a manufacturing plant in Missouri (2003), and six killed by a plant worker at Lockheed–Martin aircraft plant in Mississippi (2003). The Chicago, New York, Mississippi, and Connecticut shooters killed themselves during the incident. The Honolulu and Massachusetts shooters went to trial, both raised the insanity defense, but both were convicted.

Type IV workplace violence represents a spillover of domestic violence or intimate partner violence into the workplace, and usually women are the victims. As noted earlier, homicide is the leading cause of workplace death for women, accounting for 41 percent of all female worker fatalities (Kelleher, 1997). A good example of Type IV workplace violence is provided by the University of Iowa Injury Prevention Research Center (2001, p. 11):

> Pamela Henry, an employee of Protocall, an answering service in San Antonio, had decided in the summer of 1997 to move out of the area. The abusive behavior of her ex-boyfriend, Charles Lee White, had spilled over from her home to her workplace, where he appeared one day in July and assaulted her. She obtained and then withdrew a protective order against White, citing her plans to leave the country. On October 17, 1997, White again appeared at Protocall. This time he opened fire with a rifle, killing Henry and another female employee before killing himself.

Perpetrators of Workplace Violence

According to the FBI (Southerland *et al.*, 1997), the workplace homicide offender whose motivation is not robbery is often a disgruntled employee (Type III) who believes the job is (or was) his life, is a loner, has few friends, and lacks a support system. The target of the attack may be a person or persons (usually innocent) working within a building or structure or for an organization that symbolizes the authority (Douglas *et al.*, 1992). However, it should be emphasized that there is no precise "profile" or litmus test that will provide clear signs that an employee will become violent. Rather, it is important for employees and employers to remain alert to unstable or problematic behavior that, in combination with threatening behavior, could result in violence (see **Table 5**).

A vast majority of Type III victims are killed (often randomly) by disgruntled employees who were fired or felt mistreated by the company or agency. It seems that a particular autocratic work environment, such as found in large, impersonal bureaucratic organizations, can be a problem. However, as the examples provided by the Critical Incident Response Group (2001) indicate, no workplace seems immune. As we discussed previously, when an employee feels frustrated and angry, he or she may be more likely to strike out, and this could occur even in a benevolent work environment.

Similar to mass murderers in general, offenders who commit authority homicide—in which a figure in authority, such as a supervisor, is killed—tend to be white males who have few social supports, are socially isolated, and who blame others (externalize) for their problems and misfortune. They are often seriously depressed. Very often, the offender expects to die at the scene, either at his own hands or by the police. Authority offenders also tend to be preoccupied with weapons, accumulating a number of them over a period of time with eventual revenge or "occupational martyrdom" in mind. The weapons are often of maximum lethality, such as automatic assault weapons (e.g., AK-47) (Douglas *et al.*, 1992). In most instances, the offender is middle-aged (over 30 and under 60) (Kelleher, 1997). There is also evidence that workplace offenders tend to have a history of violent behavior, alcohol or drug abuse, and will vocalize, or otherwise act out, their violent intentions prior to the authority homicide (Kelleher, 1997).

TABLE 5   Identifying Problematic Behaviors in Coworkers Which Might Lead to Violence

- Increasing belligerence
- Ominous specific threats
- Hypersensitivity to criticism
- Recent acquisition/fascination with weapons
- Apparent obsession with a supervisor or coworker or employee grievance
- Preoccupation with violent themes
- Interest in recently publicized violent events
- Outbursts of anger
- Extreme disorganization
- Noticeable changes in behavior
- Homicidal/suicidal comments or threats

Source: Critical Incident Response Group (2001), pp. 21–22.

Summary and Conclusions

In this chapter, we have taken a closer look at types of homicides that are relatively rare but have significant impact on large numbers of victims, both directly and indirectly. Multiple murders can be divided into three main categories: serial, spree, and mass killings, with most of the latter divided into classic and family mass murders. We focused on the classic form here.

The crimes that are covered here are often investigated by police with the help of criminal profilers or investigative psychologists, terms that are often used interchangeably. Investigative psychology is actually a broader term referring to the application of psychological research and principles to the investigation of criminal behavior. It typically includes crime scene investigative methods, such as reviewing features of the modus operandi, the personation or signature, and staging. Criminal profiling focuses more on the offender, identifying personality traits, behavioral patterns, demographic features, and sometimes geographical habits.

Criminal profiling is a strategy widely used in law enforcement, particularly for multiple murders or sex crimes. In serial murders, for example, profiling is helpful particularly if the offender demonstrates some psychopathology, such as a specific method of torture. However, it may also be very useful for nonviolent crimes, such as burglaries or arsons. Profiling is a very complex enterprise, though, and unfortunately it is often based on hunches or anecdotal information. However, with increasingly larger data bases made available to professional profilers, along with scientifically rigorous methods applied to the techniques they use, there is hope that the enterprise will gain validity. Rarely does a profile provide the specific identity of an offender, but it is not intended to. As Douglas *et al.* (1986) noted, profiling tries to narrow the field to a manageable number of suspects.

The form of multiple murder that most terrorizes a community is the serial killing, particularly because it may appear that anyone can be a potential victim. Serial killers generally choose their victims for their specific characteristics, however. For example, victims may be women in their twenties, transients, preadolescent and adolescent boys, prostitutes, or, in the case of the rare female serial killers, husbands, suitors, or individuals dependent on them for care. Research indicates that the great majority of serial killers are males; however, prior assumptions that they were invariably white males may be unwarranted. Serial killers are rarely juveniles.

Attempts have been made to place serial murderers into typologies, the most useful being the four-category typology of Holmes and DeBurger (1988), who have identified the visionary, mission-oriented, hedonistic, and power/control-oriented murderers. We discussed features of each of these groups. It is important to emphasize, though, that very few well-designed and empirically-based studies of serial murders have been conducted. Virtually all available information is based on anecdotal reports, interviews, and case studies with a small number of subjects.

Mass murderers have received even less research attention. In its classic form, one or more individuals enter a scene and open fire on a group of people, such as in a restaurant, a place of worship, or a place of work. This form of mass murder is usually carefully planned, and the victims are often symbols of the murderer's discontent (e.g., the workplace or a group of women). Alternately, the group of victims includes one or more individuals whom the killer hates or blames for his misfortunes. Mass murderers are typically socially isolated and withdrawn and have inadequate interpersonal and social skills.

We discussed unique crimes that have the potential of becoming mass murders: product tampering and school and workplace violence. Although serious product tampering is rare, when it does occur, it strikes terror in consumers because the lethal product may be used by many people before it is discovered. Cyanide has been the weapon of choice because of its potency and availability. Offenders usually seek financial gain, revenge, or want to damage a competing business.

School violence is a widespread problem in the educational system, although it rarely ends in death. In the 1990s, however, an inordinate number of school shootings were reported, the most noteworthy being the Columbine incident in Littleton, Colorado, in 1999. Investigations of school shootings consistently find that peer rejection and social rejection in general were factors contributing to the eruption of violence. Cruelty to animals appeared in the background of at least half of the shooters, and fascination with guns and other weaponry was almost always present. Virtually all had communicated their intentions to other students, sometimes in very specific terms.

Recent data indicate some decline in violent incidents in schools, but we must view these statistics cautiously because school districts are often motivated to underreport them. On the other hand, the percentage of students and teachers threatened or injured with weapons neither increased nor decreased. Bullying, though, continues to be a troubling issue. Although children are far more likely to be victimized in their homes or away from school than in the school itself, any amount of violence or threats of violence is unacceptable.

The chapter ends with coverage of workplace violence, another phenomenon that may or may not end in mass murder. By all indications, however, both assaults and deaths due to assaults or other violent acts are increasing. Nevertheless, a large majority of workplace violence—including homicide—is caused by individuals coming into the workplace from the outside, not by workers themselves. Offenders are divided into four categories: those having no connection to the workplace, those who have received some service provided by the organization, those who currently or formerly worked there, and those who have some relationship with one or more employees. Again, the vast majority of violence is perpetrated by the first category, though most psychological research has focused on the third type, the disgruntled employee who kills supervisors and/or fellow workers. These individuals are not only angry but also usually socially isolated and seriously depressed. Typically, they expect or plan to die at the scene.

Key Concepts

Authority homicide
Autoeroticism
Classic mass murder
Confirmation bias
Criminal profiling
Disorganized crime scene
Equivocal death analysis
Reconstructive psychological evaluation
Family mass murder

Geographical profiling
Investigative psychology
Mass murder
Mixed crime scene
Organized crime scene
Personation
Product-tampering homicide
Psychological autopsy
Psychological profiling
Racial or ethnic profiling

Serial murder
Signature
Spree murder
Staging
Undoing
Victimological perspective
Workplace aggression
Workplace violence

Review Questions

1. Briefly describe the difference between an organized and disorganized crime scene. Discuss the profile characteristics of each.
2. Identify and discuss the motives of the four types of serial murders according to Holmes and DeBurger. What information about serial killers is provided by Fox and Levin?
3. Define geographical profiling, and identify in what ways it is useful to law enforcement.
4. Why is the victimology perspective important in understanding serial murder?
5. Define staging, and give examples of when it is most likely to occur.
6. Define investigative psychology.
7. Define racial profiling, and identify the situations it is most likely to occur.
8. List and briefly define each of the four categories of workplace violence.
9. What are the psychological characteristics of mass murderers, according to the available research?
10. According to the available research, what characteristics are school shooters most likely to have in common?

10

Sexual Assault

Sexual Assault

CHAPTER OBJECTIVES

- Define rape and its many legal complexities.
- Examine the psychological effects of rape on victims.
- Briefly review legislation to deter sex offending.
- Describe in detail the Massachusetts Treatment Center's classification system of rapists to highlight the heterogeneity of rape offenders.
- Describe the Groth typology of rape offenders.
- Identify attitudes toward rape and the extent of rape myths in society.
- Evaluate the effects of pornography on sex offending.

Sexual behavior in many societies is a subject fraught with moral codes, taboos, norm expectations, religious injunctions, myths, and unscientific conclusions. In the United States, the daring venture of Albert Kinsey and his colleagues in publishing the scientific evidence they had gathered at the Institute for Sexual Research dispelled numerous myths and corrected fallacies about sex. Many still linger, however, especially with reference to the sex offender, for whom society has little tolerance. Moreover, society often does not distinguish between types of sex offenses. "Degenerates" who expose themselves to passersby or watch unsuspecting women undressing are as likely to be feared or to attract disgust and anger as are rapists and child molesters. Often, the community clamors for the strict and speedy prosecution of the offender, who is considered a deranged or evil person driven by some inner sinister force, and from whom citizens must be protected.

Sexual offenders are frequently viewed as a homogeneous class of individuals. Research shows, however, that they vary widely in the frequency and type of sexual activity they engage in, and they differ in personal attributes such as age, background, personality, race, religion, beliefs, attitudes, and interpersonal skills (Knight, Rosenberg, & Schneider, 1985). *There is no single profile that encompasses a majority of sex offenders.* The features of their crimes also differ markedly among offenders, including time and place, the gender and age of the victim, the degree of planning the offense, and the amount of violence used or intended (Knight *et al.*, 1985). In addition, sex offenders often commit a variety of crime beyond sexual offenses, although this is more likely to be the case with rapists than with child molesters (Harris, Mazerolle, & Knight, 2009). Research also indicates that sexual reoffending by sex offenders is not as prevalent as previously assumed. In fact, there is considerable evidence to show that adult sexual offenders are more likely to be convicted for nonsexual offenses than they are for sexual offenses, both before and after a conviction for a sexual offense (Smallbone & Wortley, 2004).

WHO OFFENDS?

Surprisingly, adolescent males commit 20–30 percent of all rapes and 30–50 percent of all child molestations (Becker & Johnson, 2001). What is also surprising is that 70 percent of these adolescent sex offenders come from two-parent homes, most attend school and achieve average grades, and very few suffer from major mental disorders (Becker & Johnson, 2001). Researchers also have begun to focus on sexual offending by girls, a subject that until recently was virtually ignored (Becker & Johnson, 2001). There is also considerable evidence that prepubescent children—both boys and girls—may commit sexual offenses at a rate much higher than commonly supposed. Several studies have reported sexual aggression in children as young as 3 or 4 years of age (Araji, 1997), although their aggressive actions do not qualify as crimes because children at these ages cannot form the necessary criminal intent. In addition, a surprisingly large number of preadolescent girls are reported to be sexually aggressive toward other children, and these girls often engage in behaviors that are just as aggressive as boys' behaviors (Araji, 1997). Victims of preadolescent offenders are generally very young (averaging between ages 4 and 7), most often are female (when the offender is a male), and typically are siblings, friends, or acquaintances (Righthand & Welch, 2001).

The causes of sexual offending are neither simple nor straightforward. As the knowledge from systematic study accumulates, it is clear that this behavior is influenced by multiple, interactive factors. Past learning experiences, cognitive expectations and beliefs, conditioning, environmental stimuli, and reinforcement contingencies (both rewards and punishments) are all involved. In this chapter, we review the major research findings on potential causal factors involved in rape, particularly rape of adults.

Some studies (e.g., Revitch & Schlesinger, 1988) reveal that many sex offenders are not prone to violence or physical cruelty, but rather are timid, shy, and socially inhibited. While this may be correct for a large segment of pedophiles—those who offend against children—it is not for rapists, whose attacks often have strong aggressive features in addition to the violence that defines the act itself. That is, by definition, rape is an aggressive act. The sexual aggression of rapists can be divided into at least two major categories: instrumental and expressive. **Instrumental sexual aggression** is when the sexual offender uses just enough coercion to gain compliance from his victim. In **expressive sexual aggression**, the offender's primary aim is to harm the victim physically as well as psychologically. In some cases, the expressive aggression is "eroticized" in that the offender becomes sexually aroused in the presence of physical or psychological brutality.

Regardless of the sex offender's characteristics, motivations, and method of attack or coercion, the social and psychological costs to victims and their families are immeasurable and often devastating. A survey of 3,132 households in the Los Angeles Epidemiologic Catchment Area

(ECA) study illustrates this very well. Researchers found that over 13 percent of the individuals interviewed had been victims of sexual assault at least once in their lifetimes (Burnam *et al.*, 1988; Siegel, Sorenson, Golding, Burnam, & Stein, 1987; Sorenson, Stein, Siegel, Golding, & Burnam, 1987). Two-thirds of the sexually assaulted subjects reported two or more assaults. Moreover, lifetime sexual assault was more frequently reported by women (16.7%) than men (9.4%). In a sobering finding, 13 percent of the victims were first assaulted between the ages of 6 and 10, 19 percent between 11 and 15, 34 percent between 16 and 20, and 15 percent between 21 and 25. The experience of being sexually assaulted was associated with substantially higher risks for later onset of serious, self-destructive depression, substance abuse, numerous fears and inhibiting anxieties, and a variety of major interpersonal problems. Overall, the ECA project found that both male and female victims of sexual assault are two to four times more likely than nonvictims to develop serious psychological problems.

LEGISLATION TO DETER SEX OFFENDERS

Before proceeding into the chapter, it is important to understand that several pieces of landmark legislation have been enacted during the past decade that strongly influence how the federal and state governments view sex offenders. National data suggest that there are approximately 234,000 sex offenders under the care, custody, or control of correction agencies on any given day (Chaiken, 1998b). We caution, though, that the term *sex offender* ranges from rapists to exhibitionists. Although not all sex offenders are violent, in recent years, highly publicized, brutally violent attacks were perpetrated by convicted-but-released sex offenders on young, vulnerable victims. These incidents had an enormous influence on state and federal legislation designed to prevent similar offenses. Much of the recent legislation on sex offenders is derived from the comprehensive Violent Crime Control and Law Enforcement Act of 1994, legislation that formed the basis for the U.S. Department of Justice's strategy for dealing with violent offenders. For our purposes here, we will briefly describe three laws that are most relevant to the topics in this chapter.

During the past two decades, the U.S. Congress passed a number of laws that collectively require states to strengthen the procedures they use to keep track of sex offenders or risk the loss of federal funding. In addition, virtually all states have passed laws consistent with the federal law and sometimes more restrictive or punitive toward sex offenders. The federal and state laws also require sex offenders to register and keep law enforcement aware of their whereabouts or face the risk of federal prosecution. Some also provide for notification to schools, day-care centers, social service agencies, and in some cases the general community, if a sex offender is living in the neighborhood. In some jurisdictions, convicted sex offenders are prohibited from residing in certain districts or obtaining employment in occupations where they would come into frequent contact with children. For illustrative purposes, we discuss some of these laws below.

The Jacob Wetterling Crimes Against Children and Sexually Violent Offender Registration Act, a federal law enacted in 1994, encourages states to require convicted child molesters and sexually violent offenders to notify law enforcement of their whereabouts for 10 years after they are released from prison, parole, or community supervision. The required notification time may be longer if the offender is considered a "sexually violent predator," or one whose crimes were especially heinous. As we note shortly, a later law requires registration and updating of one's whereabouts for even longer periods. The act encourages states to adopt registration systems for convicted child molesters and other persons convicted of sexually violent crimes. The act was named in honor of 11-year-old Jacob Wetterling of St. Joseph, Minnesota, who was abducted at gunpoint by a masked man in 1989. The young boy was never found.

The second type of legislation, known as Megan's Law, requires states to release registration information to the public *when it is necessary for public safety,* a requirement often referred to as "mandatory community notification." While the Wetterling Act does not require that communities be notified of the release of sex offenders, Megan's Law specifies that local communities be so notified, although the extent of notification varies according to the offender's level of dangerousness. For example, in the case of Level 3 offenders, officials must notify the community at large; in the case of Level 2 offenders, only certain agencies (e.g., schools and day-care centers) must be notified; in the case of Level 1 offenders, a passive notification process is in effect. That is, members of the community are told if they ask. Some state versions of Megan's Law also require that persons found not guilty by reason of insanity who would otherwise qualify as convicted sex offenders also must register. Megan's Law was named after seven-year-old Megan Kanka of Hamilton Square, New Jersey, who in 1994 was assaulted, raped, and murdered by a twice-convicted pedophile living across the street.

The Pam Lychner Sexual Offender Tracking and Identification Act, enacted in 1996, amended the Violent Crime Control and Law Enforcement Act of 1994 to require the FBI to establish a national offender database and to handle sex offender registration and notification in states unable to maintain "minimally sufficient" programs on their own. Basically, the Lychner Act establishes more stringent registration requirements for sex offenders living within the community. Under the act, offenders considered the most dangerous to public safety will be required to register for life wherever they go. The Lychner Act was named for a Houston real estate agent. A twice-convicted felon, waiting for her, brutally assaulted Lychner when she went to show a vacant house. Her life was saved when her husband arrived on the scene and interrupted the attack. Tragically, Pam Lychner and her two daughters were later killed in the explosion of TWA Flight 800 off the coast of Long Island, New York, in July 1996.

Although Congress determined that states must have registration and notification laws on the books if they wished to continue to receive federal funds, it was left to the states to determine precisely how these laws would be crafted. Most state laws are modeled on the above federal statutes, with some modifications. The Adam Walsh Act that will be discussed below, however, also calls for a more unified method of registering sex offenders, thereby creating a national data basis for use by law enforcement authorities. Furthermore, information about sex offenders has now become so widely available that it is commonly on the Internet. In some communities, cable stations carry pictures of offenders along with some details of their crimes, including the ages of their victims.

In 2006, what is perhaps the most comprehensive piece of legislation related to sex offenders, the Adam Walsh Child Protection and Safety Act 9 (AWA), was signed into law. The Act is named after the eight-year-old boy who was abducted from a shopping mall in 1981 and was found murdered 16 days later. His father, John Walsh, later founded the National Center for Missing and Exploited Children and became host of the long-running Fox network show, *America's Most Wanted.* The AWA preserves the three-tier offender categorization but requires that Tier 3, the most serious offenders, update their whereabouts every three months for the rest of their lives. Tier 2 offenders must update every six months for 25 years, and Tier 1 every 12 months for 15 years. Failure to register and to update is a federal felony. Among other provisions, the AWA also sets up a national database and registry system for consistent reporting by states and increases the penalties for sex trafficking of children and engaging children in child prostitution. Since its passage, portions of the law—particularly the required provisions relating to lower tier offenders—have been challenged, and many critics believe it overbroad. At this point, however, at least one federal appeals court (the 11th circuit) has upheld its registration provisions. Even before the passage of the AWA, however, the U.S. Supreme Court in 2002 upheld provisions of the registration laws in two states, Alaska and Connecticut, making it highly likely that registration and community notification will continue far into the foreseeable future. Nevertheless, many critics of registration laws, including social science researchers, fear that they are unwise public policy, particularly as they relate to lower level sex offenders (Burchfield & Mingus, 2008; Tewksbury, 2005).

As part of the Violent Crime Control and Law Enforcement Act of 1994, Congress also passed the Violence against Women Act (VAWA), which takes a comprehensive approach to domestic violence and sexual assault through a broad array of legal reforms. This law launched the first major federal effort to address violence against women. One of the many things the VAWA does is to extend the rape shield law to protect victims from abusive inquiries regarding their private sexual conduct. Two additional federal initiatives expanded the scope of the Violent Crime Control and Law Enforcement Act of 1994. One of the initiatives makes it illegal for a U.S. citizen or permanent resident to travel in interstate or foreign commerce with the intent to engage in sexual acts with a minor that are prohibited under federal law in the United States. This law is often referred to as the "child sex tourism" offense. The second initiative, enacted in 1996, is known as the Child Pornography Prevention Act. The act stipulates that it is illegal to purchase or download any computer-generated depiction of a child engaged in sexually explicit conduct. In April 2002, the U.S. Supreme Court lifted the ban on virtual child pornography, ruling that computer generated images were not photographs of real children and therefore were protected by the 1st Amendment.

Shortly, thereafter, however, Congress passed the Exploitation of Children Today (PROTECT) Act of 2003, a modification of the original law. The revised statute states that

> It is a crime to possess, manufacture or distribute pornography containing visual depictions of (a) a real child engaging in sexual acts, or (b) a digital image, computer image, or computer generated image that is, or is indistinguishable from, that of a minor engaged in sexually explicit conduct (18 U.S. Code § 2256(8) (B) (as amended).

A number of challenges to various provisions of the Protect Act, as it is called, have been filed, but at the very least, the courts have not been sympathetic to defendants when there is proof that actual children have been exploited in pornographic representations. According to the U.S. Department of Justice, the number of commercially sexually exploited children in the United States is estimated to be between 100,000 and 3 million, including children forced into prostitution, pornography, and those trafficked into the country for sexual slavery (Curtis, Terr, Dank, Dombrowski, & Khan, 2008). In addition, the increased use of the Internet has accompanied the dramatic rise of cybercrime involving the sexual exploitation of children. We will return to this very important topic.

One other form of legislation that relates to sexual offenders are the so-called "sexual predator laws" or "sexually violent predator laws." This type of legislature allows for the civil commitment of sex offenders after they have served their prison sentence, if they are considered both mentally ill and dangerous. Many of these laws have been challenged as so broad that they capture sexual offenders who rightly should be released, perhaps with community supervision. We will discuss the controversy about these laws at the end of the chapter.

RAPE: DEFINITIONS AND STATISTICS

Definitions of rape can vary from state to state; in many states, the term *sexual assault* has replaced *rape* in the criminal statutes. About half of the 50 states do not use the word *rape* in their penal code involving sexual assault or sex offenses (Langan, Schmitt, & Durose, 2003). One state, for example, uses the term *criminal sexual conduct* to refer to all types of sex crimes. *Rape* is the term used by the FBI in the gathering of crime reporting and arrest statistics for Part I crimes.

According to the U.S. Department of Justice, rape is "unlawful sexual intercourse with a female, by force or without legal or factual consent" (U.S. Department of Justice, 1988, p. 2). The UCR defines rape somewhat differently, distinguishing forcible from statutory rape or rape by fraud. **Forcible rape** is "the carnal knowledge of a female forcibly and against her will" (Federal Bureau of Investigation, 2005b, p. 27). It includes assaults and attempts to commit rape by force or threat of force. **Statutory rape** without force and other sex offenses are excluded. Statutory rape is the carnal knowledge of a girl under the age of consent, the age at which individuals are considered competent to give consent to sexual behavior. It pertains exclusively to consensual intercourse, as opposed to other types of sexual contact (Langan *et al.*, 2003). The limitation of the previous definitions is that they are restricted to female victims. In other words, *male* rape victims are not included in the UCR tabulations. Likewise, most of the research on this crime relates to women or girls as victims; consequently, most of the material in this chapter does the same. Men and boys are also victims of rape. Therefore, though the statistics are different, the psychological effects on rape survivors are significant whether they are female or male.

The critical factor for statutory rape is the age of the victim, an arbitrary legal cutoff point below which a girl is believed not to have the maturity to consent to intercourse or understand the consequences. Age limits vary from state to state, but most set the limit at 16 or 18. Also, it is generally understood that an age span must exist between the two individuals, typically two years. Thus, if an adult male engages in sexual relations with a minor female, he may be convicted of statutory rape, even if he argues that she "consented." The same would be true of a female teacher who engages in sexual relations with her 15-year-old male student. It should be mentioned that there are a variety of state laws that define the various circumstances in which intercourse between consenting individuals is considered illegal beside statutory rape. For example, when one of the consenting individuals is married, the illegal sexual activity may be criminalized as adultery. Some states have incest laws that criminalize sexual relations between blood relatives. **Rape by fraud** is having sexual relations with a consenting adult female under fraudulent conditions. Among the most frequently cited examples is that of the psychotherapist who has sexual intercourse with a patient under the guise of offering treatment. Another rape category that is beginning to receive some attention is **marital rape.** During the past four decades, there have been dramatic changes in marital rape laws in the United States. In 1970, marital rape was legal in all 50 states, but by 1993, all 50 states had passed laws criminalizing it (Martin, Taft, & Resick, 2007). It is estimated that about 10–14 percent of married women have experienced marital rape (Martin *et al.*, 2007).

Many in the general population (including the victims themselves) do not define sexual attacks as rape unless the assailant is a stranger. Thus, if the victim is sexually assaulted by a husband or a boyfriend, she may not report the incident. Criminal justice officials, as well as the general public, often feel that marital or date rapes are unimportant because they are believed to happen so rarely, compared with stranger rape, or to be less psychologically traumatic to the victim. Some criminal prosecutors, for example, admit they are reluctant to prosecute marital or date rape cases because of concerns that juries will not believe that a woman could be raped by a husband or male friend (Kilpatrick, Best, Saunders, & Veronen, 1988). However, in a survey of the general population conducted by Kilpatrick and colleagues (1988), subjects who had been raped identified their husbands as assailants in 24 percent of the cases and male friends in 17 percent of the cases. These data suggest that over 40 percent of the rapes were committed by husbands or dates, a significant and frequently overlooked statistic in the tabulation of rape. A growing recognition of sexual assault by spouses and acquaintances has led many scholars to prefer the term *intimate partner violence*, which includes nonsexual assault as well as sexual assault.

Date or Acquaintance Rape

Date rapes (sometimes called acquaintance rapes) may be far more common than generally realized, perhaps as high as 60 percent of all rapes. Some recent data suggest that up to one-third of young adults between the ages of 16 and 24 have reported being involved in at least one abusive dating incident (Lingren, 2001). **Date rape,** a term coined in 1984, refers specifically to a sexual assault that occurs within the context of a dating relationship. In a survey conducted by Frintner and Rubinson (1993) of 925 college women, over one-fourth of the respondents had experienced sexual assault or attempted sexual assault. Nearly 83 percent of the college women who had been sexually assaulted said the attacker had been someone they knew and that most of these incidents had happened during their freshman year.

Dating patterns have changed dramatically in the twenty-first century. Many couples meet on the Internet, and both women and men initiate a first "date." Whereas males might feel less entitled to "payback" than before—when they paid expenses and provided transportation—other factors (e.g., alcohol, other drugs, sexual mores) can facilitate a rape. Date rapes also occur in the context of a casual encounter at a party or a bar. Women who are raped by acquaintances still often blame themselves for the attack or are blamed by others for arousing the date or placing themselves in vulnerable situations. In addition, sexual assault by a date or acquaintance may be more traumatizing than assault by a stranger because of the implicit trust involved.

One traumatizing aspect of date rape relates to a phenomenon pointed out by Karmen (1996), who identifies a common distinction in society between a "real rape" and a date rape. In real rapes, the presumption is that the woman is clearly assaulted if she is ambushed as an unsuspecting victim by a blitz attack by a complete stranger. It is even more convincing if the attacker is armed, leaps out of the darkness, enters her home uninvited, or imposes serious physical injury, such as knife wounds. A date rape, on the other hand, is often not considered a real rape since it occurred on an arranged date with someone she knew, agreed to go out with, or met in a social situation. Thus, the victim is less likely to be believed and more likely to be blamed (Ullman, 1999). As Ullman (2007, p. 412) observes, "These negative reactions are harmful to women's psychological functioning and may lead to or reinforce their own self-blame for being raped."

Incidence and Prevalence of Rape

From all indications, the United States has the highest incidence of rape in the world. This refers only to reported data, however. We know, for example, that in many part of the globe, violence—including violence against women—is underplayed and underreported. Saudi Arabia, Afghanistan, Somalia, Chile, and India are only some countries where sexual abuse of women and girls may be rampant (UNFPA, 2009). On the other hand, sexual assault is widely underreported in the United States as well. In the United States, an estimated 71,857 forcible rapes were reported to law enforcement agencies nationwide in 2004 (Federal Bureau of Investigation, 2008), a figure that represents 5 percent of the total violent crime reported. As mentioned in the previous section, the UCR's definition recognizes only women and girls as victims of rape. Available data suggest that about 10 percent of the rapes in this country do not conform to the UCR definition (Chaiken, 1998a). Specifically, it is estimated that in about 9 percent of the reported rapes, the victim was male. And in another 1 percent, both the offender and the victim were female. The sexual abuse scandal that shook the Catholic Church in the 1990s illustrates the difficulty in obtaining valid statistics on this crime (Terry, 2008). Furthermore, the reality of prison rape is seldom considered in official statistics.

Of course, we must recognize that the actual rape rate is greatly underestimated, partly because of some of the problems listed in the previous section, and partly because of the ordeal victims must go through just to report the incident. Victimization studies offer a revealing contrast to the police data. The National Crime Victimization Survey (NCVS) finds that about two-thirds of the rape and sexual assaults committed in the United States go unreported (Ringel, 1997). A more recent study based on data collected in the National Violence Against Women Survey (NVAWS) estimates that the number of attempted or completed rapes is four times greater than even the NCVS estimates (Tjaden & Thoennes, 2006).

Russell (1983) selected at random and interviewed 930 women living in the San Francisco area. She learned that 175 of them (19%) reported at least one completed extramarital rape, and 284 (13%) reported at least one attempted extramarital rape. Fifty percent of those reporting these incidents said they had been raped or attacked more than once, and only 8 percent said they had reported any rape incident to law enforcement authorities. An early study by Hindelang and his associates (Hindelang, Dunn, Sutton, & Aumick, 1976), designed to gather victimization rates on randomly selected households, found that only about one out of every four forcible or attempted rapes were reported to law enforcement agencies. Another early study of hitchhike rape estimated that over two-thirds went unreported (Nelson & Amir, 1975). Based on a national sample of college students from 32 U.S. colleges and universities, Koss and her colleagues (Koss, Gidycz, & Wisniewski, 1987) discovered that about 28 percent of the college women had been victims of rape or attempted rape (as defined by the UCR). More startling, however, was the finding that virtually none of the incidents were reported to the police and thus were not recorded in official crime statistics. Based on their data, Koss and her colleagues estimated that the victimization rate for women was 3,800 per 100,000, a rate drastically different from the official rates of 65–75 per 100,000.

Additional victimization data indicate that there is approximately a one in six chance that a woman will be raped at some time during her lifetime (Tjaden & Thoennes, 2006). If we include *attempted* rape, the odds for women may be as high as three to one (Russell & Howell, 1983). Native American women report significantly higher rates of rape victimization over their lifetimes than women from all other racial and ethnic background (Tjaden & Thoennes, 2006). As mentioned previously, a surprising number of women are sexually victimized while on a date. Approximately 22 percent of college women surveyed indicated they had been subjected to a forced sexual encounter (e.g., fondling, oral sex, or intercourse) by a date at some point in their lives (Dull & Giacopassi, 1987; Yegidis, 1986). Rapaport and Burkhart (1984) found that 15 percent of a sample of college men acknowledged that they had obtained sexual intercourse against their dates' will. Koss *et al.* (1987) report that about 8 percent of their sample of nearly three 3,000 college men admitted raping or attempting to rape their dates.

It is estimated that approximately 2.8 million men in the United States have forcibly raped at some point in their lives (Tjaden & Thoennes, 2006). During their lifetimes, about one out of 35 males have been forcibly raped at some point. Men are most often raped by an acquaintance.

IMPACT ON VICTIMS

It is often said that rape victims are victimized twice, once by the perpetrator and again by the criminal justice system during the investigation of the crime and, if a suspect is arrested, during the prosecution phase. Victims also may be victimized by media scrutiny and by a public that may question whether the incident happened, or denigrate the victims and attribute some blame to them. Many women who have been raped prefer the term *survivor* to victim because of its more positive connotation. To be a rape survivor suggests that one is in control and that the rapist, the criminal justice system, and the public have not succeeded at totally demolishing one's self-concept.

Psychological Effects on Victims

The psychological effects on the rape victim, both during and after the assault, are often severe and incalculable. As noted, she is frequently victimized at least twice, by the assailant and by the criminal justice process. Upon reporting the assault, she is expected to recall and describe personally stressful and humiliating events in vivid detail for law enforcement personnel who are often men. Today, increasingly more police departments take steps to ease the victim's ordeal. These include having victim advocates present, having women officers available, and/or providing rape sensitivity training for both male and female officers. In addition to the interview with representatives of law enforcement, the victim is required to undergo a medical examination to establish physical evidence of penetration and use of physical force.

If the victim is able to withstand these stressful conditions, which are sometimes exacerbated by negative reactions from parents, husband, partner, family members, friends, and even by threats from the assailant, she must then prepare for the courtroom, where her privacy is invaded and her credibility may be attacked. Rape trials are usually covered extensively by the press, although most news organizations do not reveal the victim's name or photograph her. Her reputation, however, is especially vulnerable. Ninety-two percent of the prosecutors surveyed by Chappell (1977b) asserted that victim credibility was one of the most important elements in convincing juries to convict for forcible rape. Therefore, the defense has often concentrated on the victim's prior sexual history to destroy her credibility. The strategy of disparaging the victim in this way came under attack in the 1970s and 1980s, and many states revised their evidentiary rules in an attempt to limit the use of a victim's sexual history. Virtually all states have enacted "rape shield" laws that restrict, to varying degrees, the admissibility of the victim's sexual history into the courtroom (Kilpatrick, Whalley, & Edmunds, 2000). In addition, victim assistants—whose function it is to offer support, give direct services, and advocate for victims—have been instrumental in easing the victim's burden. In tight economic times, however, these services are often severely limited. Furthermore, rape shield laws do not always provide the protection for which they were designed (Ross & Bachar, 2002); they vary from state to state (Kinports, 2002). Consequently, many victims are surprised and dismayed when they are asked questions about their social and sexual histories during adjudication, something they believed would not happen (Ross & Bachar, 2002).

Although criminal justice agencies are beginning to be more sensitive to the stressful ordeal a victim must go through, the costs are still high. If the woman reports the sexual assault to the police, it means she must devote many hours to the process of the investigation and the subsequent court proceedings (Kilpatrick *et al.*, 2002; Ross & Bachar, 2002). She must bear the costs of missed days of work, child care, and medical expenses for the physical and psychological trauma, and transportation. She may feel a need to change lifestyles, move, and install expensive security systems and locks. Sleeplessness, anxiety, and depression must also be factored into the cost equation. We discuss these issues in more detail shortly.

Situational and Victimization Characteristics

If one looks only at victimization data, rape appears to be a crime primarily committed against youth. The National Women's Study (Tjaden & Thoennes, 1998b) reported the following statistical data concerning the age of victims:

- 29 percent of all forcible rapes occurred when the victim was less than 11 years old.
- 32 percent occurred when the victim was between the ages of 11 and 17.
- 22 percent occurred between the ages of 18 and 24.
- 7 percent occurred between the ages of 25 and 29.
- 6 percent occurred when the victim was older than 29 years old.

With reference to situational characteristics, alcohol and other disinhibiting substances play a strong role; drug use is common in rapists. The substance abuse is apparent both in the personal history of the rapist and at the time of the offense. Anywhere between 42 percent and 90 percent of convicted rapists admit they were under the influence of a disinhibiting substance at the time of the sexual assault, and between 58 percent and 90 percent exhibit a history of substance abuse (Marques & Nelson, 1989; Pithers, Beal, Armstrong, & Petty, 1989).

Kilpatrick *et al.* (2000, p. 12) report cogent evidence that most of the rapists are intimate partners and not strangers. They list the following victimization information on adult women gathered from the National Women's Survey:

- 24.4 percent of the rapists were strangers.
- 21.9 percent were husbands or ex-husbands.
- 19.5 percent were boyfriends or ex-boyfriends.
- 9.8 percent were relatives.
- 14.6 percent were other nonrelatives, such as friends or neighbors.

Women's fears about being physically harmed in rape are not unfounded. While weapons, especially firearms and knives, are used in only about 25 percent of the reported assaults (U.S. Department of Justice, 1988), about one-fourth of all rape victims sustain injury serious enough to warrant medical attention or hospitalization. *Severe physical injury,* however, is relatively rare, with about 5 percent receiving serious, lasting injury (Williams & Holmes, 1981). Another 39 percent receive minor injuries, and 23 percent receive a variety of cuts and bruises (Williams & Holmes, 1981). Further study suggests that women receive more physical and psychological trauma from sexual assault by husbands than by strangers (Kilpatrick *et al.*, 1988). In addition, the psychological damage is apparently longer lasting and more damaging, resulting in serious depression, extensive fears, and problems of sexual adjustment.

Victim surveys also indicate that the most commonly used methods of force during date rapes are verbal persuasion, alcohol, or drugs. While weapons are rarely used, physical overpowering is commonly reported (Kanin, 1984). Furthermore, data suggest that date rapes occur most frequently in the male's apartment or room, with the next likely location being the female's apartment or room. Very few occur in a car or outside. About 7 percent of rape/sexual assault involved multiple offenders who were strangers to the victim (Greenfeld, 1997).

RAPE OFFENDER CHARACTERISTICS

What kind of a person rapes? How did he get that way? Why does he do it? Can the "rapist personality" be easily identified? Are rapists mentally disordered? In this section, we should keep in mind that many studies addressing these questions are based on information obtained from convicted offenders located in prisons, forensic evaluation clinics, or secure psychiatric facilities—a very biased sample, since less than 3 percent of reported rapes in the United States result in a conviction (Battelle Law and Justice Center Report, 1977).

Age

The most consistent demographic finding is that rapists tend to be young. According to UCR data for 2007, 43 percent of those *arrested* were under age 25, and 15 percent were actually under age 18 (Federal Bureau of Investigation, 2008). Five percent of the total arrests for forcible rape and 11 percent of the total arrests for other sex offenses were under age 15. The percentage of juvenile arrests for rape has largely been the same for years. The UCR data, however, represent an underestimation. As reported earlier, some studies indicate that at least 30 percent of the rapes in the United States are committed by juveniles (Cellini, 1995). In a survey of high school students, nearly half (48%) of the females reported experiencing sexual aggression, and one-third (34%) of the males admitted committing this type of offending (Maxwell, Robinson, & Post, 2003).

Offending History

Another consistent finding is that many men accused of and convicted of rape have been in perpetual conflict with society, long before the current rape offense. In a sample of 114 convicted rapists studied by Scully and Marolla (1984), 12 percent had a previous conviction for rape or attempted rape, 39 percent had previous convictions for burglary and robbery, 29 percent for kidnapping and abduction, 25 percent for sodomy, and 11 percent for first- or second-degree murder. Overall, 82 percent had a prior criminal record, but only 23 percent had been convicted of sexual offenses.

Juvenile sex offenders (JSO), who rape and sexually assault frequently, engage in a wide range of other criminal and antisocial but nonsexual behaviors. They tend to shoplift, steal, engage in firesetting, bully and intimidate, display cruelty to animals, and physically assault others. In one study, for example, more than half of violent juvenile sex offenders were abnormally cruel to animals, including their own pets (Tingle, Barnard, Robbins, Newman, & Hutchinson, 1986). In addition, JSOs who rape are more likely to commit the sexual offense along with a co-offender, commit a nonsexual offense in conjunction with the sexual assault, and have a previous arrest record (Hunter, Figueredo, Malamuth, & Becker, 2003). On the other hand, while many would fit the life-course persistent (LCP) offender category discussed, others apparently do not offend sexually into adulthood. As a result of this growing awareness, many researchers are seeking valid and reliable risk assessment measures for predicting which juveniles will and will not re-offend (Viljoen, Elkovitch, Scalora, & Ullman, 2009).

Demographics

Some recent demographic data can be found in a comprehensive study of sex offenders assessed at the Ohio Department of Rehabilitation and Correction (ODRC) (Black & Pettway, 2001). The ODRC data involved 437 sex offenders. The study found that many rapists (49%) were unemployed or had a history of seasonal or unstable employment. Interestingly, a greater proportion of child and teen molesters, compared with rapists, had stable employment prior to their arrest (% and 53%, respectively). Further, nearly two-thirds of the rapists had never been married, whereas a majority of the child molesters were married (66%).

In a follow-up study of 3,115 rapists released from prison, 1.3 percent of the rapists were arrested for a new sex crime within six months of release (Langan *et al.*, 2003). At the end of years after release, 5 percent of the rapists were rearrested for another sex crime (rape or sexual assault). Forty-one percent were arrested for another, nonsexual crime within three years release. Fifteen percent were rearrested for a violent crime (other than rape or sexual assault). Thus, rapists in this large sample had a low recidivism rate for *sexual* offenses but a very high rate for offenses *in general*.

Assumptions About Why Men Rape

Traditionally, the rapist has been considered by many clinicians the victim of "uncontrollable urges" (Edwards, 1983) or the recipient of a "disordered personality" (Scully & Marolla, 1984). As Scully and Marolla (1985) observe, the general public has traditionally attributed four fundamental causes for this behavior. They are (1) uncontrollable impulses or urges, (2) mental illness or disease, (3) momentary loss of control precipitated by unusual circumstances, and (4) victim instigation (see Table 1). Further, Scully and Marolla assert that each of these statements attribute the cause of the behavior to parameters outside of the rapist himself, and often to the victim. In other words, they believe that the cause of sexual deviations is beyond the offender's direct or immediate control. Empirical research has not supported these assumptions, however. After discussing each in brief, we outline what researchers and clinical experts have been finding.

Uncontrollable or irresistible impulse attribution refers to a psychological state wherein the normal restraints of self-control are substantially reduced or virtually eliminated by an

TABLE 1   The Four Fundamental Assumptions About Why Men Rape

Attribution	The Description
Irresistible impulse	The normal restraints of self-control and self-regulation are overwhelmed by an excessive sex drive.
Mental illness or disease	Sexual deviations are caused by mental disorders or disease.
Drug and alcohol	Offender loses control of his impulses when under the influence of certain substances.
Victim	Victim was seductive and at fault.

overwhelming sex drive. The major argument from this perspective is that high levels of sexual deprivation may cause a bubbling over of an innate, natural sex drive of such intensity that the individual loses control of his behavior and consequently can no longer help himself. Driven by this powerful, biological force, his only release is immediate sexual gratification. Symons (1979), for example, writes that men's sexual impulses are part of human nature and that men innately seek "no-cost, impersonal copulations." Presumably, if unable to obtain consensual sexual experiences, they resort to forcible rape. There is little sympathy for this perspective and, as noted above, its assumptions are not empirically supported.

Mental illness or disease attribution contends that rape—and most other sexual deviations—is symptomatic of some deep-seated sickness or mental aberration. According to this view, all sexual offenders are basically "sick" and in need of help. Inherent in this perspective is the conviction that sexually deviant behaviors are similar in causation and represent a single type of psychopathology, usually some form of character disorder (Lanyon, 1986). According to Lanyon (p. 176), this belief "tends to be the view held by the judicial system, by social service agencies, and by the general public." And as Scully and Marolla (1985) point out, "belief that rapists are or must be sick is amazingly persistent" (p. 298). Nevertheless, even if considered "sick," rapists are not excused for their offense.

An interesting development within this disease model perspective is the contention that sexual offending represents an addiction (e.g., Carnes, 1983), an approach highlighted over the last decade by the behavior and claims of some public figures in the entertainment and sports world. In a rather strange, life-imitates-art illustration, the actor David Duchovny portrays a sex addict in the television show "Californication" and was himself treated for sex addiction in 2008. Compulsive sexual behavior has been the theme of numerous literary works as well, but thus far, the American Psychiatric Association has resisted including it as a separate category in the DSM. The sexual-addiction approach to explaining sexual offending is persuasive and appealing to some, because sex offending has some obvious and compelling similarities to other forms of addiction, such as alcoholism, overeating, gambling, shoplifting, and drug abuse. Interestingly, the approach relies heavily on the same treatment strategies advocated by Alcoholics Anonymous (AA) and emphasizes the "twelve steps to recovery." Consequently, various self-help groups have appeared, such as Sex and Love Addicts Anonymous, Sexaholics Anonymous, Sexual Addicts Anonymous, and Sexual Abuse Anonymous. The basic text for Sex and Love Addicts Anonymous (Augustine Fellowship, 1986), for example, states that one's need for a close relationship with another "could be debased by addiction into a compulsive search for sex and romance, or obsessional entrapment in relationships characterized by personal neediness and hyperdependency—in patterns that could forever prevent really meeting the underlying need for authentic experience of self and other" (p. viii). Although these groups may be helpful to some individuals, their approaches should not be confused with Relapse Prevention (RP), a treatment regimen that—along with cognitive-based therapies—shows considerable promise in the reduction of sexual offending. We discuss this form of treatment near the end of this chapter.

A third popular belief, **drug attribution,** argues that one can momentarily lose control of one's urges in certain circumstances, such as through the use of drugs or alcohol. Alcohol, for example, is believed to remove social and moral constraints, leaving some individuals at the mercy of their sexual appetites. This desire simply becomes overwhelming, causing some men to attack the most convenient victim. In one study, two-thirds of the men who raped their dates attributed their assaults to excessive drinking (Kanin, 1984). They claimed the date rape was caused by their own inebriation together with a loss of judgment due to high levels of sexual excitement. One-fifth were convinced that there was no way the attack would have occurred had they been sober.

The fourth perspective, **victim attribution,** contends that the victim has, in some way, led the
[pene]trator into temptation. Rape, according to this view, is a sexual act that is promoted uncon-
[scious]ly by the female. "Nice girls don't get raped," or at least they don't "let it get out of hand."
[Hitch]hike rape, for example, is, according to this view, probably victim-precipitated rape. Because
[of the]ir unconscious desires, women unwittingly cooperate with the rapist by making themselves
[availab]le to him in various ways. In the Kanin (1984, p. 96) date rape study, two-thirds of the men
[said t]hat "although it was probably rape in the legal sense, the fault for the incident resided with the
[victim] because of her sexual conduct." According to these males, the sexual demeanor of their
[victim]s literally absolved them of guilt. Several major surveys conducted on a wide section of the
[Ameri]can population strongly suggest that many people continue to believe a victim is at least par-
[tly r]esponsible for her rape and that only certain "girls" get raped (Lottes, 1988). As we see shortly,
[howev]er, these attitudes are showing signs of change, particularly among younger respondents.

[Deni]ers and Admitters

[As not]ed earlier, empirical study has not supported the validity of these four fundamental
[assum]ptions; it does, however, support their persistence. In other words, many people continue to
[believe] that rape is caused by drugs, precipitated by the victim, or is the product of mental illness
[or the] offender's uncontrollable urges or addiction. These misconceptions are held by offenders as
[well as] others. Scully and Marolla (1984) interviewed 114 convicted rapists to obtain information
[about t]heir perceptions, motivations, and afterthoughts and found that most could be divided into
[two ma]jor groups, "admitters" and "deniers." **Admitters** essentially corroborated the story told by
[police] and victims. They are those sex offenders willing to take responsibility for this behavior.
[Denier]s' versions differed significantly from those of police and victims. The researchers identified
[adm]itters and 32 deniers. Apparently, the remainder could not be classified into either category.
[**D**]**eniers** justified their rape behavior primarily by making the victim blameworthy. Five
[themes] ran through these justifications: (1) women are seductresses, (2) women mean yes when
[they sa]y no, (3) most women eventually relax and really enjoy it, (4) nice girls don't get raped, and
[(5) the] act was a minor wrongdoing, since the victims were not physically hurt. Thirty-one
[percent] of the deniers said the victim was the aggressor; a seductress who lured them, unsuspect-
[ing, int]o sexual action. About 22 percent said the victim had not resisted enough or that her no
[rea]lly meant yes. As one offender put it, despite some struggle, "deep down inside I think she
[had it] as a fantasy come true." Most of the deniers justified their behavior by claiming not only
[that the] victim was willing, but also that she enjoyed herself, in some cases to an immense degree.
[Most o]f the deniers (69%) were also convinced that "nice girls don't get raped." Their victims,
[they sai]d, had dressed seductively, were hitchhiking, or were generally known to be "loose."
[T]he belief that bad things happen to bad people and good things happen to good people is
[called b]y psychologists the **just-world hypothesis** (Lerner, 1980). It is the simplistic belief that
[one get]s what one deserves and deserves what one gets. Just-worlders—people who are most apt
[to accep]t this hypothesis—believe that victims of misfortune or crime deserve their fate. Deniers
[felt th]at their victims should not have been in the bar alone, should not have been hitchhiking,
[or shou]ld have worn a bra. The deniers, in this sense, expressed many of the views that would be
[held] by just-worlders.

[R]eported Reasons for Sexual Assault

[The major]ity of the deniers said that their actions were not reprehensible since they believed they
[had not] physically harmed the victim. Many felt that although their behavior was not completely

proper, it should not have been considered a serious criminal offense, despite the fact that they had threatened their victims with lethal weapons.

Admitters, in contrast to deniers, regarded their behavior as morally wrong and as a serious, harmful attack on their victims. However, most of them tried to diminish their own culpability by asserting that they could not help themselves or were compelled by forces outside their control. Three themes ran through the admitters' justifications: (1) the use of alcohol and drugs, (2) emotional problems, and (3) a "nice guy" self-image. Over three-fourths said they had been under the influence of alcohol or drugs at the time of the attack and that the substance had influenced their judgment and behavior. They were convinced that the ingested substance had, in effect, reduced their awareness as well as their self-control. Normally, they said, they would not have engaged in such a disgusting act.

Forty percent of the admitters said they believed emotional problems were at the root of their rape behavior, and 33 percent specifically cited an unhappy, unstable childhood, or a marital-domestic situation. Furthermore, 80 percent of the admitters described an upsetting problem or anger-inducing event that occurred prior to the attack. Consistently, Scully and Marolla (1984) found that these men described themselves as being in a rage because of an incident involving a woman with whom they believed they were in love. By contrast, only about 20 percent of the deniers described such problems.

Most of the admitters described themselves as "nice guys," who under normal circumstances would never dream of doing such a violent thing to a woman. In other words, their actions during that violent episode did not represent their true selves. Many expressed regret and sorrow for their victim and apologized to the researchers.

CLASSIFICATION OF RAPE PATTERNS

Since such a wide variety of sexual offenders are involved in rape, some interesting attempts have been made to categorize rapists according to their behavioral patterns. Researchers at the Massachusetts (Bridgewater) Treatment Center (Cohen, Garafalo, Boucher, & Seghorn, 1971; Cohen, Seghorn, & Calmas, 1969; Knight & Prentky, 1987; Prentky & Knight, 1986) recognized that rape involves both sexual and aggressive features and tried to formulate a behavioral classification system that takes these elements into consideration.

Before we proceed, however, it is important to remind readers that classification systems are permeated with numerous problems and drawbacks. One obvious problem is that individuals do not fit neatly into a category. Furthermore, there may not be many who do. As astutely noted by Gibbons (1988), classification systems or typologies generally consist "of criminological foundations that assume that real life persons can be found in significant numbers who resemble the descriptions of offenders in the various typologies that have been put forth . . . researchers have often failed to uncover many point-for-point real-life cases of these hypothesized types of offenders" (p. 9). However, as we have noted earlier in the book, typologies or classification systems are valuable in organizing an otherwise confusing array of behaviors. They can also be useful in correctional facilities for risk management, such as deciding where to place an inmate, or in treatment programming, such as deciding what particular treatment modality might be most beneficial for an inmate. It should be stressed, however, that rape is not a unified behavior pattern but rather is a complicated, often poorly understood, individualized behavior that appears to be precipitated by a variety of internal and external stimuli.

;achusetts Treatment Center Classification System

lassachusetts Treatment Center (MTC) originally identified four major categories of rapists: placed aggression, (2) compensatory, (3) sexual aggressive, and (4) impulsive rapists. Although major categories still exist—with slight changes in nomenclature—MTC researchers have d the classification system to include various sub-categories, as will be noted shortly. **Displaced sion rapists** (also called in other classification systems **displaced anger** or **anger-retaliation** ;) are primarily violent and aggressive in their attack, displaying minimum or total absence of feeling. These men use the act of rape to harm, humiliate, and degrade the woman. The victim ally assaulted and subjected to sadistic acts like biting, cutting, or tearing. In most instances, the is a complete stranger who happens to be the best available object or stimulus for the violence, gh she may possess characteristics that attract the assailant's attention. The assault is not sexu-)using for the displaced aggression rapist, and he often demands oral manipulation or mastur- from the victim to become tumescent. Available evidence suggests that resisting this type of only makes him more violent. However, this is not meant to suggest that someone *not* resist. According to Knight and Prentky (1987), an offender must demonstrate the following teristics during the attack in order to be assigned to the displaced aggression category:

The presence of a high degree of nonsexualized aggression or rage expressed either through erbal and/or physical assault that clearly exceed what is necessary to force compliance of he victim.
Clear evidence, in verbalization or behavior, of the intent to demean, degrade, or humiliate he victim.
No evidence that the aggressive behavior is eroticized or that sexual pleasure is derived rom the injurious acts.
The injurious acts are not focused on parts of the body that have sexual significance.

Although many of these rapists are married, they are usually ambivalent toward the women : lives (Cohen *et al.*, 1971), and their relationships with women are often characterized by it irritation and periodic violence. They perceive women as being hostile, demanding, and ful. In addition, they often select as their targets for sexual assault women whom they con-:tive, assertive, and independent. The occupational history of these assailants is stable and 1ows some level of success. Usually, the work is "masculine," such as truck driving, carpen-struction, or mechanics. The attack typically follows an incident that has upset or angered ist, particularly about women and their behavior. The term *displaced aggression* is derived 1e fact that the victim rarely has played any direct role in generating the aggression and . This offender often attributes his offense to "uncontrollable impulses."
Compared with other rapists, the childhood of the displaced aggression offender is often and unstable. Many were physically and emotionally neglected. A large number were d or placed in foster homes. About 80 percent were brought up in single-parent homes.
Compensatory rapists rape in response to an intense sexual arousal initiated by stimuli in ironment, often quite specific stimuli. This type of rapist is sometimes referred to in the and research literature as the "power-reassurance," "sexual aim," "ego dystonic," or "true" nder. Aggression is not a significant feature here; the basic motivation is a desire to prove prowess and adequacy. In their day-to-day lives, compensatory rapists tend to be extremely withdrawn, and socially inept. They live in a world of fantasy that centers on images of yielding victims who will submit to pleasurable intercourse and find the rapist's perform- outstanding that they will plead for a return engagement. The compensatory rapist's

fantasies or personal versions of the world may so distort his view of the victim that he may seek further contact with her, even if she strongly resisted the sexual assault.

Although his victim is usually a stranger, the compensatory rapist has probably seen her frequently, watched her, or followed her. Specific stimuli associated with her probably excite him. For example, he may be drawn to college women but may feel the attraction would not be mutual if he approached them via a socially accepted route. He cannot face the prospect of rejection. However, if he can prove his sexual prowess, the victim will appreciate his value. If the victim vigorously resists the compensatory rapist, he is likely to flee; if she submits passively, he will rape without much force or violence. This sexually aroused passive assailant will often ejaculate spontaneously, even on mere physical contact with the victim. In general, he does not demonstrate other kinds of antisocial behavior.

The compensatory rapist is often described by others as a quiet, shy, submissive, lonely nice man. Although he is a reliable worker, his withdrawn, introverted behavior, lack of self-esteem, and low levels of need for achievement usually preclude academic, occupational, or social success. His rapes—or attempts at rape—are efforts to compensate for his sense of inadequacy, hence the category to which he is assigned. More recent research by Knight and Prentky (1987) questions the incompetence issue. They found that, compared with the other rapist types, the compensatory rapist evidenced the best heterosexual adaptation and achieved the highest employment skill level. Consequently, the term *compensatory rapist* has been replaced with the term *sexual gratification*, nonsadistic type.

The **sexual aggressive** or **sadistic rapist** is the one in whom sexual and aggressive features seem to coexist at equal or near equal levels. In order for him to experience sexual arousal, it must be associated with violence and pain, which excite him. He rapes, therefore, because of the combination of violence and sexual features in the act. He is convinced that women enjoy being forcefully raped and being dominated and controlled by men. This, he believes, is part of women's nature. Anger and aggression are not always present during the early stages of the assault, which may actually begin as a seduction. In this sense, the sexual aggressive rapist considers the victim's resistance and struggle a game, a form of protesting too much; what she really wants is to be sexually assaulted and raped. This belief appears deeply ingrained and widely accepted in many Western societies (Edwards, 1983). Consider the following remarks made by a Scottish attorney general: "M.P.s would do well to remember that rape involves an activity which was normal . . . it was part of the business of men and women that they hunted and were hunted and said 'yes' and 'no' and meant the opposite" (Edwards, 1983, p. 114).

Sexual aggressive offenders are often married, but because they display little commitment or loyalty, they also often have a history of multiple marriages, separations, and divorces. They also may be frequently involved in domestic violence. In fact, their backgrounds include antisocial behaviors beginning during adolescence or before and ranging from truancy to rape-murder. They have been severe management problems in school. Throughout their childhood, adolescence, and adulthood, they exhibit poor behavior controls and a low frustration tolerance. Their childhoods are characterized by physical abuse and neglect.

In the extreme, these rapists engage in sexual sadism much like the displaced aggression rapists: Their victims may be viciously violated, beaten, and even killed. The difference between the two types is that the sexual aggressive rapist derives intense sexual satisfaction from aggression, pain, and violence. In order to qualify for assignment to this category, the offender needs to demonstrate (1) a level of aggression or violence that clearly exceeds what is necessary to force compliance of the victim, and (2) the explicit, unambiguous evidence that aggression is sexually exciting to him.

A fourth type of rapist, the **impulsive** or **exploitative rapist,** demonstrates neither strong nor aggressive features, but engages in spontaneous rape when the opportunity presents The rape is usually carried out in the context of another crime, such as robbery or burglary. ctims simply happen to be available, and they are sexually assaulted with minimum extra-iolence or sexual feeling. Generally, this offender has a long history of criminal offenses han rape. In order to be assigned to this group, the offender must show (1) callous indif-: to the welfare and comfort of victim, and (2) the presence of no more force than is neces-gain the compliance of the victim.

ITC:R3

assachusetts Treatment Classification scheme offers a rough framework for conceptualiz-l simplifying the behaviors and motives involved in rape. However, it needs refinement construction, a process the group has been pursuing for a number of years (e.g., Knight, Knight & Prentky, 1990). After a series of analyses and further development, the new husetts Treatment Classification scheme (called the MTC:R3) finds that rape offenders w be classified into *four* major types and *nine* subtypes. Although the basic four offender -displaced aggression, sexual gratification (formerly compensatory), sexual aggressive, pulsive—are still in the equation, the researchers have also discovered there are subtle ices within the original four types. The researchers decided that four primary *motivations* e could improve the MTC significantly: *opportunity, pervasive anger, sexual gratification,* dictiveness (Knight, 1999; Knight, Warren, Reboussin, & Soley, 1998). Knight and his es (Knight *et al.*, 1998) concluded that these four motivations appeared to describe ig behavioral patterns that distinguished most rapists. The **opportunistic types** (Types 1 are similar to the impulsive rapist described earlier. Their sexual assaults appear to be ve, predatory acts as a result of being in a situation where the opportunity for the sexual rises, and they are not primarily driven by sexual fantasy or explicit anger at women. r, analysis of offender data showed that the opportunistic type can be subdivided on the their social competence (see **Figure 1**). Type 1 offenders are higher in social competence : exhibited their impulsive sexual tendencies in adulthood. Type 2 offenders, on the other e lower in social competence and first demonstrated their impulsive sexual actions dur-escence.

he **pervasive anger type** (Type 3) is similar to displaced aggression rapists but with the ce that his generalized anger pervades all areas of his life. Their pervasive anger is not lirected at women but at everyone. Consequently, they often have a long history of anti-iolent behavior of all kinds, and they tend to inflict high levels of physical injury on their especially their rape victims. In many ways, they manifest behaviors similar to the life-persistent offender. **Sexual gratification** motivations characterized four subtypes of 1 the newly developed MTC classification scheme (Types 4, 5, 6, and 7; see **Figure 1**). The rapists (Types 4 and 5) are subdivided into overt and muted types "on the basis of their sexual-aggressive fantasies are directly expressed in violent attacks or are only d" (Knight *et al.*, 1998, p. 58). The nonsadistic sexual rapists (Types 6 and 7) are subdi-1 the basis of their social competence; they are similar to the compensatory rapist d earlier in the chapter.

e new MTC:R3 also includes **vindictive offender** types (Types 8 and 9), characterized by rected exclusively at women. These types are also highly similar to the displaced aggres- described in the original MTC. "The sexual assaults of these men are distinguished by

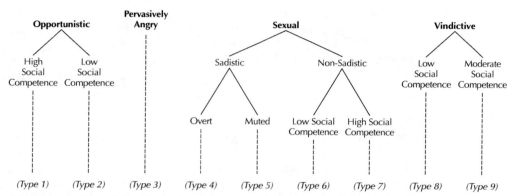

MTC:R3

PRIMARY MOTIVATION

FIGURE 1   Breakdown of Four Categorizations of Rapist Type into Non Rapist Subtypes

Source: R.A. Knight et al. Criminal Justice and Behavior, Vol. 25. P. 57, Fig. 2. Copyright © 1998 by Sage Publications, Inc. Reprinted by permission of Sage Publications, Inc.

behaviors that are explicitly intended to harm the woman physically, as well as to degrade and humiliate her" (Knight *et al.*, 1998, p. 58). Like the opportunistic and nonsadistic rapists, the vindictive types can be subdivided into high social competence and low social competence people.

Knight *et al.* (1998) postulate that these nine rape-offender classifications can help substantially in providing additional clues in crime-scene investigations. With refinement and continuing research, the MTC:R3 should ultimately enable investigators to identify "type" based on parameters gathered at the crime scene. The MTC:R3 also underscores the multiple strategies and cognitive beliefs possessed by rapists and discourages dogmatic proclamations about why rape occurs. The MTC:R3 increases the understanding of the etiology of sexual offending and helps mental health professions predict recidivism. Knight (1999) cautions, though, that while the MTC:R3 provides a useful way of classifying the many motivations of rapists, it may need considerable refinement and research to establish its validity and ultimate utility. In a recent study, Goodwill, Alison, and Beech (2009) found that the MTC:R3 does appear to have predictive validity in criminal profiling.

A frequently asked question is, To what extent should a woman fight back or resist the attack? In the past, women were often encouraged to take a passive role, under the assumption that resistance would infuriate the offender and increase the risk of further injury, even death. However, this created a double bind, because courts then required evidence that the victim had struggled! With increasing awareness of the psychological trauma experienced by many women who have survived a completed rape (Ullman, 2007), researchers began to search instead for effective strategies that could be used against perpetrators. Recent research indicates that some rape resistance strategies can be effective.

In an interesting study, Sarah Ullman and Raymond Knight (1993) examined the police reports and court testimonies of 274 women who were either raped or avoided rape by violent stranger rapists. They found that forceful resistance (fighting, screaming, fleeing, or pushing the offender) was more effective for avoiding rape than nonresistance. This strategy was

lly effective in dangerous situations in which the offender had a weapon. However,
gh the victim avoided being raped or sexually assaulted, she often received more physi-
ry when the offender had a weapon, even if the weapon was not used. On the other
nonresistance strategies were largely ineffective in avoiding rape or physical injury. In
ctims who used nonresistant strategies—such as pleading, crying, or trying to reason-
e offender—were more likely to be sexually and physically assaulted than women who
y resisted. Pleading, crying, or attempting to reason seem to encourage the offender
rther.

More recent research continues to support the view that women who fight back forcefully
re likely to avoid completed rape (see Ullman, 1997, 2007). One thing to keep in mind is
Ullman–Knight (1993) study focused on violent, stranger offenders who were commit-
exually dangerous to the MTC. Whether the same results would occur when examining
type of offender is unclear. Moreover, the MTC rape categories make it fairly clear that
isatory rapists and impulsive rapists—and possibly many sexual aggressive rapists—will
rred by a victim who struggles. However, the displaced aggression rapists are apt to
d with more violence as the victim resists. Nevertheless, it is unrealistic to think that a
would be able to detect this one type of rapist and decide not to resist. And, as Ullman
writes: "More research is needed, but concerns that sadistic rapists or other specific rapist
e.g., pervasively angry, opportunistic, nonsadistic sexual, vindictive) will inflict more
on victims who forcefully resist remain unfounded to date" (p. 420).

their comprehensive review of the research, Rosenbaum, Lurigio, and Davis (1998) iden-
r basic strategies of resistance to rape: (1) forceful physical resistance, (2) forceful verbal
ce, (3) nonforceful physical resistance, and (4) nonforceful verbal resistance. Forceful phys-
stance involves hitting, kicking, biting, using fingernails, or a weapon. Research suggests
ng this method of resistance generally helps reduce the probability of severe sexual abuse or
mpletion, but it also increases the risk that the victim will be attacked and physically
Forceful verbal resistance includes screaming, calling for help, or threatening the attacker.
his strategy reduces the probability of a rape completion, the degree of physical injury
on the victim is unclear from the research evidence. The third strategy, nonforceful physi-
ance, includes trying to flee the scene, pushing the attacker away, or shielding oneself. This
resistance reduces the probability of rape completion but has little or no effect on the
of injury received by the victim. Nonforceful verbal resistance, such as pleading, crying, or
reason with the attacker, generally leads to an increased probability of rape completion,
no effect in reducing physical injury. Overall, it appears that some type of forceful resist-
most effective in reducing a violent sexual attack and completion of a rape. To the question,
the victim forcefully resist, scream, or try to run away?" therefore, the answer in general
affirmative. Pleading for mercy or not forcefully resisting is more likely to result in a com-
pe.

Certain places and situations may put women at a greater risk of rape and affect their abil-
fectively resist an attacker" (Ullman, 2007, p. 416), and these may differ according to
the perpetrator is a stranger or an acquaintance. Sexual assaults by acquaintances most
cur indoors or in isolated locations. With respect to strangers, bars are especially risky
for women if drinking alone. Fraternity parties also sometime put women at risk. In addi-
of alcohol or drugs by one or both parties, women initiating a date, or men paying for a
ough still a common practice—all are contributing factors in developing a risky situation.
less, while women should be cognizant of these risky settings, the crime is the fault of the
tor, not the one who is attacked.

The Groth Typology

Groth (1979) has developed a typology with many similarities to the MTC scheme. The Groth proposal is based on the presumed motivations and aims that underlie almost all rapes. Rape is seen as a "pseudo-sexual act" in which sex serves merely as a vehicle for the primary motivations of power and aggression. Groth asserts, "Rape is never the result simply of sexual arousal that has no other opportunity for gratification. . . . Rape is always a symptom of some psychological dysfunction, either temporary and transient or chronic and repetitive" (p. 5). Later, he states, "Rape is always and foremost an aggressive act" (p. 12). Consequently, Groth divides rape behavior into three major categories: anger rape, power rape, and sadistic rape.

In **anger rape**, the offender uses more force than necessary for compliance and engages in a variety of sexual acts that are particularly degrading or humiliating to the woman (such as sodomy, fellatio, or even urinating on her). He also expresses his contempt for the victim through abusive and profane language. Thus, for the anger rapist, rape is an act of conscious anger and rage toward women, and he expresses his fury physically and verbally. Sex is actually dirty, offensive, and disgusting to him, and this is why he uses it to defile and degrade the victim. Very often, his attacks are prompted by some previous conflict with or humiliation by a significant woman (often a wife, a boss, or a mother). The assault is characterized by considerable physical brutality.

In **power rape**, the assailant seeks to establish power and control over his victim. Thus, the amount of force and threat used depends on the degree of submission shown by the victim. "I told her to undress and when she refused I struck her across the face to show her I meant business" (Groth, 1979, p. 26). His goal is sexual conquest, and he will try to overcome any resistance. Sexual intercourse is his way of asserting identity, authority, potency, mastery, and domination rather than strictly sexual gratification. Often the victim is kidnapped or held captive in some fashion, and she may be subjected to repeated assaults over an extended period of time. The sexual assault is sometimes disappointing to the power rapist because it fails to live up to his frequent fantasies of rape. "Everything was pleasurable in the fantasy, and there was acceptance, whereas in the reality of the situation, it wasn't pleasurable, and the girl was scared, not turned on to me" (Groth, 1979, p. 27). A good illustration of power rape may be the widely publicized case of Elizabeth Smart, who was abducted from her home at age 14, allegedly by Brian David Mitchell. She was found 9 months later, in March 2003. Mitchell has yet to be tried, in part because his attorneys maintain that he is incompetent to stand trial. In September 2009, 21-year-old Elizabeth Smart testified in a pretrial competency hearing that she was humiliated and raped repeatedly while held captive. It is said that Mitchell has refused to cooperate with clinicians attempting to evaluate his mental status (National Public Radio, October 2, 2009).

The third pattern of rape, **sadistic rape**, includes both sexual and aggressive components. In other words, aggression is eroticized. The sadistic rapist experiences sexual arousal and excitement in the victim's maltreatment, torment, distress, helplessness, and suffering. The assault usually involves bondage and torture, and he directs considerable abuse and injury on various areas of the victim's body. Prostitutes, women he considers promiscuous, or women representing symbols of something he wants to punish or destroy often incur the wrath of the sadistic rapist. The victim may be stalked, abducted, abused, and sometimes murdered.

Groth (1979) reports that over half of the offenders evaluated or treated by his agency (Connecticut Sex Offender Program) were power rapists, 40 percent were anger rapists, and only 5 percent were sadistic rapists. The similarities between Groth's scheme and the MTC typology are multiple. The anger rapist is similar to the displaced aggression rapist, the sadistic rapist is similar to the sexual aggressive rapist, and the power rapist shows many commonalities with the compensatory rapist. However, the MTC typology is far more extensive and based on ongoing research.

.OGY OR CAUSES OF RAPE

lly speaking, sexual socialization and social learning play a crucial role in the rapist's ions of what the rape accomplishes and what is "masculine." It is important to realize that ocialization (or sexual training) is rarely acquired entirely from home or school; much of it from peers, friends, the entertainment media, and experimentation. Most of us, even as , were fed misconceptions, taboos, and strategies for dealing with the opposite sex. Males arn it is "manly" to take the sexual initiative and to persist, even against resistance. Details ual conquest, related to buddies, represent the badge of masculinity and self-worth. On the and, if attempts to conquer turn into a comedy of errors, they are seen as personal failure ual inadequacy. In addition, some people (both men and women) believe that a woman be raped unless she wants to be. Others learn that women want to be dominated and con-nd that successful lovers demonstrate the "I'm-the-boss" syndrome. It is interesting to note ontext that some victims actually receive marriage proposals from their assailants (Russell,)ther rapists ask their victims to evaluate their performance during or after the act.

me researchers have proposed an **immaturity hypothesis** to account for a large portion ipe. Goldstein (1977) found that a sample of convicted sex offenders (who were mostly continued in adulthood to derive most of their sexual pleasure from fantasizing sexual they had derived from the media or from their own imagination. Average males s), by contrast, drew much of their sexual pleasure from real-life sexual encounters. n also discovered that many rapists have pervasive and obsessive preoccupations with iatters, to the point where the sexual preoccupation permeates their lives, and where r nonerotic material becomes vividly incorporated into sexual fantasies.

ildstein found that rapists, compared with the average male, relied substantially more on ation during adulthood, and that this was frequently accompanied by erotic material from the entertainment media. Furthermore, *all types* of sexual offenders had on the *ewer* contacts with erotica during their formative years than did most other males. In sexual curiosity was often repressed because of a punitive parental approach to matters)gether, these factors provide a conducive setting for sexual misconceptions and igno-should be emphasized, though, that these observations and hypotheses might not hold f the electronic and virtual media available in contemporary society.

es toward Rape

:dly, a major explanatory factor for many rapes is the attitudes about women and rape by the perpetrators. Some researchers go so far as to say that these attitudes also are iany individuals in the general population. Koss and Dinero (1988) conducted a well-survey of approximately 3,000 male students at 32 U.S. colleges and universities. were asked questions about the extent of verbal coercion and physical force they had :come sexually intimate with women without their consent. They were also questioned tudes and habits. The results indicated that highly sexually aggressive men expressed stility toward women, frequently used alcohol, frequently viewed violent and degrading)hy (in contrast to Goldstein's finding), and were closely involved with peer groups that highly sexualized and dominating views of women. In addition, the more sexually the student, the more likely he was to believe that force and coercion are legitimate in compliance in sexual relationships. The researchers concluded, "In short, the results upport for a developmental sequence for sexual aggression in which early experiences)logical characteristics establish conditions for sexual violence" (p. 144).

In summary, most rapists seem to subscribe to attitudes and ideology that encourage men to be dominant, controlling, and powerful, whereas women are expected to be submissive, permissive, and compliant. Such an orientation seems to have a particularly strong disinhibitory effect on sexually aggressive men, encouraging them to interpret the ambiguous behavior of females as come-ons, to believe that women are not really offended by coercive sexual behaviors, and to perceive rape victims as desiring and deriving gratification from being sexually assaulted (Lipton, McDonel, & McFall, 1987).

Additional evidence of rapists' deviant attitudes and beliefs comes from physiological research. Abel and his associates (Abel, Barlow, Blanchard, & Guild, 1977; Abel, Becker, Blanchard, & Djenderedjian, 1978) have found that rapists show high and nearly equal sexual arousal to audiotaped portrayals of both rape and consenting sexual acts. The degree of sexual arousal was indicated by the subject's penile tumescence, which is measured by a device called a plethysmograph. Male nonrapists, on the other hand, show significantly less penile tumescence to rape depictions. In fact, convicted rapists became highly aroused by rape depictions in which the victim experiences abhorrence and pain rather than sexual pleasure. Encouraged by these findings, Abel developed a physiological measure called the "rape index." The index is arrived at by dividing the average percentage of full penile erection to rape stimuli by the average percentage of full penile erection to consenting sexual stimuli. Avery-Clark and Laws (1984) have developed a similar indicator for pedophiles called the *Dangerous Child Abuser Index.* Today, many investigators use this measure in the diagnosis and treatment of rapists, as well as child molesters. Generally, research suggests that rapists tend to have a higher rape index than nonrapists. The overall accuracy of the penile plethysmograph and its sensitivity to extraneous factors and faking remain very much in question, however. Furthermore, some clinicians and researchers have moral objections to using this approach.

Abel and his group also discovered that some rapists became highly sexually aroused even to scenes of *nonsexual aggression,* such as a man beating a woman with his fists. Thus, it appears that some men strongly associate aggression and violence toward women with sexual arousal, a pattern very similar to that of the sexual aggressive rapist described earlier. In fact, in rapists, the intensity of this deviant arousal has been found to be positively related to the number of rapes committed and the degree of injury inflicted on victims (Abel *et al.,* 1978). Some rapists apparently find scenes that show women being beaten exciting and pleasurable. In addition, male spouse abusers may, in part, be motivated by such arousal. On the other hand, a majority of men (70%) in the general population find the presence of aggression inhibiting to sexual arousal (Malamuth, Check, & Briere, 1986). Interestingly, men in the general population who are sexually aroused by force also are more accepting of an ideology that justifies male aggression against and dominance over women. These men also admit that they would probably rape if the opportunity were presented.

The role played by fantasy and imagination in the development of sexually aggressive behavior is becoming an increasingly important topic (Laws & Marshall, 1990). Self-reports by sexual offenders find that frequent imagery and fantasy of sexually aggressive scenes is extremely important in motivating and guiding overt sexual aggression. Aggressive fantasies are particularly exciting to men convicted of rape (Abel *et al.,* 1977). Interestingly, in an SR survey of 114 college men conducted by Greendlinger and Byrne (1987), over one-third indicated they fantasize about aggressively raping a woman and 54 percent fantasize about "forcing a woman to have sex."

Related to the role played by fantasy in the development of sexual deviance is the role played by masturbation. The intrinsically physiological pleasure and arousal generated by

bation can serve as a strong bonding agent, particularly if paired repeatedly with some
ed object or person. Also, it is important to realize that there are two powerfully reinforc-
cesses in masturbatory activity: sexual arousal and the reduction of that arousal at
Fantasized or actual behaviors that are sexually arousing and that result in sexual satis-
(i.e., orgasm) are likely to increase in strength and frequency. This process is known as
rbatory conditioning" (Marshall & Barbaree, 1988). On the basis of clinical studies
eorge & Marlatt, 1989; Groth, 1979; Marshall, 1988), it appears that masturbatory
ning may play an integral part in the development of both normal and deviant sexual
r.

sum, the evidence to date indicates overwhelmingly that rapists learn to be rapists and
ch of the teaching is done by equally naive peers, parents, significant social models, and the
ment media. Rape springs from a culture, characterized by violence that communicates a
it ideology that degrades women and justifies coercive sexuality. Fortunately, most males
ly acquire a close approximation of sexual sophistication and some understanding of
s of others. Many rapists, however, seem to remain sexually and, in some ways socially,
e.

lyths

ths have received considerable research attention during the past four decades. **Rape**
e "attitudes and beliefs that are generally false but widely and persistently held, and that
deny and justify male sexual aggression against women" (Lonsway & Fitzgerald, 1994,
hey stem from the traditional view of masculinity that men should be strong, assertive,
dominant, and heterosexual (Davies, 2002). Rape myths essentially are the false beliefs
en must be dominated and coerced into sexual activity.

e myths and misogynistic (hatred of women) attitudes appear to play a major role in
sault. Many—but not all—rapists and violently sexually aggressive men tend to hold
search indicates that men who subscribe to rape myths are hostile toward women in
orbes, Adams-Curtis, & White, 2004). Furthermore, attitudes that promote the denigra-
omen may be widespread. There is distressing evidence that rapists may reflect the
nd implicit beliefs held by many others. Recall that in one study, 35 percent of male
idents on several different campuses felt there was some likelihood that they would rape
ild be sure of getting away with it (Malamuth, 1981). In another study, 60 percent of a
52 male undergraduates indicated there was some likelihood they would rape or force a
perform a sexual act against her will if given the opportunity (Briere, Malamuth, &
31).

amuth (1989) cautions, however, that one should not conclude that subjects who indi-
would sexually force a woman are necessarily "potential rapists." The scale used in his
ttraction to Sexual Aggression (ASA), is designed to measure the belief that actually
n sexual aggression would be an arousing, attractive experience. Whether they would
t belief is dictated by a myriad of factors across a wide spectrum of influences, includ-
ree of motivation to commit the act, the internal and external inhibitions present, and
unity to commit the act.

e is some recent evidence that some false beliefs and rape myths are beginning to
t least among college students. Ferro, Cermele and Saltzman (2008) report that today's
lents are less likely to hold false beliefs about rape, and are generally sympathetic toward
s. However, the students still held rape myths concerning marital rape. The participants

found it difficult to believe that rape occurs in a married relationship since a higher level of intimacy is expected between married couples. They were also reluctant to believe that the act was a violation of the wife's rights or that she would be psychologically damaged from the experience.

SEXUAL ASSAULT AND PORNOGRAPHY

The relationship between rape and pornography is shrouded with confusion and surrounded by debate. Two presidential commissions established to study the effect of pornography on crime and human behavior reached opposite conclusions. The first and most comprehensive, established in 1967, was directed not to issue recommendations unless the effects were clearcut. Because of the complexity it uncovered, the commission could not conclude whether explicit sexual material contributed significantly to sex crimes, prompting then-President Richard M. Nixon to remark that the commission was "morally bankrupt." Many have used this conclusion to support their contention that pornography is not harmful. The second National Commission on Obscenity and Pornography, which issued a report in 1984, recommended widespread restrictions of pornographic material. This commission has been extensively criticized for its lack of scientific objectivity.

Part of the problem is determining exactly what is meant by pornography. Seto, Maric, and Barbaree (2001) offer some help. First, there is the distinction between erotica and pornography. Erotica refers to "sexually explicit material that depicts adult men and women consensually involved in pleasurable, nonviolent, nondegrading, sexual interactions" (Seto et al., 2001, p. 37). Pornography may be described as depictions of sexual contact where one of the participants is portrayed as powerless or nonconsenting, or is little more than an object for the pleasure of the other participant or participants. Pornography may be further described as either physically violent or degrading and humiliating to one of the participants, usually the woman if the parties are of different sexes. Both forms of the pornography portray sexual interactions as impersonal and without affection or consideration of the actors as individuals.

Overall, Seto et al. (2001) were able to conclude from their critical review of the research literature that there is little support for a direct causal link between pornography use and sexual aggression. However, some research evidence has suggested that under *certain* conditions, pornography facilitates aggressive, sexual behavior. Studies by Donnerstein (1983) and Malamuth (Malamuth & Check, 1981; Malamuth, Haber, & Feshbach, 1980; Malamuth, Heim, & Feshbach, 1980) indicate, for example, that a general statement that pornography does not negatively influence people needs several qualifiers. In a series of ongoing experiments, Donnerstein found evidence that three factors influence the relationship between pornography and human aggression: (1) the level of arousal elicited by pornographic films, (2) the level of aggressive content, and (3) the reactions of the victims portrayed in these films and photographs. Donnerstein and others (e.g., Meyer, 1972; Zillman, 1971) angered male subjects in a variety of ways, then found that pornography shown to these aroused subjects significantly increased their aggressive behavior toward others. Because of their arousing properties, the pornographic stimuli apparently may promote aggression under certain conditions. This finding accords with Berkowitz's theory on the relationship between arousal and aggression. Anything—sexual or not—that increases the arousal level of an already aroused subject will increase aggressive behavior in situations where aggression is the dominant behavior. The increased arousal may also draw the subject away from his own internal control or self-regulatory mechanisms, thereby allowing him to be less concerned about the consequences of his behavior. Furthermore, pornography investigations reveal that if the subject was angered by a woman, he would be even more

ve toward other women after being exposed to a pornographic image or film. These find-
roborate the frequent clinical observation that prior to a rape, many rapists had been
, upset, humiliated, or insulted, often by a woman (e.g., Groth, 1979).

tremely violent stimuli, both pornographic and nonpornographic, can also facilitate
on toward women, even in nonangered males, under certain conditions. The level of vio-
the film appears significant. Portrayals of women being assaulted, even nonsexually, can
subsequent aggressive behavior by men toward women, even when the males are not
herefore, highly aggressive and violent acts depicted in the media may facilitate the rape
ome males. Since many rapists regard their act as a direct aggressive attack on women,
lms where women are physically abused may encourage and support their own violent
ons. Seto *et al.* (2001) make the point, though, that individuals who are already predis-
sexually offend are the most likely to demonstrate the strongest effects of pornographic
s on their sexual and aggressive behavior. Men who are not predisposed toward aggres-
al behavior are unlikely to be affected by pornographic materials.

e reactions of the victims portrayed in films also seem crucial. Films or photographs that
e female victim enjoying rape (common in pornography) encourage acceptance of the
th and promote violence against women (Allen, Emmers, Gebhart, & Giery, 2001;
th & Check, 1981). In fact, Allen and his colleagues (2001) found that as the level of
depicted in the pornographic material goes up, so does the acceptance of the rape myth. If,
ther hand, the victim finds the rape both painful and abhorrent (negative aggressive
phy), male observers are disinclined to act aggressively. However, several qualifiers must be
to this finding. If the male observer is already angered (aroused), seeing the victim suffer
e him more aggressive, since any arousal increase in an already aroused subject will
ubsequent aggressive behavior. The specific content of the film becomes irrelevant, as long
ts the minimum criterion of being somehow arousing. On the other hand, males who are
t or aroused before seeing a female victim suffer are less likely to aggress against women.
r some individuals, however, due to their conditioning history, pain cues are reinforcing
re repeatedly associated with sexual gratification. Precisely how they react to various
phic portrayals is unclear, but it seems reasonable to suggest that they would find depic-
ain both highly arousing and supportive of their belief that pain and sexual gratification
er. They might also conclude that the pain–pleasure relationship is inherently character-
eryone's sexual gratification and that women really enjoy being "roughed up."

e relationship between violent pornography and sexual aggression remains complex and
. Although sexually arousing nonviolent pornography should be available in a free soci-
rguably has social value, it can also be argued that violent pornography has no redeeming
harmful effects, however, are difficult to document except as they relate to a subgroup of
ls. If all violent pornography were eradicated today, sex crimes would likely decrease.
guments could be made to support universal confiscation of handguns and rifles, or ran-
nnounced drug testing of the citizenry, both of which violate the U.S. Constitution. The
which a society should be asked to barter freedom in exchange for security remains a
ut which reasonable people consistently disagree.

e commercial sexual exploitation of children by distributors via media and Internet
phic materials is a very different story, and producing, possessing, and distributing depic-
ildren engaged in sexually explicit activity is a criminal offense. Nevertheless, prosecutors
known to be overzealous in pursuing individuals who take pictures of their naked chil-
llect items depicting children in suggestive poses, when evidence of exploitation of actual
s meager. As mentioned at the beginning of the chapter, the number of truly sexually

exploited children (prostitution, pornography, sex trafficking) in the United States and across the globe is astounding, and resources might better be spent fighting this serious problem. We will cover this topic in the text on the sexual assault of children and youth. In that text, we will also cover the topic of psychological treatment of sex offenders in general. As you will learn, there is increasing evidence that the principles of psychological treatment that are effective with moderate and high-risk offenders in general (Andrews, Bonta, & Hoge, 1990) are also effective with sex offenders (Hanson, Bourgon, Helmus, & Hodgson, 2009). Related to the issue of treatment, however, is the special topic of "sexual predators" and recent efforts to keep them confined, sometimes indefinitely, under the guise of providing treatment for their disorders. Sexual predators may prey on adults or children and thus are a good transition topic.

THE (NON)MENTALLY DISORDERED SEX OFFENDER

In recent years, fueled by media accounts, the public has been particularly concerned about the crimes of the sexual offender, sometimes referred to as the sexual predator, who among other violent offenders is believed to be particularly dangerous. Furthermore, the rare but horrific serial killings may be accompanied by sexual assaults.

Until relatively recently, sexual predators were considered to be mentally disordered and were committed to civil mental institutions under laws enabling the confinement of the mentally disordered sex offender (MDSO). In most states, the MDSO was an individual either charged with or convicted of a sexual offense; he was then involuntarily committed to a civil mental institution on the basis of his mental disorder and presumed dangerousness to society.

Today the great majority of these offenders are committed under **sexually violent predator** laws, and they do not necessarily require a finding of a diagnosable mental disorder. In some jurisdictions, "mental abnormality" (a vaguer term) will suffice. This is a critically important point to make, because many if not most mental health professionals do not consider sex offenders as a group mentally disordered in the clinical sense of the term. That is, they do not meet criteria for the diagnoses such as schizophrenia, paranoia, or depression.

MDSO statutes first appeared on the scene during the early part of the twentieth century, and were then called "sexual psychopath" laws. The term *psychopath* was not really appropriate for a vast majority of these individuals, whose crimes ranged from minor to very serious acts. In most cases, the legislative intention was to provide special dispositional procedures for persons who exhibit a tendency to commit sex offenses, but each state developed its own set of procedures and definitions. Either explicitly or implicitly, the statutes depicted the sexual "psychopath" as a mentally disordered individual who was particularly dangerous to children, women, or both.

Sexual psychopath statutes were challenged in the 1960s and 1970s on a number of constitutional grounds, but particularly because they were vague and overbroad and placed individuals in mental institutions without evidence of their dangerousness. In the late 1980s and 1990s, however, these statutes were resurrected in various forms, most notably sexually violent predator legislation. That is, the term *sexual predator* or *sexually violent predator* is used in place of the outdated "sexual psychopath" terminology. For example, in 1990, the state of Washington enacted the **Sexually Violent Predator Act (SVPA)** that provides for special commitment facilities and allows for a possible lifetime commitment for sexual predators with a mental or personality disorder (Cohen, 1998). Other states quickly followed suit. In Iowa, the law authorizes involuntary civil commitment for an indefinite period of time for those mentally unstable sex offenders who are a threat to strike again. The law

...at sex offenders be evaluated near the end of their prison terms. If they are determined to be ...dators, they are confined indefinitely in a high-security treatment facility until no longer a ...ociety. Approximately 16 states have passed similar statutes, including Kansas, Washington, ...alifornia, and New York. La Fond (2003) estimates that as many as 2,209 individuals may be ...these laws. In the late 1990s, the U.S. Supreme Court gave its approval to these statutes as ...state could document (1) a history of sexually violent conduct, (2) a current mental disor- ...*mality,* (3) a risk of future sexually violent conduct, (4) a connection between the disorder ...conduct, and (5) some inability to control behavior (*Kansas v. Hendricks,* 1997; *Kansas v. Crane,* 2002).

The terms *sexually violent predator* or *sexual predator* are used purposely to avoid the traditional requirements that both mental disorder and dangerousness must be established before an individual can be committed involuntarily to a civil mental institution (Cohen, 1998). Additionally, the state wishes to be able to confine the individual for long periods, even after serving a prison term and without proof of a recent overt act (Cohen, 1998). Lawmakers reasoned that predators, by their very nature, are dangerous to society and must be kept out of circulation as long as possible. We stress again that the statutes do not necessarily require a finding of mental disorder; in some, "abnormality" is sufficient. Because clinicians recognize that many sexual offenders are not mentally disordered (Janus & Walbek, 2000), this allows their confinement even if their behavior does not meet the standard for a diagnosable mental illness. The Supreme Court has emphasized, though, that *present* dangerousness must be *established* (it cannot merely be presumed) (*Kansas v. Crane,* 2002). In other words, if you want to confine a sexual predator to a mental institution, you must prove that—at this time—he is highly likely to harm one or more individuals if not confined. In the Hendricks case, for example, Hendricks himself stated at his civil commitment hearing that he was not "cured," could not control his sexual urges, and that only death would stop him from victimizing children. Few offenders would be so forthcoming or would provide the court with so much incentive to keep them under control.

While it is understandable that the public wishes to be protected from dangerous sex offenders, both the earlier statutes and their latest incarnations have a number of flaws. The early sexual psychopath laws often attempted to intercept sexual psychopaths before they had been convicted of a crime (Morris, 1982). They were also based on the false premise that sexual offenders start with minor sexual offenses (e.g., indecent exposure, voyeurism) and move on to serious crimes of violence, like rape. While some do, most do not. The sexual predator laws of today require a conviction, but in some of these statutes the crime can range from relatively minor acts to serious offenses—again seeming to assume that the offender will move from minor to more serious acts. The early laws illustrated "a legislative capacity to conceal excessive punitiveness behind a veil of psychiatric treatment. At base lies the false assumption of a connection between sexual offenses and mental illness" (Morris, 1982, p. 136). Critics of the latest statutes argue that here, too, little has changed. Research has found that many sex offenders do not suffer from mental disorder (Janus & Walbek, 2000), yet the statutes imply that they do. Thus, individuals continue to be committed under the guise that they will receive treatment. In reality, treatment is believed to be sporadic and ineffective (Janus, 2000). Cohen (2008), citing an Illinois case, notes that less than 50 percent of the SVP population in that state was involved in core treatment. Treatment, he notes, does not seem to be a requirement of SVP commitment. The sexually violent predator statutes appear to be a questionable response to a highly disturbing problem. One better solution to the problem, according to clinical psychologists and psychiatrists, is to offer meaningful treatment in prisons or in the community for those individuals who have been convicted of sexual offenses.

Summary and Conclusions

The very serious crime of rape is widely believed to be the most underreported crime. When we consider the psychological toll it takes on its victims—or rape survivors—it is not surprising that the vast majority of rapes never come to the attention of police. We noted early in the chapter that many researchers, as well as statutes, now use the term *sexual assault*, which can encompass both penetration and a variety of behaviors that fall short of that ultimate violation.

Rape, as well as other violent sexual offenses, is committed for a variety of reasons by a variety of offenders. A major motivation appears to be to harm, derogate, or embarrass the victim. In some situations, the rapist may interpret his behavior as harmless, believing that his victims enjoy being "roughed up." Nevertheless, the effect is invariably the opposite. The psychological and social damages to the victim are incalculable.

We reviewed statistics on rape and sexual assault, as well as available demographic information about offenders and victims. Sexual assaults by husbands, dates, and intimate friends are more frequent than commonly supposed. Most rapists are young and often show a history of rape and other violent actions. Traditionally, both rape and other sexual assaults have been considered almost exclusively a male enterprise. In the 1990s, researchers began to question this assumption. Although it is still a fact that men and boys commit the great majority of sexual offenses, we can no longer ignore the reality that women and girls also commit them. Because most theory building and typologies have been developed on males, we have used the male pronoun to refer to offenders throughout the chapter. It is also important to recognize the trauma that is experienced by male rape victims.

Several attempts at typologies or classification systems of sex offenders have been made, the most notable being those developed by the Massachusetts Treatment Center and Nicholas Groth. Of the two, the MTC classification system is the most widely used and has been the one most submitted to empirical research.

Rape and other sexual behavior appear to be due, in part, to the type of socialization experiences the offender has had. He has constructed, from information received from a variety of sources and models, a belief and value system that encourages and justifies the aggressive behavior. Furthermore, most rapists have attitudes and an ideology that encourage men to be dominant, controlling, and powerful, while expecting women to be submissive, permissive, and compliant. This attitudinal pattern may be much more prevalent in society in both men and women than commonly realized. It is also a global phenomenon.

We also learned that under very high levels of arousal, any consideration of the rightness of a sexual assaulter's behavior or its consequences may be obliterated. As we saw with reference to homicide and assault, high levels of arousal reduce attention to private self-awareness and personal standards of appropriate conduct. Under high levels of excitement, along with the influence of alcohol or other drugs, some normally law-abiding persons may become rapists, or at least use the high excitement as a justification for their rape behavior. Of course, some people possess a value system that justifies rape or the resolution of interpersonal conflict through violence, regardless of their arousal level.

We ended the chapter with a brief discussion of the role of pornography in facilitating aggressive sexual behavior. In a free society, pornographic material obviously cannot be banned (although restrictions can be and are placed on the pornography that exploits children). Considering the appeal of pornography, it is clear that there is no direct causal link to rape or other sexual assault. However, research does indicate that individuals who are predisposed to commit such assault often use pornography as a stimulus. Furthermore, *violent* pornography has been shown to increase violent tendencies even in some males who were not otherwise predisposed. Thus, the effect of violent pornography on aggressive behavior is troubling.

Key Concepts

Admitters

Anger rape

Compensatory rapist

Date rape

Deniers

Displaced aggression rapists/displaced anger/anger retaliation rapists

Drug attribution

Expressive sexual aggression

Forcible rape

Impulsive rapist/exploitative rapist

Instrumental sexual aggression

Just-world hypothesis

Marital rape

Mental illness or disease attribution

Opportunity rapist

Pervasive anger rapist

Power rape

Rape by fraud

Rape myths

Sadistic rape

Sexual aggressive rapist/sadistic rapist

Sexual gratification rapist

Statutory rape

Uncontrollable or irresistible impulse attribution

Victim attribution

Vindictive rapist

Review Questions

1. Briefly describe the actions taken in the past decade by federal and state lawmakers to protect potential victims from sexual offenders.

2. Describe the five common attributions used by rapists to justify their sexual behavior.

3. What precisely is date rape, and what is the estimated incidence?

4. What is the just-world hypothesis, and how might it enter into sexual assault?

5. Define and provide examples of rape myths.

6. How did Groth classify rapists? Be sure to describe all of his classifications.

7. What are the known offender characteristics of rapists?

8. Does pornography play a crucial role in sex crimes against women and children? Briefly support your answer with reference to research findings.

9. Contrast the Massachusetts Treatment Center's original classification of rapists with its most recently revised version.

11

Sexual Assault of Children and Youth and Other Sexual Offenses

Sexual Assault of Children and Youth and Other Sexual Offenses

CHAPTER OBJECTIVES

- Define pedophilia and related concepts.
- Outline the demographic and other characteristics of child molesters.
- Review the research literature on classification systems of child molesters.
- Summarize what is known about the recidivism rates of adult and juvenile child molesters.
- Discuss the sexual deviations of exhibitionism, voyeurism, and fetishism.
- Identify treatment approaches to reducing sex offender recidivism.

In 2009, the world was shocked at the revelation that an Austrian citizen, Josef Fritzl, had held his own daughter as a sexual captive in the basement of the family home in St. Poelten, Austria, for 24 years. She had borne him seven children, who had apparently been raised as her younger brothers and sisters. Later that year, he confessed to a range of sexual crimes against his daughter and his other children. In the same year, a 28-year-old female Sunday-school teacher in Tracy, California, was arrested and charged in the abduction and death of an eight-year-old girl; shortly thereafter, child sexual abuse was added to the charges against her.

Pedophilia (from the Greek word for child lover) is the clinical term for the more commonly used terms child molestation and child sexual abuse. We must emphasize at the outset, however, that the clinical condition is not necessarily accompanied by action. When criminal action *is* involved, **pedophile** is the term often used for the offender. Pedophilia is defined in a variety of ways. The DSM-IV (1994) defines it as a condition in which, "over a period of at least 6 months, recurrent, intense sexually arousing fantasies, sexual urges, or behaviors involving sexual activity with a prepubescent child or children (generally age 13 years or younger) occur" (p. 528). The DSM-IV further specifies that some pedophiles are sexually attracted only to children (the exclusive type), whereas others are sexually attracted to both children and adults (nonexclusive type).

According to Finkelhor and Araji (1986), pedophilia is a male adult's conscious sexual interest in prepubertal children. One of two behaviors signifies that interest. Either the adult has had some sexual contact with a child (touched the child or had the child touch him with the purpose of arousing him sexually), or the adult has masturbated to sexual fantasies or images involving children. Although the second behavior is not a crime, criminal behavior may have been involved in the procuring of the images. Occasionally, researchers extend the definition to include ages 13 through 15, but most literature reserves the term **hebephilia** for sexual contact by adult males with young adolescents. However, the distinction between hebephilia and pedophilia does not appear to be clinically meaningful (Blanchard, Klassen, Dickey, Kuban, & Blak, 2001), so hebephilia is usually not considered a distinct, diagnostic category.

Traditionally, most definitions of pedophilia were restricted to sexual contact between an adult and child who are not closely related. Sexual acts between members of a family when at least one participant is a minor has traditionally been labeled incest or **intrafamilial** (within the family) **child molestation** and is most commonly perpetrated by men who molest their sexually immature daughters or stepdaughters (Rice & Harris, 2002). Sexual contact with immature family members by individuals from outside the family is called **extrafamilial child molestation.** See **Table 1** for terms and definitions.

Some mental health professionals argue that pedophilia and child molestation should refer to two different things, with the former limited to fantasies or sexual attraction to children and the latter referring to the act itself (Bartol & Bartol, 2008). In other words, as noted above, pedophilia is the condition, not the behavior. Other professionals prefer the all-encompassing term **paraphilia,** which covers other cognitions and behaviors in addition to those relating to children. The essential features of paraphilia "are recurrent sexually arousing fantasies, sexual urges, or behaviors generally involving (1) nonhuman objects, (2) the suffering or humiliation of oneself or one's partner, or (3) children or other nonconsenting persons, that occur over a period of at least 6 months" (American Psychiatric Association, 1994, p. 522). In this chapter,

TABLE 1   Terms Used in Research on Child Molestation

Term	Definition
Extrafamilial child molestation	Sexual contact with a minor child by someone *outside* the immediate family.
Intrafamilial child molestation	Sexual contact with a minor child by someone *within* the immediate family.
Pedophilia	For some researchers and clinicians, the term refers to strong sexual *attraction* toward children. Others use the term to refer to sexual *contact* with children. In this text, it will refer to the latter.
Pedophile	Someone with strong sexual attraction toward children, or someone who has frequent sexual contacts with children.
Child molester	Largely accepted term for someone who has sexual contact or sexually abuses a minor child. In this text, it will be used interchangeably with pedophile.
Hebephilia	Sexual contact by adult males with young adolescents.
Paraphilia	Sexual disorders in which sexual arousal occur almost exclusively in the presence of inappropriate objects or individuals.

however, we will continue to use the term **pedophilia** when referring to illegal sexual actions on children, ranging from sexual touching to penetration. It is important to stress, though, that not all individuals diagnosed with pedophilia commit crimes against children. Nevertheless, they are probably more likely to come to clinical attention because they have acted in accordance with their fantasies and cognitions. Later in the chapter, we will cover activities that better fall under the term paraphilia.

INCIDENCE AND PREVALENCE OF PEDOPHILIA

As with sexual offenses in general, a caveat pertaining to the statistics is necessary. Data on pedophilia are difficult to obtain, since there are no central or national objective recording systems for tabulating sexual offenses against children. Sex crimes as a group have the lowest rates of reporting of all crimes (Terry & Tallon, 2004). Most estimates of the distribution of pedophiles in the general population are derived from arrest or prison data. However, offenders may be arrested and prosecuted under a variety of statutes and for a variety of offenses, including child rape, aggravated assault, sodomy, incest, indecent exposure, or lewd and lascivious behavior. Furthermore, although the UCR lists sex offenses other than forcible rape and prostitution in its statistics on Part II crimes, it does not differentiate pedophilia from the mixture of these other possible sexual offenses.

From a national survey of about 1,200 American males (Finkelhor & Lewis, 1988), it is estimated that between 5 percent and 10 percent of the male population has engaged or will engage in child sexual abuse at some time in their lives. It is important to note, however, that this figure may include a one-time incident that—although still to be condemned—may not represent the offender's usual behavior and would not qualify him as a pedophile for purposes of this chapter. However, these data indicate that children are sexually victimized at levels that far exceed those reported for adults (see Finkelhor & Dziuba-Leatherman, 1994).

Prison data also give us an indication of the extent of the problem. Two-thirds of all prisoners in state prisons convicted of rape or sexual assault had committed their crime against a child, and in most cases the victim was female (Greenfeld, 1996). Approximately 60 percent of those convicted of child molestation had attacked victims less than 13 years old.

Nationwide tabulations of the number of victims are equally difficult to obtain. For example, the National Crime Victimization Survey only collects data from victims older than age 12, thus neglecting the victimization of young children. However, a variety of retrospective surveys of the general population indicate that from a quarter to a third of all females and a tenth or more of all males have indicated that they were molested during childhood (Finkelhor & Lewis, 1988; Peters, Wyatt, & Finkelhor, 1986). Moreover, only 35 percent of the children who are sexually victimized report it to anyone (Finkelhor, 1979). Russell (1984) found that in her survey sample, only 2 percent of all incestuous abuse cases and 6 percent of all cases of extrafamilial abuse of girls under 18 had ever been reported to the police. In a nationally representative sample of 2,030 children ages 2–17 years, Finkelhor, Ormrod, Turner, and Hamby (2005) discovered that one in 12 children or youth had experienced a sexual victimization during the year of the survey. Sexual assaults were substantially more common against girls than boys. The survey also found that the great majority of sexual victimizations were perpetrated by acquaintances.

The National Incident-Based Reporting System (NIBRS), has the potential to provide better information on the prevalence of sexual assaults on young children. Using NIBRS data between 1991 and 1996, Snyder (2006) found that 34 percent of the victims of sexual assault reported to law enforcement were under age 12. Most disturbing was the finding that one of every seven victims of sexual assault (14% of the victims) was under age six.

It is well recognized in the criminology literature that female adolescents with persistent antisocial behavior as well as adult female offenders have often experienced child sexual abuse (Ullman, 1999, 2007). Among nonoffenders, the figures are also sobering. Russell (1984) surveyed 930 randomly selected female residents of San Francisco during 1978. The purpose of the project was to obtain an estimate of the incidence and prevalence of rape and other forms of sexual assault, including the amount of sexual abuse respondents experienced as children. Twelve percent of the women said they had been sexually abused by a relative before the age of 14. Twenty-nine percent reported at least one experience of sexual abuse by a nonrelative before reaching the age of 14. Overall, 28 percent of the 930 women reported at least one incident of sexual abuse before reaching the age of 14.

The reports of perpetrators themselves indicate that numerous children are affected. Abel and his colleagues (Abel, Becker, Murphy, & Flanagan, 1981) reported that incarcerated homosexual pedophiles had, on the average 31 victims, while heterosexual pedophiles had an average of 62 victims. A Dutch study (Bernard, 1975) reported that at least half of its respondents claimed sexual contacts with at least 10 or more children. Fourteen percent of the sample—which included both arrested and nonarrested pedophiles—admitted to sexual contacts with more than 50, and 6 percent to contacts with between 100 and 300 children. Fifty-six percent of this sample indicated they had one or more "regular" sexual contacts with children. Fully 90 percent asserted that they did not want to stop their pedophilial activities.

While some of the above studies may appear dated, nothing in the recent research literature suggests that this problem has been attenuated. In a meta-analysis of studies examining victim prevalence, Bolen and Scannapieco (1999) found that 13 percent of male children had been sexually abused, and 30 percent to 40 percent of female children had been sexually abused during childhood. Both rape and molestation that did not meet the criteria for rape are included in these statistics. In summary, the amount of sexual abuse and violence against children in the United States is staggering. To what extent it is a major problem worldwide is unknown, though there are numerous anecdotal accounts, such as the example cited at the beginning of the chapter.

Situational and Victimization Characteristics

The offender, or pedophile, is almost always male, but the victim may be of either gender. As noted earlier, however, research is beginning to focus more on the sexual offending of women (Becker & Johnson, 2001; Ellis, 1998). Although the predominant view remains that men far outnumber women as perpetrators, there is growing recognition that women are not immune to committing this type of crime. We will discuss this topic again below.

Heterosexual pedophilia—male adult with female child—appears to be the more common type, with available data indicating that three-quarters of pedophiles choose female victims exclusively (Langevin, 1983; Lanyon, 1986). Homosexual pedophilia—male adult preference for male child—appears to be substantially less frequent (about 20%–23% of the reported cases). A small minority of pedophiles choose their victims from both sexes. The behavior of the pedophile or child molester is usually limited to caressing the child's body, fondling the child's genitals, and/or inducing the child to manipulate the adult's genitals. Penetration is apparently involved in only a small proportion of the total number of offenses (Seto, 2008).

The offender and the victim know one another in most instances, often very well (McCaghy, 1967; Schultz, 1975; Virkkunen, 1975). Many victims were actively seeking natural affection from their offenders, as a child seeks to be hugged or cuddled. Some victims feel kindly and lovingly toward the offender, who sometimes interprets this behavior as "seductive." Clinical observations suggest that pedophiles, as a group, tend to have positive feelings toward their victims, generally perceive them as being willing participants, and frequently victimize children living in their immediate households (Miner, Day, & Nafpaktitis, 1989). It is not uncommon for the sexual behavior between the offender and victim to have gone on for a sustained period of time. The widespread fear among many parents that their child will be abducted and sexually abused by a stranger is understandable, but in reality such cases are very rare.

Types of Sexual Contact

The form of the sexual contact seems to depend on three factors: the degree to which the offender had previous nonsexual interactions with children, the nature of the relationship between the child and the offender, and the age of each. Offenders who have had limited interaction with children are more likely to perform or to expect genital-genital and oral-genital contact, rather than to indulge only in caressing or fondling. Furthermore, the more familiar the offender and the victim are with one another, the greater the tendency for genital-genital or oral-genital contact.

There is some disagreement about the extent to which child molesters harm the child physically or use physical force. According to most research, pedophiles do not usually use overt physical coercion. McCaghy (1967) found no evidence of any kind of coercion, verbal or physical, in three-fourths of the child molestation cases he examined. Research by Groth and his colleagues (Groth, Hobson, & Gary, 1982) supports these findings. Lanyon (1986), summarizing the research, concluded that violence is involved in about 10 percent to 15 percent of child sexual abuse cases.

Some research documents more force and violence, however. Hall, Proctor, and Nelson (1988) report that 28 percent of a sample of convicted pedophiles (122 nonpsychotic patients of a state mental hospital) were officially identified as having used physical force or the threat of force beyond what was necessary to gain the victim's compliance. Marshall and Christie (1981) found that in a sample of 41 pedophiles incarcerated in Canadian federal penitentiaries, 29 had used physical force. In an earlier study of 150 pedophiles, Christie, Marshall, and Lanthier (1979) had reported that 58 percent used excessive force in their attack, and 42 percent of the child victims had sustained notable injuries. The researchers suggested that the offenders in their sample were highly sexually aroused by physical violence, significantly more so than other nonaggressive sex offenders. The reported differences in the use of violence and force by pedophiles appears to be explained by the sample used. Studies reporting a high incidence of violence or aggression focus on incarcerated, relatively hard-core offenders, while those reporting little or no violence sampled less-criminal or nonincarcerated pedophiles, generally those on probation.

Groth et al. (1982) recommend that the few offenders using violence or force and causing physical harm to the child should be labeled "child rapists." On the other hand, those offenders only using psychological pressures should be considered child molesters or pedophiles. Although Groth's suggestion has merit, researchers in this area have used pedophile or child molester as umbrella terms to cover all child sexual abusers, including those who rape their victims.

Psychological Effects of Child Sexual Victimization

Research offers strong support for the assumption that sexual abuse in childhood (both violent and nonviolent) produces long-term psychological problems in many children (Briere, 1988). Reports of depression, guilt, feelings of inferiority, substance abuse, suicide ideation, anxiety, chronic tension, sleep problems, and fears and phobias are common. Depression is the symptom most commonly reported among adults who were molested as children.

The extent of psychological damage to the child produced by sexual abuse is dependent on several factors. Groth (1978) contends that the greatest trauma occurs in children who have been victims for long periods of time, are victimized by a closely related person (such as a father or stepfather), when the victimization involves penetration, and when it is accompanied by aggression. In their careful review of the research literature on pedophilia, Browne and Finkelhor (1986) concluded that (1) younger children appear to be somewhat more vulnerable to trauma than older children, (2) the closer the relationship between offender and victim the greater the trauma, and (3) the greater the force used the greater the trauma. They also maintained, however, that there is no conclusive support for the contention that the longer and more frequent the abuse, the greater the trauma. Nor is there any clear evidence that traumas are related to the type of sexual abuse (e.g., intercourse, fondling, fellatio, cunnilingus). This suggests that "mild" abuse may be as traumatizing as intercourse, especially if the victim is young and closely related to the offender. The Browne and Finkelhor review also suggests that victims of child sexual abuse are more likely than nonvictims to be sexually assaulted again as adults.

OFFENDER CHARACTERISTICS

Many aggressive pedophiles demonstrate a large number of similarities to rapists and the prison population in general (Knight, Rosenberg, & Schneider, 1985). The most notable commonalities are the following: (1) they have problems with alcohol, (2) they have a high rate of high school failure and dropout, (3) they tend to have unstable work histories in unskilled occupations, and (4) they tend to come from the low socioeconomic class. Alcohol abuse is frequently a problem in sex offenders. While about one-third to one-half of convicted rapists have serious problems with alcohol, about one-quarter to one-third of convicted pedophiles have such problems (Knight *et al.*, 1985).

Prentky, Knight, and Lee (1997) conclude from their extensive research on the subject that the classification and diagnosis of child molesters are complicated by a high degree of variability among individuals in reference to personal characteristics, life experiences, criminal histories, and reasons or motivations for offending. Essentially, there is no single "profile" that accurately describes all child molesters. With this caveat in mind, we proceed with some commonly observed characteristics of many of the pedophiles.

Gender of the Offender

Pedophilia is primarily committed by males, but it is not exclusively a male offense. The National Center on Child Abuse and Neglect (2000) reported that 46 percent of the abusive sexual experiences encountered by children included a female perpetrator. This figure is misleading, however, in that it includes any female caretaker who "permitted acts of sexual abuse to occur" (Russell & Finkelhor, 1984). In other words, leaving the child with a boyfriend as a babysitter who in turn molests the child would be considered sexual abuse by the mother. The mother who fails to report her suspicions that her husband is sexually abusing her daughter may also be included in the statistic. If only those women who actually *committed* child sexual abuse are included, the percentage of female offenders drops to 13 percent in the case of female victims and 24 percent in the case of males (Russell & Finkelhor, 1984). More recent data suggest that 8 percent of all *arrests* for sexual assault were female (Freeman & Sandler, 2008). The number of arrests of females for sexual offenses in any given year probably represents a low figure. In cases that involved female sexual abuse, either the abuse is not reported for many years, or if reported, it is often dismissed or disbelieved (Strickland, 2008).

According to self-reported victimization data, between 4 percent and 25 percent of victims of child sexual abuse stated their abusers were female (Kaplan & Green, 1995).

Utilizing a matched sample of 780 female and male sex offenders in New York state, Freeman and Sandler (2008) determined that female sex offenders were more likely to victimize males, whereas male sex offenders were more likely to victimize females. In addition, the researchers found that male sex offenders have a far more extensive criminal history than female sex offenders. This criminal history included both sexual and nonsexual offenses. Similarly, most of the female sex offenders investigated by Vandiver and Walker (2002) had a history of only one sex offense and no other criminal history.

Findings in others studies indicate that women who become sexual abusers have themselves experienced more physical, emotional, and sexual abuse than female nonsexual offenders (Matthews, Hunter, & Vuz, 1997; Strickland, 2008). In addition, they are more likely than nonsexual offenders to come from severe deprived backgrounds, such as poor living conditions, food deprivation, and lack of medical care. These conditions of extreme deprivation and abuse are likely to sharply affect appropriate coping and interpersonal skills, self-regulation skills, emotional maturity, and feelings of self-worth. As noted by Strickland (2008), females who suffered family violence, sexual abuse, and severe deprivation may have greater difficulty in developing and maintaining appropriate interpersonal relationships. Similar findings are found in the backgrounds of male child sex abusers, especially sexual abuse (Simons, Wurtlele, & Durham, 2008). To a large extent, these forms of trauma may induce women who sexually abuse to find intimate relations with young children and adolescents.

Female sex offenders are beginning to receive considerable research and clinical attention in recent years (e.g., Freeman & Sandler, 2008; Gannon & Rose, 2008; Sandler & Freeman, 2007; Vandiver & Kercher, 2004). Since most of the documented sexual offenses committed by females involve infant, child, or adolescent victims (Strickland, 2008), female sex offenders will be covered in this chapter.

Age

Although there is considerable age variability, it is well documented that male pedophiles tend to be older, on average, than male rapists (Hanson, 2001). While about 75 percent of convicted male rapists are under 30, about 75 percent of convicted male child molesters are over that age (Henn, Herjanic, & Vanderpearl, 1976b). By contrast, Sandler and Freeman (2007) found that the average female sex offender was in her early thirties, and they most often target victims just under age 12 years. The age at which they commit their first sexual offense may also differ according to gender. Vandiver and Walker (2002) report the majority of female sex offenders committed their first sexual offense at around age 31. Groth (1978) notes that all the male child molesters he and colleagues have worked with had committed their first child molestation offense before age 40. Over 80 percent were first offenders by age 30, and about 5 percent had committed their first sexual assault before they reached adolescence. However, in addition to the statistical finding that child molesters tend to be older than most other sexual offenders, there seems to be a pattern of victim preference as a function of age. Older pedophiles (over 50) seek out immature children (age 10 or younger); younger pedophiles (under age 40) prefer girls between the ages of 12 and 15 (Revitch & Weiss, 1962). The latter offenders are technically classified as hebephiles.

Attitudes toward Victims

Perhaps because of the extremely negative attitude society displays toward child molesters, pedophiles almost always resist taking full responsibility for their offenses (McCaghy, 1967). They are motivated to disguise their thoughts and feelings about their sexual beliefs and attraction toward children. Many claim that they went blank, were too intoxicated to know what they were doing, could not help themselves, or did not know what came over them. They show a strong preference to attribute the cause of their behavior to external forces or motivating factors largely beyond their personal control.

Self-control emerges as a critical variable in cognitions of pedophiles. As outlined by Hanson (2001), low self-control refers to the tendency to respond impulsively to temptation, have little consideration of the consequences, and engage in high-risk behaviors. However, pedophiles appear to have significantly better self-control than rapists (Hanson, 2001), leading to the conclusion that the argument that pedophiles claim their behavior is outside of their control may have very little validity.

Cognitive Functions

In an important study, Cantor, Blanchard, Robichaud, and Christensen (2005) found that adult males who commit sexual offenses score significantly lower in IQ measures than adult males who commit nonsexual offenses. However, IQ differences between sexual and nonsexual offenders do not occur uniformly across sexual offender subtypes. That is, offenders who commit rape against *adults* did not differ in IQ from the nonsexual offenders. Overall, the results revealed that the younger the victim, the lower the intelligence of the offender. Consequently, the observed difference in intelligence for sexual offenders and nonsexual offenders appears to be largely due to the scores of child molesters. In fact, the IQ scores of pedophiles were, on average, two-thirds of one standard deviation below the population mean. Cantor *et al.* (2005) admonish that the results do not indicate that low IQ scores *cause* pedophilia, only that something may have happened during early childhood to limit their cognitive functioning.

Lower levels of intellectual functioning in pedophiles are associated with a stronger sexual attraction for male children and a greater interest in younger children compared with pedophiles with higher levels of intelligence (Blanchard *et al.*, 1999). Lower intelligence may limit the individual from appreciating the nature of the sexual assault or its long-term consequences.

Occupational and Socioeconomic Status

About two-thirds of those arrested and convicted for child molestation offenses come from the unskilled or semiskilled occupational groups (Gebhard, Gagnon, Pomeroy, & Christenson, 1965; McCaghy, 1967), but as with statistics on other crimes, these should be interpreted cautiously. However, other occupational groups may handle the incident quite differently to prevent additional trauma for the victim and social embarrassment for their families during the legal investigation and process. In the 1980s, the media were filled with accounts of the alarming increase in child sex abuse rates. These same accounts note that it knows no economic or social barriers. Many families deal with this issue on their own by isolating the offending family members, seeking treatment for the offender and the victim, or taking more drastic measures, including threatening or assaulting the perpetrator. Child offenders exist in all levels of society and among all occupational groups. It should be noted, however, that in many jurisdictions, treatment providers have the obligation to report instances of ongoing physical or sexual abuse, so this may affect the family's willingness to seek help.

Interpersonal and Social Skills

Prentky *et al.* (1997) assert that the more an offender's sexual preference is limited to children, the less socially competent the offender tends to be. In this context, social competence refers to the offender's

TABLE 2   General Comparisons between Pedophiles and Rapists on Important Variables

Common Characteristic[*]	Pedophiles	Rapists
Cognitive functioning	Below average	Average
Interpersonal skills	Below average	Average
Education level	Low	Average
Employment	Unstable	Stable
Age	Older	Younger
Self-control	Average	Low
Sexual recidivism	Unknown, but likely high for a small group	Lower
Offending history	Largely restricted to pedophilia	Variable and extensive
Alcohol use	Frequent problem	Less of a problem

[*] This table is intended to provide only the typical findings from the available research. It should be emphasized, however, that there are many individual exceptions to these comparisons.

social and sexual relationships with adults. Several studies (e.g., Marshall, Barbaree, & Fernandez, 1995; Marshall & Mazzucco, 1995; Prentky *et al.*, 1997) have revealed that, on average, pedophiles are inadequate socially, lack interpersonal skills, are unassertive, and have poor self-esteem. We have seen the same social, interpersonal, self-worth, and confidence factors among female sex offenders (Strickland, 2008). (See **Table 2** for a comparison of pedophile and rapist characteristics.)

Similar to other sexual offenders, the classification, diagnosis, and assessment of pedophiles are complicated by a high degree of variability among individuals in reference to personal characteristics, life experiences, criminal histories, and motives for offending (Prentky *et al.*, 1997). "There is no single 'profile' that accurately describes or accounts for all child molesters" (Prentky *et al.*, 1997, p. v). The best way to highlight the complex nature of pedophilia is through a discussion of two well-known classification systems or typologies. Like the rape typologies described, they were developed by the Massachusetts Research Center and by Groth, with the former being more research based and the latter more clinically based. In addition, like the rapist typologies discussed, they have been formulated primarily on information gathered on male offenders.

CLASSIFICATION OF CHILD OFFENDER PATTERNS

The Massachusetts Treatment Center (MTC) (Cohen, Seghorn, & Calmas, 1969; Knight, 1988; Knight *et al.*, 1985) has developed a widely cited typology of pedophile behavioral patterns. Four major pedophiliac patterns have been identified: (1) the fixated type, (2) the regressed type, (3) the exploitative type, and (4) the aggressive or sadistic type.

The **fixated** (or **immature**) **pedophile** demonstrates a long-standing, exclusive preference for children as both sexual and social companions. He has never been able to develop a mature relationship with his adult peers, male or female, and he is considered socially immature, passive, timid, and dependent by most people who know him. He feels most comfortable relating to children, whom he seeks out as companions. Sexual contact usually occurs only after the adult and child have become well acquainted. Fixated pedophiles rarely marry, and their social background lacks much evidence of dating peers or even any sustained, long-term friendship with an adult (outside of relatives). This pedophile wishes to touch, fondle, caress, and taste the child. He rarely expects genital intercourse, and very rarely does he use physical force or aggression.

The fixated pedophile generally has average intelligence. His work history is steady, although it is often work that is below his ability. His social skills are adequate for day-to-day functioning. Probably most troubling about the fixated or immature pedophile is that he is not concerned or disturbed about his exclusive preference for children as companions, nor can he see why others are concerned. Therefore, he is difficult to treat and is most likely to recidivate.

The **regressed pedophile** had a fairly normal adolescence and good peer relationships and sexual experiences, but later developed feelings of masculine inadequacy and self-doubt. Problems in the individual's occupational, social, and sexual lives followed. The regressed child offender's background commonly includes alcohol abuse, divorce, and a poor employment record. Each pedophilial act is usually precipitated by a significant jolt to the offender's sexual adequacy, either by female or male peers. For example, the pedophile may perceive other males as being more successful with women after a female acquaintance rejects him in favor of another man. Unlike the immature (or fixated) child offender, the regressed child offender usually prefers victims who are strangers and who live outside his neighborhood. The victims are nearly always female. Also unlike the fixated pedophile, he seeks genital sex with his victim. Because he feels remorseful and expresses disbelief after that act, clinicians usually find him a good prospect for rehabilitation. As long as stressful events are kept to a minimum and he learns to cope adequately with those he does have, he is unlikely to reoffend. We return to this later in the chapter when we discuss principles of effective treatment.

The **exploitative pedophile** seeks children primarily to satisfy his sexual needs. He exploits the child's weaknesses any way he can, and tries various kinds of strategies and tricks to get him or her to comply. He is usually unknown to the child and commonly tries to get the child isolated from others and his or her familiar surroundings. If necessary, he will use aggression and physical force to get the child to comply with his wishes. The exploitative offender does not care about the emotional or physical well-being of the child, but only sees the victim as a sexual object.

The exploitative offender exhibits a long history of criminal or antisocial conduct. His relationships with peers are unpredictable and stormy. He is unpleasant to be around and is often avoided by others who know him. He tends to be highly impulsive, irritable, and moody. His markedly defective interpersonal skills may be the principal reason that he chooses children as victims (Knight *et al.*, 1985). Clinicians find him difficult to treat, as his deficiencies extend to all phases of his daily life. Nevertheless, and again as will be discussed later, treatment based on certain principles may be effective.

The **aggressive** (or **sadistic**) **pedophile** is drawn to children for both sexual and aggressive reasons. Pedophiles in this group are apt to have a long history of antisocial behavior and poor adaptation to their environments. Since the primary aim is to obtain stimulation without consideration for the victim, this group often assaults the child viciously and sadistically. The more harm and pain inflicted, the more this offender becomes sexually excited. Aggressive or sadistic pedophiles are most often responsible for child abductions and murders. Clinicians find this type not only dangerous to children, but also among the most difficult to treat. Fortunately, this type is rare. Although rare, this is the type frequently portrayed in the media and is most associated—though wrongfully so—with the image of the child molester.

An example of an aggressive pedophile was Albert Fish (1870–1936), whose background is discussed by Nash (1975). Fish, called the "Moon Maniac," admitted sexually molesting more than 400 children over a span of 20 years. In addition, he confessed to six child murders and made vague reference to numerous others. He was eventually convicted of murdering a 12-year-old girl and was electrocuted in 1936. A more contemporary example might well be John Wayne Gacy Jr., who sadistically murdered 33 teenage boys and young men and buried their bodies in the cellar of his suburban Chicago home.

Fish thought the conditions of his childhood led to a "perverted" life of crime. He was abandoned at an early age and placed in an orphanage, where he first witnessed and experienced brutal acts of sadism. Fish was quoted as saying, "Misery leads to crime. I saw so many boys whipped it ruined my mind." He apparently began his career of child molesting in earnest when his wife deserted him for another man. This suggests that, like regressed offenders, aggressive offenders may begin their crimes in response to precipitating events involving rejection and feelings of sexual inadequacy.

The above are two quite distant examples of the individuals who committed a multitude of heinous acts over periods of time. The more typical cases that receive less public attention are no less troubling. Persons familiar with court and social service records (e.g., lawyers, social workers, treatment providers, juvenile justice professionals) offer chilling information about the behaviors engaged in by pedophiles and the effects on their victims. An eight-year-old girl told the court about the sexual game her stepfather played on the bed with her and her younger sister every Friday evening. In another incident, a teacher suspected a problem because a young child's leg jumped up and down with great anxiety as the end of the school day approached. It was learned that the child was being sexually abused by an after-school caretaker. Other children are forced to engage in sexual activities with their siblings or are threatened with death or grievous harm if they reveal what is occurring.

The MTC:CM3

Like the Massachusetts Treatment Center classification scheme for rapists, the MTC classification system of child molesters has also undergone some refinement in recent years. In an effort to depict more accurately the complexity involved in classifying pedophiles, the MTC:CM3 (referring to Massachusetts Treatment Center: Child Molester, Version 3) includes tentative changes to the original scheme described earlier. Specifically, three significant changes are recommended: (1) Divide the regressed and fixated types into three separate factors—degree of fixation on children, the level of social competence achieved, and the amount of contact an offender has with children, (2) incorporate into the scheme a new narcissistic offender type, and (3) partition the violence of the sexual assault into physical injury and sadistic components (Knight, 1989).

The researchers discovered that, although the regressed pedophile classification is a valid one, it was also more complicated than originally supposed. Researchers found that the regression classification could be further subdivided into the molester's style of offending, his interpersonal relationships with children, the intensity of the offender's interest, and the level of social competence achieved by the offender. For example, offenders could be classified according to their level of fixation and social competence. Level of fixation refers to the strength of an offender's sexual interest in children (Knight, Carter, & Prentky, 1989). In other words, to what extent are children the major focus of the offender's thought and attention? If children are the central focus of the offender's sexual and interpersonal fantasies and thoughts for more than six months, then the offender qualifies for high fixation. Social competence refers to the degree to which the offender can participate effectively in daily living. An offender would have high social competence if he has demonstrated at least two of the following behaviors: (1) has had a single job lasting three or more years, (2) has had a sexual relationship with an adult for at least one year, (3) has assumed responsibility in parenting a child for three or more years, (4) has been an active member in an adult-oriented organization (e.g., church group, business group) for one or more years, or (5) has had a social friendship with an adult for at least one year. The dimensions of fixation and social competence result in four types of child molesters: high fixation, low social competence (type 0); high fixation, high social competence (type 1); low fixation, low social competence (type 2); and low fixation, high social competence (type 3). The regressed type was dropped in MTC:CM3 in favor of the term "low fixation."

Research further revealed that pedophiles can also be distinguished on the basis of how much daily contact with children they seek (see **Figure 1**). A high-contact offender demonstrates regular contact with children in both sexual and nonsexual contexts (Knight *et al.*, 1989). Offenders of high contact often become involved in an occupation or recreation that brings them in considerable contact with children, such as bus drivers, schoolteachers, Boy Scout leaders, or Little League coaches. Research data revealed there are two kinds of offenders who seek more extensive involvement with children beyond their sexual offenses. The first high-contact type, the *interpersonal offender* (type 1), seeks the extensive company of children for both social and sexual needs. He sees the child as an appropriate companion in a relationship, and believes the friendship is mutually satisfying. The second type, the *narcissistic offender* (type 2), solicits the company of children only to increase his opportunities for sexual experiences. Like exploitative offenders, these offenders typically molest children they do not know and their sexual acts with children are typically genitally oriented (Knight, 1989). Furthermore, there is little or no concern about the needs, comfort, or welfare of the child (Knight *et al.*, 1989).

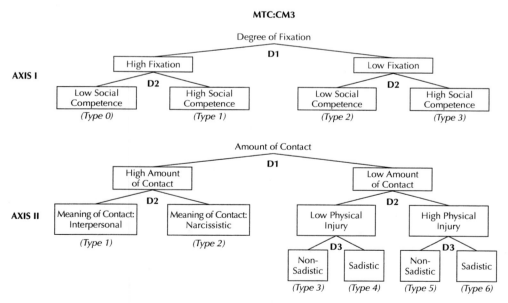

FIGURE 1   Flow Diagram of the Decision Process for Classifying Child Molesters on Axis I and Axis II on the MTC:CM3

Source: R.A. Knight et al. Journal of Interpersonal Violence, Vol. 4. P. 8, Fig. 1. Copyright © 1989 by Sage Publications, Inc. Reprinted by permission of Sage Publications, Inc.

Another group of pedophiles are low-contact seekers. Low-contact offenders' only contacts with children are in the context of sexual assault. Low-contact offenders are classified according to the amount of physical injury they administer to their victims. Two types of low-contact seekers tend to administer very little physical injury to their victims: the exploitative type and the muted sadistic type. Low injury refers to the absence of physical injury to victim and the presence of such acts as pushing, shoving, slapping, holding, or verbal threats. None of the acts of low injury results in a lasting injury (e.g., cuts, bruises, contusions). The *exploitative, nonsadistic offender* (type 3) uses no more aggression or violence than is necessary to secure victim compliance. Furthermore, the assault does not reveal evidence that sadistic actions engender sexual arousal in the offender. The *muted* or *symbolic sadistic offender* (type 4) engages in a variety of distressing, painful, and threatening acts, none of which causes significant physical injury to the child.

Finally, the MTC:CM3 classifies two offenders who have often administered a high amount of physical injury to their victims: the aggressive offender and the sadistic offender. High injury is characterized by hitting, punching, choking, sodomy, or forcing the child to ingest urine or feces (Knight *et al.*, 1989). The *aggressive, nonsadistic offender* (type 5) is similar to the aggressive pedophile described earlier except that sadism is not a primary aim of the assault. This offender is extremely angry about all things in his life and is generally violent toward people in his life, including children. The *sadistic offender* (type 6) obtains sexual pleasure from the pain, fear, and physical harm he inflicts on the child.

The newly developed MTC:CM3 helps identify offender type based on crime scene information and perhaps presents a more refined classification system of child molester or predator types. However, research beyond the MTC population is needed before investigators feel comfortable about adopting this promising scheme. Looman, Gauthier, and Boer (2001) were able to replicate the MTC:CM3 Classification System with a Canadian sample of child molesters, suggesting that the system has applicability across cultures.

The Groth Classification Model

In a classification system similar to that of the Massachusetts Treatment Center, Groth (1978; Groth & Burgess, 1977) classifies child offenders on the basis of the longevity of the behavioral patterns and the offender's psychological aims. Like Groth's rape offender groupings, though, it is less research based compared with the MTC classifications. If the sexual preference for children has existed persistently since adolescence, the person is classified as an *immature* or *fixated child offender.* The fixated child offender has been sexually attracted primarily or exclusively to significantly younger people throughout his life, regardless of what other sexual experiences he has had. Groth believes that this fixation is due to an arresting of psychological maturation, resulting from unresolved formative issues that persist and underlie subsequent development. On the other hand, if the offender has managed to develop some normalcy in his relationships with adults, but resorts to child offending when stressed or after suffering a devastating blow to his self-esteem, he is called a *regressed* child offender.

Groth has also subdivided child offenders according to their intentions or psychological aims. He identifies two basic categories: (1) sex pressure offenders, and (2) sex force offenders. In sex pressure offenses, the offender's typical modus operandi is to entice children into sexual behavior through persuasion or cajolement, or to entrap them by placing them in a situation in which they feel indebted or obligated. A child may feel he owes something to the person who taught him to swim or bought him a bike. The sex force offense, on the other hand, is characterized by threat of harm and/or the use of physical force in the commission of the offense. The offender either intimidates the child—by exploiting the child's relative helplessness, naiveté, and awe of adults—or attacks and physically overpowers his victim.

Groth finds he can further subdivide the sex force group into the *exploitative type,* in which the threat of force is used to overcome victim resistance, or the *sadistic type,* who derives great pleasure in hurting the child. The exploitative type typically employs verbal threats, restraint, manipulation, intimidation, and physical strength to overcome any resistance on the part of the child. His intent is not necessarily to hurt the child but to obtain compliance. The sadistic type, which fortunately is rare, eroticizes physical aggression and pain. He uses more force than is necessary to overpower the victim and may commit a so-called lust murder. Therefore, the physical and psychological abuse and/or degradation of the child is necessary for him to experience sexual excitement and gratification. Often, the child is beaten, choked, tortured, and violently sexually abused.

Certainly the Groth typology has strong commonalities with the MTC typology. The immature and the regressed child offenders display features of the sex pressure offender, and the aggressive child offender shows strong similarities to the sex force offender. It may be more appropriate at the present time to classify the child offender according to the degree of coercion or force he uses rather than according to personality features. The first method focuses on offender behavior, a criterion that is more objective and clearcut. The second focuses on "understanding" the behavior by assuming a variety of personality constructs. We have too little information about child offenders at this point to do that with total confidence.

Female Sex Offender Typology

Donna Vandiver and Glen Kercher (2004) have proposed a clinically useful and research-meaningful typology of female sex offenders. Utilizing 471 registered adult female sexual offenders in Texas, the researchers identified six types:

1. Heterosexual nurturers
2. Noncriminal homosexual offenders
3. Female sexual predators
4. Young adult child exploiters
5. Homosexual criminals
6. Aggressive homosexual offenders

Heterosexual nurturers were the largest group. This group victimized only males with an average age of 12. The offenders are generally in mentorship, care-taking, or teacher roles, such as the teacher-lover category in which a teacher engages in a "romantic" relationship with one of her students or a counselor with one of her clients. Many of the offenders in this group do not perceive the relationship as abusive or psychologically damaging to the child. These females appear to be motivated by a desire for intimacy to compensate for unmet emotional and social needs, and may not recognize or want to recognize the inappropriateness of the relationship. This group had a low recidivism rate.

Noncriminal homosexual offenders represented the second largest group. This group primarily preferred early adolescent females as victims (average age of 13). This offender group appeared to have many of the same characteristics as heterosexual nurturers but their victim preferences were females. Similar to heterosexual nurturers, these offenders were unlikely to have a criminal record or to recidivate.

Female sexual predators victimized both male (60 percent) and female children (40 percent) who averaged 11 years of age. This group resembled other female criminals and their sexual offending may be an offshoot of other criminal activity. In other words, they are repeat offenders committing a variety of crimes. They also had a high probability of committing another sexual offense.

Young adult child exploiters most often committed sexual assault. Their victims were frequently young with an average age of seven, and involved both genders. These offenders themselves were the youngest of the six offender groups, with an average age of 28. About half of the victims were related to the offender, sometimes the offender's own child.

The fifth group, homosexual criminals, had an extensive history of antisocial behavior. Their victims were usually female with an average age of 11. Their sexual crimes included indecency with a child, and compelling the child into prostitution or child pornography. Most of these offenders are motivated by profit rather than sexual ambitions.

Aggressive homosexual offenders represent the smallest group and were also the oldest. Their victims were generally adult females, and therefore are not relevant to the topic of this chapter. They appeared to be representative of homosexual women involved in a domestically violent relationship.

In their sample of 390 female sex offenders in New York state, Sandler and Freeman (2007) also identified six categories. In addition, their sample was very similar to Vandiver and Kercher's on demographic variables, such as offender age and race. However, Sandler and Freeman did not entirely support some of the characteristics reported in the Vandiver and Kercher typology. This is to be expected, considering that typologies that attempt to classify female sex offenders are in early stages of development.

Sandler and Freeman did find support for the heterosexual nurturer and young adult child exploiter categories found by Vandiver and Kercher, but some characteristics of the four other categories were different. One of the major differences was the gender of the victims. Sandler and Freeman discovered that many of the female sex offenders did not *consistently* victimize one gender more than the other. Because the cluster analysis did not highlight a strong victim preference as found in the Vandiver-Kercher analysis, Sandler and Freeman felt it was appropriate to label only one group as homosexual, which they called the homosexual child molester. This group, which emerged as the smallest, almost exclusively targeted female victims (91 percent).

Some of the differences in results of the two studies may be due to the substantially different criminal codes or registry requirements for sex offenders between states. In addition, the Vandiver and Kercher sample included females who may or may not have served time in prison, and their offenses were considered serious enough to warrant arrest and prosecution (Gannon & Rose, 2008). Although their sample was a forensic population, it represented a very wide range of female sexual offenders.

Although the two studies significantly advance our knowledge pertaining to female sex offenders, neither study was able to obtain additional data relating to co-offenders (Gannon & Rose, 2008). In other words, did the females offend alone or with a co-offender, such as a male partner? Gannon and Rose (2008) emphasize that this shortcoming limits strategies and programs for treating female sex offenders. In addition, neither Sandler and Freeman's nor Vandiver and Kercher's typologies examine psychological variables, such as mental health status or the victimization histories of the offenders themselves. In general, the research on female sexual offenders has focused on the demographics and the very basic details of their offending characteristics, which is extremely helpful. However, as Gannon and Rose (2008) note, there is very little research on the sexual interests, empathy, intimacy deficits, and self-regulation of female sex offenders. This research needs to be done if we are to get a better understanding of the female sex offender.

JUVENILE SEX OFFENDERS

As much as 30 percent to 50 percent of child molestation offenses (known and unknown) may be committed by adolescents (Cellini, 1995). Van Wijk, van Horn, Bullens, Bijleveld, and Doreleijers (2005) discovered that juvenile child molesters represent a very different group compared with juvenile rapists. These researchers found that juvenile child molesters demonstrate significantly more social isolation because of poorly developed social skills and very limited interactions with peers. This and other research indicates that those youngsters who molest children (individuals at least four or five years younger in age than the perpetrator) were introverted and rejected by peers from an early age. The majority of their victims (more than 60%) are younger than 12, and two-thirds of these young victims are younger than age six (Veneziano & Veneziano, 2002). Ryan, Miyoshi, Metzner, Krugman, and Fryer (1996) found that 63% of the victims of juvenile molesters were younger than age nine. Adolescent rapists, on the other hand, are more likely to select victims their own age or older (Veneziano & Veneziano, 2002). A study investigating incest cases reported that sibling offenders are more likely to have molested younger children than are nonsibling offenders (Worling, 1995).

Juvenile molesters are far more likely than juvenile rapists to have been sexually abused themselves in early childhood (Prentky, Harris, Frizzell, & Righthand, 2000). Juveniles who sexually offend against children display lower self-efficacy and self-esteem, and higher levels of depression, anxiety, and pessimism than found for other juvenile sex offenders (Hunter & Figueredo, 1999; Hunter, Figueredo, Malamuth, & Becker, 2003). They view themselves as socially inadequate and anticipate peer ridicule and rejection (Hunter *et al.*, 2003). They also show greater deficits in psychosocial functioning than other juvenile sex offenders, are less aggressive, and are more likely to offend against victims to whom they are related (Hunter *et al.*, 2003).

Female Juvenile Sex Offenders

According to the latest UCR statistics, juvenile females accounted for only 5 percent of all juveniles arrested for sex offenses (excluding forcible rape, where their rates are lower, and prostitution, where their rates are higher) (Federal Bureau of Investigation, 2008). However, the prevalence of juvenile female sexual offending is probably underreported. First, most of the research on female sex offending has focused on adult female offenders (Bumby & Bumby, 1997).

Second, as noted earlier, when female juveniles sexually offend, the victim is usually a child younger than themselves by five years or more, suggesting it is undiscovered or unlikely to be reported to protect the victim from additional trauma. Finally, research on girls who have committed sex offenses has been sparse, and existing investigations have been limited to small sample sizes and other methodological shortcomings (Becker, Hall, & Stinson, 2001; Righthand & Welch, 2001).

Fehrenbach and Monastersky (1988) found that most adolescent girls who sexually victimized young children did so while doing child care or babysitting. The victims of the 28 female sex offenders they studied were 12 years old or younger. They were mostly acquaintances (57%), followed by siblings (29%) and other relatives (14%). Mathews, Hunter, and Vuz (1997) provided data on 67 female adolescent sex offenders who ranged in age from 11 to 18. More than 90 percent of their victims were acquaintances or relatives. Each of the above two studies also found that a high percentage of the abusers (50% and 77.65%, respectively) themselves had a history of being sexually abused. These findings suggest that female juveniles who sexually offend are far more likely to have been sexually abused themselves than male juvenile sex offenders. Similarly, Bumby and Bumby (1997) found that adolescent female sex offenders tend to be depressed, have a poor self-concept, have a suicide ideation, and have most often been sexually abused during childhood.

RECIDIVISM OF PEDOPHILES

If pedophilia is learned, we would expect a fairly high incidence of recidivism. Like the national recidivism rates for most offenses, however, pedophile recidivism rates are difficult to obtain. Moreover, the second time around, the pedophile is undoubtedly more careful about detection. On the other hand, he is also more closely monitored by the criminal justice system or may be in treatment. Interestingly, therefore, some research suggests low repeat offending, particularly for nonviolent pedophiles. In general, though, research on recidivism must still be described as uncovering mixed results.

Hanson (2001) examined the recidivism rates of over 4,500 sexual offenders from diverse settings (Canada, the United States, and the United Kingdom). The data revealed a 19 percent sexual recidivism rate for extrafamilial pedophiles, compared with a sexual recidivism rate of 17 percent for rapists during an average follow-up time of five years. These figures seem low compared with the findings of other researchers. For example, in a follow-up investigation of 4,295 child molesters released from prison in 1994, Langan, Schmitt, and Durose (2003) found that 39 percent were rearrested within three years after release. However, this figure represents rearrest for any type of offense, not just sexual offenses. If we examine rearrest data for sex crime against a child, only 3.3 percent of the child molesters were rearrested within the three-year follow-up. Thus, Langan's rates are actually lower than those of Hanson. However, in a dated California study by Frisbie (1965), recidivism rates over a five-year period were reported to be 18.2 percent for heterosexual pedophiles and 34.5 percent for homosexual pedophiles.

Other types of data, including research on treatment dropout, suggest that recidivism is a significant problem. Abel and colleagues (Abel *et al.*, 1988) report that of the 192 nonincarcerated child offenders who voluntarily participated in a treatment program, the men most likely to drop out of treatment were those with a history of considerable and varied pedophilic behavior. That is, 70 percent of the frequent child offenders who demonstrated no age preference (child or adolescent) or gender preference (male or female) dropped out of treatment, usually early in the process. The treatment program consisted of 30 group sessions of 90 minutes given weekly and directed at decreasing deviant arousal, developing cognitive restructuring of distorted sexual attitudes and beliefs, and increasing subjects' social competence with adults. Interestingly, those subjects who managed to complete the program, and who had varied child offending behaviors and multiple victims, were the ones who were most likely to recidivate within one year after treatment. This should not suggest that treatment is ineffective, however. Further indications of recidivism rates of child offenders can be garnered from the 13-year outpatient treatment program described by Marshall and Barbaree (1988). This Canadian project offered psychological treatment of deviant sexual behavior on a voluntary basis to a variety of sexual offenders. Forty percent of the child offenders refused treatment. The project had access to official records (charges and convictions) throughout North America, as well as to information from "unofficial" files of local police departments and Children's Aid Societies in the towns where the offenders lived. Thirty-two percent of the untreated child offenders reoffended, compared with 14 percent of the treated offenders (a somewhat more optimistic appraisal of the effectiveness of treatment). The average follow-up period for both groups was approximately 3.5 years. Of the 26 men who recidivated, only 11 were identified "officially" (charges and convictions), whereas the remainder were identified through the "unofficial" information. Even so, the unofficial measures of recidivism were still collected by public agencies, leaving us to wonder how high the "true" unofficial recidivism rates for child offenders really are.

Recidivism of Juvenile Sex Offenders

Some investigators (Alexander, 1999; Hunter & Becker, 1999) have reported that juvenile sex offenders are significantly less likely to reoffend than adult offenders. In general, studies have reported that the juvenile offender recidivism rate for sex offenses ranges between 2 percent and 14 percent (Reitzel, 2003; Rubinstein, Yeager, Goodstein, & Lewis, 1993; Sipe, Jensen, & Everett, 1998; Waite *et al.*, 2005). Alexander (1999) found an overall sexual recidivism rate (based on rearrest) of 7 percent, with juvenile rapists having the highest sexual reoffending rate of all juvenile sex offenders. There is also considerable evidence that juvenile sex offenders who are highly impulsive and demonstrate poor self-regulation are far more likely to reoffend than those juvenile sex offenders who are evaluated as less impulsive (Waite *et al.*, 2005).

If juveniles do indeed reoffend less than adult sex offenders, this may be due to a variety of factors, including the aging out process and the availability of effective treatment. As we will note later in the chapter, extensive attention has been given to sex offender treatment in juvenile facilities, as well as in community placements. It is possible—though still speculative—that this attention is bearing fruit. As juveniles get older and move out of their living situations, they also are more likely to develop sexual relationships with persons within their own age group. Thus, they neither need nor have the same opportunity for contact with younger children.

THEORIES ON POTENTIAL CAUSES

Most explanations of pedophilia focus on a single factor as the principal cause of sexual and social preferences for children by adults. One clinical hypothesis, for example, suggests that pedophiles select children as sex objects because they are haunted by feelings of masculine and sexual inadequacy in adult relationships (e.g., Groth *et al.*, 1982). They are terrified of being ridiculed in their sexual and social behavior by the adult world. In the world of the child, they can be safely curious, awkward, and inexperienced. This observation might help explain why pedophiles rarely engage in intercourse with adults. Although this inadequacy hypothesis appears to have some validity, it fails to explain the full range and diversity of pedophilic behavior.

Finkelhor and Araji (1986) find four basic explanations for pedophilia in the research and clinical literature: emotional congruence, sexual arousal, blockage, and disinhibition theories (see **Table 2**). The most common is the *emotional congruence theories*. These theories try to explain why a person would think that relating sexually to a child is emotionally gratifying and congruent

TABLE 2   Four Theoretical Explanations for Pedophilia

Theory	Basic Premise
Emotional congruence	Pedophiles see themselves as children with childish emotional needs and interests, and therefore feel most comfortable with children.
Sexual arousal	Pedophiles become unusually sexually aroused to stimuli not typical of the other adults.
Blockage	Pedophilia is the result of unattainable sexual and emotional gratification with adults, usually because of inadequate interpersonal and social skills. They feel more comfortable socially and sexually with children.
Disinhibition	Pedophilia is the result of poor self-regulation or self-control.

with their needs. They convey the idea of a fit between the adult's emotional needs and the child's characteristics. Most congruence theories are psychoanalytic in origin and focus on "arrested psychological development." According to this perspective, pedophiles see themselves as children with childish emotional needs and dependency, and consequently they feel most comfortable with children. A similar version focuses on the low self-esteem and loss of efficacy pedophiles experience in their daily lives. Relating to a child is congruent, because the inadequate adult finally feels powerful, omnipotent, and in control of a relationship. In short, relating to a child provides a sense of mastery and control in their lives.

The second group of theories, the *sexual arousal theories,* try to explain why pedophiles become sexually aroused by certain characteristics of children. Sexual arousal is typically measured by penile tumescence to the presence of children or to sexual fantasies of children. This perspective contends that pedophiles become sexually aroused to stimuli (features of children) that, for a variety of reasons, do not generate sexual arousal in normal males. One set of theories within this group posits that it is a common childhood experience to engage in sexual play with playmates. For the pedophile, the childhood sexual play may have been particularly vivid, rewarding, stimulating, and even possibly the most sexually exciting experience he has ever had. Adult sexual play, by comparison, was less arousing, satisfying, or rewarding, perhaps even nonexistent. The pedophile's shyness, for example, may have precluded adult sexual contacts. Under these conditions, he probably took the most available sexual avenue, masturbation. The powerful reinforcing role of masturbatory behavior (masturbatory conditioning) has been demonstrated in clinical studies of most sexual offenses (Marshall, 1988). During masturbation, the pedophile's fantasies may focus on the satisfying sexual experiences he had during childhood. Repetitive masturbatory activity, therefore, reinforces the immature level of sexual behavior associated with childhood. Whereas masturbation of itself may be a normal outlet for sexual tension, for the pedophile it becomes an act that reinforces his attraction to children. Continual association between the pleasurable masturbatory activities and fantasies about childhood sexual experiences results in a strong bond between sexual arousal and children. Eventually, the children become sexual stimuli capable of arousing high levels of sexual excitation.

Another version of the sexual arousal perspective links traumatic sexual victimization to pedophilic behavior. Many researchers have found unusually high amounts of childhood sexual victimization in the background of pedophiles (Bard *et al.,* 1987). It is unclear, however, how sexual trauma, which is aversive, becomes conditioned or associated with the presumed sexual pleasures of pedophilia.

Blockage theories assume that pedophilia is the result of blockage of normal sexual and emotional gratification from adult relationships. Frustrated in his quest for normal channels of sexual gratification, the offender seeks the company of children. Blockage theories emphasize the unassertive, timid, inadequate, and awkward personalities of the pedophile, arguing that these social deficiencies make it nearly impossible for him to develop normal social and sexual relationships with adult women. When the marital relationship breaks down, for example, the pedophile may turn to his daughter as a substitute.

The fourth set of explanations focus on the loss of self-control and personal constraints on behavior. *Disinhibition theories* outline a variety of circumstances that presumably propel the offender to his deeds. Poor impulse control, excessive use of alcohol and drugs, and an assortment of stressors could all lead him over the brink to his favorite deviant sexual practices. As mentioned earlier, many pedophiles refuse to take blame, but attribute the cause of their pedophilic behavior to forces outside themselves. "I couldn't help myself" or "I don't know what came over me" are frequent pleas.

Which theoretical perspective has the inside track for the explanation of pedophilia? By itself, none can account for the multiple causes and the full range of learning experiences, beliefs, motivations, and attitudes of pedophiles. Theories that focus on cognitive aspects appear to be the most promising, just as treatment based on cognitive principles holds the most promise for preventing recidivism. Nonetheless, as Walters, Deming, and Elliott (2009, p. 1025) observe, "Cognitive factors have not received the attention they deserve from researchers in the field of sex offending."

In recent years, however, much research attention has been given to the cognitions and beliefs of child molesters, especially pertaining to their cognitive distortions. The cognitive distortion hypothesis states that child molesters hold "well-established and generalized offense-related beliefs that facilitate sexual offenses against children" (Gannon & Polaschek, 2006, p. 1001). An example would be the core belief that children are fundamentally sexual beings who enjoy and often seek out sex with adults (Ward, 2000). Another example would be the belief that children are relatively unaffected by sexual activities with adults (Gannon & Polaschek, 2006).

Gannon and her colleagues have critically examined the research and theory relating to cognitive distortions by child molesters (Gannon & Polaschek, 2006; Gannon, Ward, & Collie, 2007). Although clinical treatment of child molesters has run ahead of scientific knowledge, they conclude that there continues to be considerable confusion about the nature of these cognitive distortions. Consequently, researchers have yet to develop a comprehensive theory to explain child molesters and their motivations and beliefs. Next, we discuss a variety of other sexual activities that are far milder in their consequences for offenders and their effect on victims. Nevertheless, they are prohibited by the criminal law and thus qualify for consideration in this text. As will become clear, many of the same psychological principles discussed above are relevant here. The sexual offenses to be presented next are often classified under paraphilia disorders, as defined earlier in the chapter. To a large extent, most of the offenses described are referred to as "hands-off" offenses, indicating that there is no physical contact between the offender and the victim.

EXHIBITIONISM

Exhibitionism is the deliberate exposure of the genitals to another person to achieve sexual gratification. The DSM-IV-TR (American Psychiatric Association, 2000) criteria for exhibitionism are as follows: (1) For at least six months, a person has recurring, intense, sexually arousing fantasies or behaviors of exposing one's genitals to unsuspecting strangers, and (2) the fantasies, urges, or behaviors cause clinically significant distress or impairment in social, occupational, or other important areas of functioning. The fantasies or urges themselves are not crimes unless they are accompanied by the behavior, of course.

Several authors have reported that in some parts of the world, exhibitionism—often called indecent exposure—is the most frequent sexual offense known to the police (e.g., Murphy & Page, 2008; Wincze, 1977). The prevalence of the behavior is most likely underreported, as most victims do not report the incident to the police (Riordan, 1999). In Canada and the United States, exhibitionism—sometimes encompassed under the general class of lewd and lascivious behaviors in the legal system—accounts for about one-third of all sex crimes (Evans, 1970; Rooth, 1974), and in the United Kingdom, it accounts for one-fourth (Feldman, 1977). While exhibitionism, along with other relatively mild offenses such as voyeurism and frottage, make up a substantial number of officially recorded sex offenses, persons convicted of these offenses are rarely incarcerated (Rice, Harris, & Quinsey, 2001). In most states, exhibitionism is a misdemeanor, punishable by a fine and possibly a maximum of a year in jail. However, most courts try to avoid incarceration and instead recommend treatment alternatives. Bancroft (1976) estimates that exhibitionism is the second most common sexual deviation treated at mental health facilities in England. The major question is whether the offense leads to more serious sexual offending. At this juncture in our knowledge, the data are mixed and inconclusive (Murphy & Page, 2008). Compared with rape and pedophilia, this offense has received very little research attention, and what research is available is often very outdated. Very possibly, the paucity of research on the topic is because it is assumed that exhibitionism is simply a nuisance behavior that causes little harm to its victims. Evidence exists, however, that many victims of exposure experience traumatizing effects, and there is also some evidence that exhibitionism leads to a variety of other sexual deviations and offenses (Morin & Levinson, 2008).

Rooth (1973, 1974) argued that the practice of exposing oneself is primarily a Western phenomenon. In India, extensive surveys failed to uncover a single case (Rooth, 1974). In Japan, the incidence for one year was 59 convicted cases, compared with 2,767 in England and Wales during the same year. Rooth (1973) also suggested that exhibitionism is rare in Latin America and Third World countries.

To what extent exhibitionism is exclusively a Western phenomenon remains open to debate. Much depends on the culture and police discretion in each country. In Latin American countries, for example, it is a common sight to see men and women openly urinating in public (Rhoads & Borjes, 1981), but this of course does not qualify as exhibitionism. In an effort to determine comparable rates of exhibitionism, Rhoads and Borjes (1981) asked working women in both the United States and Guatemala how often men had exposed themselves to them in public. The survey indicated no difference in number of incidences, but the official records of the two countries were drastically different. This may reflect reluctance on the part of the Guatemalan women to report exhibitionism, since officers are likely to ridicule the victims, or it may reflect a more casual reaction to nudity in general. Across the globe, nudity itself is now common in the media, in clubs, on beaches, and in other venues both public and private. Interestingly, however, we still learn of incidents in which sculptures or other art works have been repositioned from a public window. In one highly publicized situation in the early 2000s, a painting in a government office building was covered with draperies, apparently at the request of a high-ranking government official. In general, though, as society continues to react more casually to nudity or exposure of sexual organs, exhibitionism will lose its shock value and the rates could decline.

Exhibitionists are almost always males who delight in surprising and shocking their audiences. They differ from "strippers"—both male and female—in that the former expose themselves for economic gain rather than sexual gratification. In addition, of course, persons watching strippers do so deliberately, openly, and voluntarily. Exhibitionists sometimes masturbate during the exposure, but most prefer to do so in private, immediately following their exposure.

Although exhibitionism is considered almost exclusively a male behavior, Långström and Seto (2006) discovered that it may also be a relatively common behavior in females. In Swedish national survey, Långström and Seto found that nearly one-third of the self-reported exhibitionists were females, suggesting that female exhibitionism may be more common than official or clinical data indicate.

Situational Characteristics

If the offender is not particularly brazen, he may habitually hide behind the curtain of a window in his home when school lets out and, as young girls walk by, tap on the window, quickly expose himself, and make a fast retreat behind the curtain. This is risky, however, since his identity is easily traceable. Another favorite procedure is to use a car, drive slowly by a girl or woman, open the car door, show himself, and quickly drive away. The bolder exhibitionist is often the "street flasher" who opens his coat to a selected victim, makes certain the impression registers, and then runs or walks away.

Favorite locations for exposure vary, but most exhibitionists prefer public places like parks, theaters, stores, or relatively uncrowded streets. An early Toronto study (Mohr, Turner, & Jerry, 1964) reported that 74 percent of a sample studied preferred open places, and most displayed themselves from a parked car. The remainder of the sample generally preferred their own homes, often exhibiting themselves through windows or doorways.

The overwhelming majority of exhibitionists prefer strangers for victims, and they rarely expose more than once to the same victim. Although the preferred victim is usually female, an exhibitionist will occasionally expose himself to adult males and male children. Exhibitionists who prefer adult women will usually expose to them individually, while those who prefer children will generally expose to small groups of two or three (Evans, 1970; Mohr et al., 1964). Most adult female victims are in their late teens or early twenties, supporting the theory that most exhibitionists deliberately select their victims on the basis of specific stimuli. For example, an exhibitionist may have a definite preference for exhibiting to young girls between the ages of 9 and 11 who look "naive." Another may search for a pretty face, dark hair, shapely legs, or various other physical features. Exhibitionists also tend to be consistent in the setting and time of day they choose for exposure. In fact, many are so predictable that, once the incident is reported, they are easily detected and arrested.

Offender Characteristics

Most exhibitionists begin their behavior at puberty, with a peak period occurring between ages 15 and 30 (Evans, 1970; Murphy & Page, 2008). Contrary to popular belief, onset after age 30 is extremely rare, except in men with mental impairment due to organic brain damage or some form of dementia. Compared with the general population, exhibitionists usually have at least average intelligence, educational levels, and vocational interests (Blair & Lanyon, 1981). The majority also appear to have a reliable work record (Mohr et al., 1964).

Psychosis or other mental disorders are found no more frequently in exhibitionists than in the general population (Blair & Lanyon, 1981). However, exhibitionists show an above average incidence of previous sexual offenses other than exhibitionism, including voyeurism and even attempted rape. In the main, however, exhibitionists neither assault their audience physically nor desire sexual intercourse with them. It is highly probable that if victims expressed interest in sexual activity, most exhibitionists would be frightened and confused and would flee. In most cases, the primary motive behind the exhibitionism is the sexual excitation (reinforcement) the offender receives from shocking, surprising, or mildly frightening his victims. These reactions generate considerable sexual arousal. Later, he will probably masturbate to that image. On the other hand, if his exposure fails to engender the anticipated fright or surprise, and produces instead a disinterested, noncommittal facial expression, the offender is disappointed and suffers some loss of self-esteem. It is not recommended that the victim laugh at or otherwise ridicule the exhibitionist.

Although many exhibitionists are married, most are considered socially and sexually inadequate both by themselves and by those around them. Many are introverted, shy, socially reserved individuals who feel uncomfortable in most social situations. Generally, they are described as unassertive, self-effacing, timid, and passive. A majority of exhibitionists feel the urge to expose following a blow to their fragile self-esteem, which prompts heightened feelings of inadequacy and stress.

Therefore, like other sexual offenses, exhibitionism is a learned behavioral pattern reinforced by sexual arousal and the subsequent tension reduction achieved through masturbation. Many exhibitionists indicate that their behavior was initially acquired through some preadolescent sex play or by chance. For example, the history of most exhibitionists includes a vivid memory of a young girl expressing amazement or fear at their penis, viewed either accidentally or during sexual play. Characteristically, this attention was sexually exciting to the male, and he masturbated to the imagery of the incident. This not uncommon incident by itself is usually not sufficient to establish exhibitionism. However, a repeated pairing of the memory of the event with the sexual arousal derived from masturbation may lead to a proclivity for exhibitionism in individuals who lack sufficient self-control or self-regulatory mechanisms. That is, pleasurable, repetitive masturbatory activities in the presence of this mental imagery strongly encourage eventual exposure of the penis to victims who are perceived as similar to the initial observer. If the first, real-life exposure is sexually arousing, a strongly reinforcing chain of events is established. Each time the exhibitionist exposes and receives this sequence of rewards, the behavior pattern becomes that much more firmly entrenched.

During subsequent periods of stress and inadequacy, exposure becomes an increasingly effective way of dealing with uncomfortable emotions, especially when preferred victims are available. Therefore, because exhibitionism is a learned response, it continues to be repetitive and resistant to extinction. Furthermore, exhibitionists may expose themselves countless times without complaints from victims. Irate adults usually do not report an incidence of exhibitionism unless the victim was their offspring. Even then, they may not report in order to protect the child from having to describe the incident to police.

Murphy and Page (2008) note that, from a clinical standpoint, exhibitionism can have a major impact on the offender and his family. The behavior occurs frequently, and consequently the risks for arrest are high, leading to public embarrassment and significant stress for the family. There is also some evidence that, because the behavior is partly due to poor self-regulation or self-control, the exhibitionist is arrested for other offenses (Firestone, Kingston, Wexler, & Bradford, 2006; Murphy & Page, 2008). Approximately 15 percent are arrested for other nonsexual offenses (Firestone *et al.*, 2006). Another common clinical observation that highlights self-regulation problems is that many exhibitionists exhibited a variety of behavioral disorders such as ADHD and conduct disorders in childhood (Kafka & Hennen, 2003; Lee, Jackson, Pattison, & Ward, 2002).

It is important to note that exhibitionists, in contrast to many pedophiles, often express a desire to change their behavior. Although they may expose themselves numerous times, once detected they are more likely to seek therapeutic help. Moreover, it is not uncommon for an exhibitionist to seek professional help prior to being arrested for his behavior. Reviewing the literature on treatment for sex offenders, Rice *et al.* (2001) note that motivated exhibitionists have been helped by pharmacological or other treatments designed to reduce sexual arousal together with attention to other factors that might facilitate their offending, such as depression or lack of employment. Day and Berney (2001) note that antiandrogen drugs have been shown to be effective in cases of exhibitionism, pedophilia, and fetishism in developmentally disabled individuals. There is no evidence that these individuals are any more likely than others to engage in these activities, however.

VOYEURISM AND FETISHISM

Voyeurism, also known as scoptophilia or inspectionalism, is the tendency to gain sexual excitement and gratification from observing unsuspecting others naked, undressing, or engaging in sexual activity. The term **fetishism** refers specifically to a sexual attraction to inanimate objects rather than to people. It is distinct from **partialism,** which is an exaggerated sexual interest in some part of the human anatomy not usually associated with sexual arousal, such as the knee. The individual with a fetish may become sexually aroused at the sight of boots, handbags, stockings, panties, fur, or even tailpipes on motor vehicles. The fetish object may be kissed, fondled, tasted, smelled, or just looked at.

Both voyeurism and fetishism are little more than minor sexual offenses, since they usually do not seriously harm the community. They are, of course, egregious violations of other people's privacy, because "victims" are being observed without their knowledge or their possessions are appropriated for "deviant" purposes. The United Kingdom did not make voyeurism a crime until passage in 2004 of the Sexual Offences Act of 2003 (Lavin, 2008). Canada included "peeping" in its criminal code also in 2004 (Lavin, 2008). The voyeur or the fetishist most likely runs afoul of the law when he harasses, trespasses, burglarizes, damages property, or steals objects.

Recall that the voyeur is sometimes an exhibitionist, and vice versa. However, the voyeur is even less likely than the exhibitionist to become involved in serious forms of antisocial behavior, such as rape or other forms of violence. He does not harm his victims physically, and, like the exhibitionist, he is often described as a passive, shy, introverted, submissive, and harmless person. Clinical studies reveal that he suffers from strong heterosexual anxieties and immaturity.

One observation made in a dated but widely cited study by the Queen's Bench Foundation (1978) demands attention. About 10 percent of the convicted rapists interviewed for that study stated that they had watched their victim through a window before attacking her. The authors suggested that, in light of this finding, some "peeping Toms" should be watched for possible rape tendencies. However, some distinguishing aspects about voyeurism should be noted. All but one offender had intentions of raping before observing. The one rapist who said that he did not intend to rape when he watched his victim admitted that he did intend to "have sex" with her. In addition, all but one of these offenders had weapons in their possession at the time of their arrest (knives, guns, meat fork), even though they ordinarily did not carry them. Also, forceful entry into the victim's apartment was the common approach, and the victim was often raped with extreme violence.

These rapists, therefore, probably had little in common with the typical voyeur. Their intention from the outset was to attack the victim violently. They apparently watched the victim to determine her habits, whether anyone else was at home, and the best way to get into her residence. In other words, they were stalking their victims. The typical voyeur gets his satisfaction from watching, imagining, and eventually masturbating, with no intention of having sexual contact, forced or otherwise, with the victim. It is primarily a male behavior, although there have been clinical reports of female voyeurists (Mann, Ainsworth, Al-Attar, & Davies, 2008).

Voyeurism, like other forms of sexual deviation, is a learned behavior. Although each individual has a unique approach to viewing, many voyeurs report the preadolescent experience of becoming sexually aroused while watching an unsuspecting woman undress. A common theme running through clinical studies is that the mental imagery of that scene is later coupled with sexual arousal, again perhaps satisfied through masturbation. Eventually, this conditioning produces a desire to observe different, realistic sexual scenes. Keep in mind that an important component of the sexual excitement experienced by the voyeur is his victim's *unawareness* of his presence. Erotic films or pornography, by themselves, are not likely to serve his purpose.

In contrast to voyeurism, fetishism is pursued in the privacy of one's home, without interference. It is primarily a male phenomenon. A fetish refers to the use of nonliving objects as a repeatedly and strongly preferred method of achieving sexual excitement. The fetish object is most often a woman's wearing apparel, such as undergarments, shoes, boots, or stockings. The person with a fetish typically masturbates while rubbing, holding, or smelling the fetish object or may ask the sexual partner to wear the object during their sexual encounters (DSM-IV, 1994, p. 526). Through classical conditioning, virtually any object may assume sexual significance. Gosselin and Wilson (1984) describe a study of a man who was strongly attracted to safety pins. From the age of eight, he had experienced extreme sexual pleasure from gazing at these shiny objects in the privacy of his bathroom. "When he was 23 his wife observed the complete sequence, which began with him staring at the safety pin for about a minute. This was followed by a glassy-eyed appearance, vocal humming noises, sucking movements of the lips and total immobility for another minute or two" (Gosselin & Wilson, 1984, p. 104).

As mentioned previously, most fetish objects are those worn by a woman. Chalkley and Powell (1983) found that women's underwear, stockings, and other types of lingerie were most popular for British fetish collectors. Next most common were rubber and certain rubber articles such as Mackintoshes, tubes, dolls, and paraphernalia for giving enemas.

In a carefully designed, if controversial, demonstration of fetish conditioning, Rachman (1966) showed male subjects a slide of a pair of women's black boots, followed immediately by slides of attractive, naked women (sexual arousal). After a number of such trials, the subjects became sexually excited, as measured by penile circumference, in response to the boots slide itself. There were also indications that the subjects not only became aroused by the particular boots, but also by slides of other boots and shoes as well.

Fetishism merits attention here primarily because the person with a strong attachment to an object might commit larceny or burglary to get it. Fetish objects, particularly if they are items of apparel, are not typically purchased in retail outlets. They must belong to, or have been used by, someone else. Therefore, one of the major avenues for obtaining fetishes is to steal, and, since clothes dryers are more in vogue in modern society than clotheslines, the fetishist's traditional method of stealing from the backyard clothesline has been replaced by more daring techniques. Chalkley and Powell (1983), in their British sample of 48 cases of fetishism, found that 38 percent experienced considerable excitement and sexual arousal even in the act of stealing the fetish. In this sense, it is conceivable that an indeterminant number of unexplained burglaries (when minor things are taken but more valuable items remain untouched) are a result of an impatient quest for fetishes! Some fetish burglars find sexual excitement just being in someone's house without his or her knowledge and presence. It is also not unusual for the fetish burglar to take valuable objects along with his fetish, however, either to throw off suspicion or to offer a face-saving "reasonable" explanation for the burglary if he is apprehended. In one serious fetish case described by Hazelwood and Burgess (1987), the offender admitted committing over 5,000 burglaries primarily to obtain panties to satisfy his fetish. He also estimated that he stole valuables in about one-half of these burglaries.

TREATMENT OF SEX OFFENDERS

While the research is mixed with respect to recidivism rates among sex offenders, as a general principle, they are often highly resistant to changing their deviant behavior patterns. As noted above, there are exceptions both across offender types and within an offender population.

A wide variety of treatment programs have been tried, but few have been successful in eradicating sexual offending. A 1994 survey of therapeutic services for sex offenders revealed that there were 710 adult and 684 juvenile treatment programs (Longo, Bird, Stevenson, & Fiske, 1995), compared with 297 adult and 346 juvenile treatment programs in 1985 (Knopp, Rosenberg, & Stevenson, 1986). Despite the increase in treatment programs, the success ratio remains disappointingly low (Camilleri & Quinsey, 2008; Thakker, Collie, Gannon, & Ward, 2008). After careful review of the research and clinical literature, Furby, Weinrott, and Blackshaw (1989, p. 27) concluded, "There is as yet no evidence that clinical treatment reduces rates of sex reoffenses in general and no appropriate data for assessing whether it may be differentially effective for different types of offenders." The Furby review included all variants of therapeutic approaches. Likewise, Marnie Rice *et al.* (2001, p. 302) write, "The effectiveness of sex-offender treatment has yet to be demonstrated. . . . Thus the treatment outcome literature is profoundly unhelpful in giving clues about what might be effective with particular kinds of sex offenders." Nevertheless, Rice *et al.* note that all is not hopeless. They urge clinicians to adopt individualized treatment approaches that take into account an offender's motivation. Specific interventions designed to reduce recidivism should then be undertaken. An essential component of the treatment, they point out, is ongoing supervision.

Furthermore, many psychologists who work with offenders as a group are becoming more optimistic. Most of the optimism comes from those working with child molesters (Thakker *et al.*, 2008). First, they believe that the most effective interventions, or treatment methods, are those that follow the principles of risk, need, and responsivity (**RNR**) identified by James Bonta, Robert Hoge, and Don Andrews (see, e.g., Andrews, Bonta, & Hoge, 1990; Bonta & Andrews, 2007). Second, they believe that these principles can be applied to sex offenders. Camilleri and Quinsey (2008), for example, conclude from their extensive review of treatment for child molesters that treatment so far has been ineffective because no one has developed "a method that can durably alter the central criminogenic need factor in pedophilia—sexual preference for children" (p. 203).

Before discussing how RNR principles relate to sexual offending, it is worthwhile to overview them briefly. According to Hanson *et al.* (2009, p. 867), " . . . treatments are most likely to be effective when they treat offenders who are likely to reoffend (moderate or higher risk), target characteristics that are related to reoffending (criminogenic needs), and match treatment to the offenders' learning styles and abilities (responsivity; cognitive-behavioral interventions work best)."

Interestingly, offenders who are considered low risks of reoffending are also not considered good targets for psychological treatment. This is both because they do not need the intensive attention and because scarce resources can best be applied to offenders who need them the most. Low-risk offenders can benefit from support services in the community (e.g., help with finding employment or improving social skills). Moderate and high-risk offenders, on the other hand, can benefit by psychological treatment that focuses on their criminogenic needs, defined as factors in their lives that make it more likely that they will engage in criminal activity. Examples of criminogenic needs are substance abuse problems or episodes of violent behavior. The responsivity principle is met if the treatment offered recognizes the individual strengths and abilities of the offender. Thus, to be effective, the treatment provider should be attentive to the level of risk posed by the offender, the factors in his or her life that are conducive to continued offending, and the offender's individual cognitions and learning style. Cognitive behavioral programs have fared very well when measured against this last criterion because they seek to engage the offender actively in his or her own treatment. In a meta-analysis involving 69 studies and covering close to 10,000 sexual offenders, Lösel and Schmucker (2005; Schmucker & Lösel, 2008) found that treatment programs based on cognitive behavioral principles had positive effects. Likewise, Hanson *et al.* (2009) found in another meta-analysis that a program's faithfulness to RNR principles was associated with lower recidivism in sex offenders.

Prentky *et al.* (1997) conclude that sex offender therapy can be categorized into four broad approaches. One approach is **evocative therapy,** a treatment that focuses on (1) helping offenders to understand the causes and motivations of their sexual behavior, and (2) increasing their empathy for the victims of the sexual assault. Evocative therapy may include individual, group, couples/marital, and family counseling. A second approach is **psychoeducational counseling**, which utilizes a group or class setting to remedy deficits in social and interpersonal skills. Psychoeducational strategies include anger management, the principles of relapse prevention, and other topics such as human sexuality, dating, and myths about sexuality and relationships. A third approach is **drug treatment.** This approach concentrates on "reducing sexual arousability and the frequency of deviant sexual fantasies through the use of antiandrogen and antidepressant medication" (Prentky *et al.*, 1997, p. 13). The fourth approach is **cognitive behavior therapy**. The behavioral component focuses on sexual preference, while the cognitive component focuses on changing beliefs, fantasies, attitudes, and rationalizations that justify and perpetuate sexually violent behavior. Child molesters appear to have far more cognitive distortions than men who sexually assault adult women (Camilleri & Quinsey, 2008). Prentky *et al.* (1997) suggest that the most effective approach probably resides in using some combination of the four, although which specific combination remains unclear. They agree, however, that cognitive-behavioral approaches (complemented on occasion with some medication) continue to offer the most effective technique in the temporary cessation of deviant sexual behavior in motivated individuals. Cognitive-behavior therapy argues that maladaptive sexual behaviors are learned according to the same rules as normal sexual behavior, by means of classical and/or instrumental conditioning, modeling, reinforcement, generalization, and punishment. They are, therefore, modifiable. Cognitive-behavioral therapy, compared with traditional verbal, insight-oriented therapy, has demonstrated short-term effectiveness in eliminating exhibitionism and fetishism (Kilmann, Sabalis, Gearing, Bukstel, & Scovern, 1982), some forms of pedophilia (Hall, 1995; Marshall & Barbaree, 1988), and sexual aggression and arousal (Quinsey & Marshall, 1983).

A major problem, however, is not with getting the motivated offender to stop his deviant sexual pattern, but with preventing his relapse across time and situations. This is especially the case with pedophilia. It is analogous to dieting. Most diet regimens do work in getting the motivated individual to lose weight. However, they offer little help in preventing people from eventually relapsing into old eating habits. This is why ongoing therapeutic supervision of sex offenders is critical. Although some success with cognitive-behavioral therapy with sex offenders has been established, the effects of the treatment often do not last (Brecklin & Forde, 2001; Camilleri & Quinsey, 2008).

A treatment approach showing some promise in the treatment of sex offenders is called **relapse prevention (RP)**. "RP is a self-control program designed to teach individuals who are trying to change their behavior how to anticipate and cope with the problem of relapse" (George & Marlatt, 1989, p. 2). The program emphasizes self-management; clients are considered responsible not for the cause but for the solution of the problem. And as the name implies, the program concentrates on preventing a *relapse* of deviant sexual behavior. Therefore, RP distinguishes treatment from maintenance. As stated earlier, cognitive-behavior therapy is effective in the temporary cessation of the behavior, but additional steps must be taken to make the change permanent. Cognitive behavioral therapists are well aware of this, and some employ RP to achieve this goal.

RP is specifically designed to be effective in helping the individual *maintain* the "cure." Distinctions are made between the terms *relapse* and *lapse*. "Relapse is a violation of a self-imposed rule or set of rules governing the rate or pattern of a selected target behavior" (George & Marlatt, 1989, p. 6). A *lapse* on the other hand, refers to "a single instance of violating the rule" (p. 6). "With sex offenders, the term relapse will refer to any occurrence of a sexual offense, thus connoting full-scale reestablishment of the problematic behavior. The term lapse will refer to any occurrence of willful and elaborate fantasizing about sexual offending or any return to sources of stimulation associated with the sexual offense pattern, but short of performance of the offense behavior" (p. 6).

RP, as a system of maintenance-oriented principles and interventions, has two central objectives: It teaches individuals (1) to cope effectively with "high-risk situations" (HRSs), and (2) to identify and respond to early warning signals of urges and "apparently irrelevant decisions" (AIDs). An HRS is any situation that poses a threat to the individual's sense of control over his behavior and consequently increases the probability of lapse or relapse. Examples of HRSs that may predispose an individual toward relapse include negative emotional states, such as anger and depression, interpersonal conflict, and various social pressures (George & Marlatt, 1989).

Research by Pithers and associates (Pithers, Kashima, Cumming, Beal, & Buell, 1988; Pithers, Beal, Armstrong, & Petty, 1989) has found that rapists often experience anger and use alcohol or other drugs before engaging in sexual aggression. Pedophiles, on the other hand, often experience anxiety or depression before seeking a child. A feeling of low self-esteem is experienced by both groups. These precursors reflect the beginning stages of an HRS. In other words, they psychologically predispose the individual toward a relapse.

Relapse seems to follow a sequence of events, all representing HRSs (George & Marlatt, 1989; Pithers, Marques, Gibat, & Marlatt, 1983). First, an urge, fleeting thought, or dream about committing an offense occurs. This is followed by elaborations of fantasies about committing the offense. Then, the aroused individual engages in masturbation coupled with fantasies and/or pornography related to the imagined sexual activity. The individual then plans how he is going to commit the act. Finally, the individual engages in the act. RP provides a framework within which a variety of behavioral, cognitive, educational, and skill-training techniques are used to train sex offenders to recognize and interrupt these chains of events (Marshall & Barbaree, 1988).

Critical to RP treatment intervention is the motivation of the offender. Without motivation, the program will not work. Remember, RP is aimed primarily at *maintaining* a cessation of the deviant behavior, not cessation itself. Therefore, a behavior therapy program or other conventional treatment intervention that stops the behavior must precede RP. The treatment phase normally takes a relatively short period of time. Another important point outlined by George and Marlatt (1989) is that incarceration without treatment will not prevent reoffending. They offer three reasons for this. First, externally imposed, forced control does little to encourage an offender to seek help in changing his ways. Second, the offender can still maintain attachment to his offense pattern through fantasy. Third, it is conceivable that an offender could continue to actually engage in some semblance of his offense patterns even during confinement.

RP is a relatively recent development and its long-term success has yet to be established (Marques, Wiederanders, Day, Nelson, & Van Ommeren, 2005). However, it does have substantial promise for the elimination of deviant behavior in offenders motivated to change. And as noted by Prentky *et al.* (1997, p. 14), "Continuity of treatment is considered a critical factor in managing sex offenders. Maintenance is forever, and Relapse Prevention never ends. Community-based clinical management must be supportive, vigilant, and informed by current wisdom about maximally effective maintenance."

Treatment of Juvenile Sex Offenders

While juvenile sexual offenders (JSOs) may also be treated in community settings, we focus here on the serious offenders who are most likely to be held in restrictive institutional settings. Nevertheless, it is important to keep in mind that juvenile sexual offenders—like adult sexual offenders—are often viewed as a homogeneous class of individuals. Research shows, however, that they vary widely in the frequency and type of sexual activity they engage in, and they differ in personal attributes, such as age, background, personality, race, religion, beliefs, attitudes, and social skills.

The foundation of treatment for JSOs is grounded on the premise that their deviant sexual behaviors are associated with distorted thought patterns that serve to deny, justify, minimize, and rationalize their actions (Eastman, 2004). Research reveals that sexually aggressive male juveniles subscribe to attitudes and ideology that encourage males to be dominant, controlling, and powerful, whereas females are expected to be submissive, permissive, and compliant. Such a cognitive orientation seems to have a particularly strong disinhibitory effect on sexually aggressive juveniles, prompting them to interpret ambiguous behaviors of girls or women as come-ons, to believe that they are not really offended by coercive sexual behavior, and to perceive victims as desiring and deriving gratification from being sexually assaulted (Lipton, McDonel & McFall, 1987). Thus, it would seem that cognitive behavioral programs, aimed at encouraging the offender to modify these misperceptions, would hold considerable promise.

Consequently, treatment approaches to JSOs have traditionally included treatment of denial, past victimization, attitudes and values, social skills, and arousal patterns (Kahn & LaFond, 1988; Sciarra, 1999). In addition, these treatment programs have been modeled after treatment programs designed for adult sex offenders. However, few studies have examined whether these same programs are effective in the treatment of JSOs until recently.

Currently, there is considerable ongoing research evaluating treatment programs for juveniles (Veneziano & Veneziano, 2002). These programs designed for JSOs are different from those that target adult sexual offenders. This is primarily because contemporary research suggests that juveniles are far more changeable than adults, are more influenced by the social environment, and appear to be at lower risk for sexual recidivism (Veneziano & Veneziano, 2002).

Summary and Conclusions

Following upon the chapter on serious sexual assaults of adults, the present chapter has focused upon sexual offenses against children. We used the term pedophilia to characterize these offenses but noted that the legal terms include but are not limited to child molestation, child sexual assault, and child rape. Individuals are not arrested and charged with pedophilia; this is a clinical term that covers a range of sexually related offenses against children. However, the term pedophile is now commonly used by the public and in media accounts.

Sexual assaults against children—covering a range of offenses—are disturbingly too common, although accurate statistics are difficult to obtain. Much of our information is derived not only from arrest and conviction data but also from the reports of adults who say they were victimized as children and from the perpetrators themselves. Arrest data indicate that 34 percent of all victims of sexual assault reported to law enforcement in the early 1990s were under age 12. In a related finding, some research indicates that approximately two-thirds of convicted rapists in state prisons committed their crimes against children. By their own accounts, offenders admit to molesting not one but many children, sometimes over a period of years. Other research suggests that from a quarter to a third of all women and one-tenth of men say they were sexually abused during childhood. As we discussed in the chapter, the long-term psychological effects of this victimization are often, if not typically, devastating.

We reviewed a variety of offender characteristics, including both demographic and psychological features. Aggressive pedophiles—not all are—show similarities to men who rape adults, including problems with alcohol, high school failure rates, unstable work history, and low socioeconomic status. Pedophiles as a group tend to be older than rapists, although the great majority apparently commits the first offense before age 30. Although increasingly more attention is being given to female pedophiles, pedophilia is still predominantly a male phenomenon.

The cognitive skills of pedophiles are typically lower than those of the general population. They often lack social skills and adequate self-control mechanisms. They rarely take responsibility for their offenses, preferring to attribute their behavior to external forces beyond their control. Although there have been successful treatment programs for pedophiles, program dropout rates are often high. However, many clinicians maintain that pedophiles are far easier to treat than rapists.

The Massachusetts Treatment Center has developed classification systems for the behavioral patterns of both rapists and child molesters. Both systems have undergone revision to further specify and refine some of their categories and to incorporate crime scene information. We reviewed the MTC systems in some detail, focusing on the MTC:CM3, the latest version. Similar but less elaborate classification systems proposed by Groth for both rapists and child molesters were covered as well. The MTC classification systems are the most widely used and have been the most submitted to empirical research.

We discussed some of the available research on juvenile sex offending, which is clearly a major challenge to the juvenile justice system. Distinctions are often made in the literature between juvenile molesters and juvenile rapists. For example, molesters almost invariably choose children younger than they are as victims, while rapists choose victims of about the same age or older. Molesters are also more likely than rapists to have been victims of child sexual abuse and to view themselves as socially inadequate. The topic of female juvenile sex offending is increasingly making an appearance in the literature. These offenders typically have been abused themselves and often commit their abuses while babysitting or otherwise caring for children.

A variety of explanatory theories were covered, but it is clear that no one theory or no one factor would account for the behavior of all offenders. We cannot say, for example, that all pedophiles engage in their actions because they are haunted by feelings of sexual inadequacy with adults. Theories have been placed in one of four major groups: the emotional congruence, the sexual arousal, the blockage, and the disinhibition theories. While pedophilia appears to be motivated by both sexual desire and an expectation of sexual adequacy that would not occur in sexual congress with another adult, it is engaged in for a variety of reasons by a variety of offenders.

Thus, there is no such thing as a common "molester profile." Each has his own construct system and beliefs about his behavior and motivations. Some offenders, for whatever reason, are vicious and violent; others are passive, relatively meek people who enjoy the companionship of children. It appears from the research that many, if not most, pedophiles are the latter. They apparently see themselves as sexually and interpersonally inept adults who feel more comfortable interacting with children.

We also gave some attention to the minor sexual offenses of exhibitionism and voyeurism, as well as to fetishism. Classical conditioning, particularly masturbatory conditioning, appears to play a crucial role in the development of these sexual deviations, as it does with pedophilia. Sexual arousal repeatedly linked with objects and persons seems especially important.

Although reviews of the treatment literature are not encouraging, particularly programs aimed at the most serious offenders, treatment of sexual offending can be successful if the offender's motivation to change is evident. Successful treatment strategies must not only focus on the cessation of the antisocial sexual conduct, but also on maintenance of prosocial behaviors as well. Thus, continual monitoring or supervision should be a part of the treatment regimen. Recent meta-analyses indicate that cognitive-behavioral treatment based on risk, needs, and responsivity (RNR) principles is most promising with respect to both sex offenders and offenders in general.

Key Concepts

Aggressive (sadistic) pedophile

Cognitive behavior therapy

Drug treatment

Evocative therapy

Exhibitionism

Exploitative pedophile

Extrafamilial child molestation

Fetishism

Fixated (immature) pedophile

Hebephilia
Intrafamilial child
    molestation
Paraphilia
Partialism

Pedophile
Pedophilia
Psychoeducational
    counseling
Regressed pedophile

Relapse prevention (RP)
RNR (risk, needs,
    responsivity
    principles)
Voyeurism

Review Questions

1. Define partialism and paraphilia.
2. What are the major differences between extrafamilial pedophiles and intrafamilial pedophiles?
3. List four demographic characteristics of pedophiles.
4. Outline the pedophile typologies of the MTC and the Groth system. Which is better supported by the research literature?
5. List some of the justifications that pedophiles use for their sexual behavior.
6. In what major way does a fixed pedophile differ from a regressed pedophile?
7. What three treatment principles are represented in the acronym RNR? Briefly define each.

GLOSSARY

GLOSSARY

adjudicative competence The ability to participate in a variety of court proceedings. See also, **incompetent to stand trial.**

admitters Refers to those sex offenders who are willing to take responsibility for their actions.

adolescent-limited (AL) offender An individual who usually demonstrates delinquent or antisocial behavior only during his or her teen years and then stops offending during his or her young adult years.

advantageous comparison An offender's process of convincing himself that his values and ways of life are superior to those of his victims; used to explain the cognitive restructuring that occurs in terrorism.

aggression, hostile (expressive) Aggressive behavior characterized by the intent to cause the target discomfort or pain.

aggression, instrumental Aggressive behavior characterized by the intent to gain material or financial rewards from the target.

aggressive driving Reckless behavior while driving that indicates anger, hostility, or frustration as a result of a recent incident or series of incidents in the driver's life. The aggressive driving may be prompted by minor, irritating actions of another motorist but these actions are not the root cause of the reckless behavior. Should be distinguished from **road rage.**

aggressive (sadistic) pedophile An adult drawn to children for both sexual and aggressive (violent) purposes.

ambiversion Scoring in the average range on the extraversion–introversion scale developed by Hans J. Eysenck.

amnesia Complete or partial (**limited**) memory loss of an incident, series of incidents, or some aspects of life's experiences.

anger rape A rape situation, identified by Groth, in which an offender uses more force than necessary for compliance and engages in a variety of sexual acts that are particularly degrading or humiliating to the victim.

anger retaliation rapist A classification of rapists proposed by the Massachusetts Research Center to identify those individuals who are more motivated to humiliate the victim than to gain sexual gratification. See also **displaced anger rapist.**

antisocial behavior Clinical term reserved for serious habitual behavior, especially that involving direct harm to others.

antisocial personality disorder (APD or ASP) A disorder characterized by a history of continuous behavior in which the rights of others are violated.

arson Any willful or malicious burning or attempt to burn, with or without intent to defraud, a dwelling house, public building, motor vehicle, aircraft, or personal property of another.

assault The intentional inflicting of bodily injury on another person, or the attempt to inflict such injury.

assault, aggravated Inflicting, or attempting to inflict, bodily injury on another person, with the intent to inflict serious injury.

assault, simple The unlawful, intentional inflicting of less than serious bodily injury without a deadly or dangerous weapon, or the attempt to inflict such bodily injury, again without a deadly or dangerous weapon.

attachment theory A theory developed by John Bowlby, and later expanded by Mary Salter Ainsworth, which states that infants have a strong need to establish close emotional bonds with significant others in their social environments. According to the theory, the nature of this emotional bond determines the quality of social relationships later in life.

attention deficit hyperactivity disorder (ADHD) Traditionally considered a chronic neurobiological condition characterized by developmentally poor attention, impulsivity, and hyperactivity. More contemporary perspectives see the behavioral pattern as a deficiency in interpersonal skills.

authoritarian style The approach to parenting that sets a very rigid structure on the family setting and allows little decision making by the child.

authoritative style The approach to parenting that sets firm rules yet encourages the development of autonomy in the child.

authority homicide In the context of workplace violence, the killing of a supervisor or other person in authority by an employee.

autoeroticism A term coined by Havelock Ellis that refers to the self-arousal and self-gratification of sexual arousal.

availability heuristic The cognitive shortcuts that people use to make quick inferences about their world. It is the information that is most readily available to us mentally, and is usually based extensively on the most recent material we gain from the news or entertainment media.

avoidance learning A process whereby, if a person responds in time to a warning signal, he or she avoids painful or aversive stimuli.

barricade situation In hostage-taking scenarios, a situation in which an individual has fortified him or herself in a building or residence and threatens violence, typically to the hostages.

battered woman syndrome A cluster of behavioral and psychological characteristics believed common to women who have been abused in relationships.

behaviorism A perspective that focuses on observable, measurable behavior and argues that the social environment and learning are the key determinants of human behavior.

biopsychologists Psychologists who study the biological aspects of behavior to determine which genetic and neurophysiological variables play a part. They generally see human behavior as the result of a complex interaction between the individual's physiological and social environment.

bioterrorism The category of terrorism that involves the use of bacteria, viruses, germs, and other agents.

boot camps Military-style, short-term facilities for juveniles and adults who have not committed serious crimes; most focus on instilling discipline rather than education or treatment.

boosters Professional shoplifters.

Brawner Rule A standard for evaluating the insanity defense that recognizes that the defendant suffers from a condition that substantially (1) affects mental or emotional processes, or (2) impairs behavior controls. Also called the ALI/Brawner Rule.

burglary The unlawful entry of a structure, with or without force, with intent to commit a felony or theft.

carjacking The completed or attempted theft in which a motor vehicle is taken by force or threat of force.

caveat paragraph A section of the ALI/Brawner Rule that excludes abnormality manifested only by repeated criminal or antisocial conduct. It was specifically designed to disallow the insanity defense for psychopaths.

child delinquents Children between the ages of 7 and 12 who have committed or are accused of committing a criminal act.

classical (Pavlovian) conditioning The process of learning to respond to a formerly neutral stimulus that has been paired with another stimulus that already elicits a response. Also called **Pavlovian conditioning.**

classic mass murder A situation in which an individual enters a public place or barricades himself or herself inside a public building, such as a fast-food restaurant, and randomly kills patrons and other individuals.

classical theory Theory of human behavior that emphasizes free will as a core concept.

classification In corrections, the process of placing offenders into categories for the purposes of custody and treatment.

clearance rate The proportion of reported crimes that have been "solved" through the arrest and turning over for prosecution of at least one person. Crimes also may be cleared through exceptional means.

coercion theory The belief that punitive and coercive tactics employed by parents will increase the likelihood of later aggressive behavior and family violence.

cognitions The internal processes that enable humans to imagine, to gain knowledge, to reason, and to evaluate. The attitudes, beliefs, values, and thoughts that a person holds about the environment, relationships, and him- or herself.

cognitive behavior therapy An approach to therapy that focuses on changing beliefs, fantasies, attitudes, and rationalizations that justify and perpetuate antisocial or other problematic behavior. It is often used in the treatment of sex offenders.

cognitive learning The formation and development of mental concepts, schemas, theories, attitudes, beliefs, and other mental versions of the world.

cognitive-neoassociation model A revised theory of the frustration-aggression hypothesis proposed by Leonard Berkowitz.

cognitive processes Internal mental processes that enable humans to imagine, gain knowledge, reason, and evaluate information.

cognitive restructuring A psychological process that allows one to justify committing reprehensible actions; typically involves **moral justification, euphemistic language,** and **advantageous comparison.**

cognitive scripts Mental images of how one feels he or she should act in a variety of situations.

cognitive scripts model Rowell Huesmann's theory that social behavior in general and aggressive behavior in particular are controlled largely by cognitive scripts learned through daily experiences.

community-based corrections The term for a wide variety of options that allow convicted offenders to be supervised in the community rather than incarcerated. It includes probation and parole and their variants, such as halfway houses and intensive supervision programs.

compensatory rapist An offender who rapes in response to an intense sexual arousal initiated by stimuli in the environment, often quite specific stimuli (e.g., dark-haired women). His main motive is to prove his sexual prowess.

competency to stand trial The legal requirement that a defendant is able to understand the proceedings and to help the attorney in preparing a defense. See also **incompetency to stand trial.**

compulsion An action a person feels compelled (driven) by internal thoughts to take, even though it may be irrational.

compulsive gambling A psychiatric syndrome characterized by anxiety and an insatiable, unconscious desire to lose what was gained in previous gambling.

concordance A term used in genetics to represent the degree to which related pairs of subjects both show a particular behavior or condition. It is usually expressed in percentages.

conduct disorder A diagnostic label used to identify children who demonstrate habitual misbehavior.

conformity perspective The theoretical position that humans are born basically good and generally try to do the right and just thing.

constructivist therapy Psychotherapy based on the view that the therapist must begin and work with each person's unique version of the world.

contagion effect A tendency for some people to model or copy a behavior or activity portrayed by the news or entertainment media.

controlled substance Any psychoactive drug or chemical substance whose availability is restricted, as designated by state or federal law.

copycat effect See **contagion effect.**

corporate crime Any criminal offense committed by officers or employees in which the corporation benefits.

correlation A mathematical index that reflects the nature of the relationship between two variables.

crimes against the public order See **public order offenses.**

crimes of obedience Illegal acts that are committed under the order of someone in authority.

criminal homicide A term that encompasses both murder and nonnegligent homicide.

criminalization The process whereby inmates exchange, share, and support one another's beliefs, attitudes, and feelings, which in the long run promotes criminal activity.

criminal profiling See **profiling.**

criminal psychopath A primary psychopath who engages in repetitive antisocial or criminal behavior.

criminogenic needs Those dynamic risk factors that are empirically found related to criminal behavior.

criminology The multidisciplinary study of crime.

criminology, psychiatric The branch of criminology that focuses on individual aspects of behavior, particularly internal forces and unconscious drives. Also called **forensic psychiatry.**

criminology, psychological The branch of criminology that examines the individual behavior and especially the mental processes involved in criminal behavior.

criminology, sociological The branch of criminology that examines the demographic, group, and societal variables related to crime.

cyberbullying Sending or posting harmful or cruel text or images using the Internet or other digital communication devices. Primarily a problem with school-aged children and adolescents.

cybercrime Any illegal act that involves a computer system. Also called **computer crime.**

cyberstalking Threatening behavior or unwanted advances directed at another using the Internet or other forms of online communications.

cycle of violence The continuation of violence which may occur across generations among individuals who have experienced and witnessed violence in their families. Also pertains to the violence experienced by women in domestic violence situations.

dangerousness The characteristic of individuals which render them serious threats to their own well-being or the safety of others. See also **risk assessment.**

dark figure The number of crimes that go unreported in official crime data reports.

date rape A sexual assault that occurs within the context of a dating relationship.

dehumanize To engage in actions that obscure the identity of the victim, such as excessive facial battery, or to see and treat victims like objects rather than human beings.

deindividuation A process by which individuals feel they cannot be identified, primarily because they are disguised or are subsumed within a group.

deniers Refers to those sex offenders who are unwilling to take responsibility for their actions.

delusional (paranoid) disorder Mental disorder characterized by a system of false beliefs.

delusions False beliefs about the world.

dependence In substance abuse, a condition that may be physical, psychological, or both, whereby a person develops an intense craving for (and feels he or she cannot live without) a drug.

dependent variable The variable that is measured to see how it is changed by manipulations of the independent variable.

developmental approach Examines the changes and influences (risk factors) across a person's lifetime that contribute to the formation of antisocial and criminal behavior or, alternately, that protect individuals with many risk factors in their lives.

developmental disability A status that is attributable to a cognitive or physical impairment.

developmental pathways In the study of criminal behavior, these are the various tracks individuals follow that lead to antisocial behavior. Researchers began by identifying two pathways but have now found evidence of more.

Diagnostic and Statistical Manual of Mental Disorders (DSM) The official guidebook or manual, published by the American Psychiatric Association, used to define and diagnose specific mental disorders. Now in its fourth revised edition (DSM-IV-R).

difference in degrees The perspective of human nature that argues that humans are intimately tied to their animal ancestry in important and significant ways and differ only in the extent to which they have developed through the evolutionary process. For example, this perspective might argue that human violence is a result of innate, biological needs to obtain sufficient food supplies, territory, or mates.

differential association-reinforcement (DAR) theory A theory of deviance developed by Ronald Akers that combines Skinner's behaviorism and Sutherland's differential association theory. The theory states that people learn deviant behavior through the reinforcements they receive from the social environment.

differential association theory Formulated by Edwin Sutherland, a theory of crime that states that criminal behavior is primarily due to obtaining values or messages from others, including but not limited to those who engage in crime. The critical factors include with whom a person associates, how early, for how long, how frequently, and how personally meaningful the associations are.

discriminative stimuli According to Akers, social signals or gestures transmitted by subcultural or peer groups to indicate whether certain kinds of behavior will be rewarded or punished within a particular social context.

disease attribution A position that contends that sexual assault or other crimes are the results of a mental disorder.

disorganized crime scene Demonstrates that the offender committed the crime without premeditation or planning. In other words, the crime scene indicators suggest the individual acted on impulse or in rage, or under extreme excitement.

displaced aggression rapist The rapist whose attack is violent and aggressive, displaying minimum or total absence of sexual feeling. Also called **anger-retaliation rapist.**

displaced aggression theory The theory that some aggression is directed at the target as a replacement for the individual who is the real source of the provocation.

displacement of responsibility A concept that allows an individual to deny responsibility for an action because he or she was told to perform it by someone higher in authority; also referred to as **obedience to authority** or **strong respect for authority.** See also **crimes of obedience.**

dispositions In personality theory, a term that signifies internal or personality determinants of human behavior. Dispositional theorists look to inner conflicts, beliefs, drives, personal needs, traits, or attitudes to explain behavior. See also **traits.**

dissociated state A state of mind during which the person feels detached from self and surroundings.

dissociative identity disorder A psychiatric syndrome characterized by the existence within an individual of two or more distinct personalities, any of which may be dominant at any given moment. Formerly called **multiple personality disorder (MPD).**

dizygotic twins Twins who developed from two fertilized eggs and are no more *genetically* alike than nontwins. Also called **fraternal twins.**

drug attribution With respect to sex offending, the contention that alcohol and psychoactive drugs can cause one to momentarily lose control of one's sexual urges.

drug courts Courts that specifically handle nonviolent substance abusing offenders and which are designed to help offenders recover from their drug habit and become productive citizens.

drug treatment An approach to therapy that concentrates on reducing the targeted behavior through the use of medication.

DSM See **Diagnostic and Statistical Manual.**

Durham Rule A legal standard of insanity that holds that an accused is not criminally responsible if his or her unlawful act was the product of mental disease or defect. Also known as the **Product Rule.**

duty to protect Requirement from the *Tarasoff* case that clinicians must take steps to protect possible victims from serious bodily harm as a result of threats made by the clinicians' clients. The duty to protect does not require that the clinician contact the potential victim.

duty to warn Requirement from the *Tarasoff* case that clinicians must actively warn potential victims of threats of serious bodily harm made by their clients.

dynamic risk factors Things about a person's developmental history that change over time, such as attitudes, opinions, and knowledge.

dyssocial psychopath Individual with psychopathic characteristics who is antisocial because of social learning and does not possess the features of the primary psychopath.

eldercide The killing of an older person, usually over 60.

emotional paradox The research observation that psychopaths seem to be able to talk about emotional cues but lack the ability to use them effectively in the real world.

enmeshed style A parental style in which the parent takes extraordinary control of the child's life including imposing rigid rules and seeing even trivial, minor behaviors as problematic. Typically results in harsh punishment but inconsistent discipline. Opposite of **lax style.**

equivocal death analysis See **reconstructive psychological evaluation (RPE).**

erotomania stalking In this form of stalking, the stalker usually has serious mental disorders and is considered delusional. Public figures are typically the targets.

euphemistic language Words used to make something appear more innocuous or less negative than it actually is.

evocative therapy An approach to sex offender therapy that focuses on (1) helping offenders to understand the causes and motivations of their sexual behavior, and (2) increasing their empathy for the victims of the sexual assault.

evolutionary psychology The study of the evolution of behavior using the principles of natural selection.

excitation transfer theory Theory explaining how physiological arousal can generalize from one situation to another; based on the assumption that physiological arousal, however produced, dissipates slowly over time.

executive functions Higher order mental abilities involved in goal-directed behavior. They include organizing behavior, memory, inhibition processes, and planning strategies.

exhibitionism The deliberate exposure of the genitals to another person to achieve sexual gratification. Also called **indecent exposure.**

expectancy theory A theory of motivation that takes into account both the expectancy of achieving a particular goal and the value placed on it.

experimental substance use (ESU) Experimentation—typically by adolescents—with various psychoactive substances before dependency or addiction to drugs occurs.

exploitative pedophile An adult who seeks children almost exclusively for sexual gratification.

exploitative rapist See **impulsive rapist.**

expressive aggression Aggression in which a person's primary aim is to hurt or do injury to another. Also called **hostile aggression,** it is the opposite of **instrumental aggression.**

expressive burglars Burglars who take considerable pride in developing ingenious techniques and skills for successful burglary.

expressive hostage taking Hostage-taking situation in which the offender's primary goal is to gain some control over his or her life.

expressive sexual aggression A rape situation in which the offender's primary goal is to gain some control over his life.

extinction The decline and eventual disappearance of a conditioned or learned response when it is no longer reinforced.

extrafamilial child molester A sex abuser whose victims are outside the immediate or extended family.

extraversion In Eysenck's theory, a personality dimension that represents needs for stimulation.

Factor 1 A behavioral dimension, identified through factor analysis, representing the interpersonal and emotional aspects of psychopathy.

Factor 2 A behavioral dimension representing the socially deviant lifestyle characteristics of psychopaths.

factor analysis A statistical procedure by which underlying patterns, factors, or dimensions are identified among a series of scale items.

false positive A prediction that someone will do a certain thing when he or she does not.

false negative A prediction that someone will not do a certain thing when he or she does.

family mass murder A situation in which at least three family members are killed (usually by another family member).

Fast-Track Project A theoretically-based, multisite, multicomponent prevention program for young children believed to be at high risk of long-term antisocial behavior.

Federal Bureau of Prisons (BOP) Oversees all federal penitentiaries, correctional institutions, prison camps, and medical centers in the United States other than those operated by the military.

fence An individual who accepts stolen goods and resells them.

fetishism Sexual attraction to inanimate objects.

filicide Killing of one's child older than one year.

firesetting The term used in the literature on child psychopathology for an abnormal fascination with fire accompanied by successful or unsuccessful attempts to start harmful fires.

fixated pedophile See **immature pedophile.**

forcible rape The carnal knowledge of a female, forcibly and against her will. It includes rape by force, assault to rape, and attempted rape. Although victims may be both female and male, the UCR definition limits this to female victims.

forensic psychiatry See **criminology, psychiatric.**

forensic psychology The production and application of psychological knowledge to the civil and criminal justice systems.

fraternal twins See **dizygotic twins.**

fratricide The killing of one's brother.

frustration An aversive internal state of arousal that occurs when one is prevented from responding in a way that previously produced rewards (or that one believes would produce rewards).

frustration-aggression hypothesis The theory that frustration leads to aggressive behavior. The theory has been revised several times, with most substantial changes coming from the work of Leonard Berkowitz.

fundamental attribution error A tendency to underestimate the importance of situational determinates and to overestimate the importance of personality or dispositional factors in identifying the causes of human behavior.

geographic profiling A type of profiling that focuses on the location of the crime and how it relates to the residence and/or base of operations of the offender.

good burglar Refers to the burglar who demonstrates technical skill and overall competence in burglarizing.

Guilty but Mentally Ill (GBMI) A verdict alternative in some states that allows mentally disordered defendants to be found guilty while seemingly affording them treatment for mental disorders.

habit strength A construct that refers to the strong tendency to repeat a habitual behavior that has been frequently reinforced in the past.

habituation Getting used to or adapting to a stimulus.

hallucinations Things or events that a mentally disordered person, but no others, see or perceive. Characteristic of schizophrenia and some forms of dementia.

hallucinogens Those psychoactive drugs that sometimes generate hallucinations and lead to changes in perceptions of reality. Also called **psychedelics.**

Hate Crime Statistics Act A 1990 federal statute that directs the FBI to collect data on all crimes motivated by hatred of or bias against victims based on their racial, ethnic, religious, or sexual orientation. Physical or mental disability bias was added in 1997.

hierarchy rule In the UCR program, the rule that requires that only the most serious crime in a series be reported in the crime statistics.

hebephilia The use of young adolescent girls or boys for sexual gratification by adults, usually males.

hemisphere asymmetry An unusual or abnormal balance between the two hemispheres, both in language processing and in emotional states.

hostile attribution bias The tendency to perceive hostile intent in others even when it is totally lacking.

hostile attribution model A cognitive model of aggression developed by Kenneth Dodge and colleagues. See also **hostile attributional bias.**

human trafficking The transportation and exploitation of individuals, usually for sex-related purposes and high profits. Children and women from impoverished nations or parts of the United States are particularly vulnerable.

hydraulic model A model of aggression that presumes aggressive energy accumulates in the individual and erupts in a display of violence. Also called **psychodynamic model.**

hyperactivity A behavioral pattern demonstrated by both children and adults wherein there is considerable motor activity in an attempt to gain adequate amounts of cortical stimulation.

iatrogenic A process whereby mental or physical disorders are unintentionally induced or developed in patients by physicians, clinicians, or psychotherapists.

identical twins See **monozygotic twins.**

identity theft The fraudulent use of another person's personal identification information—such as social security number, date of birth, or mother's maiden name—without that person's knowledge or permission.

imitational learning See **observational learning.**

immature pedophile A child sex abuser who demonstrates a long-standing, exclusive preference for children as both sexual and social companions. Also called **fixated pedophile.**

impulsive rapist A rapist who demonstrates neither strong sexual nor aggressive features, but engages in spontaneous rape when the opportunity presents itself. The rape is usually carried out in the context of another crime, such as robbery or burglary. Also called **exploitative rapist.**

incompetent to stand trial (IST) A judicial determination that a defendant lacks sufficient ability to understand the legal process against him or her and/or to assist a lawyer in the preparation of a defense. See also **adjudicative competence.**

independent variable The measure whose effect is being studied, and, in most scientific investigations, that is manipulated by the experimenter in a controlled fashion.

index crimes (now commonly called Part I crimes) The crimes that are of most concern, as defined by the FBI's Uniform Crime Reports, and are used to indicate the seriousness of the crime problem. The eight Part I crimes are murder and nonnegligent manslaughter, aggravated assault, robbery, forcible rape, burglary, larceny-theft, arson, and motor vehicle theft.

infanticide Although this term literally means the killing of an infant, it has become synonymous with the killing of a child by a parent.

inhalants Refers to a thousand or more different household and commercial products that can be abused by sniffing or "huffing" (inhaling though the mouth) for an intoxicating effect. They are found in organic solvents and volatile substances commonly found in adhesives, lighter fluids, cleaning solutions, and paint products.

Insanity Defense Reform Act of 1984 A law designed to make it more difficult for defendants using the insanity defense in the federal courts to be acquitted.

instrumental aggression Aggression carried out for the primary purpose of gaining material goods or other rewards rather than for the purpose of harming the victim.

instrumental hostage taking A hostage situation in which the primary goal of the offender is material or monetary gain.

instrumental learning A form of learning in which a voluntary response is strengthened or diminished by its consequences. Also called **operant conditioning.**

instrumental sexual aggression When the sexual offender uses just enough coercion to gain compliance from his victim.

interaction An important concept in psychological criminology, it refers to the mutual influence of a multitude of internal and external factors on the behavior of the individual. See also **interactionism.**

interactionism The perspective that argues that human behavior is determined or influenced by both internal (biological, psychological, cognitive) and external (social environmental) factors.

intimate partner violence Crimes committed against persons by their current or former spouses, boyfriends, or girlfriends.

intrafamilial child molester A child sex abuser whose victims are within the immediate or extended family.

invariance hypothesis Proposed by Gottfredson and Hirschi, this hypothesis refers to the observation that crime seems to decline with age, no matter when in history and no matter what culture is being considered.

investigative psychology The application of psychological research and concepts to the investigation of crime.

irrationality A basic ingredient of the insanity standard. Refers to the legal assumption that a person cannot be held criminally responsible for his or her actions if it is determined he or she could not understand the consequences of his or her behavior.

irresistible impulse attribution In sex offending, refers to a psychological state in which the normal restraints of self-control are substantially reduced or eliminated by an overwhelming sex drive.

jail A facility operated by a local government to hold persons temporarily detained, awaiting trial, or sentenced to confinement after having been convicted of a misdemeanor.

just-world hypothesis A belief that one gets what one deserves in this world.

juvenile courts Specialized courts, separate from the criminal system, that deal with status offenses, delinquency cases, and other issues relating to juveniles, such as abuse or neglect. Also called family courts in many states.

Juvenile Justice and Delinquency Prevention Act (JJDPA) Landmark federal legislation passed in 1974 that attempted to address the needs of juveniles in the juvenile justice system as well as those considered at risk of delinquency.

kleptomania The irresistible urge to steal unneeded objects. Whether there is such an urge is highly questionable.

language impairment Broad term for a variety of problems in expressing or understanding language.

lax style A parental style that does not respond sufficiently to problematic or antisocial behavior in children but rather allows it to occur without disciplinary action. Opposite of the **enmeshed style** and similar to the **permissive.**

learned helplessness A learned passive and withdrawing response in the face of perceived hopelessness, as theorized by Martin Seligman (1975).

learning perspective The theoretical position that humans are born basically neutral and behaviorally a blank slate. What they become as individuals depends on their learning experiences rather than innate predispositions.

life-course-persistent (LCP) offenders A term introduced by Terrie Moffitt to represent offenders who demonstrate a life-long pattern of antisocial behavior and who are resistant to treatment or rehabilitation.

limited amnesia A pathological inability to remember a specific episode, or small number of episodes, from the recent past.

London syndrome A behavioral pattern observed during a hostage situation at the Iranian Embassy in London. Refers to the explicit and consistent resistance and refusals by hostages to do what is expected by captors. This behavior often results in death or serious injury to the resistors.

love obsession stalking In this form of stalking, the stalker and victim are strangers or casual acquaintances. The stalker seeks a love relationship with the object of his or her obsession.

major depressive disorder General label for symptoms that include an extremely depressed state, general slowing down of mental and physical activity, and feelings of self-worthlessness.

markers A term used for the neurological indicators of a particular phenomenon, such as psychopathy.

mass murder Murdering three or more persons at a single location with no cooling-off period between murders.

matricide The killing of one's mother.

MDMA Abbreviation for a drug called "ecstasy," which is a synthetic drug that is considered a stimulant with strong psychedelic effects.

mental disorder See **mental illness.**

mental illness Term used for a variety of psychiatric diagnoses that indicate that the individual has problems in living; also referred to as **mental disorder.**

mentally disordered sex offender (MDSO) A classification established by some state legislatures to identify those mentally disordered individuals prone toward repetitive sexual attacks on children, women, or both.

mental retardation A developmental disability indicating that a person's cognitive skills are below normal in the general population.

mixed crime scene Indicates that the nature of the crime demonstrates both organized and disorganized behavioral patterns.

M'Naghten Rule An insanity standard based on the conclusion that if a defendant has a defect of reason, or a disease of the mind, so as not to know the nature and quality of his or her actions, then he or she cannot be held criminally responsible. Also called **the right and wrong test.**

modeling See **observational learning.**

models Individuals or groups of individuals in the environment whose behavior is observed and imitated.

modus operandi (MO) The actions and procedures an offender uses to commit a crime successfully.

Monitoring the Future (MTF) A self-report survey administered to high school students nationwide focusing on drug use and abuse.

monozygotic twins Twins who developed from one fertilized egg and share the same genes. Also called **identical twins.**

moral disengagement The process of freeing oneself from one's own moral standards in order to act against those standards. The unacceptable conduct is usually undertaken under orders from someone higher in authority or under high social pressure.

moral justification The process of convincing oneself that one's actions are worthy and have an ultimate moral and good purpose.

multiassaultive family A nuclear family (traditional or nontraditional) characterized by multiple incidents of violence involving more than one perpetrator.

multiple personality disorder (MPD) See **dissociative identity disorder.**

multisystemic therapy (MST) A treatment approach for serious juvenile offenders that focuses on the family while being responsive to the many other contexts surrounding the family, such as the peer group, the neighborhood, and the school.

Munchausen syndrome by proxy (MSBP) An unusual form of child abuse in which the parent (usually the mother), or parents, consistently bring a child for medical attention with symptoms falsified or directly induced by the parent or parents.

murder The felonious killing of one human being by another with malice aforethought. See also **criminal homicide.**

narcotics Psychoactive drugs that produce sleep and are derivatives of the poppy plant. Often divided into three categories depending on the amount of preparation needed: **natural, synthetic,** or **semisynthetic.** Examples are opium, heroin, and methadone, respectively.

National Crime Victimization Survey (NCVS) A government-sponsored survey of victims of crime, intended to collect data from the victim's perspective on crimes both reported and not reported to police.

National Incident-Based Reporting System (NIBRS) The FBI's system of collecting *detailed* data from law enforcement agencies on known crimes and arrests. See also **Uniform Crime Reporting.**

natural narcotics Psychoactive substances classified as narcotics that require no chemical preparation.

negative reinforcement See **reinforcement, negative.**

negligent manslaughter The unlawful killing of another through reckless or negligent behavior, without intention to kill.

neonaticide The killing of a newborn, usually under 48 hours.

neuroticism A dimension of personality that—according to Hans J. Eysenck—is characterized by a chronic level of emotional instability and proneness to psychological distress.

neurotransmitters Biochemicals directly involved in the transmission of neural impulses and without which communication would not be possible. **Serotonin** is one example.

nonconformist perspective The theoretical perspective that humans will naturally try to get away with anything they can, including illegal conduct, unless social controls are imposed.

nonindex crimes (Part II crimes) Crimes not considered as serious as Part I crimes by the FBI and on which only arrest data are gathered for UCR purposes. Examples include simple assault, fraud, embezzlement, and vandalism.

nonnegligent manslaughter The killing of a human being without premeditation but with the intention to kill in the "heat of the moment," such as under high emotional states of anger or passion.

nonshared environments An important concept in twin studies, this refers to the living experiences that are different for each twin, such as being raised by different parents.

not guilty by reason of insanity (NGRI) A legal determination that a defendant was so mentally disordered at the time of the crime that he or she cannot be held criminally responsible for his or her actions.

observational learning (modeling) The process by which individuals learn patterns of behavior by observing another person performing the action.

occupational crime (1) Any one of a variety of offenses committed by an individual through opportunity created by his or her occupation; see also, Green's four categories of **individual, organizational, professional,** and **state-authority** occupational crime. (2) The second category of **white-collar crime** (along with corporate) that refers to crimes committed by individuals for their own benefit.

Office of Juvenile Justice and Delinquency Prevention (OJJDP) The federal agency charged with overseeing juvenile justice on the national level, providing grants for juvenile research and programs, and taking a leadership role in setting policies nationwide relative to juveniles.

operant conditioning See **instrumental learning.**

opiate narcotics Psychoactive drugs that have sedative (sleep-inducing) and analgesic (pain-relieving) effects.

opportunist rapist Rapist whose sexual assault is an impulsive, predatory act that is controlled by situational and contextual factors, such as a woman being present during the commission of another crime.

organized crime scene Indicates planning and premeditation on the part of the offender. In other words, the crime scene shows signs that the offender maintained control of himself or herself and of the victim, if it is a crime against a person.

overcontrolled personality A person who has well-established inhibitions against aggressive behavior and rigidly adheres to them, but who may suddenly erupt in violence.

paranoid disorders See **delusional disorders.**

paraphilia The clinical term for a sexual condition exhibited in fantasies, urges, or behaviors involving nonhuman objects, suffering or humiliation of oneself or one's partner, or children or other nonconsenting persons.

parental monitoring Supervision by parents of their children's activities. Poor parental monitoring is a strong risk factor for delinquency.

parental practices Methods employed by parents to meet some specific goal they would like to have their children achieve.

parental styles Seemingly nongoal-directed approaches displayed by parents, although the goals may be implicit.

parricide The killing of a parent.

Part 1 crime See **index crimes.**

Part 2 crime See **nonindex crimes.**

partialism An exaggerated sexual interest in some part of the human anatomy not usually associated with sexual arousal, such as a heel or elbow.

patricide The killing of one's father.

passive-aggressive behavior Hostile behavior that does not directly inflict physical harm, such as refusing to speak to someone against whom one holds a grudge.

Pavlovian conditioning See **classical conditioning.**

pedophile The clinical term for an adult who uses children for sexual gratification and companionship.

pedophilia The use of children by adults for sexual gratification and companionship.

permissive style a relaxed parenting style characterized by few demands, controls, or limits.

personation See **signature.**

pervasive anger type A rapist characterized by anger directed toward virtually everyone he knows.

plasticity The characteristic of the brain that allows both its structure and its function to be profoundly responsive to experiences, particularly during early life.

positive reinforcement See **reinforcement, positive.**

positivist theory Theory that argues prior experiences or influences determine present behavior.

postpartum blues The common mood swings, crying spells, irritability, and anxiety that occur in 50–80 percent of women after giving birth.

postpartum depression More severe than postpartum blues, this affects 7–17 percent of childbearing women. Symptoms may include depression, loss of appetite, loss of interest in the newborn, and in life activities. May represent a recurring mood swing across the woman's life cycle.

postpartum psychosis A rare but severe mental disorder believed to be linked to childbirth; symptoms are similar to those of serious bipolar depression.

posttraumatic stress disorder (PTSD) A cluster of behavioral patterns that result from a psychologically distressing event outside the usual range of human experience.

power rape A rape situation, identified by Groth, in which the assailant seeks to establish power and control over his victim. Thus, the amount of force and threats used depends on the degree of submission shown by the victim.

primary prevention An intervention program designed to prevent behavior or disorders before any signs of the behavioral pattern develops. Also called **universal prevention.**

primary psychopath Robert Hare's classification of the "true" psychopath. That is, the individual who demonstrates those physiological and behavioral features that represent psychopathy—in contrast to **secondary psychopaths,** who commit antisocial acts because of severe emotional problems or inner conflicts, and **dyssocial psychopaths,** who are antisocial because of social learning.

prisonization The process by which inmates adopt and internalize the prisoner subculture within a particular correctional facility.

prisons Correctional facilities operated by state and federal governments to hold persons convicted of felonies and sentenced generally to terms of more than one year.

proactive aggression Similar to **instrumental aggression,** actions undertaken to obtain a specific goal. In children, refers to insensitive actions such as bullying, name-calling, and coercive actions.

product-tampering homicide A rare death or deaths occurring as the result of one or more individuals tampering with a product, usually for revenge or economic gain.

profiling The process of identifying personality traits, behavioral tendencies, and demographic variables of an offender based on characteristics of the crime. See also **psychological profiling.**

prostitution Offering or agreeing to engage in, or engaging in, a sex act with another in exchange for a fee.

psychedelics The category of psychoactive drugs that produce elevated mood, hallucinations, and altered states of consciousness. Also called **hallucinogens.**

psychiatric criminology See **criminology, psychiatric.**

psychoactive drugs Drugs that exert their primary effect on the brain, thus altering mood or behavior.

psychodynamic model The theoretical perspective that argues that human behavior can be best explained through the use of psychological forces and pressures. See also **hydraulic model.**

psychoeducational counseling An approach to therapy that utilizes a group or class setting to remedy deficits in social and interpersonal skills.

psychological autopsy Postmortem analysis often reserved for cases in which suicide occurred or is suspected or alleged. The psychological autopsy is frequently done to determine the reasons and precipitating factors for the death.

psychological criminology See **criminology, psychological.**

psychological profiling The psychological description of a person or persons, whether or not suspected of or involved in criminal activity.

psychometric approach The perspective that human characteristics, attributes, and traits can be measured and quantified.

psychometric intelligence (PI) A more contemporary designation of intelligence as measured by intelligence or IQ tests. However, the term is not yet widely used in comparison with "IQ."

psychopath An individual who demonstrates a distinct behavioral pattern that differs from the general population in its level of sensitivity, empathy, compassion, and guilt. See also **primary psychopath.**

psychopathic factor I Of the two behavioral dimensions of psychopathy, this reflects the interpersonal and emotional components, such as callousness and manipulation of others.

psychopathic factor II Of the two behavioral dimensions of psychopathy, this reflects a socially deviant lifestyle, such as impulsiveness, excessive need for stimulation, and lack of realistic goals.

Psychopathy Checklist (PCL) and Psychopathy Checklist-Revised (PCL-R). Developed by Robert Hare, currently the best-known instrument for the measurement of criminal psychopathy. Additional versions include the **Psychopathy Checklist—Screening Version,** the **P-Scan: Research Version,** and the **Psychopathy Checklist, Youth Version (PCL:YV).**

psychophysiology The study of the dynamic interactions between behavior and the autonomic nervous system.

psychosis A severe form of mental disorder characterized by hallucinations, delusions, and other indications of loss of contact with reality.

psychotechnology Methods of permanently altering brain tissue through surgical, electrical (direct current), or chemical means.

psychoticism A personality dimension, proposed by Eysenck, characterized by cold cruelty, social insensitivity, unemotionality, high risk taking, troublesome behavior, and a dislike of others.

public order offenses Nonviolent offenses that disrupt the peace and tranquility of a community (e.g., public inebriation, disturbing the peace, vagrancy).

punishment An event by which a person receives a noxious, painful, or aversive stimulus, usually as a consequence of behavior.

pyromania A psychiatric term for an irresistible urge to set fires along with an intense fascination (usually sexual) with fire. The existence of this behavioral phenomenon has been brought into serious question by the available research.

racial profiling Police-initiated action that relies on the race, ethnicity, or national origin rather than the behavior of an individual or on other information that leads the police to suspect him or her of criminal activity.

radical environmental groups Environmental activists who have used terrorist tactics to draw attention to dangers to the environment.

rape by fraud The act of having sexual relations with a supposedly consenting adult female under fraudulent conditions, such as when a physician or psychotherapist has sexual intercourse with a patient under the guise of "effective treatment."

rape myths A variety of mistaken beliefs about the crime of rape and its victims held by many men and women.

rational reconstruction A mental process whereby an individual engages in a reinterpretation of past behavior through which he or she recasts activities in a manner consistent with "what should have been" rather than "what was." The term in this book was used specifically for explaining research on burglary.

reactive aggression Spontaneous aggression, possibly in response to provocation. In children, hot-blooded aggressive acts, such as temper tantrums and emotionally driven vengeful hostility.

reality therapy Treatment based on the view that the patient must face reality and take full responsibility for his or her behavior.

recidivism A return to criminal activity (usually measured by arrest) after being convicted of a criminal offense.

reconstructive psychological evaluation (RPE) Reconstruction of the personality profile and cognitive features (especially intentions) of deceased individuals.

reductionism A research approach that argues that in order to understand highly complex events or phenomenon, one must start examining the simplest parts first.

regressed pedophile A male who had fairly normal relationships with adults but later reverted to children for sexual and social companionship because of feelings of inadequacy.

reinforcement Anything that increases the probability of responding.

reinforcement, negative The reward received for avoiding a painful or aversive condition, or stimuli.

reinforcement, positive The acquisition of something desired as a result of one's behavior.

relapse prevention (RP) A method of treatment primarily designed to prevent a relapse of an undesired behavioral pattern.

relative deprivation A concept developed by Gresham Sykes for explaining economic crime. It refers to the perceived discrepancy between what an individual has and what he or she would like to have. It is a condition that is especially prominent when people of wealth and people of poverty live in close proximity.

repeat burglary Refers to the observation that some burglars burglarize the same place repeatedly.

residential treatment Juvenile training school or rehabilitation center where youths are incarcerated for extended periods of time. Usually considered the "last stop" for youths.

right and wrong test See **M'Naghten Rule.**

right-wing terrorists Extremist groups that adhere to an antigovernment or racist ideology and often engage in a variety of hate crimes and violence.

risk assessment The enterprise in which clinicians offer probabilities that a given individual will engage in violent or otherwise antisocial behavior based on known factors relating to the individual.

ritualized aggression The symbolic display of aggressive intentions or strength without actual physical combat or conflict.

road rage Anger at another motorist expressed in highly reckless driving and, in some cases, attempts to harm the other motorist. To be distinguished from **aggressive driving,** in which the actions of the other motorist are not the direct cause of the reckless behavior.

robbery The taking or attempt to take anything of value from the care, custody or control of another by force or the threat of force.

Rohypnol Sometimes referred to as a date-rape drug, it is a powerful depressant commonly abused by young adults and adolescents.

rumination The focused attention on one's own thoughts and feelings that, if excessive, can lead to aggression against others.

sadistic pedophile See **aggressive pedophile.**

sadistic rape A rape situation, identified by Groth, in which the offender experiences sexual arousal and excitement as a result of the victim's torment, distress, helplessness, and suffering. The assault usually involves bondage and torture, and the rapist directs considerable abuse and injury on various areas of the victim's body.

sadistic rapist See **sexually aggressive rapist.**

schizophrenia Mental disorder characterized by severe breakdowns in thought patterns, emotions, and perceptions.

secondary prevention An intervention program designed for individuals who demonstrate early signs or indications of behavioral problems or antisocial behavior. Also called **selective prevention.**

secondary psychopath Individual with psychopathic characteristics, but who commits antisocial acts because of severe emotional problems or inner conflicts. Distinct from **primary psychopath.**

sedative-hypnotic compounds Psychoactive drugs that depress central nervous system functioning, generally reducing anxiety and tension.

selective prevention See **secondary prevention.**

self-regulation The ability to control one's behavior in accordance with internal cognitive standards.

self-regulatory mechanisms The personal characteristics that help one to control one's behavior, usually attained through social learning.

self-serving bias A tendency to attribute positive things that happen to us to our abilities and personalities, and to attribute negative events to some cause outside ourselves or beyond our control.

semantic aphasia A characteristic found in psychopaths whereby the words they speak are devoid of emotional sincerity.

semisynthetic narcotics See **narcotics.**

serial murder Incidents in which an individual (or individuals) kill a number of individuals (usually a minimum of three) over time.

serotonin A chemical by which nerve cells communicate with one another. Low levels of this chemical may be related to aggressive behavior.

sexual aggressive rapist A rapist who demonstrates both sexual and aggressive features in his attack. In order for him to experience sexual arousal, it must be associated with violence and pain, which excite him. Also called **sadistic rapist.**

sexual gratification rapist Rapist whose motivation is hypothesized to be sexual, marked by the presence of protracted sexual or sadistic fantasies that influence as well as sustain the rape. These offenders have in common some form of enduring sexual preoccupation.

Sexually Violent Predator Act A law that allows states to place restrictive conditions on sex offenders believed to represent heightened danger to the public. Some statutes allow civil commitment of sexually violent predators after they have completed their prison sentences.

sexual sadism A deviation characterized by torture and/or killing and mutilation of other persons in order to achieve sexual gratification.

shaken baby syndrome (SBS) A form of child abuse in which an adult (usually male) shakes a baby so hard that it causes significant brain damage or death.

shared environment An important concept in twin studies, this refers to the prenatal and life experiences that are common to both twins, such as being raised by the same biological parents.

siblicide The killing of one's brother or sister; **sororicide** is the killing of one's sister; **fratricide** is the killing of one's brother.

signature Any behavior that goes beyond what is necessary to commit the crime. Also called **personation.**

simple obsession stalking The form in which the stalker seeks power and control after a failed relationship with the victim; often associated with past domestic violence.

simulation Research conducted in a laboratory setting that is designed to mimic as closely as possible the "real world."

situationism A theoretical perspective that argues that environmental stimuli control behavior.

snitches Amateur shoplifters.

social class Socioeconomic status typically based predominantly on refers to one's economic position in society, based primarily on family income. Also referred to as socioeconomic status.

social control theory A theory proposed by Travis Hirschi that contends that crime and delinquency occur when an individual's ties to the conventional order or normative standards are weak or largely nonexistent.

social learning theory A theory of human behavior based on learning from watching others in the social environment. This leads to an individual's development of his or her own perceptions, thoughts, expectancies, competencies, and values.

socialized offender A person who violates the law consistently because of learning the behavioral patterns from his or her social environment.

sociological criminology See **criminology, sociological.**

sociopath A person who is repetitively in conflict with the law, apparently with very limited capacity to learn from past experience. Distinct from Hare's concept of primary psychopath.

sororicide See **sibicide.**

spree murder The killing of three or more individuals without any cooling-off period, usually at two or more locations.

staging The intentional alteration of a crime scene prior to the arrival of the police.

stalking Conduct directed at a specific person that involves repeated physical or visual proximity, nonconsensual communication, or verbal, written, or implied threats sufficient to cause fear in a reasonable person.

static risk factors Things about a person's developmental history that cannot change, such as prenatal injuries, child abuse, or criminal parents. Also called historical factors.

status offenses A class of illegal behavior that only persons with certain characteristics or status can commit. Used almost exclusively to refer to the behavior of juveniles. Examples include running away from home, violating curfew, buying alcohol, or skipping school.

statutory rape Rape for which the age of the victim is the crucial distinction, on the premise that a victim below a certain age (usually 16) cannot validly consent to sexual intercourse with an adult.

stimulants A broad drug classification that refers to those psychoactive drugs that "stimulate" the central nervous system and elevate mood.

stimulus A person, event, or situation that elicits behavior.

Stockholm syndrome A term coined after a hostage situation in Sweden in 1973, it refers to the phenomenon of hostages becoming attracted to their captors. In the original incident, an escaped convict held four bank employees in Stockholm in the bank vault for 131 hours. One of the bank employees eventually married her hostage taker.

strain theory A prominent sociological explanation for crime based on Robert Merton's theory that crime and delinquency occur when there is a perceived discrepancy between the materialistic values and goals cherished and held in high esteem by a society and the availability of the legitimate means for reaching these goals.

street culture A variety of conduct norms, particularly in urban areas, that are conducive to robbery and other street crimes. Examples of these norms are disdain for conventional living, a hedonistic pursuit of sensory stimulation, and lack of future orientation.

strong-arm robbery A robbery in which the main weapon used is one's own body rather than guns, knives, or other weapons.

substance abuse A pattern of drug use characterized by recurrent negative or adverse consequences as a result of repeated ingestion of the drug.

succumbers In hostage-taking situations, refers to those hostages who, after release, have considerable difficulty dealing with the aftereffects of the incident.

supermax prisons See **ultramax prisons.**

survivors In hostage-taking situations, refers to those hostages who are able to return to a meaningful existence with little evidence of long-term depression, nightmares, or serious stress-induced illness.

synthetic narcotics See **narcotics.**

temperament A natural mood disposition determined largely by genetic and biological influences.

territoriality The tendency to attack violators of one's personal space.

terrorism The unlawful use of force or violence against persons or property to intimidate or coerce a government, the civilian population, or any segment thereof, in furtherance of political or social objectives.

tertiary prevention Intervention strategy designed to reduce or eliminate behavioral problems or antisocial behavior that is fully developed in individuals. Treatment or counseling of convicted offenders is an example of tertiary prevention.

theory An integrated set of principles that describes, predicts, and explains some phenomena and that guides research.

theory of moral disengagement Proposed by Bandura, it supposes that we must disengage our own moral values before committing a criminal act.

theory verification A process whereby a scientific theory is tested through observation and analysis. If the process falsifies the theory, the theory must be revised to account for the observed events.

tolerance In substance use, the condition in which only increasing dosages of the drug produce the desired effect.

traits Relatively stable and enduring tendencies to behave in a particular way across time and place. Traits are believed by some psychologists to be the basic building blocks of personality.

treatment In juvenile justice, a term reserved for psychologically-based programs designed to reduce serious, persistent, delinquent, or antisocial behavior.

tripartite conceptual model Identifies three main categories of drug related crimes. Proposed by Paul Goldstein.

true negative The correct prediction that someone will not do a certain act.

true positive The correct prediction that someone will do a certain act (e.g., commit another violent crime).

ultramax prisons Extremely high-security prisons, or units within a prison, in which prisoners are held in isolation, often for 23 hours a day and for extended periods of time.

uncontrollable attribution See **irresistible impulse attribution.**

undercontrolled personality A person who has few inhibitions against aggressive behavior and frequently engages in violence when frustrated or provoked.

undoing A behavioral pattern found at the crime scene whereby the offender tries to psychologically "undo" the murder.

Uniform Crime Reporting (UCR) The FBI's system of gathering data from law enforcement agencies on the crimes that come to their attention and on arrests. See also **NIBRS.**

variable Any entity that can be measured.

vengeance stalkers These stalkers do not seek a relationship with their victims but rather are trying to elicit a response or change of behavior from the victim.

victim attribution The tendency to blame the victim; may be especially prevalent in cases of sexual assault.

victimological perspective A proposal that suggests we can gain substantial amounts of knowledge on offender characteristics by also studying the nature and possibly the behavior of the victims selected by offenders.

victimology The scientific study of the causes, circumstances, individual characteristics, and social contexts associated with crime victims.

vindictive rapist Rapist whose attack is driven by his central and focused hatred of women.

volitional prong The part of the insanity defense that requires acceptance of the possibility that a defendant could not control his or her behavior to conform to the requirements of the law. The volitional prong is not recognized in federal law or the law of many states.

voyeurism The tendency to gain sexual excitement and gratification from observing unsuspecting others naked, undressing, or engaging in sexual activity.

weapons effect Suggestion that the mere presence of a weapon leads a witness or victim to concentrate on the weapon itself rather than other features of the crime.

white-collar crime A broad term, coined in 1939 by Edwin Sutherland, that refers to illegal acts committed by those of high social status in the process of their employment. Contemporary definitions often divide it into corporate crime and individual or occupational crime. See also **occupational crime.**

wilderness and adventure programs Rehabilitative approaches for adjudicated delinquents (and preventive approaches for some youngsters at risk) that focus on skills building and the development of self-esteem.

workplace aggression A term for the conduct, usually on the part of employees, that qualifies as emotional harm or minor physical harm to other employees. Distinct from workplace violence.

workplace violence The aggressive actions, including deaths, that occur at the workplace, not necessarily caused by those who work within the organization.

REFERENCES

Abadinsky, H. (1993). *Drug abuse* (2nd ed.). Chicago: Nelson-Hall.

Abel, G. G., Barlow, D. H., Blanchard, E. B., & Guild, D. (1977). The components of rapists' sexual arousal. *Archives of General Psychiatry, 34,* 895–903.

Abel, G. G., Becker, J. V., Blanchard, E. B., & Djenderedjian, A. (1978). Differentiating sexual aggressives with penile measures. *Criminal Justice and Behavior, 5,* 315–332.

Abel, G. G., Becker, J. V., Murphy, W. D., & Flanagan, B. (1981). Identifying dangerous child molesters. In R. B. Stuart (Ed.), *Violent behavior: Social learning approaches to prediction, management and treatment.* New York: Brunner/Mazel.

Abel, G. G., Mittelman, M., Becker, J. V., Rathner, J., & Rouleau, J. (1988). Predicting child molesters' response to treatment. In R. A. Prentky & V. L. Quinsey (Eds.), *Human sexual aggression: Current perspectives.* New York: New York Academy of Sciences.

Abrahamsen, D. (1952). *Who are the guilty?* Westport, CT: Greenwood Press.

Abrahamsen, D. (1960). *The psychology of crime.* New York: Columbia University Press.

Achenbach, T. M., & Edelbrock, C. (1983). *Manual for the child behavior checklist and revised child behavior profile.* Burlington, VT: University of Vermont.

Acoca, L., & Austin, J. (1996). *The hidden crisis: The women offenders sentencing study and alternative sentencing recommendations project.* San Francisco: National Council on Crime and Delinquency.

Acoca, L., & Dedel, K. (1998). *No place to hide: Understanding and meeting the needs of girls in the California juvenile justice system.* San Francisco, CA: National Council on Crime and Delinquency.

Adams, D. (1992). Biology does not make men more aggressive than women. In K. Bjorkquist & P. Niemela (Eds.), *Of mice and women: Aspects of female aggression.* San Diego, CA: Academic Press.

Adamson, L. A., & Thompson, R. A. (1998). Coping with interparental verbal conflict by children exposed to spouse abuse from nonviolent homes. *Journal of Family Violence, 13,* 213–232.

Adler, F. (1975). *Sisters in crime.* New York: McGraw-Hill.

Adler, J. (2002, February 25). The "thrill" of theft: It's not just movies stars. *Newsweek,* p. 52.

Adler, R., Nunn, R., Northam, E., Lebnan, V., & Ross, R. (1994). Secondary prevention of childhood firesetting. *Journal of the American Academy of Child and Adolescent Psychiatry, 33,* 1194–1202.

Adshead, G. (2002). Three degrees of security: Attachment and forensic institutions. *Criminal Behaviour and Mental Health, 12,* S31–S45.

Ailworth, E. (2003, June 18). Another tampered jar of baby food. *Los Angeles Times,* p. B-3. Adsheada.

Ainsworth, M. D. (1979). Infant-mother attachment. *American Psychologist, 34,* 932–937.

Ainsworth, M. D., Blehar, M. C., Waters, E., & Wall, S. (1979). *Patterns of attachment: A psychological study of the strange situation.* Hillsdale, NJ: Erlbaum.

Akers, R. L. (1977). *Deviant behavior: A social learning approach* (2nd ed.). Belmont, CA: Wadsworth.

Akers, R. L. (1985). *Deviant behavior: A social learning approach* (3rd ed.). Belmont, CA: Wadsworth.

Akers, R. L., & Cochran, J. K. (1985). Adolescent marijuana use: A test of three theories of deviant behavior. *Deviant Behavior, 6,* 323–346.

Akers, R. L., & Lee, G. (1996). A longitudinal test of social learning theory: Adolescent smoking. *Journal of Drug Issues, 26,* 317–343.

Albanese, J. S. (1995). *White-collar crime in America.* Englewood Cliffs, NJ: Prentice Hall.

Alexander, M. A. (1999). Sexual offender treatment efficacy revised. *Sexual Abuse: A Journal of Research and Treatment, 11,* 101–116.

Alison, L. J., & Canter, D. V. (1999). Professional, legal and ethical issues in offender profiling. In D. V. Canter & L. J. Alison (Eds.), *Profiling in policy and practice*. Aldershot, UK: Ashgate.

Alison, L., Bennell, C., Ormerod, D., & Mokros, A. (2002). The personality paradox in offender profiling: A theoretical review of the processes involved in deriving background characteristics from crime scene actions. *Psychology, Public Policy, and Law, 8,* 115–135.

Alison, L. J., Smith, M. D., Eastman, O., & Rainbow, L. (2003). Toulmin's philosophy of argument and its relevance to offending profiling. *Psychology, Crime & Law, 9,* 173–183.

Alison, L. J., Smith, M. D., & Morgan, K. (2003). Interpreting the accuracy of offender profiles. *Psychology, Crime & Law, 9,* 185–195.

Allen, M., Emmers, T., Gebhardt, L., & Giery, M. A. (2001). Exposure to pornography and acceptance of rape myths. *Journal of Communication, 45,* 5–53.

Allen, N. B., Lewinsohn, P. M., & Seeley, J. R. (1998). Prenatal and perinatal influences on risk for psychopathology in childhood and adolescence. *Development and Psychopathology, 10,* 513–529.

Alvord, M. K., & Grados, J. J. (2005). Enhancing resilience in children: A protective approach. *Professional Psychology: Research and Practice, 3,* 238–245.

American Bar Association. (1979). *Juvenile justice standards project*. Chicago: Author.

American Psychiatric Association (APA). (1994). *Diagnostic and statistical manual of mental disorders* (DSM-IV). Washington, DC: Author.

American Psychiatric Association (APA). (2000). *Diagnostic and statistical manual of mental disorders—revised* (DSM-IV-R). Washington, DC: Author.

American Psychological Association. (2003). *Violence and the family: Report of the APA Presidential Task Force on Violence and the Family—executive summary*. APA Online. Available: www.apa.org/pi/pii/viol&fam.html.

Amir, M. (1971). *Patterns in forcible rape*. Chicago: University of Chicago Press.

Amsel, A. (1958). The role of frustrative nonreward in noncontinuous reward situations. *Psychological Bulletin, 55,* 102–119.

Andershed, H., Kerr, M., Stattin, H., & Levander, S. (2002). Psychopathic traits in non-referred youths: A new assessment tool. In E. Blauuw & L. Sheridan (Eds.), *Psychopaths: Current international perspectives*. The Hague, Netherlands: Elsevier.

Anderson, C. A. (2004). An update on the effects of playing violent video games. *Journal of Adolescence, 27,* 113–122.

Anderson, C. A., & Bushman, B. J. (2001). Effects of violent games on aggressive behavior, aggressive cognition, aggressive effect, physiological arousal, and prosocial behavior: A meta-analytic review of the scientific literature. *Psychological Science, 12,* 353–359.

Anderson, C. A., & Bushman, B. J. (2002). Human aggression. *Annual Review of Psychology, 53,* 27–51.

Anderson, C. A., & Dill, K. E. (2000). Video games and aggressive thoughts, feelings, and behavior in the laboratory and in life. *Journal of Personality and Social Psychology, 78,* 772–790.

Anderson, C. A., Sakamoto, A., Gentile, D. A., Ihori, N., Shibuya, A., Yukawa, S., et al. (2008). Longitudinal effects of violent video games on aggression in Japan and the United States. *Pediatrics, 122,* 1067–1072.

Andreasen, N. C. (2001). *Brave new brain: Conquering mental illness in the era of the genome*. New York: Oxford University Press.

Andreasen, N. C., & Carpenter, W. T. (1993). Diagnosis and classification of schizophrenia. *Schizophrenia Bulletin, 19,* 199–214.

Andrew, J. M. (1978). Laterality on the tapping test among legal offenders. *Journal of Clinical Psychology, 7,* 149–150.

Andrew, J. M. (1980). Are left-handers less violent? *Journal of Youth and Adolescence, 9,* 1–9.

Andrews, D. A., & Bonta, J. (1994). *The psychology of criminal conduct*. Cincinnati, OH: Anderson.

Andrews, D. A., Bonta, J., & Hoge, R. D. (1990). Classification for effective rehabilitation: Rediscovering psychology. *Criminal Justice and Behavior, 17,* 19–52.

Ansbro, M. (2008). Using attachment theory with offenders. *Probation Journal, 55*, 231–244.

Appelbaum, P. S., Jick, R. Z., Grisso, T., Givelbar, D., Silver, E., & Steadman, H. J. (1993). Use of post-traumatic stress. *Psychiatry, 150*, 229–234.

Appelbaum, P. S., Robbins, P. C., & Monahan, J. (2000). Violence and delusions: Data from the MacArthur Violence Risk Assessment Study. *American Journal of Psychiatry, 157*, 566–572.

Araji, S. (1997). *Sexually aggressive children: Coming to understand them.* Thousand Oaks, CA: Sage.

Arata, C. M., Stafford, J., & Tims, M. S. (2003). High school drinking and its consequences. *Adolescence, 38*, 567–579.

Archer, J. (2004). Sex differences in aggression in real-world settings: A meta-analytic review. *Review of General Psychology, 8*, 291–322.

Ardrey, R. (1966). *The territorial imperative.* New York: Athenum.

Arena, M. P., & Arrigo, B. A. (2005). Social psychology, terrorism, and identity: A preliminary re-examination of theory, culture, self, and society. *Behavioral Sciences & the Law, 23*, 485–506.

Arkow, P. (1998). The correlations between cruelty to animals and child abuse and the implications for veterinary medicine. In R. Lockwood & F. R. Ascione (Eds.), *Cruelty to animals and interpersonal violence: Readings in research and application.* West Lafayette, IN: Purdue University Press.

Arrestees Drug Abuse Monitoring Program. (1999, April). *1998 annual report on marijuana use among arrestees.* Washington, DC: National Institute of Justice.

Arrestees Drug Abuse Monitoring Program. (2000, June). *1999 annual report on drug use among adult and juvenile arrestees.* Washington, DC: National Institute of Justice.

Arseneault, L., Tremblay, R. E., Boulerice, B., & Saucier, J-F. (2002). Obstetrical complications and violent delinquency: Testing two developmental pathways. *Child Development, 73*, 496–508.

Asbridge, M., Smart, R. G., & Mann, R. E. (2006). Can we prevent road rage? *Trauma, Violence, & Abuse, 7*, 109–121.

Ascione, R. R. (1997). *Animal welfare and domestic violence.* Logan, UT: Utah State University.

Ashford, J. B., Sales, B. D., & Reid, W. H. (2001). Introduction. In J. B. Ashford, B. D. Sales, & W. H. Reid (Eds.), *Treating adult and juvenile offenders with special needs.* Washington, DC: American Psychological Association.

Associated Press. (2006, May 17). Miami flagged for worst road rage. *Times Union*, p. A7.

Au Coin, K. (2003a). Family violence against older adults. In Canadian Centre for Justice Statistics (Ed.), *Family violence in Canada: A statistical profile 2003.* Ottawa: Canadian Centre for Justice Statistics.

Au Coin, K. (2003b). Violence and abuse against children and youth by family members. In Canadian Centre for Justice Statistics (Ed.), *Family violence in Canada: A statistical profile 2003.* Ottawa: Canadian Centre for Justice Statistics.

Augustine Fellowship. (1986). *Sex and love addicts anonymous.* Boston: Author.

Ault, R., & Reese, J. T. (1980). A psychological assessment of criminal profiling. *FBI Law Enforcement Bulletin, 49*, 22–25.

Avery-Clark, C. A., & Laws, D. R. (1984). Differential erection response patterns of sexual child abusers to stimuli describing activities with children. *Behavior Therapy, 15*, 71–83.

Babcock, J. C., Waltz, J., Jacobson, N. S., & Gottman, J. M. (1993). Power and violence: The relation between communication patterns, power discrepancies, and domestic violence. *Journal of Consulting and Clinical Psychology, 61*, 40–50.

Bacigal, R. J. (2002). Assault and battery. In K. L. Hall (Ed.), *The Oxford companion to American law.* New York: Oxford University Press.

Bagwell, C. L. (2004). Friendships, peer networks, and antisocial behavior. In J. B. Kupersmidt & K. A. Dodge (Eds.), *Children's peer relations: From development to intervention.* Washington, DC: American Psychological Association.

Bakker, E. (2006). *Jihadi terrorists in Europe, their characteristics and the circumstances in which they joined the jihad: An exploratory study.* The Hague: Clingendael Institute.

Ball, J. C., Shaffer, J. W., & Nurco, D. N. (1983). The day-to-day criminality of heroin addicts in Baltimore—a study in the continuity of offense rates. *Drug and Alcohol Dependence, 12,* 119–142.

Bamfield J. (1994). Electronic article surveillance: Management learning in curbing theft. In M. Gill (Ed.), *Crime at work: Studies in security and crime prevention.* Leiscester, UK: Perpetuity Press.

Bancroft, H. (1976). Behavioral treatments of sexual deviations. In N. H. Leitenberg (Ed.), *Handbook of behavioral modifications and behavioral therapy.* Englewood Cliffs, NJ: Prentice Hall.

Bandura, A. (1965). Influence of models' reinforcement contingencies on the acquisition of imitative responses. *Journal of Personality and Social Psychology, 1,* 589–595.

Bandura, A. (1973a). *Aggression: A social learning analysis.* Englewood Cliffs, NJ: Prentice Hall.

Bandura, A. (1973b). Social learning theory of aggression. In J. F. Knutson (Ed.), *The control of aggression.* Chicago: Aldine.

Bandura, A. (1978). The self-system in reciprocal determinism. *American Psychologist, 33,* 344–358.

Bandura, A. (1983). Psychological mechanisms of aggression. In R. G. Geen & E. I. Donnerstein (Eds.), *Aggression: Theoretical and empirical reviews* (Vol. 1). New York: Academic Press.

Bandura, A. (1986). *Social foundations in thought and action: A social cognitive theory.* Englewood Cliffs, NJ: Prentice Hall.

Bandura, A. (1989). Human agency in social cognitive theory. *American Psychologist, 44,* 1175–1184.

Bandura, A. (1990). Selective activation and disengagement of moral control. *Journal of Social Issues, 46,* 27–46.

Bandura, A. (1991). Social cognitive theory or moral thought and action. In M. W. Kurtines & J. L. Gewirtz (Eds.), *Handbook of moral behavior and development: Vol. I. Theory.* Hillsdale, NJ: Erlbaum.

Bandura, A. (1997). *Self-efficacy: The exercise of control.* New York: Freeman.

Bandura, A. (1999). Moral disengagement in the perpetration of inhumanities. *Personality and Social Psychology Review, 3,* 193–209.

Bandura, A. (2004). The role of selective moral disengagement in terrorism and counterterrorism. In F. M. Moghaddam & A. J. Marsella (Eds.), *Understanding terrorism: Psychosocial roots, consequences, and interventions.* Washington, DC: American Psychological Association.

Bandura, A., Barbaranelli, C., Caprara, G. V., & Pastorelli, C. (1996). Mechanisms of moral disengagement in the exercise of moral agency. *Journal of Personality and Social Psychology, 71,* 364–374.

Bandura, A., Caprara, G. V., Barbaranelli, C., Pastorelli, C., & Regalia, C. (2001). Sociocognitive self-regulatory mechanisms governing transgressive behavior. *Journal of Personality and Social Psychology, 80,* 125–135.

Bandura, A., & Huston, A. (1961). Identification as a process of incidental learning. *Journal of Abnormal and Social Psychology, 63,* 311–318.

Bandura, A., Ross, D., & Ross, S. (1963). Vicarious reinforcement and imitative learning. *Journal of Abnormal and Social Psychology, 67,* 601–607.

Bandura, A., & Walters, R. H. (1959). *Adolescent aggression.* New York: Ronald Press.

Bank, L., & Patterson, G. R. (1992). The use of structural equation modeling in combining data from different types of assessment. In J. C. Rosen & P. McReynolds (Eds.), *Recent advances in psychological assessment. Vol. 8.* New York: Plenum Press.

Barash, J., Tranel, D., & Anderson, S. W. (2000). Acquired personality disturbances associated with bilateral damage to the ventromedial prefrontal region. *Developmental Neuropsychology, 18,* 355–381.

Bard, L. A., Carter, D. L., Cerce, D. D., Knight, R. A., Rosenberg, R., & Schneider, B. (1987). A descriptive study of rapists and child molesters: Developmental, clinical, and criminal characters. *Behavioral Sciences & the Law, 5,* 203–220.

Bardone, A. M., Moffitt, T. E., & Caspi, A. (1996). Adult mental health and social outcomes of adolescent girls with depression and conduct disorder. *Development and Psychopathology, 8,* 811–829.

Barker, M. (2000). The criminal range of small-town burglars. In D. Canter & L. Alison (Eds.), *Profiling property crimes.* Dartmouth, UK: Ashgate.

Baron, R. A. (1977). *Human aggression.* New York: Plenum.

Baron, R. A. (1983). The control of human aggression: An optimistic perspective. *Journal of Social and Clinical Psychology, 1,* 97–119.

Baron, R. A., & Byrne, D. (1977). *Social psychology* (2nd ed.). Boston: Allyn and Bacon.

Barry, T. D., Barry, C. T., Deming, A. M., & Lochman, J. E. (2008). Stability of psychopathic characteristics in childhood. *Criminal Justice and Behavior, 35,* 244–262.

Bartholow, B. D., Sestir, M. A., & Davis, E. B. (2005). Correlates and consequences of exposure to video game violence: Hostile personality, empathy, and aggressive behavior. *Personality and Social Psychology Bulletin, 31,* 1573–1586.

Bartol, C. R., & Bartol, A. M. (1998). *Delinquency and justice: A psychosocial approach* (2nd ed.). Upper Saddle River, NJ: Prentice Hall.

Bartol, C. R., & Bartol, A.M. (2004). *Psychology and law: Theory, research, and application* (3rd ed.). Belmont, CA: Wadsworth/Thomson.

Bartol, C. R., & Bartol, A. M. (2008). *Introduction to forensic psychology* (2nd edition). Thousand Oaks, CA: Sage.

Bates, J. E., & McFadyen-Ketchum, S. (2000). Temperament and parent-child relations as interacting factors in children's behavioral adjustment. In V. Molfese & D.L. Molfese (Eds.), *Temperament and personality development across the life span.* Mahway, NJ: Lawrence Erlbaum Associates.

Bates, J. E., Pettit, G. S., Dodge, K. A., & Ridge, B. (1998). Interaction of temperamental resistance to control and restrictive parenting in the development of externalizing behavior. *Developmental Psychology, 34,* 982–995.

Battelle Law and Justice Center Report. (1977). *Forcible rape: An analysis of the legal issue.* Washington, DC: National Institute of Law Enforcement and Criminal Justice.

Baum, K. (2006, April). *Identity theft, 2004.* Washington, DC: U.S. Department of Justice, Bureau of Justice Statistics.

Baumer, T. L., & Rosenbaum, D. P. (1984). *Combating retail theft: Programs and strategies.* Boston: Butterworth.

Baumrind, D. (1991a). Parenting styles and adolescent development. In J. Brooks-Gunn, R. Lerner, & A. C. Petersen (Eds.), *The encyclopedia of adolescence.* New York: Garland.

Baumrind, D. (1991b). The influence of parenting style on adolescent competence and substance use. *Journal of Early Adolescence, 11,* 56–95.

Beatty, D. (2001). Stalking. In G. Coleman, M. Gaboury, M. Murray, & A. Seymour (Eds.), *1999 National Victim Assistance Academy.* Washington, DC: U.S. Department of Justice.

Beaver, K. M., Ratchford, M., & Ferguson, C. J. (2009). Evidence of genetic and environmental effects on the development of low self-control. *Criminal Justice and Behavior, 36,* 1148–1162.

Beck, A. J. (2000, August). *Prisoners in 1999.* Washington, DC: Bureau of Justice Statistics.

Becker, J. V., Hall, S. R., & Stinson, J. D. (2001). Female sexual offenders: Clinical, legal and policy issues. *Journal of Forensic Psychology Practice, 1,* 29–50.

Becker, J. V., & Johnson, B. R. (2001). Treating juvenile sex offenders. In J. B. Ashford, B. D. Sales, & W. H. Reid (Eds.), *Treating adult and juvenile offenders with special needs.* Washington, DC: American Psychological Association.

Becker, K. D., Stuewig, J., Herrera, V. M., & McCloskey, L. A. (2004). A study of firesetting and animal cruelty in children: Family influences and adolescent outcomes. *Journal of the American Academy of Child and Adolescent Psychiatry, 43,* 905–913.

Benda, B. B. (2005). Introduction: Boot camps revisited: Issues, problems, prospects. *Journal of Offender Rehabilitation, 40,* 1–25.

Bennell, C., & Canter, D. V. (2002). Linking commercial burglaries by modus operandi: Tests using regression and ROC analysis. *Science and Justice, 42,* 153–162.

Bennell, C., & Jones, N. J. (2005). Between a ROC and a hard place: A method for linking serial burglaries using an offender's modus operandi. *Journal of Investigative Psychology and Offender Profiling, 2,* 23–41.

Bennett, D. S., Bendersky, M., & Lewis, M. (2002). Children's intellectual and emotional-behavioral adjustment at 4 years as a function of cocaine exposure, maternal characteristics, and environmental risk. *Developmental Psychology, 38,* 648–658.

Bennett, T., Holloway, K., & Farrington, D. (2008). The statistical association between drug misuse and crime: A meta-analysis. *Aggression and Violent Behavior, 13,* 107–118.

Bennett, T., & Wright, R. (1984). *Burglars on burglary: Prevention and the offender.* Brookfield, VT: Gower.

Bereczkei, T. (2000). Evolutionary psychology: A new perspective in the behavioral sciences. *European Psychologist, 5,* 175–190.

Bergman, L. R., & Andershed, A. (2009). Predictors and outcomes of persistent or age-limited registered criminal behavior: A 30-year longitudinal study of a Swedish urban population. *Aggressive Behavior, 35,* 164–178.

Berkowitz, L. (1962). *Aggression: A social-psychological analysis.* New York: McGraw-Hill.

Berkowitz, L. (1969). The frustration-aggression hypothesis revisited. In L. Berkowitz (Ed.), *Roots of aggression.* New York: Atherton Press.

Berkowitz, L. (1973). Words and symbols as stimuli to aggressive responses. In J. F. Knutson (Ed.), *The control of aggression.* Chicago: Aldine.

Berkowitz, L. (1983). The experience of anger as a parallel process in the display of impulsive, "angry" aggression. In R. G. Geen & E. I. Donnerstein (Eds.), *Aggression: Theoretical and empirical reviews* (Vol. 1). New York: Academic Press.

Berkowitz, L. (1989). Frustration-aggression hypothesis: Examination and reformulation. *Psychological Bulletin, 106,* 59–73.

Berkowitz, L. (1994). Guns and youth. In L. E. Eron, J. H. Gentry, & P. Schlegel (Eds.), *Reason to hope: A psychosocial perspective on violence and youth.* Washington, DC: American Psychological Association.

Berkowitz, L., & LePage, A. (1967). Weapons as aggression-eliciting stimuli. *Journal of Personality and Social Psychology, 7,* 202–207.

Berlyne, D. E. (1960). *Conflict, arousal, and curiosity.* New York: McGraw-Hill.

Bernard, F. (1975). An inquiry among a group of pedophiles. *Journal of Sex Research, 11,* 242–255.

Bernasco, W. (2006). Co-offending and the choice of target areas in burglary. *Journal of Investigative Psychology and Offending Profiling, 3,* 139–155.

Bernstein, A., Newman, J. P., Wallace, J. F., & Luh, K. E. (2000). Left hemisphere activation and deficient response modulation in psychopaths. *Psychological Science, 11,* 414–418.

Berrueta-Clement, J. R., Schweinhart, L. J., Barnett, W. S., & Weikart. D. P. (1987). The effects of early educational intervention in adolescence and early adulthood. In J. D. Burhcard & S. N. Burchard (Eds.), *Prevention of delinquent behavior.* Newbury Park, CA: Sage.

Beyer, K., Mack, S. M., & Shelton, J. L. (2008). Investigative analysis of neonaticide: An exploratory study. *Criminal Justice and Behavior, 35,* 522–535.

Beyers, J. M., Bates, J. E., Pettit, G. S., & Dodge, K. A. (2003). Neighborhood structure, parenting processes, and the development of youths' externalizing behaviors: A multilevel analysis. *American Journal of Community Psychology, 31,* 35–53.

Bhal, K. T., & Leekha, N. D. (2008). Exploring cognitive moral logics using grounded theory: The case of software piracy. *Journal of Business Ethics, 81,* 635–646.

Binder, A. (1988). Juvenile delinquency. *Annual Review of Psychology, 39,* 253–282.

Björkqvist, K., Lagerspetz, M. J., & Kaukianinen, A. (1992). Do girls manipulate and boys fight? Developmental trends in regard to direct and indirect aggression. *Aggressive Behavior, 18,* 117–127.

Black, H. C. (1990). *Black's law dictionary.* St. Paul, MN: West Publishing.

Black, M. S., & Pettway, C. (2001, December). *Profile of ODRC offenders assessed at the sex offender risk reduction center.* Columbus, OH: Ohio Office of Policy, Bureau of Research.

Blackburn, R. (1993). *The psychology of criminal conduct: Theory, research and practice.* Chichester, UK: Wiley.

Blackburn, R. (1998). Criminality and the interpersonal circle in mentally disordered offenders. *Criminal Justice and Behavior, 25,* 155–176.

Blair, C. D., & Lanyon, R. I. (1981). Exhibitionism: An etiology and treatment. *Psychological Bulletin, 89,* 439–463.

Blair, R. J. R., Peschardt, K. S., Budhani, S., Mitchell, D. G. V., & Pine, D. S. (2006). The development of psychopathy. *Journal of Child Psychology and Psychiatry, 47,* 262–275.

Blanchard, R., Klassen, P., Dickey, R., Kuban, M. E., & Blak, T. I. (2001). Sensitivity and specificity of the phallometric test for pedophilia in nonadmitting sex offenders. *Psychological Assessment, 13,* 118–126.

Blanchard, R., Watson, M. S., Choy, A., Dickey, R., Klassen, P., Kuban, M., & Ferren, D. J. (1999). Pedophiles: Mental retardation, maternal age, and sexual orientation. *Archives of Sexual Behavior, 28,* 111–127.

Blanco, C., Grant, J., Petry, N. M., Simpson, H. B., Alegria, A., Liu, S-M., et al. (2008). Prevalence and correlates of shoplifting in the United States: Results from the National Epideiologic Survey on Alcohol and Related Conditions (NESARC). *American Journal of Psychiatry, 155,* 905–913.

Blitstein, J. L., Murray, D. M., Lytle, L. A., Birnbaum, A. S., & Perry, C. L. (2005). Predictors of violent behavior in an early adolescent cohort: Similarities and differences across genders. *Health Education and Behavior, 32,* 175–194.

Blonigen, D. M., Carlson, S. R., Krueger, R. F., & Patrick, C. J. (2003). A twin study of self-reported psychopathic traits. *Personality and Individual Differences, 35,* 179–197.

Blonigen, D. M., Hicks, B. M., Krueger, R. F., Iacono, W. G., & Patrick, C. J. (2005). Psychopathic personality traits: Heritability and genetic overlap with internalizing and externalizing psychopathology. *Psychological Medicine, 35,* 637–648.

Blumenthal, D. R. (1999). *The banality of good and evil: Moral lessons from the Shoah and Jewish tradition.* Washington, DC: Georgetown University Press.

Blumer, D. (1976). Epilepsy and violence. In D. J. Madden & J. R. Lion (Eds.), *Rage • hate • assault • and other forms of violence.* New York: Spectrum Publishing.

Blumer, H., Sutter, A., Ahmed, S., & Smith, R. (1967). *ADD center final report: The world of youthful drug use.* Berkeley, CA: University of California Press.

Boehnert, C. E. (1989). Characteristics of successful and unsuccessful insanity pleas. *Law and Human Behavior, 13,* 31–39.

Bolen, R. M., & Scannapieco, M. (1999). Prevalence of child sexual abuse: A corrective metanalysis. *Social Service Review, 73,* 281–313.

Bolt, D. M., Hare, R. D., Vitale, J. E., & Newman, J. P. (2004). A multigroup item response theory analysis of the Psychopathy Checklist—Revised. *Psychological Assessment, 16,* 155–168.

Bonanno, G. A. (2004). Loss, trauma, and human resilience: Have we underestimated the human capacity to thrive after extremely aversive events? *American Psychologist, 59,* 20–28.

Bongers, I. L., Koot, H. M., van der Ende, J., & Verhulst, F. C. (2003). The normative development of child and adolescent problem behavior. *Journal of Abnormal Psychology, 112,* 179–192.

Bonnie, R. J., & Grisso, T. (2000). Adjudicative competence and youthful offenders. In T. Grisso & R. G. Schwartz (Eds.), *Youth on trial.* Chicago: University of Chicago Press.

Bonta, J., & Andrews, D. A. (2007). *Risk-need-responsivity model for offender assessment and rehabilitation (corrections research user report no. 2007–06).* Ottawa, Canada: Public Safety Canada.

Bonta, J., & Cormier, R. B. (1999). Corrections research in Canada: Impressive progress and promising prospects. *Canadian Journal of Criminology, 41,* 235–245.

Bonta, J., Law, M., & Hanson, K. (1998). The prediction of criminal and violent recidivism among mentally disordered offenders: A meta-analysis. *Psychological Bulletin, 123,* 123–142.

Borduin, C. M. (1994). Innovative models of treatment and service delivery in the juvenile justice system. *Journal of Clinical Child Psychiatry, 23,* 19–21.

Borduin, C. M., Mann, B. J., Cone, L. T., Henggeler, S. W., Fucci, B. R., Blaske, D. M., et al. (1995). Multisystemic treatment of serious juvenile offenders: Long-term prevention of criminality and violence. *Journal of Consulting and Clinical Psychology, 63,* 569–578.

Borduin, C. M., Schaeffer, C. M., & Heiblum, N. (2009). A randomized clinical trial of multisystemic therapy with juvenile sexual offenders: Effects on youth social ecology and criminal activity. *Journal of Consulting and Clinical Psychology, 77*, 26–37.

Borum, R. (1996). Improving the clinical practice of violence risk assessment. *American Psychologist, 51*, 945–956.

Borum, R., & Gelles, M. (2005). Al-Qaeda's operational evolution: Behavioral and Organizational Perspectives. *Behavioral Sciences & the Law, 23*, 467–483.

Borum, R., & Strentz, T. (1993, April). The borderline personality: Negotiation strategies. *FBI Law Enforcement Bulletin*, 6–10.

Bottcher, J., & Ezell, M. E. (2005). Examining the effectiveness of boot camps: A randomized experiment with a long-term follow up. *Journal of Research in Crime and Delinquency, 42*, 309–332.

Boudreau, J., Kwan, Q., Faragher, W., & Denault, G. (1977). *Arson and arson investigation.* Washington, DC: USGPO.

Bourque, B. B., Cronin, R. C., Felker, D. B., Pearson, F. R., Han, M., & Hill, S. M. (1996). *Boot camps for juvenile offenders: An implementation evaluation of three demonstration programs.* Research in Brief. Washington, DC: National Institute of Justice.

Bowker, L. H. (1983). *Beating wife-battering.* Lexington, MA: Lexington Books.

Bowlby, J. (1969). *Attachment and loss: Vol. 1. Attachment.* New York: Basic Books.

Boykin, A. W. (1986). The triple quandary and the schooling of Afro-American children. In U. Neisser (Ed.), *The school achievement of minority children.* Hillsdale, NJ: Erlbaum.

Boykin, A. W. (1994). Harvesting talent and culture: African-American children and educational reform. In R. Rossi (Ed.), *Schools and students at risk.* New York: Teachers College Press.

Bracey, D. H. (1982). Concurrent and consecutive abuse: The juvenile prostitute. In B. R. Price and N. Sokoloff (Eds.), *The criminal justice system and women.* New York: Clark Boardman.

Bradford, J. M. W. (1982). Arson: A clinical study. *Canadian Journal of Psychiatry, 27*, 188–193.

Braga, A. A., & Kennedy, D. M. (2001). The illicit acquisition of firearms by youth and juveniles. *Journal of Criminal Justice, 29*, 397–388.

Brandt, J. R., Kennedy, W. A., Patrick, C. J., & Curtain, J. J. (1997). Assessment of psychopathy in a population of incarcerated adolescent offenders. *Psychological Assessment, 9*, 429–435.

Brantley, A. G., & Kosky, R. H., Jr. (2005, January). Serial murder in the Netherlands: A look at motivation, behavior, and characteristics. *FBI Law Enforcement Bulletin*, 26–32.

Braun, J. M., Kahn, R. S., Froehlich, T., Auinger, P., & Lanphear, B. P. (2006, December). Exposure to environmental toxicants and attention deficit hyperactivity disorder in U.S. children. *Environmental Health Perspectives, 114*, 1904–1909.

Bray, C. (2009, March 12). Madoff pleads guilty to massive fraud. *The Wall Street Journal*, pp. 1, 9.

Brecklin, L. R., & Forde, D. R. (2001). A meta-analysis of rape education programs. *Violence and Victims, 16*, 303–321.

Brennan, P. A., Grekin, E. R., & Mednick, S. A. (1999). Maternal smoking during pregnancy and adult male criminal outcomes. *Archives of General Psychiatry, 56*, 215–219.

Brennan, P. A., Hall, J., Bor, W., Najman, J. M., & Williams, G. (2003). Integrating biological and social processes in relation to early-onset persistent aggression in boys and girls. *Developmental Psychology, 39*, 309–323.

Brennan, P. A., Mednick, S. A., & Hodgins, S. (2000). Major mental disorders and criminal violence in a Danish birth cohort. *Archives of General Psychiatry, 53*, 1033–1039.

Brenner, V., & Fox, R. A. (1999). An empirically derived classification of parenting practices. *The Journal of Genetic Psychology, 160*, 343–356.

Brent, D. A. (1989). The psychological autopsy: Methodological issues for the study of adolescent suicide. *Suicide and Life Threatening Behavior, 19*, 43–57.

Brier, N. (1989). The relationship between learning disability and delinquency: A review and reappraisal. *Journal of Learning Disabilities, 22*, 546–553.

Briere, J. (1988). The long-term clinical correlates of childhood sexual victimization. In R. A. Prentky & V. L. Quinsey (Eds.), *Human sexual aggression: Current perspectives.* New York: New York Academy of Sciences.

Briere, J., Malamuth, N., & Ceniti, J. (1981). Self-assessed rape proclivity: Attitudinal and sexual correlates. Paper presented at APA Meeting, Los Angeles, CA.

Brodsky, S. L. (1973). Psychologists in the criminal justice system. Urbana, IL: University of Illinois Press.

Brodsky, S. L. (1977). Criminal and dangerous behavior. In D. Rimm & J. Somervill (Eds.), Abnormal psychology. New York: Academic Press.

Broidy, L. M., Nagin, D. S., Tremblay, R. E., Bates, J. E., Brame, B., Dodge, K. A., et al. (2003). Developmental trajectories of childhood disruptive behaviors and adolescent delinquency: A six-site, cross-national study. Developmental Psychology, 39, 222–245.

Brookman, F., & Nolan, J. (2006). The dark figure of infanticide in England and Wales: Complexes of diagnosis. Journal of Interpersonal Violence, 21, 869–889.

Brown, B. B., & Harris, P. B. (1989). Residential burglary victimization: Reactions to the invasion of a primary territory. Journal of Environmental Psychology, 9, 119–132.

Brown, J. S., & Farber, I. E. (1951). Emotions conceptualized as intervening variables—with suggestions toward a theory of frustration. Psychological Bulletin, 48, 465–495.

Brown, T. L., Borduin, C. M., & Henggeler, S. W. (2001). Treating juvenile offenders in community settings. In J. B. Ashford, B. D. Sales, & W. H. Reid (Eds.), Treating adult and juvenile offenders with special needs. Washington, DC: American Psychological Association.

Browne, A. (1987). When battered women kill. New York: Free Press.

Browne, A., & Finkelhor, D. (1986). Impact of child sexual abuse: A review of the research. Psychological Bulletin, 99, 66–77.

Browning, K., & Loeber, R.. (1999, February). Highlights of findings from the Pittsburgh Youth Study. OJJDP Fact Sheet. Washington, DC: U.S. Department of Justice, Office of Juvenile Justice and Delinquency Prevention.

Brownlie, E. B., Beitchman, J. J., Escobar, M., Young, A., Atkinson, L., Johnson, C., Wilson, B., & Douglas, L. (2004). Early language impairment and young adult delinquent and aggressive behavior. Journal of Abnormal Child Psychology, 32, 453–467.

Brunet, B. L., Reiffenstein, R. J., Williams, T., & Wong, L. (1985–1986). Toxicity of phencyclidine and ethanol in combination. Alcohol and Drug Research, 6, 341–349.

Brussel, J. A. (1978). Casebook of a crime psychiatrist. New York: Bernard Geis Associates.

Bryant, J., & Zillmann, D. (Eds.). (2002). Media effects: Advances in theory and research (2nd ed.). Mahwah, NJ: Erlbaum.

Buckle, A., & Farrington, D. P. (1994). Measuring shoplifting by systematic observation: A replication study. Psychology, Crime & Law, 1, 133–141.

Bumby, K. M., & Bumby, N. H. (1997). Adolescent female sexual offenders. In J. R. Cellini & B. Schwartz (Eds.), The sex offender: New insights, treatment innovations and legal developments (Vol. 2). Kingston, NJ: Civil Research Institute.

Bumpass, E. R., Fagelman, F. D., & Birx, R. J. (1983). Intervention with children who set fires. American Journal of Psychotherapy, 37, 328–345.

Burchfield, K. B., & Mingus, W. (2008). Not in my neighborhood: Assessing registered sex offenders' experiences with local social capital and social control. Criminal Justice and Behavior, 35, 356–374.

Bureau of International Narcotics and Law Enforcement Affairs. (2000, March). International narcotics control strategy report, 1999. Washington, DC: U.S. Department of State. Available: www.state.gov/www/global/narcotics.

Bureau of Justice Assistance. (2000, April). Emerging judicial strategies for the mentally ill in the criminal caseload: Mental health courts. Washington, DC: U.S. Department of Justice.

Bureau of Justice Statistics. (2000, June). Drugs and crime facts: Drug use and crime. Washington, DC: Author. Available: www.ojp.usdoj.gov/bjs/dcf/duc.htm.

Bureau of Justice Statistics. (2005, November 20). School violence rate stable: Lowest level in a decade. Washington, DC: U.S. Department of Justice, Author.

Bureau of Justice Statistics. (2006, June). Prison statistics: Summary findings. Washington, DC: U.S. Department of Justice, Author.

Bureau of Labor Statistics. (2004). *Census of fatal occupational injuries.* Washington, DC: U.S. Department of Labor.

Burger, J. M. (2009). Replicating Milgram: Would people still obey today? *American Psychologist, 64,* 1–11.

Burgess, A. W., Garbarino, C., & Carlson, M. I. (2006). Pathological teasing and bullying turned deadly: Shooters and suicide. *Victims and Offenders, 1,* 1–14.

Burgess, R. L., & Akers, R. L. (1966). A differential association-reinforcement theory of criminal behavior. *Social Problems, 14,* 128–147.

Burnam, M. A., Stein, J. A., Golding, J. M., Siegel, J. M., Sorenson, S. B., Forsythe, A. B., et al. (1988). Sexual assault and mental disorders in a community population. *Journal of Consulting and Clinical Psychology, 56,* 843–850.

Busch, K G., & Weissman, S. H. (2005). The intelligence community and the war on terror: The role of behavioral science. *Behavioral Sciences & the Law, 23,* 559–571.

Bushman, B. J., & Anderson, C. A. (2001). Is it time to pull the plug on the hostile versus instrumental aggression dichotomy. *Psychological Review, 108,* 273–279.

Bushman, B. J., Bonacci, A. M., Pederson, W. C., Vasquez, E. A., & Miller, N. (2005). Chewing on it can chew you up: Effects of rumination on triggered displaced aggression. *Journal of Personality and Social Psychology, 88,* 969–983.

Buss, A. H. (1971). Aggression pays. In J. L. Singer (Ed.), *The control of aggression and violence.* New York: Academic Press.

Buss, D. M., & Shackelford, T. K. (1997). Human aggression in evolutionary psychological perspective. *Clinical Psychology Review, 17,* 605–619.

Butler, R. A. (1954). Curiosity in monkeys. *Scientific American* (Reprint #426). San Francisco: W. H. Freeman.

Buzawa, E. S., & Buzawa, C. G. (1996). *Domestic violence: The criminal justice response* (2nd ed.). Thousand Oaks, CA: Sage.

Cacioppo, J. T., Berntson, G. G., Sheridan, J. F., & McClintock, M. K. (2000). Multilevel integrative analyses of human behavior: Social neuroscience and the complementing nature of social and biological approaches. *Psychological Bulletin, 6,* 829–843.

Cairns, R. B., Cairns, B. D., Neckerman, H. J., Ferguson, L. L., & Gariépy, J. L. (1989). Growth and aggression: I. Childhood to early adolescence. *Developmental Psychology, 25,* 320–330.

Cale, E. M. (2006). A quantitative review of the relations between the "Big 3" higher order personality dimensions and antisocial behavior. *Journal of Research in Personality, 40,* 250–284.

California Division of Occupational Safety and Health. (1995). *Guidelines for workplace security.* San Francisco: California Department of Industrial Relations.

Callahan, L. A., McGreevy, M. A., Circincione, C., & Steadman, H. J. (1992). Measuring the effects of guilty but mentally ill (GBMI) verdict. *Law and Human Behavior, 16,* 447–462.

Callahan, L. A., Steadman, H. J., McGreevy, M. A., & Robbins, P. C. (1991). The volume and characteristics of insanity defense pleas: An eight-state study. *Bulletin of Psychiatry and the Law, 19,* 331–338.

Cameron, M. O. (1964). *The booster and the snitch.* New York: Free Press.

Camilleri, J. A., & Quinsey, V. L. (2008). Pedophilia: Assessment and treatment. In D. R. Laws & W. T. O'Donohue (Eds.), *Sexual deviance: Theory, assessment, and treatment.* New York: Guilford.

Campbell, A. (1993). *Men, women, and aggression.* New York: Basic Books.

Campbell, A. (2006). Sex differences in direct aggression: What are the psychological mediators. *Aggression and Violent Behavior, 22,* 237–264.

Campbell, B. J. (1996). *Validity and use of evidence concerning battering and its effects in criminal trials.* Washington, DC: U.S. Department of Justice, Violence Against Women Office.

Campbell, M. A., Porter, S., & Santor, D. (2004). Psychopathic traits in adolescent offenders: An evaluation of criminal history, clinical, and psychosocial correlates. *Behavioral Sciences & the Law, 22,* 23–47.

Canadian Government's Commission of Inquiry. (1971). *The non-medical use of drugs: Interim report.* London: Penguin Books.

Canfield, R. L., Henderson, C. R., Cory-Slechta, A. A., Cox, C., Jusko, T. A., & Lanphear, B. P. (2003). Intellectual impairment in children with blood lead concentrations below 10 microgram per deciliter. *New England Journal of Medicine, 348,* 1517–1526.

Canter, D., & Alison, L. (2000). Profiling property crimes. In D. Canter & L. Alison (Eds.), *Profiling property crimes.* Burlington, VT: Ashgate.

Canter, D. V., Alison, L. J., Alison, E., & Wentink, N. (2004). The organized/disorganized typology of serial murder: Myth or model? *Psychology, Public Policy, and Law, 10,* 293–320.

Canter, D. V., & Fritzon, K. (1998). Differentiating arsonists: A model of firesetting actions and characteristics. *Legal and Criminological Psychology, 3,* 73–96.

Canter, S. (1973). Personality traits in twins. In G. Claridge, S. Canfree, & W. I. Hume (Eds.), *Personality differences and biological variations: A study of twins.* Oxford, UK: Pergamon Press.

Cantor, J. M., Blanchard, R., Robichaud, L. K., & Christensen, B. K. (2005). Quantitative reanalysis of aggregate date on IQ in sexual offenders. *Psychological Bulletin, 131,* 555–568.

Caputo, G. A. (2004). Treating sticky fingers: An evaluation of treatment and education for shoplifters. *Journal of Offender Rehabilitation, 38,* 49–68.

Carlson, B. E. (1991). Outcomes of physical abuse and observation of marital violence among adolescents in placement. *Journal of Interpersonal Violence, 6,* 526–534.

Carlson, M., Marcus-Newhall, A., & Miller, N. (1990). Effects of situational aggression cues: A quantitative review. *Journal of Personality and Social Psychology, 58,* 622–633.

Carnegie Council on Adolescent Development. (1995). *Great transitions: Preparing American Youth for a new century.* New York: Carnegie Corporation of New York.

Carnes, P. (1983). *Out of the shadows: Understanding sexual addiction.* Minneapolis, MN: Compcare Publications.

Carraher, T. N., Carraher, D., & Schliemann, A. D. (1985). Mathematics in the streets and schools. *British Journal of Developmental Psychology, 3,* 21–29.

Carrasco, M., Barker, E. D., Tremblay, R. E., & Vitaro, F. (2006). Eysenck's personality dimension as predictors of male adolescent trajectories of physical aggression, theft and vandalism. *Personality and Individual Differences, 41,* 1309–1320.

Carter, D. L., & Katz, A. J. (1996). *Computer crime: An emerging challenge for law enforcement.* Washington, DC: U.S. Department of Justice. Available: www.fbi.gov/leb/dec961.txt.

Casey-Cannon, S., Hayward, C., & Gowen, K. (2001). Middle-school girls' reports of peer victimization: Concerns, consequences, and implications. *Professional School Counseling, 5,* 138–148.

Caspi, A., Wright, B. R. E., Moffitt, T. E., & Silva, P. A. (1998). Early failure in the labor market: Childhood and adolescent predictors of unemployment in the transition to adulthood. *American Sociological Review, 63,* 424–451.

Catalano, R., Haggerty, K., Oesterle, S., Fleming, C., & Hawkins, J. D. (2004). The importance of bonding to school for healthy development: Findings from the Social Development Research Group. *Journal of School Health, 74,* 252–261.

Catalano, S. M. (2005). *Crime victimization, 2004.* Washington, DC: U.S. Department of Justice, National Crime Victimization Survey.

Cellini, H. R. (1995). Assessment and treatment of the adolescent sexual offender. In B. Schwartz & H. R. Cellini (Eds.), *The sex offender: Corrections, treatment and legal practice* (Vol. 1). Kingston, NJ: Civil Research Institute.

Center, D. B., Jackson, N., & Kemp, D. (2005). A test of Eysenck's antisocial behavior hypothesis employing 11–15-year-old students dichotomous for PEN and L. *Personality and Individual Differences, 38,* 393–402.

Center, D. B., & Kemp, D. E. (2002). Antisocial behaviour in children and Eysenck's theory of personality: An evaluation. *International Journal of Disability, Development and Education, 49,* 353–366.

Chaiken, J. M. (1998a, April). Learning more from national data collection programs. *National*

Conference on Sex Offender Registries. Sacramento, CA: SEARCH group. Available: www.ojp.usdoj.gov/bjs/pub/.

Chaiken, J. M. (1998b, April). Foreword. *National Conference on Sex Offender Registries.* Sacramento, CA: SEARCH group. Available: www.ojp.usdoj.gov/bjs/pub/.

Chalkley, A. J., & Powell, G. E. (1983). The clinical description of forty-eight cases of clinical fetishism. *British Journal of Psychiatry, 142,* 292–295.

Chamberlain, P. (1996). Treatment foster care for adolescents with conduct disorders and delinquency. In P. S. Jensen & D. Hibbs (Eds.), *Psychological treatment with research with children and adolescents.* Rockville, MD: National Institute of Mental Health.

Chappell, D. (1977a). *Forcible rape: A national survey of the response by police (LEAA).* Washington, DC: USGPO.

Chappell, D. (1977b). *Forcible rape: A national survey of the response by prosecutors (LEAA).* Washington, DC: USGPO.

Chapple, C. L. (2003). Examining intergenerational violence: Violent role modeling or weak parental controls? *Violence and Victims, 18,* 143–159.

Chen, Y-H., Arria, A., & Anthony, J. C. (2003). Firesetting in adolescents and being aggressive, shy, and rejected by peers: New epidemiologic evidence from a national sample survey. *Journal of the American Academy of Psychiatry and Law, 31,* 44–52.

Chermak, S. M., Freilich, J. D., & Shemtob, Z. (2009). Law-enforcement training and the domestic far right. *Criminal Justice and Behavior, 36* (in press).

Chesney-Lind, M., & Shelden, R. (1998). *Girls, delinquency, and juvenile justice* (2nd ed.). Belmont, CA: West/Wadsworth.

Chesno, F. A., & Kilmann, P. R. (1975). Effects of stimulation intensity on sociopathic avoidance learning. *Journal of Abnormal Psychology, 84,* 144–150.

Child Abuse Prevention Center. (1998). *Shaken baby syndrome fatalities in the United States.* Ogden, UT: Author.

Chilosi, A. M., Cipriani, P., Pecini, C., Brizzolara, D., Blagi, L., Montanaro, D., **et al.** (2008). Acquired focal brain lesions in childhood: Effects on

development and reorganization of language. *Brain & Language, 106,* 211–225.

Chimbos, P. D. (1973). A study of breaking and entering offenses in "Northern City," Ontario. *Canadian Journal of Criminology and Corrections, 15,* 316–325.

Christiansen, K. O. (1977). A review of studies of criminality among twins. In S. Mednick & K. O. Christiansen (Eds.), *Biosocial bases of criminal behavior.* New York: Gardiner Press.

Christie, M. M., Marshall, W. L., & Lanthier. R. D. (1979). *A descriptive study of incarcerated rapists and pedophiles.* Ottawa, ON: Report to the Solicitor General of Canada.

Chung, I-J, Hill, K. G., Hawkins, J. D., Gilchrist, L. D., & Nagin, D. S. (2002). Childhood predictors of offense trajectories. *Journal of Research in Crime and Delinquency, 39,* 60–90.

Churgin, M. M. (1983). The transfer of inmates of mental health facilities: Developments in the law. In J. Monahan & H. J. Steadman (Eds.), *Mentally disordered offenders.* New York: Plenum.

Cicero, T. J., Inciardi, J. A., & Muñoz, A. (2005). Trends in abuse of OxyContin® and other opioid analgesics in the United States: 2002–2004. *The Journal of Pain, 6,* 662–672.

Cillessen, A. H. N., & Mayeux, L. (2004). Sociometric status and peer group behavior: Previous findings and current directions. In J. B. Kupersmidt & K. A. Dodge (Eds.), *Children's peer relations: From development to intervention.* Washington, DC: American Psychological Association.

Cirincione, C., & Jacobs, C. (1999). Identifying insanity acquittals: Is it easier? *Law and Human Behavior, 23,* 487–497.

Claridge, G. (1973). Final remarks. In G. Claridge, S. Canter, & W. I. Hume (Eds.), *Personality differences and biological variations.* Oxford, UK: Pergamon Press.

Clark, J. P., & Hollinger, R. C. (1983). *Theft by employees in work organizations.* Washington, DC: USGPO.

Clark, K. B. (1971). The pathos of power: A psychological perspective. *American Psychologist, 26,* 1047–1057.

Cleckley, H. (1976). *The mask of sanity* (5th ed.). St. Louis, MO: Mosby.

Clinard, M. B., & Quinney, E. R. (1980). *Criminal behavior systems: A typology.* New York: Holt, Rinehart & Winston.

Cochrane, R. E., Grisso, T., & Frederick, R. I. (2001). The relationship between criminal charges, diagnoses, and psychological opinions among federal defendants. *Behavioral Science & the Law, 19,* 565–582.

Cocozza, J. J., & Steadman, H. J. (1976). The failure of psychiatric prediction of dangerousness: Clear and convincing evidence. *Rutgers Law Review, 29,* 1084–1101.

Cohen, D., & Strayer, J. (1996). Empathy in conduct-disordered and comparison youth. *Developmental Psychology, 32,* 988–998.

Cohen, F. (1998). *The mentally disordered inmate and the law.* Kingston, NJ: Civic Research Institute.

Cohen, F. (2000). *The mentally disordered inmate and the law: 2000–2001 supplement.* Kingston, NJ: Civic Research Institute.

Cohen, F. (2008). *The mentally disordered inmate and the law* (2nd ed.). Kingston, NJ: Civic Research Institute.

Cohen, M., Seghorn, T., & Calmas, W. (1969). Sociometric study of the sex offender. *Journal of Abnormal Psychology, 74,* 249–255.

Cohen, M. L., Garafalo, R., Boucher, R., & Seghorn, T. (1971). The psychology of rapists. *Seminars in Psychiatry, 3,* 307–327.

Cohen, N. J., Menna, R., Vallance, D. D., Barwick, M., Im, N., & Horodezky, N. B. (1998). Language, social cognitive processing, and behavioral characteristics of psychiatrically disturbed children with previously identified and suspected language impairments. *Journal of Child Psychology and Psychiatry, 39,* 853–864.

Cohen, P., Cohen, J., & Brook, J. (1993). An epidemiological study of disorders in late childhood and adolescence—II. Persistent disorders. *Journal of Child Psychology and Psychiatry, 34,* 869–877.

Cohn, V. (1986). Crack use. *NIDA Notes, 1,* 6.

Coie, J. D. (2004). The impact of negative social experience on the development of antisocial behavior.

In J. B. Kupersmidt & K. A. Dodge (Eds.), *Children's peer relations: From development to intervention.* Washington, DC: American Psychological Association.

Coie, J. D., Belding, M., & Underwood, M. (1988). Aggression and peer rejection in childhood. In B. Lahey & A. Kazdin (Eds.), *Advances in clinical child psychology* (Vol. 2). New York: Plenum.

Coie, J. D., Dodge, K., & Kupersmith, J. (1990). Peer group behavior and social status. In S. R. Asher & J. D. Coie (Eds.), *Peer rejection in childhood.* Cambridge, UK: Cambridge University Press.

Coie, J. D., & Miller-Johnson, S. (2001). Peer factors and interventions. In R. Loeber & D. P. Farrington (Eds.), *Child delinquents: Development, intervention, and service needs.* Thousand Oaks, CA: Sage.

Coleman, J. C. (1976). *Abnormal psychology and modern life* (5th ed.). Glenview, IL: Scott, Foresman.

Coleman, J. W. (1998). *The criminal elite* (4th ed.). New York: St. Martin's Press.

Coles, E., Freitas, T., & Tweed, R. (1996). Assessment of understanding by people manifesting mental retardation: A preliminary report. *Perceptual and Motor Skills, 83,* 187–192.

Colwell, M. J., Pettit, G. S., Meece, D., Bates, J. E., & Dodge, K. A. (2001). Cumulative risk and continuity in nonparental care from infancy to early adolescence. *Merrill-Palmer Quarterly, 47,* 207–234.

Comer, R. J. (2004). *Abnormal psychology* (5th ed.). New York: Worth.

Committee on Preventive Psychiatry. (1999). Violent behavior in children and youth: Preventive intervention from a psychiatric perspective. *Journal of the American Academy of Child and Adolescent Psychiatry, 38,* 235–241.

Commons, M. L., & Goodheart, E. A. (2007). Consider stages of development in preventing terrorism: Does government building fail and terrorism result when developmental stages of governance are skipped? *Journal of Adult Development, 14,* 91–111.

Conduct Problems Prevention Research Group. (1999). Initial impact of the Fast Track prevention trail for conduct problems: I. The high-risk sample. *Journal of Consulting and Clinical Psychology, 67,* 631–647.

Conduct Problems Prevention Research Group. (2004). The fast track experiment: Translating the developmental model into a prevention design. In J. B. Kupersmidt & K. A. Dodge (Eds.), *Children's peer relations: From development to intervention.* Washington, DC: American Psychological Association.

Conklin, J. E. (1977). *"Illegal but not criminal."* Englewood Cliffs, NJ: Prentice Hall.

Connell, D. (1996, November). *Driver aggression.* Washington, DC: Automobile Association Group Public Policy Road Safety Unit.

Cook, S. E. (2000). Forced prostitution. In N. H. Rafter (Ed.), *Encyclopedia of women and crime.* Phoenix: Oryx Press.

Cooke, D. J., & Michie, C. (1997). An item response theory analysis of the Hare Psychopathy Checklist-Revised. *Psychological Assessment, 9,* 3–14.

Cooke, D. J., & Michie, C. (2001). Refining the construct psychopathy: Toward a hierarchical model. *Psychological Assessment, 13,* 171–188.

Cooke, D. J., Michie, C., Hart, S. D., & Clark, D. A. (2004). Reconstructing psychopathy: Clarifying the significance of antisocial and socially deviant behavior in the diagnosis of psychopathic personality disorder. *Journal of Personality Disorders, 18,* 337–357.

Cooke, D. J., Michie, C., Hart, S. D., & Hare, R. D. (1999). Evaluation of the screening version of the Hare Psychopathy Checklist—Revised (PCL:SV): An item response theory analysis. *Psychological Assessment, 11,* 3–13.

Coordinating Council on Juvenile Justice and Delinquency Prevention. (1996). *Combating violence and delinquency: The national juvenile justice action plan.* Washington, DC: USGPO.

Copeland, J., & Dillon, P. (2005). The health and psycho-social consequences of ketamine use. *International Journal of Drug Policy, 16,* 122–131.

Copes, H., & Cherbonneau, M. (2006). The key to auto theft. *British Journal of Criminology, 46,* 1–18.

Cornell, D. G. (1989). Causes of juvenile homicide: A review of the literature. In E. P. Benedek & D. G. Cornell (Eds.), *Juvenile homicide.* Washington, DC: American Psychiatric Press.

Corrado, R. R., Vincent, G. M., Hart, S. D., & Cohen, I. M. (2004). Predictive validity of the Psychopathy Checklist: Youth Version for general and violent recidivism. *Behavioral Sciences & the Law, 22,* 5–22.

Coscina, D. V. (1997). The biopsychology of impulsivity: Focus on brain serotonin. In C. D. Webster & M. A. Jackson (Eds.), *Impulsivity: Theory, assessment, and treatment.* New York: Guilford Press.

COT. (2007, June 7). *Lone-wolf terrorism.* The Hague, Netherlands: COT, Instituut voor Veiligheids- en Crisismanagement.

Cowan, P. A., & Cowan, C. P. (2004). From family relationships to peer rejection to antisocial behavior in middle childhood. In J. B. Kupersmidt & K. A. Dodge (Eds.), *Children's peer relations: From development to intervention.* Washington, DC: American Psychological Association.

Cowley, G. (1993, July 26). The not-young and the restless. *Newsweek,* pp. 48–49.

Cressey, D. R. (1953). *A study in the social psychology of embezzlement: Other people's money.* Glencoe, IL: Free Press.

Crick, N. R. (1995). Relational aggression: The role of intent attributions, feelings of distress, and provocation type. *Development and Psychopathology, 7,* 313–322.

Crick, N. R., & Grotpeter, J. K. (1995). Relational aggression, gender, and social-psychological adjustment. *Child Development, 66,* 710–722.

Crick, N. R., & Zahn-Waxler, C. (2003). The development of psychopathology in females and males: Current progress and future challenges. *Development and Psychopathology, 15,* 719–742.

Crider, R. (1986). Phencyclidine: Changing abuse patterns. In D. H. Clovet (Ed.), *Phencyclidine: An update.* Rockville, MD: National Institute of Drug Abuse.

Critchley, M. (1951). *The trial of Neville George Clevely Heath.* London: William Hodge.

Critchlow, B. (1986). The powers of John Barleycorn: Beliefs about the effects of alcohol on social behavior. *American Psychologist, 41,* 751–764.

Critchton, R. (1959). *The great imposter.* New York: Random House.

Critical Incident Response Group. (2001). *Workplace violence: Issues in response.* FBI Critical Incident Response Group, National Center for the Analysis of Violent Crime, Quantico, VA.

Crocker, A. G., & Hodgins, S. (1997). The criminality of noninstitutionalized mentally retarded persons: Evidence from a birth cohort followed to age 30. *Criminal Justice and Behavior, 24,* 432–454.

Cromwell, P. F., Olson, J. F., & Avary, D. W. (1991). *Breaking and entering: An ethnographic analysis of burglary.* Newbury Park, CA: Sage.

Cromwell, P. F., & Thurman, Q. (2003). The devil made me do it: Use of neutralizations by shoplifters. *Deviant Behavior, 24,* 535–550.

Crowe, R. R. (1974). An adoptive study of antisocial personality. *Archives of General Psychiatry, 31,* 785–791.

Crowe, S.L., & Blair, R. J. R. (2008). The development of antisocial behavior: What can we learn from functioning neuroimaging studies? *Development and Psychopathology, 20,* 1145–1159.

Cruise, K. R., Colwell, L. H., Lyons, P. M., & Baker, M. D. (2003). Prototypical analysis of adolescent psychopathy: Investigating the juvenile justice perspective. *Behavioral Sciences & the Law, 21,* 829–846.

Cruise, K. R., & Rogers, R. (1998). An analysis of competency to stand trial: An integration of case law and clinical knowledge. *Behavioral Sciences & the Law, 16,* 35–50.

Culberton, F. M., Feral, C. H., & Gabby, S. (1989). Pattern analysis of Wechlser Intelligence Scale for Children-Revised profiles of delinquent boys. *Journal of Clinical Psychology, 45,* 651–660.

Cunnien, A. J. (1985). Pathological gambling as an insanity defense. *Behavioral Sciences & the Law, 3,* 85–101.

Curtis, R., Terry, K., Dank, M., Dombrowski, K., & Khan, B. (2008, September). *Commercial sexual exploitation of children in New York City, (Vol. 1).* New York: Center for Court Innovation and John Jay College of Criminal Justice.

Dabbs, J. M., Jr., Carr, T. S., Frady, R. L., & Riad, J. K (1995). Testosterone, crime, and misbehavior among 692 male prison inmates. *Personality and Individual Differences, 18,* 627–633.

Dabbs, J. M. Jr., Riad, J. K., & Chance, S. E. (2001). Testosterone and ruthless homicide. *Personality and Individual Differences, 31,* 599–603.

Dabney, D. A., Dugan, L., Topalli, V., & Hollinger, R. C. (2006). The impact of implicit stereotyping on offender profiling: Unexpected results from an observational study of shoplifting. *Criminal Justice and Behavior, 33,* 646–674.

Dåderman, A. M., & Kristiansson, M. (2003). Degree of psychopathy: Implications for treatment in male juvenile delinquents. *International Journal of Law and Psychiatry, 26,* 310–315.

Dahlberg, L. L., & Potter, L. B. (2001). Youth violence: Developmental pathways and prevention challenges. *American Journal of Preventive Medicine, 20* (1s), 3–14.

Dalbert, C. (1999). The world is more just for me than generally: About the Personal Belief in a Just World Scale's validity. *Social Justice Research, 12,* 79–98.

Dalbert, C., & Filke, E. (2007). Belief in a personal just world, justice judgments, and their functions for prisoners. *Criminal Justice and Behavior, 34,* 1516–1527.

Dalgaard, O. S., & Kringlen, E. (1976). A Norwegian twin study of criminality. *British Journal of Criminology, 16,* 213–233.

Damon, W. (2004). What is positive youth development? *Annals, AAPSS, 591,* 13–24.

Daniels, D. N., & Gilula, M. F. (1970). Violence and the struggle for existence. In D. Daniels, M. Gilula, & F. Ochberg (Eds.), *Violence and the struggle for existence.* Boston: Little, Brown.

Darby, P. J., Allan, W. D., Kashani, J. H., Hartke, K. L., & Reid, J. C. (1998). Analysis of 112 juveniles who committed homicide: Characteristics and a closer look at family abuse. *Journal of Family Violence, 13,* 365–375.

Darling, N., & Steinberg, L. (1993). Parenting style as context: An integrative model. *Psychological Bulletin, 113,* 487–496.

David, P. R. (1974). *The world of the burglar.* Albuquerque, NM: University of New Mexico Press.

Davies, M. (2002). Male sexual assault victims: A selected review of the literature and implications for support services. *Aggression and Violent Behavior, 7,* 203–214.

Davis, M. G., Lundman, R. J., & Martinez, R. (1991). Private corporate justice: Store police, shoplifters, and civil recovery. *Social Problems, 38,* 395–411.

Dawkins, M. P. (1997). Drug use and violent crime among adolescents. *Adolescence, 32,* 395–405.

Dawson, J. M., & Langan, P. A. (1994). *Murder in families.* Washington, DC: Bureau of Justice Statistics.

Day, K., & Berney, T. (2001). Treatment and care for offenders with mental retardation. In Ashford, J. B., Sales, B. D., & Reid, W. H. (Eds.), *Treating adult and juvenile offenders with special needs.* Washington, DC: American Psychological Association.

Day, R., & Wong, S. (1996). Anomalous perceptual asymmetries for negative emotional stimuli in the psychopath. *Journal of Abnormal Psychology, 105,* 648–652.

Deal, M. M. (2003). Product tampering. In E. Hickey (Ed.), *Encyclopedia of murder & violent crime.* Thousand Oaks, CA: Sage.

Deal, M. M., & Hickey, E. W. (2003). Helter-Skelter. In E. Hickey (Ed.), *Encyclopedia of murder & violent crime.* Thousand Oaks, CA: Sage.

Decker, S. H., Pennel, S., & Caldwell, A. (1997). *Illegal firearms: Access and use by arrestees.* Washington, DC: U.S. Department of Justice, National Institute of Justice.

Decker, S. H., Wright, R., Redfern, A., & Smith, D. (1993). A woman's place is in the home: Females and residential burglary. *Justice Quarterly, 10,* 143–163.

Deem, D., & Murray, M. (2000). Financial crime. In G. Coleman, M. Gaboury, M. Murray, & A. Seymour (Eds.), *1999 National Victim Assistance Academy.* Washington, DC: U.S. Department of Justice.

Dehue, F., Bolman, C., & Völlink, T. (2008). Cyberbullying: Youngsters' experiences and parental perception. *Cyberpsychology & Behavior, 11,* 217–223.

de Kemp, R. A. T., Overbeek, G., de Wied, M., Engels, R. C. M. E., & Scholte, R. H. J. (2007). Early adolescent empathy, parental support, and antisocial behavior. *The Journal of Genetic Psychology, 168,* 5–18.

Dekovic, M., Janssens, J. M. A. M., & Van As, N. M. C. (2003). Family predictors of antisocial behavior in adolescence. *Family Process, 42,* 223–235.

Delgado-Escueta, A., Mattson, R., & King, L. (1981). The nature of aggression during epileptic seizures. *New England Journal of Medicine, 305,* 711–716.

Delisi, M., & Scherer, A. M. (2006). Multiple homicide offenders: Offense characteristics, social correlates, and criminal careers. *Criminal Justice and Behavior, 33,* 367–391.

DeLisi, M. (2009). (Ed.). Biosocial Criminology. Special issue, *Criminal Justice and Behavior, 36* (November).

DeLisi, M., Umphress, Z. R., & Vaughn, M. G. (2009). The criminology of the amygdala. *Criminal Justice and Behavior, 36,* 1231–1241.

D'Emilio, J., & Freedman, E. B. (1988). *Intimate matters: A history of sexuality in America.* New York: Harper & Row.

DeMatteo, D. (2007). Legal update: The Supreme Court rules on the insanity defense and capital sentencing procedures. *American Psychology-Law Society Newsletter, 27*(1), 1, 5.

Department of Health and Human Services. (2003, September). *Overview of findings from the 2002 national survey on drug use and health.* Rockville, MD: Substance Abuse and Mental Health Services, Office of Applied Studies.

Dern, H., Dern, C., Horn, A., & Horn, U. (2009). The fire behind the smoke: A reply to Snook and colleagues. *Criminal Justice and Behavior, 36,* 1085–1090.

Devapriam, J., Raju, L. B., Singh, N., Collacott, R., & Bhaumik, S. (2007). Arson: Characteristics and predisposing factors in offenders with intellectual disabilities. *The British Journal of Forensic Practice, 9,* 23–27.

Developments in the Law. (1974). Civil commitment of the mentally ill. *Harvard Law Review, 87,* 1190–1406.

DeWall, C. N., Twenge, J. M., Gitter, S. A., & Baumeister, R. F. (2009). It's the thought that counts: The role of hostile cognition in shaping aggressive responses to social exclusion. *Journal of Personality and Social Psychology, 96,* 45–59.

Diamanduros, T., Downs, E., & Jenkins, S. J. (2008). The role of school psychologists in the assessment, prevention, and intervention of cyberbullying. *Psychology in the Schools, 45,* 693–704.

DiCataldo, F., & Everett, M. (2008). Distinguishing juvenile homicide from violent juvenile offending. *International Journal of Offender Therapy and Comparative Criminology, 52*, 158–174.

Dietrich, K. N., Ris, M. D., Succop, P. A., Berger, O. G., & Bornschein, R. L. (2001). Early exposure to lead and juvenile delinquency. *Neurotoxicology and Teratology, 23*, 511–518.

Dietz, T. L. (1998). An examination of violence and gender role portrayals in video games: Implications for gender socialization and aggressive behavior. *Sex Roles, 38*, 425–442.

Dill, K. E., Anderson, C. A., Anderson, K. B., & Deuser, W. E. (1997). Effects of aggressive personality on social expectations and social perceptions. *Journal of Research in Personality, 31*, 272–292.

Dill, K. E., & Dill, J. C. (1998). Video game violence: A review of the empirical literature. *Aggression and Violent Behavior, 3*, 407–428.

DiLonardo, R. L. (1996). Defining and measuring the economic benefit of electronic article surveillance. *Security Journal, 7*, 3–9.

Diserens, C. M. (1925). Psychological objectivism. *Psychological Review, 32*, 121–152.

Dishion, T. J., & Andrews, D. W. (1995). Preventing escalation in problem behaviors with high-risk young adolescents: Immediate and 1-year outcomes. *Journal of Consulting and Clinical Psychology, 63*, 538–548.

Dishion, T. J., & Loeber, R. (1985). Male adolescent marijuana and alcohol use: The role of parents and peers revisited. *American Journal of Drug and Alcohol Abuse, 11*, 11–25.

Ditzler, T. F. (2004). Malevolent minds: The teleology of terrorism. In F. M. Moghaddam & A. J. Marsella (Eds.), *Understanding terrorism: Psychosocial roots, consequences, and interventions.* Washington, DC: American Psychological Association.

Dix, G. E. (1980). Clinical evaluation of the "dangerous" if "normal" criminal defendants. *Virginia Law Review, 66*, 523–581.

Dobson, V., & Sales, B. (2000). The science of infanticide and mental illness. *Psychology, Public Policy, and Law, 6*, 1098–1112.

Dodge, K. A. (1986). A social information processing model of social competence in children. In M. Perlmutter (Ed.), *The Minnesota symposium on child psychology.* Hillsdale, NJ: Erlbaum.

Dodge, K. A. (1991). The structure and function of reactive and proactive aggression. In D. J. Pepler & K. H. Rubin (Eds.), *The development and treatment of childhood aggression.* Hillsdale, NJ: Erlbaum.

Dodge, K. A. (1993a). The future of research on the treatment of conduct disorder. *Development and Psychopathology, 5*, 311–319.

Dodge, K. A. (1993b). Social-cognitive mechanisms in the development of conduct disorder and depression. *Annual Review of Psychology, 44*, 559–584.

Dodge, K. A. (2001). The science of youth violence prevention: Progressing from developmental epidemiology to efficacy to effectiveness in public policy. *American Journal of Preventive Medicine, 20* (1S), 63–70.

Dodge, K. A. (2003). Do social information-processing patterns mediate aggressive behavior? In B. B. Lahey, T. E. Moffitt, & A. Caspi (Eds.), *Causes of conduct disorder and juvenile delinquency.* New York: Guilford Press.

Dodge, K. A., Bates, J. E., & Pettit, G. S. (1990). Mechanisms in the cycle of violence. *Science, 250*, 1678–1683.

Dodge, K. A., & Coie, J. D. (1987). Social information processing factors in reactive and proactive aggression in children's peer groups. *Journal of Personality and Social Psychology, 53*, 1146–1158.

Dodge, K. A., Greenberg, M. T., Malone, P. S., & Conduct Problems Prevention Research Group. (2008). Testing an idealized dynamic cascade model of the development of serious violence in adolescence. *Child Development, 79*, 1907–1927.

Dodge, K. A., Laird, R., Lochman, Zelli, A., & Conduct Problems Prevention Research Group. (2002). Multi-dimensional latent construct analysis of children's social information-processing patterns: Correlations with aggressive behavior problems. *Psychological Assessment, 14*, 60–73.

Dodge, K. A., Lochman, J. E., Harnish, J. D., Bates, J. E., & Pettit, G. S. (1997). Reactive and proactive aggression in school children and psychiatrically impaired chronically assaultive youth. *Journal of Abnormal Psychology, 106,* 37–51.

Dodge, K. A., & Pettit, G. S. (2003). A biopsychological model of the development of chronic conduct problems in adolescence. *Developmental Psychology, 39,* 349–371.

Doerner, W. G. (1988). The impact of medical resources on criminally induced lethality: A further examination. *Criminology, 26,* 171–179.

Doerner, W. G., & Speir, J. C. (1986). Stitch and sew: The impact of medical resources upon criminally induced lethality. *Criminology, 24,* 319–330.

Doley, R. (2003). Pyromania: Fact or fiction? *British Journal of Criminology, 43,* 797–807.

Dollard, J., Doob, L. W., Miller, N. E., Mowrer, O. H., & Sears, R. R. (1939). *Frustration and aggression.* New Haven, CT: Yale University Press.

Donnerstein, E. (1983). Erotica and human aggression. In R. G. Geen & E. I. Donnerstein (Eds.), *Aggression: Theoretical and empirical reviews* (Vol. 2). New York: Academic Press.

d'Orban, P. T., & O'Connor, A. (1989). Women who kill their parents. *British Journal of Psychiatry, 154,* 27–33.

Doren, D. M. (2002). *Evaluating sex offenders.* Thousand Oaks, CA: Sage.

Douglas, J. E., Burgess, A. W., Burgess, A. G., & Ressler, R. K. (1992). *Crime classification manual.* New York: Lexington Books.

Douglas, J. E., Burgess, A. W., Burgess, A. G., & Ressler, R. K. (2006). *Crime classification manual* (2nd ed.). San Francisco: Jossey-Bass.

Douglas, J. E., & Munn, C. (1992a). The detection of staging and personation at the crime scene. In J. E. Douglas, A. W. Burgess, A. G. Burgess, & R. K. Ressler (Eds.), *Crime classification manual.* New York: Lexington Books.

Douglas, J. E., & Munn, C. (1992b). Modus operandi and the signature aspects of violent crime. In J. E. Douglas, A. W. Burgess, A. G. Burgess, & R. K. Ressler (Eds.), *Crime classification manual.* New York: Lexington Books.

Douglas, J. E., & Munn, C. (1992c, February). Violent crime scene analysis. *FBI Law Enforcement Bulletin,* 1–10.

Douglas, J. E., Ressler, R. K., Burgess, A. W., & Hartman. C. R. (1986). Criminal profiling from crime scene analysis. *Behavioral Sciences & the Law, 4,* 401–421.

Douglas, K. S., Herbozo, S., Poythress, N. G., Belfrage, H., & Edens, J. F. (2006). *Psychological Services, 3,* 97–116.

Douglas, V. I. (2004). Cognitive deficits in children with attention deficit hyperactivity disorder: A long-term follow up. *Canadian Psychology, 46,* 23–31.

Drug Enforcement Administration. (2000). *Drugs of abuse.* Washington, DC: U.S. Department of Justice. Available: www.usdoj.gov/dea/concern/abuse.

Drug Enforcement Administration. (2005). *Drugs of abuse, 2005 edition.* Washington, DC: U.S. Department of Justice.

DSM-IV. (1994). *Diagnostic and statistical manual of mental disorders* (4th ed.). Washington, DC: American Psychiatric Association.

DSM-IV-R. (2000). *Diagnostic and statistical manual of mental disorders* (4th ed.). Washington, DC: American Psychiatric Association.

Duhaime, A., Christian, C. W., Rorke, L. B., & Zimmerman, R. A. (1998). Nonaccidental head injury in infants: The "shaken-baby syndrome." *New England Journal of Medicine, 338,* 1822–1829.

Dull, R. T., & Giacopassi, D. J. (1987). Demographic correlates of sexual and dating attitudes: A study of date rape. *Criminal Justice and Behavior, 14,* 175–193.

Dunn, C. S. (1976). *The patterns and distribution of assault incident characteristics among social areas.* Albany, NY: Criminal Justice Research Center, Analytic Report 14.

Durand, V. M., & Barlow, D. H. (2000). *Abnormal psychology: An introduction.* Belmont, CA: Wadsworth.

Durose, M. R., Harlow, C. W., Langan, P. A., Motivans, M., Rantala, R. R., & Smith, E. L. (2005, June). *Family violence statistics: Including statistics on strangers and acquaintances.* Washington, DC: U.S. Department of Justice, Bureau of Justice Statistics.

Dvorak, J. A. (2000, December 21). *Kansas launches racial profiling study. Kansas City Star,* pp. 1, 11.

Easterbrook, J. A. (1959). The effect of emotion on cue utilization and the organization of behavior. *Psychological Review, 66,* 183–201.

Eastman, B. J. (2004). Assessing the efficacy of treatment for adolescent sex offenders: A cross-over longitudinal study. *Prison Journal, 84,* 472–485.

Eaton, J., & Polk, K. (1961). *Measuring delinquency.* Pittsburgh, PA: University of Pittsburgh Press.

Ebert, B. W. (1987). Guide to conducting a psychological autopsy. *Professional Psychology: Research and Practice, 18,* 52–56.

Eccles, J., & Robinson, D. N. (1984). *The wonder of being human: Our brain and our mind.* New York: Free Press.

Eck, J. (2000) Preventing crime at places. In L. W. Sherman, D. Gottfresson, D. MacKenzie, J. Eck, P. Reuter, & S. Bushway (Eds.), *Preventing crime: What works, what doesn't, what's promising.* A Report to the United State Congress. Available: www.ncjrs.org/works.

Eddy, J. M. (2003). *Conduct disorders: The latest assessment and treatment strategies.* Kansas City, MO: Compact Clinicals.

Edens, J. F., Guy, L. S., & Fernandez, K. (2003). Psychopathic traits predict attitudes toward a juvenile capital murderer. *Behavioral Sciences & the Law, 21,* 807–828.

Edens, J. F., Petrila, J., & Buffington-Vollum, J. K. (2001). Psychopathy and the death penalty: Can the Psychopathy Checklist-Revised identify offenders who represent "a continuing threat to society?" *Journal of Psychiatry and Law, 29,* 433–481.

Edens, J. F., Skeem, J. L., Cruise, K. R., & Cauffman, E. (2001). Assessment of "juvenile psychopathy" and its association with violence: A critical review. *Behavioral Sciences & the Law, 19,* 53–80.

Edleson, J. L. (1999). Children's witnessing of adult domestic violence. *Journal of Interpersonal Violence, 14,* 839–870.

Edwards, S. (1983). Sexuality, sexual offenses, and conception of victims in the criminal justice process. *Victimology: An International Journal, 8,* 113–128.

Efran, M. G., & Cheyne, J. A. (1974). Affective concomitants of the invasion of shared space:

Behavioral, physiological, and verbal indicators. *Journal of Personality and Social Psychology, 29,* 219–226.

Eisenberg, N., & Fabes, R. A. (1998). Prosocial development. In W. Damon (Series Ed.) & N. Eisenberg (Vol. Ed.), *Handbook of child psychology: Vol 3. Social, emotional and personality development* (5th ed.). New York: Wiley.

Eisenhower, M. S. (Chairman). (1969). *Commission statement on violence in television entertainment programs.* Washington, DC: USGPO.

Elliott, D. S. (1989). Criminal justice procedures in family violence crimes. In L. Ohlin & M. Tonry (Eds.), *Family violence* (Vol. 11). Chicago: University of Chicago Press.

Elliott, D. S., Dunford, T. W., & Huizinga, D. (1987). The identification and prediction of career offenders utilizing self-reported and official data. In J. D. Burchard & S. N. Burchard (Eds.), *Prevention of delinquent behavior.* Newbury Park, CA: Sage.

Elliott, D. S., & Menard, S. (1996). Delinquent friends and delinquent behavior: Temporal and developmental patterns. In J. D. Hawkins (Ed.), *Delinquency and crime: Current theories.* New York: Cambridge University Press.

Ellis, C. A., & Lord, J. (2001). Homicide. In G. Coleman, M. Gaboury, M. Murray, & A. Seymour (Eds.), *1999 National Victim Assistance Academy.* Washington, DC: U.S. Department of Justice.

Ellis, L. (1998). Why some sexual assaults are not committed by men: A biosocial analysis. In P. Anderson & C. Struckman-Johnson (Eds.), *Sexually aggressive women.* New York: Guilford.

Else-Quest, N. M., Hyde, J. S., Goldsmith, H. H., & Van Hulle, C. A. (2006). Gender differences in temperament: A meta-analysis. *Psychological Bulletin, 132,* 33–72.

Emery, R. E., & Laumann-Billings, L. (1998). An overview of the nature, causes, and consequences of abusive family relationships. *American Psychologist, 53,* 121–135.

Epstein, J. F., & Gfroerer, J. C. (1997, August). *Heroin abuse in the United States.* Rockville, MD: Substance Abuse and Mental Health Services Administration.

Erhardt, D., & Hinshaw, S. P. (1994). Initial sociometric impressions of attention-deficit hyperactivity disorder and comparison boys: Predictions from social behaviors and from nonbehavioral variables. *Journal of Consulting and Clinical Psychology, 62,* 833–842.

Erickson, R. (1996). *Armed robbers and their crimes.* Seattle, WA: Athena Research Corporation.

Ericson, N. (2001, June). *Addressing the problem of juvenile bullying.* Washington, DC: U.S. Department of Justice, Office of Juvenile Justice and Delinquency Prevention.

Eron, L. D., & Huesmann, L. P. (1984). The relation of prosocial behavior to the development of aggression and psychopathology. *Aggressive Behavior, 10,* 201–211.

Eron, L. D., & Slaby, R. G. (1994). Introduction. In L. D. Eron, J. H. Gentry, & P. Schlegel (Eds.), *Reason to hope: A psychosocial perspective on violence and youth.* Washington, DC: American Psychological Association.

Eskridge, C. W. (1983). Prediction of burglary: A research note. *Journal of Criminal Justice, 11,* 67–75.

Eslea, M., Menesini, E., Morita, Y., O'Moore, M., Mora-Merchán, J. A., Pereira, B., et al. (2003). Friendship and loneliness among bullies and victims: Data from seven countries. *Aggressive Behavior, 30,* 71–83.

Evans, D. (1970). Exhibitionism. In C. G. Costello (Ed.), *Symptoms of psychopathology: A handbook.* New York: Wiley.

Evans, G. W. (2004). The environment of childhood poverty. *American Psychologist, 59,* 77–92.

Ewing, C. P. (1990). Psychological self-defense: A proposed justification for battered women who kill. *Law and Human Behavior, 14,* 579–594.

Eysenck, H. J. (1964). *Crime and personality.* London: Routledge & Kegan Paul.

Eysenck, H. J. (1967). *The biological basis of personality.* Springfield, IL: Charles C Thomas.

Eysenck, H. J. (1971). *Readings in extraversion-introversion. Vol. 2. Fields of application.* New York: Wiley-Interscience.

Eysenck, H. J. (1973). *The inequality of man.* San Diego, CA: EDITS Publishers.

Eysenck, H. J. (1977). *Crime and personality* (2nd ed.). London: Routledge & Kegan Paul.

Eysenck, H. J. (1981). *A model for personality.* New York: Springer.

Eysenck, H. J. (1983). Personality, conditioning, and antisocial behavior. In W. S. Laufer & J. M. Day (Eds.), *Personality theory, moral development, and criminal behavior.* Lexington, MA: Lexington Books.

Eysenck, H. J. (1996). Personality and crime: Where do we stand? *Psychology, Crime & Law, 2,* 143–152.

Eysenck, H. J., & Gudjonsson, G. H. (1989). *The causes and cures of criminality.* New York: Plenum.

Eysenck, H. J., & Rachman, S. (1965). *The causes and cures of neurosis.* San Diego, CA: Robert R. Knapp.

Eysenck, S. B., & Eysenck, H. J. (1970). Crime and personality: An empirical study of the three-factor theory. *British Journal of Criminology, 10,* 225–239.

Fagan, J. (1989). Cessation of family violence. In L. Ohlin & M. Tonry (Eds.), *Family violence* (Vol. 11). Chicago: University of Chicago Press.

Falkenbach, D. M. Poythress, N. G., & Heide, K. M. (2003). Psychopathic features in a juvenile diversion population: Reliability and predictive validity of two self-report measures. *Behavioral Sciences & the Law, 21,* 787–805.

Fantuzzo, J. W., Boruch, R., Abdullahi, B., Atkins, M., & Marcus, S. (1997). Domestic violence and children: Prevalence and risk in five major U.S. cities. *Journal of American Academy of Child and Adolescent Psychiatry, 36,* 116–122.

Fantuzzo, J. W., DePaola, L. M., Lambert, L., Martino, T., Anderson, G., & Sutton, S. (1991). Effects of interparental violence on the psychological adjustment and competencies of young children. *Journal of Consulting and Clinical Psychology, 59,* 258–265.

Farrell, G., Phillips, C., & Pease, K. (1995). Like taking candy, why does repeat victimization occur? *British Journal of Criminology, 35,* 384–399.

Farrington, D. P. (1991). Childhood aggression and adult violence: Early precursors and later life outcomes. In D. J. Pepler & K. H. Rubin (Eds.), *The development and treatment of childhood aggression.* Hillsdale, NJ: Erlbaum.

Farrington, D. P. (1995). Crime and physical health: Illnesses, injuries, accidents, and offending in the Cambridge study. *Criminal Behaviour and Mental Health, 5,* 278.

Farrington, D. P. (2005a). The importance of child and adolescent psychopathy. *Journal of Abnormal Child Psychology, 33,* 489–497.

Farrington, D. P. (2005b). Family background and psychopathy. In C. J. Patrick (Ed.), *Handbook of psychopathy.* New York: Guilford.

Farrington, D. P., Bowen, S., Buckle, A., Burns-Howell, T., Burrows, J., & Speed, M. (1993). An experiment on the prevention of shoplifting. In R. V. Clarke (Ed.), *Crime prevention studies* (Vol. 1). Monsey, NY: Criminal Justice Press.

Farrington, D. P., & Burrows, J. N. (1993). Did shoplifting really decrease? *British Journal of Criminology, 33,* 57–59.

Farrington, D. P., Ttofi, M. M., & Coid, J. W. (2009). Development of adolescence-limited, late-onset, and persistent offenders from age 8 to age 48. *Aggressive Behavior, 35,* 150–163.

Faupel, C. E. (1991). *Shooting dope: Career patterns of hard-core heroin users.* Gainesville, FL: University of Florida Press.

Federal Bureau of Investigation. (1985, August). Crime scene and profile characteristics of organized and disorganized murders. *FBI Law Enforcement Bulletin, 54,* 18–25.

Federal Bureau of Investigation. (1992). *Killed in the line of duty: A study of selected felonious killings of law enforcement officers.* Washington, DC: U.S. Department of Justice.

Federal Bureau of Investigation. (1997). *Uniform Crime Reports—1996.* Washington, DC: U.S. Department of Justice.

Federal Bureau of Investigation. (1999). *The FBI's national drug strategy.* Washington, DC: U.S. Department of Justice.

Federal Bureau of Investigation. (2002). *Uniform Crime Reports—2001.* Washington, DC: U.S. Department of Justice.

Federal Bureau of Investigation. (2003). Special report: Bank robbery in the United States. *Uniform Crime Reports—2002.* Washington, DC: U.S. Department of Justice.

Federal Bureau of Investigation. (2005a). *Serial murder: Multi-disciplinary perspectives for investigators.* Washington, DC: Behavioral Analysis Unit-2, National Center for the Analysis of Crime.

Federal Bureau of Investigation. (2005b). *Crime in the United States 2004: Uniform Crime Reports.* Washington, DC: U.S. Department of Justice.

Federal Bureau of Investigation. (2008). *Crime in the United States 2007: Uniform Crime Reports.* Washington, DC: U.S. Department of Justice.

Federal Interagency Forum on Child and Family Statistics. (2005). *America's children: Key national indicators of well-being 2005.* Washington, DC: Author.

Fehrenbach, P. A., & Monasterky, C. (1988). Characteristics of female sexual offenders. *American Journal of Orthopsychiatry, 58,* 148–151.

Fehrenbach, P. A., Smith, W., Monastersky, C., & Deisher, R. W. (1986). Adolescent sexual offenders: Offender and offense characteristics. *American Journal of Orthopsychiatry, 56,* 225–233.

Feinberg, G. (1984). Profile for the elderly shoplifter. In E. S. Newman, D. J. Newman, & M. L. Gewirtz (Eds.), *Elderly criminals.* Cambridge, MA: Oelgeschlager, Gunn & Hain.

Feldman, M. P. (1977). *Criminal behavior: A psychological analysis.* London: Wiley.

Feldman, R., & Klein, P. S. (2003). Toddler's self-regulated compliance to mothers, caregivers, and fathers: Implications for theories of socialization. *Developmental Psychology, 39,* 680–692.

Felthous, A. R. (2001). Introduction to this issue: The clinician's duty to warn or protect. *Behavioral Sciences & the Law, 19,* 321–324.

Fenichel, O. (1945). *The psychoanalytic theory of neurosis.* New York: W. W. Norton.

Ferguson, C. A., Rueda, S. M., Cruz, A. M., Ferguson, D. E., Fritz, S., & Smith, S. M. (2008). Violent video games and aggression: Causal relationship or byproduct of family violence and intrinsic violence motivation? *Criminal Justice and Behavior, 35,* 311–332.

Ferro, C., Cermele, J., & Saltzman, A. (2008). Current perceptions of marital rape: Some good and not-so-good news. *Journal of Interpersonal Violence, 23,* 764–779.

Feshbach, S. (1964). The function of aggression and the regulation of aggressive drive. *Psychological Review, 71*, 257–272.

Festinger, L., Pepitone, A., & Newcomb, T. (1952). Some consequences of de-individuation in a group. *Journal of Abnormal and Social Psychology, 47*, 382–389.

Feucht, T. W., & Kyle, G. M. (1996, November). Methamphetamine use among adult arrestees: Findings of the DUF program. *NIJ Research in Brief*. Washington, DC: U.S. Department of Justice.

Fields, G. (2006, September 26). Police are changing how they confront the mentally ill. *The Wall Street Jorunal*, pp. A1, A11.

Finckenauer, J. O., & Schrock, J. (2000). *Human trafficking: A growing criminal market in the U.S.* Washington, DC: National Institute of Justice, International Center. Available: www.ojp.usdoj.gov/nij/international/ht.html.

Finkelhor, D. (1979). *Sexually victimized children*. New York: Free Press.

Finkelhor, D., & Araji, S. (1986). Explanations of pedophilia: A four factor model. *The Journal of Sex Research, 22*, 145–161.

Finkelhor, D., & Dziuba-Leatherman, J. (1994). Children as victims of violence: A national survey. *Pediatrics, 94*, 413–420.

Finkelhor, D., & Lewis, I. A. (1988). An epidemiologic approach to the study of child molestation. In R. A. Prentky & V. L. Quinsey (Eds.), *Human sexual aggression: Current perspectives*. New York: New York Academy of Sciences.

Finkelhor, D., Ormrod, R., Turner, H., & Hamby, S. L. (2005). The victimization of children and youth: A comprehensive, national survey. *Child Maltreatment, 10*, 5–25.

Firestone, P., Bradford, J. M., Greenberg, D. M., & Larose, M. R. (1998). Homicidal sex offenders: Psychological, phallometric, and diagnostic features. *Journal of the American Academy of Psychology and Law, 26*, 537–552.

Firestone, P., Kingston, D. A., Wexler, A., & Bradford, J. M. (2006) Long-term follow-up of exhibitionists: Psychological, phallometric, and offense characteristics. *Journal of the American Academy of Psychiatry and the Law, 34*, 349–359.

Fishbein, D. (2001). *Biobehavioral perspectives in criminology*. Belmont, CA: Wadsworth/Thomson Learning.

Fiske, D. E., & Maddi, S. R. (1961). *Functions of varied experience*. Homewood, IL: Dorsey.

Fite, P. J., Stoppelbein, L., & Greening, L. (2009). Proactive and reactive aggression in a child psychiatric inpatient population: Relations to psychopathic characteristics. *Criminal Justice and Behavior, 36*, 481–493.

Fitzgerald, L. F. (2003). Sexual harassment and social justice: Reflections and distance yet to go. *American Psychologist, 11*, 915–924

Fitzhugh, K. B. (1973). Some neuropsychological features of delinquent subjects. *Perceptual and Motor Skills, 36*, 494.

Flannery, D. J., Williams, L. L., & Vazsonyi, A. T. (1999). Who are they with and what are they doing? Delinquent behavior, substance abuse, and early adolescence after school time. *American Journal of Orthopsychiatry, 69*, 247–253.

Flor-Henry, P. (1973). Psychiatric syndromes considered as manifestations of lateralized temporal-limbic dysfunction. In L. V. Latiner & K. E. Livingston (Eds.), *Surgical approaches in psychiatry*. Lancaster, UK: Medical and Technical Publishing.

Flor-Henry, P., & Yeudall, L. T. (1973). Lateralized cerebral dysfunction in depression and in aggressive criminal psychopathy. *International Research Communications, 7*, 31.

Flynn, E. E. (1983). Crime as a major social issue. *American Behavioral Scientist, 27*, 7–42.

Fontaine, N., Carbonneau, R., Vitaro, F., Barker, E. D., & Tremblay, R. E. (2009). Research review: A critical review of studies on the developmental trajectories of antisocial behavior in females. *Journal of Child Psychology and Psychiatry, 50*, 363–385.

Fontaine, R. G. (2008). Reactive cognitive, reaction emotion: Toward a more psychologically-informed understanding of reactive homicide. *Psychology, Public Policy, and Law, 14*, 243–261.

Fontaine, R. G., & Dodge, K. A. (2006). Real-time decision making and aggressive behavior in youth: A heuristic model of response evaluation and decision (RED). *Aggressive Behavior, 32*, 604–624.

Forbes, G. B., Adams-Curtis, L. E., & White, K. B. (2004). First- and second-generation measures of sexism, rape myths and related beliefs, and hostility toward women. *Violence Against Women, 10*, 236–261.

Forehand, R., Wierson, M., Frame, C. L., Kemptom, T., & Armistead, L. (1991). Juvenile firesetting: A unique syndrome or an advanced level of antisocial behavior? *Behavioral Research and Therapy, 29*, 125–128.

Forney, W. S., Forney, J. C., & Crutsinger, C. (2005). Developmental stages of age and moral reasoning as predictors of juvenile delinquents' behavioral intention to steal clothing. *Family and Consumer Sciences Research Journal, 34*, 110–126.

Forrstrom-Cohen, B., & Rosenbaum, A. (1985). The effects of parental marital violence on young adults: An exploratory investigation. *Journal of Marriage and Family, 47*, 467–472.

Forth, A. E., & Burke, H. C. (1998). Psychopathy in adolescence: Assessment, violence, and developmental precursors. In D. J. Cooke, A. E. Forth, & R. D. Hare (Eds.), *Psychopathy: Theory, research and implications for society.* Boston: Kluwer Academic.

Forth, A. E., Kosson, D. S., & Hare, R. D. (2003). *Psychopathy Checklist-Youth Version: Technical manual.* Toronto: Multi-Health Systems.

Fothergill, K. E., & Ensminger, M. E. (2006). Childhood and adolescent antecedents of drug and alcohol problems: A longitudinal study. *Drug and Alcohol Dependence, 82*, 61–76.

Fox, J. A., & Levin, J. (2003). Mass murder: An analysis of extreme violence. *Journal of Applied Psychoanalytic Studies, 5*, 47–64.

Fox, R. G. (1971). The XYY offender: A modern myth? *Journal of Criminal Law, Criminology, and Police Science, 62*, 59–73.

Franke, D. (1975). *The torture doctor.* New York: Avon.

Frederick, R. I. (2000). Mixed group validation: A method to address the limitations of criterion group validation in research on malingering detection. *Behavioral Science & the Law, 18*, 693–718.

Freedman, J. L., Sears, D. O., & Carlsmith, J. J. (1978). *Social psychology* (3rd ed.). Englewood Cliffs, NJ: Prentice Hall.

Freeman, N. J., & Sandler, J. C. (2008). Female and male sex offenders: A comparison of recidivism and risk factors. *Journal of Interpersonal Violence, 23*, 1394–1413.

Freilich, J. D., Chermak, S. M., & Caspi, D. (2009). Critical events in the life trajectories of domestic extremist white supremacist groups: A case study analysis of four violent organizations. *Criminology and Public Policy, 8*, 497–530.

French, J. D. (1957). The reticular formation. *Scientific American, 196*, 54–60.

Frick, P. J. (1998). Callous-unemotional traits and conduct problems: Applying the two-factor model of psychopathy to children. In D. J. Cooke, A. E. Forth, & R. D. Hare (Eds.), *Psychopathy: Theory, research and implications for society.* Boston: Kluwer Academic.

Frick, P. J., Bodin, S. D., & Barry, C. T. (2000). Psychopathic traits and conduct problems in community and clinic-referred samples of children: Further development of the psychopathy screening device. *Psychological Assessment, 12*, 382–393.

Frick, P. J., & Hare, R. D. (2001). *The Antisocial Process Screening Device.* Toronto: Multi-Health Systems.

Frick, P. J., & Morris, A. S. (2004). Temperament and developmental pathways to conduct problems. *Journal of Clinical Child and Adolescent Psychology, 33*, 54–68.

Frick, P. J., O'Brien, B. S., Wootton, J., & McBurnett, K. (1994). Psychopathy and conduct problems in children. *Journal of Abnormal Psychology, 103*, 700–707.

Frick, P. J., & White, S. F. (2008). Research review: The importance of callous-unemotional traits for developmental models of aggressive and antisocial behavior. *Journal of Child Psychology and Psychiatry, 49*, 359–375.

Frieze, I. H., & Browne, A. (1989). Violence in marriage. In L. Ohlin & M. Tonry (Eds.), *Family violence* (Vol. 11). Chicago, IL: University of Chicago Press.

Frintner, M., & Rubinson, L. (1993). Acquaintance rape: The influence of alcohol, fraternity membership and sports team membership. *Journal of Sex Education and Therapy, 19*, 272–284.

Frisbie, L. V. (1965). Treated sex offenders who reverted to sexually deviant behavior. *Federal Probation, 29,* 52–57.

Fung, M. T., Raine, A., Loeber, R., Lynam, D. R., Steinhauser, S. R., Venables, P. H., & Stouthamer-Loeber, M. (2005). Reduced electrodermal activity in pychopathy-prone adolescents. *Journal of Abnormal Psychology, 114,* 187–196.

Funk, J. B., Baldacci, H. B., Pasold, T., & Baumgarnder, J. (2004). Violence exposure in real-life, video games, television, movies, and the internet: is there desensitization? *Journal of Adolescence, 27,* 23–39.

Funk, J. B., & Buchman, D. D. (1996). Playing violent video and computer games and the adolescent self-concept. *Journal of Communications,* Spring, 84–89.

Furby, L., Weinrott, M. R., & Blackshaw, L. (1989). Sex offender recidivism: A review. *Psychological Bulletin, 105,* 3–30.

Fuselier, G. D. (1999, July). Placing the Stockholm syndrome in perspective. *FBI Law Enforcement Bulletin,* 9–12.

Fuselier, G. D., & Noesner, G. W. (1990, July). Confronting the terrorist hostage taker. *FBI Law Enforcement Bulletin,* 6–11.

Gabrielli, W. F., & Mednick, S. A. (1983). Genetic correlates of criminal behavior. *American Behavioral Scientist, 27,* 59–74.

Gacono, C. B., Nieberding, R. J., Owen, A., Rubel, J., & Bodholdt, R. (1997). Treating conduct disorder, antisocial, and psychopathic personalities. In J. B. Ashford, B. D. Sales, & W. H. Reid (Eds.), *Treating adult and juvenile offenders with special needs.* Washington, DC: American Psychological Association.

Gacono, C. B., Nieberding, R. J., Owen, A., Rubel, J., & Bodholdt, R. (2001). Treating conduct disorder, antisocial, and psychopathic personalities. In J. B. Ashford, B. D. Sales, & W. H. Reid (Eds.), *Treating adult and juvenile offenders with special needs.* Washington, DC: American Psychological Association.

Galovski, T. E., & Blanchard, E. B. (2002). The effectiveness of a brief psychological intervention on court-referred and self-referred aggressive drivers. *Behavior and Research Therapy, 40,* 1385–1402.

Galovski, T. E., & Blanchard, E. B. (2004). Road rage: A domain for psychological intervention. *Aggression and Violent Behavior, 9,* 105–127.

Ganley, A. L., & Schechter, S. (1996). *Domestic violence: A national curriculum for children's protective services.* San Francisco: Family Violence Prevention Fund.

Gannon, T. A., Collie, R. M., Ward, T., & Thakker, J. (2008). Rape: Psychopathology, theory and treatment. *Clinical Psychology Review, 28,* 982–1008.

Gannon, T. A., & Polaschek, D. L. L. (2006). Cognitive distortions in child molesters: A re-examination of key theories and research. *Clinical Psychology Review, 26,* 1000-1019.

Gannon, T. A., & Rose, M. R. (2008). Female child sexual offenders: Towards integrating theory and practice. *Aggression and Violent Behavior, 13,* 442–461.

Gannon, T. A., Ward, T., & Collie, R. (2007). Cognitive distortions and child molesters: Theoretical and research developments over the past two decades. *Aggression and Violent Behavior, 12,* 402-416.

Garbarino, J. (1989). The incidence and prevalence of child maltreatment. In L. Ohlin & M. Tonry (Eds.), *Family violence* (Vol. 11). Chicago: University of Chicago Press.

Garbarino, J., & Asp, C. E. (1981). *Successful schools and competent students.* Lexington, MA: Lexington Books.

Garcia, M. M., Shaw, D. S., Winslow, E. B., & Yaggi, K. E. (2000). Destructive sibling conflict and the development of conduct problems in young boys. *Developmental Psychology, 36,* 44–53.

Gardner, T. J. (1985). *Crime law: Principles and cases.* St. Paul, MN: West Publishing.

Garofalo, J. (1977). *Public opinion about crime: The attitudes of victims and nonvictims in selected cities.* Washington, DC: USGPO.

Garside, R. B. & Klimes-Dougan, B. (2002). Socialization of discrete negative emotions: Gender differences and links with psychological distress. *Sex Roles: A Journal of Research, 14,* 115–129.

Gaynor, J. (1996). Firesetting. In M. Lewis (Ed.), *Child and adolescent psychiatry: A comprehensive textbook.* Baltimore, MD: Williams & Wilkins.

Gebhard, P. H., Gagnon, J. H., Pomeroy, W. B., & Christenson, C. V. (1965). *Sex offenders.* New York: Harper & Row.

Geis, G. (1988). From Deuteronomy to deniability: A historical perlustration on white-collar crime. *Justice Quarterly, 5,* 7–32.

Geis, G. (1997). Preface. In G. Green, *Occupational crime* (2nd ed.). Chicago: Nelson-Hall.

Gelinas, D. J. (1993, October 3). *Recognizing and treating dissociative processes trauma survivors.* Professional workshop sponsored by Vermont Trauma Institute, Burlington, VT.

Gelles, R. J. (1982). Domestic criminal violence. In M. E. Wolfgang & N. A. Weiner (Eds.), *Criminal violence.* Beverly Hills, CA: Sage.

Gelles, R. J. (1997). *Intimate violence in families.* Thousand Oaks, CA: Sage.

Gelles, R. J., & Straus, M. A. (1979). Determinants of violence in the family: Toward a theoretical integration. In W. R. Burr, F. I. Nye, & I. L. Reiss (Eds.), *Contemporary theories about the family.* New York: Free Press.

Gendreau, P., Little, T., & Goggin, C. (1996). A meta-analysis of the predictors of adult offender recidivism: What works! *Criminology, 34,* 575–607.

Gentile, D. A., Lynch, P. J., Linder, J. R., & Walsh, D. A. (2004). The effects of violent video game habits on adolescent hostility, aggressive behaviors, and school performance. *Journal of Adolescence, 27,* 5–22.

Gentile, D. A., & Walsh, D. A. (2002). A normative study of family media habits. *Journal of Applied Developmental Psychology, 23,* 157–178.

George, W. H., & Marlatt, G. A. (1989). Introduction. In D. R. Laws (Ed.), *Relapse prevention with sex offenders.* New York: Guilford Press.

Gerbner, G., Gross, L., Morgan, M., & Signorielli, N. (1981). Health and medicine on television. *The New England Journal of Medicine, 305,* 901–904.

Gerler, E. R., Jr. (2007). What the Amish taught us. *Journal of School Violence, 6,* 1–2.

Getz, J. G., & Bray, J. H. (2005). Predicting heavy alcohol use among adolescents. *American Journal of Orthopsychiatry, 75,* 102–116.

Gibbens, T. C. (1957). Female offenders. *British Journal of Delinquency, 8,* 23–25.

Gibbons, D. C. (1977). *Society, crime and criminal careers* (3rd ed.). Englewood Cliffs, NJ: Prentice Hall.

Gibbons, D. C. (1988). Some critical observation on criminal types and criminal careers. *Criminal Justice and Behavior, 15,* 8–23.

Giddan, J. J., Milling, L., & Campbell, N. B. (1996). Unrecognized language and speech deficits in preadolescent psychiatric patients. *American Journal of Orthopsychiatry, 66,* 85–92.

Glueck, S., & Glueck, E. (1950). *Unraveling juvenile delinquency.* New York: Harper & Row.

Goetting, A. (1993). Patterns of homicide among children. In A. V. Wilson (Ed.), *Homicide: The victim/offender connection.* Cincinnati, OH: Anderson.

Gold, L. H. (1962). Psychiatric profile of the firesetter. *Journal of Forensic Sciences, 7,* 404–417.

Gold, M. S. (1984*). 800-cocaine.* New York: Bantam.

Golding, S. L., Skeem, J. L., Roesch, R., & Zapf, P. A. (1999). The assessment of criminal responsibility: Current controversies. In I. B. Weiner & A. K. Hess (Eds.), *Handbook of forensic psychology* (2nd ed.). New York: Wiley.

Goldman, M. J. (1991). Kleptomania: Making sense of the nonsensical. *American Journal of Psychiatry, 148,* 986–995.

Goldstein, J. H. (1975). *Aggression and crimes of violence.* New York: Oxford University Press.

Goldstein, M. (1974). Brain research and violent behavior. *Archives of Neurology, 30,* 1–34.

Goldstein, M. J. (1977). A behavioral scientist looks at obscenity. In B. D. Sales (Ed.), *The criminal justice system* (Vol. 1). New York: Plenum.

Goldstein, N. E., Arnold, D. H., Rosenberg, J. L., Stowe, R. M., & Ortiz, C. (2001). Contagion of aggression in day care classrooms as a function of peer and toddler responses. *Journal of Educational Psychology, 93,* 708–719.

Goldstein, P. J. (1985). The drugs-violence nexus: A tri-partite conceptual framework. *Journal of Drug Issues, 15,* 493–506.

Goles, T., Jayatilaka, B., George, B., Parsons, L., Chambers, V., Taylor, D., et al. (2008). Softlifting: Exploring determinants of attitude. *Journal of Business Ethics, 77*, 481–499.

Golub, A. L., & Johnson, B. D. (1997, July). *Crack's decline: Some surprises across U.S. cities.* NIJ Research in Brief. Washington, DC: U.S. Department of Justice.

Goodwill, A. J., Alison, L. J., & Beech, A. R. (2009). What works in offender profiling? A comparison of typological, thematic, and multivariate models. *Behavioral Sciences & the Law, 27*, 507–529.

Gordon, R. (1983). An operational definition of prevention. *Public Health Reports, 98*, 107–109.

Gorenstein, E. E. (1982). Frontal lobe functions in psychopaths. *Journal of Abnormal Psychology, 91*, 368–379.

Gorman-Smith, D., & Loeber, R. (2005). Are developmental pathways in disruptive behaviors the same for girls and boys? *Journal of Child and Family Studies, 14*, 15–27.

Gorman-Smith, D., Tolan, P. H., Huesmann, L. R., & Zelli, A. (1996). The relation of family functioning to violence among inner-city minority youths. *Journal of Family Psychology, 10*, 115–129.

Gosselin, C., & Wilson, G. (1984). Fetishism, sadomasochism and related behaviours. In K. Howells (Ed.), *The psychology of sexual diversity.* London: Basil Blackwell.

Gottfredson, G. D., Gottfredson, D. C., Payne, A. A., & Gottfredson, N. C. (2005). School climate predictors of school disorder: Results from a national study of delinquency prevention in schools. *Journal of Research in Crime and Delinquency, 42*, 412–444.

Gottman, J. M. (2001). Crime, hostility, wife battering, and the heart: On the Meehan *et al.* (2001) failure to replicate the Gottman *et al.* (1995) typology. *Journal of Family Psychology, 15*, 409–414.

Gove, W. R., & Crutchfield, R. D. (1982). The family and delinquency. *Sociological Quarterly, 23*, 301–319.

Grafman, J., Schwab, K., Warden, D., Pridgen, A., Brown, H. R., & Salazar, A. M. (1996). Frontal lobe injuries, violence and aggression: A report of the Vietnam Head Injury Study. *Neurology, 46*, 1231–1238.

Grann, M. (2000). The PCL-R and gender. *European Journal of Psychological Assessment, 16*, 147–149.

Grant, V. (1977). *The menacing stranger.* New York: Dover.

Green, G. S. (1997). *Occupational crime* (2nd ed.). Chicago; Nelson-Hall.

Greendlinger, V., & Byrne, D. (1987). Coercive sexual fantasies of college men as predictors of self-reported likelihood to rape and overt sexual aggression. *Journal of Sex Research, 23*, 1–11.

Greenfeld, L. A. (1996, March). *Child victimization: Violent offenders and their victims.* Washington, DC: U.S. Department of Justice, Bureau of Justice Statistics.

Greenfeld, L. A. (1997, February). *Sex offenses and offenders: An analysis of data on rape and sexual assault.* Washington, DC: U.S. Department of Justice, Bureau of Justice Statistics.

Greenfeld, L. A. (1998, April). *Alcohol and crime: An analysis of national data on the prevalence of alcohol involvement in crime.* Washington, DC: U.S. Department of Justice.

Greenwald, H. (1958). *The call girl.* New York: Ballantine Books.

Gregorie, T. (2000). Workplace violence. In G. Coleman, M. Gaboury, M. Murray, & A. Seymour (Eds.), *1999 National Victim Assistance Academy.* Washington, DC: U.S. Department of Justice.

Gretton, H. M., McBride, M., Hare, R. D., O'Shaughnessy, R., & Kumka, G. (2001). Psychopathy and recidivism in adolescent sex offenders. *Criminal Justice and Behavior, 28*, 427–449.

Grimes, T., & Bergen, L. (2008). The epistemological argument against a causal relationship between media violence and sociopathic behavior among psychologically well viewers. *American Behavioral Scientist, 51*, 1137–1154.

Grisso, T. (1986). *Evaluating competencies: Forensic assessments and instruments.* New York: Plenum.

Grossman, D., & DeGaetano, G. (1999). *Stop teaching our kids to kill: A call to action against TV, movie and video game violence.* New York: Crown Publishing Group.

Groth, A. N. (1978). Patterns of sexual assault against children and adolescents. In A. W. Burgess, A. N. Groth, L. L. Holmstrom, & S. M. Sgroi (Eds.),

Sexual assault of children and adolescents. Lexington, MA: Lexington Books.

Groth, A. N. (1979). *Men who rape: The psychology of the offender.* New York: Plenum.

Groth, A. N., & Burgess, A. W. (1977). Motivational intent in the sexual assault of children. *Criminal Justice and Behavior, 4,* 253–271.

Groth, A. N., Hobson, W. F., & Gary, T. S. (1982). The child molester: Clinical observation. *Journal of Social Work and Human Sexuality, 1,* 129–144.

Gudjonsson, G. H., Einarsson, E., Bragason Ö. Ó., & Sigurdsson, J. F. (2006). Personality predictors of self-reported offending in Icelandic students. *Psychology, Crime & Law, 12,* 383–393.

Guerette, R. T. (2002). Geographical profiling. In D. Levinson (Ed.), *Encyclopedia of crime and punishment.* Thousand Oaks, CA: Sage.

Guerra, N. G., Huesmann, L. R., Tolan, P. H., Van Acker, R., & Eron, L. D. (1995). Stressful events and individual beliefs as correlates of economic disadvantage and aggression among urban children. *Journal of Consulting and Clinical Psychology, 63,* 518–528.

Guerra, N., Tolan, P. H., & Hammond, W. R. (1994). Prevention and treatment of adolescent violence. In L. R. Eron, J. H., Gentry, & P. Schlegel (Eds.), *Reason to hope: A psychological perspective on violence and youth.* Washington, DC: American Psychological Association.

Gunter, B. (2008). Media violence: Is there a case for causality? *American Behavioral Scientist, 51,* 1061–1122.

Gurley, J. R., & Marcus, D. K. (2008). The effects of neuroimaging and brain injury on insanity defenses. *Behavioral Sciences & the Law, 26,* 85–97.

Guymer, A. C., Mellor, D., Luk, E. S., & Pearse, V. (2001). The development of a screening questionnaire for childhood cruelty to animals. *Journal of Child Psychology and Psychiatry, 42,* 1057–1063.

Guze, S. B. (1976). *Criminality and psychiatric disorders.* New York: Oxford University Press.

Haapasalo, J., & Petaja, S. (1999). Mothers who killed or attempted to kill their child: Life circumstances, childhood abuse, and types of killing. *Violence and Victims, 14,* 219–239.

Haft, M. G. (1976). Hustling for rights. In L. Crites (Ed.), *The female offender.* Lexington, MA: Lexington Books.

Häkkänen, H. & Laajasalo, T. (2006). Homicide crime scene behaviors in a Finnish sample of mentally ill offenders. *Homicide Studies, 10,* 33–54.

Häkkänen, H., Puolakka, P., & Santtila, P. (2004). Crime scene actions and offender characteristics in arsons. *Legal and Criminological Psychology, 9,* 197–214.

Hall, D. M. (1998). The victims of stalking. In J. R. Meloy (Ed.), *The psychology of stalking: Clinical and forensic perspectives.* San Diego, CA: Academic Press.

Hall, G. C. N. (1995). Sexual offender recidivism revisited: A meta-analysis of recent treatment studies. *Journal of Consulting and Clinical Psychology, 63,* 802–809.

Hall, G. C. N., Proctor, W. C., & Nelson, G. M. (1988). Validity of physiological measures of pedophilic sexual arousal in a sexual offender population. *Journal of Consulting and Clinical Psychology, 56,* 118–122.

Halleck, S. L. (1967). *Psychiatry and the dilemmas of crime.* New York: Harper & Row.

Hallett, B. (2004). Dishonest crimes, dishonest language: An argument about terrorism. In F. M. Moghaddam & A. J. Marsella (Eds.), *Understanding terrorism: Psychosocial roots, consequences, and interventions.* Washington, DC: American Psychological Association.

Hämäläinen, T., & Haapasalo, J. (1996). Retrospective reports of childhood abuse and neglect among violent and property offenders. *Psychology, Crime & Law, 3,* 1–13.

Hammond, W. R., & Yung, B. (1994). African Americans. In L. D. Eron, J. H. Gentry, & P. Schlegel (Eds.), *Reason to hope: A psychosocial perspective on violence and youth.* Washington, DC: American Psychological Association.

Hampson, J. E., Rahman, M. A., Brown, B., Taylor, M. E., & Donaldson, C. J. (1998). Project SELF: Beyond resilience. *Urban Education, 33,* 6–33.

Haney, C., & Zimbardo, P. (1998). The past and future of U.S. prison policy: Twenty-five years after the Stanford prison experiment. *American Psychologist, 53,* 709–727.

Haney, C. W. (1983). The good, the bad, and the lawful: An essay on psychological injustice. In W. S. Laufer & J. M. Day (Eds.), *Personality theory, moral development, and criminal behavior.* Lexington, MA: Lexington Books.

Hanson, R. K. (2001). *Age and sexual recidivism: A comparison of rapists and child molesters.* Ottawa, Ontario: Solicitor General Canada.

Hanson, R. K., Bourgon, G., Helmus, L., & Hodgson, S. (2009). The principles of effective correctional treatment also apply to sexual offenders: A meta-analysis. *Criminal Justice and Behavior, 36,* 865–891.

Harbin, H. T., & Madden, D. J. (1979). Battered parents: A new syndrome. *American Journal of Psychiatry, 136,* 1288–1291.

Hare, R. D. (1965a). A conflict and learning theory analysis of psychopathic behavior. *Journal of Research in Crime and Delinquency, 2,* 12–19.

Hare, R. D. (1965b). Acquisition and generalization of a conditioned-fear response in psychopathic and nonpsychopathic criminals. *Journal of Psychology, 59,* 367–370.

Hare, R. D. (1968). Psychopathy, autonomic functioning, and the orienting response. *Journal of Abnormal Psychology, 73,* 1–24.

Hare, R. D. (1970). *Psychopathy: Theory and research.* New York: Wiley.

Hare, R. D. (1976). Anxiety, stress and psychopathy. In G. Shean (Ed.), *Dimensions in abnormal psychology.* Chicago: Rand McNally.

Hare, R. D. (1980). A research scale for the assessment of psychopathy in criminal populations. *Personality and Individual Differences, 1,* 111–119.

Hare, R. D. (1984). Performance of psychopaths on cognitive tasks related to frontal lobe function. *Journal of Abnormal Psychology, 93,* 133–140.

Hare, R. D. (1991). *The Hare Psychopathy Checklist-Revised.* Toronto, ON: Multi-Health Systems.

Hare, R. D. (1993). *Without conscience: The disturbing world of the psychopaths among us.* New York: Pocket Books.

Hare, R. D. (1996). Psychopathy: A clinical construct whose time has come. *Criminal Justice and Behavior, 23,* 25–54.

Hare, R. D. (1998). Emotional processing in psychopaths. In D. J. Cooke, R. D. Hare, & A. Forth (Eds.), *Psychopathy: Theory, research, and implications for society.* The Netherlands: Kluwer Academic Publishers.

Hare, R. D. (2003). *The Hare Psychopathy Checklist—Revised* (2nd ed.). Toronto: Multi-Health Systems.

Hare, R. D., Clark, D., Grann, M., & Thornton, D. (2000). Psychopathy and the predictive validity of the PCL-R: An international perspective. *Behavioral Sciences & the Law, 18,* 623–645.

Hare, R. D., & Connolly, J. F. (1987). Perceptual asymmetries and information processing in psychopaths. In S. A. Mednick, T. E. Moffitt, & S. A. Stack (Eds.), *The causes of crime: New biological approaches.* Cambridge, UK: Cambridge University Press.

Hare, R. D., & Craigen, D. (1974). Psychopathy and physiological activity in a mixed-motive game. *Psychophysiology, 11,* 197–206.

Hare, R. D., Forth, A. E., & Stachan, K. E. (1992). Psychopathy and crime across the life span. In R. D. Peters, R. J. McMahon, & V. L. Quinsey (Eds.), *Aggression and violence throughout the life span.* Newbury Park, CA: Sage.

Hare, R. D., Hart, S. D., & Harpur, T. J. (1991). Psychopathy and the DSM-IV criteria for antisocial personality disorder. *Journal of Abnormal Psychology, 100,* 391–398.

Hare, R. D., & McPherson, L. M. (1984). Violent and aggressive behavior by criminal psychopaths. *International Journal of Law and Psychiatry, 7,* 35–50.

Hare, R. D., & Neumann, C. S. (2008). Psychopathy as a clinical and empirical construct. *Annual Review of Clinical Psychology, 4,* 217–246.

Hare, R. D., & Quinn, M. (1971). Psychopathy and autonomic conditioning. *Journal of Abnormal Psychology, 77,* 223–239.

Harmon, R. B., Rosner, R., & Wiederlight, M. (1985). Women and arson: A demographic study. *Journal of Forensic Sciences, 10,* 467–477.

Harpur, T. J., Hakstian, A., & Hare, R. D. (1988). Factor structure of the Psychopathy Checklist. *Journal of Consulting and Clinical Psychology, 56,* 741–747.

Harris, D. A. (1999, June). *Driving while Black: Racial profiling on our nation's highways.* New York: American Civil Liberties Union. Available: www.aclu.org/profiling/report/index.html.

Harris, D. A., Mazerolle, P., & Knight, R. A. (2009). Understanding male sexual offending: A comparison of general and specialist theories. *Criminal Justice and Behavior, 36,* 1051–1069.

Hart, S. D., Cox, D. N., & Hare, R. D. (1995). *The Hare Psychopathy Checklist: Screening Version.* Toronto, ON: Multi-Health Systems.

Hart, S. D., & Dempster, R. J. (1997). Impulsivity and psychopathy. In C. D. Webster & M. A. Jackson (Eds.), *Impulsivity: Theory, assessment and treatment.* New York: Guilford.

Hart, S. D., & Hare, R. D. (1997). Psychopathy: Assessment and association with criminal conduct. In D. M. Stoff, J. P. Maser, & J. Breiling (Eds.), *Handbook of antisocial behavior.* New York: Wiley.

Hart, S. D., Hare, R. D., & Forth, A. E. (1993). Psychopathy as a risk marker for violence: Development and validation of a screening version of the Revised Psychopathy Checklist. In J. Monahan & H. Steadman (Eds.), *Violence and mental disorder: Development in risk assessment.* Chicago: University of Chicago Press.

Hart, C. H., Nelson, A. A., Robinson, C. C., Olsen, S. F., & McNeilly-Choque, M. K. (1998). Overt and relational aggression in Russian nursery-school-age children: Parenting style and marital linkages. *Developmental Psychology, 34,* 687–697.

Hastings, P. D., Zahn-Waxler, C., Usher, B., Robinson, J., & Bridges, D. (2000). The development of concern for others in children with behavior problems. *Developmental Psychology, 36,* 531–546.

Hawes, D. J., & Dadds, M. R. (2005). The treatment of conduct problems in children with callous-unemotional traits. *Journal of Consulting and Clinical Psychology, 73,* 737–741.

Hawkins, D. L., Pepler, D. J., & Craig, W. M. (2001). Naturalistic observations of peer interventions in bullying. *Social Development, 10,* 512–527.

Hawkins, S. R., Graham, P. W., Williams, J., & Zahn, M. A. (2009, January). *Resilient girls: Factors that protect against delinquency.* Washington, DC: U.S. Department of Justice, Office of Justice Programs.

Hazelwood, R. R., & Burgess, A. W. (1987, September). An introduction to the serial rapist. *FBI Law Enforcement Bulletin,* 16–24.

Heaven, P. C. L., Newbury, K., & Wilson, V. (2004). The Eysenck psychoticism dimension and delinquent behaviours among non-criminals: Changes across the lifespan? *Personality and Individual Differences, 36,* 1817–1825.

Hebb, D. O. (1955). Drives and the C.N.S. (Conceptual Nervous System). *Psychological Review, 62,* 243–254.

Heckel, R. V., & Shumaker, D. M. (2001). *Children who murder: A psychological perspective.* Westport, CT: Praeger.

Heide, K. (1993). Adolescent parricide offenders: Synthesis, illustration and future directions. In A. V. Wilson (Ed.), *Homicide—the victim/offender connection.* Cincinnati, OH: Anderson.

Heide, K. M. (2003). Youth homicide: A review of the literature and blueprint for action. *International Journal of Offender Therapy and Comparative Criminology, 47,* 6–36.

Heilbrun, K., Marczyk, G. R., & Dematteo, D. (2002). *Forensic mental health assessment: A casebook.* New York: Kluwer Academic.

Hellmich, C. (2008). Creating the ideology of Al Qaeda: From hypocrites to Salafi-Jihadists. *Studies in Conflict & Terrorism, 31,* 111–124.

Hemphill, J. F., & Hare, R. D. (2004). Some misconceptions about the Hare PCL-R and risk assessment: A reply to Gendreau, Goggin, and Smith. *Criminal Justice and Behavior, 31,* 203–243.

Hemphill, J. F., Hare, R. D., & Wong, S. (1998). Psychopathy and recidivism: A review. *Legal and Criminological Psychology, 3,* 139–170.

Hendricks, N. J., Ortiz, C. W., Sugie, N., & Miller, J. (2007). Beyond the numbers: Hate crimes and cultural trauma within Arab American immigrant communities. *International Review of Victiminology, 14,* 95–113.

Henggeler, S. W. (1996). Treatment of violent juvenile offenders—we have the knowledge. *Journal of Family Psychology, 10,* 137–141.

Henggeler, S. W., & Borduin, C. M. (1990). *Family therapy and beyond: A multisystemic approach to treating the behavior problems of children and adolescents*. Pacific Grove, CA: Brooks/Cole.

Henggeler, S. W., Melton, G. B., & Smith, L. A. (1992). Family preservation using multisystemic therapy—an effective alternative to incarcerating serious juvenile offenders. *Journal of Consulting and Clinical Psychology, 60,* 953–961.

Henggeler, S. W., Melton, G. B., Smith, L. A., Schoenwald, S. K., & Hanley, J. (1993). Family preservation using multisystemic therapy: Long-term follow-up to a clinical trial with serious juvenile offenders. *Journal of Child and Family Studies, 2,* 283–293.

Henker, B., & Whalen, C. K. (1989). Hyperactivity and attention deficits. *American Psychologist, 44,* 216–244.

Henn, F. A., Herjanic, M., & Vanderpearl, R. H. (1976a). Forensic psychiatry: Profiles of two types of sex offenders. *American Journal of Psychiatry, 133,* 694–696.

Henn, F. A., Herjanic, M., & Vanderpearl, R. H. (1976b). Forensic psychiatry: Diagnosis of criminal responsibility. *The Journal of Nervous and Mental Disease, 162,* 423–429.

Henry, B., Caspi, A., Moffitt, T. E., & Silva, P. A. (1996). Temperament and familial predictors of violent and nonviolent criminal conviction: Age 3 to age 18. *Developmental Psychology, 32,* 614–623.

Henry, B. C., & Sanders, C. E. (2007). Bullying and animal abuse: Is there a connection? *Society and Animals, 15,* 107126.

Hepburn, L. M., & Hemenway, D. (2004). Firearm availability and homicide: A review of the literature. *Aggression and Violent Behavior, 9,* 417–429.

Hepworth, W., & Towler, A. (2004). The effects of individual differences and charismatic leadership on workplace aggression. *Journal of Occupational Health Psychology, 9,* 176–185.

Herpertz, S. C., & Sass, H. (2000). Emotional deficiency and psychopathy. *Behavioral Sciences & the Law, 18,* 567–580.

Herzberg, J. L., & Fenwick, P. B. C. (1988). The aetiology of aggression in temporal lobe epilepsy. *British Journal of Psychiatry, 153,* 50–55.

Hetherington, E. M., & Parke, R. D. (1975). *Child psychology: A contemporary viewpoint.* New York: McGraw-Hill.

Hewitt, C. (2003). *Understanding terrorism in America: From the Klan to al Qaeda.* New York: Routledge.

Hickey, E. (1991). *Serial killers and their victims.* Pacific Grove, CA: Brooks/Cole.

Hickey, E. W. (1997). *Serial murderers and their victims* (2nd ed). Belmont, CA: Wadsworth.

Hill, H. M., Soriano, F. I., Chen, S. A., & LaFromboise, T. D. (1994). Sociocultural factors in the etiology and prevention of violence among ethnic minority youth. In L. D. Eron, J. H. Gentry, & P. Schlegel (Eds.), *Reason to hope: A psychosocial perspective on violence and youth.* Washington, DC: American Psychological Association.

Hill, L. G., Lochman, J. E., Coie, J. D., & Geenberg, M. T. (2004). Effectiveness of early screening for externalizing problems: Issues of screening accuracy and utility. *Journal of Consulting and Clinical Psychology, 72,* 809–820.

Hill, N. E., Castellino, D. R., Lansford, J. E., Nowlin, P., Dodge, K. A., Bates, J. E. et al. (2004). Parent-academic involvement as related to school behavior, achievement, and aspirations: Demographic variations across adolescence. *Child Development, 75,* 1491–1509.

Hill, P. (1960). *Portrait of a sadist.* New York: Avon.

Hill, R. W., Langevin, R., Paitich, D., Handy, L., Russon, A., & Wilkinson, L. (1982). Is arson an aggressive act or a property offense? *Canadian Journal of Psychiatry, 27,* 648–654.

Hillbrand, M., Alexandre, J. W., Young, J. L., & Spitz, R. T. (1999). Parricide: Characteristics of offenders and victims, legal factors, and treatment issues. *Aggression and Violent Behavior, 4,* 179–190.

Hindelang, M. J. (1974). Decisions of shoplifting victims to invoke the criminal justice process. *Social Process, 21,* 580–593.

Hindelang, M. J., Dunn, C. S., Sutton, L. P., & Aumick, A. (1976). *Sourcebook of criminal justice statistics, 1975.* Washington, DC: USGPO.

Hinduja, S. (2008). Deindividuation and Internet software piracy. *Cybercrime and Behavior, 11,* 391–398.

Hinduja, S., & Patchin, J. (2008). Cyberbullying: An exploratory analysis of factors related to offending and victimization. *Deviant Behavior, 29*, 129–156.

Hinshaw, S. P. (1992). Externalizing behavior problems and academic underachievement in childhood and adolescence: Causal relationships and underlying mechanisms. *Psychological Bulletin, 111*, 127–155.

Hirschi, T. (1969). *Causes of delinquency.* Berkeley: University of California Press.

Hirschi, T., & Hindelang, M. J. (1977). Intelligence and delinquency. *American Sociological Review, 42*, 571–587.

Hockenbury, D. H., & Hockenbury, S. E. (2004). *Discovering psychology* (3rd edition). New York: Worth.

Hochstedler, E. (Ed.). (1984). *Corporations as criminals.* Beverly Hills, CA: Sage.

Hodgins, S. (2001). The major mental disorders and crime: Stop debating and start treating and preventing. *International Journal of Law and Psychiatry, 24*, 427–446.

Hodgins, S., Cree, A., & Mak, T. (2008). From conduct disorder to severe mental illness: Associations with aggressive behaviour, crime and victimization. *Psychological Medicine, 38*, 975–987.

Hoeve, M., Smeenk, W., Loeber, R., Stouthamer-Loeber, M., van der Laan, P. H., Gerris, J. R. M. et al. (2007). Long-term effects of parenting and family characteristics on delinquency of male young adults. *European Journal of Criminology, 4*, 161–194.

Hoffman, B. (1993). *"Holy terror": The implications of terrorism motivated by a religious imperative* (RAND Research Paper P-7834). Santa Monica, CA: RAND.

Hoffman, B. (2002). Rethinking terrorism and counterterrorism since 9/11. *Studies in Conflict and Terrorism, 25*, 303–316.

Hoffman, J. J., Hall, R. W., & Bartsch, T. W. (1987). On the relative importance of "psychopathic" personality and alcoholism measures of frontal lobe dysfunction. *Journal of Abnormal Psychology, 96*, 158–160.

Hoffman, K. L., Kiecolt, K. J., & Edwards, J. N. (2005). Physical violence between siblings: A theoretical and empirical analysis. *Journal of Family Issues, 26*, 1103–1130.

Hofmann, F. G. (1975). *A handbook on drug and alcohol abuse: The biomedical aspects.* New York: Oxford University Press.

Hoge, S. K., Poythress, N., Bonnie, R., Monahan, J., Eisenberg, M., & Feucht-Haviar, T. (1997). The MacArthur adjudicative competence study: Diagnosis, psychopathology, and competence-related abilities. *Behavioral Sciences & the Law, 15*, 329–345.

Hoge, S. K., Poythress, N., Bonnie, R., Eisenberg, M., Monahan, J., Feucht-Haviar, T., & Oberlander, L. (1996). Mentally ill and non-mentally ill defendants' abilities to understand information relevant to adjudication: A preliminary study. *Bulletin of the American Academy of Psychiatry and the Law, 24*, 187–197.

Holtfreter, K., & Cupp, R. (2007). Gender and risk assessment: The empirical status of the LSI-R for women. *Journal of Contemporary Criminal Justice, 23*, 363–382.

Hollinger, R. (1986). Acts against the workplace: Social bonding and employee deviance. *Deviant Behavior, 7*, 53–75.

Hollister-Wagner, G. H., Foshee, V. A., & Jackson, C. (2001). Adolescent aggression: Models of resilience. *Journal of Applied Social Psychology, 31*, 445–466.

Holmes, C. T. (1989). Grade level retention effects: A meta-analysis of research studies. In L. A. Shepard & M. L. Smith (Eds.), *Flunking grades: Research and policies on retention.* Philadelphia: Falmer Press.

Holmes, R. M., & DeBurger, J. (1988). *Serial murder.* Newbury Park, CA: Sage.

Holmes, R. M., & Holmes, S. T. (1998). *Serial murder* (2nd ed.). Thousand Oaks, CA: Sage.

Holmes, S. T., Hickey, E., & Holmes, R. M. (1991). Female serial murderesses: Constructing differentiating typologies. *Journal of Contemporary Criminal Justice, 7*, 245–256.

Holt, S. E., Meloy, J. R., & Stack, S. (1999). Sadism and psychopath in violent and sexual violent offenders. *Journal of the American Academy of Psychiatry and Law, 27*, 23–32.

Holtzworth-Monroe, A., & Stuart, G. L. (1994). Typologies of male batterers: Three subtypes and the differences among them. *Psychological Bulletin, 116*, 476–497.

Home Office. (1986). *Criminal statistics: England and Wales 1985.* London: HMSO.

Horgan, J. (2005). *The psychology of terrorism.* London: Routledge.

Horning, D. N. M. (1970). Blue-collar theft: Conceptions of property, attitudes toward pilfering, and work group norms in a modern industrial plant. In E. O. Smigel & H. L. Ross (Eds.), *Crimes against bureaucracy.* New York: Van Nostrand Reinhold.

Hornung, C. A., McCullough, B. C., & Sugimoto, T. (1981). Status relationships in marriage: Risk factors in spouse abuse. *Journal of Marriage and the Family, 43,* 675–692.

Hotaling, G. T., & Straus, M. A. (1989). Intrafamily violence, and crime and violence outside the family. In L. Ohlin & M. Tonry (Eds.), *Family violence* (Vol. 11). Chicago, IL: University of Chicago Press.

Howes, C., & Olenick, M. (1986). Family and child care influences on toddlers' compliance. *Child Development, 57,* 202–216.

Hubbard, J. A., Dodge, K. A., Cillessen, A. H. N., Coie, J. D., & Schwartz, D. (2001). The dyadic nature of social information processing in boys' reactive and proactive aggression. *Journal of Personality and Social Psychology, 80,* 268–280.

Hudson, M. I. (1986). Elder maltreatment: Current research. In K. A. Pillemer & R. S. Wolf (Eds.), *Elder abuse: Conflict in the family.* Dover, MA: Auburn House.

Huesmann, L. R. (1988). An information processing model for the development of aggression. *Aggressive Behavior, 14,* 13–24.

Huesmann, L. R. (1997). Observational learning of violent behavior: Social and biosocial processes. In A. Raine, P. A. Brennan, D. P. Farrington, & S. A. Mednick (Eds.), *Biosocial bases of violence.* New York: Plenum.

Huesmann, L. R. (1998). The role of social information processing and cognitive schema in the acquisition and maintenance of habitual aggressive behavior. In R. G. Geen & E. Donnerstein (Eds.), *Human aggression: Theories, research, and implications for social policy.* San Diego, CA: Academic Press.

Huesmann, L. R. (2007). The impact of electronic media violence: Scientific theory and research. *Journal of Adolescent Health, 41,* Supplement, S6–S13.

Huesmann, L. R., Moise-Titus, J., Podolski, C., & Eron, L. D. (2003). Longitudinal relations between children's exposure to TV violence and their aggressive and violent behavior in young adulthood: 1977–1992. *Developmental Psychology, 39,* 201–221.

Hughes, H. M. (1988). Psychological and behavioral correlates of family violence in child witnesses and victims. *American Journal of Orthopsychiatry, 58,* 77–90.

Hughes, H. M., & Barad, S. J. (1983). Psychological functioning of children in a battered women's shelter: A preliminary investigation. *American Journal of Orthopsychiatry, 53,* 525–531.

Hughes, H. M., Parkinson, D., & Vargo, M. (1989). Witnessing spouse abuse and experiencing physical abuse: A "double whammy"? *Journal of Family Violence, 4,* 197–209.

Huizinga, D., & Jakob-Chien, C. (1998). The contemporaneous co-occurrence of serious and violent juvenile offending and other problem behaviors. In R. Loeber & D. P. Farrington (Eds.), *Serious & violent juvenile offenders: Risk factors and successful interventions.* Thousand Oaks, CA: Sage.

Hunter, J. A., & Becker, J. V. (1999). Motivators of adolescent sex offenders and treatment perspectives. In J. Shaw (Ed.), *Sexual aggression.* Washington, DC: American Psychiatric Press.

Hunter, J. A., & Figueredo, A. J. (1999). Factors associated with treatment compliance in a population of juvenile sex offenders. *Sex Abuse: A Journal of Research and Treatment, 11,* 49–67.

Hunter, J. A., Figueredo, A. J., Malamuth, N. M., & Becker, J. V. (2003). Juvenile sex offenders: Toward the development of a typology. *Sexual Abuse: A Journal of Research and Treatment, 15,* 27–48.

Hutchings, B., & Mednick, S. A. (1975). Registered criminality in the adoptive and biological parents of registered male criminal adoptees. In R. R. Fieve, D. Rosenthal, & H. Brill (Eds.), *Genetic research in psychiatry.* Baltimore, MD: Johns Hopkins University Press.

Icove, D. J., & Estepp, M. H. (1987, April). Motive-based offender profiles of arson and fire-related crime. *FBI Law Enforcement Bulletin,* 17–23.

Inaba, D. S., & Cohen, W. E. (1993). *Uppers, downers, all arounders: Physical and mental effects of psychoactive drugs* (2nd ed.). Ashland, OR: CNS Productions.

Inciardi, J. A. (1970). The adult firesetter, a typology. *Criminology, 3,* 145–155.

Inciardi, J. A. (1980). Women, heroin, and property crime. In S. K. Datesman & F. R. Scarpitti (Eds.), *Women, crime and justice.* New York: Oxford University Press.

Inciardi, J. A. (1981). Crime and alternative patterns of substance abuse. In S. E. Gardner (Ed.), *Drug and alcohol abuse.* Rockville, MD: National Institute on Drug Abuse.

Inciardi, J. A. (1986). *The war on drugs: Heroin, cocaine, crime and public policy.* Palo Alto, CA: Mayfield Publishing.

The Informant. (2003). Newsletter of National White Collar Crime Center (August issue). Richmond, VA: National White Collar Crime Center.

Ingram, G. L., Gerard, R. E., Quay, H. C., & Levison, R. B. (1970). An experimental program for the psychopathic delinquent: Looking in the "correctional wastebasket." *Journal of Research in Crime and Delinquency, 7,* 24–30.

Insight Canada Research. (1998). *Prevalence of problem and pathological gambling in Ontario using the South Oaks Gambling Screen.* Ottawa, ON: Canadian Foundation on Compulsive Gambling. Available: www.cfcg.on.ca.

International Arrestees Drug Abuse Monitoring Program. (2000). *Comparing drug use rates of detained arrestees in the United States and England.* Washington, DC: U.S. Department of Justice.

Internet Crime Complaint Center. (2008). *Annual report on Internet crime.* Available: www. Ic3.gov.

Ishikawa, S. S., & Raine, A. (2004). Prefrontal deficits and antisocial behavior: A causal model. In B. B. Lahey, T. E. Moffitt, & A. Caspi (Eds.), *Causes of conduct disorder and juvenile delinquency.* New York: Guilford.

Ishikawa, S. S., Raine, A., Lencz, T., Bihrle, S., & Lacasse, L. (2001). Autonomic stress reactivity and executive functions in successful and unsuccessful criminal psychopaths from the community. *Journal of Abnormal Psychology, 110,* 423–432.

Jackson, C., & Foshee, V. A. (1998). Violence-related behaviors of adolescents: Relations with responsive and demanding parenting. *Journal of Adolescent Research, 13,* 343–359.

Jackson, H. F., Glass, C., & Hope, S. (1987). A functional analysis of recidivistic arson. *British Journal of Clinical Psychology, 26,* 175–185.

Jackson, R. L., Neumann, C. S., & Vitacco, M. J. (2007). Impulsivity, anger, and psychopathy: The moderating effect of ethnicity. *Journal of Personality Disorders, 21,* 289–304.

Jackson, R. L., Rogers, R., Neumann, C. S., & Lambert, P. L. (2002). Psychopathy in female offenders: An investigation of its underlying dimensions. *Criminal Justice and Behavior, 29,* 692–704.

Jacobs, B. A., Topalli, V., & Wright, R. (2003). Carjacking, streetlife and offender motivation. *British Journal of Criminology, 43,* 673–688.

Jacobs, G. D., & Snyder, D. (1996). Frontal brain asymmetry predicts affective style in men. *Behavioral Neuroscience, 110,* 3–6.

Jacobs, P. A., Brunton, M., Melville, H. M., Brittain, R. P., & McClemont, W. F. (1965). Aggressive behavior, mental subnormality and the XYY male. *Nature, 208,* 1351–1352.

Jaffee, S. R., Caspi, A., Moffitt, T. E., Dodge, K. A., Rutter, M., Taylor, A., et al. (2005). Nature x nurture: Genetic vulnerabilities interact with physical maltreatment to promote conduct problems. *Development and Psychopathology, 17,* 67–84.

James, D. J., & Glaze, L. E. (2006, September). *Mental health problems of prison and jail inmates.* Washington, DC: U.S. Department of Justice, Bureau of Justice Statistics.

James, J. (1976). Motivations for entrance into prostitution. In L. Crites (Ed.), *The female offender.* Lexington, MA: Lexington Books.

James, J. (1978). The prostitute as victim. In J. R. Chapman & M. Gates (Eds.), *The victimization of women.* Beverly Hills, CA: Sage.

Janofsky, M. (June 16, 1993). *Reports of needles in soda cans climb.* New York Times. Available: www.query.nytimes.com/gst/fullpage.html?sec=health&res=9F0CE2D8143EF935A25755.

Janus, E. S. (2000). Sexual predator commitment laws: Lessons for law and the behavioral sciences. *Behavioral Sciences & the Law, 18,* 5–21.

Janus, E. S., & Walbek, N. H. (2000). Sex offender commitments in Minnesota: A descriptive study of second generation commitments. *Behavioral Sciences & the Law, 18,* 343–374.

Jarvik, L. F., Klodin, V., & Matsuyama, S. S. (1973). Human aggression and the extra Y chromosome. *American Psychologist, 28,* 674–682.

Jarvis, G., & Parker, H. (1989). Young heroin users and crime. *British Journal of Criminology, 29,* 175–185.

Jeffrey, C. R. (1965). Criminal behavior and learning theory. *Journal of Criminal Law, Criminology and Police Science, 56,* 294–300.

Jenkins, P. (1988). Serial murder in England 1940–1985. *Journal of Criminal Justice, 16,* 1–15.

Jenkins, P. (1993). Chance or choice: The selection of serial murder victims. In A. V. Wilson (Ed.), *Homicide: The victim/offender connection.* Cincinnati, OH: Anderson.

Jenson, B. (1996 May). *Cyberstalking: Crime, enforcement and personal responsibility in the on-line world.* Available: www. law.ucla.edu/Classes/Archive.S96/340/cyberlaw.htm.

Johns, J. H., & Quay, H. C. (1962). The effect of social reward on verbal conditioning in psychopathic military offenders. *Journal of Consulting Psychology, 26,* 217–220.

Johnsen, M. (2008, October 20). Pinched by economy retail crime on the rise. *Drug Store News,* pp. 1, 6, 42.

Johnson, R. (1996). *Hard time: Understanding and reforming the prison* (2nd ed.). Belmont, CA: Wadsworth.

Johnston, L. D., O'Malley, P. M., Bachman, J. G., & Schulenberg, J. E. (2006). *Monitoring the future national results on adolescent drug use: Overview of key findings, 2005.* Bethesda, MD: National Institute on Drug Abuse.

Joiner, T. E. (1994). Contagious depression: Existence, specificity to depressed symptoms, and the role of reassurance seeking. *Journal of Personality and Social Psychology, 67,* 287–296.

Joint, M. (1995, March). *Road rage.* Washington, DC: Automobile Association Group Public Policy Road Safety Unit.

Jolin, A. (1994). On the backs of working prostitutes: Feminist theory and prostitution policy. *Crime and Delinquency, 40,* 69–83.

Jolliffe, D., & Farrington, D. P. (2006). Examining the relationship between low empathy and bullying. *Aggressive Behavior, 32,* 540–550.

Jolliffe, D., & Farrington, D. P. (2007). Examining the relationship between low empathy and self-reported offending. *Legal and Criminological Psychology, 12,* 265–286.

Jones, A. P., Laurens, K. R., Herba, C. M., Barker, G. J., & Viding, E. (2009). Amygdala hypoactivity to fearful faces in boys with conduct problems and callous-unemotional traits. *American Journal of Psychiatry, 166,* 95–102.

Jones, C., & Aronson, E. (1973). Attribution of fault to a rape victim as a function of respectability of the victim. *Journal of Personality and Social Psychology, 26,* 415–419.

Jones, J. G., Butler, H. L., Hamilton, B., Perdue, J. D., Stern, H. P., & Woody, R. C. (1986). Munchausen syndrome by proxy. *Child Abuse and Neglect, 10,* 33–40.

Jones, S., Cauffman, E., Miller, J. D., & Mulvey, E. (2006). Investigating different factor structures of the Psychopathy Checklist: Youth Version (PCL:YV) confirmatory factor analytic findings. *Psychological Assessment, 18,* 33–48.

Julien, R. M. (1975). *A primer of drug action.* San Francisco: W. H. Freeman.

Julien, R. M. (1992). *A primer of drug action* (6th ed.). New York: W. H. Freeman.

Junger, M., West, R., & Timman, R. (2001). Crime and risk behavior in traffic: An example of cross-situational consistency. *Journal of Research in Crime and Delinquency, 38,* 439–459.

Kafrey, D. (1980). Playing with matches: Children and fire. In D. Canter (Ed.), *Fires and human behaviour.* Chichester, UK: Wiley.

Kafka, M. P., & Hennen, J. (2003). Hypersexual desire in males: Are males with paraphilias different from males with paraphilia-related disorders? *Sexual Abuse: A Journal of Research and Treatment, 4,* 307–321.

Kahn, T. J., & LaFond, M. A. (1988). Treatment of the adolescent sex offender. *Child and Adolescent Social Work, 5,* 135–148.

Kandel, D., Yamaguchi, K., & Chen, K. (1992). Stages of drug involvement from adolescence to adulthood:

Further evidence for the gateway theory. *Journal of Studies on Alcohol, 53,* 447–457.

Kandel, E., Mednick, S. A., Kirkegaard-Sorenson, L., Hutchings, B., Knop, J., Rosenberg, R., & Schulsinger, F. (1988). IQ as a protective factor for subjects at high risk for antisocial behavior. *Journal of Consulting and Clinical Psychology, 56,* 224–226.

Kanin, E. J. (1984). Date rape: Unofficial criminals and victims. *Victimology, 9,* 95–108.

Kaplan, M. S. & Green, A. (1995). Incarcerated female sexual offenders: A comparison of sexual histories with eleven female nonsexual offenders. *Sexual Abuse, 7,* 287–300.

Karmen, A. (1996). *Crime victims: An introduction to victimology* (3rd ed.). Belmont, CA: Wadsworth.

Karmen, A. (2001). *Crime victims* (4th ed.). Belmont, CA: Wadsworth/Thomson Learning.

Katz, J. (1988). *Seduction of crime: Moral and sensual attractions in doing evil.* New York: Basic Books.

Kazdin, A. E. (1987). Treatment of antisocial behavior in children: Current status and future directions. *American Psychologist, 48,* 127–141.

Kazdin, A. E. (1989). Developmental psychopathology: Current research, issues, and directions. *American Psychologist, 44,* 180–187.

Kazdin, A. E. (1994). Psychotherapy for children and adolescents. In A. E. Bergrin & S. LO. Garfield (Eds.), *Handbook of psychotherapy and behavior change* (4th ed.). New York: Wiley.

Kelleher, M. D. (1997). *Profiling the lethal employee: Case studies of violence in the workplace.* Westport, CT: Praeger.

Kelley, T. M., Kennedy, D. B., & Homant, R. J. (2003). Evaluation of an individualized treatment program for adolescent shoplifters. *Adolescence, 38,* 725–733.

Kelman, H. C., & Hamilton, V. L. (1989). *Crimes of obedience: Toward a social psychology of authority and responsibility.* New Haven, CT: Yale University Press.

Kempe, C. H., Silverman, F. N., Steele, B. B., Droegemueller, W., & Silver, H. K. (1962). The battered-child syndrome. *Journal of the American Medical Association, 181,* 17–24.

Kemp, D. E., & Center, D. B. (2003). An investigation of Eysenck's antisocial behavior hypothesis in general education students and students with behavior disorders. *Personality and Individual Differences, 35,* 1359–1371.

Kendall, P. C., & Hammen, C. (1995). *Abnormal psychology.* Boston: Houghton Mifflin.

Kerlinger, F. (1973). *Foundations of behavioral research* (2nd edition). New York: Holt, Rinehart & Winston.

Kerns, K. A., Aspelmeier, J. E., Gentzler, A. L., & Grabill, C. M. (2001). Parent-child attachment and monitoring in middle childhood. *Journal of Family Psychology, 15,* 69–71.

Kiehl, K. A. (2006). A cognitive neuroscience perspective on psychopathy: Evidence for paralimbic system dysfunction. *Psychiatry Research, 142,* 107–128.

Kiehl, K. A., Smith, A. M., Hare, R. D., Mendrek, A., Forster, B. B., Brink, J. et al. (2001). Limbic abnormalities in affective processing by criminal psychopaths as revealed by functional magnetic resonance imaging. *Biological Psychiatry, 50,* 677–684.

Kilgore, K., Snyder, J., & Lentz, C. (2000). The contribution of parental discipline, parental monitoring, and school risk to early-onset conduct problems in African American boys and girls. *Developmental Psychology, 36,* 835–845.

Kilmann, P. R., Sabalis, R. F., Gearing, M. L., Bukstel, L. H., & Scovern, A. W. (1982). The treatment of sexual paraphilias: A review of the outcome research. *Journal of Sex Research, 18,* 193–252.

Kilpatrick, D. G., Best, C. L., Saunders, B. E., & Veronen, L. J. (1988). Rape in marriage and in dating relationships: How bad is it for mental health? In R. A. Prentky & V. L. Quinsey (Eds.), *Human sexual aggression: Current perspectives.* New York: New York Academy of Sciences.

Kilpatrick, D. G., Whalley, A., & Edmunds, C. (2000). Sexual assault. In A. Seymour, M. Murray, J. Sigmon, M. Hook, C. Edmunds, M. Gaboury, & G. Coleman (Eds.), *2000 National Victim Assistance Academy.* Washington, DC: U.S. Department of Justice.

Kilpatrick, D. G., Whalley, A., & Edmunds, C. (2002). Sexual assault. In A. Seymour, M. Murray,

J. Sigmon, M. Hook, C. Edmunds, M. Gaboury, & G. Coleman (Eds.), *2002 National Victim Assistance Academy*. Washington, DC: U.S. Department of Justice.

Kinports, K. (2002). Sex offenses. In K. L. Hall (Ed.), *The Oxford companion to American law*. New York: Oxford University Press.

Kivivuori, J. (1998). Delinquent phases: The case of temporally intensified shoplifting behaviour. *British Journal of Criminology, 38*, 663–680.

Kivivuori, J. (2007). Crime by proxy: Coercion and altruism in adolescent shoplifting. *British Journal of Criminology, 47*, 817–833.

Klassen, D., & O'Connor, W. (1988). Crime, inpatient admissions, and violence among male mental patients. *International Journal of Law and Psychiatry, 11*, 305–312.

Klassen, D., & O'Connor, W. (1990). Assessing the risk of violence in released mental patients: A cross-validation study. *Psychological Assessment: A Journal of Consulting and Clinical Psychology, 1*, 75–81.

Klaus, P. (1999, March). *Carjackings in the United States, 1992–1996*. Washington, DC: U.S. Department of Justice, Bureau of Justice Statistics.

Klaus, P. (2000, January). *Crimes against persons age 65 or older, 1992–97* (NCJ 176352). Washington, DC: U.S. Department of Justice, Bureau of Justice Statistics.

Klaus, P. (2004, July). *Carjacking, 1993–2002*. Washington, DC: U.S. Department of Justice, National Crime Victimization Survey.

Kleber, H. D. (1988). Epidemic cocaine abuse: America's present, Britain's future. *British Journal of Addiction, 83*, 1359–1371.

Klemke, L. W. (1992). *The sociology of shoplifting: Boosters and snitches today*. Westport, CT: Praeger.

Klinteberg, B., Magnusson, D., & Schalling, D. (1989). Hyperactive behavior in childhood and adult impulsivity: A longitudinal study of male subjects. *Personality and Individual Differences, 10*, 43–50.

Knight, R. A. (1988). A taxonomic analysis of child molesters. In R. A. Prentky & V. L. Quinsey (Eds.), *Human sexual aggression: Current perspectives*. New York: New York Academy of Science.

Knight, R. A. (1989). An assessment of the concurrent validity of a child molester typology. *Journal of Interpersonal Violence, 4*, 131–150.

Knight, R. A. (1999). Validation of a typology for rapists. *Journal of Interpersonal Violence, 14*, 303–330.

Knight, R. A., Carter, D. L., & Prentky, R. A. (1989). A system for the classification of child molesters: Reliability and application. *Journal of Interpersonal Violence, 4*, 3–23.

Knight, R. A., & Prentky, R. A. (1987). The developmental antecedents and adult adaptations of rapist subtypes. *Criminal Justice and Behavior, 14*, 403–426.

Knight, R. A., & Prentky, R. A. (1990). Classifying sexual offenders: The development and corroboration of taxonomic models. In W. L. Marshall, D. R. Laws, & H. E. Barbaree (Eds.), *The handbook of sexual assault: Issues, theories, and treatment of the offender*. New York: Plenum.

Knight, R. A., & Prentky, R. A. (1993). Exploring characteristics for classifying juvenile sex offenders. In H. E. Barbaree, W. L. Marshall, & S. M. Hudson (Eds.), *The juvenile sex offender*. New York: Guilford.

Knight, R. A., Rosenberg, R., & Schneider, B. A. (1985). Classification of sexual offenders: Perspectives, methods, and validation. In A. W. Burgess (Ed.), *Rape and sexual assault*. New York: Garland.

Knight, R. A., Warren, J. I., Reboussin, R., & Soley, B. J. (1998). Predicting rapist type from crime-scene variables. *Criminal Justice and Behavior, 25*, 46–80.

Knopp, F. H., Rosenberg, J., & Stevenson, W. (1986). *Report on nationwide survey of juvenile and adult sex-offender treatment programs and providers*. Syracuse, NY: Safer Society Press.

Kochanska, G., Friesenborg, A. E., Lange, L. A., & Martel, M. M. (2004). Parents' personality and infants' temperament as contributors to their emerging relationship. *Journal of Personality and Social Psychology, 86*, 744–759.

Kocsis, R. N., Cooksey, R. W., & Irwin, H. J. (2002). Psychological profiling of offender characteristics from crime behaviors in serial rape offenses. *International Journal of Offender Therapy and Comparative Criminology, 46*, 144–169.

Koenen, M. A., & Thompson, J. W. (2008). Filicide: Historical review and prevention of child death by parent. *Infant Mental Health Journal, 29,* 61–75.

Kohlberg, L. (1976). Moral stages and moralization: The cognitive development approach. In T. Licona (Ed.), *Moral development and behavior.* New York: Holt, Rinehart, & Winston.

Kohlberg, L. (1977). The child as a moral philosopher. In CRM, *Readings in developmental psychology today.* New York: Random House.

Koivisto, H., & Haapasalo, J. (1996). Childhood maltreatment and adulthood in psychopathy in light of file-based assessments among mental state examinees. *Studies on Crime and Crime Prevention, 5,* 91–104.

Kokko, K., & Pulkkinen, L. (2005). Stability of aggressive behavior from childhood to middle age in women and men. *Aggressive Behavior, 31,* 485–497.

Kolko, D. (Ed). (2002). *Handbook on firesetting in children and youth.* Boston: Academic Press.

Kolko, D. J., & Kazdin, A. E. (1989). The children's firesetting interview with psychiatrically referred and nonreferred children. *Journal of Abnormal Child Psychology, 17,* 609–624.

Kolko, D. J., Kazdin, A. E., & Meyer, E. C. (1985). Aggression and psychopathology in childhood firesetters: Parent and child reports. *Journal of Consulting and Clinical Psychology, 53,* 377–385.

Korman, A. (1974). *The psychology of motivation.* Englewood Cliffs, NJ: Prentice Hall.

Kornhauser, R. R. (1978). *Social sources of delinquency.* Chicago: University of Chicago Press.

Koson, D. F., & Dvoskin, J. (1982). Arson: A diagnostic study. *Bulletin of the American Academy of Psychiatry and the Law, 10,* 39–49.

Koss, M. P., & Dinero, T. E. (1988). Predictors of sexual aggression among a national sample of male college students. In R. A. Prentky and V. L. Quinsey (Eds.), *Human sexual aggression: Current perspectives.* New York: New York Academy of Sciences.

Koss, M. P., Gidycz, C. A., & Wisniewski, N. (1987). The scope of rape: Incidence and prevalence of sexual aggression and victimization in a national sample of higher education students. *Journal of Consulting and Clinical Psychology, 55,* 162–170.

Kosson, D. S. (1998). Divided visual attention to psychopathic and nonpsychopathic offenders. *Personality and Individual Differences, 24,* 373–391.

Kosson, D. S., Smith, S. S., & Newman, J. P. (1990). Evaluating the construct validity of psychopathy in black and white male inmates: Three preliminary studies. *Journal of Abnormal Psychology, 99,* 250–259.

Kosson, D. S., Suchy, Y., Mayer, A. R., & Libby, J. (2002). Facial affect recognition in criminal psychopaths. *Emotion, 2,* 398–411.

Kovacs, M. (1996). Presentation and course of major depressive disorder during childhood and later years of the life span. *Journal of the American Academy of Child and Adolescent Psychiatry, 35,* 705–715.

Kozol, H. L., Boucher, R. L., & Garofalo, P. F. (1972). The diagnosis and treatment of dangerousness. *Crime and Delinquency, 8,* 371–392.

Kraemer, G. W., Lord, W. D., & Heilbrun, K. (2004). Comparing single and serial homicide offenses. *Behavioral Sciences & the Law, 22,* 325–343.

Krahé, B. (2005). Predictors of women's aggressive driving behavior. *Aggressive Behavior, 31,* 537–546.

Krahé, B. & Möller, I. (2004). Playing violent electronic games, hostile attributional style, and aggression-related norms in German adolescents. *Journal of Adolescence, 27,* 53–69.

Kramer, R. C. (1984). Corporate criminality: The development of an idea. In E. Hochstedler (Ed.), *Corporations as criminals.* Beverly Hills, CA: Sage.

Krasnovsky, T., & Lane, R. (1998). Shoplifting: A review of the literature. *Aggression and Violence Behavior, 3,* 219–235.

Kratzer, L., & Hodgins, S. (1999). A typology of offenders: A test of Moffitt's theory among males and females from childhood to age 30. *Criminal Behavior and Mental Health, 9,* 57–73.

Krisberg, B. (1992). Youth crime and its prevention: A research agenda. In I. M. Schwartz (Ed.), *Juvenile justice and public policy.* New York: Lexington Books.

Krisberg, B. (1995). The legacy of juvenile corrections. *Corrections Today, 57,* 122–126.

Krisberg, B., & Howell, J. C. (1998). The impact of the juvenile justice system and prospects for graduated sanctions in a comprehensive strategy. In R. Loeber & D. P. Farrington (Eds.), *Serious & violent juvenile offenders: Risk factors and successful interventions.* Thousand Oaks, CA: Sage.

Krisberg, B., & Schwartz, I. (1983). Rethinking juvenile justice. *Crime and Delinquency, 29,* 333–364.

Krohn, M. D., Akers, R. L., Radosevich, M. J., & Lanza-Kaduce, L. (1982). Norm qualities and adolescent drinking and drug behavior: The effects of norm quality and reference group on using and abusing alcohol and marijuana. *Journal of Drug Issues, 4,* 343–360.

Krueger, R. F., Caspi, A., Moffitt, T. E., White, J., & Stouthamer-Loeber, M. (1996). Delay of gratification, psychopathology, and personality: Is low self-control specific to externalizing problems? *Journal of Personality, 64,* 107–129.

Kruesi, M. J. P. (1979). Cruelty to animals and CSF 5HIAA. *Psychiatry Research, 28,* 115–116.

Kruesi, M. J. P., & Jacobsen, T. (1997). Serotonin and human violence: Do environmental mediators exist? In A. Raine, P. A. Brennan, D. P. Farrington, S. A. Mednick (Eds.), *Biological bases of violence.* New York: Plenum.

Kruesi, M. J. P., Rapoport, J., Hamburger, S., Hibbs, E., Potter, W., Levane, M., et al. (1990). Cerebrospinal fluid monoamine metabolites, aggression, and impulsivity in disruptive behavior disorders of children and adolescents. *Archives of General Psychiatry, 47,* 419–426.

Kruglanski, A. W., & Fishman, S. (2006). The psychology of terrorism: "Syndrome" versus "tool" perspectives. *Terrorism and Political Science, 18,* 193–215.

Kuhnley, E. J., Hendren, R. L., & Quinlan, D. M. (1982). *Journal of the American Academy of Child Psychiatry, 21,* 560–563.

Kulka, R. A., Schlenger, W. E., Fairbank, J. A., Jordan, B. K., Hough, R. L., Marmar, C. R., et al. (1991). Assessment of post-traumatic stress disorder in the community: Prospects and pitfalls from recent studies of Vietnam veterans. *Psychological Assessment: A Journal of Consulting and Clinical Psychology, 4,* 547–560.

Laajasalo, T., & Häkkänen, H. (2006). Excessive violence and psychotic symptomatology among homicide offenders with schizophrenia. *Criminal Behaviour and Mental Health, 16,* 242–253

Labato, A. (2000). Criminal weapon use in Brazil: A psychological analysis. In D. Canter & L. Alison (Eds.), *Profiling property crimes.* Dartmouth, UK: Ashgate.

Lacourse, E., Nagin, D., Tremblay, R. E., Vitaro, F., & Claes, M. (2003). Developmental trajectories of boys' delinquent group membership and facilitation of violent behaviors during adolescence. *Developmental and Psychopathology, 15,* 183–197.

La Fon, D. S. (2002). The psychological autopsy. In B. E. Turvey (Ed.), *Criminal profiling: An introduction to behavioral evidence analysis.* San Diego, CA: Academic Press.

La Fond, J. Q. (2003). Outpatient commitment's next frontier: Sexual predators. *Psychology, Public Policy, and Law, 9,* 159–182.

Lahey, B. B., Loeber, R., Hart, E. L., Frick, P. J., Applegate, B., Zhang, Q., Green, S. M., & Russo, M. (1995). Four-year longitudinal study of conduct disorder in boys: Patterns and predictors of persistence. *Journal of Abnormal Psychology, 104,* 83–93.

Lahey, B. B., & Waldman, I. D. (2003). A developmental propensity model of the origins of conduct problems during childhood and adolescence. In B. B. Lahey, T. E. Moffitt, and A. Caspi (Eds.), *Causes of conduct disorder and juvenile delinquency.* New York: Guilford.

Laird, R. D., Jordan, K., Dodge, K. A., Pettit, G. S., & Bates, J. E. (2001). Peer rejection in childhood, involvement with antisocial peers in early adolescence, and the development of externalizing problems. *Development and Psychopathology, 13,* 337–354.

Laird, R. D., Pettit, G. S., Bates, J. E., & Dodge, K. A. (2003). Parents' monitoring—relevant knowledge and adolescents' delinquent behavior: Evidence of correlated developmental changes and reciprocal influences. *Child Development, 74,* 752–768.

Laird, R. D., Pettit, G. S., Dodge, K. A., & Bates, J. E. (2005). Peer relationship antecedents of delinquent behavior in late adolescence: Is there evidence of demographic group differences in developmental processes. *Development and Psychopathology, 17,* 127–144.

Lamb, H. R., Weinberger, L. E., & Gross, B. H. (2004). Mentally ill persons in the criminal justice system: Some perspectives. *Psychiatric Quarterly, 75*, 107–126.

Lambie, I., McCardle, S., & Coleman, R. (2002). Where there's smoke there's fire: Firesetting behaviour in children and adolescents. *New Zealand Journal of Psychology, 31*, 73–79.

Lamontagne, Y., Boyer, R., Hetu, C., & Lacerte-Lamontagne, C. (2000). Anxiety, significant losses, depression, and irrational beliefs in first-offence shoplifters. *Canadian Journal of Psychiatry, 45*, 63–66.

Lance, D. (1988, April). Product tampering. *FBI Law Enforcement Bulletin*, 20–23.

Landy, D., & Aronson, E. (1969). The influence of the character of the criminal and his victim on the decisions of simulated jurors. *Journal of Experimental Social Psychology, 5*, 141–152.

Langan, P. A., Schmitt, E. L., & Durose, M. R. (2003, November). *Recidivism of sex offenders released from prison in 1994*. Washington, DC: U.S. Department of Justice, Bureau of Justice Statistics.

Lang, S., af Klinteberg, B., & Alm, P.-O. (2002). Adult pschopathy and violent behavior in males with early neglect and abuse. *Acta Pschiatrica Scandinavica, 106*, 93–100.

Lange, J. (1929). *Verbrechen als sochicksal*. Leizig, Germany: Georg Thieme Verlag.

Langer, E. J., & Miransky, J. (1983). Burglary (non) prevention. In E. J. Langer (Ed.), *The psychology of control*. Beverly Hills, CA: Sage.

Langevin, R. (1983). *Sexual strands*. Hillsdale, NJ: Erlbaum.

Långström, N., & Seto, M. C. (2006). Exhibitionistic and voyeuristic behavior in a Swedish national population survey. *Archives of Sexual Behavior, 35*, 427–435.

Lansford, J. E., Deater-Deckard, K., Dodge, K. A., Bates, J. E., & Pettit, G. S. (2004). Ethnic differences in the link between physical discipline and later adolescent externalizing behaviors. *Journal of Child Psychology and Psychiatry, 45*, 801–812.

Lansford, J. E., Dodge, K. A., Pettit, G. S., Bates, J. E., Crozier, I., & Kaplow, J. (2002). Long-term effects of early child physical maltreatment on psychological, behavioral, and academic problems in adolescence: A 12-year prospective study. *Archives of Pediatrics and Adolescent Medicine, 156*, 824–830.

Lanyon, R. I. (1986). Theory and treatment in child molestation. *Journal of Consulting and Clinical Psychology, 54*, 176–182.

Lavin, M. (2008). Voyeurism: Psychopathology and theory. In D. R. Laws & W. T. O'Donohue (Eds.), *Sexual deviance: Theory, assessment, and treatment*. New York: Guilford.

Laws, D. R., & Marshall, W. L. (1990). A conditioning theory of the etiology and maintenance of deviant sexual preference and behavior. In W. L. Marshall, D. R. Laws, & H. E. Barbaree (Eds.), *Handbook of sexual assault*. New York: Plenum.

Leach, E. (1973). Don't say "boo" to a goose. In A. Montagu (Ed.), *Man and aggression* (2nd ed.). London: Oxford University Press.

Leary, M. R., Kowalski, R. M., Smith, L., & Phillips, S. (2003). Teasing, rejection, and violence: Case studies of the school shootings. *Aggressive Behavior, 29*, 202–214.

Lee, J. K. P., Jackson, H. J., Pattison, P., & Ward, T. (2002). Developmental risk factors for sexual offending. *Child Abuse and Neglect, 26*, 73-92.

Legras, A. M. (1932). *Psychese en Criminaliteit bij Twellingen*. Utrecht, Neth.: Keminken ZOON N. V.

Lemon, N. K. D. (1994, December). *Domestic violence & stalking: A comment on the Model Anti-Stalking Code proposed by the National Institute of Justice*. Duluth, MN: Battered Women's Justice Project.

Lerner, M. J. (1980). *The belief in a just world: A fundamental delusion*. New York: Plenum.

Lerner, M. J., & Miller, D. T. (1978). Just world research and the attribution process: Looking back and ahead. *Psychological Bulletin, 85*, 1030–1051.

Lerner, M. J., & Simmons, C. H. (1966). Observer's reaction to the "innocent victim": Compassion or rejection? *Journal of Personality and Social Psychology, 4*, 203–210.

Lesch, K. P., & Merschdorf, U. (2000). Impulsivity, aggression, and serotonin: A molecular psychobiological perspective. *Behavioral Sciences & the Law, 18*, 581–604.

Letkemann, P. (1973). *Crime as work.* Englewood Cliffs, NJ: Prentice Hall.

Letourneau, E. J., & Miner, M. H. (2005). Juvenile sex offenders: A case against the legal and clinical status quo. *Sexual Abuse: A Journal of Research and Treatment, 17,* 293–312.

Levant, R. F. (2002). Psychology responds to terrorism. *Professional Psychology: Research and Practice, 33,* 507–509.

Levant, R. F., Barbanel, L., & DeLeon, P. H. (2004). Psychology's response to terrorism. In F. M. Moghaddam & A. J. Marsella (Eds.), *Understanding terrorism: Psychosocial roots, consequences, and interventions.* Washington, DC: American Psychological Association.

Leve, L. D., & Chamberlain, P. (2004). Female juvenile offenders: Defining an early-onset pathway for delinquency. *Journal of Child and Family Studies, 13,* 439–452.

Levin, B. (1976). Psychological characteristics of firesetters. *Fire Journal, 70,* 36–41.

Levine, S. A., & Jackson, C. J. (2004). Eysenck's theory of crime revisited: Factors or primary scales? *Journal of Legal and Criminological Psychology, 9,* 135–152.

Lewin, T. (2001, January 1). New state laws tackle familiar national issues. *New York Times.* Available: www.nytimes.com/2001/01/01/politics/01laws.html.

Lewis, C. F., Baranoski, M. V., Buchanan, J. A., & Benedek, E. P. (1998). Factors associated with weapon use in maternal filicide. *Journal of Forensic Sciences, 43,* 613–618.

Lewis, C. F., & Bunce, S. C. (2003). Filicidal mothers and the impact of psychosis on filicide. *Journal of the American Academy of Psychiatry and the Law, 31,* 459–470.

Lewis, D. O., Lovely, R., Yeager, C., Ferguson, G., Friedman, M., Sloane, G., et al. (1988). Intrinsic and environmental characteristics of juvenile murderers. *Journal of the American Academy of Child and Adolescent Psychiatry, 27,* 582–587.

Lewis, D. O., Moy, E., Jackson, L. D., Aarsonson, R., Restifo, N., Serra, S., et al. (1985). Biopsychological characteristics of children who later murder: A prospective study. *American Journal of Psychiatry, 142,* 1161–1167.

Li, Q. (2006). Cyberbullying in schools: A research on gender differences. *School Psychology International, 27,* 157–170.

Lidzba, K., & Staudt, M. (2008). Development and (re)organization of language after early brain lesions: Capacities and limitation of early brain plasticity. *Brain & Language, 106,* 165–166.

Lightsey, O. R., Jr. (2006). Resilience, meaning, and well-being. *Counseling Psychologist, 34,* 96–107.

Lilienfeld, S. O., Gershon, J., Duke, M., Marion, L., & de Waal, F. B. M. (1999). A preliminary investigation of the construct of psychopathic personality (psychopathy) in chimpanzees (*Pan troglodytes*). *Journal of Comparative Psychology, 113,* 365–375.

Linedecker, C., & Burt, W. (1990). *Nurses who kill.* New York: Pinnacle Books.

Lingren, H. G. (2001). *Dating violence and acquaintance assault.* Nebraska Cooperative Extension. University of Nebraska: Lincoln

Lipsey, M. W., & Wilson, D. B. (1998). Effective interventions with serious juvenile offenders: A synthesis of research. In R. Loeber & D. P. Farrington (Eds.), *Serious and violent juvenile offenders: Risk factors and successful intervention.* Thousand Oaks, CA: Sage.

Lipton, D. N., McDonel, E. C., & McFall, R. M. (1987). Heterosocial perception in rapists. *Journal of Consulting and Clinical Psychology, 55,* 17–21.

Litwack, T. R., & Schlesinger, L. B. (1999). Dangerous risk assessments: Research, legal, and clinical considerations. In A. K. Hess & I. B. Weiner (Eds.), *The handbook of forensic psychology* (2nd ed.). New York: Wiley.

Liu, J., Raine, A., Venables, P. H., & Mednick, S. A. (2004). Malnutrition at age 3 years and externalizing behavior at ages 8, 11, and 17 years. *American Journal of Psychiatry, 161,* 2005–2013.

Lizotte, A., & Sheppard, D. (2001, July). *Gun use by male juveniles: Research and prevention.* Washington, DC: U.S. Department of Justice, office of Juvenile Justice and Delinquency Prevention.

Lochman, J. G., & Conduct Problems Prevention Research Group. (1995). Screening of child behavior problems for prevention programs at school entry. *Journal of Consulting and Clinical Psychology, 63,* 549–559.

LoCicero, A., & Sinclair, S. J. (2008). Terrorism and terrorist leaders: Insights from developmental and ecological psychology. *Studies in Conflict & Terrorism, 31,* 227–250.

Loeber, R. (1990). Development and risk factors of juvenile antisocial behavior and delinquency. *Clinical Psychology Review, 10,* 1–41.

Loeber, R., Farrington, D. P., & Petechuk, D. (2003, May). Child delinquency: Early intervention and prevention. *Child Delinquency Bulletin Series.* Washington, DC: U.S. Department of Justice, Office of Juvenile Justice and Delinquency Prevention.

Loeber, R., Farrington, D. P., Stouthamer-Loeber, M., & Van Kammen, W. B. (1998). *Antisocial behavior and mental health problems: Explanatory factors in childhood and adolescence.* Mahmah, NJ: Lawrence Erlbaum.

Loeber, R., Lahey, B. B., & Thomas, C. (1991). The diagnostic conundrum of oppositional defiant disorder and conduct disorder. *Journal of Abnormal Psychology, 100,* 379–390.

Loeber, R., Pardini, D., Homish, D. L., Wei, E. H., Crawford, A. M., Farrington, D., et al. (2005). The prediction of violence and homicide in young men. *Journal of Consulting and Clinical Psychology, 73,* 1074–1088.

Loeber, R., & Stouthamer-Loeber, M. (1998). Development of juvenile aggression and violence: Some common misconceptions and controversies. *American Psychologist, 53,* 242–259.

Loehlin, J. C. (1992). *Genes and environment in personality development.* Newbury Park, CA: Sage.

Lombardo, V. S., & Lombardo, E. F. (1991). The link between learning disabilities and juvenile delinquency: Fact or fiction? *International Journal of Biosocial and Medical Research, 13,* 112–117.

Longo, R. F., Bird, S., Stevenson, W. F., & Fiske, J. A. (1995). *1994 nationwide survey of treatment programs and models.* Brandon, VT: Safer Society Program and Press.

Lonsway, K. A., & Fitzgerald, L. F. (1994). Rape myths: In review. *Psychology of Woman Quarterly, 18,* 133–164.

Looman, J., Gauthier, C., & Boer, D. (2001). Replication of the Massachusetts Treatment Center child molester typology in a Canadian sample. *Journal of Interpersonal Violence, 16,* 753–767.

Lorber, M. F. (2004). Psychophysiology of aggression, psychopathy, and conduct problems: A meta-analysis. *Psychological Bulletin, 130,* 531–552.

Lorenz, A. R., & Newman, J. P. (2002). Deficient response modulation and emotion processing in low-anxious caucasian psychopathic offenders: Results from a lexical decision task. *Emotion, 2,* 91–104.

Lorenz, K. (1966). *On aggression.* New York: Harcourt Brace Jovanovich.

Lösel, F., & Schmucker, M. (2005). The effectiveness of treatment for sexual offenders: A comprehensive meta-analysis. *Journal of Experimental Criminology, 1,* 117–146.

Lottes, I. L. (1988). Sexual socialization and attitudes toward rape. In A. W. Burgess (Ed.), *Rape and sexual assault II.* New York: Garland Publishing.

Loukas, A., Zucker, R. A., Fitzgerald, H. F., & Krull, J. L. (2003). Developmental trajectories of descriptive behavior problems among sons of alcoholics: Effects of parent psychopathology, family conflict, and child under control. *Journal of Abnormal Psychology, 112,* 119–131.

Lubenow, G. C. (1983, June 27). When kids kill their parents. *Newsweek,* 35–36.

Lumley, V. A., McNeil, C. B., Herschell, A. D., & Bahl, A. B. (2002). An examination of gender differences among young children with disruptive behavior disorders. *Child Study Journal, 32,* 89–100.

Luxenburg, J. (2000). Prostitution. In N. H. Rafter (Ed.), *Encyclopedia of women and crime.* Phoenix, AZ: Oryx Press.

Lykken, D. T. (1955). *A study of anxiety in the sociopathic personality* (Doctoral dissertation, University of Minnesota). Ann Arbor, MI: University Microfilms, No. 55–944.

Lykken, D. T. (1957). A study of anxiety in the sociopathic personality. *Journal of Abnormal and Social Psychology, 55,* 6–10.

Lykken, D. T. (1978). The psychopath and the lie detector. *Psychophysiology, 15,* 137–142.

Lykken, D. T., & Venables, P. H. (1971). Direct measurement of skin conductance: A proposal for standardization. *Psychophysiology, 8,* 856–872.

Lynam, D. R. (1997). Pursuing the psychopath: Capturing the fledging psychopath in a nomological net. *Journal of Abnormal Psychology, 106,* 425–438.

Lynam, D. R. (1998). Early identification of the fledgling psychopath: Locating the psychopathic child in the current nomenclature. *Journal of Abnormal Psychology, 107,* 566–575.

Lynam, D. R., Caspi, A., Moffitt, T. E., Loeber, R., & Stouthamer-Loeber, M. (2007). Longitudinal evidence that psychopathy scores in early adolescence predict adult psychopathy. *Journal of Abnormal Psychology, 116,* 155–165.

Lynam, D. R., Moffitt, T., & Stouthamer-Loeber, M. (1993). Explaining the relation between IQ and delinquency: Class, race, test motivation, school failure, or self control? *Journal of Abnormal Psychology, 102,* 187–196.

Maccoby, E. E. (1986). Social groupings in childhood. In D. Olweus, J. Block, & M. Radke-Yarrow (Eds.), *Development of antisocial and prosocial behavior: Research, theories, and issues.* New York: Academic Press.

MacCoun, R., Kilmer, B., & Reuter, P. (2003, July). *Research on drugs-crime linkages: The next generation. NIJ Special Report: Toward a drug and crime research agenda for the 21st century.* Washington, DC: National Institute of Justice.

MacDonald, J. M. (1977). *Bombers and firesetters.* Springfield, IL: C C Thomas.

MacKay, S., Henderson, J., Del Bove, G., Marton, P., Warling, D., & Root, C. (2006). Fire interest and antisociality as risk factors in the severity and persistence of juvenile firesetting. *Journal of the American Academy of Child and Adolescent Psychiatry, 45,* 1077–1084.

MacKenzie, D. L., & Hebert, E. (Eds.). (1995). *Correctional boot camps: A tough intermediate sanction.* Washington, DC: National Institute of Justice.

MacKenzie, D. L., Layton, D., Soural, C., Sealock, M., & Bin Kashen, M. (2001). Effects of correctional boot camps on offending. *The Annals of the American Academy of Political and Social Sciences, 78,* 126–143.

Maikovich, A. K. (2005). A new understanding of terrorism using cognitive dissonance principles. *Journal for the Theory of Social Behaviour, 35,* 373–397.

Maker, A. H., Kemmelmeier, M., & Peterson, C. (1998). Long-term psychological consequences in women witnessing parental physical conflict and experiencing abuse in childhood. *Journal of Interpersonal Violence, 13,* 574–589.

Malamuth, N. M. (1981). Rape proclivity among males. *Journal of Social Issues, 37,* 138–157.

Malamuth, N. M. (1989). The attraction to sexual aggression scale: Part one. *Journal of Sex Research, 26,* 26–49.

Malamuth, N. M., & Check, J. V. P. (1981). The effects of violent-sexual movies: A field experiment. *Journal of Research in Personality, 15,* 436–446.

Malamuth, N. M., Check, J. V. P., & Briere, J. (1986). Sexual arousal in response to aggression: Ideological, aggressive, and sexual correlates. *Journal of Personality and Social Psychology, 50,* 330–340.

Malamuth, N. M., Haber, S., & Feshbach, S. (1980). Testing hypothesis regarding rape: Exposure to sexual violence, sex differences, and the "normality" of rape. *Journal of Research in Personality, 14,* 121–137.

Malamuth, N. M., Heim, M., & Feshbach, S. (1980). The sexual responsiveness of college students to rape depictions: Inhibitory and disinhibitory effects. *Journal of Personality and Social Psychology, 38,* 399–408.

Manchak, S. M., Skeem, J. L., Douglas, K. S., & Siranosian, M. (2009). Does gender moderate the predictive utility of the Level of Service Inventory-Revised (LSI-R) for serious violent offenders? *Criminal Justice and Behavior, 36,* 425–442.

Mann, C. R. (1993). Maternal filicide of preschoolers. In A. V. Wilson (Ed.), *Homicide: The victim/offender connection.* Cincinnati, OH: Anderson.

Mann, R. E., Ainsworth, F., Al-Attar, Z., & Davies, M. (2008). Voyeurism: Assessment and treatment. In D. R. Laws & W. T. O'Donohue (Eds.), *Sexual deviance: Theory, assessment, and treatment.* New York: Guilford.

Marleau, J. D., Millaud, F., Auclair, N. (2003). A comparison of parricide and attempted parricide: A study of 39 psychotic adults. *International Journal of Law and Psychiatry, 26,* 269–279.

Marques, J. K., & Nelson, C. (1989). Elements of high-risk situations for sex offenders. In D. R. Laws (Ed.), *Relapse prevention with sex offenders.* New York: Guilford.

Marques, J. K., Wiederanders, M., Day, D. M., Nelson, C., & Van Ommeren, A. (2005). Effects of a relapse prevention program on sexual recidivism: Final results from California's Sex Offender Treatment and Evaluation Project (SOTEP). *Sexual Abuse: A Journal of Research and Treatment, 17,* 79–107.

Marsella, A. J. (2004). Reflections on international terrorism: Issues, concepts, and directions. In F. M. Moghaddam & A. J. Marsella (Eds.), *Understanding terrorism: Psychosocial roots, consequences, and interventions.* Washington, DC: American Psychological Association.

Marsh, L., & Krauss, G. L. (2000). Aggression and violence in patients with epilepsy. *Epilepsy & Behavior, 1,* 160–168.

Marshall, C. E., Benton, D., & Brazier, J. M. (2000). Elder abuse: Using clinical tools to identify clues of mistreatment. *Geriatrics, 55,* 42–53.

Marshall, L. A., & Cooke, D. J. (1999). The childhood experiences of psychopaths: A retrospective study of familial and societal factors. *Journal of Personality Disorders, 13,* 211–225.

Marshall, W. L. (1988). The use of sexually explicit stimuli by rapists, child molesters, and nonoffenders. *Journal of Sex Research, 25,* 267–288.

Marshall, W. L., & Barbaree, H. E. (1988). An outpatient treatment program for child molesters. In R. A. Prentky and V. L. Quinsey (Eds.), *Human sexual aggression: Current perspectives.* New York: New York Academy of Sciences.

Marshall, W. L., Barbaree, H. E., & Fernandez, M. (1995). Some aspects of social competence in sexual offenders. *Sexual Abuse, 7,* 113–127.

Marshall, W. L., & Christie, M. M. (1981). Pedophilia and aggression. *Criminal Justice and Behavior, 8,* 145–158.

Marshall, W. L., & Mazzucco, A. (1995). Self-esteem and parental attachments in child molesters. *Sexual Abuse, 7,* 229–285.

Martin, E. K., Taft, C. T., & Resick, P. A. (2007). A review of marital rape. *Aggression and Violent Behavior, 12,* 329–347.

Maslow, A. H. (1954). *Motivation and personality.* New York: Harper.

Mason, K.L. (2008). Cyberbullying: A preliminary assessment for school personnel. *Psychology in the Schools, 45,* 323–348.

Matheny, A. P. (1989). Children's behavioral inhibition over age and across situations: Genetic similarity for a trait during change. *Journal of Personality, 57,* 215–235.

Mathews, J. K., Hunter, J. A., & Vuz, I. (1997). Juvenile female sexual offenders: Clinical characteristics and treatment issues. *Sexual Abuse: A Journal of Research and Treatment, 9,* 187–199.

Maxwell, C. D., Robinson, A. L., & Post, L. A. (2003). The nature and predictors or sexual victimization and offending among adolescents. *Journal of Youth and Adolescence, 32,* 465–478.

Maxwell, J. C. (2004). *Patterns of club drug use in the U.S., 2004.* Austin, TX: The Center for Excellence in Drug Epidemiology, The Gulf Coast Addition Technology Transfer Center, University of Texas.

Mayes, L. C. (1999). Developing brain and in utero cocaine exposure: Effects on neural ontogeny. *Development and Psychopathology, 11,* 685–714.

Mazerolle, P., Brame, R., Paternoster, R., Piquero, A., & Dean, C. (2000). Onset age, persistence, and offending versatility: Comparisons across gender. *Criminology, 38,* 1143–1172.

Mazulis, A. H., Hyde, J. S., & Clark, R. (2004). Father involvement moderates the effect of maternal depression during a child's infancy on child behavior problems in kindergarten. *Journal of Family Psychology, 18,* 575–588.

McCabe, K. M., Hough, R., Wood, P. A., & Yeh, M. (2001). Childhood and adolescent onset conduct disorder: A test of the developmental taxonomy. *Journal of Abnormal Child Psychology, 29,* 305–316.

McCabe, K. M., Rodgers, C., Yeh, M., & Hough, R. (2004). Gender differences in childhood onset conduct disorder. *Development and Psychopathology, 16,* 179–192.

McCaghy, C. H. (1967). Child molesters: A study of their careers as deviants. In M. Clinard & R. Quinney (Eds.), *Criminal behavior systems: A typology.* New York: Holt, Rinehart & Winston.

McCaghy, C. H. (1980). *Crime in American society.* New York: Macmillan.

McCarthy, J. (2003, November 29). Police link 2 shootings on stretch of highway. *Boston Globe,* pp. 1, 13.

McClearn, G. E., & DeFries, J. C. (1973). *Introduction to behavioral genetics.* San Francisco: W. H. Freeman.

McClelland, G. M., Teplin, L. A., & Abram, K. M. (2004, June). Detection and prevalence of substance abuse among juvenile detainees. *Juvenile Justice Bulletin.* Washington, DC: Office of Justice Programs, Office of Juvenile Justice and Delinquency Prevention.

McClosky, L. A., Figueredo, A. J., & Koss, M. P. (1995). The effects of systemic family violence on children's mental health. *Child Development, 66,* 1239–1261.

McCord, D. (1987). Syndromes, profiles and other mental exotica: A new approach to the admissibility of nontraditional psychological evidence in criminal cases. *Oregon Law Review, 66,* 19–108.

McCord, W., McCord, J., & Zola, I. K. (1959). *Origins of crime: A new evaluation of the Cambridge-Somerville Youth Study.* New York: Columbia University Press.

McElroy, S. L., Pope, H. G., Hudson, J. I., Keck, P. E., & White, K. L. (1991). Kleptomania: A report of 20 cases. *American Journal of Psychiatry, 148,* 652–657.

McGinley, H., & Paswark, R. A. (1989). National survey of the frequency and success of the insanity plea and alternate pleas. *Journal of Psychiatry and Law, 17,* 205–221.

McKee, G. R., & Shea, S. J. (1998). Maternal filicide: A cross-national comparison. *Journal of Clinical Psychology, 54,* 679–687.

McKenzie, C. (1995). A study of serial murder. *International Journal of Offender Therapy and Comparative Criminology, 39,* 3–10.

McKnight, L. R., & Loper, A. B. (2002). The effect of risk and resilience factors on the prediction of delinquency in adolescent girls. *School Psychology International, 23,* 186–198.

McShane, D. A., & Plas, J. M. (1984a). Response to a critique of the McShane & Plas review of American Indian performance on the Wechsler Intelligence Scales. *School Psychology Review, 13,* 83–88.

McShane, D. A., & Plas, J. M. (1984b). The cognitive functioning of American Indian children: Moving from the WISC to the WISC-R. *School Psychology Review, 13,* 61–73.

Meadows, S. (2006, July 17). Murder on their minds. *Newsweek,* pp. 28–29.

Mechoulam, R. (1970). Marihuana chemistry. *Science, 168,* 1159–1166.

Mednick, S. A., Gabrielli, W. F., & Hutchings, B. (1984). Genetic influences in criminal convictions: Evidence from an adoption cohort. *Science, 234,* 891–894.

Mednick, S. A., Gabrielli, W. F., & Hutchings, B. (1987). Genetic factors in the etiology of criminal behavior. In S. A. Mednick, T. E. Moffitt, & S. A. Stack (Eds.), *The causes of crime: New biological approaches.* Cambridge, UK: Cambridge University Press.

Megargee, E. I. (1982). Psychological determinants and correlates of criminal violence. In M. E. Wolfgang & N. A. Weinder (Eds.), *Criminal violence.* Beverly Hills, CA: Sage.

Meloy, J. R. (1998). The psychology of stalking. In J. R. Meloy (Ed.), *The psychology of stalking: Clinical and forensic perspectives.* San Diego, CA: Academic Press.

Melton, G. B., Petrila, J., Poythress, N. G., & Slobogin, C. (1997). *Psychological evaluations for the courts: A handbook for mental health professionals and lawyers* (2nd ed.). New York: Guilford.

Mercy, J., & Salzman, L. (1989). Fatal violence among spouses in the United States, 1986–1987. *American Journal of Public Health, 79,* 595–599.

Merry, S., & Hansent, L. (2000). Intruders, pilferers, raiders, and invaders: The interpersonal dimension of burglary. In D. Canter & L. Alison (Eds.), *Profiling property crimes.* Dartmouth, UK: Ashgate.

Merton, r. K. (1957). *Social theory and social structure* (Revised edition). New York: The Free Press.

Merz-Perez, L., Heide, K. M., & Silverman, I. J. (2001). Childhood cruelty to animals and subsequent violence against humans. *International Journal of Offender Therapy and Comparative Criminology, 45,* 556–573.

Messner, S., & Rosenfeld, R. (1994). *Crime and the American dream.* Belmont, CA: Wadsworth.

Meyer, C. L., & Oberman, M. (2001). *Mothers who kill their children: Understanding the acts of moms from Susan Smith to the "prom mom."* New York: University Press.

Meyer, T. P. (1972). The effects of sexually arousing and violent films on aggressive behavior. *Journal of Sex Research, 8,* 324–333.

Miczek, K. A., DeBold, J. F., Haney, M., Tidey, J., Vivian, J., & Weerts, E. M. (1994). Alcohol, drugs of abuse, aggression, and violence. In A. J. Reiss & J. A. Roth (Eds.), *Understanding and preventing violence. Vol. 3. Social influences.* Washington, DC: National Academy Press.

Middlebrook, P. M. (1974). *Social psychology and modern life.* New York: Knopf.

Milgram, S. (1963). Behavioral study of obedience. *Journal of Abnormal and Social Psychology, 67,* 371–378.

Milgram, S. (1974). *Obedience to authority.* New York: Harper & Row.

Milgram, S. (1977). *The individual in a social world.* Reading, MA: Addison-Wesley.

Miller, J. L. (1991). Prostitution in contemporary American society. In E. Graverholtz & M. A. Koralewski (Eds.), *Sexual coercion: A sourcebook on its nature, causes, and prevention.* Lexington, MA: Lexington Books.

Miller, L. (2006). The terrorist mind I: A psychological and political analysis. *International Journal of Offender Therapy and Comparative Criminology, 50,* 121–138.

Miller, M., Hennenway, D., & Solop, D. (2002). Road rage in Arizona: Armed and dangerous. *Accident Analysis and Prevention, 34,* 807–814.

Miller, N., Pedersen, W. C., Earleywine, M., & Pollack, V. E. (2003). A theoretical model of triggered displaced aggression. *Personality and Social Psychology Review, 7,* 75–97.

Miller, P. A., & Eisenberg, N. (1988). The relation of empathy to aggressive and externalizing antisocial behavior. *Psychological Bulletin, 103,* 324–344.

Miller, R. D. (2003). Hospitalization of criminal defendants for evaluation of competence to stand trial or for restoration of competence: Clinical and legal issues. *Behavioral Sciences & the Law, 21,* 369–391.

Miller-Johnson, S., Coie, J. D., Maumary-Gremaud, A., Bierman, K., & the Conduct Problems Prevention Research Group. (2002). Peer rejection and aggression and early starter models of conduct disorder. *Journal of Abnormal Child Psychology, 30,* 217–230.

Miner, M. H., Day, D. M., & Nafpaktitis, M. K. (1989). Assessment of coping skills: Development of situational competency test. In D. R. Laws (Ed.), *Relapse prevention with sex offenders.* New York: Guilford.

Miron, M. S., & Goldstein. A. P. (1978). *Hostage.* Kalamazoo, MI: Behaviordelia.

Mischel, W. (1976). *Introduction to personality* (2nd ed.). New York: Holt, Rinehart & Winston.

Mizell, L. (1995). *Aggressive driving.* Washington, DC: AAA Foundation for Traffic Safety.

Moffitt, T. E. (1990a). The neuropsychology of juvenile delinquency: A critical review. In M. Tonry & N. Morris (Eds.), *Crime and justice: A review of research.* Chicago: University of Chicago Press.

Moffitt, T. E. (1990b). Juvenile delinquency and attention deficit disorder: Boys' developmental trajectories from age 13 to age 15. *Child Development, 61,* 893–910.

Moffitt, T. E. (1993a). Adolescence-limited and life-course-persistent antisocial behavior: A developmental taxonomy. *Psychological Review, 100,* 674–701.

Moffitt, T. E. (1993b). The neuropsychology of conduct disorder. *Development and Psychopathology, 5,* 135–151.

Moffitt, T. E. (2003). Life-course-persistent and adolescent-limited antisocial behavior: A 10-year research review and research agenda. In B. B. Lahey, T. E. Moffitt, and A. Caspi (Eds.), *Causes of conduct disorder and juvenile delinquency.* New York: Guilford.

Moffitt, T. E. (2005). The new look of behavioral genetics in developmental psychopathology: Gene-environment interplay in antisocial behaviors. *Psychological Bulletin, 131*, 533–534.

Moffitt, T. E. (2006). Life-course-persistent versus adolescence-limited antisocial behavior. In D. Cicchetti & D. J. Cohen (Eds.), *Developmental psychopathology. Vol. 3: Risk, disorder, and adaptation* (2nd ed.). Hoboken, NJ: Wiley.

Moffitt, T. E., & Caspi, A. (2001). Childhood predictors differentiate life-course persistent and adolescence-limited antisocial pathways among males and females. *Development and Psychopathology, 13*, 355–375.

Moffitt, T. E., Caspi, A., Dickson, N., Silva, P., & Stanton, W. (1996). Childhood-onset versus adolescent-onset antisocial conduct problems in males: Natural history from age 3 to age 18. *Development and Psychopathology, 8*, 399–424.

Moffitt, T. E., Caspi, A., Fawcett, P., Brammer, G. L., Raleigh, M., Yuwiler, A., et al. (1997). Whole blood serotonin and family background relate to male violence. In A. Raine, P. A. Brennan, D. P. Farrington, S. A. Mednick (Eds.), *Biological bases of violence.* New York: Plenum.

Moffitt, T. E., Caspi, A., Harrington, H., & Milne, B. J. (2002). Males on the life-course-persistent and adolescence-limited antisocial pathways: Follow-up at age 26 years. *Development and Psychopathology, 14*, 179–207.

Moffitt, T. E., Caspi, A., Rutter, M., & Silva, P. A. (2001). *Sex differences in antisocial behaviour: Conduct disorder delinquency, and violence in the Dunedin Longitudinal Study.* New York: Cambridge University Press.

Moffitt, T. E., Lynam, D. R., & Silva, P. A. (1994). Neuropsychological tests predicting persistent male delinquency. *Criminology, 33*, 111–139.

Moffitt, T. E., & Silva, P. A. (1988). Self-reported delinquency, neuropsychological deficit, and history of attention deficit disorder. *Journal of Abnormal Child Psychology, 16*, 553–569.

Moghaddam, F. M., & Marsella, A. J. (2004a). Preface. In F. M. Moghaddam & A. J. Marsella (Eds.), *Understanding terrorism: Psychosocial roots, consequences, and interventions.* Washington, DC: American Psychological Association.

Moghaddam, F. M., & Marsella, A. J. (2004b). Introduction. In F. M. Moghaddam & A. J. Marsella (Eds.), *Understanding terrorism: Psychosocial roots, consequences, and interventions.* Washington, DC: American Psychological Association.

Monahan, J. (1996). Violence prediction: The past twenty years and the next twenty years. *Criminal Justice and Behavior, 23*, 107–120.

Mohr, J. W., Turner, R. E., & Jerry, N. B. (1964). *Pedophilia and exhibitionism.* Toronto, ON: University of Toronto Press.

Moll, K. D. (1974). *Arson, vandalism and violence: Law enforcement problems affecting fire departments (LEAA).* Washington, DC: USGPO.

Monahan, J. (1976). The prevention of crime. In J. Monahan (Ed.), *Community mental health and the criminal justice system.* New York: Pergamon Press.

Monahan, J. (1981). *Predicting violent behavior.* Beverly Hills, CA: Sage.

Monahan, J. (1984). The prediction of violent behavior: Toward a second generation of theory and policy. *American Journal of Psychiatry, 141*, 10–15.

Monahan, J. (1992). Mental disorder and violent behavior: Perceptions and evidence. *American Psychologist, 47*, 511–521.

Monahan, J., & Geis, G. (1976). Controlling "dangerous" people. *Annals of the American Academy of Political and Social Science, 423*, 142–151.

Monahan, J., Steadman, H. J., Silver, E., Appelbaum, P. S., Robbins, P. C., Mulvey, E. P., et al. (2001). *Rethinking risk assessment: The MacArthur study of mental disorder and violence.* New York: Oxford University Press.

Monahan, J., & Walker, L. (1990). *Social science and law: Cases and materials* (2nd ed.). Westbury, NY: Foundation Press.

Monahan, J., & Walker, L. (1994). *Social science and law: Cases and materials* (3rd ed.). Waterbury, NY: Foundation Press.

Monahan, T. P. (1957). Family status and the delinquent child: A reappraisal and some new findings. *Social Forces, 35*, 250–258.

Montagu, A. (1973). *Man and aggression* (2nd ed.). London: Oxford University Press.

Montagu, A. (1976). *The nature of human aggression.* New York: Oxford University Press.

Moore, R. H. (1984). Shoplifting in middle America: Patterns and motivational correlates. *International Journal of Offender Therapy and Comparative Criminology, 28,* 53–64.

Morawetz, T. H. (2002). Homicide. In K. L. Hall (Ed.), *The Oxford companion to American law.* New York: Oxford University Press.

Moreland, J. (2000). Toxicity of drug abuse—amphetamine designer drugs (ecstasy): Mental effects and consequences of a single dose. *Tox Letters,* 147–152.

Morgan, A. B., & Lilienfeld, S. O. (2000). A meta-analytic review of the relation between antisocial behavior and neuropsychological measures of executive function. *Clinical Psychology Review, 20,* 113–146.

Morgan, J. P., & Zimmer, L. (1997). The social pharmacology of smokeable cocaine: Not all it's cracked up to be. In C. Reinarman & H. G. Levine (Eds.), *Crack in America: Demon drugs and social justice.* Berkeley, CA: University of California Press.

Morin, J. W., & Levenson, J. S. (2008). Exhibitionism: Assessment and treatment. In D. R. Laws & W. T. O'Donohue (Eds.), *Sexual deviance: Theory, assessment, and treatment.* New York: Guilford.

Morris, D. (1967). *The naked ape.* New York: McGraw-Hill.

Morris, N. (1982). *Madness and the criminal law.* Chicago: University of Chicago Press.

Morris, N., & Miller, M. (1985). Prediction of dangerousness. In M. Tonry & N. Morris (Eds.), *Crime and justice: An annual review of research.* Chicago: University of Chicago Press.

Morrissey, T. W. (2009). Multiple child-care arrangements and young children's behavioral outcomes. *Child Development, 80,* 59–76.

Morse, S. J. (1978). Behavior, morals, and science: An analysis of mental health law. *Southern California Law Review, 51,* 527–654.

Morse, S. J. (1985). Excusing the crazy: The insanity defense reconsidered. *Southern California Law Review, 58,* 777–836.

Morse, S. J. (1986). Why amnesia and the law is not a useful topic. *Behavioral Sciences & the Law, 4,* 99–102.

Mott, J. (1986). Opioid use and burglary. *British Journal of Addiction, 81,* 671–677.

Mounts, N. S. (2002). Parental management of adolescent peer relationships in context: The role of parenting style. *Journal of Family Psychology, 16,* 58–69.

Moyer, K. E. (1976). *The psychobiology of aggression.* New York: Harper & Row.

Mueller, C. W. (1983). Environmental stressors and aggressive behavior. In R. G. Geen & E. I. Donnerstein (Eds.), *Aggression: Theoretical and empirical reviews* (Vol. 2). New York: Academic Press.

Mulder, R. T., Wells, J. E., Joyce, P. R., & Bushnell, J. A. (1994). Antisocial women. *Journal of Personality Disorders, 8,* 279–287.

Müller, J. L., Sommer, M., Wagner, V., Lange, K., Taschler, H., Röder, C. H. et al. (2003). Abnormalities in emotion processing within cortical and subcortical regions in criminal psychopaths: Evidence from a functional magnetic resonance imaging study using pictures with emotional content. *Biological Psychiatry, 54,* 152–162.

Mulvey, E. P., Arthur, M. W., & Reppucci, N. D. (1993). The prevention and treatment of juvenile delinquency: A review of the research. *Clinical Psychology Review, 13,* 133–167.

Mumley, D. L., Tillbrook, C. E., & Grisso, T. (2003). Five year research update (1996–2000): Evaluations for competence to stand trial (adjudicative competence). *Behavioral Sciences & the Law, 21,* 329–350.

Mumola, C. J. (1999). *Substance abuse and treatment, state and federal prisoners.* Washington, DC: Bureau of Justice Statistics.

Murphy, G. H., & Clare, C. H. (1996). Analysis of motivation in people with mild learning disabilities (mental handicap) who set fires. *Psychology, Crime, & Law, 2,* 153–164.

Murphy, W. D., Coleman, E. M., & Haynes, M. R. (1986). Factors related to coercive sexual behavior with a nonclinical sample of males. *Violence and Victims, 1,* 255–278.

Murphy, W. D., & Page, I. J. (2008). Exhibitionism: Psychopathology and theory. In D. R. Laws & W. T. O'Donohue (Eds.), *Sexual deviance: Theory, assessment, and treatment.* New York: Guilford.

Murray, J. B. (1997). Munchausen syndrome/Munchausen syndrome by proxy. *The Journal of Psychology, 131,* 343–350.

Murray, J. P. (2008). Media violence: The effects are both real and strong. *American Behavioral Scientist, 51,* 1212–1230.

Murrie, D. C., Boccaccini, M. T., Zapf, P. A., Warren, J. I., & Henderson, C. E. (2008). Clinician variations in findings of competence to stand trial. *Psychology, Public Policy, and Law,14,* 177–193.

Murrie, D. C., & Cornell, D. G., Kaplan, S., McConville, D., & Levy-Elkon, A. (2004). Psychopathy scores and violence among juvenile offenders: A multi-measure study. *Behavioral Sciences & the Law, 22,* 49–67.

Myers, D. G. (1996). *Social psychology* (5th ed.). New York: McGraw-Hill.

Myers, W. C. (1992). What treatments do we have for children and adolescents who have killed. *Bulletin of the American Academy of Psychiatry and Law, 20,* 47–58.

Myers, W. C. (1994). Sexual homicide by adolescents. *Journal of the American Academy of Child and Adolescent Psychiatry, 33,* 962–969.

Myers, W. C. (2004). Serial murder by children and adolescents. *Behavioral Sciences & the Law, 22,* 357–374.

Myers, W. C., & Mutch, P. J. (1992). Language disorders in disruptive behaviour disordered homicidal youth. *Journal of Forensic Sciences, 37,* 919–922.

Myers, W. C., & Scott, K. (1998). Psychotic and conduct disorder symptoms in juvenile murderers. *Homicide Studies, 2,* 160–175.

Myers, W. C., Scott, K., Burgess, A. W., & Burgess, A. G. (1995). Psychopathology, biopsychosocial factors, crime characteristics, and classification of 25 homicidal youths. *Journal of the American Academy of Child and Adolescent Psychiatry, 34,* 1483–1489.

Nachshon, I. (1983). Hemisphere dysfunction in psychopathy and behavior disorders. In M. Myslobodsky (Ed.), *Hemisyndromes: Psychobiology, neurology, psychiatry.* New York: Academic Press.

Nachshon, I., & Denno, D. (1987). Violent behavior and cerebral hemisphere function. In S. A. Mednick, T. E. Moffitt, & S. A. Stack (Eds.), *The causes of crime: New biological approaches.* Cambridge, UK: Cambridge University Press.

Nagin, D. S., & Land, K. C. (1993). Age, criminal careers, and population heterogeneity: Specification and estimation of a nonparametric mixed Poisson model. *Criminology, 31,* 163–189.

Narag, R. E., Pizarro, J., & Gibbs, C. (2009). Lead exposure and its implications for criminological theory. *Criminal Justice and Behavior, 36,* 954–973.

Nash, J. R. (1975). *Bloodletters and badmen: Book 3.* New York: Warner Books.

National Cable Television Association. (1998). *National Television Violence Study* (Vol. 3). Thousand Oaks, CA: Sage.

National Center for Education Statistics. (2005). *Executive summary: Indicators of school crime and safety, 2003.*Available: www.nces.ed.gov/pubs2004/crime03.

National Center for Juvenile Justice. (2003, July). *Juvenile court statistics 1999.* Washington, DC: U.S. Department of Justice, Office of Juvenile Justice and Delinquency Prevention.

National Center for Victims of Crime (NCVC). (2000). *Cyberstalking.* Available: www.ncvc/special/ cyber_stk.htm.

National Center on Child Abuse and Neglect. (2000). *Study findings: National study of the incidence and severity of child abuse and neglect.* Washington, DC: U.S. Department of Health and Human Services.

National Center on Elder Abuse. (1999). *Types of elder abuse in domestic settings.* Washington, DC: Author.

National Commission on Marihuana and Drug Abuse. (1972). *Marihuana: A signal of misunderstanding.* (Appendix, Vol. 1). Washington, DC: USGPO.

National Commission on Marihuana and Drug Abuse. (1973). *Drug use in America: Problem in perspective* (2nd report). Washington, DC: USGPO.

National Drug Control Policy. (2001). *2001 Annual Report.* Washington, DC: U.S. Office of National Drug Control Policy.

National Drug Intelligence Center. (2001, January). *OxyContin diversion and abuse.* Washington, DC: Author.

National Drug Intelligence Center. (2006, June 5). *Fentanyl: Situation Report.* Washington, DC: U.S. Department of Justice.

National Highway Traffic Safety Administration. (2005, March). *Alcohol involvement in fatal motor vehicle traffic crashes, 2003.* Springfield, VA: Author.

National Information Support and Referral Service. (1998). Available: www.ojp.usdoij.gov/nisrs.

National Institute of Health. (1999, June). *NIDA news release: Long-term brain injury from use of "ecstasy."* Rockville, MD: National Institute of Drug Abuse. Available: www.nida.nih.gov/ MedAdv/99/NR-614b.html.

National Institute on Alcohol Abuse and Alcoholism. (1990). *Alcohol and health: Neuroscience.* Rockville, MD: USGPO.

National Institute on Alcohol Abuse and Alcoholism. (1997, October). Alcohol, violence, and aggression. *Alcohol Alert.* Rockville, MD: USGPO.

National Institute on Drug Abuse. (1978). Drug abuse and crime. In L. D. Savitz & N. Johnson (Eds.), *Crime in society.* New York: Wiley.

National Institute on Drug Abuse. (1999, May). *Cocaine: Abuse and addiction.* Rockville, MD: USGPO. Available: www.nida.nih.gov/researchreports/cocaine/cocaine.html.

National Institute on Drug Abuse. (2000, June). *Epidemiologic trends in drug abuse.* Rockville, MD: USGPO. Available: www.nida.gov/CEWG/AdvancedRep/6_20ADV/0600adv.html.

National Institute on Drug Abuse. (2002). *Methamphetamine: Abuse and addiction.* Rockville, MD: U.S. Department of Health and Human Services.

National Institute on Drug Abuse. (2004, November). *Cocaine: Abuse and addiction.* Rockville, MD: U.S. Department of Health and Human Services.

National Institute on Drug Abuse. (2005). *Hallucinogens and dissociative drugs.* Rockville, MD: U.S. Department of Health and Human Services.

National Institute on Drug Abuse and University of Michigan. (2005, December). *Monitoring the Future National Survey results on drug use, 1975–2003. Volume II: College students & Adults ages 19–45.* Washington, DC: National Institute on Drug Abuse.

Naudts, K., & Hodgins, S. (2005, December 29). Neurobiological correlates of violent behavior among persons with schizophrenia. *Schizophrenia Bulletin,* 1–11.

Nee, C., & Taylor, M. (1988). Residential burglary in the Republic of Ireland: A situational perspective. *Howard Journal, 27,* 105–116.

Needleman, H. L., McFarland, C., Ness, R. B., Fienberg, S. E., & Tobin, M. J. (2002). Bone lead levels in adjudicated delinquents: A case control study. *Neurotoxicology and Teratology, 24,* 711–717.

Neighbors, C., Vietor, N. A., & Knee, C. R. (2002). A motivational model of driving anger and aggression. *Personality and Social Psychology Bulletin, 28,* 324–335.

Neisser, U., Boodoo, G., Bouchard, T., Boykin, A. W., Brody, N., Ceci, S. J., **et al.** (1996). Intelligence: Knowns and unknowns. *American Psychologist, 51,* 77–101.

Nelson, C. A., & Bloom, F. E. (1997). Child development and neuroscience. *Child Development, 68,* 970–987.

Nelson, D. R., Hammen, C., Brennan, P. A., & Ullman, J. B. (2003). The impact of maternal depression in adolescent adjustment: The role of expressed emotion. *Journal of Consulting and Clinical Psychology, 71,* 935–944.

Nelson, D. W. (2003). *On adolescent crime: Trend to end fad justice.* Baltimore, MD: Annie E. Casey Foundation Newsletter.

Nelson, S., & Amir, M. (1975). The hitchhike victim of rape: A research report. In I. Drapkin & E. Viano (Eds.), *Victimology: A new focus* (Vol. 5). Lexington, MA: Lexington Books.

Nettler, G. (1984). *Explaining crime* (3rd ed.). New York: McGraw-Hill.

Neugebauer, R., Hoek, H. W., & Susser, E. (1999). Prenatal exposure to wartime famine and development of antisocial personality disorder in early adulthood. *Journal of the American Medical Association, 4,* 479–481.

Neuman, J. H., & Baron, R. A. (1998). Workplace violence and workplace aggression: Evidence concerning specific forms, potential causes, and preferred targets. *Journal of Management, 24,* 391–419.

Neumann, C. S., Hare, R. D., & Newman, J. P. (2007). The superordinate nature of Psychopathy Checklist-Revised. *Journal of Personality Disorders, 21,* 102–107.

Neumann, C. S., Kosson, D. S., Forth, A. E., & Hare, R. D. (2006). Factor structure of the Hare Psychopathy Checklist: Youth Version (PCL:YV) in incarcerated adolescents. *Psychological Assessment, 18,* 142–154.

Newcomb, A. F., Bukowksi, W. M., & Pattee, L. (1993). Children's peer relations: A meta-analytic review of popular, rejected, neglected, controversial and average sociometric status. *Psychological Bulletin, 113,* 99–128.

Newman, J. P. (1987). Reaction to punishment in extroverts and psychopaths: Implications for the impulsive behavior of disinhibited individuals. *Journal of Research in Personality, 21,* 464–480.

Newman, J. P., & Kosson, D. S. (1986). Passive avoidance learning in psychopathic and nonpsychopathic offenders. *Journal of Abnormal Psychology, 95,* 252–256.

Newman, J. P., Patterson, C. M., Howland, E. W., & Nichols, S. L. (1990). Passive avoidance in psychopaths: The effects of reward. *Personality and Individual Differences, 11,* 1101–1114.

Newman, J. P., Patterson, C. M., & Kosson, D. S. (1987). Response preservation in psychopaths. *Journal of Abnormal Psychology, 96,* 145–148.

Newman, J. P., Schmitt, W. A., & Voss, W. D. (1997). The impact of motivationally neutral cues on psychopathic individuals: Assessing the generality of the response modulation hypothesis. *Journal of Abnormal Psychology, 106,* 563–575.

Nicholls, T. L., Ogloff, J. R. P., Brink, J., & Spidel, A. (2005). Psychopathy in women: A review of its clinical usefulness for assessing risk for aggression and criminality. *Behavioral Sciences & the Law, 23,* 779–802.

Nicholls, T. L., & Petrila, J. (2005). Gender and psychopathy: An overview of important issues and introduction to the special issue. *Behavioral Sciences & the Law, 23,* 729–741.

Nicholson, R. A., & Kugler, K. E. (1991). Competent and incompetent criminal defendants: A quantitative review of comparative research. *Psychological Bulletin, 109,* 355–370.

Nicholson, R. A., & Norwood, S. (2000). The quality of forensic psychological assessments, reports, and testimony: Acknowledging the gap between promise and practice. *Law and Human Behavior, 24,* 9–44.

Nietzel, M. T. (1979). *Crime and its modification: A social learning perspective.* New York: Pergamon.

Nigg, J. T., & Huang-Pollock, C. L. (2003). An early-onset model of the role of executive functions and intelligence in conduct disorder/delinquency. In B. B. Lahey, T. E. Moffitt, and A. Caspi (Eds.), *Causes of conduct disorder and juvenile delinquency.* New York: Guilford.

Nisbett, R. E. (2005). Heredity, environment, and race differences in IQ. *Psychology, Public Policy, and Law, 11,* 302–310.

Noesner, G. W., & Dolan, J. T. (1992, August). First responder negotiation training. *FBI LawEnforcement Bulletin,* 1–4.

Nordström, A., Dahlgren, L., & Kullgren, G. (2006). Victim relations and factors triggering homicides committed by offenders with schizophrenia. *Journal of Forensic Psychiatry & Psychology, 17,* 192–203.

Obeidallah, D. A., & Earls, F. J. (1999). *Adolescent girls: The role of depression in the development of delinquency.* Washington, DC: National Institute of Justice.

Odgers, C. L., Moffitt, T. E., Broadbent, J. M., Dickson, N., Hancox, R. J., Harrington, H., et al. (2008). Female and male antisocial trajectories: From childhood origins to adult outcomes. *Development and Psychopathology, 20,* 673–716.

Odgers, C. L., Reppucci, N. D., & Moretti, M. M. (2005). Nipping psychopathy in the bud: An examination of the convergent, predictive, and theoretical utility of the PCL-YV among adolescent girls. *Behavioral Sciences & the Law, 23,* 743–763.

O'Donnell, J., Hawkins, J. D., & Abbott, R. D. (1995). Predicting serious delinquency and substance abuse among aggressive boys. *Journal of Consulting and Clinical Psychology, 63,* 529–537.

Office of Applied Studies. (2004). *Drug abuse warning network, 2003.* Rockville, MD: U.S. Department of Health and Human Services.

Office of National Drug Control Policy. (1999a, November). *Gamma hydroxybutyrate (GHB).* Washington, DC: Executive Office of the President. Available: www.whitehousedrugpolicy.gov.

Office of National Drug Control Policy. (1999b, May). *Methamphetamine.* Washington, DC: Executive Office of the President. Available: www.whitehouse-drugpolicy.gov.

Office of National Drug Control Policy. (1999c, April). *Drug data summary.* Available: www.whitehouse-drugpolicy.gov.

Office of National Drug Control Policy. (2000, June). *MDMA.* Washington, DC: Executive Office of the President. Available: www.whitehouse drugpolicy.gov.

Office of National Drug Control Policy. (2003a, February). *Rohypnol.* Washington, DC: Executive Office of the President. Available: www.whitehouse-drugpolicy.gov.

Office of National Drug Control Policy. (2003b, November). *Methamphetamine.* Washington, DC: Author.

Office of National Drug Control Policy. (2003d, November). *Drug data summary.* Washington, DC: Author.

Office of National Drug Control Policy. (2003e, October). *Marijuana.* Washington, DC: Author.

Office of National Drug Control Policy. (2005, November). *Marijuana.* Washington, DC: Author.

Office of National Drug Control Policy. (2006a, July). *Marijuana.* Washington, DC: Author.

Office of National Drug Control Policy. (2006b, July). *Methamphetamine.* Washington, DC: Author.

Office of National Drug Control Policy. (2006c, June). *Cocaine.* Washington, DC: Author.

Office of National Drug Control Policy. (2006d, June). *MDMA.* Washington, DC: Author.

Office of National Drug Control Policy. (2006e, May). *Heroin.* Washington, DC: Author.

Office of National Drug Control Policy. (2006f, July). *OxyContin.* Washington, DC: Author.

Office of National Drug Control Policy. (2006g, July). *Club drugs.* Washington, DC: Author.

Offord, D. R., Boyle, M. C., & Racine, Y. A. (1991). The epidemiology of antisocial behavior in childhood and adolescence. In D. J. Pepler & K. H. Rubin (Eds.), *The development and treatment of childhood aggression.* Hillsdale, NJ: Erlbaum.

Offord, D. R., Chmura Kraemeer, H., Kazdin, A. E., Jensen, P. S., & Harrington, R. (1998). Lowering the burden of suffering from child psychiatric disorder: Trade-offs among clinical, targeted, and universal interventions. *Journal of the American Academy of Child & Adolescent Psychiatry, 37,* 686–694.

Ogloff, J. R., & Wong, S. (1990) Electrodermal and cardiovascular evidence of a coping response in psychopaths. *Criminal Justice and Behavior, 17,* 231–245.

Ohlin, L. E., & Tonry, M. (1989). Family violence in perspective. In L. Ohlin & M. Tonry (Eds.), *Family violence* (Vol. 11). Chicago: University of Chicago Press.

Oliver, B. R., & Plomin, R. (2007). Twins' early development study (TEDS): A multivariate, longitudinal genetic investigation of language, cognition and behavior problems from childhood through adolescence. *Twin Research and Human Genetics, 10,* 96–105.

Olson, C. K. (2004). Media violence research and youth violence data: Why do they conflict? *Academic Psychiatry, 28,* 144–150.

Olson, S. L., Sameroff, A. J., Kerr, D. C. R., Lopez, N. L., & Wellman, H. M. (2005). Developmental foundations of externalizing problems in young children: The role of effortful control. *Development and Psychopathology, 17,* 25–45.

Olweus, D. (1997). Bully/victim problems in school: Facts and intervention. *European Journal of Psychology of Education, 12,* 495–510.

Ondrovik, J., & Hamilton, D. (1991). Credibility of victims diagnosed as multiple personality: A case study. *American Journal of Forensic Psychology, 9,* 13–17.

O'Neill, M. L., Lidz, V., & Heilbrun, K. (2003). Adolescents with psychopathic characteristics in a substance abusing cohort: Treatment process and outcomes. *Law and Human Behavior, 27,* 299–313.

Orne, M. T., Dinges, D. F., & Orne, E. C. (1984). On the differential diagnosis of multiple personality in the forensic context. *International Journal of Clinical and Experimental Hypnosis, 32,* 118–169.

Orris, J. B. (1969). Visual monitoring performance in three subgroups of male delinquents. *Journal of Abnormal Psychology, 74,* 227–229.

Osgood, W. D., O'Malley, P. M., Bachman, G. G., & Johnstone, L. D. (1989). Time trends and urge trends in arrests and self-reported illegal behavior. *Criminology, 27*, 389–415.

O'Toole, M. E. (2000). *The school shooter: A threat assessment perspective.* Quantico, VA: Critical Incident Response Group, National Center for the Analysis of Violent Crime.

Pagani, L. S., Tremblay, R. G., Nagin, D., Zoccolilo, M., Vitaro, F., & McDuff, P. (2004). Risk factor models for adolescent verbal and physical aggression toward mothers. *International Journal of Behavioral Development, 28*, 528–537.

Pagelow, M. D. (1989). The incidence and prevalence of criminal abuse of other family members. In L. Ohlin & M. Tonry (Eds.), *Family violence* (Vol. 11). Chicago: University of Chicago Press.

Pardini, D., & Loeber, R. (2008). Interpersonal callousness trajectories across adolescence: Early social influences and adult outcomes. *Criminal Justice and Behavior, 35*, 173–196.

Parker, H., & Newcombe, R. (1987). Heroin use and acquisitive crime in an English community. *British Journal of Sociology, 38*, 331–350.

Parker, J. G., & Asher, S. R. (1987). Peer relations and later personal adjustment: Are low-accepted children at risk? *Psychological Bulletin, 102*, 357–389.

Patchin, J. W., & Hinduja, S. (2006). Bullies move beyond the schoolyard: A preliminary look at cyberbullying. *Youth Violence and Juvenile Justice, 4*, 148–169.

Patrick, C. J., Bradley, M. M., & Lang, P. J. (1993). Emotion in the criminal psychopath: Start reflex modulation. *Journal of Abnormal Psychology, 102*, 82–92.

Patrick, C. J., Zempolich, K.A., & Levenston, G. K. (1997). Emotionality and violent behavior in psychopaths: A biosocial analysis. In A. Raine, P. A. Brennan, D. P. Farrington, & S. A. Mednick (Eds.), *Biosocial bases of violence.* New York: Plenum.

Patterson, G. R. (1982). *Coercive family processes.* Eugene, OR: Castalia Press.

Patterson, G. R. (1986). Performance models for antisocial boys. *American Psychologist, 41*, 432–444.

Patterson, G. R., & Yoerger, K. (2002). A developmental model for early- and late-onset delinquency. In J. B. Reid, G. R. Patterson, & J. J. Snyder (Eds.), *Antisocial behavior in children and adults: A developmental analysis and the Oregon model for intervention.* Washington, DC: American Psychological Association.

Paull, D. (1993). *Fitness to stand trial.* Springfield, IL: C C Thomas.

Pearl, P. T. (1995). Identifying and responding to Munchausen syndrome by proxy. *Early Child Development and Care, 106*, 177–185.

Penfield, W. (1975). *The mystery of the mind.* Princeton, NJ: Princeton University Press.

Penrod, S. (1983). *Social psychology.* Englewood Cliffs, NJ: Prentice Hall.

Pepler, D. J., & Slaby, R. G. (1994). Theoretical and development perspectives on youth and violence. In L. D. Eron, J. H. Gentry, & P. Schlegel (Eds.), *Reason to hope: A psychosocial perspective on violence and youth.* Washington, DC: American Psychological Association.

Perkins, C. A. (2003). *Weapon use and violent crime.* Washington, DC: U.S.Department of Justice, Bureau of Justice Statistics.

Peters, S. D., Wyatt, G. E., & Finkelhor, D. (1986). Prevalence. In D. Finkelhor (Ed.), *Sourcebook on child sexual abuse.* Beverly Hills, CA: Sage.

Petraitis, J., Flay, B. R., & Miller, T. Q. (1995). Reviewing theories of adolescent substance abuse: Organizing pieces in the puzzle. *Psychological Bulletin, 117*, 67–86.

Petras, H., Schaeffer, C. M., Ialongo, N., Hubbard, S., Muthén., Lambert, S. F., Poduska, J., & Kellam, S. (2004). When the course of aggressive behavior in childhood does not predict antisocial behavior outcomes in adolescence and young adulthood: An examination of potential explanatory variables. *Development and Psychopathology, 16*, 919–941.

Pettit, G. S., Laird, R. D., Bates, J. E., & Dodge, K. A. (1997). Patterns of after-school care in middle childhood: Risk factors and developmental outcomes. *Merrill-Palmer Quarterly, 43*, 515–538.

Pfiffner, L.J., McBurnett, K., Rathouz, P. I., & Judice, S. (2005). Family correlates of oppositional and conduct disorder in children with attention deficit/hyperactivity disorders. *Journal of Abnormal Child Psychology, 33*, 551–563.

Piaget, J. (1948). *The moral judgment of the child.* New York: Free Press.

Piazza, J. A. (2009). Is Islamist terrorism more dangerous? An empirical study of group of ideology, organization, and goal structure. *Terrorism and Political Violence, 21*, 62–88.

Pillemer, K., & Finkelhor, D. (1988). The prevalence of elder abuse: A random sample survey. *Gerontologist, 28*, 51–57.

Pillemer, K., & Suitor, J. J. (1988). Elder abuse. In V. B. van Hasselt, R. L. Morrison, A. S. Morrison, A. S. Bellak, & M. Hersen (Eds.), *Handbook of family violence.* New York: Plenum.

Pillmann, F., Rohde, A., Ullrich, S., Draba, S., Sannemueller, U., & Marnerous, A. (1999). Violence, criminal behavior, and the EEG: Significance of left hemispheric focal abnormalities. *Journal of Neuropsychiatry & Clinical Neurosciences, 11*, 454–457.

Pincus, J. H. (1980). Can violence be a manifestation of epilepsy? *Neurology, 30*, 304–306.

Pinizzotto, A. J. (1984). Forensic psychology: Criminal personality profiling. *Journal of Police Science and Administration, 12*, 32–40.

Pinizzotto, A. J., & Finkel, N. J. (1990). Criminal personality profiling: An outcome and process study. *Law and Human Behavior, 14*, 215–234.

Pithers, W. D., Beal, L. S., Armstrong, J., & Petty, J. (1989). Identification of risk factors through clinical interviews and analysis of records. In D. R. Laws (Ed.), *Relapse prevention with sex offenders.* New York: Guilford.

Pithers, W. D., Kashima, K. M., Cumming, G. F., Beal, L. S., & Buell, M. M. (1988). Relapse prevention of sexual aggression. In R. A. Prentky & V. L. Quinsey (Eds.), *Human sexual aggression: Current perspectives.* New York: New York Academy of Sciences.

Pithers, W. D., Marques, J. K., Gibat, C. C., & Marlatt, G. A. (1983). Relapse prevention with sexual aggressives. In J. G. Greer & I. R. Stuart (Eds.), *The sexual aggressor: Current perspectives on treatment.* New York: Van Nostrand Reinhold.

Pleck, E. (1989). Criminal approaches to family violence, 1640–1980. In L. Ohlin & M. Tonry (Eds.), *Family violence* (Vol. 11). Chicago: University of Chicago Press.

Plomin, R. (1986). *Development, genetics, and psychology.* Hillsdale, NJ: Erlbaum.

Plummer, D. L., & Graziano, W. G. (1987). Impact of grade retention on the social development of elementary school children. *Developmental Psychology, 23*, 267–275.

Podnieks, E., Pillemer, K., & Nicolson, J. P. (1990). *National survey on abuse of the elderly in Canada: Final report.* Toronto, ON: Ryerson Polytechnic Institute.

Pope, C. E. (1977a). *Crime-specific analysis: An empirical examination of burglary offender characteristics (LEAA).* Washington, DC: USGPO.

Pope, C. E. (1977b). *Crime-specific analysis: The characteristics of burglary incidents (LEAA).* Washington, DC: USGPO.

Pope, C. E. (1977c). *Crime-specific analysis: An empirical examination of burglary offense and offense characteristics (LEAA).* Washington, DC: USGPO.

Popper, K. R. (1968). *The logic of scientific discovery.* New York: Harper & Row.

Porter, C. L., Hart, C. H., Yang, C., Robinson, C. C., Olsen, S. F., Zeng, Q., et al. (2005). A comparative study of child temperament and parenting in Beijing, China and the western United States. *International Journal of Behavioral Development, 29*, 541–551.

Porter, L. E., & Alison, L. J. (2006). Behavioural coherence in group robbery: A circumplex model of offender and victim interactions. *Aggressive Behavior, 32*, 330–342.

Porter, S., Birt, A. R., & Boer, D. P. (2001). Investigation of the criminal and conditional release histories of Canadian federal offenders as a function of psychopathy and age. *Law and Human Behavior, 25*, 647–661.

Porter, S., Fairweather, D., Drugge, J., Herve, H., Birt, A. R., & Boer, D. (2000). Profiles of psychopathy in incarcerated sexual offenders. *Criminal Justice and Behavior, 27*, 216–233.

Porter, S., Woodworth, M., Earle, J., Drugge, J., and Boer, D. (2003). Characteristics of sexual homicides committed by psychopathic and nonpsychopathic offenders. *Law and Human Behavior, 27,* 459–470.

Posner, J. K., & Vandell, D. L. (1999). After-school activities and the development of low-income urban children: A longitudinal study. *Developmental Psychology, 35,* 868–879.

Post, J. M., & Gold, S. N. (2002). The psychology of the terrorist: An interview with Jerrold M. Post. *Journal of Trauma Practice, 1,* 83–100.

Postmes, T., & Spears, R. (1998). Deindividuation and antinormative behavior: A meta-analysis. *Psychological Bulletin, 123,* 238–259.

Potoczniak, M. J., Mourot, J. E., Crosbie-Burnett, M., & Potoczniak, D. J. (2003). Legal and psychological perspectives on same-sex domestic violence: A multisystematic approach. *Journal of Family Violence, 17,* 252–259.

Poulin, F., & Boivin, M. (2000). Reactive and proactive aggression: Evidence of a two-factor model. *Psychological Assessment, 12,* 115–122.

Power, R. (2000, Spring). 2000 CSI/FBI computer crime and security survey. *Computer Security: Issues & Trends, 6*(1).

Powers, R. (2002, March). Apocalypse of adolescence. *Atlantic Monthly,* pp. 58, 60–65.

Poythress, N. G., Otto, R. K., Darkes, J., & Starr, L. (1993). APA's expert panel in the Congressional review of the USS Iowa incident. *American Psychologist, 48,* 8–15.

Prentky, R. A., Harris, B., Frizzell, K., & Righthand, S. (2000). An actuarial procedure of assessing risk in juvenile sex offenders. *Sexual Abuse: A Journal of Research and Treatment, 12,* 71–93.

Prentky, R. A., & Knight, R. A. (1986). Impulsivity in the life style and criminal behavior of sexual offenders. *Criminal Justice and Behavior, 13,* 141–164.

Prentky, R. A., Knight, R. A., & Lee, A. F. S. (1997). *Child sexual molestation: Research issues.* NIJ Research Report. Rockville, MD: National Criminal Justice Reference Service. Available: www.ncjrs.org/txtfiles/163390.txt.

President's Commission on Law Enforcement and Administration of Justice. (1967). *The challenge of crime in free society.* Washington, DC: USGPO.

Price, W. H., & Whatmore, P. B. (1967). Behaviour disorders and patterns of crime among XYY males identified at a maximum security hospital. *British Medical Journal, 1,* 533–536.

PRIDE Surveys. (2003). *2002–2003 PRIDE surveys national summary, grades 6 through 12.* Bowling Green, KY: Author.

Prinstein, M. J., Boergers, J., & Vernberg, E. M. (2001). Overt and relational aggression in adolescents: Social-psychological adjustment of aggressors and victims. *Journal of Clinical Child Psychology, 30,* 479–491.

Prinstein, M. J., & La Greca, A. M. (2004). Childhood peer rejection and aggression predictors of adolescent girls' externalizing and health risk behaviors: A 6-year longitudinal study. *Journal of Consulting and Clinical Psychology, 72,* 103–112.

Putnam, C. T., & Kirkpatrick, J. T. (2005, May). Juvenile firesetting: A research overview. *Juvenile Justice Bulletin* (NCJ 207606). Washington, DC: U.S. Department of Justice, Office of Juvenile Justice and Delinquency Prevention.

Puzzanchera, C. M. (2009, April). *Juvenile arrests 2007.* Washington, DC: U.S. Department of Justice, Office of Juvenile Justice and Delinquency Prevention.

Puzzanchera, C. M., Stahl, A. L., Finnegan, T. A., Tierney, N., & Snyder, H. N. (2004, December). *Juvenile court statistics 2000.* Washington, DC: Office of Juvenile Justice and Delinquency Prevention, National Center for Juvenile Justice.

Quay, H. C. (1964). Dimensions of personality in delinquent boys as inferred from the factor analysis of case history data. *Child Development, 35,* 479–484.

Quay, H. C. (1965). Psychopathic personality: Pathological stimulation-seeking. *American Journal of Psychiatry, 122,* 180–183.

Quay, H. C. (1987). Intelligence. In H. C. Quay (Ed.), *Handbook of juvenile delinquency.* New York: Wiley.

Queen's Bench Foundation. (1978). The rapist and his crime. In L. D. Savitz & N. Johnson (Eds.), *Crime in society.* New York: Wiley.

Quinet, K. (2007). The missing missing: Toward a quantification of serial murder victimization in the United States. *Homicide Studies, 11,* 319–339.

Quinsey, V. L., Chaplin, T. C., & Upfold, D. (1989). Arsonists and sexual arousal to firesetting: Correlation unsupported. *Journal of Behaviour Therapy and Experimental Psychiatry, 20,* 203–209.

Quinsey, V. L., Harris, G. T., Rice, M. E., & Cormier, C. (2006). *Violent offenders: Appraising and managing risk* (2nd ed.). Washington, DC: American Psychological Association.

Quinsey, V. L., & Marshall, W. L. (1983). Procedures for reducing inappropriate sexual arousal: An evaluation review. In J. G. Greer & I. R. Stuart (Eds.), *The sexual aggressor.* New York: Van Nostrand Reinhold.

Quinsey, V. L., Rice, M. E., & Harris, G. T. (1995). Actuarial prediction of sexual recidivism. *Journal of Interpersonal Violence, 10,* 85–105.

Quinsey, V. L., Skilling, T. A., Lalumière, M. L., & Craig, W. M. (2004). *Juvenile delinquency: Understanding the origins of individual differences.* Washington, DC: American Psychological Association.

Rabkin, J. G. (1979). Criminal behavior of discharged mental patients: A critical appraisal of the research. *Psychological Bulletin, 86,* 1–27.

Rabrenovic, G. (2007). Introduction: Responding to hate violence: New challenges and solutions. *American Behavioral Scientist, 51,* 143–148.

Rachman, S. J. (1966). Sexual fetishism: An experimental analogue. *Psychological Record, 16,* 293–296.

Raine, A. (1993). *The psychopathology of crime: Criminal behavior as a clinical disorder.* San Diego, CA: Academic Press.

Raine, A. (2002). Biosocial studies of antisocial and violent behavior in children and adults: A review. *Journal of Abnormal Child Psychology, 30,* 311–326.

Raine, A., Brennan, P., & Mednick, S. A. (1997). Interaction between birth complications and early maternal rejection in predisposing individuals to adult violence: Specificity to serious, early-onset violence. *American Journal of Psychiatry, 134,* 1265–1271.

Raine, A., Venables, P. H., & Williams, M. (1995). High autonomic arousal and electrodermal orienting at age 15 years as protective factors against criminal behavior at age 29 years. *American Journal of Psychiatry, 152,* 1595–1600.

Raine, A., Venables, P. H., & Williams, M. (1996). Better autonomic arousal and faster electrodermal half-recovery time at age 15 years as possible protective factors against crime at age 29 years. *Developmental Psychology, 32,* 624–630.

Ramirez, D., McDevitt, J., & Farrell, A. (2000, November). *A resource guide on racial profiling data collection systems: Promising practices and lessons learned.* Boston: Northeastern University Press. Available: www.usdoj.gov.

Ramirez, J. M. (2003). Hormones and aggression in childhood and adolescence. *Aggression and Violent Behavior, 8,* 621–644.

Ramirez, J. R., Crano, W. D., Quist, R., Burgoon, M., Alvaro, E. M., & Grandpre, J. (2004). Acculturation, familism, parental monitoring, and knowledge as predictors of marijuana and inhalant use in adolescents. *Psychology of Addictive Behavior, 18,* 3–11.

Rantala, R. R. (2004). *Cybercrime against businesses.* Washington, DC: U.S. Department of Justice, Bureau of Justice Statistics.

Rapaport, K., & Burkhart, B. R. (1984). Personality and attitudinal characteristics of sexually coercive college males. *Journal of Abnormal Psychology, 93,* 216–221.

Räsänen, P., Tiihonen, J., Isohanni, M. Rantakallio, P., Lehtonen, J., & Moring, J. (1998). Schizophrenia, alcohol abuse, and violent behavior: A 26-year follow-up study of an unselected birth cohort. *Schizophrenia Bulletin, 24,* 432–441.

Rasche, C. (1993). Given reason for violence in intimate relationships. In A. Wilson (Ed.), *Homicide.* Cincinnati, OH: Anderson.

Raskin, D. C., & Hare, R. D. (1978). Psychopathy and detection of deception in a prison population. *Psychophysiology, 15,* 126–136.

Ray, O. (1972). *Drugs, society and human behavior.* St. Louis, MO: C. V. Mosby.

Ray, O. (1983). *Drugs, society and human behavior* (3rd ed.). St. Louis, MO: C. V. Mosby.

Rehder, W., & Dillow, G. (2003). *Where the money is: True tales from the bank robbery capital of the world.* New York: Norton.

Reid, J. B. (1993). Prevention of conduct disorder before and after school entry: Relating interventions to developmental findings. *Development and Psychopathology, 5,* 243–262.

Reiman, J. (1995). *The rich get richer and the poor get prison* (4th ed.). Needham Heights, MA: Allyn & Bacon.

Reiss, A. J., & Roth, J. A. (Eds.) (1993). *Understanding and preventing violence.* Washington, DC: National Academy Press.

Reitzel, L. R. (2003, January). Sexual offender update: Juvenile sexual offender recidivism and treatment effectiveness. *Correctional Psychologist, 35*(1), 3–4.

Rengert, G., & Wasilchick, J. (1985). *Suburban burglary: A time and place for everything.* Springfield, IL: Charles C Thomas.

Rennison, C. M. (2003, February). *Intimate partner violence, 1993–2001* (NCJ 197838). Washington, DC: U.S. Department of Justice, Bureau of Justice Statistics.

Rennison, C. M., & Rand, M. R. (2003, August). *Criminal victimization, 2002.* Washington, DC: U.S. Department of Justice, Bureau of Justice Statistics.

Rennison, C. M., & Welchans, S. (2000, May). *Intimate partner violence.* Washington, DC: U.S. Department of Justice.

Resnick, P. J. (1969). Child murder by parents. *American Journal of Psychiatry, 126,* 325–334.

Resnick, P. J. (1970). Murder of the newborn: A psychiatric review of neonaticide. *American Journal of Psychiatry, 126,* 1414–1420.

Revitch, E., & Schlesinger, L. B. (1988). Clinical reflections on sexual aggression. In R. A. Prentky & V. L. Quinsey (Eds.), *Human sexual aggression: Current perspectives.* New York: New York Academy of Sciences.

Revitch, G., & Weiss, R. G. (1962). The pedophiliac offender. *Diseases of the Nervous System, 23,* 73–78.

Rhee, S. H., & Waldman, I. D. (2002). Genetic and environmental influences on antisocial behavior: A meta-analysis of twin and adoption studies. *Psychological Bulletin, 128,* 490–529.

Rhoads, J. M., & Borjes, E. D. (1981). The incidence of exhibitionism in Guatemala and U.S. *British Journal of Psychiatry, 139,* 242–244.

Rice, M. E. (1997). Violent offender research and implications for the criminal justice system. *American Psychologist, 52,* 414–423.

Rice, M. E., & Harris, G. T. (1991). Firesetters admitted to a maximum security psychiatric institution. *Journal of Interpersonal Violence, 6,* 461–475.

Rice, M. E., & Harris, G. T. (2002). Men who molest their sexually immature daughters: Is a special explanation required? *Journal of Abnormal Psychology, 111,* 329–339.

Rice, M. E., Harris, G. T., & Cormier, C. A. (1992). An evaluation of a maximum security therapeutic community for psychopaths and other mentally disordered offenders. *Law and Human Behavior, 16,* 399–412.

Rice, M. E., Harris, G. T., & Quinsey, V. L. (2001). Research on the treatment of adult sex offenders. In J. B. Ashford, B. D. Sales, & W. H. Reid (Eds.), *Treating adult and juvenile offenders with special needs.* Washington, DC: American Psychological Association.

Richard, A. (1999, November). *International trafficking in women to the United States: A contemporary manifestation of slavery and organized crime.* Washington, DC: Center for the Study of Intelligence.

Richards, H., Casey, J., & Lucente, S. (2003). Psychopathy and treatment response to incarcerated female substance abusers. *Criminal Justice and Behavior, 30,* 251–276.

Righthand, S., & Welch, C. (2001, March). *Juveniles who have sexually offended: A review of the professional literature.* Washington, DC: Office of Juvenile Justice and Delinquency Prevention.

Riley, S. (1998). Competency to stand trial adjudication: A comparison of female and male defendants. *Journal of the American Academy of Psychiatry and the Law, 26,* 223–240.

Ringel, C. (1997, November). *Criminal victimization in 1996: Changes 1995–1996 with trends 1993–1996.* Washington, DC: U.S. Department of Justice.

Riordan, S. (1999). Indecent exposure: The impact upon the victim's fear of sexual crime. *Journal of Forensic Psychiatry, 10,* 309–316.

Ritvo, E., Shanok, S. S., & Lewis, D. O. (1983). Firesetting and nonfiresetting delinquents. *Child Psychiatry and Human Development, 13,* 259–267.

Robbins, E., & Robbins, L. (1964). Arson with special reference to pyromania. *New York State Journal of Medicine, 2,* 795–798.

Roberts, A. R. (2002). Preface. In A. R. Roberts (Ed.), *Handbook of domestic violence intervention strategies: Policies, programs, and legal remedies.* New York: Oxford University Press.

Roberts, A. R., Zgoba, K. M., & Shahidullah, S. M. (2007). Recidivism among four types of homicide offenders: An exploratory analysis of 336 homicide offenders in New Jersey. *Aggression and Violent Behavior, 12,* 493–507.

Roberts, L., & Indermaur, D. (2005). Boys and rage: Driving-related violence and aggression in Western Australia. *Australian & New Zealand Journal of Criminology, 38,* 361–380.

Robins, L. N., & Regier, D. A. (1991). *Psychiatric disorders in America: The epidemiologic catchment area study.* New York: Free Press.

Roche, P. Q. (1958). *The criminal mind: A study of communication between criminal law and psychiatry.* New York: Grove Press.

Roche, T. (2006, July 7). Andrea Yates: More to the story. *Time.* Available: www.time.com/time/nation/article/0,8599,218445,00html.

Rodman, H., & Grams, P. (1967). *Juvenile delinquency and the family: A review and discussion.* Task Force Report: Juvenile delinquency and youth crime. Washington, DC: USGPO.

Roe-Sepowitz, D. (2007). Adolescent female murderers: Characteristics and treatment implications. *American Journal of Orthopsychiatry, 77,* 489–496.

Roesch, R., Zapf, P. A., Golding, S. L., & Skeem, J. L. (1999). Defining and assessing competency to stand trial. In A. K. Hess & I. B. Weiner (Eds.), *The handbook of forensic psychology* (2nd ed.). New York: Wiley.

Rogers, R. (1997). *Clinical assessment of malingering and deception* (2nd ed.). New York: Guilford.

Rogers, R. (2000). The uncritical acceptance of risk assessment in clinical practice. *Law and Human Behavior, 24,* 595–605.

Rogstad, J. E., & Rogers, R. (2008). Gender differences in contributions of emotion to psychopathy and antisocial personality disorder. *Clinical Psychology Review, 28,* 1472–1484.

Roizen, J. (1997). Epidemiological issues in alcohol-related violence. In M. Galanter (Ed.), *Recent developments in alcoholism* (Vol. 13). New York: Plenum.

Root, C., MacKay, S., Henderson, J., Del Bove, G., & Warling, D. (2008). The link between maltreatment and juvenile firesetting: Correlates and underlying mechanisms. *Child Abuse & Neglect, 32,* 161–176.

Rooth, G. (1973). Exhibitionism outside Europe and America. *Archives of Sexual Behavior, 2,* 351–363.

Rooth, G. (1974). Exhibitionists around the world. *Human Behavior, 3,* 61.

Rose, A. J., Swenson, L. P., & Waller, E. M. (2004). Overt and relational aggression and perceived popularity: Developmental differences in concurrent and prospective relations. *Developmental Psychology, 40,* 378–387.

Rosecan, J. S., Spitz, H. I., & Gross, B. (1987). Contemporary issues in the treatment of cocaine abuse. In H. I. Spitz & J. S. Rosecan (Eds.), *Cocaine abuse: New directions in treatment and research.* New York: Brunner/Mazel.

Rosenbaum, D. P., Lurigio, A. J., & Davis, R. C. (1998). *The prevention of crime: Social and situational strategies.* Belmont, CA: West/Wadsworth.

Rosenbaum, M. (1989). *Just saw what? An alternative view on solving America's drug problem.* San Francisco: National Council of Crime and Delinquency.

Rosenfeld, B., & Ritchie, K. (1998). Competence to stand trial: Clinician reliability and the role of offense severity. *Journal of Forensic Sciences, 43,* 151–157.

Rosenthal, D. (1970). *Genetic theory and abnormal behavior.* New York: McGraw-Hill.

Rosenthal, D. (1971). *Genetics of psychopathology.* New York: McGraw-Hill.

Rosenthal, D. (1975). Heredity in criminality. *Criminal Justice and Behavior, 2,* 3–21.

Rosoff, S. M., Pontell, H. N., & Tillman, R. (1998). *Profit without honor: White-collar crime and the looting of America.* Upper Saddle River, NJ: Prentice Hall.

Ross, M. P., & Bachar, K. J. (2002). Rape. In D. Levinson (Ed.), *Encyclopedia of crime and punishment* (Vol. 3). Thousand Oaks, CA: Sage.

Rossmo, D. K. (1997). Geographic profiling. In J. L. Jackson & D. A. Bekerain (Eds.), *Offender profiling: Theory, research, and practice*. Chichester, UK: Wiley.

Roth, J. A. (1996). *Psychoactive substances and violence*. Washington, DC: U.S. Department of Justice. Available: www.ncjrs.org/txtfile/psycho.txt.

Rowe, D. C., & Gulley, B. (1992). Sibling effects on substance abuse and delinquency. *Criminology, 35*, 217–233.

Rowe, D. C., Rodgers, D. C., & Meseck-Bushey, S. (1992). Sibling delinquency and the family environment: Shared and unshared influences. *Child Development, 63*, 57–67.

Rubin, B. (1972). Predictions of dangerousness in mentally ill criminals. *Archives of General Psychiatry, 27*, 397–407.

Rubin, K. H., Bukowski, W., & Parker, J. G. (1998). Peer interactions, relationships, and groups. In W. Damon (Series Ed.) & N. Eisenberg (Vol. Ed.), *Handbook of child psychology: Vol. 3. Social, emotional, and personality development* (5th ed.). New York: Wiley.

Rubin, K. H., Burgess, K. B., Dwyer, K. M., & Hastings, P. d. (2003). Predicting preschoolers' externalizing behaviors from toddler temperament, conflict, and maternal negativity. *Developmental Psychology, 39*, 164–176.

Rubinsky, E. W., & Brandt, J. (1986). Amnesia and criminal law: A clinical overview. *Behavioral Sciences & the Law, 4*, 27–46.

Rubinstein, M., Yeager, C. A., Goodstein, C., & Lewis, D. O. (1993). Sexually assaultive male juveniles: A follow-up. *American Journal of Psychiatry, 150*, 262–265.

Ruby, C. L. (2002). Are terrorists mentally deranged? *Analyses of Social Issues and Public Policy, 2*, 15–26.

Ruchkin, V. (2002). Family impact on violent youth. In R. R. Corrado, R. Roesch, S. D. Hart, & J. K. Gierowski (Eds.), *Multi-problem violent youth: A foundation for comparative research on needs, interventions, and outcomes*. Amsterdam: IOS Press.

Ruffolo, M. C., Sarri, R., & Goodkind, S. (2004). Study of delinquent, diverted, and high-risk adolescent girls: Implications for mental health intervention. *Social Work Research, 28*, 237–245.

Russell, A., Hart, C. H., Robinson, C. C., & Olsen, S. F. (2003). Children's sociable and aggressive behaviour with peers: A comparison of the US and Australia, and contributions of temperament and parental styles. *International Journal of Behavioral Development, 27*, 74–86.

Russell, D. (1973). Emotional aspects of shoplifting. *Psychiatric Annals, 3*, 77–86.

Russell, D. E. H. (1975). *The politics of rape: The victim's perspective*. New York: Stein & Day.

Russell, D. E. H. (1983). The prevalence and incidence of forcible rape and attempted rape of females. *Victimology: An International Journal, 7*, 81–93.

Russell, D. E. H. (1984). *Sexual exploitation*. Beverly Hills, CA: Sage.

Russell, D. E. H., & Finkelhor, D. (1984). The gender gap among perpetrators of child sexual abuse. In D. E. H. Russell (Ed.), *Sexual exploitation*. Beverly Hills, CA: Sage.

Russell, D. E. H., & Howell, N. (1983). The prevalence of rape in the United States revisited. *Signs: Journal of Women in Culture and Society, 8*, 688–695.

Rutter, M. (1997). Individual differences and levels of antisocial behavior. In A. Raine & P. A. Brennan (Eds.), *Biological bases of violence*. New York: Plenum.

Rutter, M. (2005). Commentary: What is the meaning and utility of the psychopathy concept? *Journal of Abnormal Child Psychology, 33*, 499–503.

Rutter, M., Giller, H., & Hagell, A. (1998). *Antisocial behavior by young people*. Cambridge, UK: Cambridge University Press.

Ryan, G., Miyoshi, T. J., Metzner, J. L., Krugman, R. D., & Fryer, G. E. (1996). Trends in a national sample of sexually abusive youths. *Journal of the American Academy of Child and Adolescent Psychiatry, 33*, 17–25.

Sageman, M. (2004). *Understanding terrorist networks*. Philadelphia: University of Pennsylvania Press.

Salekin, R. T. (2002). Psychopathy and therapeutic pessimism: Clinical lore or clinical reality? *Clinical Psychology Review, 22*, 79–112.

Salekin, R. T., Brannen, D. N., Zalot, A. A., Leistico, A-M, & Neumann, C. S. (2006). Factor structure of psychopathy in youth: Testing the applicability of the new four-factor model. *Criminal Justice and Behavior, 33,* 135–157.

Salekin, R. T., & Frick, P. J. (2005). Psychopathy in children and adolescents: The need for a developmental perspective. *Journal of Abnormal Child Psychology, 33,* 403–409.

Salekin, R. T., Leistico, A-M. R., Trobst, K. K., Schrum, C. L., & Lochman, J. E. (2005). Adolescent psychopathy and personality theory—the interpersonal circumplex: Expanding evidence of a nomological net. *Journal of Abnormal Child Psychology, 33,* 445–460.

Salekin, R. T., & Lochman, J. E. (2008). Child and adolescent psychopathy: The search for protective factors. *Criminal Justice and Behavior, 35,* 159–172.

Salekin, R. T., Rogers, R., & Machin, D. (2001). Psychopathy in youth: Pursuing diagnostic clarity. *Journal of Youth and Adolescence, 30,* 173–195.

Salekin, R. T., Rogers, R., & Sewell, K. W. (1997). Construct validity of psychopathy in a female offender sample: A multitrait-multimethod evaluation. *Journal of Abnormal Psychology, 106,* 576–585.

Salekin, R. T., Rogers, R., Ustad, K. L., & Sewell, K. W. (1998). Psychopathy and recidivism among female inmates. *Law and Human Behavior, 22,* 109–128.

Salekin, R. T., Ziegler, T. A., Larrea, M. A., Anthony, V. L., & Bennett, A. D. (2003). Predicting psychopathy with two Millon Adolescent Psychopathy scales. The importance of egocentric and callous traits. *Journal of Personality Assessment, 80,* 154–163.

Salisbury, E. J. & Van Voorhis, P. (2009). Gendered pathways: An empirical investigation of women probationers' paths to incarceration. *Criminal Justice and Behavior, 35,* 541–566.

Saltaris, C. (2002). Psychopathy in juvenile offenders: Can temperament and attachment be considered as robust developmental precursors? *Clinical Psychology Review, 22,* 729–752.

Sameroff, A. J., Peck, S. C., & Eccles, J. S. (2004). Changing ecological determinants of conduct problems from early adolescence to early childhood. *Development and Psychopathology, 16,* 873–896.

Sampson, R. J., & Lauritsen, J. L. (1994). Violent victimization and offending: Individual, situational and community-level risk factors. In A. T. Reiss Jr.

& J. Roth (Eds.), *Understanding and preventing violence: Social Influences* (Vol. 3). Washington, DC: National Academy Press.

Sandler, J. C., & Freeman, N. J. (2007). Typology of female sex offenders: A test of Vandiver and Kercher. *Sex Abuse, 19,* 73–89.

Saner, H., & Ellickson, P. (1996). Concurrent risk factors for adolescent violence. *Journal of Adolescent Health, 19,* 94–103.

Santa Clara Criminal Justice Pilot Project. (1972). *Burglary in San Jose.* Springfield, VA: U.S. Department of Commerce.

Santiago, G. B. (2002). Latina battered women: Barriers to service delivery and cultural considerations. In A. R. Roberts (Ed.), *Handbook of domestic violence intervention strategies: Policies, programs, and legal remedies.* New York: Oxford University Press.

Santtila, P., Häkkänen, H., Alison, L., & Whyte, C. (2003). Juvenile firesetters: Crime scene actions and offender characteristics. *Legal and Criminological Psychology, 8,* 1–20.

Sarangi, S., & Alison, L. (2005). Life story accounts of left wing terrorists in India. *Journal of Investigative Psychology and Offender Profiling, 2,* 69–86.

Sarasalo, E., Bergman, B., & Toth, J. (1996). Personality traits and psychiatric and somatic morbidity among kleptomaniacs. *Acta Psychiatrica Scandinavica, 94,* 358–364.

Sarasalo, E., Bergman, B., & Toth, J. (1997). Kleptomania-like behaviour and psychosocial characteristics among shoplifters. *Legal and Criminological Psychology, 2,* 1–10.

Sarbin, T. R. (1979). The myth of the criminal type. In T. R. Sarbin (Ed.), *Challenges to the criminal justice system: The perspective of community psychology.* New York: Human Services Press.

Satterfield, J. H., Swanson, J., Schell, A., & Lee, F. (1994). Prediction of antisocial behavior in attention-deficit hyperactivity disorder boys from aggression/defiance scores. *Journal of the American Academy of Child and Adolescent Psychiatry, 33,* 185–191.

Saulnier, K., & Perlman, D. (1981). The actor-observer bias is alive and well in prison: A sequel to Wells. *Personality and Social Psychology, 7,* 559–564.

Saunders, D. G., & Azar, S. T. (1989). Treatment programs for family violence. In L. Ohlin & M. Tonry (Eds.), *Family violence* (Vol. 11). Chicago: University of Chicago Press.

Saunders, E. B., & Awad, G. A. (1991). Adolescent female firesetters. *Canadian Journal of Psychiatry, 36,* 401–404.

Savage, J. (2008). The role of exposure to media violence in the etiology of violent behavior: A criminologist weighs in. *American Behavioral Scientist, 51,* 1123–1136.

Savage, J., & Yancey, C. (2008). The effects of media violence exposure on criminal aggression: A meta-analysis. *Criminal Justice and Behavior, 35,* 772–791.

Scaret, D., & Wilgosh, L. (1989). Learning disabilities and juvenile delinquency: A causal relationship? *International Journal for the Advancement of Counselling, 12,* 113–123.

Scarr, S. (1998). American child care today. *American Psychologist, 53,* 95–108.

Scelfo, J. (2005, June 13). Bad girls go wild: A rise in girl-on-girl violence is making headlines nation-wide and prompting scientists to ask why. *Newsweek.* Available: wwwnewsweek.com/id/50082.

Schauer, E. J., & Wheaton, E. M. (2006). Sex trafficking into the United States: A literature review. *Criminal Justice Review, 31,* 146–169.

Schachter, S. (1971). *Emotion, obesity and crime.* New York: Academic Press.

Schachter, S., & Latane, B. (1964). Crime, cognition, and the autonomic nervous system. In M. R. Jones (Ed.), *Nebraska symposium on motivation.* Lincoln, NE: University of Nebraska Press.

Schacter, D. L. (1986a). On the relation between genuine and simulated amnesia. *Behavioral Sciences & the Law, 4,* 47–64.

Schacter, D. L. (1986b). On the relation between genuine and simulated amnesia. *Behavioral Sciences & the Law, 4,* 47–64.

Schaeffer, C. M., & Borduin, C. M. (2005). Long-term follow-up to a randomized clinical trial of multisys-temic therapy with serious and violent juvenile offenders. *Journal of Consulting and Clinical Psychology, 73,* 445–453.

Schaffer, M., Clark, S., & Jeglic, E. L. (in press). The role of empathy and parenting style in the develop-ment of antisocial behaviors. *Crime & Delinquency.*

Scherer, D. G., Brondino, M. J., Henggeler, S. W., Melton, G. B., & Hanley, J. H. (1994). Multisystemic family preservation therapy: Preliminary findings from a study of rural and minority serious adoles-cent offenders. *Journal of Emotional and Behavioral Disorders, 2,* 198–206.

Schlosser, E. (2001). *Fast food nation: The dark side of the all-American meal.* Boston: Houghton Mifflin.

Schmideberg, M. (1953). Pathological firesetters. *Journal of Criminal Law, Criminology and Police Science, 44,* 30–39.

Schmucker, M., & Lösel, F. (2008). Does sexual offender treatment work? A systematic review of outcome evaluation. *Psicothema, 20,* 10–19.

Schneider, J. L. (2005). Stolen-goods markets. *British Journal of Criminology, 45,* 129–140.

Scholtz, D. C., Girard, M. L., & Vanderpool, M. A. (2008). *The development of a psychological screening program for sniper selection.* Director Human Resources Research and Evaluation, National Defence Headquarters, Ottawa, Ontario, Canada.

Schrager, L., & Short, J. (1978). Toward a sociology of organizational crime. *Social Problems, 25,* 407–419.

Schuller, R. A., & Vidmar, V. (1992). Battered woman syndrome evidence in the courtroom: A review of the literature. *Law and Human Behavior, 16,* 272–292.

Schulsinger, F. (1972). Psychopathy: Heredity and environment. *International Journal of Mental Health, 1,* 190–206.

Schultz, L. G. (1975). *Rape victimology.* Springfield, IL: Charles C Thomas.

Schuster, M. A., Stein, B. D., Jaycox, L. H., Collins, R. L., Marshall, G. N., & Elliott, M. N. (2001). A national survey of stress reactions after the September 11, 2001, terrorist attacks. *New England Journal of Medicine, 345,* 1507–1512.

Schwartz, J. P., Hage, S. M., Bush, I., & Burns, L. K. (2006). Unhealthy parenting and potential media-tors as contributing factors to future intimate violence: A review of the literature. *Trauma, Violence, & Abuse, 7,* 206–221.

Schwartz, I. M. (1989). (In) *Justice for juveniles: Rethinking the best interests of the child.* Lexington, MA: Lexington Books.

Sciarra, D. (1999). Assessment and treatment of adolescent sex offenders: A review from a cross-cultural perspective. *Journal of Offender Rehabilitation, 28,* 103–118.

Scientific American. (1999). *The Scientific American book of the brain.* New York: Author.

Scully, D., & Marolla, J. (1984). Convicted rapists' vocabulary of motive: Excuses and justifications. *Social Problems, 31,* 530–544.

Scully, D., & Marolla, J. (1985). Rape and vocabularies of motive: Alternative perspectives. In A. W. Burgess (Ed.), *Rape and sexual assault.* New York: Garland Publishing.

Seagrave, D., & Grisso, T. (2002). Adolescent development and measurement of juvenile psychopathy. *Law and Human Behavior, 26,* 219–239.

Sears, R., Maccoby, E., & Levin, H. (1957). *Patterns of child rearing.* Evanston, IL: Row, Peterson.

Séguin, J. R., Nagin, D., Asaad, J-M., & Tremblay, R. E. (2004). Cognitive-neuropsychological function in chronic physical aggression and hyperactivity. *Journal of Abnormal Psychology, 113,* 603–613.

Seligman, M. E. (1975). *Helplessness: On depression, development, and death.* San Francisco: W. H. Freeman.

Selkin, J. (1987). *Psychological autopsy in the courtroom.* Denver, CO: Author.

Selkin, J. (1994). Psychological autopsy: Scientific psychohistory or clinical intuition? *American Psychologist, 49,* 74–75.

Sellbom, M., & Verona, E. (2007). Neuropsychological correlates of psychopathic traits in a non-incarcerated sample. *Journal of Research in Personality, 41,* 276–294.

Sellin, T. (1970). A sociological approach. In M. E. Wolfgang, L. Savitz, & N. Johnson (Eds.), *The sociology of crime and delinquency* (2nd ed.). New York: Wiley.

Serin, R. C., & Amos, N. L. (1995). The role of psychopathy in the assessment of dangerousness. *International Journal of Law & Psychiatry, 18,* 231–238.

Serin, R. C., Peters, R. D., & Barbaree, H. E. (1990). Predictors of psychopathy and release outcome in a criminal population. *Psychological Assessment, 2,* 419–422.

Serin, R. C., & Preston, D. L. (2001). Managing and treating violent offenders. In J. B. Ashford, B. D. Sales, & W. H. Reid (Eds.), *Treating adult and juvenile offenders with special needs.* Washington, DC: American Psychological Association.

Seto, M. C. (2008). Pedophilia: Psychopathology and theory. In D. R. Laws & W. T. O'Donohue (Eds.), *Sexual deviance: Theory, assessment, and treatment* (2nd edition). New York: Guilford.

Seto, M. C., & Barbaree, H. E. (1999). Psychopathy, treatment behavior, and sex offender recidivism. *Journal of Interpersonal Violence, 14,* 1235–1248.

Seto, M. C., Maric, A., & Barbaree, H. E. (2001). The role of pornography in the etiology of sexual aggression. *Aggression and Violent Behavior, 6,* 35–53.

Sevecke, K., Pukrop, R., Kosson, D. S., & Krischer, M. K. (2009). Factor structure of the Hare Psychopathy Checklist: Youth Version in German female and male detainees and community adolescents. *Psychological Assessment, 21,* 45–56.

Seymour, A. (2001). Victimization of the elderly. In G. Coleman, M. Gaboury, M. Murray, & A. Seymour (Eds.), *1999 National Victim Assistance Academy.* Washington, DC: U.S. Department of Justice.

Shain, R., & Phillips, J. (1991). The stigma of mental illness: Labeling and stereotyping in the news. In L. Wilkins & P. Patterson (Eds.), *Risky business: Communicating issues of science, risk, and public policy.* Westport, CT: Greenwood Press.

Shaw, D. S., Gilliom, M., Ingoldsby, E. M., & Nagin, D. S. (2003). Trajectories leading to school-age conduct problems. *Developmental Psychology, 39,* 189–200.

Shaw, D. S., Owens, E. B., Giovannelli, J., & Winslow, E. B. (2001). Infant and toddler pathways leading to early externalizing disorders. *Journal of the American Academy of Child and Adolescent Psychiatry, 40,* 36–43.

Sherman, L. W., & Berk, R. A. (1984). The specific deterrent effects of arrest for domestic assault. *American Sociological Review, 49,* 261–272.

Shields, J. (1962). *Monozygotic twins brought up apart and together.* Oxford, UK: Oxford University Press.

Shneidman, E. S. (1994). The psychological autopsy. *American Psychologist, 49,* 75–76.

Short, J. F., & Nye, I. (1957). Reported behavior as a criterion of deviant behavior. *Social Problems, 5,* 207–213.

Shover, N. (1972). Structures and careers in burglary. *Journal of Criminal Law, Criminology and Police Science, 63,* 540–548.

Showers, J. (1999). *Never never never shake a baby: The challenges of shaken baby syndrome.* Alexandria, VA: National Association of Children's Hospitals and Related Institutions.

Shumaker, D. M., & Prinz, R. J. (2000). Children who murder: A review. *Clinical Child and Family Psychology Review, 3,* 97–115.

Sickmund, M. (2004, June). *Juveniles in corrections.* (NCJ 202885). Washington, DC: U.S. Department of Justice, Office of Juvenile Justice and Delinquency Prevention.

Sickmund, M. (2009, June). *Delinquency cases in juvenile court, 2005.* Washington, DC: U.S. Department of Justice, Office of Juvenile Justice and Delinquency Prevention.

Siegel, A., & Kohn, L. (1959). Permissiveness, permission, and aggression: The effect of adult presence or absence on aggression in children's play. *Child Development, 30,* 131–141.

Siegel, J. M., Sorenson, S. B., Golding, J. M., Burnam, M. A., & Stein, J. A. (1987). The prevalence of childhood sexual assault: The Los Angeles Epidemiological Catchment Area Project. *American Journal of Epidemiology, 126,* 1141–1153.

Sieh, E. W. (1987). Garment workers: Perceptions of inequity and employee theft. *British Journal of Criminology, 27,* 174–190.

Siever, L. J. (2008). Neurobiology of aggression and violence. *American Journal of Psychiatry, 165,* 429–442.

Silberman, E. K., & Weingartner, H. (1996). Hemispheric lateralization of functions related to emotion. *Brain and Cognition, 5,* 322–353.

Silke, A. (2003). The psychology of suicidal terrorism. In A. Silke (Ed.), *Terrorists, victims and society: Psychological perspectives on terrorism and its consequences.* Chichester, UK: Wiley.

Silke, A. (2008). Holy warriors: Exploring the psychological processes of Jihadi radicalization. *European Journal of Criminology, 5,* 99–123.

Silverman, R. A., & Mukhergee, S. K. (1987). Intimate homicide: An analysis of violent social relationships. *Behavioral Sciences & the Law, 5,* 37–47.

Silvern, L., Karyl, J., Waelde, L., Hodges, W. F., Starek, J., Heidt, E., et al. (1995). Retrospective reports of parental partner abuse: Relationships to depression, trauma symptoms and self-esteem among college students. *Journal of Family Violence, 10,* 177–202.

Silverthorn, P., & Frick, P. J. (1999). Developmental pathways to antisocial behavior: The delayed-onset pathway in girls. *Development and Psychopathology, 11,* 101–126.

Simon, R. J. (1983). The defense of insanity. *Journal of Psychiatry and Law, 11,* 183–201.

Simon, R. J., & Aaronson, D. E. (1988). *The insanity defense.* New York: Praeger.

Simon, R. J., & Cockerham, W. (1977). Civil commitment, burden of proof, and dangerous acts: A comparison of the perspectives of judges and psychiatrists. *Journal of Psychiatry and Law, 5,* 571–594.

Simonelli, C. J., Mullis, T., & Rohde, C. (2005). Scale of negative family interactions: A measure of parental and sibling aggression. *Journal of Interpersonal Violence, 20,* 792–803.

Simons, D. A., Wurtele, S. K., & Durham, R. L. (2008). Developmental experiences of child sexual abusers and rapists. *Child Abuse & Neglect, 32,* 549–560.

Simons, R. L., Lin, K. H., & Gordon, L. C. (1998). Socialization in the family of origin and male dating violence: A prospective study. *Journal of Marriage and the Family, 60,* 467–478.

Simourd, D. J., & Hoge, R. D. (2000). Criminal psychopathy: A risk-and-need perspective. *Criminal Justice and Behavior, 27,* 256–272.

Simpson, P. M., Banerjee, D., & Simpson, C. L., Jr. (1994). Softlifting: A model of motivating factors. *Journal of Business Ethics, 13,* 431–438.

Singer, M. I., Miller, D. B., Guo, S., Flannery, D. J., Frierson, T., & Slovack, K. (1999). Contributors to violent behavior among elementary and middle school children. *Pediatrics, 104,* 878–884.

Sipe, R., Jensen, E. L., & Everett, R. S. (1998). Adolescent sexual offenders grown up: Recidivism in young adulthood. *Criminal Justice and Behavior, 25,* 109–124.

Sitnikova, T., Goff, D., & Kuperberg, G. R. (2009). Neurocognitive abnormalities during comprehension of real-world, goal-directed behaviors in schizophrenia. *Journal of Abnormal Psychology, 118,* 256–277.

Skeem, J. L., & Cauffman, E. (2003). Views of the downward extension: Comparing the youth version of the Psychopathy Checklist with the Youth Psychopathic Traits Inventory. *Behavioral Sciences & the Law, 21,* 737–770.

Skeem, J. L., Edens, J. F., Camp, J., & Colwell, L. H. (2004). Are there ethnic differences in levels of psychopathy? A meta-analysis. *Law and Human Behavior, 28,* 505–527.

Skeem, J. L., Edens, J. F., & Colwell, L. H. (2003, April). Are there racial differences in levels of psychopathy? A meta-analysis. *Paper presented at the 3rd annual conference of the International Association of Forensic Mental Health Services,* Miami, FL.

Skeem, J. L., Edens, J. F., Sanford, G. M., & Colwell, L. H. (2003). Psychopathic personality and racial/ethnic differences reconsidered: A reply to Lynn (2002). *Personality and Individual Differences 35,* 1439–1462.

Skeem, J. L., Emke-Francis, P., & Louden, J. L. (2006). Probation, mental health, and mandated treatment: A national survey. *Criminal Justice and Behavior, 33,* 158–184.

Skeem, J. L., & Golding, S. (1998). Community examiners' evaluations of competence to stand trial: Common problems and suggestions for improvements. *Professional Psychology: Research and Practice, 29,* 357–367.

Skeem, J. L., Monahan, J., & Mulvey, E. P. (2002). Psychopathy, treatment involvement, and subsequent violence among civil psychiatric patients. *Law and Human Behavior, 26,* 577–603.

Skeem, J. L., Poythress, N., Edens, J., Lilienfeld, S., & Cale, E. (2003). Psychopathic personality or personalities? Exploring potential variants of psychopathy and their implications for risk assessment. *Aggression and Violent Behavior, 8,* 513–546.

Skilling, T. A., Quinsey, V. L., & Craig, W. M. (2001). Evidence of a tax on underlying serious antisocial behavior in boys. *Criminal Justice and Behavior, 28,* 450–470.

Skinner, B. F. (1964). Behaviorism at fifty. In T. W. Wann (Ed.), *Behaviorism and phenomenology.* Chicago: University of Chicago Press.

Skogan, W. G. (1977). Dimensions of the dark figure of unreported crime. *Crime and Delinquency, 23,* 41–50.

Skrzpek, G. J. (1969). The effects of perceptual isolation and arousal on anxiety, complexity preference, and novelty preference in psychopathic and neurotic delinquents. *Journal of Abnormal Psychology, 74,* 321–329.

Slavkin, M. L. (2001). Enuresis, firesetting, and cruelty to animals: Does the ego triad show predictive validity? *Adolescence, 36,* 461–467.

Slobogin, C. (1985). The guilty but mentally ill verdict: An idea whose time should not have come. *George Washington Law Review, 53,* 494–580.

Slobogin, C. (1999). The admissibility of behavioral science information in criminal trials: From primitivism to *Daubert* to voice. *Psychology, Public Policy, and Law, 5,* 100–119.

Slovenko, R. (1989). The multiple personality: A challenge to legal concepts. *The Journal of Psychiatry and Law, 17,* 681–719.

Smallbone, S. W., & Wortley, R. K. (2004). Criminal diversity and paraphilic interests among adult males convicted of offenses against children. *International Journal of Offender Therapy and Comparative Criminology, 48,* 175–188.

Smart, R. G. (1986). Cocaine use and problems in North America. *British Journal of Criminology, 28,* 109–128.

Smart, R. G., Asbridge, M., Mann, R. E., & Adlaf, E. M. (2003). Psychiatric distress among road rage victims and perpetrators. *Canadian Journal of Psychiatry, 48,* 681–688.

Smigel, E. O. (1970). Public attitudes toward stealing as related to the size of the victim organization. In E. O. Smigel & H. L. Ross (Eds.), *Crimes against bureaucracy.* New York: Van Nostrand Reinhold.

Smith, B. L., & Morgan, K. D. (1994). Terrorists right and left: Empirical issues in profiling American terrorists. *Studies in Conflict and Terrorism, 17,* 39–57.

Smith, D. (2002, June). Helping mentally ill offenders. *Monitor on Psychology, 33,* 64.

Smith, E. J. (2006). The strength-based counseling model. *The Counseling Psychologist, 34,* 13–79.

Smith, G. A., & Hall, J. A. (1982). Evaluating Michigan's guilty but mentally ill verdict: An empirical study. *Michigan Journal of Law Reform, 16,* 75–112.

Smith, P. K., Mahdavi, J., Carvalho, M., Fisher, S., Russell, S., & Tippett, N. (2008). Cyberbullying: Its nature and impact in secondary school pupils. *Journal of Child Psychology and Psychiatry, 49,* 376–385.

Smith, S., & Hudson, R. (1995). A quick screening test of competency to stand trial for defendants with mental retardation. *Psychological Reports, 78,* 234.

Smith, S. S., & Newman, J. P. (1990). Alcohol and drug abuse-dependence disorder in psychopathic and nonpsychopathic criminal offenders. *Journal of Abnormal Psychology, 99,* 430–439.

Smithey, M. (1998). Infant homicide: Victim-offender relationship and causes of death. *Journal of Family Violence, 13,* 285–287.

Smithey, M. (2002). Infanticide. In D. Levinson (Ed.), *Encyclopedia of crime and punishment* (Vol. 2). Thousand Oaks, CA: Sage.

Snook, B., Cullen, R. M., Bennell, C., Taylor, P. J., & Gendreau, P. (2008). The criminal profiling illusion: What's behind the smoke and mirrors? *Criminal Justice and Behavior, 35,* 1257–1276.

Snook, B., Eastwood, J., Gendreau, P., Goggin, C., & Cullen, R. M. (2007). Taking stock of criminal profiling: A narrative review and meta-analysis. *Criminal Justice and Behavior, 34,* 437–453.

Snyder, H. N. (2001). Epidemiology of official offending. In R. Loeber & D. P. Farrington (Eds.), *Child delinquents: Development, intervention, and service needs.* Thousand Oaks, CA: Sage.

Snyder, H. N. (2006, December). *Juvenile arrests 2004.* Washington, DC: U.S. Department of Justice, Office of Juvenile Justice and Delinquency Prevention.

Snyder, H. N. (2008, August). *Juvenile arrests 2005.* Washington, DC: U.S. Department of Justice, Office of Juvenile Justice and Delinquency Prevention.

Snyder, H. N., Espiritu, R. C., Huizinga, D., Loeber, R., & Petechuk, D. (2003, March). Prevalence and development of child delinquency. *Child Delinquency Bulletin Series* (NCJ193411). Washington, DC: U.S. Department of Justice, Office of Juvenile Justice and Delinquency Prevention.

Snyder, H. N., Sickmund, M., & Poe-Yamagata, E. (2000). *Juvenile transfer to criminal court in the 1990s: Lessons learned from four studies.* Washington, DC: Office of Juvenile Justice and Delinquency Prevention.

Snyder, J., & Patterson, G. (1987). Family interaction and delinquent behavior. In H. C. Quay (Ed.), *Handbook of juvenile delinquency.* New York: Wiley.

Snyder, J., Reid, J., & Patterson, G. (2003). A social learning model of child and adolescent antisocial behavior. In B. B. Lahey, T. E. Moffitt, & A. Caspi (Eds.), *Causes of conduct disorder and juvenile delinquency.* New York: Guilford.

Sorenson, S. B., Stein, J. A., Siegel, J. M., Golding, J. M., & Burnam, M. A. (1987). The prevalence of adult sexual assault: The Los Angeles Epidemiological Catchment Area Project. *American Journal of Epidemiology, 126,* 1154–1164.

Southerland, M. D., Collins, P. A., & Scarborough, K. E. (1997). *Workplace violence.* Cincinnati, OH: Anderson.

Spaccarelli, S., Coatsworth, J. D., & Bowden, B. S. (1995). Exposure to serious family violence among incarcerated boys: Its association with violent offending and potential mediating variables. *Violence and Victims, 10,* 163–182.

Spain, S. E., Douglas, K. S., Poythress, N. G., & Epstein, M. (2004). The relationship between psychopathic features, violence, and treatment outcomes: The comparison of three youth measures of psychopathic features. *Behavioral Sciences & the Law, 22,* 85–102.

Spallone, P. (1998). The new biology of violence: New geneticisms for old? *Body and Society, 4,* 47–65.

Sperry, R. (1983). *Science and moral priority.* New York: Columbia University Press.

Spinrad, T. L., Eisenberg, N., & Bernt, F. (2007). Introduction to the special issues on moral development: Part I. *The Journal of Genetic Psychology, 168,* 101–104.

Spinelli, M. G. (2001). A systematic investigation of 16 cases of neonaticide. *American Journal of Psychiatry, 158,* 811–813.

Stadolnik, R. F. (2000). *Drawn to the flame: Assessment and treatment of juvenile firesetting behavior.* Sarasota, FL: Professional Resources Press.

Stagg, V., Wills, G. D., & Howell, M. (1989). Psychopathology in early childhood witnesses of family violence. *Topics in Early Childhood Special Education, 9,* 73–87.

Staller, J. A. (2006). Diagnostic profiles in outpatient child psychiatry. *American Journal of Orthopsychiatry, 76,* 98–102.

Stanger, C., Achenbach, T. M., & Verhulst, F. C. (1997). Accelerated longitudinal comparisons of aggressive versus delinquent syndromes. *Development and Psychopathology, 9,* 43–58.

Stark, C., Paterson, B., Henderson, T., Kidd, B., & Godwin, M. (1997). Counting the dead. *Nursing Times, 93,* 34–37.

Stark, E. (2002). Preparing for expert testimony in domestic violence cases. In A. R. Roberts (Ed.), *Handbook of domestic violence intervention strategies: Policies, programs, and legal remedies.* New York: Oxford University Press.

Stattin, H., & Klackenberg-Larsson, I. (1993). Early language and intelligence development and their relationship to future criminal behavior. *Journal of Abnormal Psychology, 102,* 369–378.

Stattin, H., & Magnusson, D. (1991). Stability and change in criminal behaviour up to age 30. *The British Journal of Criminology, 31,* 327–346.

Staub, E. (2001). Genocide and mass killing: Their roots and prevention. In D. J. Christie, R. V. Wagner, & D. D. Winter (Eds.), *Peace, conflict, and violence: Peace psychology for the 21st century.* Upper Saddle River, NJ: Prentice-Hall.

Staub, E. (2004). Understanding and responding to group violence: Genocide, mass killing, and terrorism. In F. M. Moghaddam & A. J. Marsella (Eds.), *Understanding terrorism: Psychosocial roots, consequences, and interventions.* Washington, DC: American Psychological Association.

Steadman, H. J. (1976). Predicting dangerousness. In D. J. Madden & J. R. Lion (Eds.), *Rage • hate •* *assault • and other forms of violence.* New York: Spectrum Publishers.

Steadman, H. J. (1979). *Beating a rap? Defendants found incompetent to stand trial.* Chicago: University of Chicago Press.

Steadman, H. J., & Cocozza, J. J. (1974). *Careers of the criminally insane.* Lexington, MA: Lexington Books.

Steadman, H. J., Fabisiak, S., Dvoskin, J., & Holobean, E. (1987). A survey of mental disability among state prison inmates. *Hospital and Community Psychiatry, 38,* 1086–1090.

Steadman, H. J., McGreevy, M. A., Morrissey, J. P., Callahan, L. A., Robbins, P. C., & Cirincione, C. (1993). *Before and after Hinckley: Evaluating insanity defense reform.* New York: Guilford Press.

Steadman, H. J., Mulvey, E. P., Monahan, J., Robbins, P. C., Appelbaum, P. S., Grisso, T., et al. (1998). Violence by people discharged from acute psychiatric inpatient facilities and by others in the same neighborhoods. *Archives of General Psychiatry, 55,* 393–401.

Steffan, J. S., & Morgan, R. D. (2005, February). Meeting the needs of mentally ill offenders: Inmate service utilization. *Corrections Today,* pp. 38–43.

Steinman, K. J. (2005). Drug selling among high school students: Related risk behaviors and psychosocial characteristics. *Journal of Adolescent Health, 36,* 71–79.

Steinmetz, S. K. (1981). A cross-cultural comparison of sibling violence. *International Journal of Family Psychiatry, 2,* 337–351.

Stern, K. R. (2001, May). A treatment study of children with attention deficit hyperactivity disorder. *OJJDP Fact Sheet.* Washington, DC: U.S. Department of Justice, Office of Juvenile Justice and Delinquency Prevention.

Sternberg, R. J. (2003). A duplex theory of hate: Development and application of terrorism, massacres, and genocide. *Review of General Psychology, 7,* 299–328.

Stevens, M. J. (2005). What is terrorism and can psychology do anything to prevent it? *Behavioral Sciences & the Law, 23,* 507–526.

Stewart, M. A., & Culver, K. W. (1982). Children who set fires: The clinical picture and a follow-up. *British Journal of Psychiatry, 140,* 357–363.

Stickle, T., & Blechman, E. (2002). Aggression and fire: Antisocial behavior in firesetting and nonfiresetting juvenile offenders. *Journal of Psychopathology and Behavioral Assessment, 24,* 177–193.

Stone, A. (1975). *Mental health law: A system in transition.* Washington, DC: USGPO.

Stone, M. H. (1998). Sadistic personality in murders. In T. Millon, E. Simonsen, M. Burket-Smith, & R. Davis (Eds.), *Psychopathy: Antisocial, criminal, and violent behavior.* New York: Guilford.

Stouthamer-Loeber, M., Loeber, R., Wei, E., Farrington, D., & Wilkström, P. H. (2002). Risk and promotive effects in the explanation of persistent serious delinquency in boys. *Journal of Consulting and Clinical Psychology, 70,* 111–123.

Stouthamer-Loeber, M. Wei, E., Loeber, R., & Masten, A. S. (2004). Desistence from persistent serious delinquency in the transition to adulthood. *Development and Psychopathology, 16,* 897–918.

Strasser, F. (1989, August 7). One nation, under siege. *National Law Journal,* S2–S3, S15.

Straus, M. (1991). Discipline and deviance: Physical punishment of children and violence and other crime in adulthood. *Social Problems, 38,* 133–154.

Straus, M. A., & Gelles, R. J. (1990). *Physical violence in American families.* New Brunswick, NJ: Transaction Publishers.

Strentz, T. (1987, November). A hostage psychological survival guide. *FBI Law Enforcement Bulletin,* pp. 1–7.

Stretesky, P. B., & Lynch, M. J. (2001). The relationship between lead exposure and homicide. *Archives of Pediatrics and Adolescent Medicine, 155,* 579–582.

Stretesky, P. B., & Lynch, M. J. (2004). The relationship between lead and crime. *Journal of Health and Social Behavior, 45,* 214–219.

Strickland, S. M. (2008). Female sex offenders: Exploring issues of personality, trauma, and cognitive distortions. *Journal of Interpersonal Violence, 23,* 474–489.

Strote, J., Lee, J. E., & Wechsler, H. (2002). Increasing MDMA use among college students: Results of a national survey. *Journal of Adolescent Health, 30,* 64–72.

Substance Abuse and Mental Health Administration. (2005, September). *2004 National Survey on Drug Abuse and Mental Health.* Rockville, MD: U.S. Department of Health and Human Services, Author.

Substance Abuse and Mental Health Administration. (2006, March). *State estimates of substance use from the 2003–2004 national surveys on drug use and health.* Rockville, MD: U.S. Department of Health and Human Services, Author.

Substance Abuse and Mental Health Administration. (2009, April). *Nonmedical use of Adderall® among full-time college students.* Rockville, MD: U.S. Department of Health and Human Services, Author.

Surette, R. (1999). *Media, crime, and criminal justice* (2nd ed.). Belmont, CA: West/Wadsworth.

Sutherland, E. H. (1947). *Principles of criminology* (4th ed.) Philadelphia: Lippincott.

Sutherland, E. H. (1949). *White-collar crime.* New York: Holt, Rinehart & Winston.

Sutherland, E. H. (1983). *White-collar crime: The uncut version.* New Haven, CT: Yale University Press.

Sutherland, E. H., & Cressey, D. R. (1974). *Criminology* (9th ed.). Philadelphia: Lippincott.

Sutherland, E. H., & Cressey, D. R. (1978). *Criminology* (10th ed.). Philadelphia: Lippincott.

Sutherland, E. H., Cressey, D. R., & Luckenbill, D. F. (1992). *Principles of criminology* (11th ed.). Dix Hills, NY: General Hall.

Sutker, P. B., & Allain, A. N. (1983). Behavior and personality assessment in men labeled adaptive sociopaths. *Journal of Behavioral Assessment, 5,* 65–79.

Sutker, P. B., Uddo-Crane, M., & Allain, A. N. (1991). Clinical and research assessment of posttraumatic stress disorder: A conceptual overview. *Psychological Assessment: A Journal of Consulting and Clinical Psychology, 3,* 520–530.

Sutton, R. M., & Douglas, K. M. (2005). Justice for all, or all for me? More evidence of the importance of the self-other distinction in just-world beliefs. *Personality and Individual Differences, 39,* 637–645.

Sutton, S. K., Vitale, J. E., & Newman, J. P. (2002). Emotion among women with psychopathy during picture perception. *Journal of Abnormal Psychology, 111,* 610–619.

Swahn, M. H., & Donovan, J. E. (2004). Correlates and predictors of violent behavior among adolescent drinkers. *Journal of Adolescent Health, 34,* 480–492.

Sykes, G. M. (1956). *Crime and society.* New York: Random House.

Sykes, G. M., & Matza, D. (1957). Techniques of neutralization: A theory of delinquency. *American Sociological Review, 22,* 664–670.

Symons, D. (1979). *The evolution of human sexuality.* New York: Oxford University Press.

Tappan, P. W. (1947). Who is the criminal? *American Sociological Review, 12,* 100–110.

Tarolla, S. M., Wagner, E. F., Rabinowitz, J., & Tubman, J. G. (2002). Understanding and treating juvenile offenders: A review of current knowledge and future directions. *Aggression and Violent Behavior, 7,* 125–143.

Taylor, D. M., & Louis, W. (2004). Terrorism and the quest for identity. In F. M. Moghaddam & A. J. Marsella (Eds.), *Understanding terrorism: Psychosocial roots, consequences, and interventions.* Washington, DC: American Psychological Association.

Taylor, J., Iacono, W. G., & McGue, M. (2000). Evidence for a genetic etiology of early-onset delinquency. *Journal of Abnormal Psychology, 109,* 634–643.

Taylor, M., & Nee, C. (1988). The role of cues in simulated residential burglary. *British Journal of Criminology, 28,* 396–401.

Taylor, P. J., Leese, M., Williams, D., Butwell, M., Daly R., & Larkin, E. (1998). Mental disorder and violence: A special (high security) hospital study. *British Journal of Psychiatry, 172,* 477–484.

Tedeschi, R. G., & Kilmer, R. P. (2005). Assessing strengths, resilience, and growth to guide clinical interventions. *Professional Psychology: Research and Practice, 36,* 230–237.

Tengström, A., Hodgins, S., Grann, M., Långström, N., & Kullgren, G. (2004). Schizophrenia and criminal offending: The role of psychopathy and substance use disorders. *Criminal Justice and Behavior, 31,* 367–391.

Teplin, L. (1984). Criminalizing mental disorder. *American Psychologist, 39,* 794–803.

Teplin, L. (1990). The prevalence of severe mental disorder among male urban jail detainees: Comparisons with the epidemiologic catchment area program. *American Journal of Public Health, 80,* 663–669.

Teplin, L. (2000, October). Psychiatric disorders in youthful offenders. *National Institute of Justice Journal,* 30–32.

Terrorism Research Center. (1997). *The basics: Combating terrorism.* Alexandria, VA: Author.

Terry, K. J. (2008). Stained glass: The nature and scope of child sexual abuse in the Catholic church. *Criminal Justice and Behavior, 35,* 549–569.

Terry, K. J., & Tallon, J. (2004). *Child sexual abuse.* New York: John Jay College Research Team, John Jay College of Criminal Justice.

Tewksbury, R. (2005). Collateral consequences of sex offender registration. *Journal of Contemporary Criminal Justice, 21,* 67–81.

Thakker, J., Collie, R. M., Gannon, T., & Ward, T. (2008). Rape: Assessment and treatment. In D. R. Laws & W. T. O'Donohue (Eds.), *Sexual deviance: Theory, assessment, and treatment.* New York: Guilford.

Thomas, A., & Chess, S. (1977). *Temperament and development.* New York: Brunner/Mazel.

Thompson, K. M. (1990). Refacing inmates: A critical appraisal of plastic surgery programs in prison. *Criminal Justice and Behavior, 17,* 448–466.

Thompson, R. A. (1998). Early sociopersonality development. In W. Damon & N. Eisenberg (Eds.), *Handbook of child psychology. Vol. 3. Social, emotional, and personality development* (5th ed.). New York: Wiley.

Thompson, R. A., & Nelson, C. A. (2001). Developmental science and the media: Early brain development. *American Psychologist, 56,* 5–15.

Thorley, G. (1984). Review of follow-up and follow-back studies of childhood hyperactivity. *Psychological Bulletin, 96,* 116–132.

Thornberry, T. P., & Burch, J. H. H. (1997). *Gang membership and delinquent behavior.* Washington, DC: U.S. Department of Justice, Office of Juvenile Justice and Delinquency Prevention.

Thornberry, T. P., Huizinga, D., & Loeber, R. (1995). The prevention of serious delinquency and violence: Implication from the program of research on the causes and correlates of delinquency. In J. C. Howell, B. Krisberg, J. D. Hawkins, & J. Wilson (Eds.), *Sourcebook on serious violent and chronic juvenile offenders.* Thousand Oaks, CA: Sage.

Thornberry, T. P., & Jacoby, J. E. (1979). *The criminally insane: A community follow-up of mentally ill offenders.* Chicago: University of Chicago Press.

Thornberry, T. P., & Krohn, M. D. (2005). Applying interactional theory to the explanation of continuity and change in antisocial behavior. In D. P. Farrington (Ed.), *Integrated developmental and life-course theories of offending.* New Brunswick, NJ: Transaction.

Thornberry, T. P., Krohn, M., Lizotte, A. J., & Chard-Wierschem, D. (1993). The role of juvenile gangs in facilitating delinquent behavior. *Journal of Research in Crime and Delinquency, 30,* 55–87.

Tingle, D., Barnard, G. W., Robbins, L., Newman, G., & Hutchinson, D. (1986). Childhood and adolescent characteristics of pedophiles and rapists. *International Journal of Law and Psychiatry, 9,* 103–116.

Tinklenberg, J. R., & Stillman, R. C. (1970). Drug use and violence. In D. Daniels, M. Gilula, & F. Ochberg (Eds.), *Violence and the struggle for existence.* Boston: Little, Brown.

Tinklenberg, J. R., & Woodrow, K. M. (1974). Drug use among youthful assaultive and sexual offenders. In S. H. Frazier (Ed.), *Aggression.* Baltimore, MD: Williams & Wilkins.

Tittle, C. R. (1980). *Sanctions and social deviance: The question of deterrence.* New York: Praeger.

Tittle, C. R., & Villemez, W. J. (1977). Social class and criminality. *Social Forces, 56,* 474–502.

Tjaden, P. (1997, November). *The crime of stalking: How big is the problem?* NIJ Research Preview. Washington, DC: U.S. Department of Justice.

Tjaden, P., & Thoennes, N. (1997). *Stalking in America: Findings from the National Violence Against Women Survey.* Denver, CO: Center for Policy Research.

Tjaden, P., & Thoennes, N. (1998a). *Stalking in America: Findings from the National Violence Against Women Survey.* Washington, DC: U.S. Department of Justice.

Tjaden, P., & Thoennes, N. (1998b). *Prevalence, incidence, and consequences of violence against women: Findings from the National Violence Against Women Survey.* Washington, DC: U.S. Department of Justice.

Tjaden, P., & Thoennes, N. (2006, January). *Extent, nature, and consequences of rape victimization: Findings from the National Violence Against Women Survey.* Washington, DC: U.S. Department of Justice.

Toch, H. (2008). (Ed.), Special issue: The disturbed offender in confinement. *Criminal Justice and Behavior, 35.*

Tolan, P. H., Gorman-Smith, D., & Henry, D. B. (2003). On developmental ecology of urban males' youth violence. *Developmental Psychology, 39,* 274–279.

Tolan, P. H., & Thomas, P. (1995). The implications of age of onset for delinquency II: Longitudinal data. *Journal of Abnormal Child Psychology, 23,* 157–169.

Tomarken, A. J., Davidson, R. J., Wheeler, R. E., & Doss, R. C. (1992). Individual differences in anterior brain asymmetry and fundamental dimensions of emotion. *Journal of Personality and Social Psychology, 62,* 676–687.

Tonglet, M. (2001). Consumer misbehaviour: An exploratory study of shoplifting. *Journal of Consumer Behaviour, 1,* 336–354.

Torres, A. N., Boccaccini, M. T., & Miller, H. A. (2006). Perceptions of the validity and utility of criminal profiling among forensic psychologists and psychiatrists. *Professional Psychology: Research and Practice, 37,* 51–58.

Tran, H., & Weinraub, M. (2006). Child care effects in context. Quality, stability, and multiplicity in nonmaternal child care arrangements during the first 15 months of life. *Developmental Psychology, 42,* 566–582.

Trasler, G. (1987). Some cautions for the biological approach to crime causation. In S. A. Mednick, E. Moffitt, & S. A. Stack (Eds.), *The causes of crime: New biological approach.* Cambridge, UK: Cambridge University Press.

Tremblay, R. E., & Craig, W. (1995). Developmental crime prevention. In M. Tonry & D. P. Farrington (Eds.), *Building a safer society: Strategic approaches to crime prevention.* Chicago: University of Chicago Press.

Tremblay, R. E., LeMarquand, D., & Vitaro, F. (1999). The prevention of oppositional defiant disorder and conduct disorder. In H. C. Quay & A. F. Hogan (Eds.), *Handbook of disruptive behavior disorders*. New York: Kluwer Academic/Plenum Publishers.

Tremblay, R. E., Vitaro, F., Gagnon, C., Piche, C., & Royer, N. (1992). A prosocial scale for the Preschool Behaviour Questionnaire: Concurrent and predictive correlates. *International Journal of Behavioral Development, 15*, 227–245.

Tsang, J. (2002). Moral rationalization and the integration of situational factors and psychological processes in immoral behavior. *Review of General Psychology, 6*, 25–50.

Tucker, D. M. (1981). Lateral brain function, emotion and conceptualization. *Psychological Bulletin, 89*, 19–46.

Turrell, S. C. (2000). A descriptive analysis of same-sex relationship violence for a diverse sample. *Journal of Family Violence, 15*, 281–293.

Turvey, B. (2002). *Criminal profiling: An introduction to behavioral evidence analysis* (2nd ed.). San Diego, CA: Academic Press.

Turvey, B. (2008). *Criminal profiling: An introduction to behavioral evidence analysis* (3rd ed.). San Diego, CA: Elsevier.

Tuvblad, C., Eley, T. C., & Lichtenstein, P. (2005). The development of antisocial behaviour from childhood to adolescence: A longitudinal twin study. *European Child and Adolescent Psychiatry, 14*, 216–225.

Tyler, J., Darville, R., & Stalnaker, K. (2001). Juvenile boot camps: A descriptive analysis of program diversity and effectiveness, *Social Science Journal, 38*, 445–460.

Tyner, E. A., & Fremouw, W. J. (2008). The relation of methamphetamine use and violence: A critical review. *Aggression and Violent Behavior, 13*, 285–297.

Ullman, A., & Straus, M. A. (2003). Violence by children against mothers in relation to violence between parents and corporal by parents. *Journal of Comparative Family Studies, 34*, 41–64.

Ullman, S. E. (1997). Review and critique of empirical studies of rape avoidance. *Criminal Justice and Behavior, 24*, 177–204.

Ullman, S. E. (1999). Social support and recovery from sexual assault: A review. *Aggression and Violent Behavior: A Review Journal, 4*, 343–358.

Ullman, S. E. (2007). A 10-year update of "Review and critique of empirical studies of rape avoidance." *Criminal Justice and Behavior, 34*, 411–429.

Ullman, S. E., & Knight, R. A. (1993). The efficacy of women's resistance strategies in rape situations. *Psychology of Women Quarterly, 17*, 23–38.

Ullrich, S., Farrington, D. P., & Coid, J. W. (2008). Psychopathic personality traits and life-success. *Personality and Individual Differences, 44*, 1162–1171.

Underwood, R. C., & Patch, P. C. (1999). Siblicide: A descriptive analysis of sibling homicide. *Homicide Studies, 3*, 333–348.

UNFPA. (2009). *Programming to address violence against women: 8 case studies*. New York: Author.

U.S. Bomb Data Center. (2008). *Fact sheet*. Washington, DC: Bureau of Alcohol, Tobacco, Firearms, and Explosives.

U.S. Bureau of the Census. (2001). *2000 census of population and housing*. Washington, DC: USGPO.

U.S. Bureau of the Census. (2002). *Who's minding the kids? Child care arrangements*. Washington, DC: USGPO.

U.S. Conference of Majors. (1998). *A status report on hunger and homelessness in America's cities: 1998*. Washington, DC: Author.

U.S. Department of Health and Human Services. (2003, April 1). *Child abuse prevention: An overview*. Washington, DC: Author.

U.S. Department of Justice. (1976). *Bomb summary— 1975*. Washington, DC: USGPO.

U.S. Department of Justice. (1988). *Report to the nation on crime and justice: The data* (2nd ed.). Washington, DC: USGPO.

U.S. Department of Justice. (1989). *Criminal victimization in the United States, 1987*. Washington, DC: USGPO.

U.S. Department of Justice. (1998). *Inhalants*. Washington, DC: Author.

U.S. Department of Justice. (1999). *Cyberstalking: A new challenge for law enforcement and industry*. Washington, DC: Author. Available: www.usdoj.gov/criminal/cybercrime/cyberstalking.htm.

U.S. Department of Justice. (2000a). *Terrorism in the United States–1998.* Washington, DC: Author.

U.S. Department of Justice. (2000b). *The structure of family violence: An analysis of selected incidents.* Washington, DC: Author.

U.S. Department of Justice. (2002a, October). *Highlights from the NISMART Bulletin.* Washington, DC: U.S. Department of Justice, Office of Juvenile Justice and Delinquency Prevention.

U.S. Department of Justice. (2002b, October). *Nonfamily abducted children: National estimates and characteristics.* Washington, DC: U.S. Department of Justice, Office of Juvenile Justice and Delinquency Prevention.

U.S. Fire Administration. (2004). *Arson and juveniles: Responding to the violence.* Washington, DC: Federal Emergency Management Agency, National Fire Data Center.

University of Iowa Injury Prevention Research Center. (2001). *Workplace violence: A report to the nation.* Iowa City: Author.

Valenstein, E. S. (1973). *Brain control.* New York: Wiley.

van Beijsterveldt, C. E. M., Bartels, M., Hudziak, J. J., & Boomsma, D. I. (2003). Causes of stability of aggression from early childhood to adolescence: A longitudinal genetic analysis in Dutch twins. *Behavior Genetics, 33,* 591–605.

Van Dam, C., Janssens, J. M. A. M., & De Bruyn, E. E. J. (2006). PEN, Big Five, juvenile delinquency and criminal recidivism. *Personality and Individual Differences, 39,* 7–19.

Vandebosch, H., & Van Cleemput, K. (2008). Defining cyberbullying: A qualitative research into the perceptions of youngsters. *Cyberpsychology & Behavior, 11,* 499–503.

Vandell, D. L., & Posner, J. K. (1999). Conceptualization and measurement of children's after-school environments. In S. L. Freidman & T. D. Wachs (Eds.), *Measuring environment across the life-span: Emerging methods and concepts.* Washington, DC: American Psychological Association.

Vandersall, T. A., & Wiener, J. M. (1970). Children who set fires. *Archives of General Psychology, 22,* 63–71.

Vandiver, D. M., & Kercher, G. (2004). Offender and victim characteristics of registered female sexual offenders in Texas: A proposed typology of female sexual offenders. *Sexual Abuse: A Journal of Research and Treatment, 16,* 121–137.

Vandiver, D. M., & Walker, J. T. (2002). Female sex offenders: An overview and analysis of 40 cases. *Criminal Justice Review, 27,* 284–300.

van Lier, P. A. C., Vuijk, P., & Crijen, A. M. (2005). Understanding mechanisms of change in the development of antisocial behavior: The impact of a universal intervention. *Journal of Abnormal Psychology, 33,* 521–533.

van Lier, P. A. C., Wanner, B., & Vitaro, F. (2007). Onset of antisocial behavior affiliation with deviant friends and childhood maladjustment: A text of the childhood- and adolescent-onset models. *Development and Psychopathology, 19,* 167–185.

van Wijk, A., van Horn, J., Bullens, R., Bijleveld, C., & Doreleijers, T. (2005). Juvenile sex offenders: A group on its own? *International Journal of Offender Therapy and Comparative Criminology, 49,* 25–36.

Vaughn, M. G., DeLisi, M., Beaver, K. M., & Howard, M. O. (2008). Toward a quantitative typology of burglars: A latent profile analysis of career offenders. *Journal of Forensic Sciences, 53,* 1387–1392.

Vaughn, M. G., DeLisi, M., Beaver, K. M., & Wright, J. P. (2009). DAT1 and 5HTT are associated with pathological criminal behavior in a nationally representative sample of youth. *Criminal Justice and Behavior, 36,* xx

Veenstra, R., Lindenberg, S., Oldehinkel, A. J., De Winter, A. F., & Ormel, J. (2005). Bullying and victimization in elementary schools: A comparison of bullies, victims, bully/victims, and uninvolved preadolescents. *Developmental Psychology, 41,* 672–682.

Veenstra, R., Lindenberg, S., Oldehinkel, A. J., De Winter, A. F., & Ormel, J. (2006). Temperament, environment, and antisocial behavior in a population sample of preadolescent boys and girls. *International Journal of Behavioral Development, 30,* 422–432.

Veneziano, C., & Veneziano, L. (2002). Adolescent sex offenders: A review of the literature. *Trauma, Violence, & Abuse, 3,* 247–260.

Verlinden, S., Hersen, M., & Thomas, J. (2000). Risk factors in school shootings. *Clinical Psychology Review, 20,* 3–56.

Verona, E., Joiner, T. E., Johnson, F., & Bender, T. W. (2006). Gender specific gene-environment interactions on laboratory-assessed aggression. *Biological Psychology, 71,* 33–41.

Verona, E., Patrick, C. J., & Joiner, T. E. (2001). Psychopathy, antisocial personality, and suicide risk. *Journal of Abnormal Psychology, 110,* 462–470.

Vetter, H. J., & Silverman, I. J. (1978). *The nature of crime.* Philadelphia, PA: W. B. Saunders.

Victoroff, J. (2005). The mind of the terrorist: A review and critique of psychological approaches. *Journal of Conflict Resolution, 49,* 3–42.

Viding, E., Blair, R., James, R., Moffitt, T. E., & Plomin, R. (2005). Evidence for substantial genetic risk for psychopathy in 7-year-olds. *Journal of Child Psychology and Psychiatry, 46,* 592–597.

Vien, A., & Beech, A. R. (2006). Psychopathy: Theory, measurement, and treatment. *Trauma, Violence, & Abuse, 7,* 155–174.

Viljoen, J. L., Elkovitch, N., Scalora, M. J., & Ullman, D. (2009). Assessment of reoffense risk in adolescents who have committed sexual offenses: Predictive validity of the ERASOR, PCL:YV, YLS/CMI, and Static-99. *Criminal Justice and Behavior, 36,* 981–1000.

Viljoen, J. L., & Grisso, T. (2007). Prospects for remediating juveniles' adjudicative incompetence. *Psychology, Public Policy, and Law, 13,* 87–114.

Vijoen, J. L., O'Neill, M. L., & Sidhu, A. (2005). Bullying behaviors in female and male adolescent offenders: Prevalence, types, and association with psychosocial adjustment. *Aggressive Behavior, 31,* 521–536.

Viljoen, J. L., & Wingrove, T. (2007). Adjudicative competence in adolescent defendants: Judges' and defense attorneys' views of legal standards for adolescents in juvenile and criminal court. *Psychology, Public Policy, and Law, 13,* 204–229.

Vincent, G. (2006). Psychopathy and violence risk assessment in youth. *Child and Adolescent Psychiatric Clinics of North America, 15,* 407–428.

Vincent, G. M., Odgers, C. L., McCormick, A. V., & Corrado, R. R. (2008). The PCL:YV and recidivism in male and female juveniles: A follow-up into young adulthood. *International Journal of Law and Psychiatry, 31,* 287–296.

Vincent, K. R. (1991). Black/white IQ difference? *Journal of Clinical Psychology, 47,* 266–270.

Virkkunen, M. (1975). Victim-precipitated pedophilia offenses. *British Journal of Criminology, 15,* 175–180.

Virkkunen, M., & Linnoila, M. (1993). Brain serotonin, Type II alcoholism and impulsive violence. *Journal of Studies on Alcohol* (Supplement), *11,* 163–169.

Vitacco, M. J., Neumann, C. S., & Jackson, R. L. (2005). Testing a four-factor model of psychopathy and its association with ethnicity, gender, intelligence, and violence. *Journal of Consulting and Clinical Psychology, 73,* 466–476.

Vitacco, M. J., Van Rybroek, G. J., Rogstad, J. E., Erickson, S. K., Tripp, A., Harris, L., **et al.** (2008). Developing services for insanity acquittees conditionally released into the community: maximizing success and minimizing recidivism. *Psychological Services, 5,* 118–125.

Vitale, J., Smith, S. S., Brinkley, C. A., & Newman, J. P. (2002). The reliability and validity of the Psychopathy Checklist-Revised in a sample of female offenders. *Criminal Justice and Behavior, 29,* 202–231.

Vitale, J. E., Newman, J. P., Serin, R. C., & Bolt, D. M. (2005). Hostile attributions in incarcerated adult male offenders: An exploration of diverse pathways. *Aggressive Behavior, 31,* 99–115.

Vitale, J. E., Smith, S. S., Brinkley, C. A., & Newman, J. P. (2002). The reliability and validity of the Psychopathy Checklist-Revised in a sample of female offenders. *Criminal Justice and Behavior, 29,* 202–231.

Vitaro, F., & Brendgen, M. (2005). Proactive and reactive aggression: A developmental perspective. In R. E. Tremblay, W. W. Hartrup, & J. Archer (Eds.), *The developmental origins of aggression.* New York: Guilford.

Vitaro, F., Brendgen, M., & Barker, E. D. (2006). Subtypes of aggressive behaviors: A developmental perspective. *International Journal of Behavioral Development, 30,* 12–19.

Vitaro, F., & Tremblay, R. P. (1994). Impact of a prevention program on aggressive children's friendships and social adjustment. *Journal of Abnormal Child Psychology, 22,* 457–476.

Vold, G. B. (1958). *Theoretical criminology.* New York: Oxford University Press.

Vossekuil, B., Fein, R., Reddy, M., Borum, R., & Modzeleski, W. (2002). *The final report and findings of the Safe School Initiative: Implications for the prevention of school attacks in the United States.* Washington, DC: U.S. Secret Service and Department of Education.

Waaktaar, T., Christie, H. J., Borge, A. I. H., & Torgerson, S. (2004). How can young people's resilience be enhanced? Experiences from a clinical intervention project. *Clinical Child Psychology and Psychiatry, 9,* 167–183.

Wachi, T., Watanabe, K., Yokota, K., Suzuki, M., Hoshino, M., Sato, A., et al. (2007). Offender and crime characteristics of female serial arsonists in Japan. *Journal of Investigative Psychology and Offender Profiling, 4,* 29–52.

Wagner, R. V., & Long, K. R. (2004). Terrorism from a peace psychology perspective. In F. M. Moghaddam & A. J. Marsella (Eds.), *Understanding terrorism: Psychosocial roots, consequences, and interventions.* Washington, DC: American Psychological Association.

Waite, D., Keller, A., McGarvey, E. L., Wieckowski, E., Pinkerton, R., & Brown, G. L. (2005). Juvenile sex offender re-arrest rates for sexual, violent nonsexual, and property crimes. *Sexual Abuse: A Journal of Research and Treatment, 17,* 313–331.

Wakefield, J. C. (1992). Disorder as harmful dysfunction: A conceptual critique of DSM-III-R's definition of mental disorder. *Psychological Review, 99,* 232–247.

Wakschlag, L. S., & Hans, S. L. (2002). Maternal smoking during pregnancy and conduct problems in high-risk youth: A developmental framework. *Development and Psychopathology, 14,* 351–369.

Walker, J. S., & Gudjonsson, G. H. (2006). The Maudsley Violence Questionnaire: Relationship to personality and self-reported offending. *Personality and Individual Differences, 40,* 795–806.

Walker, K. L., & Chestnut, D. (2003). The role of ethnocultural variables in response to terrorism. *Cultural Diversity and Ethnic Minority Psychology, 9,* 251–262.

Walker, L. E. (1979). *The battered woman.* New York: Harper Colophon Books.

Walker, S. (2001). *Sense and nonsense about crime and drugs* (5th ed.). Belmont, CA: Wadsworth/Thomson Learning.

Wallace, H. (1996). *Family violence: Legal, medical, and social perspectives.* Boston: Allyn & Bacon.

Wallace, H., & Seymour, A. (2001). Domestic violence. In G. Coleman, M. Gaboury, M. Murray, & A. Seymour (Eds.), *1999 National Victim Assistance Academy.* Washington, DC: U.S. Department of Justice.

Wallerstein, J. S., & Wyle, J. (1947). Our law-abiding law breakers. *Probation, 25,* 107–112.

Walsh, A. (2005). African Americans and serial killing in the media. *Homicide Studies, 9,* 271–291.

Walsh, D. (1980). *Break-ins: Burglary from private homes.* London: Constable.

Walters, G. C., & Grusec, J. E. (1977). *Punishment.* San Francisco: W. H. Freeman.

Walters, G. D. (2003). Predicting institutional adjustment and recidivism with the Psychopathy Checklist factor scores: A meta-analysis. *Law and Human Behavior, 27,* 541–558.

Walters, G. D., Deming, A., & Elliott, W. N. (2009). Assessing criminal thinking in male sex offenders with the Psychological Inventory of Criminal Thinking Styles. *Criminal Justice and Behavior, 36,* 1025–1036.

Ward, T. (2000). Sexual offenders' cognitive distortions as implicit theories. *Aggression and Violent Behavior, 7,* 53–68.

Ward, T., & Hudson, S. M. (2000). Sexual offenders' implicit planning: A conceptual model. *Sexual Abuse: A Journal of Research and Treatment, 12,* 189–202.

Ward. T., Hudson, S. M., Marshall, W. L., & Siegert, R. (1995). Attachment style and intimacy deficits in sexual offenders: A theoretical framework. *Sexual Abuse: A Journal of Research and Treatment, 7,* 317–335.

Warren, J. I., Burnette, M. L., South, S. C., Chauhan, P., Bale, R., Friend, R. et al. (2003). Psychopathy in women: Structural modeling and comorbidity. *International Journal of Law and Psychiatry, 26,* 223–242.

Warren, J. I., Rosenfeld, B., Fitch, W. L., & Hawk, G. (1997). Forensic mental health clinical evaluation: An analysis of interstate and intersystemic differences. *Law and Human Behavior, 21,* 377–390.

Washington Post. (1993, October 12). Guns at home. *Washington Post Health Section,* pp. 12–15.

Wasserman, G. A., & Seracini, A. M. (2001). Family risk factors and interventions. In R. Loeber & D. P. Farrington (Eds.), *Child delinquents: Development, intervention, and service needs.* Thousand Oaks, CA: Sage.

Watson, R. I. (1973). Investigation into deindividuation using a cross-cultural survey technique. *Journal of Personality and Social Psychology, 25,* 342–345.

Webb, J. A., Bray, J. H., Getz, J. G., & Adams, G. (2002). Gender, perceived parental monitoring, and behavioral adjustment: Influences on adolescent alcohol use. *American Journal of Orthopsychiatry, 72,* 392–400.

Webster, C. D., Douglas, K. S., Eaves, D., & Hart, S. D. (1997). Assessing risk to violence to others. In C. D. Webster & M. A. Jackson (Eds.), *Impulsivity: Theory, assessment and treatment.* New York: Guilford.

Webster, C. D., Harris, G. T., Rice, M. E., Cormier, C., & Quinsey, V. L. (1994). *The violence prediction scheme: Assessing dangerousness in high-risk men.* Toronto, ON: University of Toronto Press.

Webster, C. D., & Menzies, R. J. (1993). Supervision in the deinstitutionalized community. In S. Hodgins (Ed.), *Mental disorder and crime.* Newbury Park, CA: Sage.

Weiler, B. L., & Widom, C. S. (1996). Psychopathy and violent behaviour in abused and neglected young adults. *Criminal Behaviour and Mental Health, 6,* 253–271.

Weis, J. G. (1989). Family violence methodology and design. In L. Ohlin & M. Tonry (Eds.), *Family violence* (Vol. 11). Chicago: University of Chicago Press.

Weis, J. G., & Sederstrom, J. (1981). *The prevention of serious delinquency. What to do?* Washington, DC: U.S. Department of Justice.

Weis, R., & Toolis, E. E. (2008). Military style residential treatment for disruptive adolescents: A critical review and look to the future. In A. M. Columbus (Ed.), *Advances in psychology research* (Vol. 56). Hauppauge, NY: Nova Science Publishers.

Weisbrot, D. M. (2008). Prelude to school shooting? Assessing threatening behaviors in childhood and adolescence. *Journal of the American Academy of Child & Adolescent Psychiatry, 47,* 847–852.

Weisel, D. L. (2007, March). *Bank robbery.* Washington, DC: U.S. Department of Justice, Office of Community Oriented Policing Services.

Weiss, R. D., & Mirin, S. M. (1987). *Cocaine.* Washington, DC: American Psychiatric Press.

Wenk, E. A., Robison, J. O., & Smith, G. W. (1972). Can violence be predicted? *Crime and Delinquency, 18,* 393–402.

Wessler, S., & Moss, M. (2001, October). *Hate crimes on campus: The problem and efforts to confront it.* Washington, DC: U.S. Department of Justice, Office of Justice Programs.

Wheatman, S. R., & Shaffer, D. R. (2001). On finding for defendants who plead insanity: The crucial impact of dispositional instructions and opportunity to deliberate. *Law and Human Behavior, 25,* 167–183.

Wheeler, R. W., Davidson, R. J., & Tomarken, A. J. (1993). Frontal brain asymmetry and emotional reactivity: A biological substrate of affective style. *Psychophysiology, 30,* 82–89.

Whitcomb, D. (2001). Child victimization. In G. Coleman, M. Gaboury, M. Murray, & A. Seymour (Eds.), *1999 National Victim Assistance Academy.* Washington, DC: U.S. Department of Justice.

White, J. L., Moffitt, T. E., Earls, F., Robins, L., & Silva, P. A. (1990). How early can we tell? Predictors of childhood conduct disorder and delinquency. *Criminology, 28,* 507–533.

White, J. L., Moffitt, T. E., & Silva, P. A. (1989). A prospective replication of the protective effects of IQ in subjects at high risk for juvenile delinquency. *Journal of Consulting and Clinical Psychology, 57,* 719–724.

Whitehill, M., DeMyer-Gapin, S., & Scott, T. G. (1976). Stimulation seeking in antisocial preadolescent children. *Journal of Abnormal Psychology, 85,* 101–104.

Wicker, T. (1976). *Time to die.* New York: Ballatine.

Widiger, T. A., Frances, A. J., Pincus, H. A., Davis, W. W., & First, M. B. (1991). Toward an empirical classification of the DSM-IV. *Journal of Abnormal Psychology, 100,* 280–288.

Widom, C. S. (1978). A methodology for studying non-institutionalized psychopaths. In R. D. Hare & D. Schalling (Eds.), *Psychopathic behavior: Approaches to research.* Chichester, UK: Wiley.

Widom, C. S. (1992, September). The cycle of violence. *Research in Brief.* Washington, DC: U.S. Department of Justice.

Widom, C. S. (2000, January). Childhood victimization: Early adversity, later psychopathology. *National Institute of Justice Journal,* 3–9.

Widom, C. S., & Newman, J. P. (1985). Characteristics of noninstitutionalized psychopaths. In J. Gunn & D. Farrington (Eds.), *Current research in forensic psychiatry and psychology* (Vol. 2). New York: Wiley.

Wiesen, A. E. (1965). *Differential reinforcing effects of onset and offset of stimulation on the operant behavior of normals, neurotics, and psychopaths.* Doctoral dissertation, University of Florida. Ann Arbor, MI: University Microfilms, No. 65–9625.

Wiesner, M., Kim, H. K., & Capaldi, D. M. (2005). Developmental trajectories of offending: Validation and prediction to young adult alcohol use, drug use, and depressive symptoms. *Development and Psychopathology, 17,* 251–270.

Wiesner, M., & Windle, M. (2004). Assessing covariates of adolescent delinquency trajectories: A latent growth mixture modeling approach. *Journal of Youth and Adolescence, 33,* 431–432.

Wilczynski, A. (1997). Mad or bad? Child-killers, gender, and the courts. *British Journal of Criminology, 37,* 419–436.

Wike, T. L., & Fraser, M. W. (2009). School shootings: Making sense of the senseless. *Aggression and Violent Behavior, 14,* 162–169.

Williams, F. P., & McShane, M. D. (2004). *Criminological theory* (4th ed.). Upper Saddle River, NJ: Prentice Hall.

Williams, J. E., & Holmes, K. A. (1981). *The second assault: Rape and public attitudes.* Westport, CT: Greenwood Press.

Williams, W., & Miller, K. S. (1981). The processing and disposition of incompetent mentally ill offenders. *Law and Human Behavior, 5,* 245–261.

Williamson, S., Hare, R. D., & Wong, S. (1987). Violence: Criminal psychopaths and their victims. *Canadian Journal of Behavioral Science, 19,* 454–462.

Wilson, D. J. (2000). *Drug use, testing, and treatment in jails.* Washington, DC: Bureau of Justice Statistics.

Wilson, J. Q., & Herrnstein, R. J. (1985). *Crime and human nature.* New York: Simon & Schuster.

Wincze, J. P. (1977). Sexual deviance and dysfunction. In D. Rimm & J. Somervill (Eds.), *Abnormal psychology.* New York: Academic Press.

Windle, M., & Wiesner, M. (2004). Trajectories of marijuana use from adolescence to young adulthood: Predictors and outcomes. *Development and Psychopathology, 16,* 1007–1027.

Wolf, B. C., & Lavezzi, W. A. (2007). Paths to destruction: The lives and crimes of two serial killers. *Journal of Forensic Science, 52,* 199–203.

Wolf, R. S. (1992). Victimization of the elderly: Elder abuse and neglect. *Reviews in Clinical Gerontology, 2,* 269–276.

Wolfe, D. A. (1985). Child-abusive parents: An empirical review and analysis. *Psychological Bulletin, 97,* 462–582.

Wolfe, D. A., Jaffe, P. G., Wilson, S. K., & Zak, L. (1985). Children of battered women: The relation of child behavior to family violence and maternal stress. *Journal of Consulting and Clinical Psychology, 53,* 657–665.

Wolford, M. R. (1972). Some attitudinal, psychological and sociological characteristics of incarcerated arsonists. *Fire and Arson Investigator, 16,* 8–13.

Wong, M. T. H., Lumsden, J., Fenton, G. W., & Fenwick P. B. C. (1994). Epilepsy and violence in mentally abnormal offenders in a maximum security mental hospital. *Journal of Epilepsy, 7,* 253–258.

Wong, S. (2000). Psychopathic offenders. In S. Hodgins & R. Muller-Isberner (Eds.), *Violence, crime and mentally disordered offenders: Concepts and methods for effective treatment and prevention.* New York: Wiley.

Wood, J. J., Cowan, P. A., & Baker, B. L. (2002). Behavior problems and peer rejection in preschool boys and girls. *Journal of Genetic Psychology, 163,* 72–89.

Woodworth, M. & Porter, S. (2001). Historical foundations and current applications of criminal profiling in violent crime investigations. *Expert Evidence, 7,* 241–264.

Woodworth, M. & Porter, S. (2002). In cold blood: Characteristics of criminal homicides as a function of psychopathy. *Journal of Abnormal Psychology, 111,* 436–445.

Worling, J. R. (1995). Adolescent sibling incest offenders: Differences in family and individual functioning when compared to adolescent nonsibling sex offenders. *Child Abuse & Neglect, 19,* 633–643.

Wright, J., & Hensley, C. (2003). From animal cruelty to serial murder: Applying the graduation hypothesis. *International Journal of Offender Therapy and Comparative Criminology, 47,* 71–88.

Wright, J. C., Huston, A. C., Vandewater, E. A., Bickman, D. S., Scantlin, R. M., Kotler, J. A., et al. (2001). American children's use of electronic media in 1997: A national survey. *Applied Developmental Psychology, 22,* 31–47.

Wright, J. D., & Rossi, P. H. (1994). *Armed and considered dangerous: A survey of felons and their firearms.* New York: Aldine De Gruyter.

Wright, R., Brookman, F., & Bennett, T. (2006). The foreground dynamics of street robbery in Britain. *British Journal of Criminology, 46,* 1–15.

Wright, R. T., & Decker, S. (1997). *Armed robbers in action: Stickup and street culture.* Boston: Northeastern University Press.

Xie, H., Farmer, T. W., & Cairns, B. D. (2003). Different forms of aggression among inner-city African-American Children: Gender, configurations, and school social networks. *Journal of School Psychology, 41,* 355–375.

Yang, Y., Raine, A., Lencz, T., Bihrle, S., LaCasse, L., & Colletti, P. (2005). Volume reduction in prefrontal gray matter in unsuccessful criminal psychopaths. *Biological Psychiatry, 57,* 1103–1108.

Yates, E. (1986). The influence of psychosocial factors on nonsensical shoplifting. *International Journal of Offender Therapy and Comparative Criminology, 30,* 203–211.

Yegidis, B. L. (1986). Date rape and other forced sexual encounters among college students. *Journal of Sex Education and Therapy, 12,* 51–54.

Yesavage, J. A., Benezech, M., Ceccaldi, P., Bourgeois, M., & Addad, M. (1983). Arson in mentally ill and criminal populations. *Journal of Clinical Psychiatry, 44,* 128–130.

Young, S., Fox, N. A., & Zahn-Waxler, C. (1999). Relations between temperament and empathy. *Developmental Psychology, 35,* 1189–1197.

Yu, J., Evans, P. C., & Perfetti, L. (2004). Road aggression among drinking drivers: Alcohol and non-alcohol effects on aggressive driving and road rage. *Journal of Criminal Justice, 32,* 421–430.

Zahn, M. A., Brumbaugh, S., Steffensmeier, D., Feld, B. C. Morash, M., Chesney-Lind, M. et al. (2008, May). *Violence by teenage girls: Trends and context.* Washington, DC: U.S. Department of Justice, Office of Juvenile Justice and Delinquency Prevention.

Zahn, M. A., Hawkins, S. R., Chiancone, J., & Whitworth, A. (October, 2008). *The Girls Study Group—Charting the way to delinquency prevention for girls.* Washington, DC: U.S. Department of Justice, Office of Juvenile Justice and Delinquency Prevention.

Zawitz, M. W., & Strom, K. J. (2000, October). *Firearm injury and death from crime, 1993–1997.* Washington, DC: U.S. Department of Justice.

Zigler, E., Taussig, C., & Black, K. (1992). Early childhood intervention: A promising prevention for juvenile delinquency. *American Psychologist, 47,* 997–1006.

Zillmann, D. (1971). Excitation transfer in communication-mediated aggressive behavior. *Journal of Experimental Social Psychology, 7,* 419–434.

Zillmann, D. (1979). *Hostility and aggression.* Hillsdale, NJ: Erlbaum.

Zillmann, D. (1983). Arousal and aggression. In R. G. Geen & E. I. Donnerstein (Eds.), *Aggression: Theoretical and empirical reviews* (Vol. 1). New York: Academic Press.

Zillmann, D. (1988). Cognitive-excitation interdependencies in aggressive behavior. *Aggressive Behavior, 14,* 51–64.

Zimbardo, P. G. (1970). The human choice. Individuation, reason, and order versus deindividuation, impulse, and chaos. In W. J. Arnold & D. Levine (Eds.), *Nebraska symposium on motivation 1969.* Lincoln, NE: University of Nebraska Press.

Zimbardo, P. G. (1973). The psychological power and pathology of imprisonment. In E. Aronson & R. Helmreich (Eds.), *Social psychology.* New York: Van Nostrand.

Zipper, P., & Wilcox, D. K. (2005, April). The importance of early intervention. *FBI Law Enforcement Bulletin, 74,* 3–9.

Zoccoulillo, M. (1993). Gender and the development of conduct disorder. *Development and Psychopathology, 5,* 65–78.

Zorza, J. (1991). Woman battering: A major cause of homelessness. *Clearinghouse Review, 25*(4).

Zucker, R. A., Fitzgerald, H. E., Refior, S. K., Puttler, L. I., Pallas, D. M., & Ellis, D. A. (2000). The clinical and social ecology of childhood for children of alcoholics: Description of a study and implications for a differentiated social policy. In H. E. Fitzgerald, B. M. Lester, & B. S. Zuckerman (Eds.), *Children of addiction: Research, health, and public policy issues* New York: RoutledgeFalmer.

Index